Models of Human Memory

CONTRIBUTORS

HARLEY A. BERNBACH

ROBERT A. BJORK

EDWARD A. FEIGENBAUM

JAMES G. GREENO

WALTER KINTSCH

JOHN MORTON

BENNET B. MURDOCK, JR.

DONALD A. NORMAN

JUDITH S. REITMAN

WALTER REITMAN

DAVID E. RUMELHART

RICHARD M. SHIFFRIN

ROSEANNE G. SPEELMAN

GEORGE SPERLING

WAYNE A. WICKELGREN

Models
Human Me

EDITED BY

DONALD A. NORMAN

University of California, San Diego

ACADEMIC PRESS New York and London

ACADEMIC PRESS, INC.
111 Fifth Avenue, New York, New York 10003

United Kingdom Edition published by
ACADEMIC PRESS, INC. (LONDON) LTD.
Berkeley Square House, London W1X 6BA

LIBRARY OF CONGRESS CATALOG CARD NUMBER: 79-91427

PRINTED IN THE UNITED STATES OF AMERICA

CONTENTS

IV. MECHANISMS OF STORAGE AND RETRIEVAL

10. Repetition and Rehearsal Mechanisms in Models for Short-Term Memory

Robert A. Bjork

11. Models for Free Recall and Recognition

Walter Kintsch

12. Memory Search

Richard M. Shiffrin

V. INFORMATION PROCESSING AND MEMORY

13. Information Processing and Memory

Edward A. Feigenbaum

LIST OF CONTRIBUTORS

Numbers in parentheses indicate the pages on which the authors' contributions begin.

HARLEY A. BERNBACH (103), Cornell University, Ithaca, New York

ROBERT A. BJORK (307), University of Michigan, Ann Arbor, Michigan

EDWARD A. FEIGENBAUM (451), Stanford University, Stanford, California

JAMES G. GREENO (257), The University of Michigan, Ann Arbor, Michigan

WALTER KINTSCH (331), University of Colorado, Boulder, Colorado

JOHN MORTON (203), Applied Psychology Research Unit, Cambridge, England

BENNET B. MURDOCK, JR. (285), University of Toronto, Ontario, Canada

DONALD A. NORMAN (1, 19, 511), University of California, San Diego, California

JUDITH S. REITMAN (117), University of Michigan, Ann Arbor, Michigan

WALTER REITMAN (469), University of Michigan, Ann Arbor, Michigan

DAVID E. RUMELHART (19), University of California, San Diego, California

RICHARD M. SHIFFRIN (375), Indiana University, Bloomington, Indiana

ROSEANNE G. SPEELMAN* (151), Bell Telephone Laboratories, Incorporated, Murray Hill, New Jersey

GEORGE SPERLING (151), Bell Telephone Laboratories, Incorporated, Murray Hill, New Jersey

WAYNE A. WICKELGREN† (65), Massachusetts Institute of Technology, Cambridge, Massachusetts

* Present address: Seton Hill College, Greensburg, Pennsylvania.

† Present address: University of Oregon, Eugene, Oregon.

PREFACE

When this book was first conceived, I assumed that the authors' contributions would represent a fairly standard set of descriptions of mathematical and computer models of human memory. Fortunately, I was wrong. The papers have turned out to be much more general than that, and, as a result, much more interesting and much more important. In fact, several papers in the volume hint at the difficulties we psychologists have gotten ourselves into by our rigid conceptualization of memory processes. One paper—appropriately placed last so that it serves as an epilogue—asks openly whether many of the preceding papers have not been something of a waste of time. Regardless of the answer, it would seem about time that we took the question seriously.

A few years ago, most of the quantitative models of memory were based upon the formal representation of some learning theory, or some sort of information–processing analysis of the storage and retrieval of items in memory. Now, however, we find increasing emphasis on cognitive processes with increasing concern about the rules and strategies used by subjects in storing and retrieving information. More and more, the processes involved in memory are being described in terms very similar to those used to describe the processes of perception, of thinking, and of problem-solving. We find the tools from linguistic theories of semantics, from computer studies of list structures, from general considerations of retrieval and organization, and from a sort of systems analysis of the way that the different processes involved in the human memory system interact with one another.

This collection has come about because the time seemed ripe for it. A number of us have been working on models of memory, and although we do communicate with one another, it seemed that it would serve a valuable purpose to compile a set of papers that would be useful as a reference to current theory and as a textbook. The fact that the end product is somewhat different than was contemplated proves its need. Many of us are reasonably satisfied with the progress of the first generation of memory models (call them the mechanistic generation) and we are stumbling toward a way of describing the models of the second generation (call these the cognitive generation). This book, then, both summarizes and predicts. In both cases it appears to be timely and worthwhile.

I have urged the contributors to be informal in their presentation so that the chapters will illustrate personal idiosyncrasies as well as formal, logical reasoning. Thus, I have asked the authors to write in the first person singular, to expand upon their ideas where desirable, and to state their own philosophies of theory building and speculations of things to come. The result of so much individuality produces a somewhat uneven collection of papers in that each new chapter introduces a new writing style, a new first person to contend with, and a rather different method of presentation. Hopefully, the virtues of informality will outweigh the lack of literary consistency and scientific decorum, or even preciseness. The aim here is to give the reader an up-to-date picture of modern models of human memory, complete with the personalities of the authors.

Throughout the writing of the chapters there has been a good deal of communication among the participants. Most authors provided rough manuscripts for one another early in the process of compiling the book. In addition, most of us gathered together at the first annual meeting of the Mathematical Psychology Meetings (see the *Journal of Mathematical Psychology,* 1968, **5**, 496–499) where we exchanged ideas, both in informal discussions and in a more formal panel discussion which lasted until the heat wave then in progress at Stanford brought the proceedings to an end. The final papers were not collected for another eight months, leaving time for more thought and revision. In addition, most of the papers have received critical evaluation and reviews from selected readers, both named and anonymous. (Authors, of course, often disagreed with these comments, and ignored them.)

Hopefully, all this intercommunication, refereeing, and informality has produced a readable set of manuscripts which are related to one another and which will convey to you, the reader, some of the excitement we feel about the potential developments in the study of human memory. We all feel that this area of research is about ready to yield to the onslaught of our attacks. Part of our goal in these chapters, therefore, is to tell you why and how we study the problems and to give sufficient information that someone in the audience may take the next step.

A word about level: our hope is that the articles are sufficiently complete that they can be understood by the graduate or advanced undergraduate student who has some background in the literature of human memory. Mathematical sophistication should not be necessary in order to follow the ideas. Even the paper with the most frightening set of equations has been written so that the ideas underlying the model can be obtained without any understanding of the equations. To understand the mathematical papers, the reader ought to be reasonably familiar with the material covered in Atkinson, Bower, and Crother's *Introduction to Mathematical Learning Theory* (New York: Wiley, 1965). In addition, we have all assumed that the reader is familiar with current theories and experiments on human memory.

A number of people have helped in the preparation of this volume. Many of the authors spent extra time discussing the overall organization of the material in addition to commenting upon specific chapters, both voluntarily and when coerced to serve as referees. In addition to the authors, I wish to thank Peter Dean, Dominic Massaro, David Krantz, and one anonymous reader for reviewing particular chapters.

La Jolla, California DONALD A. NORMAN

Models of Human Memory

1

Introduction: Models of Human Memory

Donald A. Norman
University of California, San Diego

The Basic Stages of the Memory System

In recent years, we have reached a rather general consensus about the stages of processing that are involved in human memory. This consensus is reflected in the development of a new class of psychological theories that differs radically from the more traditional approach to the same problems. This new approach, often called "Human Information Processing," is a direct result of an attempt to view memory as a complex system with many interacting stages, rather than as something that mediates between the presentation of a stimulus to the subject and his eventual response. Proponents of these theories have not hesitated to suggest what different mechanisms might exist in the human, especially when the logic or formal requirements of their particular model required them. Of course, it turns out that different theorists often demand different mechanisms, with the theoretical demands of their models far outstripping the interpretations that can be supported by the existing experimental data, but even so, there is rather good agreement about a number of essential features of the system.

The general picture of human information processing is this. First, newly presented information would appear to be transformed by the sensory system into its physiological representation (which may already involve a substantial amount of processing on the initial sensory image), and this representation is stored briefly in a sensory information storage system. Following this sensory storage, the presented material is identified and encoded into a new format and retained temporarily in a different storage system, usually called short-term memory. Then, if extra attention is paid to the material, or if it is rehearsed frequently enough, or if it gets properly organized, the information is transferred to a more permanent memory system (or, in some models, the rate at which it decays decreases substantially). In general, the capacity of this more permanent storage is so large that information that is stored there must be organized in an efficient manner if it is ever to be retrieved. Then, finally, when it is necessary to retrieve information from memory, decision rules must be used, both to decide exactly how to get access to the desired information and then to decide exactly what response should be made to the information that has been retrieved.

Most of the authors of the chapters in this volume agree with this general picture, although each chapter emphasizes different aspects of the system and different chapters usually make different assumptions about the details of the processes. Most authors assume that there are three different types of memory storage systems: a sensory information storage, a short-term memory, and a long-term memory. Everyone accepts the need for a sensory information storage. Some, however, do not believe that there is any need to distinguish between short- and long-term memory (Bernbach, Chapter 4; Murdock, Chapter 9). Others feel that the distinction between short- and long-term memory is too crude and there is, in fact, an intermediate-term memory between the other two, making a total of four memory systems in all (Wickelgren, Chapter 3). Whether there be two memory systems or four, everyone does agree that newly presented material is forgotten rather rapidly unless it is rehearsed, but there is quite a bit of disagreement over why the forgetting takes place. Some authors claim that items decay with the passage of time, others claim that forgetting results as a result of interference from the presentation of other material. Some postulate a mixture of both time decay and interference, and still a few others cannot quite make up their minds. Similarly, although everyone agrees that with extra rehearsal, attention, or organization, material is forgotten very slowly, if at all, there is disagreement over why; is the information transferred to a more permanent memory system, has its rate of decay simply slowed up, or did its initial strength value simply increase substantially?

History

The models appear to have three different historical roots: mathematical learning theory, signal detection theory, and computer processes.

Mathematical Learning Theory

Mathematical learning theory has provided the tools of stochastic analysis which allow us to describe the fate of an item as it passes through the various stages of memory. It is extremely difficult to distinguish among models of learning and models of memory: in some sense, the former concentrate on what is retained, the latter on what is forgotten. The real combination of the two areas started when learning theorists discovered that they had to allow material to be forgotten as well as learned, that is, to make the transition backwards in the states of learning.

The first models of learning to introduce this memory loss were published by Atkinson and Crothers (1964), who found that the ability of their learning model to handle an experiment in paired-associate learning was improved substantially by the addition of both a short-term memory state and forgetting. By now, it is common practice to include consideration of the effects of short-term memory in learning models. In general, this is done by assuming that there are several different states of learning. Items start out in an initial state of no knowledge from which a correct response can be made only by guessing. As the subject learns the material presented to him, this learning is represented in the model by transitions to states of intermediate or complete knowledge. Usually (but not always) items in intermediate states are not permanent in that they can return to other intermediate states or even to the initial state. Items that make it to the final, learned state, stay there more permanently: in the Markov model, the final state is often an absorbing state. These state models, then, describe the transitions that occur among the various stages of learning and memory. A number of the models in these chapters show the influence of learning theory.

Signal Detection Theory

Signal detection theory has provided us both with a tool for describing the decision processes of the subjects and also with an important analogy. Thus, although Kintsch (Chapter 11) points out that it is misleading to talk of a signal detection model of memory because we have borrowed only the decision aspects of the theory, it should be emphasized that we have also benefited by the analogy between the mechanisms involved in trying to recognize a weak, fading trace in the memory system and those involved in recognizing a weak acoustical signal that is masked by noise. In both cases, we assume that the decision process gets some measure of the information contained in the signal or memory trace, and from this it must decide what the information represents. The psychophysicist has the advantage that he can specify the parameters of the signal and noise distributions with great precision, whereas we cannot. Yet the analogy is important and useful.

The decision process used in signal detection theory is actually common to a number of fields. It forms the framework of statistical decision theory and it has been used in psychological theories at least since Thurstone's law of categorical judgment (1927) and to some extent, Hull (1943). Nevertheless, it seems fair to say that the historical origins of the decision aspects of most memory models come directly from the communication theories that comprise signal detection theory. The assumptions and history of detection theory in psychology, including its application to memory, are reviewed in the book by Green and Swets (1966). The first clear statement and experimental demonstration of the way that detection theory might be useful in the study of recognition memory for words came in a technical report by James Egan (1958). The method was also applied to a study of recognition memory for tones by Irwin Pollack (1959), but it then took until 1964 and 1965 for the next group of papers devoted to the use of detection theory analysis of recognition memory for words to get published: one paper in 1964 (Pollack, Norman, and Galanter, 1964), and two in 1965 (Murdock, 1965; Norman and Wickelgren, 1965).

One other major contribution of the detection theory approach is the recognition that it is both necessary and possible to separate different stages of processing. Thus, detection theorists clearly separate the process of extracting information from the signal from the process of making a response based on that information. This distinction is now widely accepted, so much so that in this book the distinction has been enlarged to separate the processes of acquisition, sensory storage, and perception of the items presented to the subject from the short-, intermediate-, and long-term memories of those items, from the rules and procedures used to organize that material in memory, and, finally, from the strategies and procedures used to retrieve stored information and make an appropriate response.

Computer Models

Computer models of memory take at least three different forms. One results simply from the fact that the computer can be used as a computational tool. Thus, whenever the mathematical expression for a proposed system of memory becomes too complex, it often seems more sensible and direct to construct a simulation of the system on the computer, rather than to oversimplify the mathematical formulation. When used in this way, the computer makes no fundamental contribution to the model.

The other contributions are of a more fundamental influence. The second influence of computers is as a model of a successful information processing system. This alone would not necessarily be of more than passing interest because each new advance in technology seems to spawn an immediate set of possible brain mechanisms, from clockwork gears, to pneumatic constructions, through telephone switchboards, large sets of relays, and now, computer circuits. The particular interest in today's computer analogies results from the fact that a science of information processing has been formed, so that many of the principles devised for efficient information processing are extremely general and apply to any system, not just those constructed of electronic and mechanical devices.

Thus, one lesson that has been learned is that there is a problem in synchronizing the operation of the computational processes with the rather random and chaotic arrival of external information. The general solution to this problem is to impose some sort of storage device at every interconnection of an input or output with the information processor.

Another lesson is that many of the operations of getting information into and out of the environment are routine, even though they may also be sophisticated, so that it makes sense to save the capacity of the central processor by providing external peripheral processing devices that can handle these tasks without additional assistance. In humans, we can compare the sensory information storage systems with the input–output buffers and the stimulus-analyzing mechanisms that operate on the sensory inputs and the elaborate motor control systems that control our outputs with the peripheral processors. The student of information processing devices cannot help but find numerous other analogies between the mechanisms required for efficient operation of information systems with the mechanisms used by humans. This point is discussed in more detail in the chapter by Feigenbaum (Chapter 13).

Many of the models in this book have borrowed from the concepts of the information processing field. We talk about the encoding of information and the temporary or working storage of information. We talk of passing information from one system to another much as we might speak of passing actual physical objects. All this comes naturally from the various sciences that have developed around the technology of computers. The phrase "process model" will be used to describe models that result from this second influence of computers.

The third influence of computers results from the study of algorithms and rules. It is only natural that these analytical tools be natural devices for the study and simulation of human performance. This approach to the study of human skills owes its modern origins to the group of workers at the Carnegie Institute of Technology (now called Carnegie-Mellon University) and the work of Newell, Simon, and Shaw on list-processing languages for computers and heuristic problem solving (see the review by Newell and Simon, 1963). One major development of this group was a new concept in computer languages: list processing. This work, which culminated in the language IPL-V (Newell, 1961) is the predecessor of most modern list processing and string manipulation languages, such as the SNOBOL described and used by Judith Reitman (see the Appendix to Chapter 5). In general, this approach to the study of human processes emphasizes how a human uses rules and strategies to solve the problems confronting him.

Although the information processing models of this volume deal rather well with many of the processes involved in the initial analysis of incoming sensory signals and in the description of short-term memory, they do not attempt to describe performance with material that has been organized by the subject. Yet, there is increasing evidence that subjects, in fact, attempt to organize and make sense out of all material presented to them, even in tasks where the experimenter feels this to be difficult or impossible. It is clear that long-term memory structures depend heavily upon the organization of the material contained within it, and it is quite clear that linguistic performance depends upon the application of rules to the syntactic and semantic structure of language, rather than simple associations among previously encountered items. Kintsch (in Chapter 11) reviews these arguments in some detail and proposes a direction in which we might start in our attempts to describe the organization of verbal material in long-term memory. Walter Reitman (Chapter 14) points out that if we observe subjects who are performing experiments in memory, we cannot escape the conclusion that they are struggling with the material to be learned, not by an attempt to memorize the items by rote, but by their attempts to find some rule or structure which they can apply to the material. Shiffrin (Chapter 12) discusses in some detail the search process used by a human as he attempts to retrieve information from memory. This view of human memory is strongly supported by the arguments and the discussions in Chapter 13 by Feigenbaum.

Future Models

The models in this book stand at a crucial point in our understanding of the processes of human memory. As you will note, a reasonable variety of topics are discussed by the various chapters and a variety of analytical techniques are used with a good deal of emphasis on the relevance of the underlying psychological concepts. What appears to have been achieved is a respectable set of models capable of handling reasonably well many of the experimental phenomena of memory and perception. In addition, we have enough sophistication about the processes of memory to be able to speculate about the direction in which future studies will lead us.

Perhaps the most encouraging aspect of these speculations is the increasing realization that we must eventually come to understand the strategies and rules used by subjects if we eventually are to understand human memory. This emphasis on what a subject actually is doing (as opposed to a description, no matter how elaborate, of his observable behavior) is a refreshing throwback to the psychology of the late 19th and early 20th centuries. But we now have an increased sophistication about the meaning of strategies, rules, algorithms, and heuristics. Primarily due to the development of communication, computer, and information sciences, we now realize that the rules followed by a system (that is, the program) are often more important than the physical structure of which the system is constructed.

Before embarking on a wild search for strategies that might be relevant, however, a number of basic issues do need to be decided. We need to know more about the way that permanently stored material is encoded in memory; does it reside as an image of the actual item or as lists of attributes that can simply be reexcited and examined anew; does it require an active reconstructive effort before it can be used? What about the address structure of memory? Are items stored once or many times, in temporal sequence or according to their relations to previously acquired information, or none of these? Do we retrieve material by parallel access schemes, by a content-addressable search, or by a serial list-processing mode? In fact, although it could hardly be false to claim that we need to answer the basic questions before we can go on to study the realization of a subject's strategies in memory, it is well to remember that we cannot even start that task until we determine what these basic questions are. So far, we have just the sketchiest of ideas.

The future would appear to bring forth several new directions of work. We expect increasing emphasis to be placed on the study of the rules and strategies of subjects. But first we need to have many more experimental studies than now exist. It would be useful to have imaginative new experimental techniques as well, for there would appear to be many limitations of the trust one can apply to protocols that subjects generate: not only is it not safe to trust a subject's introspection of what he is doing, but these verbal records must necessarily be incomplete generalizations of the actual occurrences (see Walter Reitman's discussion in Chapter 14). Then, after we have learned some more facts, we need new analytical techniques, perhaps along the lines suggested by Feigenbaum (Chapter 13), Kintsch (Chapter 11), Walter Reitman (Chapter 14), and Shiffrin (Chapter 12). Computer techniques and increasing use of list processing and string manipulation languages will play important roles in these theoretical developments.

In addition to this increasing research on the structure of stored material and the strategies involved in the use of memory, we need somehow to make the other models compatible with the computer work. Thus, the information processing models that concentrate on mathematical descriptions of the processing of information from one stage of analysis to the next must eventually show how the transfer of material to more permanent storage (by whatever mechanism that is assumed) leads to the strategies and organizational schemes that we know are used by subjects. In turn, the computer models must take into account the limitations on speed and processing capacity of the early stages of perception and memory which are now so ably described by the process-type models.

Supplementary Papers

The chapters in this book contain a reasonably complete sample of current work on models of human memory. Several of the authors of chapters in this volume discuss models that are reasonably different from the versions which they studied several years ago, so that many of the earlier, fundamental papers have been simply assumed already to be known by the reader. Wherever this is the case, of course, the earlier papers are summarized and/or adequately referenced. There are several major examples of models that have not been covered in this book, however, namely the multicomponent model of Bower and the rehearsal-buffer model of Atkinson and Shiffrin. The serious student of the models in this book should also read these two papers. The papers are to be found in the series edited by Spence and Spence (1967, 1968), *The Psychology of Learning and Motivation:* Bower's model is in Volume 1 (1967) and Atkinson and Shiffrin's model is in Volume 2 (1968). In addition to these two papers, Volume 3 of the series, edited by Spence and Bower (1969), also contains several chapters highly relevant to the papers contained in this book.

Organization

This book contains samples of a wide variety of models of human memory. Although each paper differs in subject matter and in the particular philosophy used by each author, all the papers overlap considerably with one another. Indeed, although the table of contents and the section headings suggest a neat separation of the papers into discrete topics, you will find that the actual papers do not reflect the neatness of the artificial organization. To organize these papers properly would require a multidimensional representation: a structure that is not allowed by present-day printing practices.

The classification of papers used in this book attempts to follow the substantive areas discussed in each paper. Such classification is always incorrect in details. Hopefully, it is accurate enough to serve as a guide through the topics of this book. We start in Part I with the discussion of general systems: the interactions among perception and short- and long-term memory. In this part, four different papers explore how the many different operations involved in memory might depend upon and interact with each other. In Part II, two specific discussions of the representation of verbal material are presented: one for storage of the individual phonemes of verbal material in short-term memory, the other for the way in which perceptual information interacts with memory for the recognition of words. Part III presents two statements about the nature of the relationship between the learning of associations and memory, both based around a Markovian description of the states of learning and memory.

In Part IV, we examine particular mechanisms involved in memory: mechanisms for storage and retrieval, for rehearsal and interference, for recall and recognition. These papers differ from those of Part I primarily by their specificity. Rather than dealing with the memory system as a whole, they treat components of the system in detail: rehearsal, repetition, and interference in short-term memory; the structure of long-term memory; the nature of retrieval. Finally, in Part V, some of the general considerations involved in information processing models are discussed.

Part I: Memory Systems

The four chapters of this section present rather general discussions of possible systems for and representations of the processes of memory. Donald Norman and David Rumelhart (Chapter 2) discuss how information might be represented initially by the perceptual system as a multicomponent vector of features. This perceptual vector is then translated by a "naming process" into a different multicomponent memory vector of attributes which is retained in either (or both) short- or long-term memory.

Wayne Wickelgren (Chapter 3) is not so concerned with these details of the processing as with the specification of the various functional processes of memory. He proposes a generalized version of a strength theory of memory with four different types of memories: a very short-term, a short-term, an intermediate-term, and a long-term memory. For each memory, Wickelgren reviews the evidence which caused him to postulate its existence and discusses four different phases of the memory trace: acquisition, consolidation, decay, and retrieval.

Harley Bernbach's paper (Chapter 4) contrasts sharply with Wickelgren's, for he suggests that only one memory system is necessary to account for the phenomena observed in studies of short-, intermediate-, and long-term memories. Bernbach proposes a system in which repeated presentations or attention paid to an item increases the number of replications of the representation of that item in a single memory system. In this system, differences which are observed in the apparent rate of decay of material result from differences in the number of replications that exist of that material.

Judith Reitman (Chapter 5) presents a general description of a queuing model for information processing. She discusses how limitations in the rate at which information can be processed at one stage of the memory system can cause information from the preceding stages to pile up in a queue just prior to the stage at which the limitation occurs. Thus, some information is lost before it can be processed. Although Reitman illustrates the model by an examination of short-term memory, she also shows how the general arguments apply to all stages involved in the processing of the information in human memory.

Part II: Phoneme Storage and Word Recognition

These two papers present a detailed description of two different aspects of the way that meaningful verbal material is processed by the memory system. In the first paper (Chapter 6), George Sperling and Roseanne Speelman consider the way by which we might retain a short-term memory for items. They propose that the processing of verbal material, whether presented visually or acoustically, uses an auditory short-term memory that has a limited capacity measured in phonemes (or possibly a more basic linguistic unit). With this model, Sperling and Speelman discuss a number of phenomena, including why we can retain a longer string of letters that sound different from one another than of letters that sound similar.

In the other paper (Chapter 7), John Morton proposes a functional model for the recognition of words. This model includes sensory analysis systems, a cognitive system (equivalent to long-term memory) from which the effects of context exert their effect on recognition, and a response buffer in which a number of items are held to allow efficient programming of the mechanisms that are responsible for articulation of the spoken words. Evidence from both sensory sources and contextual sources is combined by the basic response unit which Morton terms a *logogen*. The temporal characteristics of the units accounts for the way that information from them is used in short-term memory paradigms. The auditory analysis system uses acoustic coding; the response buffer uses articulatory coding.

Part III: Memory for Associations

In the first paper of this Section (Chapter 8), James Greeno discusses the differences between the traditional theory for the formation of associative connections and an approach which he characterizes as the storage-retrieval theory. The storage-retrieval theory hypothesizes that in the memorization of a simple association there are two distinct operations that must be performed: storing the stimulus-response pair as a unit and learning to retrieve the stored memory structure. After some speculation on the possible mechanisms of storage and retrieval, Greeno examines the results of some paired-associate experiments by means of a two-stage Markov model. By proper interpretation of the psychological operations underlying the parameters of the model, especially the way in which individual parameters vary with changes in the experiment, it is possible to support the storage-retrieval model over the more traditional models.

In the next paper (Chapter 9), Bennet Murdock discusses a two-state Markov model of short-term memory for paired associates. The model postulates two opposing processes, forgetting and reminiscence, and two different states of memory, accessible and nonaccessible. To extend this model to confidence-rating data, Murdock considers the decision processes which might map the underlying states into the observed responses. The two states are represented as partially overlapping distributions which might be binomial, Poisson, or geometric exponential. These distributions are associated with encoding, storage, and retrieval processes, respectively. Finally, he suggests that the d' measure of signal detection theory may, in type II (recall) paradigms in short-term memory, be more a measure of discriminability than of trace strength.

Part IV: Mechanisms of Storage and Retrieval

The three chapters in this Section all discuss specific aspects of the mechanisms of memory. In the first chapter of the section (Chapter 10), Robert Bjork presents a discussion about the roles of rehearsal and repetition in short-term memory. Bjork discusses the general ways in which these operations have been represented (or might be represented) in theoretical models of memory. Then, by means of a critical evaluation of the experimental literature he attempts to see whether it is possible to choose among the various alternative theoretical representations of repetition and rehearsal.

In Chapter 11, Walter Kintsch both performs a critical review of the theoretical and empirical distinctions between retrieval of learned items by recognition and by recall and provides a basic framework for discussing the way in which material is organized within the memory system. In the process of the discussion, Kintsch proposes a two-process theory of recognition and recall and a marker model of long-term memory in which the organization of stored material is based upon semantic structures.

The nature of retrieval is considered by Richard Shiffrin in Chapter 12. He presents a general theory of retrieval as a recursive search. A search model is applied to data from a variety of free-recall paradigms, and tentative extensions are made to paired-associate paradigms and to a number of current memory variables of interest. Shiffrin demonstrates how forgetting can be predicted as a (perhaps) transient failure in the search, even though information may be stored permanently in long-term memory. Thus, this chapter provides a natural counterpart to Greeno's (Chapter 8), whereas Greeno proposes that improved performance results from "learning to retrieve," Shiffrin deals with forgetting as "failure to retrieve." Both Kintsch and Shiffrin analyze a good deal of the literature dealing with the clustering of material in subjects' responses and the effect of explicit categorization of the material that is to be learned on the subjects' performance. Both Kintsch and Shiffrin provide us with models of the organizational and retrieval processes, with Kintsch's chapter focusing on the organization of memory, and Shiffrin's chapter focusing on the process of retrieval.

Part V: Information Processing and Memory

In this final part of the book, Edward Feigenbaum (Chapter 13) and Walter Reitman (Chapter 14) provide critical discussions of the implications of general information processing considerations on human cognition in general and memory in specific. Feigenbaum describes some of the concepts of information processing that have come into psychology as a result of developments in computer hardware and languages. An illustration of the way that these concepts can be used for a description of processes involved in human learning and memory is provided by a brief description of the postulates and operation of a simulation model developed by Feigenbaum, called EPAM. He concludes with a discussion of structure of long-term memory and of the virtues of viewing the retrieval of information from memory as a problem solving process.

In the final chapter of the book, Walter Reitman reconsiders some current ideas about the aims and methods of research on memory. His discussion gains its perspective from studies of thinking, problem solving, and pattern recognition, especially those using information processing and computer-simulation concepts and techniques and it focuses upon relations between memory and other aspects of cognitive activity. Reitman suggests that memory is not easily segregated from other cognitive functions. Thus, models explaining memory behavior solely in terms of a small number of hypothetical memory processes are likely to be of limited value in the long run. Reitman proposes that we treat memory behavior as the product of an information processing network that utilizes complex strategy systems and substantial information structures. This metaphor suggests several research goals. We can study the strategy and rule systems subjects use in coping with memory tasks. We can seek to relate strategy learning and strategy choices to individual and task variables. We can try to find out how strategy systems are organized and built up from underlying basic processes.

Appendix: Serial Position Curves

Because so many of the papers in this book test the same set of serial position curves, the data from two of the most popular sets (the numbers have not been published before) are collected together in the Appendix of the book.

I

MEMORY SYSTEMS

2

A System for Perception and Memory[1]

Donald A. Norman
David E. Rumelhart
University of California, San Diego

There is a good deal of agreement about the nature of the psychological processes that transform a physical image into a meaningful psychological form. The basic picture assumed by a number of investigators contains separate mechanisms for sensation, perception, short- and long-term memory, and retrieval from memory.

First, a visual or auditory signal is transformed into a sensory representation by the appropriate sense organs. Then, a sensory storage system maintains an image of that signal for a short time after the physical signal ends. This sensory image reflects many of the characteristics of the physical signal although some transformations have presumably already taken place. If the signal was a printed or spoken word, we know that it is identified very rapidly. Our primary impression of a

[1] This research was supported by Grant NB07454 from the National Institute of Neurological Diseases, National Institutes of Health.

meaningful signal is of its meaning, rather than of its physical characteristics. There is a good deal of evidence that this identification has already been performed by the time the signal enters short-term memory, for the immediate memory of an item often is more related to its psychological encoding than to its actual, physical form. Thus, somewhere between the sensory storage system and short-term memory, the sensory image has its critical features analyzed, identified, and interpreted.

In addition to these steps of analysis, it is convenient to distinguish two different forms of memory: short- and long-term. Material in short-term memory decays rapidly so that it has essentially disappeared if eight or ten new items enter the memory after it or 10–20 seconds elapse. Material is more permanently stored in long-term memory, but the likelihood that an item in short-term memory will get into long-term memory depends upon the attention paid to the item and the types of operations performed on it.

The justification for this picture comes from a number of sources. Some of the arguments are presented in the other chapters of this book. Some come from the papers of Atkinson and Shiffrin (1968), Conrad (1963, 1964), Norman (1968, 1969), Sperling (1960), and Waugh and Norman (1965, 1968). Most of the arguments are reviewed and summarized in the books by Neisser (1967) and Norman (1969).

Many of the individual stages of this analysis process have been studied in detail. In fact, a number of different models of the individual stages now exist, with different models emphasizing different aspects of the information flow. In this chapter, we attempt to put together one consistent model of the entire process. Our goal is to emphasize the interaction of the stages, but to do this, we must make specific models of each individual process. As we worked out the details of the model, we discovered that many of the steps necessary for tying together the different pieces were never well specified by the existing models of the individual system. As we tried to put together the overall process, we discovered that our requirement of consistency forced us into some awkward situations. As a result, some of the parts of our system do not work as well as they ought to. The justification for our model, therefore, is that in addition to handling most data adequately, we describe the relationships necessary for one model to operate across the entire process. We are able to show how the various systems might interact: how perception affects memory, how context affects perception, and how perceptual and retrieval strategies affect performance.

The General System

The system can conveniently be separated into two sections: perception and memory. By perception, we include those processes involved in the initial transduction of the physical signal into some sensory image, the extraction of relevant features from the sensory image, and the identification of that list of features with a previously learned structure. By memory, we mean the processes that act to retain the material that was sent to it from the perceptual system.

Several different aspects of the memory system need to be distinguished from one another. First, we need to distinguish between short- and long-term traces. Second, we need to specify the mechanism that causes some material to be transferred from its temporary or short-term state into one that is more permanent or long-term. Third, we need to specify the retrieval cues that subjects use when trying to answer the questions about the material that the experimenter asks of them.

The flow of information within the system is illustrated in Fig. 1. In this section of the chapter, we describe the general characteristics of each of the individual processes. In the next section of the chapter,

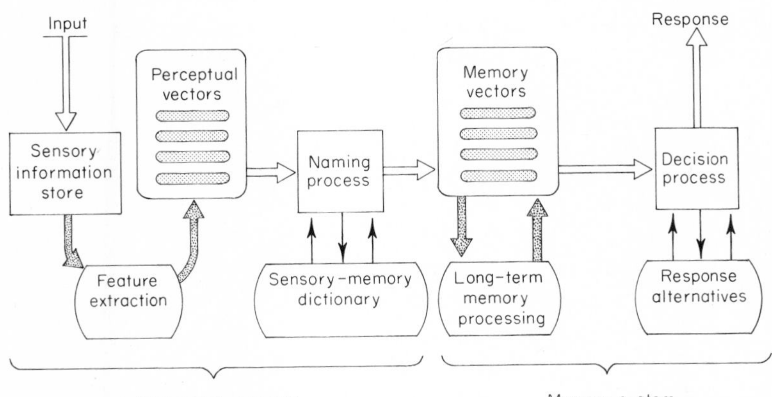

FIG. 1. Outline of the general system. Physical inputs are stored in their sensory form by the SIS while critical features are extracted from each item and placed in the appropriate perceptual vectors. The vectors of perceptual features are transformed into vectors of memory attributes by the naming system. The type of response is based on the question asked of the decision process, the set of possible response alternatives, and the attributes remaining in each memory vector, either temporarily (as STM attributes), or more permanently (as LTM attributes).

we derive the mathematical description of each process. In the last section of the chapter, we compare the predictions of the model with data from the experimental literature.

Perception

THE SENSORY IMAGE

The sensory system transforms the physical signal into a sensory image; this image resides temporarily in a sensory storage system, while the perceptual system attempts to extract sufficient characteristics from it that it can be identified unambiguously. We assume that the image resides in the sensory memory for the duration of the signal presentation, after which it decays exponentially. The need for a sensory memory has been well documented for visual processing and there is growing suspicion that it may be required for auditory processing as well.

We assume that we can represent information by means of a list of its features or attributes. That is, visual material might be represented by a list of its spatial properties, spoken speech by a list of its phonemes or distinctive features, and permanently stored material by a list of its relationships with other material. These lists are represented in the model as vectors, with the individual features or attributes comprising the elements of the vector.

FEATURE EXTRACTION

The problem of identifying the physical signal can be considered to be that of attaching a previously learned name to each particular acoustical or visual input. The simplest way of doing this is to use a dictionary that matches physical features with psychological names. We assume that the naming usually takes place in a rush, with the perception of the physical signal being incomplete and noisy, and with several things competing for attention simultaneously. The rate at which many people read, for example, far exceeds the rate that would be possible were every letter examined completely.

Requiring the naming system to use a dictionary based upon actual physical features would lead to extreme difficulties in pattern recognition (see Neisser, 1967, Chapter 3). It would seem more reasonable to suppose that a good deal of feature extraction precedes the dictionary match. In this chapter, we do not consider the details of the way by which features might be extracted from the incoming signals. Rather, we assume that some sort of stimulus-analyzing mechanism extracts generalized features and presents them to the naming system. This process continues either until the naming system manages to identify the signal unambiguously or until the image of the signal has disappeared from the sensory system. Thus, we can characterize the processing of incoming sensory information as something of a race between the amount of time that information is available in the sensory memory and the amount of time needed to acquire sufficient number of features so that the new material may be properly perceived and encoded.

So far, nothing much of what we have said is new. It all follows naturally from a standard information-processing approach to perception. The first new assumption concerns the way by which the system handles multiple inputs. We know that performance is degraded when too many items are presented simultaneously (or serially so rapidly that their processing overlaps). We represent this degradation by requiring the feature extraction mechanism to slow up as more signals arrive. Basically, we assume that the rate at which features are extracted from any signal depends inversely upon the total number of signals requiring processing at that moment. It is as if there were only one feature extraction mechanism that could find at the most ν features per second. If there were a total of L items present at once, the mechanism would have to divide its attention among all of them, so that each individual signal would have only an average of ν/L features extracted per second. (In general, we assume all items are attended to equally, with a correction for the clarity of the image, which will be discussed later.) This much of the system, a sensory memory and a feature extraction mechanism with a restriction on its processing rate, turns out to be sufficient to describe many aspects of perceptual experiments. Details and further justification of this part of the model may be found in Rumelhart (1970). Note that we are proposing a parallel extraction process, whereas many models now in the literature assume serial processes. There is reasonably strong evidence for parallel processes, however, one line simply being the fact that this model gives a good description of the data from the relevant experiments. In addition, Sperling (1967, p. 290, Fig. 3c and footnote 3) provides good evidence for a parallel process, as do Eriksen and Spencer (1969) and Wolford, Wessel, and Estes (1968).

NAMING

There are many possible mechanisms that might be used to match the features extracted by the perceptual system with those in the dictionary. Moreover, although it is clear that it should be possible to reduce the amount of the dictionary that needs to be examined by contextual or instructional cues, it is not clear which of the numerous possible schemes provide the best description of the actual process. In this paper we assume a simple matching scheme, first described by Bower in his multicomponent model of memory (Bower, 1967). Basically, we assume that the naming system matches the vector of features provided to it by the naming system with all of the relevant dictionary items. If one dictionary item matches more features correctly than all the others, then it is used to provide the name. If several dictionary items match the features equally well, then the strategy used depends upon whether the subject wishes to be conservative or liberal in his perceptions.

A conservative subject (the usual case) will refuse to make a choice any time the perception is ambiguous, thus leading to a failure of the naming system. The liberal subject (for example, one who is forced to make a response) will guess randomly among the several dictionary items that have the best match to the perceptual features. Failure to provide a name (in the conservative scheme) does not mean that the subject is unaware of the possible alternatives. It means that in these cases the response to the question "What was presented?" will be "I don't know." Misperception can be observed only with the liberal naming strategy.

Thus, perception of a physical input (of a given signal to noise ratio) can be enhanced in three ways. The first way is to increase the duration of the stimulus presentation. This gives the perceptual system more time to build up the features of the perceptual vector. A second way is to decrease the number of stimulus items being analyzed by the perceptual system at any moment. This increases the rate at which the perceptual vector is developed. The third way is to decrease the number of possible stimulus items that the subject expects to be presented to him. This decreases the number of features needed in the perceptual vector to distinguish unambiguously among the possible stimulus items.

This model of perception assumes that subjects are always aware of the stimulus alternatives which might be presented to them. This assumption need not pose any problem. In many experiments, subjects are explicitly told what the class of stimuli will be. In others, the restrictions are implicit in the nature of the task required of them. In experiments with grammatical material, for example, the syntax and semantics of English effectively restrict the number of possible words that could be present at any location in a sentence. Even where the stimulus alternatives can come from a set as large as the entire English vocabulary, no particular problem exists for the model. The model, however, will predict that the subject will require long, clear stimulus exposures before he is able to recognize a word which is ranked low in his expectations. None of these factors are inconsistent with the known facts of perception.

Memory

We represent the output of the naming dictionary as an ordered list of attributes. These attributes, formed into a memory vector, contain the name of the stimulus item. The first real difficulty comes in deciding exactly what these memory elements represent. Our first thoughts were to assume that the attributes contained the name of the item, and the more attributes that were retained, the better. Unfortunately, this simple idea does not work when we try to decide upon a set of decision rules for recognition and recall that can operate on the same memory elements. Kintsch, in Chapter 11, argues forcefully that an extremely critical distinction between recognition and recall methods of testing memory lies in their reliance on the organization imposed upon the items. A recognition test tends to be independent of the organization of memory, primarily because the to-be-remembered item is provided by the experimenter at the time of test. Recall, however, requires the subject to recreate the original item.

Our solution to the problem is to invoke an ill-defined concept: context. We assume, as do Kintsch and many others, that when we talk about meaningful material, the item that is to be remembered is already stored before the experiment begins. Thus, the information that is to be learned does not really concern the nature of the verbal material. Rather, it is the fact that this particular item was presented within the context of the experiment that must be retained. Thus, we suggest that the primary items of interest in the memory store are the contextual cues: a slightly different cue for each different item that is presented. We do not know just what this contextual cue is, but it clearly is an essential component of the retrieval process. Similar concepts are in-

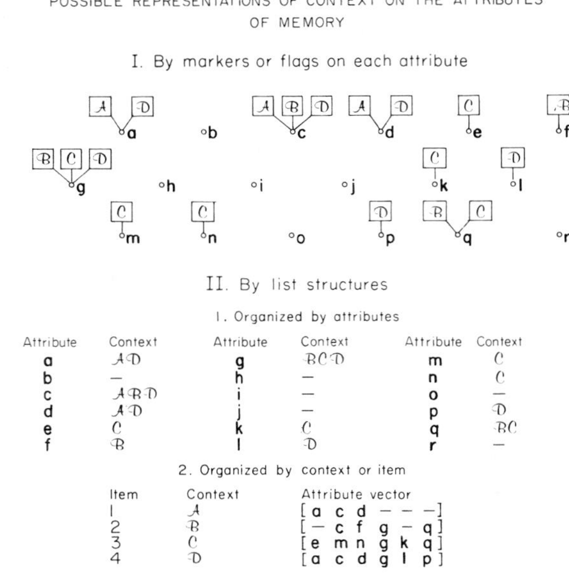

Attribute	Context	Attribute	Context	Attribute	Context
a	AD	g	BCD	m	C
b	—	h	—	n	C
c	ABD	i	—	o	—
d	AD	j	—	p	D
e	C	k	C	q	BC
f	B	l	D	r	—

Item	Context	Attribute vector
1	A	[a c d — — —]
2	B	[— c f g — q]
3	C	[e m n g k q]
4	D	[a c d g l p]

FIG. 2. Amplification of the way that contextual cues are associated with memory attributes.

troduced by Kintsch in Chapter 11 and by Shiffrin in Chapter 12 with his specification of the proper "search set."

We represent the storage of material by assuming that each possible individual attribute of a memory vector has one specific representation in storage. Any vector that contains this attribute must refer to the same representation. The attributes themselves need not be entered into storage, for they are already there. Rather, each attribute has attached to it information about the contexts in which it has occurred (see Fig. 2). (In this figure, lower case boldface letters, **a-r**, represent attributes, while upper case script letters, $\mathscr{A}$–$\mathscr{D}$, represent context.)

When a subject is asked to recall material, he does so by going to the information about the context in which the attributes were originally stored. He then tries to retrieve all the individual attributes. If the link between any attribute and its context is missing, then, for the purposes of the memory system, that attribute is missing. Then, from all those attributes the subject has been able to recover with the contextual cues, he tries to recreate what the item must have been.

When the subject is asked whether he recognizes an item, he does so by checking its attributes with their representatives in storage. Only if an attribute contains the proper contextual information will he say that he remembers it. If a sufficient number of attributes contain the proper contextual material, the subject responds that he recognized the item.

Note that by this scheme of memory, we do not actually store the items that are presented to us. Rather, we store information about the context in which the attributes have appeared. In recall, we assume that we are given the contextual information, and we use that to try to recreate the individual attributes. In recognition, we are given the attributes, and we try to recover the contextual information. We talk as if we store, remember, and retrieve individual attributes. Actually, we operate only on their links and associations.

RECOGNITION

In a recognition experiment, the subject is given a test item and asked to state whether it is *old* or *new*. We assume that he does this by checking the context associated with each attribute of the test item. The task is illustrated in Fig. 2, where we present the test item consisting of the context $\mathscr{D}$ and the attributes **a**, **c**, **d**, **g**, **l**, and **p**. Could these attributes have been presented earlier under context $\mathscr{A}$, $\mathscr{B}$, or $\mathscr{C}$? We see that three attributes of the test item are consistent with context $\mathscr{A}$, two with $\mathscr{B}$, one with $\mathscr{C}$, and (obviously), all 6 with the test item context, $\mathscr{D}$. The test item could not have belonged to either context $\mathscr{B}$ or $\mathscr{C}$, however, because these contexts are also associated with attributes outside of (and therefore inconsistent with) the test item. The question for the subject then reduces to this: Could the test item be represented by $\mathscr{A}$?

We assume that the subject answers *Yes* if a sufficient number of attributes in the test item can be matched with a consistent context. Note, that if this critical number is three or less, the subject will answer *Yes* in the example shown in Fig. 2. It is quite possible, of course, that the test item had not been presented, so that the *Yes* response is incorrect. It is also possible that the test item $\mathscr{D}$, was actually presented, but as $\mathscr{F}$, not $\mathscr{A}$. In this case, the *Yes* response, although correct, would be given for the wrong reason.

The probability of making a false recognition is the probability that c or more attributes of the test item match one of the memory vectors for an item that was actually presented. The probability of responding *Yes* correctly is given by the probability that either c or more attributes of the correct memory vector are remembered or, failing that, that c or more attributes of one of the other vectors exactly match the test item.

RECALL

When we wish the subject to recall an item, we provide a cue or the context and ask him to provide the item that belongs in that context. Normally, we suppose that subjects do not recall an item unless it can be identified unambiguously.

Consider, as an example, that we provide the subject with context $\mathscr{A}$ (see Fig. 2). From $\mathscr{A}$, he can recover the attributes **a**, **c**, and **d**. Before these attributes can be used to generate a response, however, they must be completed to give the entire memory vector. This is done by entering the three retained attributes into the dictionary of possible responses to see if they uniquely identify the item. If so, the proper response can be given; if not, the subject has the choice of either remaining quiet or of guessing among the several possible memory vectors that contain the attributes **a**, **c**, and **d**. If the list of vectors is taken to be the dictionary (for illustrative purposes), the subject could not tell whether the attributes of $\mathscr{A}$ belong to item 1 or 4.

This scheme for both recognition and recall assumes several things about memory. For one, it is necessary to have a content-addressable storage system. That is, given a list of attributes, we can find them in storage without requiring any lengthy search process. Similarly, we can go to the contextual material when necessary. In the experiments discussed here, we assume that the contextual material is always available and is always found; hence, the model does not discuss any of the problems that might be encountered were this not the case.

SHORT- AND LONG-TERM MEMORY

An item enters short-term memory from the perceptual system (actually, from the naming process) as a vector of attributes. As more items enter short-term memory, some of the attributes of the vector are lost or degraded in quality, and, therefore, cannot always be retrieved. (It is important to remember that when we speak of storing or losing an attribute, we are actually referring to the storage and loss of a connection between an attribute and its context. Throughout this paper, the first statement is used as an abbreviation for the second.)

The development of the long-term memory trace is assumed to proceed in a fashion very similar to the development of the perceptual vector. We assume that long-term memory differs from short-term memory primarily in the permanence with which the contextual information is attached to the individual attributes. In addition, it is likely that the contextual information is more complete in its references to and organization of related material, but although these factors are often very important, we will not consider them further here.

There are several ways in which long-term processes might operate on the individual attributes of the memory vector. Part of the problem of dealing with the permanent build-up of the memory trace is that the process can be changed by the strategies used by the subject. For example, it is quite possible that the subject might rehearse only one particular item which has been presented to him, ignoring all the others. In this case, the model ought to show how this one item receives a rather large increment in long-term strength, while all other items receive very little or none. For the present purposes, however, we assume that each item receives roughly equal treatment by the subject. This long-term memory model will not be appropriate for situations in which subjects systematically deviate from an equal treatment strategy. We ignore completely categorization and mnemonics, even though these play a major role in long-term memory. These situations will require specific models.

In general, however, we assume that information about attributes has a chance of becoming stored permanently only while that attribute still resides in short-term storage. When information is retrieved, all that matters is the number of attributes that are still retained: no distinction is made between short- and long-term storage. In the typical experiment on memory, when material is retrieved, some of the attributes may be stored only temporarily and some permanently. We assume the subject uses all the information available to him to piece together as accurate a reconstruction of the original item as is possible. Note that with this scheme, the likelihood that the attributes of an item will become stored permanently depend, in part, upon how long the item has resided in short-term memory. Thus, both the parameters of short-term memory and the temporal course of the experiment affect long-term memory.

History

Much of what we present here borrows heavily from the work of our predecessors. One basic feature of this system is a representation of the various physiological images by means of vectors with many components. This representation was originally introduced by Bower (1967) and his work plays a crucial role in the development of the entire system. The description of the perceptual stage—the manner by which the initial perceptual vector is formed—is new: It is described in more detail by Rumelhart (1970). The description of the short-term memory process can be considered to be a combination of the multicomponent model of Bower and the memory trace strength model of Wickelgren and Norman (1966). The descriptions of the control and decision systems that are involved both in transferring material from the perceptual to the short-term memory stage and from the short-term to long-term memory stage and also in determining subjects' responses borrows heavily from all of the sources mentioned, as well as from the work of Atkinson and Shiffrin (1968). Thus, although we do introduce a number of new concepts here, the important aspect of this model is the way we have been able to incorporate descriptions of several different stages of information processing into one overall system.

The Formal Model[2]

Perception

The first problem is to get information from the physical stimulus into some form that can be interpreted by the naming system. We assume that at the onset of physical stimulation a representation of the physical stimulus is registered in a sensory information store (SIS). The information in the store starts to decay as soon as the physical stimulus is turned off. Whenever information is available in the SIS, a pattern recognizer extracts information from the image in an attempt to construct the perceptual vector. The rate at which this extraction occurs is determined by the clarity of the stored information and by how much is stored. Hence, as the image becomes degraded the rate of information extraction by the pattern recognizer slows down. The naming process takes over when enough features have been extracted from the perceptual image to specify the stimulus uniquely or after the information in the SIS has decayed away.

[2] This section has been organized so that the reader who does not wish to follow the mathematical arguments can simply skim them, concentrating his effort on the prose sections.

These assumptions can be stated more explicitly as follows:

P1. At the onset of physical stimulation, a sensory representation of the signal enters the SIS.

P2. When the signal is turned off, the information in the SIS fades away exponentially with time constant μ (seconds).

P3. We represent the perceptual image by a vector of N_P features. During each small unit of time Δt, it is assumed that one feature of the signal is extracted with probability $\Delta p(t)$, where

$$\lim_{\Delta t \to 0} \frac{\Delta p(t)}{\Delta t} = \nu(t) = \begin{cases} 0 & t \leqslant 0 \\ \nu & 0 < t \leqslant T \\ \nu e^{-(t-T)/\mu} & T < t \end{cases} \tag{1}$$

and T is the duration of the signal.

From these assumptions, we can calculate the probability that exactly i features have been extracted by time t. Denote this probability $P[N(t) = i]$, where $N(t)$ is the number of features discovered (or counted) by time t. It follows that the counting process $\{N(t),\ t \geqslant 0\}$ is a truncated nonhomogeneous Poisson process with intensity function $\nu(t)$ (Rumelhart, 1970). It is easy to show that for a truncated Poisson process

$$P[N(t) = i] = \begin{cases} e^{-m(t)} \dfrac{\{m(t)\}^i}{i!} & i < N_P \\ \displaystyle\sum_{j=N_P}^{\infty} e^{-m(t)} \dfrac{\{m(t)\}^j}{j!} & i = N_P \end{cases} \tag{2}$$

where $m(t)$, the mean number of features extracted by time t, is given by

$$m(t) = \int_0^t \nu(t)\ dt = \begin{cases} \nu T & t \leqslant T \\ \nu\{T + \mu[1 - e^{-(t-T)/\mu}]\} & T < t. \end{cases}$$

Furthermore, if we take the limit as $t \to \infty$, we get the distribution of the number of features that can be extracted from a single T second signal exposure:

$$\lim_{t \to \infty} P[N(t) = i] = P[N = i] = \begin{cases} e^{-m} \dfrac{m^i}{i!} & i < N_P \\ \displaystyle\sum_{j=N_P}^{\infty} e^{-m} \dfrac{m^j}{j!} & i = N_P \end{cases} \tag{3}$$

where

$$m = \int_0^{\infty} \nu(t)\ dt = \nu(T + \mu).$$

These calculations have been done for the case where a single item is presented and the subject is given unlimited time to attempt to identify it. In most experimental situations, however, the situation is not that simple. Often, items are presented simultaneously (as in the visual case), or at least serially at a rapid rate. When this occurs, the subject must select some strategy of dividing his attention among the various items that he is attempting to process. The next two sections deal with this problem. First, we consider the case of simultaneous or parallel input.

SIMULTANEOUS PRESENTATION

Simultaneous input of several different items occurs most often with visual presentation. The problem we face here is to decide how the feature extraction mechanism divides its attention among the several signals present in the SIS. With simultaneous presentation, we simply assume that the attention is divided equally among the L stimulus items. Thus, the probability of attending to the kth item, θ_k, is simply $1/L$.

Before proceeding with the model it is useful to introduce the concept of an input channel. An independent input channel refers to the particular set of physical features of the stimulus ensemble such as spatial position, in the case of vision, or frequency range, in the case of audition, which allows us to separate the items of interest. For example, in the tachistoscopic experiments of Sperling (1960), because the subjects were aware of the positions in which each stimulus item might be presented, each position represented an independent input channel.

We now calculate the probability that we get i or more counts in the kth channel, by time t. To do this, define a counting function $N_k(t)$ which gives the number of features extracted in the interval 0 to t. It is well known that a Poisson process with intensity ν, in which each event is recorded with probability p, leads to a Poisson process with intensity parameter νp (cf. Parzen, 1962, pp. 47–48). A similar result obtains for a nonhomogeneous Poisson process, even when the attention parameter (θ_k in this case) depends on time (Rumelhart, 1970). That is, the probability that i or more attributes have been extracted from input channel k by time t is given by a nonhomogeneous Poisson process with intensity function

$$\nu_k(t) = \theta_k\, \nu(t)$$

with the mean value function m_k given by

$$m_k = \int_0^\infty \nu_k(t)dt = \frac{\nu(T+\mu)}{L}. \tag{4}$$

Thus,

$$P[N_k \geqslant i] = \sum_{j=i}^{\infty} e^{-m_k} \frac{\{m_k\}^j}{j!} \qquad i \leqslant N_P \tag{5}$$

and zero elsewhere.

In a partial report experiment, at some time t_c after the stimulus presentation, the subject receives a cue instructing him to report on only a subset of the items (channels). We assume that as soon as he receives the instruction, the subject is able to assign all of his attention to the cued subset of channels. In terms of the attention function θ_k, if S of the L channels are cued at time t_c,

$$\theta_k(t) = \begin{cases} 1/L & t \leqslant t_c \\ 1/S & t_c < t. \end{cases}$$

Thus, the mean value function for the partial report situation can be written

$$m_k = \int_0^\infty \theta_k(t)\nu(t)\, dt$$

$$= \begin{cases} (\nu/L)t_c + (\nu/S)[(T-t_c)+\mu] & t_c \leqslant T \\ (\nu/L)\{T+\mu[1-e^{-(t_c-T)/\mu}]\} + (\nu/S)\mu e^{-(t_c-T)/\mu} & T < t_c. \end{cases} \tag{6}$$

SEQUENTIAL PRESENTATION

Sequential presentation is the natural procedure with auditory stimuli. The problem for the perceptual theory is to decide how a subject should divide his attention between the information remaining in the SIS from previous presentations and the information about the item which is currently being presented. The assumption adopted here is that the subject attends to an input proportionally to the relative clarity of its representation in the SIS.

Let there be L different stimulus items, with the kth item presented at time t_k for duration T_k. From assumptions P1 and P2, the clarity of the kth item is proportional to unity while it is being presented and proportional to $\exp[-(t-t_k-T_k)/\mu]$ thereafter. Thus, the attention parameter, $\theta_k(t)$, becomes

$$\theta_k(t) = \begin{cases} 0 & t \leqslant t_k \\ \dfrac{1}{1 + \sum_{i=1}^{c(t)-1} e^{-(t-t_i-T_i)/\mu}} & t_k < t \leqslant t_k + T_k \\ \dfrac{e^{-(t-t_k-T_k)/\mu}}{\sum_{i=1}^{c(t)} e^{-(t-t_i-T_i)/\mu}} & t_k + T_k < t, \end{cases} \tag{7}$$

where $c(t) = k$ for $t_k < t \leqslant t_{k+1}$. (Note that for simultaneous presentation all the t_i's $= t_k$ and all the T_i's $= T_k$, leading to $\theta_k(t) = 1/L$, as assumed in the previous section.)

We can now write the intensity function for the truncated nonhomogeneous Poisson process which counts the number of features discovered from the kth item in the list, $\nu_k(t)$:

$$\nu_k(t) = \begin{cases} 0 & t \leqslant t_k \\ \theta_k(t)\nu & t_k < t \leqslant t_k + T_k \\ \theta_k(t)\nu e^{-(t-t_k-T_k)/\mu} & t_k + T_k < t. \end{cases} \tag{8}$$

The probability that exactly i features are extracted from the kth item is thus given by (3), where

$$m_k = \int_0^\infty \nu_k(t)\ dt, \tag{9}$$

and $\nu_k(t)$ is given by (8).

FIXED RATE OF PRESENTATIONS

In the normal experiment, items are presented at a fixed rate. In this case, $t_k = (k - 1)R$, where R is the interitem time in seconds. For slow presentations or long stimulus durations the perceptual system will perform without error and, therefore, we can simply bypass the computations entirely. With short durations of the stimulus, we can write explicitly the solution to (9) if we allow each of the T_k's to approach 0. In this case,

$$m_k = \int_{t_k}^\infty \frac{e^{-(t-t_k)/\mu}}{\sum_{j=1}^{c(t)} e^{-(t-t_j)/\mu}} \nu e^{-(t-t_k)/\mu}\ dt. \tag{10}$$

This reduces to

$$m_k = \nu(e^{R/\mu} - 1)e^{2(k-1)R/\mu} \int_{(k-1)R}^{\infty} \frac{e^{-t/\mu}}{e^{c(t)R/\mu} - 1}\, dt.$$

If we approximate the discrete function $c(t)$ by the continuous function $c(t) = 1 + t/R$, $0 \leqslant t \leqslant t_L$, and L thereafter:

$$m_k = \mu\nu e^{2kR/\mu}(1 - e^{-R/\mu})\{[e^{-LR/\mu}/(e^{LR/\mu} - 1)] - e^{-kR/\mu} + e^{-LR/\mu} + \ln[(1 - e^{-LR/\mu})/(1 - e^{-kR/\mu})]\}. \qquad (11)$$

THE NAMING PROCESS

The job of the naming process is to transform the set of features extracted by the perceptual mechanism into a form meaningful to the memory system. This task is accomplished by matching, as best it can, the perceptual features extracted by the pattern recognizer against the features belonging to each of the set of possible stimuli it has been told to expect. Thus, the naming system incorporates a dictionary that gives the rules for transforming each particular perceptual vector into its corresponding memory vector. In general, the perceptual vector is far from complete, and there is considerable overlap among the set of stimuli that are expected. If the features present in the perceptual vector match unambiguously with only one dictionary vector, there is no problem in determining the proper name. However, if several dictionary vectors match the perceptual vector equally well, the subject has a choice of strategies to follow. In the *conservative naming strategy*, we assume that the perceptual vector can be named if and only if it matches exactly one dictionary vector. In the *liberal naming strategy* we assume that whenever several dictionary vectors match the perceptual vector equally well, the subject chooses randomly among those alternatives.

THE CONSERVATIVE NAMING STRATEGY

This assumption implies that when the stimulus presented is among the set of expected stimuli, the subject will either name the item correctly or will send notice to the memory system that an uninterpretable vector has been received.

Let the number of possible dictionary alternatives be denoted by A. Then the probability of a correct name is simply the probability that none of the A − 1 incorrect dictionary alternatives match the perceptual vector on as many features as the correct one. In order to compute these probabilities, we need to have some measure of stimulus overlap. The more similar the perceptual representations of the stimulus items the more features they have in common. Let the probability that any given feature is shared by any two stimulus items be σ_p. Thus, when $\sigma_p = 1$, the two perceptual vectors are identical; when $\sigma_p = 0$, there is no overlap among the items and, hence, no confusion can occur.

Now, consider the item entering the naming system through the kth input channel. If exactly i of the N_p features have been extracted, the perceptual vector matches the vector corresponding to the correct item in all i places. The system will thus name correctly if none of the other $A - 1$ vectors matches all i features of the perceptual vector. An incorrect item can have i matches only if the features of this (distractor) item happen to match the features of the correct item in exactly those i places: the probability that this can happen is $\sigma_p{}^i$. Thus, the probability that none of the $A - 1$ alternatives have as many as i matches is $(1 - \sigma_p{}^i)^{A-1}$. As in the preceding section, let N_k be the number of features extracted from the kth input channel; then, the probability that the kth item is correctly named, Π_k, is given by

$$\Pi_k = \sum_{i=1}^{N_p} (1 - \sigma_p{}^i)^{A-1} P[N_k = i], \tag{12}$$

where $P[N_k = i]$ is given by Eqs. 3 and 6 for parallel input and by Eqs. 3 and 8 for serial input.

Under certain conditions (12) can be nicely reduced. First consider the term $(1 - \sigma_p{}^i)^{A-1}$. In many conditions, A is reasonably large; in this case we notice that

$$\lim_{A\to\infty} (1 - \sigma_p{}^i)^{A-1} = \lim_{A\to\infty} \left[1 - \frac{(A-1)\,\sigma_p{}^i}{A-1}\right]^{A-1} = e^{-(A-1)\sigma_p{}^i},$$

if $\sigma_p{}^i \to 0$ in such a way that $(A - 1)\sigma_p{}^i$ is constant (for fixed i). This approximation works well for values of A as small as 8 or 10. Thus, (12) can be rewritten as

$$\Pi_k \approx \sum_{i=1}^{N_p} e^{-(A-1)\sigma_p{}^i}\, P[N_k = i]. \tag{13}$$

It is useful now to look at the function $\exp[-(A - 1)\sigma_p{}^i]$ as a function of A, σ_p and i (Fig. 3). Note how sharply it varies with i, especially for smaller values of σ_p. It is almost a step function, suggesting a further approximation to (13). We let $\Pi_k = 0$ for all values of i less than some critical number c_p and let $\Pi_k = 1$ or all values of i greater than or equal

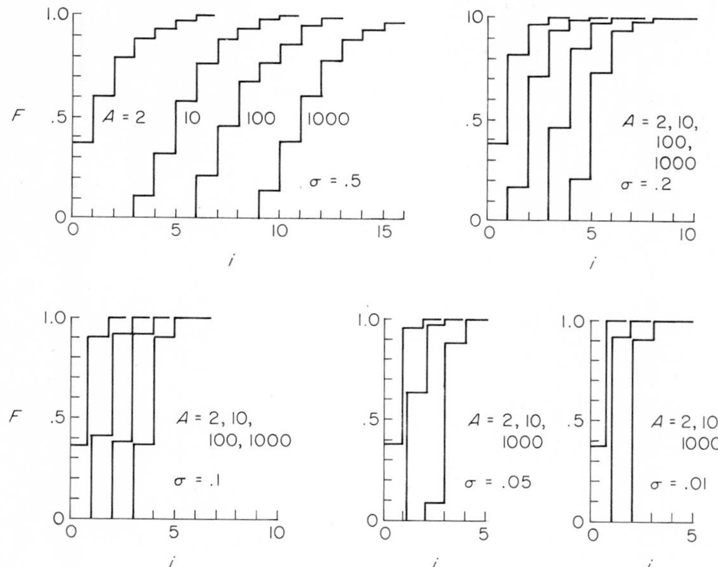

FIG. 3. The function $F = e^{-(A-1)}\ \sigma^i$ vs. i. For small values of σ and reasonable values of A, F can be approximated by a step function.

to c_p. That is,

$$\Pi_k \approx \sum_{i=c_p}^{N_p} P[N_k = i]. \tag{14}$$

We let c_p be that integer just larger than the point of maximum acceleration on the curves in Fig. 3. This value may readily be obtained from the second derivative of $\exp[-(A-1)\sigma_p{}^i]$ with respect to i. We find that

$$c_p = [\ln(A-1)/-\ln \sigma_p], \tag{15}$$

where $[x]$ denotes the next integer greater or equal to x. Table 1 compares value of Π_k given by (14) to those given by (12) for various values of σ_p, A, and m_k (the Poisson rate parameter for the distribution of N_k). This Table confirms our expectation that for fairly small values of σ_p the approximation is valid.[3]

[3] The accuracy of the approximation shown in Table 1 (and Table 2) applies only when the term within the brackets of Eq. 15 is close to an integral value. Otherwise, the approximation suffers from the need to use an integral value for c_p. One way of overcoming this difficulty is to approximate the Poisson distribution for $P[N_k = i]$ with a gamma distribution, allowing the summation of Eq. 14 to be replaced with an integral and allowing c_p to take on the exact (real) solution to Eq. 15.

TABLE 1
Conservative Naming: A Comparison of the Conservative Strategy with the Criterion Approximation

				Probability of a correct response	
A	σ_p	Criterion	m_k	Conservative strategy	Criterion approximation
100	.03	2	1.0	.27	.26
			2.0	.58	.59
			3.0	.79	.80
	.14	3	2.0	.31	.32
			3.0	.55	.58
			4.0	.73	.76
	.48	7	5.0	.22	.24
			7.0	.48	.55
			9.0	.71	.79
10	.001	1	1.0	.63	.63
			2.0	.86	.86
			3.0	.95	.95
	.18	2	1.0	.27	.26
			2.0	.55	.59
			3.0	.75	.80
	.51	4	3.0	.31	.35
			4.0	.47	.57
			5.0	.61	.73
4	.03	1	0.5	.37	.39
			1.0	.60	.63
			1.5	.75	.78
	.43	2	1.0	.23	.26
			2.0	.47	.59
			3.0	.65	.80

THE LIBERAL NAMING STRATEGY

In some experiments, the subject may always be required to respond, even if he must guess. In this case, the liberal naming strategy seems appropriate. We assume that the subject guesses by selecting the name randomly from among the h response alternatives that exactly match whatever features he has in the perceptual vector. (In the conservative strategy, we assume that he chooses a name if and only if $h = 1$.) Under this procedure, there will be false naming. If j of the $A - 1$ incorrect dictionary items (distractor items) match on all N_k of the features extracted from the kth input channel, then the guess is correct with probability $1/(j + 1)$. Thus, the probability that the kth item is correctly named, Π_k, is given by

$$\Pi_k = \sum_{i=0}^{N_P} \sum_{j=0}^{A-1} \frac{1}{j+1} \binom{A-1}{j} [\sigma_p{}^i]^j [1 - \sigma_p{}^i]^{A-1-j} P[N_k = i]$$

$$= \sum_{i=0}^{N_P} \frac{1 - (1 - \sigma_p{}^i)^A}{A\, \sigma_p{}^i} P[N_k = i]. \qquad (16)$$

As before, $P[N_k = i]$ is given by (3) and (6) for parallel input and (3) and (8) for serial input.

It turns out that the same approximation used for conservative naming can be applied to liberal naming. That is, we can approximate Eq. (16) by Eq. 14. This is true because the expression $[1 - (1 - \sigma_p{}^i)^A]/A\sigma_p{}^i$ looks very similar to the function plotted in Fig. 3, except for a slight displacement to the left for larger values of σ_p and, except for the fact that its minimum value (when $i = 0$) is $1/A$, rather than $\exp[-(A - 1)]$. For small values of A, a useful approximation for the liberal model is

$$\Pi_k \approx P_k + (1 - P_k)/A, \qquad (17)$$

where P_k is the approximation of Eq. (14). This is illustrated in Table 2.[4] This, of course, is the standard (threshold) guessing model.

TABLE 2
Comparison of Liberal and Conservative Strategies with Their Approximations[a]

	Probability of correct response			
	Conservative		Liberal	
m_k	True values	Criterion approximation	True values	Criterion approximation
.05	.05	.05	.17	.17
.1	.09	.10	.21	.21
.2	.17	.18	.28	.28
.6	.43	.45	.51	.52
.8	.53	.53	.59	.61
1.4	.73	.75	.77	.78

[a] For $A = 8$, $\sigma_p = .01$, Criterion = 1.

[4] This approximation suffers when the term within brackets of Eq. (15) is not near an integral value. See footnote 3, p. 37.

Memory

New items are presented to the memory system by the naming process, sequentially in lists of length L with each item containing N_m attributes. With probability Π_k the item presented to memory has been correctly named. There is usually considerable overlap among attributes of the various items under consideration. We let the probability that an attribute of the memory vector of one item also occurs in a second item be σ_m.

Most of the difficulties presented by the analyses of memory come from the response strategies. The details of the growth and decay of the memory traces are relatively straightforward, although in some cases, they do not lead to simple solutions. We suppose that the operation of the memory system is analogous to that of the perceptual system. That is, after the naming system places a memory vector into the short-term store (STM), the relationships between the attributes of the STM vector and their contexts are extracted and made more permanent by long-term mechanisms that operate in a manner completely analogous to the pattern recognition system. Thus, the rate at which the relationships between attributes and context of a particular STM vector can be made permanent depends upon both the clarity of the STM image and the total number of attributes that are being operated on.

In the perceptual system, it was natural to assume that information in the sensory storage system decayed as a function of time. In short-term memory, however, the choice is not made so readily. Although it is clear that some type of decay is necessary in STM, there is disagreement in the literature over the nature of the decay: does it result from the passage of time or do items presently in STM decay only when new items are entered into the system? It turns out to be more natural to do our computations in the framework of a STM image that decays in time. However, even though our derivations for the memory system will use the assumption of time decay, it is a simple matter to convert the results to an item-dependent decay. Because of the ease with which both assumptions can be followed, we state the results for both here, allowing the final choice to be made by a consideration of the data. Note, however, that even if the assumption of time-dependent decay is not made, time plays important roles in both perception and the transfer of material from STM to longer-term storage. Thus, even in experiments dealing primarily with STM, factors such as rate of presentation will play important roles, regardless of which assumption about STM decay is used.

TIME-DEPENDENT DECAY

The assumptions can be stated more explicitly as follows:

M1. When an item is interpreted by the naming system a psychological representation of that item (the memory vector), is stored in STM.

M2. Following entrance of an item into STM the clarity of the attributes decay exponentially with time constant γ (seconds). The probability that an attribute can be recognized at any given time is assumed to be proportional to the clarity of that attribute.

M3. The instantaneous rate at which attributes of the kth item are transferred to LTM, $\lambda_k(t)$, is assumed to be proportional to the clarity of the information held in STM about that item and the amount of attention allotted to that item. That is, we assume that attributes are transferred to LTM at a Poisson rate with intensity function

$$\lambda_k(t) = \lambda\theta_k(t)e^{-t/\gamma}, \tag{18}$$

where $\theta_k(t)$ is the proportion of total attention allotted to item k at time t and λ (without subscripts) is the basic rate parameter that would apply if there were only one item to be transferred.

Suppose that the kth item of the list of L entered STM at time t_k. We want to know how many attributes of item k are recognizable in STM at time t. Denote this number $N_S(t,t_k)$. From assumption M2, we know that the probability that any given attribute is recognizable at time t is $\exp[-(t - t_k)/\gamma]$. Thus, the probability that exactly j are recognizable at time t, $P[N_S(t,t_k) = j]$, is given by the binomial probability law with parameters N_m and $\exp[-(t - t_k)/\gamma]$,

$$P[N_S(t,t_k) = j] = \binom{N_m}{j}\left[e^{-(t-t_k)/\gamma}\right]^j\left[1 - e^{-(t-t_k)/\gamma}\right]^{N_m-j} \quad t \geqslant t_k. \tag{19}$$

Before we can write the total number of attributes retained we must consider those in LTM as well. Let $N_L(t,t_k)$ be the number of attributes of the kth item transferred from STM to LTM during the time interval t_k to t. Then the counting process $\{N_L(t,t_k),\ t \geqslant t_k\}$ is a truncated nonhomogeneous Poisson process with intensity function $\lambda_k(t)$ given by (18).

The problem at this point is to decide how the subject allots his attention to the various items in memory. We assume here, as in perception, that he works on each item in proportion to the relative clarity of its representation in STM. Thus,

$$\theta_k(t) = e^{-(t-t_k)/\gamma} \Big/ \left[\sum_{j=1}^{c(t)} e^{-(t-t_j)/\gamma} \right], \tag{20}$$

where $c(t) = k$ for $t_k \leqslant t < t_{k+1}$. We write the mean value function $m_k(t)$ as

$$m_k(t) = \int_{t_k}^{t} \lambda_k(t)\ dt. \tag{21}$$

Thus, the probability that j or more features from item k have been transferred into LTM by time t, $P[N_L(t,t_k) \geqslant j] = \sum_{i=j}^{\infty} e^{-m_k(t)} \frac{\{m_k(t)\}^i}{i!}$.

We are now ready to calculate the distribution that we really want, namely, the distribution of the number of attributes retained in either LTM or STM at time t. It is useful to define $N_{SO}(t,t_k)$ as the number of attributes recognizable from STM but *not* LTM for the kth item at time t. Then

$$P\{N_L(t,t_k) = i,\ N_{SO}(t,t_k) = j\} = \begin{cases} e^{-m_k(t)} \dfrac{\{m_k(t)\}^i}{i!} \dbinom{N_m - i}{j} [e^{-(t-t_k)/\gamma}]^j & \\ \quad \times [1 - e^{-(t-t_k)/\gamma}]^{N_m - i - j} & i < N_m \\ \displaystyle\sum_{i=N}^{\infty} e^{-m_k(t)} \frac{\{m_k(t)\}^i}{i!} & i = N_m. \end{cases} \tag{22}$$

Now let $N_{SL}(t,t_k)$ be the number of attributes retained by *either* STM or LTM

$$P\{N_{SL}(t,t_k) = l\} = \sum_{\substack{i,j \\ i+j=l}} P\{N_L(t,t_k) = i,\ N_{SO}(t,t_k) = j\}$$

and the moment generating function of $\{N_{SL}(t,t_k),\ t - t_k \geqslant 0\}$, $M_k(\Theta)$, is

$$M_k(\Theta) = \sum_{i=0}^{N_m} \sum_{j=0}^{N_m - i} e^{(i+j)\Theta} P\{N_L(t,t_k) = i,\ N_{SO}(t,t_k) = j\}.$$

Carrying out the summation leads to

$$M_k(\Theta) = [1 + e^{(t-t_k)/\gamma}(e^{\Theta} - 1)]^{N_m}\ e^{-m_k(t)}$$

$$\sum_{i=0}^{N_m - 1} \frac{\{m_k(t) e^{\Theta} [1 + e^{-(t-t_k)/\gamma}(e^{\Theta} - 1)]^{-1}\}^i}{i!} + e^{N_m \Theta} \sum_{i=N_m}^{\infty} \frac{\{m_k(t)\}^i}{i!}.$$

When $m_k(t)$ is small relative to N_m the second term becomes negligible and the upper limit on the summation in the first term can be extended to ∞; then

$$M_k(\Theta) \approx [1 + e^{-(t-t_k)/\gamma}(e^{\Theta} - 1)]^{N_m} e^{m_k(t)} \{e^{\Theta}[1 + e^{-(t-t_k)/\gamma}(e^{\Theta} - 1)]^{-1} - 1\}. \quad (23)$$

Thus, the expected value and variance of $N_{SL}(t,t_k)$ are

$$E[N_{SL}(t,t_k)] \approx N_m e^{-(t-t_k)/\gamma} + m_k(t)\ [1 - e^{-(t-t_k)/\gamma}] \quad (24)$$

and

$$\mathrm{Var}[N_{SL}(t,t_k)] \approx N_m e^{-(t-t_k)/\gamma}\ [1 - e^{-(t-t_k)/\gamma}] + m_k(t)[1 - e^{-(t-t_k)/\gamma}][1 - 2e^{-(t-t_k)/\gamma}]. \quad (25)$$

If we let N_m get large as γ goes to zero such that $N_m \exp[-(t - t_k)/\gamma]$ is constant (for fixed t), then (23) reduces to the moment generating function of a Poisson:

$$M_k(\Theta) \approx e^{[m_k(t)+N_m e-(t-t_k)/\gamma][e^{\Theta}_m-1]} \quad (26)$$

with a mean of

$$m_k(t) + N_m e^{-(t-t_k)/\gamma}. \quad (27)$$

Thus, $N_{SL}(t)$ can often be approximated by a Poisson distribution whose mean, given by (27), is simply the sum of an STM and an LTM component.

Before using the distributions for $N_{SL}(t,t_k)$ to compute the probabilities of correct recall, we digress for a moment to consider the effect of changing the assumption of STM decay in time to STM decay by item interference.

ITEM-DEPENDENT DECAY

Substitute the following for assumption M2 in the preceding section:

M2′. Whenever a new item enters STM there is a reduction in the clarity of all the attributes retained in STM by some amount proportional to the clarity of the image at that time. Let ρ be the constant of proportionality.

We can translate all of the equations of the preceding section to conform with this assumption readily. First, the function $c(t)=k$ *for* $t_k \leqslant t \leqslant t_{k+1}$ gives us the number of the last item to enter memory before time t. Then it is easy to show that the clarity of an attribute of item k at time t is $\rho^{c(t)-k}$. Hence, it follows that Eq. 19, the distribution of the number of attributes that can be recognized from STM becomes

$$P[N_S(t,t_k)=j]=\binom{N_m}{j}\,[\rho^{c(t)-k}]^j[1-\rho^{c(t)-k}]^{N_m-j}\qquad t\geqslant t_k. \tag{28}$$

This equation differs from (19) only in that $\rho^{c(t)-k}$ is substituted for $e^{-(t-t_k)/\gamma}$ in every case. These two functions are, of course, very similar when items enter memory at a constant rate. This substitution into all of the equations of the preceding section leads to the proper result.

FIXED PRESENTATION RATE

Under a fixed rate of presentation, several further results can be obtained. Each item in the list of L is presented for R seconds with the test of memory given at time $t_{L+1}=LR$. For the time-decay model, we have

$$m_k(LR)=\lambda\gamma\, e^{2kR/\gamma}(1-e^{-R/\gamma})\left\{[e^{-LR/\gamma}-e^{-(L+1)R/\gamma}]/(e^{LR/\gamma}-1)\right.$$
$$\left.-\,e^{-kR/\gamma}+e^{-LR/\gamma}+\ln\left[\frac{(1-e^{-LR/\gamma})}{(1-e^{-kR/\gamma})}\right]\right\}. \tag{29}$$

When the item-decay model is used, Eq. 29 can be written as

$$m_k(LR)=(R/-\ln\rho)\,\lambda\rho^{-2k}(1-\sigma)\left\{[(-\rho^L\ln\rho)/(\rho^{-L}-1)]\right.$$
$$\left.-\,\rho^k+\rho^L+\ln\left[\frac{(1-\rho^L)}{(1-\rho^k)}\right]\right\}. \tag{30}$$

Hence, for fixed presentation rate the two assumptions about decay are indistinguishable. With varying rates of presentation, however, one of the two models will have to vary ρ (or γ) in order to fit the data. These results are completely consistent with intuition. The best way to distinguish time decay from item decay is to vary the rate of presentation.

Further Simplifications

It is possible to simplify the computation for the mean value function for $N_L(t,t_k)$ (the number of attributes transferred to LTM during the interval of time t_k to t) for the part of the serial position curve past the primacy effect when the rate of presentation of the items is constant throughout the trial.

When rate of presentation is fixed, $t_k=(\text{k}-1)R$ (where R is the inter-item time in seconds). Then, for large k, the summation in the denominator of (20) reduces to $1/[1-\exp(-R/\gamma)]$. Thus, the integral can be solved readily, giving a form much simpler than that of (29) which includes the primacy effect, namely:

$$m_k(t) = \frac{(1 - e^{-R/\gamma})[1 - e^{-2(L-k)R/\gamma}]}{2/\gamma}. \tag{31}$$

[Note that $t - t_k$ is usually $t_{L+1} - t_k = (L + 1 - k)R$.] We find, therefore, that $N_{SL}(t,t_k)$ is Poisson with mean

$$a(1 - e^{-2(t-t_k)/\gamma}) + N_m e^{-(t-t_k)/\gamma},$$

where

$$a = \frac{(1 - e^{-R/\gamma})}{2/\gamma}.$$

Thus, the flat (asymptotic) portion of the serial position curve—the section that is affected by neither primacy nor recency—has a value of $m_k(t) = a$. Moreover, when R/γ is small (i.e., $e^{-R/\gamma} \geqslant 0.8$), then

$$a \approx \frac{\lambda R/\gamma}{2/\gamma} = \frac{\lambda R}{2}.$$

The same result obtains when we use the assumption of item-dependent decay. Equation 31 applies directly with the substitution of ρ for $e^{-R/\gamma}$ (and, therefore, $-\ln \rho/R$ for $1/\gamma$. When $\rho \geqslant 0.8$

$$a \approx \lambda\, R(1 - \rho)/2(1 - \rho) = \lambda\, R/2.$$

Thus, the asymptotic value of the serial position curve has the same relationship to rate of presentation under either assumption about memory: time-dependent decay or item-dependent decay. The asymptote is independent of list length. In practice, of course, the asymptote is reached only for very large serial positions and, therefore, very long list lengths.

Primacy

We can do a similar simplification of the serial position curve for the primacy (early) portion. We let the list length (L) be arbitrarily large (in Eq. 29). Thus,

$$m_k(t) = 2ae^{2kR/\gamma}[\ln(1 - e^{-kR/\gamma}) + e^{-kR/\gamma}] \tag{32}$$

under the assumption of decay in time and

$$m_k(t) = 2a\rho^{-2k}[\ln(1 - \rho^k) + \rho^k] \tag{33}$$

under the assumption of item-dependent decay. The important result is that the relationship of the entire part of the primacy section of the serial position curve to the asymptotic value of the curve (which is simply a) depends only upon the short-term memory parameter γ (in the case of time-dependent decay) or ρ (in the case of item-dependent decay) and is independent of list length and other parameters. Thus, we can normalize the serial position curves simply by dividing all the values of m_k by the asymptotic value, a.

The primacy relationship also offers us a simple way of distinguishing time- from item-dependent decay. Rate of presentation affects the primacy relationship with time-dependent decay but not with item-dependent decay.

THE RESPONSE PROCESS

In the preceding sections we have calculated the properties of the acquisition and retention processes. Now we need to specify how the subject makes use of the memory trace in answering the test questions put to him by the experimenter. From our previous calculations, we start out knowing the probability that the kth item was correctly perceived (Π_k) and, under the assumption of correct perception, the distribution of the number of attributes in the memory trace at any time t, $[N_{SL}(t,t_k)]$. Here we compute the probability that a subject can *recall* or *recognize* the kth item. We are able to apply the response rules correctly only to situations where a single response is required of the subject. This is because we have not yet included any method of accounting for the loss of attributes in the memory trace caused by previous test items in situations where the subject must make several responses (see the discussions of these points in Norman and Waugh, 1968; Waugh and Norman, 1965). In general, however, we ignore these constraints when the time comes to compare the theoretical predictions with actual results.

Recall

As we have discussed earlier, the subject's task is to recall an item which belongs to the context provided to him by the experimenter. We assume he does this by attempting to regenerate the correct response from the i memory attributes which are still retained (i.e., from the i attributes that are still associated with the proper context, see Fig. 2). This is done by matching the vectors in the memory, attribute by attribute, with the vectors of all the possible responses. From this point on, the process is formally identical to that of naming. Hence, we consider both the situation where the subject responds only when the matching process leads to an unambiguous response—*conservative recall*—and also the situation where the subject guesses selectively whenever there is ambiguity—*liberal* or *forced-choice recall.*

The equations for conservative and liberal recall are identical to the corresponding equations for conservative and liberal naming Eqs. 12–17, with the following obvious substitutions:

$$\left.\begin{array}{l} P_k \text{ (Recall)} \\ N_m \\ \sigma_m \\ P[N_{SL}(t,t_k) = i] \end{array}\right\} \quad \text{for} \quad \left\{\begin{array}{l} \Pi_k \\ N_p \\ \sigma_p \\ P[N_k = i]. \end{array}\right.$$

This means that we can approximate the results by the criterion or threshold strategy; the probability that the subject can correctly recall an item is given by the probability that the number of attributes of its memory trace exceeds some critical number.

Recognition

In a recognition experiment the subject is given a test item and asked to state whether it is *old* or *new*(n). We assume that he does this by checking the context associated with each attribute of the test item.

The probability of making a false recognition is the probability that c or more attributes of the test item match one of the L memory vectors. The probability that i elements of the vector for item j match the corresponding attributes of the test item is $\sigma_m{}^i P[N_{SL}(t,t_j) = i]$. The probability of responding *yes* (Y) to at least one of the L vectors is the probability that not all of the vectors had less than c attributes that exactly matched the test item:

$$P(Y \mid n) = 1 - \prod_{j=1}^{L} \left\{ 1 - \sum_{i=c}^{N_m} \sigma_m{}^i \, P[N_{SL}(t,t_j) = i] \right\}. \tag{34}$$

The probability of responding Y when the test item is the same as the kth item of the list, $P(Y \mid k)$, is given by the probability that either c or more attributes of the kth memory vector are remembered or, failing that, that c or more attributes of one of the vectors exactly match the test item. Thus,

$$P(Y \mid k) = \sum_{i=c}^{N_m} P[N_{SL}(t,t_k) = i] + P(Y \mid n - k) \sum_{i=0}^{c-1} P[N_{SL}(t,t_k) = i], \tag{35}$$

where $P(Y|n-k)$ is given by (34), except that in the product term, $j \neq k$.

Unfortunately, we reach more mathematical complexities with recognition than with recall. This is quite unlike other models of memory wherein it invariably occurs that the recognition experiment is easier to analyze than the recall experiment. With the present model, although some reduction of Eqs. 34 and 35 is possible, there appears to be no simplification of these equations that yields any insight into the predictions for recognition. We thus leave this subject to future work.

It is possible to simplify the situation greatly; however, if we can get rid of the overlapping of processing which occurs in transferring information from STM to LTM. It seems to be possible to get this result experimentally by proper instruction of the subjects. The critical instruction is something like this: "Think only of the last item presented to you. When a new item is presented, think only of it and not of any of the earlier ones." This type of instruction was first used by Waugh and Norman (1965) and seems to be reasonably successful in eliminating the primacy portion of the serial position curve (see also Wickelgren's discussion of these instructions in Chapter 3).

If these instructions are followed successfully, then we can simplify the term $P[N_{SL}(t,t_j) = i]$ in (34). From (26) and (27) we know that this term is well approximated by a Poisson distribution with a mean value function of $m_k(t) + N_m \exp[-(t-t_k)/\gamma]$. The first part of the mean value function represents the STM component and so it should not be affected by these instructions about rehearsal. The LTM component should be constant for all serial positions. Thus, from (18) and (21), for all k

$$\theta_k(t) = \begin{cases} 1 & t_k \leqq t < t_{k+1} \\ 0 & \text{otherwise} \end{cases}$$

and

$$m_k(t) = \lambda\gamma\ [1 - e^{-R/\gamma}] \qquad t \geqslant R. \tag{36}$$

Since $m_k(t)$ is constant across serial positions, it is clear that the mean number of attributes retained should vary only because of STM and will thus increase monotonically with serial position.

Several comparisons are now possible between the recognition theory just developed and the strength theory proposed by Wickelgren and Norman (1966). First, in strength theory, the operating characteristics result from two normal distributions; hence, when plotted on normal–normal probability graph paper they are straight lines. If the two distributions are assumed to have the same standard deviations (the usual assumption), then the operating characteristics will have a slope of one. Second, in the simplest version of the trace-decay formulation of strength theory, the memory trace decays exponentially with the number of items intervening between presentation of the critical item and its test. Wickelgren and Norman called the trace strength of the kth item in a list of L items $d(k,L)$. This measure is equivalent to the d' statistic of signal detection theory. Although it is possible to determine the analytical transformation from the parameters of the present theory to the $d(k,L)$ measure, it is easiest to determine the correspondences between the theories by drawing the operating characteristics and measuring the appropriate strength statistics from the curves.

The predictions of the multicomponent theory are shown in Fig. 4. The results are clear. The present model agrees with strength theory in predicting straight lines for the memory operating characteristics

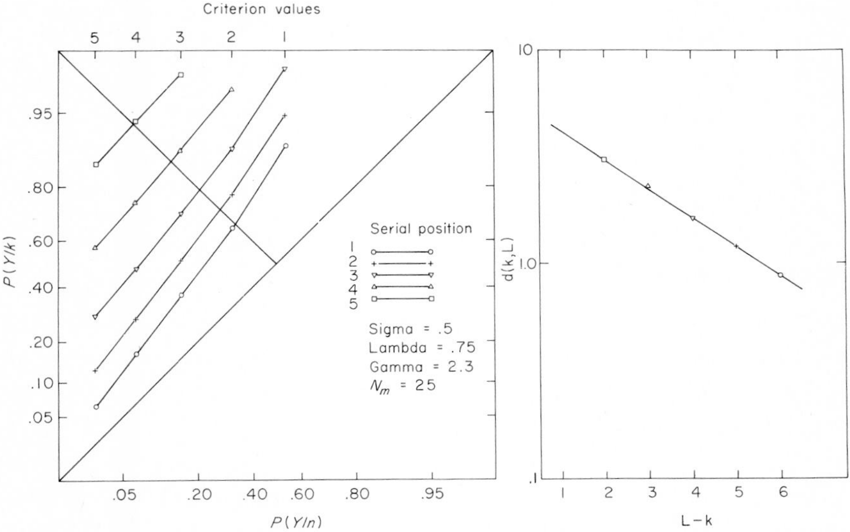

FIG. 4. Operating characteristics and strength decay for recognition memory. The left panel shows the operating characteristics of the recognition theory plotted on normal–normal probability paper. The lines are approximately linear: the slopes do deviate from unity. The operating characteristic was calculated by moving the criterion (c) through the values 1–5 as shown on the top of the figure. The right panel shows the strength statistic taken from the operating characteristics. Memory-trace strength decays exponentially with serial position. All curves were computed assuming nonoverlapping processing of items (the nonrehearsal instructions); the parameters are the same used to fit the data of Fig. 11.

and for giving an exponential decay of memory trace strength (shown by the linear decay of trace strength in the semilogarithmic plot of Fig. 4). The slopes of the operating characteristics, however, clearly deviate from unity.

The recognition model of this chapter would then appear to be capable of handling the results of a number of recognition experiments, or at least those in which it can reasonably be assumed that the effects of LTM are constant with serial position. In other situations, it is probably necessary to use computer simulations of the model in order to determine the exact predictions. The present model also is in substantial agreement with the predictions of strength theory. This point is illustrated with some actual data in the next section of the paper.

Tests of the System

The Perceptual Process

In some experiments we can assume that retention is essentially perfect and that we can, in effect, observe the output of the naming system directly. A broad class of perceptual experiments fall into this category. One such set of experiments is those involving tachistoscopic presentation of visual material in which the subject's task is simply to recognize briefly exposed letters of the alphabet.

SIMULTANEOUS PRESENTATION

To illustrate the types of functions predicted by the model for simultaneous presentations of L items with the criterion approximation to the conservative naming strategy, we present two figures taken from the paper by Rumelhart (1970). These illustrate two aspects of the experiments reported by Sperling (1960). Figure 5 shows the data reported by Sperling on the number of letters of a display his subjects were able to report after a 50 msec exposure. The solid line with slope of unity illustrates perfect performance; the lowest solid lines indicate the predictions of the perceptual theory. The predictions were obtained by using Eqs. 4 and 5.

PARTIAL REPORT

Sperling demonstrated that more letters were available to the subjects than indicated by the full report situation illustrated by Fig. 5. He presented an instruction tone at various times after the termination of the 50 millisecond display exposure and showed that subjects could improve their performance substantially by concentrating on the row of letters cued by the tone. Sperling's data for his individual subjects and our predictions are shown in Figs. 5 and 6. In terms of our Eq. 6, T is the display duration (.050 sec), L is the total number of letters in the display (12 in Fig. 6), S is the number of letters in a row (3 or 4 in these experiments, depending upon display size), and t_c is the delay of the instruction tone in seconds. The predictions shown in Figs. 5 and 6 come from application of Eqs. 5 and 6 with the criterion approximation used for Fig. 5.

The parameters used in Figs. 5 and 6 for both full and partial report experiments were held constant for a given subject across all experimental conditions. For the five subjects, the criterion value was always around 2.0, ν varied from 25.0 (subject ROR) to 70.0 (RNS), and μ

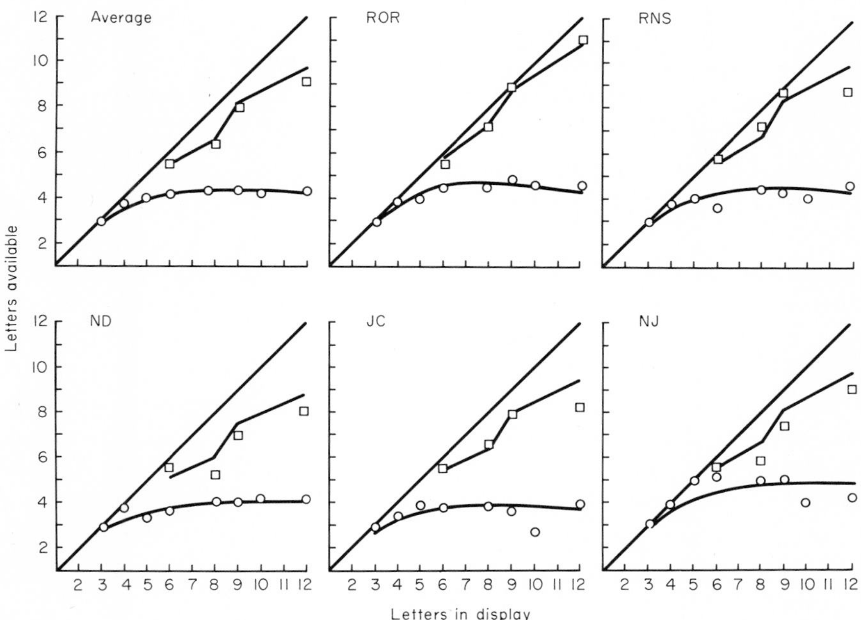

FIG. 5. Total numbers of letters available after a .050 sec visual presentation with both full and partial report procedures. Data from Sperling (1960); the figure is from Rumelhart (1970).

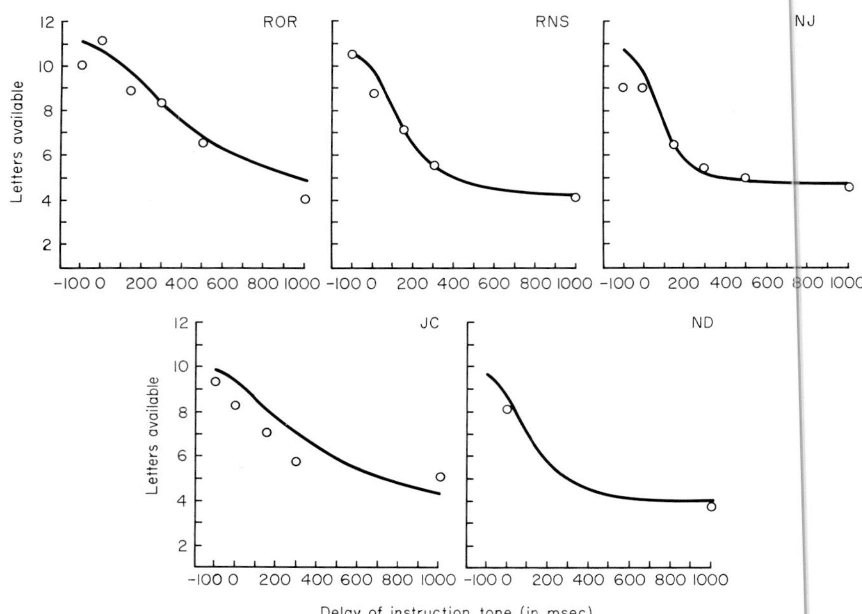

FIG. 6. Number of letters available in the partial report experiment from a .050 sec visual presentation of a display. Data are for individual subjects. We assume that subjects attended equally to all 12 letters of the display until the arrival of the instruction tone, when they concentrated on the row of four letters indicated by the tone. For any given subject, the model parameters are held constant for all experimental conditions of Figs. 5 and 6. Data are from Sperling (1960); the figure is from Rumelhart (1970).

varied from .106 sec (*NJ*) to .399 sec (JC). (See the paper by Rumelhart for more details.)

SEQUENTIAL PRESENTATION

To illustrate the predictions of the perceptual system for sequentially presented items, we mimic the experimental procedure used by Yntema, Wozencraft, and Klem (1964). They presented lists of computer-spoken digits and required subjects to recall as many digits as possible. In their experiment, each digit lasted exactly .100 sec, the lists contained 5, 7, or 9 digits, and they were presented at the rate of 2, 4, 8, and 10 digits/sec (.500, .250, .125, and .100 sec/digit).

The predictions of the perceptual system are illustrated in Fig. 7. We compute the probability of extracting a critical number of features from each digit in the list, using Eqs. 3 and 11. The curves clearly show that the accuracy of perception can follow the classical bowed serial position curve. Although these curves are qualitatively similar to the data of Yntema *et al.*, there is no reason to make any formal comparison, for the operations of the memory system must also have contributed to their experimental results.

The predictions shown in Fig. 7 are also very similar to the results obtained by Norman (1966: Fig. 4) on the retention (and perception) of the last three digits from lists of lengths 3–15 items presented at rates of 1, 4, 7, and 10 digits/sec.

The predictions of the perceptual system for simultaneous presentation have been explored in more detail by Rumelhart (1970) and discussed previously. In general, the perceptual system gives a good description of the results from experiments in visual perception with simultaneously presented material, with full and partial report, and with and without backward masking.

When many items get through the perceptual system, the model predicts that there will be serial position effects caused both by perceptual

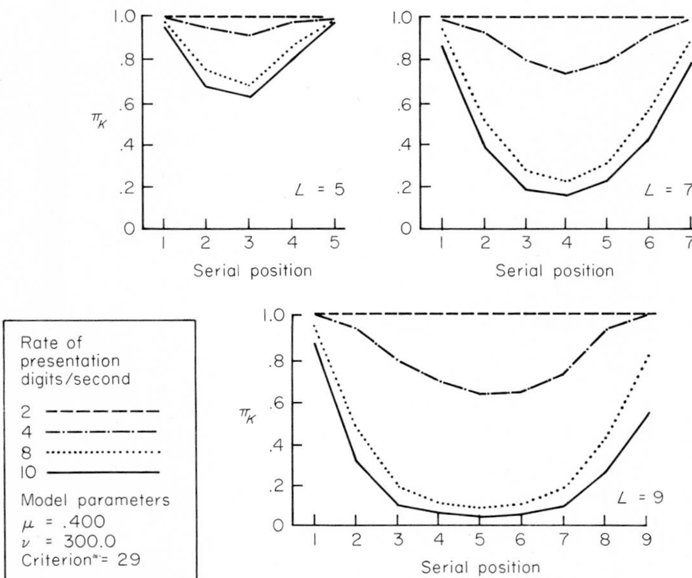

FIG. 7. Probability of correctly perceiving an item in a list of rapidly presented digits. The conditions are chosen to mimic the experiment of Yntema *et al.* (1964), with lists of length 5, 7, and 9 presented at rates of 2, 4, 8, and 10 digits/sec.

and memory factors. Unfortunately, were we to examine the effects of both these factors on performance, we would have a model with eight parameters. Although it may very well be that all eight parameters are meaningful and necessary to handle these types of experiments, use of this many parameters at this early stage of development of the model allows too much freedom in fitting data for comfort. In addition, it is difficult to estimate parameter values for such a model, for the eight dimensions of the space relating goodness-of-fit to the parameter values requires an uneconomically long amount of computer time to explore. Hence, although it would be nice to fit data such as those reported by Yntema *et al.* (1964), it seems wise to avoid it for the time being.

The Memory Process

TIME VS. ITEM DECAY

One of the first tests we can make is of the difference between the predictions of time and item decay in short-term memory. A convenient set of data to use for this comparison comes from a free recall experiment performed by Murdock (1962) (see the Appendix to this book). Murdock had groups of subjects recall freely as many words as they could from lists of various lengths of unrelated English words presented at rates of one and two seconds per word. Of particular interest here is the comparison of the recall of words of list length 20 at the two rates: the only list length tested at both rates of presentation.

Before we start, one caution is necessary. Murdock tested the memory of his subjects by the method of free recall. That is, he let them recall all the words they could, in whatever order they chose. As a result, there is considerable response interference present because the recall of the first few words affected the memory for other words. This has its major effect on the probability of recall of the last few words in the list; the probabilities obtained for these words are lower than the actual probability that the words were in memory at the end of the list (see Norman and Waugh, 1968). The model developed here assumes that recall of one item has no effect on the others. That is, it is as if each item recalled were the first in the list.

The comparison of the predicted values of recall with the experimental results for these two lists are shown in Fig. 8. The theoretical predictions were obtained by minimizing the chi-square measure of fit of theory to data. The minimization technique used was to establish a coarse grid of

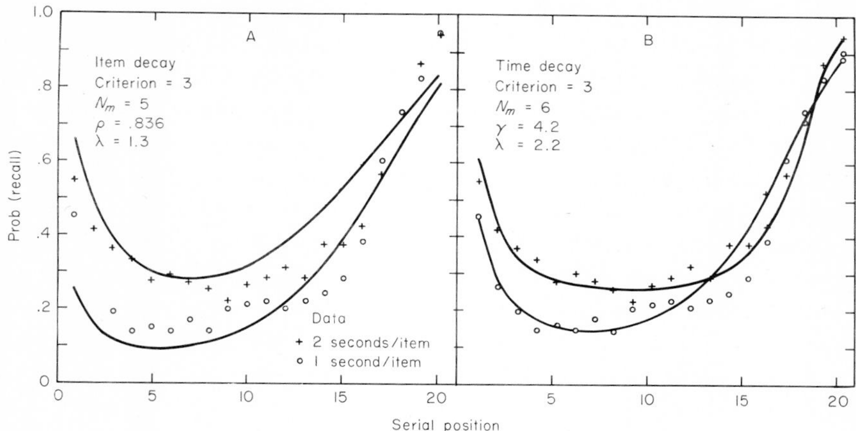

FIG. 8. Item-decay and time-decay fits of free recall serial position curves. The data are from Murdock (1962) and show free recall results from lists of 20 items presented at rates of 1 and 2 sec per item. In each half of the figure all model parameters were held constant in fitting the two rates of presentation.

parameter values in the four-dimensional space of parameters, find the location of the minimum, and then place a finer grid around that point. This procedure was repeated until no further improvement seemed near. Because of the unknown nature of the parameter space (and the subjective judgments used in following the minima on the time-shared computer console), we have no guarantee that the minimization was the correct one rather than some local value.

Our results are unequivocal. The time-decay model does a reasonable job of describing these data; the item-decay model is unsatisfactory. Because we did not completely trust these results, we studied the various parts of the curves individually. First, we looked only at the recency section of the curves by examining only the last ten points. Then, we examined only the primacy section of the curves by examining only the first 10 points. (The primacy evaluation should not suffer from the problems of response interference, since order of recall has little or no effect on the early items of lists.) But in all cases the verdict was clear. Time decay yes, item decay no.

This result is not altogether pleasing. One of us (DER) expected it. The other (DAN) has argued previously (Norman, 1966; Waugh and Norman, 1965, 1968) that material in short-term memory decays primarily as a result of interference from other material, and very little by the effects of time. Unfortunately, these present results are quite unequivocal. There is still the possibility, of course, that an inappropriate set of parameters has been used for the item-decay comparison. This would be true if local minima in the parameter space misled us in our search. Whether this is true or not, we cannot say. Let us simply point out that the search was clearly biased in favor of item decay. An alternative explanation is that the issue of item or time decay is model dependent. This particular model favors time decay; another model might favor item decay. Again, we cannot decide this issue here, except to say that this is also an unsatisfactory resolution of the problem, since the previous arguments in favor of item decay were made in the absence of a formal model. Given the finding that the time-decay model is so much superior to the item-decay model, we use the time-decay model for all further analyses.

FREE RECALL

With the parameters selected for Murdock's lists of length 20, we now examine the predictions for all the lists. Both predictions and actual data are shown in Fig. 9. Qualitatively, there is good agreement among the predictions and data.[5] In detail, however, there is substantial error. For one, some sections of the curves are very far off. For another, the theory predicts that the recall of the first item in the list should be affected only by rate of presentation and be entirely independent of the list length. This prediction is not met by the data. (An analysis of other data shows that in free recall situations, in general, the recall of the first item in the list does depend upon list length.)

PHILLIPS, SHIFFRIN, AND ATKINSON

A much more realistic test of the memory model is provided by the results of an experiment by Phillips, Shiffrin, and Atkinson (1967) (see the Appendix to this book). This experiment is extremely relevant, for it was performed in order to test the model of Atkinson and Shiffrin (1968), which has many of the constraints of the present one. Thus, while we had to overlook the problem of response interference in order to test the model with free recall data, no such problem exists with the data of Phillips *et al.*, for they only asked their subjects for one response per trial.

The experimental procedure, in brief, was to show a card to a subject

[5] We thank Bennet Murdock, Jr. for giving us the detailed data for these experiments.

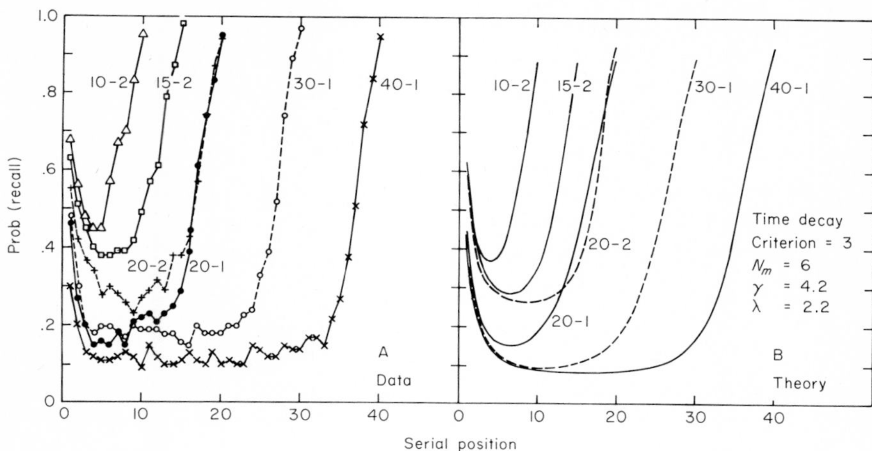

FIG. 9. Data and time-decay predictions for free recall serial position curves. The data are from Murdock (1962). The parameters used in the model are the same used for fitting the curves of length 20 in Fig. 8B.

briefly and then lay it face down, in a row in front of the subject. Then, the experimenter would point at (the back of) one card, and the subject was required to recall which item it represented. This represents the condition of liberal (or forced-choice) recall. Each card could represent only one of four alternatives: thus, in our model, $A = 4$.

The fit of the liberal recall model to the data is shown in Fig. 10. Our model contains the same number of parameters as the model of Atkinson and Shiffrin, so it is interesting to compare our fit with theirs. The model of Atkinson and Shiffrin predicts perfect performance for all list lengths of 5 and less. Hence, they ignored these lists in computing their goodness-of-fit. Looking at lists of length 6 and greater, Atkinson and Shiffrin got a chi-square score of 44.3 with 42 degrees of freedom, compared to a chi-square of 46.7 for our model, with the same number of degrees of freedom: a slight difference in favor of their model. (We estimated parameters by the same iterative procedure described in our discussion of the free recall data.) Our model predicts the results of list length 5 better than does theirs, however, so that we conclude that the two models are approximately equal in their ability to describe these data. (See also Fig. 1 in Chapter 4 by Bernbach.) Our ability to predict these data indicates that our alibi for the Murdock data (that the recall model was not designed for the free recall situation) may be justified. Note

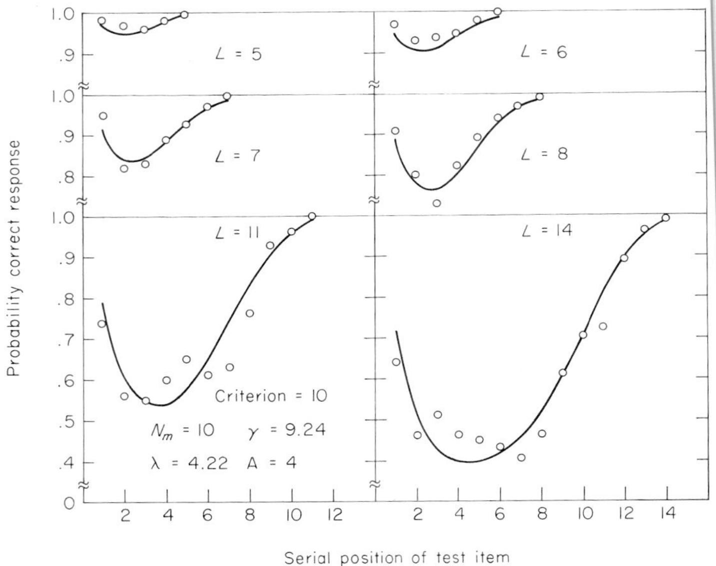

FIG. 10. Data and predictions for response probabilities for the forced recall experiment of Phillips *et al.* (1967). (Note that unlike other graphs of these same data, these are plotted in the conventional fashion, with serial position 1 corresponding to the *first* item of the list.)

that although we have used the time-decay version of the model to fit these data, the predictions from the item-decay version would also fit equally well. Rate of presentation was not varied in this experiment; hence, the predictions of the item- and time-decay theories are identical.

RECOGNITION

Results from an experiment by Wickelgren and Norman (1966) were used to test the recognition model. These results were used for two reasons. First, the data are already well described by the strength theory of Wickelgren and Norman, so that it is interesting to compare the description of the present model. Second, the data were collected with the use of instructions to avoid rehearsing any item but the one that had last been presented. As we have already seen, to the extent that subjects are capable of following this instruction, the recognition model can be greatly simplified.

In the experiment, lists of three-digit numbers were presented to the subjects at the rate of one three-digit number every second. At the end of L numbers, a tone was presented to signal the end of the list and then, without pause, a three-digit test number was presented. The subject's task was to say whether the test number had previously occurred in the list. List lengths from 2 through 7 items were used. The experiment (and the actual data) are described in more detail in the original paper.

The comparison of the data for *S*4 for all list lengths with the present theory is shown in Fig. 11. (*S*4 was the only subject who showed no primacy effect.) The curve at the bottom shows false alarm rate [*P*(yes | new)] as a function of list length; the curves at the top show hit rate [*P*(yes | old)] for the 6 different list lengths as a function of serial position of the test item in the list. On the whole, the fit is good. In fact, the fit for this model is certainly as good as that of the original strength

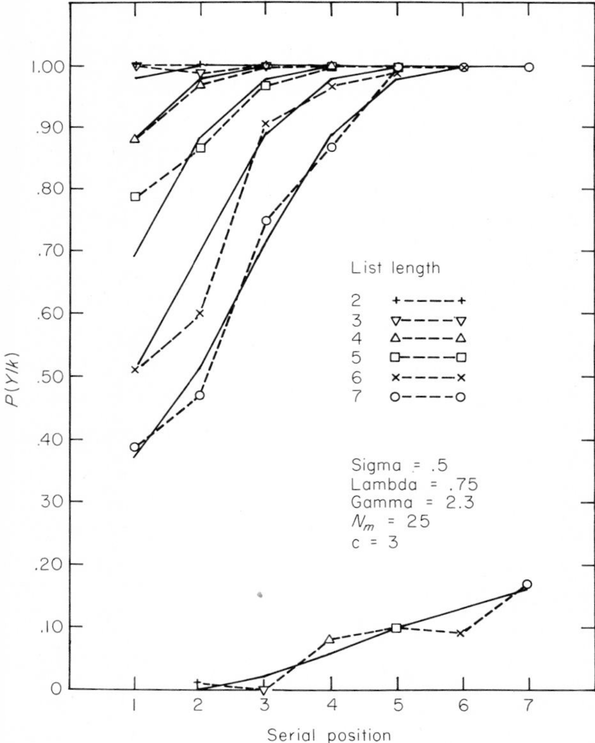

FIG. 11. Data and predictions for hit and false-alarm probabilities for Subject S4 of Wickelgren and Norman (1966) at six different list lengths. The bottom curves show false-alarm rate as a function of list length; the top six curves show hit rate as a function of the serial position of the test item.

theory. Moreover, in the strength theory analysis of these data, the false-alarm rates were used to estimate one of the parameters, and so could not be predicted by the theory. We see, however, that the present theory does a good job of describing the rise in false-alarm rate found with increasing list length.

Discussion

In the construction of this system for perception and memory a number of different types of assumptions have been made. Some, like the assumption of separate processes of sensory storage, naming, short- and long-term memory, and response determination, are essential to the system and could not be modified without changing our basic premises. Others, such as the assumptions that rate of construction of the perceptual and long-term vectors depend upon the number of items being processed simultaneously, are extremely important, but could be modified easily without changing the spirit of the model. Finally, some assumptions such as the exponential form of memory decay, were chosen primarily for mathematical convenience and have no real importance.

At this point, it is useful to review the model, stressing the important points, discussing its virtues and deficits, and pointing out the parts that need testing and the parts that need the most development.

THE NAMING SYSTEM

One major innovation is the introduction of the naming system between perception and memory. This system lets us incorporate several important features into the model. Most important, it specifies one possible mechanism for performing the transformation between the forms of representation of the sensory and memory images.

There are two implications that have not yet been explored. One is the temporal relations of the transformations, the other is the dependence of the accuracy of transformation on restrictions in the set of possible signals. With latency predictions (which follow directly from the Poisson arrival times used in the model) one would hope to be able to account for such data as those of Posner and Mitchell (1967) and Cohen (1968) on response time to make judgments of physical and name identity and those of Aaronson (1968) on the difference in processing time between detecting and remembering rapidly presented items.

If the search through the dictionary is assumed to be performed sequentially, the model will handle Sternberg's (1967) results. Sternberg measured the times required for his subjects to decide whether a stimulus item was part of a previously learned set of possibilities. He found a linear relationship between response latency and size of the set of alternatives. If we equate the slope of the linear function with the rate at which the naming system tests each dictionary item and the intercept with the time required to construct the perceptual vector (plus the times required for such fixed components as motor movements), we predict that changes in clarity (S/N ratio) of the critical item would change only the intercept of the function and not the slope. This was what Sternberg found for trained subjects, with a slight change in slope when the subjects were inexperienced.

How the naming system might be used in the encoding of nonsense forms (i.e., items without names) is not clear. In some situations it might be bypassed, making the memory vector identical to the perceptual vector. In other situations the subject might try to name components of the sensory image, leading to description lists such as suggested by Glanzer and Clark (1963) or the encoding strategies of Harris and Haber (1963) and Haber (1964).

We have deliberately avoided defining the unit of "item," either in the stimulus or dictionary. Thus, we would assume units to be defined primarily by the instructions to the subject (either explicitly stated or self-constructed), so that units might be visual segments, letters, or even words, depending upon the situation.

The method of reducing the dictionary size in the naming system is, of course, arbitrary. It is similar in many ways to standard restriction of set used in signal detection theory (Green and Swets, 1967) or the method used by Bower in his multicomponent model (1967). It is similar in spirit, although it differs in detail, from the strength notions of Broadbent (1967), Morton (1969 and Chapter 7) and Norman (1968), although their models might simply be considered continuous representations of the all-or-none dictionary list used here.

SENSORY INFORMATION STORE

Although the notion of a sensory information storage system is essential to our argument, many of its details are not. Two different aspects of the storage system require discussion. One is the type of memory decay. The other is the assumed slow-up of processing with trace decay and numbers of items in the SIS.

We assume exponential decay in time of features in SIS. Such an assumption appears to work well, but it could be replaced by a variety of other decay functions. For example, we could assume an all-or-none process, with the SIS lasting for exactly μ sec after the physical signal. Or we could assume that in any instant of time after the signal turned off, the probability of keeping the image in SIS was $d\mu$ (with $d\mu/dt$ constant as $dt \to 0$). Either assumption would maintain many features of our exponential decay. In fact for some purposes, they would all be equivalent.

In a similar vein, some restriction on processing rate for an individual item as the SIS trace decays and as more items are presented is an essential feature of this model. Presumably, other restrictions in rate (or attention factor) would work as well as or better than the one we use. To this time, however, none of the other systems we have been able to devise work very well.

One possible criticism of the attention parameter is its equality across stimulus items with no mention of the possible effects of the subject's biases or strategies. There is a natural way to incorporate selection biases into the system, namely, by multiplying each θ_k by a bias term, β_k (with $0 \leqslant \beta_k \leqslant 1$ and $\Sigma\beta_k = 1$). In fact, this approach has already been used to describe the partial report experiment.

MEMORY

Many of the assumptions of the memory system are problematical. The choice of a vector notation for the attributes in memory follow directly from the reasons given by Bower. The choice of method used to build up the long-term attributes is somewhat arbitrary, but as with the buildup of the perception image, we know of no other procedure that works as well. The continual decrease in the rate at which the long-term attributes become more permanent as more items enter the memory system seems to be a reasonable way in which to describe proactive effects and hence, the primary portion of the serial position curve. In many respects, this assumption is very similar to the scheme adopted by Atkinson and Shiffrin (1968).

It is clear that there are several major deficiencies in the memory system, primarily because there are no statements about either organizational factors or about the encoding of sequential information. Because of this, we are forced to restrict the model to situations that use simple, homogeneous lists of stimulus items. A good deal of work needs to be done testing and modifying the various assumptions that have been made. Hopefully, it will be possible to simplify many of the computations. It would be desirable to complete the discussion of retrieval methods by completing the discussion of recognition and adding descriptions of other tasks, such as paired-associates, the probe technique, and continuous memory experiments. Before free recall can be described successfully, it will be necessary to determine the effects of response interference on memory and also to add some theory of the order in which subjects recall what they remember.

In spite of these problems, we consider the model to be successful in its main goal of providing a complete description of many aspects of sensation, perception, memory, and retrieval. We have been able to show how each of the processes might interact with the others. The model appears to handle many of the qualitative phenomena associated with perception and memory, and it does not do too badly quantitatively, although there are some definite difficulties. Thus, there is some reason for our optimism about the general framework of the system.

References

AARONSON, D. The temporal course of perception in an immediate recall task. *Journal of Experimental Psychology*, 1968, **76**, 129–140.

ATKINSON, R. C., AND SHIFFRIN, R. M. Human memory: A proposed system and its control processes. In K. W. Spence and J. T. Spence (Eds.), *Advances in the psychology of learning and motivation research and theory*. Vol. II. New York: Academic Press, 1968.

BOWER, G. H. A multicomponent theory of the memory trace. In K. W. Spence and J. T. Spence (Eds.), *Advances in the psychology of learning and motivation research and theory*. Vol. I. New York: Academic Press, 1967.

BROADBENT, D. E. Word frequency effect and response bias. *Psychological Review*, 1967, **74**, 1–15.

COHEN, G. A. A comparison of semantic, acoustic, and visual criteria for matching of word pairs. *Perception & Psychophysics*, 1968, **4**, 203–204.

CONRAD, R. Acoustic confusions and memory span for words. *Nature*, 1963, **197**, 1029–1030.

CONRAD, R. Acoustic confusions in immediate memory. *British Journal of Psychology*, 1964, **55**, 75–83.

ERIKSEN, C. W., AND SPENCER, T. Rate of information processing in visual perception: Some results and methodological considerations. *Journal of Experimental Psychology*, 1969, **79** (Monogr., Part 2), Whole No. 2).

GLANZER, M., AND CLARK, W. H. Accuracy of perceptual recall: An analysis of organization. *Journal of Verbal Learning and Verbal Behavior*, 1963, **2**, 289–299.

GREEN, D. M., AND SWETS, J. A. *Signal detection theory and psychophysics*. New York: Wiley, 1966.

HABER, R. N. The effects of coding strategy on perceptual memory. *Journal of Experimental Psychology*, 1964, **68**, 357–362.

HARRIS, C. S., AND HABER, R. N. Selective attention and coding in visual perception. *Journal of Experimental Psychology*, 1963, **65**, 328–333.

MORTON, J. The interaction of information in word recognition. *Psychological Review*, 1969, **76**, 165–178.

MURDOCK, B. B., JR. The serial effect of free recall. *Journal of Experimental Psychology*, 1962, **64**, 482–488.

NEISSER, U. *Cognitive psychology*. New York: Appleton-Century-Crofts, 1967.

NORMAN, D. A. Acquisition and retention in short-term memory. *Journal of Experimental Psychology*, 1966, **72**, 369–381.

NORMAN, D. A. Toward a theory of memory and attention. *Psychological Review*, 1968, **75**, 522–536.

NORMAN, D. A. *Memory and attention*. New York: Wiley, 1969.

NORMAN, D. A., AND WAUGH, N. C. Stimulus and response interference in recognition memory experiments. *Journal of Experimental Psychology*, 1968, **78**, 551–559.

PARZEN, E. *Stochastic processes*. San Francisco, California: Holden-Day, 1962.

POSNER, M. I., AND MITCHELL, R. F. Chronometric analysis of classification. *Psychological Review*, 1967, **74**, 392–409.

PHILLIPS, J. L., SHIFFRIN, R. M., AND ATKINSON, R. C. Effects of list length on short-term memory. *Journal of Verbal Learning and Verbal Behavior*, 1967, **6**, 303–311.

RUMELHART, D. E. A multicomponent theory of the perception of briefly exposed visual displays. *Journal of Mathematical Psychology*, 1970, in press.

SPERLING, G. The information available in brief visual presentation. *Psychological Monographs*, 1960, **74** (Whole No. 498).

SPERLING, G. Successive approximations to a model for short-term memory. In A. F. Sanders (Ed.), *Attention and performance*. Amsterdam: North-Holland Publ., 1967, pp. 242–285. (Special edition of *Acta Psychologica*, 1967, **27**, 285–292.)

STERNBERG, S. Two operations in character recognition: Some evidence from reaction time measurements. *Perception & Psychophysics*, 1967, **2**, 45–53.

WAUGH, N. C., AND NORMAN, D. A. Primary memory. *Psychological Review*, 1965, **72**, 89–104.

WAUGH, N. C., AND NORMAN, D. A. The measure of interference in primary memory. *Journal of Verbal Learning and Verbal Behavior*, 1968, **7**, 617–626.

WICKELGREN, W. A., AND NORMAN, D. A. Strength models and serial position in short-term recognition memory. *Journal of Mathematical Psychology*, 1966, **3**, 316–347.

WOLFORD, G. L., WESSEL, D. L., AND ESTES, W. K. Further evidence concerning scanning and sampling assumptions of visual detection models. *Perception & Psychophysics*, 1968, **3**, 439–444.

YNTEMA, D. B., WOZENCRAFT, F. T., AND KLEM, L. Immediate serial recall of digits presented at very high rates. Paper presented at the Psychonomic Society Meetings, Niagara Falls, Ontario, 1964.

3

Multitrace Strength Theory[1]

Wayne A. Wickelgren[2]
Massachusetts Institute of Technology

[1] This work was supported by grant, MH 08890-05, from the National Institute of Mental Health, U. S. Public Health Service.
[2] Now at the University of Oregon.

There are many levels at which one can attempt to formulate a theory of memory, ranging from theories of the biochemical and biophysical bases of memory, through anatomical and physiological bases of memory, and finally, through psychological theories of memory. There are also many different sublevels within each of these three major categories of levels. By a theoretical level, I mean the degree of detail with which the memory process is described. One is attempting to describe the memory process in more detail at a molecular level than at a neuronal level than at a psychological (functional, behavioral) level.

Ultimately, we want adequate theories of memory at molecular, neuronal, and psychological levels. It may turn out to be possible to derive the psychological theory from the neuronal theory and the neuronal theory from the molecular theory. Alternatively, one or both of these derivations may be too complicated to be worth the effort. This is not our concern at present.

The concern of the present paper is to develop a possibly adequate theory of memory at a psychological level. The theory, called multitrace strength theory, is rather detailed in that it analyzes the memory trace into components and phases, but both the componential and phase analyses are less detailed (mechanistic) than some might desire. However, multitrace strength theory will attempt to achieve complete generality with respect to the basic functional properties of memory.

The basic properties of multitrace strength theory are as follows: each event and each association between two events is characterized by a vector of unidimensional strength measures for each of four possible time traces (very-short-term memory, VSTM: short-term memory, STM; intermediate-term memory, ITM; and long-term memory, LTM) in each of an unknown number of modalities (visual, auditory, speech-motor, abstract-verbal, etc.).

Each trace in each modality passes through four phases (acquisition, consolidation, decay, and retrieval). The acquisition phase refers to the period of presentation or active rehearsal of events during which the memory traces are initiated. However, acquisition is considered to refer to the establishment of potential traces, not usable (retrievable) traces. The conversion from potential traces to usable traces is accomplished by the consolidation process, which may be a matter of hours or days for LTM, but is on the order of tens of seconds or seconds for ITM and tenths of seconds for STM. After a usable trace has consolidated, it decays exponentially to zero at a rate that may depend on the experimental conditions.

In retrieval, the strengths of all traces in all modalities for an event or association are combined into a single total strength. It is this (unidimensional) total strength which is judged in the retrieval-decision process. In recognition, only the total strength of the test event or association is judged in relation to a criterion to determine the "yes-no" response. In multiple-choice or recall, the total strengths of all alternatives are compared, and the alternative with the maximum strength is selected.

An exponential approach to a limit is chosen as the general form of the acquisition and retrieval functions, and a delayed unit step or ramp function is chosen to represent consolidation. However, the choice of these functional forms is rather arbitrary on the basis of present evidence.

Some consideration is given to the nature of the coding for events and associations in different modalities by making provision for similarity functions between pairs of events and pairs of associations. As an example of event similarity, the letter names "B" and "D" are more similar in phonetic STM than "B" and "S." As an example of the positional similarity of two associations, the similarity between a direct forward association and a direct backward association is greater than the similarity between a direct forward association and a remote backward association.

Comparison to Other Theories

Multitrace strength theory is an extension of the strength theory proposed by Wickelgren and Norman (1966) for item recognition memory. The principal similarities are: (a) the characterization of memory traces by real-valued strengths, with noise added separately, similar to the learning theories of Hull (1943, 1952) and Spence (1956, 1960), (b) the criterion decision rule for recognition memory, first used for this purpose by Egan (1958), (c) the provision for more than one memory trace, (d) the distinction between acquisition, decay, and retrieval phases of memory traces, (e) the additive combination of traces, (f) the provision for strength generalization due to event similarity, and (g) exponential decay.

The principal extensions are: (a) the subdivision of the acquisition phase into acquisition of potential strength and consolidation of retrievable strength, (b) the assumption of an ITM, distinct from STM and LTM, with an approximate specification of its consolidation time and decay rate, (c) the specification of many modalities of memory, (d) the formulation of order memory and its generalization properties, which is a modification of an earlier strength theory of order memory (Wickelgren, 1967a), (e) the specification of the maximum decision rule for recall, which follows Green and Moses (1966), Norman (1966), Kintsch (1968), Wickelgren (1968a), and Norman and Wickelgren (1969), and (f) the particular functions chosen for acquisition, consolidation, and retrieval.

Markov (finite state) models with STM and LTM states (Atkinson and Crothers, 1964; Bernbach, 1965; Calfee and Atkinson, 1965; Waugh and Norman, 1965; Greeno, 1967; Chapter 8) use a very different underlying (state) representation of the memory trace than multitrace strength theory. However, they share the basic idea that there is more than one memory trace, with the different traces having different forgetting (decay) properties. Of course, since no Markov model specifies states corresponding to the VSTM, STM, ITM, and LTM traces in multitrace strength theory, there is far from complete agreement on the number of traces. Furthermore, Markov models necessarily restrict an event or association to be in one state at a time, that is, an event or association could not be in both STM and LTM unless a new compound state is defined. This is clumsy. Also, if one wants to get many gradations of trace strength, this either requires a large increase in the number of states or defining distributions associated with each state (Bernbach, 1967; Kintsch, 1967; Murdock, Chapter 9). Neither alternative seems attractive to me.

Markov models of memory make essentially the same distinction between acquisition, decay, and retrieval phases of memory as multitrace strength theory. However, when consolidation is discussed in the context of a Markov model of memory (Bower, 1967a; Greeno, 1967), consolidation means transfer from STM to LTM. The assumption that an STM trace is "converted" into an LTM trace is not necessarily true, and, in fact, some physiological evidence suggests (though it does not prove) that LTM is consolidated independently from STM (or ITM) in rats

(Albert, 1966b). Multitrace strength theory is formulated so as to be able to accommodate either possibility, and, in any case, it is quite easy to have a decaying ITM component at the same time as a consolidating LTM component. This can be represented with a Markov model, but it is awkward.

Recently, a new class of models (Bower, 1967a; Atkinson and Shiffrin, 1965, 1968; Atkinson, Brelsford, and Shiffrin, 1967) has emerged out of the Markov model tradition. These models, called "multiprocess models" by Atkinson *et al.* (1967), postulate VSTM and add considerable structural detail to STM, LTM, the transfer from STM to LTM, and the maintenance of an STM trace by rehearsal. Perhaps the three most basic features of the multiprocess models are: (a) the rehearsal buffer representation of STM, (b) the search representation of LTM, and (c) the distinction between memory structure and control processes such as rehearsal and recoding that can operate on the memory structure. In special cases, multiprocess models can be reduced to Markov models, but multiprocess models have far more flexibility. In particular, traces for a single event can be in both STM and LTM and can have different numbers of copies or degrees of strength. Multiprocess models most often maintain a basically discrete characterization of memory traces, while strength models use a continuous characterization. More important, multiprocess models have been much more concerned with the control processes of rehearsal in STM, and search processes in LTM, than has strength theory. Multitrace strength theory places much greater emphasis on memory structure: the number of traces, acquisition, consolidation, decay, and elementary retrieval-decision processes.

The multicomponent model of Bower (1967b) and the model proposed in this volume by Norman and Rumelhart (Chapter 2) differ from multitrace strength theory by analyzing an item into discrete attributes (components, features) and assuming that memory traces are formed for each attribute. Multitrace strength theory is currently designed to take a continuous similarity-space approach to item analysis.

Information processing models of memory such as EPAM (Feigenbaum, 1963; Chapter 13; Simon and Feigenbaum, 1964) and the model of Judith Reitman (Chapter 5) differ from multitrace strength theory primarily in : (a) their greater emphasis on control processes such as rehearsal and search and (b) in their choice of programming languages as the language for precise expression of the theory, rather than more conventional axiomatic mathematics.

Assumptions of Multitrace Strength Theory

Four Phases

The time course of a memory trace M under conditions K has 4 phases: acquisition of potential strength, $A(t_A)$, consolidation of actual strength, $C(t)$, decay of strength, $D(t)$, and retrieval of strength, $R(t_R)$. Events or the rehearsal of prior events initiate acquisition, and each phase follows after the other in the order: acquisition, consolidation, decay, and retrieval, with overlap being possible between two adjacent phases. Judged strength of a memory trace $M = A(t_A)\, C(t)\, D(t)\, R(t_R) + X$, where X is a normally distributed random variable: $X \sim N[0,\sigma]$. The functions A, C, D, and R and the parameter σ are functions of M and K; t_A is the acquisition (presentation or rehearsal) time, t is the delay since the onset or offset of the acquisition period, and t_R is the time allowed for retrieval.

Four Traces per Modality

In each modality of memory, there are as many as four traces with different time courses: very-short-term memory (V), short-term memory (S), intermediate-term memory (I), and long-term memory (L).

Many Modalities

Every sensory, motor, and cognitive modality of performance is a modality of memory.

Event Memory

An occurring event i initiates all four memory traces in each relevant modality for that event and for any other event j in proportion to η_{ij}, its similarity to j in that modality.

Order Memory

A sequence of events, $i = 1, \ldots, n$, initiates all four memory traces in relevant modalities for each direct forward association $i \rightarrow i + 1$ and for each other association $i \rightarrow j (j \neq i + 1)$ in proportion to a weighted linear combination of $\eta_{i+1,j}$ (event associative response generalization),

$\eta_{j-1,i}$ (event associative stimulus generalization), and π_{ij} (positional similarity to a direct forward association). For ungrouped coding, π_{ij} is a monotone decreasing function of $|i-j|$, and $\pi_{i,i+z} > \pi_{i,i-z}$.

Additive Combination of Traces in Retrieval

The sum of all trace strengths in all modalities (total strength) is judged in retrieval.

Criterion Decision Rule for Event and Order Recognition

A subject responds "yes" if the total strength of a test event or test association exceeds a criterion. Confidence ratings are obtained by partitioning the total strength dimension by further criteria. Under conditions K, criteria c_{iK} are normally distributed random variables, $c_{iK} \sim N[0,\sigma_K]$.

Maximum Decision Rule for Recall and Multiple-Choice

A subject chooses the event with the greatest total strength of association to the cue event.

Bounded Exponential Acquisition

$A(t_A) = \alpha(1 - e^{-\theta t_A})$, where α and θ depend on M and K.

Delayed Consolidation

$$C(t) = \begin{cases} 0 & \text{for } t < \tau \\ [(t-\tau)/(\epsilon-\tau)]^{\varphi} & \text{for } \tau \leqslant t \leqslant \epsilon \\ 1 & \text{for } t > \epsilon, \end{cases}$$

where τ, ϵ, and φ depend on M and K. For present purposes, we can assume $\varphi = 1$ so that $C(t)$ is a ramp function from $t = \tau$ to $t = \epsilon$.

Exponential Decay

$$D(t) = \begin{cases} 1 & \text{for } t < \tau \text{ or } \epsilon \\ e^{-\beta(t-\tau)} & \text{for } t \geqslant \tau \text{ or } \epsilon, \end{cases}$$

where β depends on M and K.

Bounded Exponential Retrieval

$$R(t_R) = \rho(1 - e^{-\psi t_R}),$$

where ρ and ψ depend on M and K.

Restrictions in Testing Strength Theory

The foregoing theory is intended to be formulated with sufficient flexibility to be able to handle known behavioral and neurobehavioral (ablation, stimulation, and pharmacological effects on behavior) phenomena of memory, with appropriate choices of the acquisition, consolidation, decay, retrieval, and decision parameters for each trace for any set of conditions. As with any general scientific theory, the predictions of the theory will be very hard to derive for the vast majority of conditions and so only carefully selected conditions are suitable for testing the theory. For ease in testing multitrace strength theory, the important restrictions on conditions are the following:

(*a*) The test event should be sufficiently simple that subjects handle it as a unit, making a single absolute or comparative judgment, not a sequence of elementary decisions combined into an overall decision by means of complicated logical reasoning. In principle, when we have some understanding of the elementary syntactic and semantic units of a phrase, sentence, or sequence of thoughts, stimuli, or responses, and when we know more about the cognitive processes in logical reasoning, then strength theory should be applicable to memory for phrases, sentences, and complex thought, sensory, or motor sequences. However, at present, no application of strength theory to such complex events is possible.

(*b*) For the same purpose of encouraging single-stage decisions, the time for the "yes–no," rating, multiple-choice, or recall response should be very limited, and rapid responding should be encouraged.

(*c*) Only a single response should be required in the retrieval-decision period in order to avoid delay and/or interference effects in the retrieval-decision period, though these effects need not be too difficult to analyze within strength theory. However, if the correctness of previous responses influences later responses, one could get stochastic processes that would needlessly add to the complexity of strength theory. Single test methods, especially probe methods (e.g., Murdock, 1961a, 1962a; Waugh and Norman, 1965; Norman, 1966; Wickelgren and Norman,

1966) are certainly to be preferred, and complete recall methods, with the order of recall uncontrolled, are too messy to be quantitatively analyzable with strength theory.

(*d*) Recognition tests are theoretically simpler to analyze with strength theory than recall or multiple-choice tests, and so recognition tests are preferable. However, much work must be done with recall to determine the relationship between recall and recognition memory. Omissions greatly complicate the strength-theory analysis of recall experiments. So omissions should not be allowed in recall (or recognition), at least until we understand recall without omissions much better than we do at present.

(*e*) Conscious rehearsal of events to be remembered must be strictly controlled by telling the subject what to rehearse (think of) at every moment. Any controlled method of rehearsal is analyzable by strength theory, but it is easiest to analyze conditions in which the subjects are thinking only of the current event or pair of events and never thinking of previous events. The reason for controlling rehearsal is that strength theory requires that we know at all times what phase of the memory process each event-trace is in. Naturally, control of conscious rehearsal will be less than perfect, but conscientious subjects appear to be able to control rehearsal quite adequately. A small amount of rehearsal will not affect strength decay curves very much and part of the effect is handled by the random noise factor X in the four-phase assumption. The remaining effect of a small probability of uncontrolled rehearsal can be reduced further by increasing the number of events that have to be remembered, since the only time that rehearsal affects the strength decay curve is when a subject rehearses the event to be tested later. Thus, probe methods are superior to presenting and testing a single item. In principle, one could model uncontrolled rehearsal within the context of strength theory. However, this greatly increases the computational complexity of strength theory, and I do not see what one would learn from this that one would not learn much more easily from controlled rehearsal.

(*f*) As we learn more about the properties of different traces in different modalities (particularly the decay rates and what they depend upon), we should try to set up conditions so as to study one trace in one modality at a time. In some cases, it may be possible to study one trace under conditions where the other traces are lower in their contribution to the total strength by a factor of 100 or more yielding simple exponential decay functions (e.g., Wickelgren and Norman, 1966). In other cases, we may have to settle for factors of around 10 (e.g., Wickelgren, 1969).

However, every effort should be made to secure strength decay curves that are very close to simple exponential decay functions, because their precise analysis requires far fewer different delay conditions than decay curves that must be fit by the sum of two exponentials.

Note that, with the exception of (f), all the other restrictions on tests of multitrace strength theory are concerned with controlling the "strategy" or "control process" of the subject in acquisition, rehearsal during the storage interval, and retrieval. Experiments on human or animal learning or memory, which have not carefully controlled these acquisition, storage, and retrieval strategies may provide qualitative tests of multitrace strength theory, but quantitative evaluation is generally difficult in these cases. Since verbal instructional control of human strategies is probably much easier to achieve than control of animal strategies by pretraining, all quantitative behavioral tests of strength theory to be mentioned in this chapter will be on human beings, though some qualitative neurobehavioral findings with animals will also be mentioned. However, there is no reason why strength theory could not be applied to animal learning and memory, at some future time.

Completeness of Multitrace Strength Theory

Although multitrace strength theory applies to all memory situations, it requires the estimation of many, possibly different, parameters in every situation to which it is applied. Obviously, there must be some parameter invariance over different situations and, failing this, some simple functions for predicting parameters in one situation from parameters in other situations. Efforts to determine parameter invariance and other simple parameter functions, within the context of multitrace strength theory, have not proceeded far enough to justify including any such assumptions in the foregoing statement of the general assumptions of multitrace strength theory. However, the available findings on parameter functions will be discussed later, along with some indications of how multitrace strength theory might be completed to include these functions.

Predictions and Empirical Adequacy of Multitrace Strength Theory

One of the features of a mathematical theory that gives it great generality with a small number of axioms is the combining power of the axioms with themselves and with the more general axioms of mathematics. In general, the predictions of the theory are theorems derived from several axioms. While this is a desirable feature of a theory, it does make testing the theory somewhat more complicated. Ideally, it would be desirable to test each assumption independently of the others, but this is rarely possible. However, one can attempt to approach this ideal as closely as possible. The present section discusses some of the predictions of multitrace strength theory that have been tested to date, pointing out which assumptions are being tested by each prediction.

Four Traces

Present evidence does not require one to postulate four separate traces with different memory properties. But present evidence does require at least two memory traces, and there is suggestive evidence for four traces.

The evidence that compels the assumption of at least two memory traces is that human beings with bilateral mesial temporal ablations can have completely normal short-term memory (STM) with very little ability to form new long-term memories (LTM) (Scoville and Milner, 1957; Milner, 1966; Wickelgren, 1968b). In terms of the present four-trace system, the cut is probably between STM (delays of 1–20 sec) and intermediate-term memory, ITM (delays of 20 sec to minutes or hours), but this is not completely clear. A huge mass of neurobehavioral data on the effects of various drugs, spreading depression, and dc potentials applied to the brain also strongly supports the hypothesis that there are at least two memory traces, though some of these data are more complex to interpret than the neurological data. (See Agranoff and Davis, 1968; Albert, 1966a, 1966b, 1966c; Barondes and Cohen, 1968; Deutsch, Hamburg, and Dahl, 1966; Flexner and Flexner, 1968; for recent representative articles.) Finally, trace strength decay curves for normal subjects often have two components, a rapidly decaying component and a more slowly decaying component (Waugh and Norman, 1965; Wickelgren, 1969).

The argument for distinguishing ITM from STM is that human beings with mesial temporal lesions show pronounced deficits in the level of ITM compared to normal subjects. These deficits appear for delays greater than about 4 sec in those tasks where normal subjects show a very slowly decaying (ITM) component of the trace lasting for minutes, tens of minutes, or more (Milner, 1966).

The argument for distinguishing this ITM from LTM is that many of the neurobehavioral studies indicate that LTM requires a consolidation period on the order of hours or days to be established. (Agranoff and Davis, 1968; Albert, 1966a, 1966b, 1966c; Deutsch *et al.*, 1966; provide some recent examples.) The ITM which is severely impaired in the subjects with mesial temporal lesions must be established in seconds, so this ITM could not be the same trace as LTM.

The argument for distinguishing between STM and ITM is stronger than the argument for distinguishing between ITM and LTM because the latter argument requires generalizing from various species of animals to humans. However, there is a factor of about 10^7 between the strength decay rates of the fastest decaying STM and the slowest decaying LTM, according to a rough calculation, and only part of this seems to be explainable on the basis of variation in the STM and LTM decay rates. Thus, there appears to be a hole which ITM could fill in normal retention curves. The evidence for three traces, STM, ITM, and LTM is not as definitive as that for distinguishing at least two traces, STM and ITM-LTM, but the three trace theory does seem more plausible than the two trace theory.

The evidence for the very-short-term memory (VSTM) trace is scant indeed, but it seems safest to consider the memory for visual or auditory material that has not been attended-to (e.g., Sperling, 1960, 1963; Averbach and Sperling, 1961; Broadbent, 1958) to be a different kind of memory until and unless it is proven otherwise.

Exponential Decay

One of the most important successes of strength theory is that, so far, strength decay functions have turned out to be either simple exponentials (Wickelgren and Norman, 1966; Wickelgren, 1967a, 1968b, 1970, and much unpublished data) or the sum of two exponentials (Wickelgren, 1969). For example, Wickelgren and Norman (1966) found simple exponential decay of the strength of the STM trace in a probe study of items (three-digit numbers) in all serial positions of lists from two to seven items long. The probe was a single item from the previous list presented immediately after the end of the list. Thus, the temporal delay between presentation and test is the number of subsequent items times the presentation time for each item (1 second in this study). Semilogarithmic plots of these strength decay curves are shown in Fig. 1. Consistent with the assumption of exponential decay, these strength decay curves are well fit by straight lines on semilog plots.

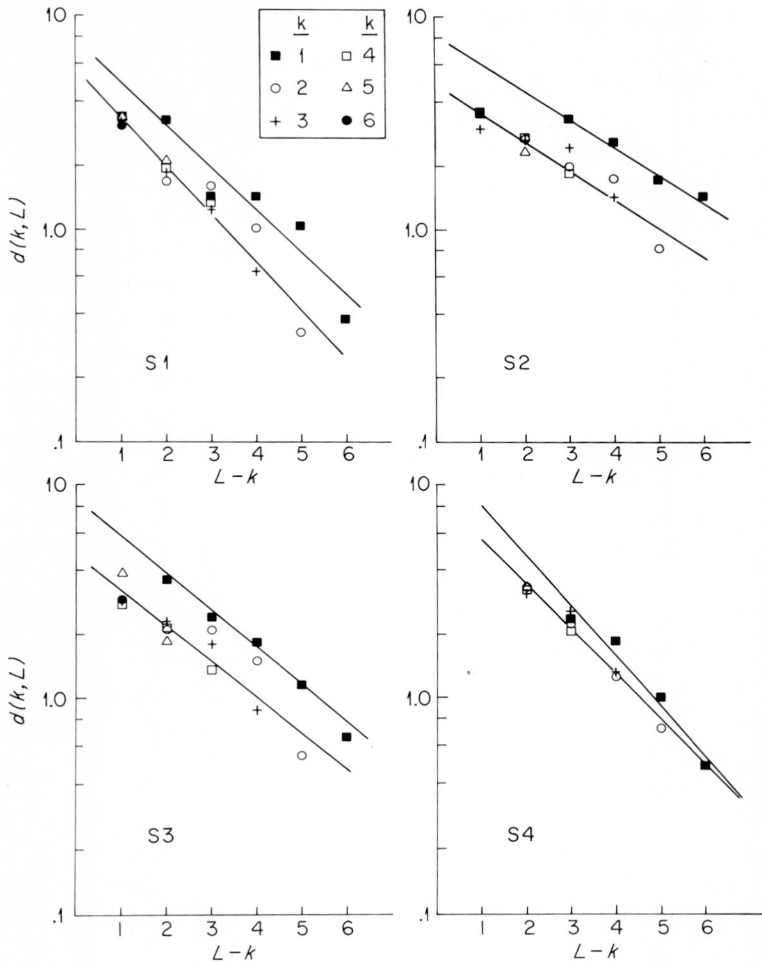

FIG. 1. The $d(k, L)$ values for each serial position (k), in lists of length $L = 2$–7, as a function of the number of subsequent items (L-k). L-k is also equal to the delay in seconds. The two straight lines in each plot are the least-squares fits to the data. The upper line is the fit to the first items ($k = 1$) and the lower line is the fit for all the other items ($k > 1$).

Furthermore, while the first item established a stronger trace in STM, it had approximately the same rate of decay as subsequent items in the list.

Probability decay curves are usually S-shaped with rate of decay first increasing and then decreasing. Strength theory may be able to account for all memory decay curves using one or two component traces at any given delay, though there are three different possible combinations of two traces, VSTM and STM, STM and ITM, ITM, and LTM.

The importance of this cannot be overemphasized. When the decay (forgetting) rate is not constant as a function of delay (under conditions which are homogeneous during all delays), it is extremely difficult to make meaningful comparisons among decay rates as a function of different conditions. When one has an analysis of the total memory trace into one or two components with each component having a constant decay rate at every delay, one has a general framework for memory and can hope for some success in determining the more specific laws of acquisition, consolidation, decay, and retrieval for each memory trace in each modality. Without such a framework, one is just stumbling in the dark.

STM and ITM

Since both STM and ITM are consolidated in seconds or tenths of a second, they are both potentially present whether the number of presentations is one or many. The basic idea that many studies have substantial amounts of both STM and ITM was first expressed in the Markov-model framework by Atkinson and Crothers (1964) and Waugh and Norman (1965). Using this theory, Waugh and Norman (1965) analyzed the decay curves for many tasks into two components. Multitrace strength also yields such an analysis, although it is somewhat different from a Markov analysis.

Besides being able to analyze a composite trace decay curve into components, it is also very desirable to design experiments so that only STM or ITM is being studied in an experiment. How can this be done, according to multitrace strength theory?

Studying ITM independently of STM is simple: just make use of the fact that ITM decays much more slowly than STM. Do not use immediate retention tests. Do use a variety of longer retention intervals on the order of minutes and hours. At least the first 20 sec of the retention interval should be filled with rehearsal preventing activity to eliminate the STM traces, but it is also highly desirable to do all one can to minimize rehearsal throughout the entire span of any retention interval. Finally, although some kinds of material and tasks give substantial levels of ITM with a single presentation of a few seconds per item, ITM often requires numerous presentations to build up to a substantial level. According to the present theory, all verbal learning tasks with filled (rehearsal-preventing) retention intervals of minutes or hours are studying verbal ITM.

Studying STM independently of ITM also makes use of the fact that ITM decays much more slowly than STM, but it makes use of this fact in a somewhat subtler way. If one uses a small population of items, say digits, letters, or a small set of words, over and over again on closely spaced trials, the ITM traces for all items and perhaps also all associations between items will be approximately equal. Only the STM trace will differentiate the items or associations on the last trial from those on previous trials. Thus, since ITM traces are equal for correct and incorrect events, one is studying only the STM traces on all trials after the first few.

Another potential way to study STM independently of ITM is to present material to be remembered so rapidly that the ITM trace does not have time to be acquired or cannot be consolidated. There is some reason to think this may be possible, but it is too early to tell for sure.

Free Recall. The present theory of STM and ITM explains many phenomena. First, it explains the two-component decay curves for free recall (e.g., Deese and Kaufman, 1957; Murdock, 1962b; Waugh, 1962) in a manner very similar to the analysis done with a different theory by Waugh and Norman (1965).

Continuous Recognition Memory. Second, it explains the large, slowly decaying component in continuous (steady-state) verbal recognition memory studies (Shepard and Teghtsoonian, 1961; Shepard and Chang, 1963; Donaldson and Murdock, 1968). In a simple yes–no continuous recognition memory study that I have done, items (words or a complex pattern composed of three consonants followed by three digits, abbreviated CCC–DDD) were presented at a rate of 3.5 sec per item. Subjects indicated whether or not they had seen an item previously, with delays between presentation and test ranging from immediate to about 12 minutes. The strength decay curves (log strength vs. delay) for one subject in this experiment are shown in Fig. 2. The straight lines are the theoretical, exponentially decaying, STM and ITM traces. The curved theoretical lines represent the total memory strength (sum of STM and ITM strengths). The component traces were derived under the assumptions that (*a*) STM decay rates are identical for words and CCC–DDD complexes, (*b*) ITM decay rates are identical for words and CCC–DDD complexes, (*c*) STM consolidates essentially immediately for both kinds of items, and (*d*) ITM consolidates linearly over

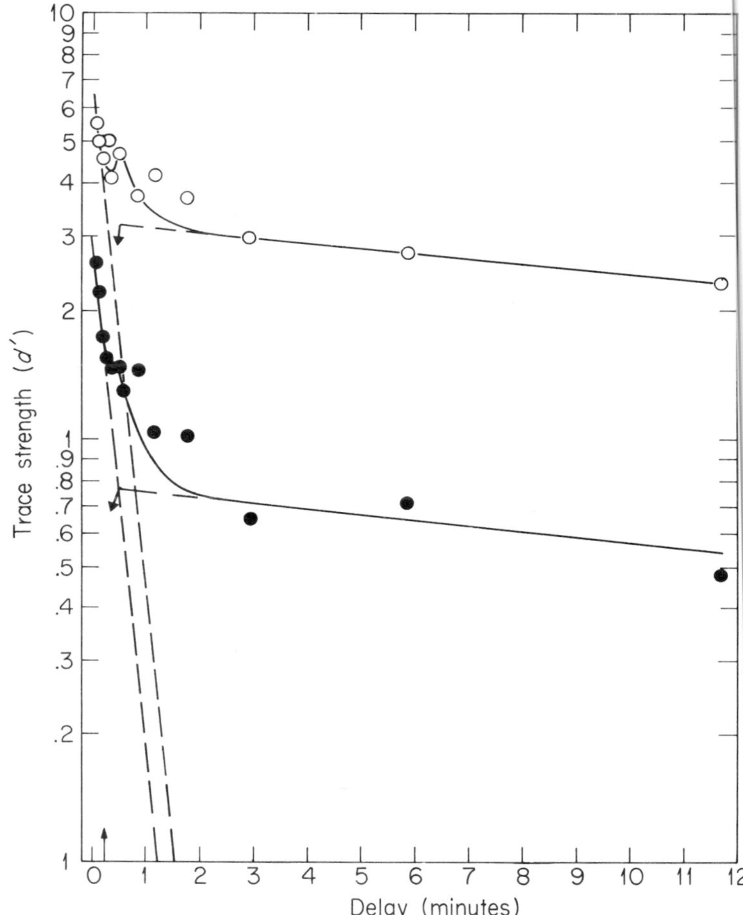

FIG. 2. Strength-decay curves for one subject in a continuous recognition memory task for words or CCC–DDD complexes. The dashed lines represent the best-fitting STM and ITM components of the trace, with the ITM component assumed to be consolidating over the period from 10 to 30 sec after presentation. The solid lines represent the total memory strength, the sum of the STM and ITM strengths.

the period from 10 to 30 sec following presentation for both kinds of items.

Note that depending on the form and rate of the consolidation function for ITM in relation to the rate of decay for STM, one can obtain short sections of the decay curve for total strength which are increasing in strength (reminiscence), though this need not occur and would not generally occur over a very long period of time. The fit of multitrace strength theory to these data is quite good with the exception of a few points at delays between 1 and 2 minutes. These modest deviations between theory and data could be due to averaging over items with very different STM or ITM decay curves, and work is in progress to determine if this is happening.

However, it is clear that, at least within the context of strength theory, the data in Fig. 1 and the continuous recognition data of Shepard and Teghtsoonian (1961) cannot possibly be fit by a single exponentially decaying trace. Rather, what seems to be required is to assume that performance is mediated by two traces, one with a decay rate similar to (though somewhat slower than) that found in probe studies of STM (Wickelgren and Norman, 1966; Wickelgren, 1970) and one with a decay rate slower by a factor of 10^2.

A study in progress on a subject with a bilateral mesial temporal lesion indicates that he has a normal or slightly reduced STM component in continuous recognition memory tasks, but has a much reduced ITM component in these tasks. This provides further support for the hypothesis that continuous recognition memory studies are studying both STM and ITM, and these studies should not be lumped together, willy-nilly, with pure STM studies that use a small population of items over and over again in rapid proximity.

Most continuous recognition memory studies using a large population of items have employed very slow presentation rates (around 5 seconds per item) though Howe (1967) got a moderate amount of ITM for pictures presented at 1.5 sec per picture. It is possible that acquisition of the ITM trace, while very rapid, is nevertheless on the order of a second or more (possibly varying with the type of material and the conditions of presentation). On the other hand, the STM trace clearly can be acquired in tenths of a second, since good STM is obtained for lists of items presented at four items per second. Thus, presenting one three-digit number per second, as in Wickelgren and Norman (1966) or four words per second in an unpublished study of mine appears to produce little or no ITM. This permits study of STM with larger populations of items.

Furthermore, use of a small population of events does not guarantee an uncomplicated study of STM, if the rate of presentation is slow enough to permit use of complicated coding or rehearsal strategies. This appears to have occurred in a continuous recognition memory study by Katz (1966) which employed a rather small population of associations (20 letter–number pairs), but used a very slow rate of presentation (8 seconds for each test plus new presentation of a pair). Katz (1966) instructed his subjects not to rehearse prior pairs, but this was not sufficient to eliminate the more slowly decaying component of the memory trace in his situation.

Recognition Memory for Pitch. Third, the present theory of STM and ITM explains the two-component trace-strength decay curves, invariably found for normal subjects in short-term recognition memory for pitch, using the delayed comparison procedure (Wickelgren, 1966a, 1969). The only subject who has not shown some ITM in this situation is a neurological subject with a bilateral mesial temporal lesion (Wickelgren, 1968b). The level of the ITM trace for normal subjects in this situation is generally fairly low, but given the frequency of presenting each tone from the rather small population of tones (usually 10 or 20 tones), this is probably reasonable. Here again, we find that some ITM can be formed for each item from a small population of items, when the rate of presenting new items to be learned is slow enough (on the order of one new item ever 10–40 sec in my pitch-memory experiments). Since the rate of decay of ITM for different kinds of materials under different conditions is not well established, it is not yet possible to make a definitive quantitative check on whether the level of ITM found in these pitch-memory studies is reasonable or not. On the basis of the estimated rate of decay for the ITM trace obtained from one experiment in Wickelgren (1969) and other unpublished studies, the level of ITM found in the pitch-memory studies appears to be of about the right order of magnitude, but further studies are necessary to clinch the point.

Three-Phase Studies. Fourth, multitrace strength theory explains the frequent (but not invariable) presence of a more slowly decaying component of the verbal memory trace in the "three-phase" or "distractor" (Murdock, 1967) design originated by Brown (1958) and Peterson and Peterson (1959). In this design, a single item or short list of items is presented followed by rehearsal-preventing activity followed by a test of some or all of the items in the short list.

In the three-phase design, acquisition (perhaps including some or all of the consolidation), storage (decay, perhaps preceded by some consolidation), and retrieval-decision phases are all distinguished to the subject and independently manipulable by the experimenter. This is the advantage of the three-phase method over the probe (two-phase) method, which confounds acquisition and storage, and the continuous (one-phase) method, which confounds all three. Probe and continuous methods have compensating advantages for certain purposes, and, as will be apparent from the present discussion, the three-phase design has some disadvantages, so no one should conclude that one of these methods is always to be preferred.

Just as in the delayed comparison of pitch studies (which use the three-phase design), the frequency with which each item is presented to be learned has generally been much lower than in probe studies. Thus, according to the present theory, it is not surprising that strength decay curves for three-phase recall studies (Peterson and Peterson, 1959; Murdock, 1961b; Hellyer, 1962; Melton, 1963) frequently require both an STM and an ITM component to achieve a good fit. In Figs. 3 and 4, strength decay curves have been plotted for the three-phase recall study of Hellyer (1962) and the vocal rehearsal condition of the Peterson and Peterson (1959) study. The parameter is the number of repetitions or amount of rehearsal time prior to beginning the backward counting that filled the delay interval. These strength-decay curves were derived from the probability decay curves by assuming that the consonant trigrams to be remembered came from a population of about 1000 and that all incorrect trigrams had approximately equal strength.

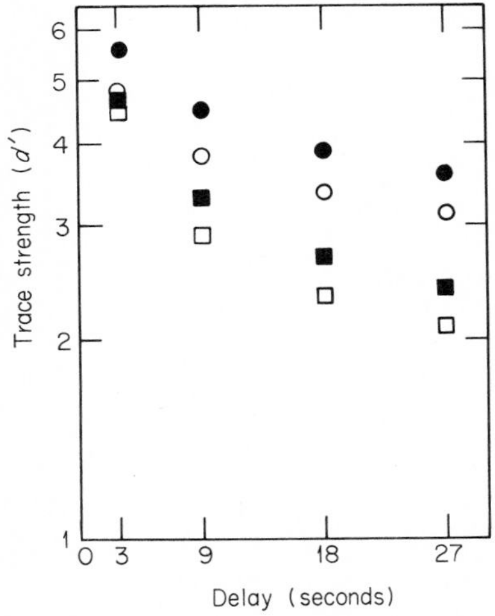

FIG. 3. Strength-decay curves for three-phase recall of consonant trigrams as a function of the number of repetitions (from Hellyer, 1962).

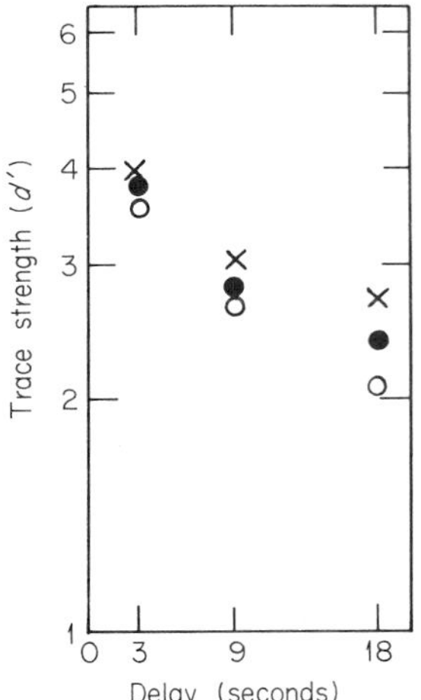

FIG. 4. Strength-decay curves for three-phase recall of consonant trigrams, as a function of rehearsal time (from Peterson and Peterson, 1959).

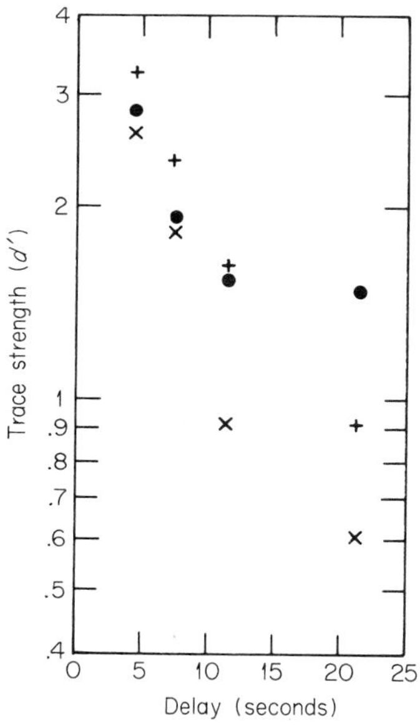

FIG. 5. Strength-decay curves for three subjects in three-phase recognition of a single consonant letter.

The same deviation from simple exponential decay is found in recognition memory, where it is not necessary to make assumptions about population size or equivalence of incorrect strength distributions. See Fig. 5 for the strength decay curves of three subjects in an unpublished study of mine where single letters were presented and tested for recognition memory after delays filled with rapid backward counting.

For a variety of reasons (the main one being the absence of really long delays with the three-phase method), it is not yet possible to draw quantitative conclusions regarding the rates of decay for verbal STM and ITM in three-phase situations. However, there is every reason to hope that the strength decay rates for STM and ITM in three-phase studies will be consistent with the STM decay rates found in probe studies and the STM and ITM decay rates found in continuous studies.

Proactive Interference in STM. Fifth, multitrace strength theory explains why the decay of the memory trace for once presented material is much slower on the first few trials of an STM experiment (Keppel and Underwood, 1962) or on the first few trials after the type of material is changed (Wickens, Born, and Allen, 1963; Loess, 1968). According to the present theory, this "proactive interference" effect is due to the first few trials having substantial levels of ITM, in addition to STM. On later trials, the ITM for items on previous trials has not decayed very much, and competition from these items in a recall test substantially reduces the value of the ITM component of the trace for items on later trials, since the cues for each trial are not very distinct. According to multitrace strength theory, the contribution of the ITM trace to the discriminability of correct and incorrect items on the previous trial decreases rapidly over the first few trials of an experiment to an asymptote that depends on the average time between successive presentations of the same item. Many factors affect the average time between successive presentations of the same item: the number of items presented per trial, the size of the item population, and the intertrial interval.

In accord with the prediction of multitrace strength theory, longer intertrial intervals are known to produce less "proactive interference" from previous trials (better memory) in "STM" experiments where few items are presented to be learned on each trial (Peterson and Gentile, 1965). According to the theory, intrusions from items in the same position on previous trials should decrease with increasing distance from the present trial, measuring distance in either time or trials, and this prediction is also known to be valid (Melton and Von Lackum, 1941;

Conrad, 1959, 1960; Peterson and Gentile, 1965; Peterson and James, 1967).

The one possibly discrepant finding is that Conrad (1960) found no net improvement in memory performance with longer intertrial intervals, though he did find intrusions from items in the same position on the previous trial to decrease with intertrial interval. The reasons for this discrepant finding are not clear. However, it is likely that Conrad's (1960) experiment involved very little ITM compared to the experiment of Peterson and Gentile (1965), since Conrad presented a much longer list to be remembered and presented it at a fairly rapid rate (two items per second).

Finally, it should be noted that all of the STM "proactive interference" studies have used recall to test retention. It should be possible to analyze the "proactive interference" effect much more precisely with recognition, carefully controlling the similarity of incorrect test items to items correct for previous trials.

VSTM and STM

If there is an auditory or visual VSTM that should be distinguished from STM, then probably the last item or two in a list, when tested immediately, should not be considered in fitting an STM trace to the strength decay curve.

ITM and LTM

Besides the neurobehavioral evidence for distinguishing ITM and LTM, strength decay curves for visual memory (Shepard, 1967; Nickerson, 1968) show a much more rapid decay in the first week or two than from two weeks to one year. Until more is known concerning the rate of decay of the ITM trace and the rate of consolidation of the LTM trace for different types of materials and conditions, one must be cautious in interpreting retention data at delays of two hours to two weeks. At some delays in this interval, one either gets substantial overlap of ITM and useful LTM or else it should be possible to show reminiscence between carefully selected delays.

Incidentally, if one does get reminiscence here, it suggests that the LTM trace consolidates independently of the ITM trace, at least to some extent.

Four Phases

The distinction between the acquisition, decay (storage), and retrieval-decision phases of memory seems to be necessarily valid for any device with memory. In the present formulation of multitrace strength theory, acquisition refers to establishing a potential, but not yet usable, memory trace. Consolidation converts this potential trace into an actual (usable) trace. The distinction between acquisition and consolidation is somewhat questionable for VSTM and STM, and the evidence is not yet conclusive for distinguishing acquisition and consolidation in ITM. However, the neurobehavioral evidence just cited seems to indicate a relatively substantial consolidation phase for LTM.

Consolidation of VSTM and STM in all modalities may proceed simultaneously with acquisition or occur so rapidly after acquisition that there is no need to recognize it as a separate phase of these memory traces. However, this is easily handled by the present theory through choice of a consolidation function that approaches asymptote so quickly that it is essentially a step function for our purposes. If this is so, then the only advantage of including a consolidation phase in VSTM and STM is to be able to handle all four traces in the same framework. Alternatively, we may, one day, find phenomena that require STM consolidation times of seconds or tenths of a second. Multitrace strength theory can handle either eventuality.

Independence from Irrelevant Strengths

The principal qualitative component of the criterion decision rule for recognition memory is the assumption of "independence from irrelevant strengths" (similar to the analogously named notions of Arrow, 1951; Luce, 1959). The assumption is that in a recognition test, the subject judges only the strength of the test event (item or association), without considering the strength of other events. This assumption means that there is no retrieval interference (competition) in a recognition test, an assumption made without proof by many workers in verbal learning.

I have not been able to think of a good test of this assumption for item memory, but a powerful test is possible for order memory. The test is to determine if the strength discriminability of a correct A–B association from an incorrect A–D association is affected by the presence or absence of a strong A–C association. According to strength theory, the difference in strength of A–B and A–D associations should be unaffected by the strength of an "irrelevant" A–C association. This strong prediction of strength theory appears to be valid, at least for STM (Wickelgren, 1967a; Bower and Bostrom, 1968). Since the assumption of the independence from irrelevant strengths applies only to the retrieval-decision phase of recognition memory, proving it for STM very strongly indicates that it holds when ITM or LTM traces are being judged also.

However, a successful test, of the type discussed above, of the assumption of independence from irrelevant strengths in retrieval requires that there also be no reduced acquisition or consolidation and and no increased decay of an A–B association when preceded or followed by an A–C association. This equivalence of acquisition, consolidation and decay for A–B, A–C and A–B, C–D is known to be false for verbal ITM (e.g., McGovern, 1964; Postman, 1965) and LTM (Houston, 1967). In these verbal learning studies, the effect is usually called "unlearning," though "storage interference" might be a better term, if recognition tests show that the effect holds when the "irrelevant" A–C association is presented before the A–B association. "Unlearning" is a fine term for a retroactive interference effect, but not for an effect due to proactive interference.

The report by Houston (1968) of an unlearning effect in STM did not use a recognition test and also employed a paradigm conducive to the presence of large ITM traces, according to the classification scheme presented here.

Either no storage interference (unlearning) occurs in STM or, more likely, as stated by Wickelgren (1967a), the strength in STM of an A–B association is impaired as much by C–D pairs as by A–C pairs among the prior and subsequent items. There is quite solid evidence that the number of subsequent items plays an important role in decay in STM, even when the temporal delay between presentation and test is held constant and rehearsal is presumed to be minimal (Waugh and Norman, 1965; Norman, 1966). The Waugh and Norman (1965) and Norman (1966) studies were recall studies, and so could be affected by retrieval interference. However, I have evidence showing that the number of intervening items also plays an important role, in addition to temporal delay, using a recognition test of STM (Wickelgren, 1970).

Invariance of Decay Rates

Although the decay rate for a single trace for a particular subject appears to be invariant with delay, it does not appear to be invariant under other conditions. For example, in a probe recognition study, I have found decay in STM to be a function of both temporal delay and the number of intervening items, making the rate of decay in STM different for different rates of presenting the items to be learned (Wickelgren, 1970). Furthermore, the rate of temporal decay of the STM trace in three-phase or continuous memory tasks appears to be somewhat slower than the rate of temporal decay in probe memory tasks, though it may be possible to account for this under the rubric of "rate of presentation of new material to be learned."

Analyzing these tasks in terms of the number of intervening items, rather than temporal delay, fails to produce invariance in STM decay rates, and, in my opinion, item decay functions provide a far less satisfactory framework in which to analyze what STM decay rates depend upon than do temporal decay functions (one example of this is found in Wickelgren, 1970).

Examples of the lack of invariance of strength decay rates for ITM and LTM can undoubtedly also be found in verbal learning studies, where a number of factors appear to affect decay rate, such as the amount and similarity of interpolated learning and the degree of learning of the original list. However, virtually all of the relevant studies were done using recall to measure retention, and permitting omissions. Such studies are very difficult to analyze with strength theory. Furthermore, intrusion frequencies are often not reported in enough detail to make any strength-theory analysis possible. One exception is the set of recognition-matching studies on unlearning that were referred to already.

Finally, there is an intuitive argument against invariance of the STM, ITM, and LTM decay rates, which derives from the factor of 10^7 between the decay rates of the fastest decaying STM and the slowest decaying LTM. Intuitively, it seems as if some memories last for seconds, others for minutes, others for hours, others for days, others for weeks or months, and others for years. To make memories last for each of these different periods of time, even with three traces, would require factors of e^{100} or e^{1000} in degree of acquisition above that required for perfect performance with an immediate retention test. This is undoubtedly a biophysical and biochemical impossibility for the nervous system. If such smooth variation in the duration of different memories is to be achieved by the nervous system with three traces, it must be done by varying the decay rate for one or more traces, not the degree of acquisition. This variability of decay rate is precisely what Melton (1963) claims for a single-trace theory.

Form of the Acquisition, Consolidation, and Retrieval Functions

No deep significance is attached to the form I have chosen for these functions: (*a*) exponential approach to a positive limit, starting from zero for the acquisition and retrieval functions and (*b*) a delayed, bounded ramp function for consolidation.

The assumption of zero starting value in acquisition and consolidation means that, in separated multiple-presentation situations, we are always focusing on the increment in trace strength contributed by the last presentation. At present, this seems to me to be the simplest way to handle multiple presentation. However, it should be noted that this requires us to consider some aspects of the history of prior presentations as part of the conditions that determine the parameters in these acquisition and consolidation functions. This could be a mess.

The upper bound on the degree of acquisition, consolidation, and retrieval is a completely reasonable constraint. The provision for some delay before consolidation begins is probably absolutely necessary for ITM and LTM, but slight delays may also be found in the onsets of other processes.

The degree of empirical support for the chosen form of these functions is almost nonexistent. Some weak evidence that the form of the acquisition function is approximately an exponential approach to a limit was found in a study of STM for pitch (Wickelgren, 1969).

Spacing of Multiple Presentation

The effects of the spacing of multiple presentations have been admirably reviewed by Bjork (Chapter 10), and this review will not be repeated here. I will content myself with three empirical generalizations that Bjork has derived from previous experimental studies, citing one representative study to support each generalization: (*a*) Massed presentations lead to superior memory at delays of less than 4 sec (Peterson, Hillner, and Saltzman, 1962); (*b*) Spaced presentations lead to superior memory at delays of 8 sec or more (Peterson *et al.*, 1962); (*c*) As the delay between presentations increases from 0 to somewhere between 16 and 32 sec, memory assessed 16 sec after the second presentation increases, but as the delay between presentations increases beyond this point memory (still assessed 16 sec after the second presentation) decreases (Peterson, Wampler, Kirkpatrick, and Saltzman, 1963).

These three effects are nicely explained by multitrace strength theory. First, the beneficial effects of massed presentation are obtained at just those brief delays at which the STM component of the total memory trace is most important. Since the STM trace consolidates and decays rapidly, one expects optimal STM from massed presentation. Second, the advantages of spaced presentation appear when ITM is beginning to play a much larger role in memory performance. It is quite reasonable to suppose that ITM requires a much longer consolidation time than STM and that the optimal level of ITM would be obtained from two presentations, when the second presentation occurred after the first had had time to consolidate. Third, one expects to find an optimal spacing time at around the time consolidation of the first presentation is complete or almost complete, because the ITM trace does decay after it consolidates. Although it may be a complete coincidence, the improvement in ITM performance with spacing appears to be greater than 16 and less than 32 sec, and in the section on continuous recognition memory studies, there seemed to be some advantage in assuming that consolidation of ITM took place over the period from 10 to 30 sec following presentation.

Independence of the Phases

This is sort of a "catch-all" title under which to include a lot of formally similar, but substantively different, properties (of an extended version of strength theory) about which little is known at present. As formulated in the present paper, multitrace strength theory, while making many definite predictions, still has considerable flexibility in many other predictions because of the unstated dependencies of acquisition, consolidation, decay, retrieval, and noise parameters on the conditions K. When one has not even specified the aspects of the experimental conditions that influence each parameter, this leaves a lot of flexibility. A completely extended version of multitrace strength theory must specify all of these parameter functions. When this is done, an important factor in evaluating the simplicity of strength theory will be the degree to which the parameters for each phase depend only upon the conditions during that phase, in addition to depending on the type of trace.

For example, one would like the decay rate for a particular trace to be independent of the degree of acquisition and consolidation. This has been found in STM for pitch (Wickelgren, 1969), where acquisition was manipulated by varying either the duration of the standard tone or the frequency difference between the standard tone and the comparison tone. In verbal STM, Wickelgren and Norman (1966) found the same decay rate for the first item in a list as for other items, even though the first item had a higher degree of learning. Unpublished data of mine in verbal ITM (1–12 minutes) and verbal LTM (weeks to years) also show decay rate to be independent of degree of acquisition.

Less is known concerning acquisition functions, but Wickelgren (1969) has found the acquisition function in STM for pitch to have approximately the same form and rate of approach to a limit, irrespective of the delay time.

Relation between Event and Order Memory

Essentially nothing is known about the relation between event and order memory. If the same kinds of traces mediate both event and order memory, then there ought to be a considerable degree of functional form and parameter invariance. Failing complete parameter invariance there might be other simple relations between comparable parameters for item and order memory.

Relation between Recognition, Multiple-Choice, and Recall

It would also be very desirable if the functional form and parameters of acquisition, consolidation, decay, retrieval, and noise were invariant over recognition, multiple-choice, and recall methods of testing memory. Failing complete invariance, there might still be some fairly simple relations that would enable an extended version of multitrace strength theory to predict performance on one test from performance on another test. Little is known about the relations between parameters for recall, multiple-choice, and recognition. However, for verbal STM, Norman (1966) obtained some support for the invariance of STM decay rate across recall and recognition.

When all the relations between two tests of memory are known for all phases of memory, it is then possible to predict performance on one test from performance on the other test. Even assuming that the basic memory traces are identical for two methods of testing retention, there are still a number of possible complications in making these predictions, which are discussed more extensively in Wickelgren (1968a) and Norman and Wickelgren (1969). First, there is the question of whether the retrieval noise is the same for two different methods of testing retention, especially when the number of traces to be retrieved is different. Second, there is the question of whether there is a noise source in recall and multiple-choice comparable to the criterion noise in recognition. Third, there is the question of whether there is increased time for decay when the number of traces to be retrieved is increased. Fourth, there is the question of whether noise distributions for different traces are uncorrelated.

Considering all these possible complications, it is surprising that two rather straightforward strength theory predictions of multiple-choice from recognition have been completely successful, in what was probably verbal ITM in one case (Green and Moses, 1966) and a mixture of verbal ITM and STM in the other case (Kintsch, 1968). The relation between recognition, multiple-choice, and recall was not quite so simple in a study of verbal STM by Norman and Wickelgren (1969).

Systematic Errors in Event Memory

Errors in recall or recognition of items (events) using verbal STM tend to be phonetically similar to the correct item (Conrad, 1964; Wickelgren, 1965a, 1965b, 1965c, 1966b, 1966c). Errors for more obviously compound items, such as digit pairs (Norman and Wickelgren, 1965; Wickelgren, 1966d), are also more frequent for compound items that have elements in common with the correct items. There appear to be two basic approaches to a mathematical theory of this kind of data: the discrete component approach (such as the multicomponent theory of Bower, 1967b, or Norman and Rumelhart, Chapter 2) and the generalization gradient (similarity space) approach taken by the present version of multitrace strength theory.

Accounting for systematic error data with multitrace strength theory can be done at two levels. At the more superficial level, the similarity parameters, η_{ij}, for all pairs of items can be estimated from the data, and a variety of predictions, such as invariances of decay rates and other rate parameters, can be tested. At a deeper level, one could attempt to extend multitrace strength theory to include a theory of the similarity parameters, deriving them from some underlying space characteristic of the modality of the memory trace. Ideally, there should be some relation between the memory similarity space for a modality and the perceptual similarity space for the same modality. But since multitrace strength theory has been (successfully) tested against error data only at the more superficial level and only in the case of STM for pitch (Wickelgren, 1969), this is all far in the future.

Systematic Errors in Order Memory

In testing memory for the item that followed another item in a list, errors tend to be from similar serial positions to that of the correct item, and the similarity function π_{ij} can be one dimensional in ungrouped coding of a list (Norman, 1966) or two dimensional in grouped coding of a list (Wickelgren, 1964, 1967b).

In addition, there is evidence for systematic errors based on item-to-item associations: (*a*) stimulus generalization (a similar item, or the same item in a different position, evoking the response appropriate to the cue item, Wickelgren, 1965d, 1966e) and (*b*) response generalization (the cue item evoking response items that are similar to the response item, Conrad, 1964; Wickelgren, 1965a, 1965b, 1965c, 1966c). These item-to-item associative effects should be handled by the same event similarity functions, η_{ij}, as before. In the absence of any evidence on how positional similarity, stimulus generalization, and response generalization are to be combined, I have just assumed a weighted average.

Latency in Memory Judgments

The present statement of multitrace strength theory does not make predictions about the latency distributions of responses in recognition, multiple-choice, and recall. A beginning effort to handle latencies with strength theory was made by Norman and Wickelgren (1969). At present, little can be said concerning the ultimate success of such an extension of strength theory.

Noise and Operating Characteristics

For reasons of simplicity, multitrace strength theory is a real-variable theory almost everywhere, with zero-mean random variables added at two places: (*a*) in the four-trace assumption, to handle the sum of the noise in acquisition, consolidation, decay, and retrieval and (*b*) in the criterion decision rule, to handle criterion noise. Both random variables are assumed to be normally distributed, but only the unimodality property of the (normal) probability density functions is important at the present level of precision in theories of memory.

Strength theory follows Thurstonian scaling (Thurstone, 1927; Torgerson, 1958) and signal detection theory (Tanner and Swets, 1954; Swets, Tanner, and Birdsall, 1961; Green and Swets, 1966) in using the standard deviation of the total noise in all phases of the process as the unit by which strengths are measured. Assuming that only one trace is substantially above zero under the conditions K, this means that in recognition the unit of strength measurement is $(\sigma_{MK}^2 + \sigma_K^2)^{1/2}$ and in recall or multiple-choice the unit of strength measurement is σ_{MK}. Since K is a subscript standing for all of the conditions of the memory task, there is no assurance that the unit of strength measurement remains constant across different conditions. In particular, one cannot be sure that σ_{MK} for recognition equals σ_{MK} for recall or multiple-choice, even when all other aspects of the conditions are identical. In addition, there is the σ_K term for recognition, which may have no analogue in the maximum decision rule for recall and multiple-choice (though a criterion-noise term can be incorporated into the maximum rule). When σ_{MK} is not invariant over different conditions, one must be careful to measure all strengths with the same unit. Sometimes it is necessary to estimate $\sigma_{MK_i}/\sigma_{MK_j}$ ratios. Problems in using the standard deviation of the noise as the unit of psychological measurement are discussed at length in Wickelgren (1968a).

Strength theory also follows Thurstonian scaling and signal-detection theory in having no true zero strength. Only the difference in trace strength between two conditions is meaningful, and this difference is measured in units of the noise in one of the conditions, i.e., $D(K_i, K_j) = (M_{K_i} - M_{K_j})/\sigma_{MK_j}$. Usually, one looks at the difference in strength between a correct item or association and an incorrect item or association. This difference can be thought of as the discriminability of correct and incorrect events (items or associations), and this discriminability is formally identical to d' in signal detection theory and the analogous concept in Thurstonian scaling.

Thus, strength is measured on an interval scale. The criterion and maximum decision rules found in Thurstonian scaling, signal detection theory, and strength theory both imply measurement on an interval scale, and one which uses the standard deviation of the total noise as the unit of measurement.

Testing the assumption that the noise is normally (unimodally) distributed, determining the ratios of noise standard deviations under different conditions, and determining the strength discriminability values for pairs of conditions are all most easily accomplished with a special plot called an operating characteristic (OC). Descriptions and proofs of the properties of OC's can be found in Green and Swets (1966) in the context of signal detection theory and in Wickelgren and Norman (1966) and Wickelgren (1968a) in the context of strength theory of memory.

OC's are only applicable to recognition, two-alternative multiple-choice, or two-alternative recall experiments, and are most efficiently and accurately derived from experiments using confidence ratings, in addition to the "yes–no" or other two-choice response. Everyone grants that ratings are the most efficient method of generating OC's. Some people think that ratings are less accurate than other methods of generating OC's, but the reverse is more likely to be true (Wickelgren, 1968a). For these reasons, OC's in memory experiments testing strength theory have always been derived from ratings.

In almost all tests of strength theory to date, the assumption of normally distributed noise has been validated by the absence of any systematic deviation of the OC's from straight lines on normal–normal plots. Systematic deviations of OC's from that expected for overlapping unimodal distributions have occurred in only two cases.

Once was in STM for pairs of digits from a serial list, where it appeared that about half of the old (presented) pairs were not distinguishable in trace strength from new pairs, leading to a bimodal distribution of trace strength for old pairs (Norman and Wickelgren, 1965). This is presumably due to the fact that the subjects coded the list into nonoverlapping pairs, leading to an incremented trace for coded pairs and little or no increment for uncoded pairs. This two-state (nonnormal) acquisition noise source can be eliminated by a variety of methods. Two methods which are known to work are to use paired-associate presentation so that pairs are never tested unless they were in fact coded as pairs

(Murdock, 1965) or just to present a single pair to be remembered (Wickelgren, 1966d).

The second case was in "higher-same-lower" judgments of recognition memory for pitch, where the deviation of the OC from a straight line was predicted by strength theory on the grounds that these judgments, under the conditions of that experiment, resulted from a multistage decision procedure, whose forced unidimensional representation led to bimodal distributions (Wickelgren, 1969). In tens of other experiments on recognition memory for pitch, one obtains OC's indicating no departure from unimodality (normality) in the underlying distributions.

The point is that there is no reason to doubt that the uncontrollable internal noise in the memory system is approximately normally distributed. When gross departures from normally distributed noise have been detected by OC's, it has been possible to determine the reasons. Since the reasons have nothing to do with the intrinsic nature of the memory system, but rather depend on the subjects' strategies (acquisition or decision, in the two cases), it is possible to study the same memory traces under conditions where the noise is normally distributed, as required in the Thurstonian scaling used by strength theory. There is no reason to think that this will not always be possible.

Now that a maximum likelihood method of estimating the intercept and slope parameters and testing goodness-of-fit for single rating OC's has been developed for rating data (Dorfman and Alf, 1968), it will probably be possible to definitely reject the assumption of normally distributed noise in many cases with a large enough sample. In my opinion, little will be gained from this, since the normal distribution assumption is merely a computational convenience, not an essential part of strength theory, and it is my guess that the accuracy of strength theory in predicting trace strength differences can not be improved substantially by assuming other noise distributions. Certainly, nothing will be gained from a mere rejection of the normal distribution assumption, without deriving a distribution that works better.

Conclusion

The present paper has demonstrated how multitrace strength theory handles a variety of memory phenomena. Emphasis has been placed on human studies of STM and ITM, because that is where the most appropriate experiments have been done to test strength theory. However, the theory is applicable to all phenomena of learning and memory, and to my knowledge, there are no phenomena that contradict multitrace strength theory. Nevertheless, much testing of the basic framework remains to be done, especially for VSTM, ITM, and LTM in a variety of modalities, and much theoretical work remains to be done to complete the theory. It remains to be seen how simple and accurate the theory will be, when it is more complete and more extensively tested.

References

AGRANOFF, B. W., AND DAVIS, R. E. Evidence for stages in the development of memory. In F. D. Carlson (Ed.), *Physiological and biochemical aspects of nervous integration.* Englewood Cliffs, New Jersey: Prentice-Hall, 1968.

ALBERT, D. J. The effect of spreading depression on the consolidation of learning. *Neuropsychologia,* 1966, **4,** 49–64. (a)

ALBERT, D. J. The effects of polarizing currents on the consolidation of learning. *Neuropsychologia,* 1966, **4,** 65–77. (b)

ALBERT, D. J. Memory in mammals: Evidence for a system involving nuclear ribonucleic acid. *Neuropsychologia,* 1966, **4,** 79–92. (c)

ARROW, K. J. *Social choice and individual values.* New York: Wiley, 1951.

ATKINSON, R. C., BRELSFORD, J. W., AND SHIFFRIN, R. M. Multiprocess models for memory with applications to a continuous presentation task. *Journal of Mathematical Psychology,* 1967, **4,** 277–300.

ATKINSON, R. C., AND CROTHERS, E. J. A comparison of paired-associate learning models having different acquisition and retention axioms. *Journal of Mathematical Psychology,* 1964, **1,** 285–315.

ATKINSON, R. C., AND SHIFFRIN, R. M. Mathematical models for memory and learning. Technical Report 79, Institute for Mathematical Studies in the Social Sciences, Stanford University, 1965. [In D. P. Kimble (Ed.), *Proceedings of the third conference on learning, remembering, and forgetting.* New York: New York Academy of Sciences, to be published.]

ATKINSON, R. C., AND SHIFFRIN, R. M. Human memory: A proposed system and its control processes. In K. W. Spence and J. T. Spence (Eds.), *Advances in the psychology of learning and motivation research and theory.* Vol. 2. New York: Academic Press, 1968.

AVERBACH, E., AND SPERLING, G. Short-term storage of information in vision. In C. Cherry (Ed.), *Information theory.* London and Washington, D.C.: Butterworth, 1961. Pp. 196–211.

BARONDES, S. H., AND COHEN, H. D. Memory impairment after subcutaneous injection of acetoxycycloheximide. *Science,* 1968, **160,** 556–557.

BERNBACH, H. A. A forgetting model for paired-associate learning. *Journal of Mathematical Psychology,* 1965, **2,** 128–144.

BERNBACH, H. A. Decision processes in memory. *Psychological Review,* 1967, **74,** 462–480.

BOWER, G. H. A descriptive theory of memory. In D. P. Kimble (Ed.), *Proceedings of the second conference on learning, remembering, and forgetting.* New York: New York Academy of Sciences, 1967, Pp. 112–185. (a)

BOWER, G. H. A multicomponent theory of the memory trace. In K. W. Spence and J. T. Spence (Eds.), *Advances in the psychology of learning and motivation research and theory.* Vol. I. New York: Academic Press, 1967. (b)

BOWER, G. H., AND BOSTRUM, A. Absence of within-list PI and RI in short-term recognition memory. *Psychonomic Science,* 1968, **10**, 211–212.

BROADBENT, D. E. *Perception and communication.* New York: MacMillan (Pergamon), 1958.

BROWN, J. Some tests of the decay theory of immediate memory. *Quarterly Journal of Experimental Psychology,* 1958, **10**, 12–21.

CALFEE, R. C., AND ATKINSON, R. C. Paired-associate models and the effects of list length. *Journal of Mathematical Psychology,* 1965, **2**, 254–265.

CONRAD, R. Errors of immediate memory. *British Journal of Psychology,* 1959, **50**, 349–359.

CONRAD, R. Serial order intrusions in immediate memory. *British Journal of Psychology,* 1960, **51**, 45–48.

CONRAD, R. Acoustic confusions in immediate memory. *British Journal of Psychology,* 1964, **55**, 75–84.

DEESE, J., AND KAUFMAN, R. A. Sequential effects in recall of unorganized and sequentially organized material. *Journal of Experimental Psychology,* 1957, **54**, 180–187.

DEUTSCH, J. A., HAMBURG, M. D., AND DAHL, H. Anticholinesterase-induced amnesia and its temporal aspects. *Science,* 1966, **151**, 221–223.

DONALDSON, W., AND MURDOCK, B. B., JR. Criterion change in continuous recognition memory. *Journal of Experimental Psychology,* 1968, **76**, 325–330.

DORFMAN, D. D., AND ALF, E., JR. Maximum likelihood estimation of parameters of signal detection theory—rating scale data. Mathematical Psychology Meetings, Stanford, California, 1968.

EGAN, J. P. Recognition memory and the operating characteristic. Technical Report Contract No. AF 19(604)–1962, Indiana University, 1958.

FEIGENBAUM, E. A. Simulation of verbal learning behavior. In E. A. Feigenbaum and J. Feldman (Eds.), *Computers and thought.* New York: McGraw-Hill, 1963.

FLEXNER, L. B., AND FLEXNER, J. B. Intracerebral saline: Effect on memory of trained mice treated with puromycin. *Science,* 1968, **159**, 330–331.

GREEN, D. M., AND MOSES, F. L. On the equivalence of two recognition measures of short-term memory. *Psychological Bulletin,* 1966, **66**, 228–234.

GREEN, D. M., AND SWETS, J. A. *Signal detection theory and psychophysics.* New York: Wiley, 1966.

GREENO, J. G. Paired-associate learning with short-term retention: Mathematical analysis and data regarding identification of parameters. *Journal of Mathematical Psychology,* 1967, **4**, 430–472.

HELLYER, S. Frequency of stimulus presentation and short-term decrement in recall. *Journal of Experimental Psychology,* 1962, **64**, 650.

HOUSTON, J. P. Unlearning of specific associations in the A–B, C–D paradigm. *Journal of Experimental Psychology,* 1967, **74**, 254–258.

HOUSTON, J. P. Unlearning and spontaneous recovery in short-term memory. *Journal of Verbal Learning and Verbal Behavior,* 1968, **7**, 251–253.

HOWE, M. J. A. Recognition memory for photographs in homogeneous sequences. *Perceptual and Motor Skills,* 1967, **24**, 1181–1182.

HULL, C. L. *Principles of behavior.* New York: Appleton-Century-Crofts, 1943.

HULL, C. L. *A behavior system.* New Haven, Connecticut: Yale University Press, 1952.

KATZ, L. A technique for the study of steady-state short-term memory. *Psychonomic Science,* 1966, **4**, 361–362.

KEPPEL, G., AND UNDERWOOD, B. J. Proactive inhibition in short-term retention of single items. *Journal of Verbal Learning and Verbal Behavior*, 1962, **3**, 153–161.

KINTSCH, W. Memory and decision aspects of recognition learning. *Psychological Review*, 1967, **74**, 496–504.

KINTSCH, W. An experimental analysis of single stimulus tests and multiple-choice tests of recognition memory. *Journal of Experimental Psychology*, 1968, **76**, 1–6.

LOESS, H. Short-term memory and item similarity. *Journal of Verbal Learning and Verbal Behavior*, 1968, **7**, 87–92.

LUCE, R. D. *Individual choice behavior*. New York: Wiley, 1959.

MCGOVERN, J. B. Extinction of associations in four transfer paradigms. *Psychological Monographs*, 1964, **78**, (16, Whole No. 593).

MELTON, A. W. Implications of short-term memory for a general theory of memory. *Journal of Verbal Learning and Verbal Behavior*, 1963, **2**, 1–21.

MELTON, A. W., AND VON LACKUM, W. J. Retroactive and proactive inhibition in retention: Evidence for a two-factor theory of retroactive inhibition. *American Journal of Psychology*, 1941, **54**, 157–73.

MILNER, B. Amnesia following operation on the temporal lobes. In C. W. M. Whitty and O. L. Zangwill (Eds.), *Amnesia*. London and Washington, D. C.: Butterworth, 1966.

MURDOCK, B. B., JR. Short-term retention of single paired-associates. *Psychological Reports*, 1961, **8**, 280. (a)

MURDOCK, B. B., JR. The retention of individual items. *Journal of Experimental Psychology*, 1961, **62**, 618–625. (b)

MURDOCK, B. B., JR. Direction of recall in short-term memory. *Journal of Verbal Learning and Verbal Behavior*, 1962, **1**, 119–124. (a)

MURDOCK, B. B., JR. The serial position effect in free recall. *Journal of Experimental Psychology*, 1962, **64**, 482–488. (b)

MURDOCK, B. B. JR. Signal-detection theory and short-term memory. *Journal of Experimental Psychology*, 1965, **70**, 443–447.

MURDOCK, B. B., JR. Distractor and probe techniques in short-term memory. *Canadian Journal of Psychology*, 1967, **21**, 25–36.

NICKERSON, R. S. A note on long-term recognition memory for pictorial material. *Psychonomic Science*, 1968, **11**, 58.

NORMAN, D. A. Acquisition and retention in short-term memory. *Journal of Experimental Psychology*, 1966, **72**, 369–381.

NORMAN, D. A., AND WICKELGREN, W. A. Short-term recognition memory for single digits and pairs of digits. *Journal of Experimental Psychology*, 1965, **70**, 479–489.

NORMAN, D. A., AND WICKELGREN, W. A. Strength theory of decision rules and latency in short-term memory. *Journal of Mathematical Psychology*, 1969, **6**, 192–208.

PETERSON, L. R., AND GENTILE, A. Proactive interference as a function of time between tests. *Journal of Experimental Psychology*, 1965, **70**, 473–478.

PETERSON, L. R., HILLNER, K., AND SALTZMAN, D. Supplementary report: Time between pairings and short-term retention. *Journal of Experimental Psychology*, 1962, **64**, 550–551.

PETERSON, L. R., AND JAMES, L. H. Successive tests of short-term retention. *Psychonomic Science*, 1967, **8**, 423–424.

PETERSON, L. R., AND PETERSON, M. J. Short-term retention of individual verbal items. *Journal of Experimental Psychology*, 1959, **58**, 193–198.

PETERSON, L. R., WAMPLER, R., KIRKPATRICK, M., AND SALTZMAN, D. Effect of spacing presentations on retention of a paired associate over short intervals. *Journal of Experimental Psychology*, 1963, **66**, 206–209.

POSTMAN, L. Unlearning under conditions of successive interpolation. *Journal of Experimental Psychology*, 1965, **70**, 237–245.

SCOVILLE, W. B., AND MILNER, B. Loss of recent memory after bilateral hippocampal lesions. *Journal of Neurology, Neurosurgery, and Psychiatry*, 1957, **20,** 11–21.

SHEPARD, R. N. Recognition memory for words, sentences, and pictures. *Journal of Verbal Learning and Verbal Behavior*, 1967, **6,** 156–163.

SHEPARD, R. N., AND CHANG, J. J. Forced-choice tests of recognition memory under steady-state conditions. *Journal of Verbal Learning and Verbal Behavior*, 1963, **2,** 93–101.

SHEPARD, R. N., AND TEGHTSOONIAN, M. Retention of information under conditions approaching a steady state. *Journal of Experimental Psychology*, 1961, **62,** 302–309.

SIMON, H. A., AND FEIGENBAUM, E. A. An information processing theory of some effects of similarity, familiarity, and meaningfulness in verbal learning. *Journal of Verbal Learning and Verbal Behavior*, 1964, **3,** 385–396.

SPENCE, K. W. *Behavior theory and conditioning*. New Haven, Connecticut: Yale University Press, 1956.

SPENCE, K. W. *Behavior theory and learning: Selected papers*. Englewood Cliffs, New Jersey: Prentice-Hall, 1960.

SPERLING, G. The information available in brief visual presentations. *Psychological Monographs*, 1960, **74,** (11, Whole No. 498).

SPERLING, G. A model for visual memory tasks. *Human Factors*, 1963, **5,** 19–31.

SWETS, J. A., TANNER, W. P., JR., AND BIRDSALL, T. G. Decision processes in perception. *Psychological Review*, 1961, **68,** 301–340.

TANNER, W. P., JR., AND SWETS, J. A. A decision making theory of visual detection. *Psychological Review*, 1954, **61,** 401–409.

THURSTONE, L. L. A law of comparative judgment. *Psychological Review*, 1927, **34,** 273–286.

TORGESON, W. S. *Theory and methods of scaling*. New York: Wiley, 1958.

WAUGH, N. C. The effect of intralist repetition on free recall. *Journal of Verbal Learning and Verbal Behavior*, 1962, **1,** 95–99.

WAUGH, N. C., AND NORMAN, D. A. Primary memory. *Psychological Review*, 1965, **72,** 89–104.

WICKELGREN, W. A. Size of rehearsal group and short-term memory. *Journal of Experimental Psychology*, 1964, **68,** 413–419.

WICKELGREN, W. A. Acoustic similarity and intrusion errors in short-term memory. *Journal of Experimental Psychology*, 1965, **70,** 102–108. (a)

WICKELGREN, W. A. Similarity and intrusions in short-term memory for consonant-vowel digrams. *Quarterly Journal of Experimental Psychology*, 1965, **17,** 241–246. (b)

WICKELGREN, W. A. Distinctive features and errors in short-term memory for English vowels. *Journal of the Acoustical Society of America*, 1965, **38,** 583–588. (c)

WICKELGREN, W. A. Short-term memory for repeated and nonrepeated items. *Quarterly Journal of Experimental Psychology*, 1965, **17,** 14–25. (d)

WICKELGREN, W. A. Consolidation and retroactive interference in short-term recognition memory for pitch. *Journal of Experimental Psychology*, 1966, **18,** 250–259. (a)

WICKELGREN, W. A. Short-term recognition memory for single letters and phonemic similarity of retroactive interference. *Quarterly Journal of Experimental Psychology*, 1966, **18,** 55–62. (b)

WICKELGREN, W. A. Distinctive features and errors in short-term memory for English consonants. *Journal of the Acoustical Society of America*, 1966, **39,** 388–398. (c)

WICKELGREN, W. A. Numerical relations, similarity, and short-term recognition memory for pairs of digits. *British Journal of Psychology*, 1966, **57,** 263–274. (d)

WICKELGREN, W. A. Associative intrusions in short-term recall. *Journal of Experimental Psychology*, 1966, **72,** 853–858. (e)

WICKELGREN, W. A. Exponential decay and independence from irrelevant associations in short-term recognition memory for serial order. *Journal of Experimental Psychology*, 1967, **73**, 165–171. (a)

WICKELGREN, W. A. Rehearsal grouping and hierarchical organization of serial position cues in short-term memory. *Quarterly Journal of Experimental Psychology*, 1967, **19**, 97–102. (b)

WICKELGREN, W. A. Unidimensional strength theory and component analysis of noise in absolute and comparative judgments. *Journal of Mathematical Psychology*, 1968, **5**, 102–122. (a)

WICKELGREN, W. A. Sparing of short-term memory in an amnesic patient: Implications for strength theory of memory. *Neuropsychologia*, 1968, **6**, 235–244. (b)

WICKELGREN, W. A. Associative strength theory of recognition memory for pitch. *Journal of Mathematical Psychology*, 1969, **6**, 13–61. (a)

WICKELGREN, W. A. Time, interference, and rate of presentation in short-term recognition memory for items. *Journal of Mathematical Psychology*, 1970, in press. (b)

WICKELGREN, W. A., AND NORMAN, D. A. Strength models and serial position in short-term recognition memory. *Journal of Mathematical Psychology*. 1966, **3**, 316–347.

WICKENS, D. D., BORN, D. G., AND ALLEN, C. K. Proactive inhibition and item similarity in short-term memory. *Journal of Verbal Learning and Verbal Behavior*, 1963, **2**, 440–445.

4

A Multiple-Copy Model for Postperceptual Memory

Harley A. Bernbach
Cornell University
Ithaca, New York

Introduction

While the formal models of verbal learning and memory developed in the early and middle 1960's were primarily limited to the simple association learning task, a number of recent theorists have considered the details of the retention process, with an emphasis on short-term memory experiments. The existence of this volume attests to that fact. A perusal of this volume will show that many of these models share a common characteristic; most postulate multiple-store memory systems. This may be a premature retreat from parsimony, however. This chapter presents a model for postperceptual verbal memory that postulates a single memory store, with multiple copies, called *replicas*, created in memory by rehearsal processes. This replica model has been shown capable of explaining data from a wide variety of experiments in human memory and learning (Bernbach, 1970). Further, as will be shown here, the replica model is also capable of explaining data commonly cited as evidence for separate short and longer-term memory systems.

Before proceeding, it is necessary to define some boundary conditions. The model is concerned with the storage and retention of readily perceived verbal units, i.e., items that have been presented for a long enough time period that their perception and coding is virtually assured. The model is not concerned with that memory which is part of the perceptual process, specifically the very short-term sensory storage, generally lasting less than one second, that was studied by Sperling (1960). Similarly, the model is not concerned with whatever memory is involved in response processes, such as how to draw the letters when making a written nonsense syllable response. Further, the model is not intended to handle the effects of context or structure (as in remembering sentences), but rather to deal with items that one can reasonably assume are treated as independent units by the memory system. Thus, the model will deal with experiments on the short-term retention and learning of items such as nonsense syllables, paired-associates, and the like.

In this paper, the model is first described in detail as it applies to a single experimental task, short-term retention of individual items from short lists. Then, following a brief discussion of the relationship between short-term memory and learning, the issue of single vs. multiple memory systems is taken up. This paper can best be considered to be an outline and brief discussion of the replica model. The brevity comes about because this presentation follows very closely in time a fuller discussion of the model in Volume III of the series on *The Psychology of Learning and Motivation* (Bernbach, 1970). Full explication of many of the points raised in this paper can usually be found in the other presentation, although some of the issues are discussed more completely here than there. The discussion in this volume is complete enough, however, so that the casual reader will be able to understand all the important features of the replica model.

The Replica Model for Serial Position in Short-Term Memory

The Phillips, Shiffrin, and Atkinson Experiment

The model will be presented here in the context of an experiment by Phillips, Shiffrin, and Atkinson (1967) on the effect of list length on short-term retention of individual items. This experiment shows several of the important features of short-term memory data. However, it is simple enough for a three-parameter mathematical model to be formulated (from the more general replica model) to account for its results.

The experiment consisted of a long series of discrete trials. On each trial a set of playing cards (the "list") was shown to the subject, one at a time. The cards each contained a color patch, either black, white, blue, or green. The size of the set, or list length, L, was varied across trials, and values of L of 3, 4, 5, 6, 7, 8, 11, and 14 were used. The L cards were shown to the subject one at a time, and then laid face down on the table so that the color was not visible. The test consisted of the experimenter pointing to a card and asking the subject to state its color.

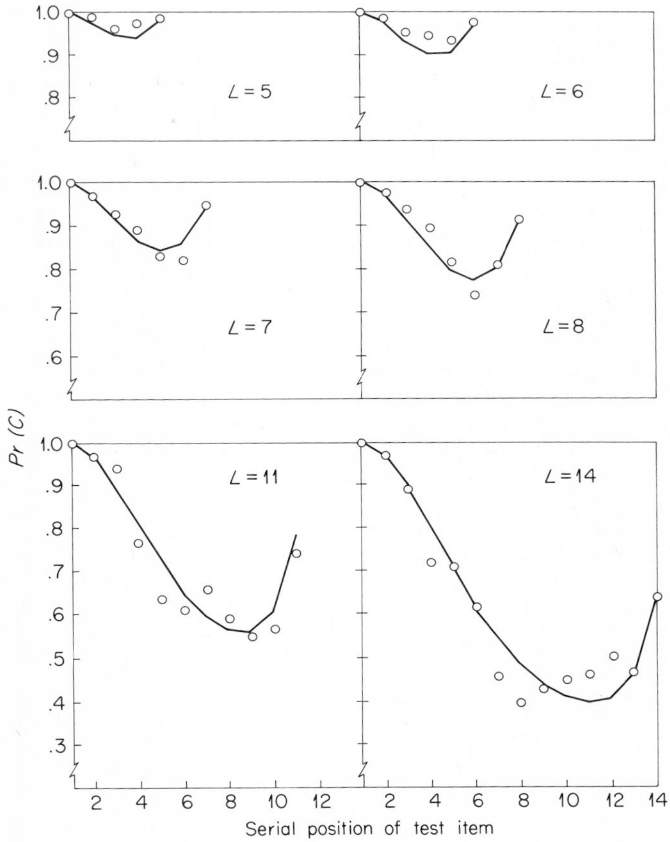

FIG. 1. Observed and theoretical probabilities of a correct response as a function of serial position for several values of list length, L (data from Phillips *et al.*, 1967). Note that serial position is counted from the end of the list, so that recall performance for the last item of each list is shown in position 1.

The results for all list lengths except three and four are shown as the open circles on Fig. 1. Recall performance was perfect at all serial positions on the two shortest lists. The serial positions are numbered so that 1 represents the most recent item, or the last one in the list, and L is the first item in the list. The most apparent characteristics of these data are a strong, S-shaped recency effect, with the probability correct at serial position 1 equal to 1.0 for all list lengths, and a marked primacy effect.

The Replica Model

REPLICATION

The assumptions of the replica model for this experiment are as follows: When each item is presented, an internal representation of it called a *replica* is stored in memory. During the time remaining before presentation of the next item, the subject engages in two consecutive activities. The first is specific rehearsal of the presented item. This rehearsal is covert and possibly below the level of the subject's awareness. Each rehearsal results in the storage of an additional replica of the item. The number of rehearsals, at the time of presentation k_p is a random variable having a Poisson distribution with parameter λ_p.

In addition to the number of times that each item is rehearsed during its presentation (k_p), items are also rehearsed later, during the presentation of the remaining items of the list. This extra, general, rehearsal takes place among all the items which have been presented to that point and which have not yet been forgotten. On each general rehearsal, the subject chooses an item at random and adds a replica of that item to its stack of items in memory. Thus, if there are k_r general rehearsals, and J is the number of items from the list that are remembered, the presentation of an item results in the storage of $1 + k_p + k_r/J$ replicas of the item. As before, both k_p and k_r are assumed to be Poisson distributed random variables with parameters λ_p and λ_r, respectively.

The probability of correct response is assumed to be 1.0 if there are one or more replicas of the tested item in memory at the time of the test, and chance otherwise. The number of replicas has no effect on response probability, unless there are *no* replicas, just as it has no effect on the probability that an item will be chosen for general rehearsal. The number of replicas is assumed to affect memory only with regard to the probability of forgetting.

FORGETTING

Forgetting is assumed to result from storage interference upon presentation of other items. Specifically, it is assumed for each item in memory that, with probability δ, a single replica is lost whenever a new item is presented and stored. Because of the response assumptions described above, however, an item is not "forgotten" until all of its replicas have been lost. The value of δ will probably be a function of such factors as the similarity of items to one another.

THE COMPLETE MODEL

The events assumed to occur by the model may be summarized in the following way:

1. When an item is first presented, a single replica of it is stored in memory.
2. Presentation is followed immediately by rehearsal of the item, causing k_p additional replicas to be stored. k_p has a Poisson distribution with parameter λ_p.
3. This rehearsal of the item that was presented is followed by k_r general rehearsals of all the items presented to this time which have not yet been forgotten. With each general rehearsal, one additional replica of the item that is rehearsed gets stored in memory. If there are J items that have not yet been forgotten, each item receives an average of k_r/J rehearsals. k_r has a Poisson distribution with parameter λ_r.
4. Whenever a new item is presented, with probability δ any or all of the other items in memory may lose exactly one replica.
5. At the time the subject's memory is tested, it is assumed that he performs perfectly as long as he retains at least one replica of the item tested. Otherwise, he must guess among the set of response alternatives.

This set of assumptions for the replica model is not as arbitrary as it may appear in this brief presentation. The rationale behind each of the assumptions has been discussed in detail elsewhere, however. The purpose here is only to describe the model and its behavior, and compare that behavior with data. The reader who is interested in a more detailed discussion of the fundamental assumptions underlying the model is referred to the discussion in Bernbach (1970).

It does seem worthwhile here, however, to point out those features of the model that are particularly important in explaining the main characteristics of the experimental results in the Phillips *et al.* (1967) study. For example, the recency effect follows from the assumptions regarding forgetting. Since the model assumes that loss of replicas occurs on presentation of other items, the probability of forgetting an item must be an increasing function of the number of other items intervening between its presentation and test. Thus, the last item in the list shows no forgetting, and recall performance then drops off for earlier items. The recency curve is S shaped. That is, the last few items in the list decay more slowly than earlier items. This is because of the assumption that, at most, one replica of an item can be lost on presentation of each interfering item. That is, it follows from the rehearsal assumptions that there is some probability that an item will have more than one replica in memory after its presentation. If there is more than one replica, however, then forgetting (loss of all replicas) cannot occur until a minimum of that same number of other items is presented. These processes hold up the recall of the last few items in the list. The resulting S shape can be seen clearly in the theoretical curves of Fig. 1.

Primacy is caused by the assumption about general rehearsal of the list. The first item in the list gets the most benefit from this rehearsal, in terms of storing additional replicas and building up a corresponding resistance to forgetting. This benefit from being early in the list becomes less effective as more items are presented. For example, on general rehearsal after the first presentation, the first item has k_r additional replicas stored. After the second item is presented, the second item and the first *each* get $k_r/2$ replicas, on the average, from general rehearsal. This rehearsal feature is at the very heart of the replica model and is the feature that is most responsible for the model's ability to do without separate short- and long-term memory systems. This will be further discussed later; first let us consider the detailed fit of the model to the Phillips *et al.* (1967) data.

Test of the Model

The parameters of the model were estimated by the common χ^2 minimization technique. That is, values of the parameters were chosen such that the model gave the best fit to the six curves, *simultaneously*, according to a minimum χ^2 criterion. Since analytic solutions for the model's predictions are not currently available, an approximation method was used to generate these predictions. A vector W was defined, whose cell entry w_i represents the probability that there are exactly $i - 1$ replicas in memory, and the maximum value of i was held to ten in order to make the grid search procedure feasible in terms of computer time. In effect, we had a random walk model, with states w_i and absorbing barriers at w_1 and w_{10}.

The operations assumed by the replica model were applied to the vector W in order. Thus, when an interfering event is assumed by the model to occur, W is transformed to W' by applying the formula,

$$w'_i = \delta w_{i+1} + (1 - \delta) w_i, \tag{1}$$

for values of i from two to eight. The other entries are similarly determined, but reflect the absorbing barriers at w_1 and w_{10}. As another example, rehearsal of an item leads to transformation of its probability vector by the formula,

$$w'_i = w_{i-1}. \tag{2}$$

Again, the appropriate exceptions for the absorbing barriers are made, that is,

$$w'_1 = 0, \tag{3}$$

and

$$w'_{10} = w_9 + w_{10}. \tag{4}$$

The probability of forgetting is simply the value of w_1 at the time of test, i.e., the probability that the number of replicas is zero. The probability of a correct response is then obtained from the equation,

$$Pr(C) = 1 - w_1(1 - \tag{5}$$

where g, the guessing rate, is equal to $\frac{1}{4}$ in this experiment.

This approximation procedure can be considered to be a difference equation statement of the various processes used in the model. The effects of rehearsal, Eqs. 2 through 4, are applied to the vector W with frequencies that depend upon the parameters λ_p and λ_r and the number of nonforgotten items (J) present at the time the transformations are used. The approximation is then carried out with a systematic set of parameter values (a gridding procedure) and the predictions compared with the data by the χ^2 statistic. The best-fitting predictions are shown in Fig. 1, and the value of χ^2 was 46.9 with 48 degrees of freedom.

There remains the question of whether the approximation used is very close to the actual replica model. To test this, a computer simulation of the model's performance in this task was developed (with the assistance of John Brelsford). Five thousand simulated subjects were run once on each list, by computer, and their performance compared with the approximation's predictions. The correspondence was extremely close: the largest deviation between predicted and simulated probabilities was .018, and the average deviation was only .005. Apparently, at least in this case, the procedure used accurately approximated the performance of the actual model. The replica model, then, appears to fit the data extremely well.

The parameter values indicate that almost every time a new item was presented in this experiment, every other item in memory lost one replica. Moreover, during the 2-sec interval allowed for the presentation of each new item subjects rehearsed the presented item an average of 2.7 times and then rehearsed all the items an average of 2.8 times. Thus, about $5\frac{1}{2}$ rehearsals occurred during the 2-sec presentation interval, along with the initial coding and storing of the item. This rehearsal seemed to be split equally between the item which was just presented and all the items. These rates of rehearsal and division of attention seem to be very reasonable.

Short-Term Memory and Simple Verbal Learning

Repeated Presentations

It is well known (e.g., Hellyer, 1962) that repeated presentations of an item in short-term memory are an aid to retention. On the basis of this, one might claim that simple verbal learning is simply a demonstration of the effect of repetition on short-term retention. The replica model lends itself quite naturally to this view. If rehearsal of an item causes the addition of more replicas, and therefore greater resistance to forgetting, it seems reasonable to suppose that repeated presentations would have a similar effect. That is, it is entirely consistent for the replica model to assume that repeated presentations lead to creation of more replicas, and this assumption has led to an excellent fit of the model to data like that of Hellyer's, i.e., less forgetting at all retention intervals in short-term memory for single items (Bernbach, 1970).

The replica model treats paired-associate learning, for example, as an extension of this result. That is, several replicas of an item are stored on its first presentation (the exact number is probabilistic as before, though it must be at least one). By the time an item is tested, its probability vector with regard to the number of replicas has shifted down due to the presentation of other items, in a manner similar to that shown in Eq. 1. The probability that the item is forgotten is the probability that there are no replicas, so that response performance will be at the chance level. Thus, the probability of a correct response is just the probability that at least one replica remains at the time of test. On the second presentation of an item, additional replicas are stored, so the probability of forgetting is less after the second presentation-to-test interval than it was after the first. Using the probability of a correct response as the response measure, a learning curve will thus be built up with additional trials.

Paired-Associate Learning

The question remains of whether the specific assumptions of the replica model are sufficient with regard to learning to describe the data from actual paired-associate learning experiments. The question can be answered in a general fashion by examining some other models which are known to describe paired-associate learning well. What we shall do, then, is to show that the replica model is at least equivalent to a wide class of other models in its ability to handle data. We do this by simulating a paired-associate experiment with the replica model and then attempting to fit those simulated results with another model that has ample evidence for its adequacy. This approach is helped by a very useful result. The model which we examine is a three-state Markov model of paired-associate learning proposed by Atkinson and Crothers (1964). Greeno (1967) has shown that the Atkinson and Crothers model is the prototype of a class of isomorphic three-state models. Thus, by looking at this one model, we look at all such three-state models.

Atkinson and Crothers assumed that an item must be in one of three states at the time of test, states G, S, or L. In G, the guessing state, items were assumed to be forgotten (or simply unknown if they were new) so that response performance was at a chance level. States S and L represented short- and long-term memory, respectively, in the Atkinson and Crothers model, and forgetting was possible from state S only. Learning consisted of a move to state L, from which no further forgetting could occur. The model is completely represented by the following state transition matrix and response probability vector.

$$\begin{array}{c} \\ L \\ S \\ G \end{array} \begin{array}{c} \begin{array}{ccc} L & \qquad S & \qquad G \end{array} \\ \begin{bmatrix} 1 & 0 & 0 \\ a & (1-a)\,(1-f) & (1-a)f \\ a & (1-a)\,(1-f) & (1-a)f \end{bmatrix} \end{array} \quad \begin{array}{c} Pr\ (\text{corr}) \\ \begin{bmatrix} 1 \\ 1 \\ g \end{bmatrix} \end{array}$$

Models of this form have proven to give excellent descriptions of the details of data from paired-associate learning experiments using simple verbal materials.

Unfortunately, the replica model lends itself no more readily to analytic solutions for its predictions in paired-associate learning than in the Phillips *et al.* (1967) experiment. Therefore, a grid search to fit actual paired-associate data seemed prohibitive in terms of computer time. Instead, a set of data was generated by the replica model, using arbitrarily chosen parameters, and the three-state Markov model was fit to those "data" (Bernbach, 1970). The fit was remarkably good as shown in Tables 1 and 2, which compare the models' predictions for the learning curve and for the eight complete response sequences on trials 2–4.

This close correspondence of the two models can be given the interpretation that a three-state model is an adequate approximation to the complete replica model for relatively gross paired-associate learning data. Note, however, that the three-state model can not handle details like the S-shaped recency curve.

There are several reasons why the three-state model is a good approximation to the replica model. We simply identify state G of the Markov model with the situation in which an item has no replicas in memory. Similarly, state L represents those items which have enough replicas that the probability of forgetting is very small. The remaining items are all grouped into state S, and the parameters of the three-state

TABLE 1
Predicted Values of the Learning Curve

	Probability of a correct response	
Trial	Replica model	Three-state model
1	.000	.000
2	.402	.411
3	.607	.595
4	.731	.722
5	.812	.809
6	.866	.868
7	.904	.909
8	.931	.938
9	.949	.957
10	.963	.971

TABLE 2
Predicted Proportions of Response Sequences

Sequence			Replica model	Three-state model
Trial 2	Trial 3	Trial 4		
Correct	Correct	Correct	.347	.374
Correct	Correct	Error	.006	.013
Correct	Error	Correct	.024	.014
Correct	Error	Error	.034	.020
Error	Correct	Correct	.208	.224
Error	Correct	Error	.034	.020
Error	Error	Correct	.143	.141
Error	Error	Error	.204	.195

Markov model are some kind of average values of transitions between these "states." In any case, the similarity of these models' predictions suggests that the replica model can account for simple paired-associate learning data, since it is known that the three-state model can do so.

Multiprocess Models

As mentioned in the introduction, it is very common to find a separate short-term memory store, having its own set of properties, in addition to what is called long-term memory in most models of human memory. Occasionally, we even come across an intermediate-term memory, or the like. Obviously, it is not possible to prove that such separate systems do not exist, just as it is not possible to prove any null hypothesis. On the other hand, it does not seem reasonable to assume that memory is multiprocess if there is no evidence that this is true. Considerable data have been collected that is claimed as evidence for a separate short-term store. We have not seen any postperceptual memory data, however, that are not explained just as well by the single-store replica model. Examples will be given here of some different kinds of such "evidence."

First, it should be noted that the assumptions of the replica model regarding rehearsal mechanisms are not gratuitous ones. Considerable evidence for such rehearsal processes has been presented (Bernbach, 1969), and even some multistore models provide for such rehearsal (e.g., Atkinson and Shiffrin, 1968). This is important because it is the rehearsal assumptions of the replica model that are most responsible for its ability to do without a short-term store.

The three-state Markov model developed by Atkinson and Crothers (1964) has a state S labeled "short-term store." This state is needed for the model to work properly, particularly when considering the effect of different lengths of the presentation-to-test interval (e.g., Bjork, 1966). But the replica model interprets this state as representing a short-term *effect*, not a separate process. Items in state S simply do not have enough replicas yet to appear learned. Nevertheless, the state S and L have no different basic properties. In each, for example, an interfering item causes the loss of exactly one replica with probability δ, and so on.

Another kind of evidence for a short-term store is the nonzero asymptotes in forgetting functions that were observed in short-term retention of individual paired associates (Murdock, 1963). The asymptotic probability of a correct response was interpreted as the proportion of items that had gone into long-term memory rather than short-term memory when they were presented. The forgetting function, then, was assumed to represent forgetting from short-term memory. The replica model is completely consistent with these data about asymptotes, however. Because of its assumptions about rehearsal, the model can be considered to be a random-walk process, with the number of replicas as the "state." Further, because it has one absorbing barrier at the state representing no replicas (since the subject cannot rehearse an item he has forgotten), this random walk is of the class called the "gambler's ruin." As demonstrated by Feller (1957, Chapter 14), such a model can have a nonzero asymptote if it has appropriate parameter values.

The third kind of evidence comes from studies involving behavioral observation after various kinds of physiological manipulations, such as drugs, brain damage, and the like. Let us consider one example. Atkinson and Shiffrin (1968) claimed to be convinced of the existence of a separate short-term store because of a series of reports by Milner (1959, 1966). Basically, she found that a particular kind of hippocampal lesion led to a syndrome in human patients such that they could not learn new verbal material on a long-term basis, though they could retain such material for short time periods. Previously acquired long-term memories were not lost. In Atkinson and Shiffrin's words, "Apparently, a short-term store remains to the patients, but the lesions have produced a breakdown either in the ability to store new information in long-term store or to retrieve new information from it" (Atkinson and Shiffrin, 1968). They go on to conclude that Milner's findings "give strong support to the hypothesis of distinct short- and long-term memory stores."

The explanation of Milner's findings in terms of the replica model is extremely straightforward. The lesion could well have interfered with the patient's rehearsal mechanisms, which are primarily covert (Bernbach, 1970). In this case, early memories would be untouched, since they had already built up a considerable number of replicas. (The model places no limit on how many replicas may be stored.) Some short-term memory would remain, since the patients could create replicas on presentation and either by repetition or by overt rehearsal. With nonfunctioning covert rehearsal mechanisms, however, they could not store enough replicas to give the appearance of having learned material permanently. A similar argument, based on rehearsal mechanisms, can be applied to all of the neuropsychological data that we have seen regarding this issue.

We have shown three different kinds of "evidence" for a separate short-term store. Atkinson and Shiffrin have already suggested, as we have, that the first (state S) may be only a short-term *effect*, rather than a separate memory store (Atkinson and Shiffrin, 1968). Similarly, Murdock (1967 and Chapter 9) has pointed out that his asymptote could be explained by a single-store model, so long as movement up (in the direction of learning) is permitted during the retention interval, along with forgetting. Although there has been no widespread backing down with regard to the alleged neuropsychological evidence as yet, it is this author's opinion that this event is to be eagerly awaited, so that we can all get down to the important task of attempting to develop a further understanding of the processes operating in the single memory store.

Concluding Remarks

In this paper, the basic features of the replica model have been presented and applied to data. The model has far more generality than might appear from this brief review; it has also been applied to several common short-term memory procedures, as well as to simple learning paradigms, and it has been shown compatible with data on confidence ratings in both recognition memory and recall. The success of the replica model in handling these postperceptual memory data, as well as data specifically claimed as evidence that memory is multiprocess, suggests strongly that the retreat from parsimony involved in assuming a separate short-term memory store, with its own set of properties, may be very premature.

References

Atkinson, R. C., and Crothers, E. J. A comparison of paired-associate learning models having different acquisitions and retention axioms. *Journal of Mathematical Psychology*, 1964, **1**, 285–315.

Atkinson, R. C., and Shiffrin, R. M. Human memory: A proposed system and its control processes. In K. W. Spence and J. T. Spence (Eds.), *The psychology of learning and motivation: Advances in research and theory.* Vol. II. New York: Academic Press, 1968. Pp. 89–195.

Bernbach, H. A. Replication processes in human memory and learning. In J. T. Spence and G. H. Bower (eds.), *The psychology of learning and motivation: Advances in research and theory.* Vol. III. New York: Academic Press, 1970.

Bjork, R. A. Learning and short-term retention of paired-associates in relation to specific sequences of interpresentation intervals. Technical Report No. 106, Institute for Mathematical Studies in the Social Sciences, Stanford University, 1966.

Feller, W. *An introduction to probability theory and its applications.* Vol. I. New York: Wiley, 1957.

Greeno, J. G. Paired-associate learning with short-term retention: Mathematical analysis and data regarding identification of parameters. *Journal of Mathematical Psychology*, 1967, **4**, 430–472.

Hellyer, S. Supplementary report: Frequency of stimulus presentation and short-term decrement in recall. *Journal of Experimental Psychology*, 1962, **64**, 650.

Milner, B. The memory defect in bilateral hippocampal lesions. *Psychiatric Research Reports*, 1959, **11**, 43–58.

Milner, B. Neuropsychological evidence for differing memory processes. Abstract for the symposium on short-term and long-term memory. *Proceedings of the 18th International Congress of Psychology*, Moscow, 1966.

Murdock, B. B. Jr. Short-term memory and paired-associate learning. *Journal of Verbal Learning and Verbal Behavior*, 1963, **2**, 320–328.

Murdock, B. B., Jr. Theoretical note: A fixed-point model for short-term memory. *Journal of Mathematical Psychology*, 1967, **4**, 501–506.

Phillips, J. L., Shiffrin, R. M., and Atkinson, R. C. The effects of list length on short-term memory. *Journal of Verbal Learning and Verbal Behavior*, 1967, **6**, 303–311.

Sperling, G. The information available in brief visual presentations. *Psychological Monographs*, 1960, **74**, Whole No. 498.

5

Computer Simulation of an Information-Processing Model of Short-Term Memory

Judith S. Reitman[1]
University of Michigan

Information Processing Models

The problem is attention, information overload, and the loss of items in memory.

Much more information is presented to the human memory system than is ever remembered or even noticed. Somewhere in the system,

[1] I wish to thank Arthur W. Melton and David Meier for their initial encouragement. In addition, I wish to thank Robert Bjork, J. E. Keith Smith, and especially Walter R. Reitman for their continuous assistance. Gordon H. Bower and Edward A. Feigenbaum were kind enough to critique an early draft. And I want to further thank Donald A. Norman for the great amount of time he spent on careful readings which produced many fruitful suggestions.

The research was partially supported by a USPHS Grant GM-1231 to The University of Michigan and USPHS Grant MH12160.

items are lost; somewhere there is a limited capacity. Those items that are lost, however, are not random items. We attend to and subsequently remember the important things, and disregard the irrelevant and unimportant. Some sort of priority scheme determines which items are important, and which are not. This priority scheme follows prescriptions determined by the human's prior knowledge of what is to be expected of him in a later situation. His current strategies determine what he will notice and what he will eventually remember. Since this limited capacity and these strategies interact, it is useful to study them simultaneously to shed light on the structure of the memory system, its components, processes, and interconnections. The model in this paper is designed to explore the sources of systematic loss due to the limits of the system and the specification of the priority schemes involved.

I first present an informal schema for thinking about the various processes involved in learning and memory. It serves here as a framework on which to hang the postulates of the model that follows. I am here concerned with the main aspects of the memory system, the structure and timing, rather than the details of the processing mechanisms. Briefly, the system is made up of a series of component processes and their respective stores (see Fig. 1). Items enter the system through the senses, and remain in a sensory register for a fraction of a second. The items may either be passed on to the next process or lost through a very rapid decay. The next process is a recognizing mechanism, a "naming mechanism" for verbal material. Once named, the item lines up to be

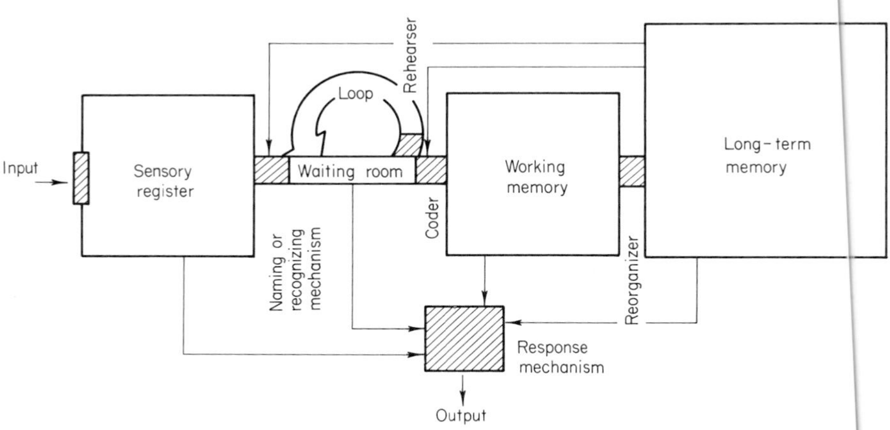

FIG. 1. Proposed structure of memory.

coded. By coded I mean stored in a working memory, a store so called because it contains not only the new items but also other relevant information from the long-term memory. When all input items have been processed through the system or the current task is interrupted, a reorganizing process goes to work disassembling the working memory in order to save the significant parts for permanent storage in the long-term memory.

Bower's Queuing Model of Short-Term Memory

Bower (1967), in a postscript to a descriptive model of memory, indicated that mathematical queuing theory is relevant to the timing characteristics of this type of system. In exploring such a model, Bower focuses his attention on the coding process that puts items into permanent memory. (We could postulate that this is the coding process as labeled in Fig. 1, though Bower makes no distinction between the working memory and the permanent long-term memory.) This coding process, he says, works much like a "server" and the incoming items behave like "customers," servers and customers being the basic elements of queuing theory. When customers enter the system at a faster rate than the server can handle, the customers must line up behind the server, and wait their turn to be served. Bower postulates that the queued items do not wait in line forever; they drop out or decay in strength at a rate which fits an exponential distribution. The server is postulated to process items at a rate that follows the same exponential distribution. Prediction of the fate of each incoming item follows from mathematical manipulation. The results fit the classical bowed serial position curve, as well as the changes in this curve which occur with changes in the rate of input of the items (cf. Murdock, 1962, reproduced in the Appendix to this book and on page 57.

There are several mathematical complications that have limited the possibility of extension of Bower's model. We consider three (see Cox and Smith, 1961). The first is that the rate of loss of items in the queue is assumed to have the same distribution as the serving rate. There is an important case for which this assumption is false. It may be that as we lower the meaningfulness of items, the time to code each item increases while the waiting items are more quickly lost to decay. The parameters of the two distributions seem to be inversely related rather than constantly equal.

The second complication is the problem of queues in series. The mathematical description of a queue whose items arrive at times determined by the processing rate of a preceding server is extremely complicated. Only in extreme cases are results easily obtained. Thus, Bower is currently restricted to exploration of a single queue with no present hope of hooking up to the other processes involved in the system (e.g., the sensory gate, the naming mechanism).

The above two complications, equal exponential distributions and a single queue, are postulated in Bower's model for the sake of mathematical simplicity. Mathematical manipulation grows quickly out of hand when these conditions are not met. The third complication involves an unsolved problem in queuing theory. It is the problem of equality and independence of the items. Here in Bower's case, the customers must be assumed to be noninteracting in order for the exponential distribution to hold. This rules out clustering of items and the noticing of distinctive or unusual items out of order. This restriction must be relaxed if we are to understand the complex behavior of the learning human being. Present limitations of mathematical queuing theory have restricted the possibility of meaningful analytic extension of Bower's model.

Feigenbaum's EPAM *and the "Anchor-Point Strategy"*

One approach to modeling which can help us out of the restrictions discussed above is the computer simulation approach. The approach can lead to demonstration of significant implications without the simplifying assumptions Bower was required to make for mathematical manipulation. A program can specify *priorities* for "preferred customers" in the queue. It can produce output that demonstrates the behavior generated by a postulated *series* of queues. It also can make evident effects due to fluctuations in the rates of processing and decay that follow from variations in the type of material presented. If specification of these parameters is simple, such a model can be explored with paper and pencil. But when these processes become complex, the computer's speed, accuracy, and memory become invaluable.

One priority scheme for coding items described in computer simulation terms can be found in a paper by Feigenbaum and Simon (1962), which discusses the implications of EPAM for a general theory of memory (see also Feigenbaum, Chapter 13). EPAM (Elementary Perceiver And Memorizer) is a program that embodies processes for discriminating incoming items from each other and for storing in a net the relevant information about them. These processes are alleged to be central to learning.

"Anchor-point strategy" in EPAM is a priority scheme of the following form. A subject selects a unique item, called an "anchor point," from his immediate memory or short-term store, and processes it first. Next he chooses the item closest to that item on some dimension, then the next closest, and so forth. If there is more than one anchor point, the selection process moves randomly among them, selecting all anchor points first, then all items next to anchor points, then all items a distance of two away, etc.

In the conditions of most verbal learning experiments, in which all items are nonsense trigrams with very little chance for the appearance of really distinct items, the anchor points are defined by positional cues, the beginning and end of the list. Predictions that are based on these experimental conditions indicate that in a list of similar and independent items, the items would be remembered from the ends toward the middle. We note that this produces the classical bowed serial position curve. Unlike the Bower model, the priority scheme goes on to account for clustering effects and ease of learning certain items in a list of items with mixed meaningfulness. Specifically, it allows a fit to the data of von Restorff (1933) who found that a single item printed in red embedded in a list of black printed items will be remembered far better than would be expected on the basis of its serial position in the list.

In following out the argument of the Feigenbaum and Simon anchor point strategy, there is one point that is quite unclear. Though all the predictions are based on the order of coding of items, the authors never state explicitly how items are *lost*. Implicit in their argument is a notion of the decay of items, but the actual postulate is missing.

In modeling the memory process, I have, I believe, extracted the essentials of both approaches. The idea that items "line up" for processing into permanent storage comes from both models. From Bower: the loss of items in the queue is due to a decay with time. From Feigenbaum and Simon: the modeling of a queuing system is formally defined in an information processing model.

A Working Model for the Learning Process

The learning process is made up of a series of component processes. These components include a *sensory gate,* which allows entrance of sensory bundles to the total system at a very fast rate; a *recognizing* mechanism, which attaches to these sensory bundles descriptive names as well as measures of the ease of remembering each item and its current importance; a discriminator and image builder called the *coder,* which takes the named bundles and discriminates them from previously learned items and stores relevant information about them in a temporary netlike structure; and finally, a *reorganizer,* which disassembles the temporary net and saves significant parts of it in the permanent memory.

Each of these mechanisms in series takes an increasingly longer time to process an item. Consequently, queues arise in front of each mechanism where items approach at a faster rate than it can handle. Queues can occur at every possible bottleneck in the system. Let me illustrate a postulated series of queues. Suppose we present items to a subject at a very fast rate, say ten per second. Although all the items are seen by the subject, he is able to recognize only a fraction of them. This may indicate that the recognizing mechanism has a certain maximum rate of handling items and that if the items are presented faster than this rate, they must line up and wait. While items wait, they are subject to various loss factors, among them being decay and interference. Suppose the recognizing mechanism continues working, passing recognized items on to the next processor, the coder. As we stated earlier, we assume the coder, as a higher-level processor, is slower than the recognizing mechanism. Thus, items passed on from the recognizer arrive at the coder at a faster rate than the coder can handle. These recognized but not coded items line up as did the original items and are subject to another set of analogous loss factors. It follows then that any item that can be remembered has had enough relative priority in the system to be processed before being destroyed by any set of relevant decay and interference factors.

It is my belief that the behavior of the items in the queues follow certain laws of regularity, and the main purpose of this model is to investigate these queue regularities. Specifically, I am interested in the *priorities* that each mechanism utilizes in choosing items to be processed, in the *decay* of an item with time, and in the *interference* an item may experience from succeeding items. Although I expect all queues to work in analogous ways, I want to concentrate on one in particular. The one seemingly most accessible queue is the one tapped most often in data collected under the heading of short-term memory. This is the queue that forms in front of the mechanism that codes items for storage in the working memory.

In order to explore the regularities of this queue, we must assume several things about the operation of the rest of the system. We have a limited set of tools with which to explore all or any part of the system. We can control only things like the type of material to be learned, the rate of presentation, and the type of response required. There are some assumptions we must make about these tools in order to claim that the responses are elicited because of the behavior of only a certain part of the system.

How do we know which part of the system we are tapping? If we want to tap only one queue, we must make sure, as sure as we can, that the responses reflect that and only that queue. First, we postulate that the retrieval process can get information from *anywhere* in the system. If a queue exists, something can be retrieved from it; if an item is stored, it is retrievable. If we want the responses to represent the behavior of one queue, therefore, we must try to create only one queue. We want to create a queue in front of the coder and not in front of any other process. We do this by manipulating the type of material and the rate at which it is presented so that it is reasonable to assume that the material is processed without queues by all mechanisms *except* the coder. The material must be such that it will pass through all early mechanisms, but be too fast and/or too hard to be processed by the coder at the rate at which it arrives. Since each mechanism in turn is slower than its predecessor, it is sufficient to find a rate that will be slow enough to allow the material to pass through the recognizing mechanism, but fast enough to prevent the subject from learning it all perfectly the first time through. We can detect whether items queue in front of the recognizing mechanisms by the existence of perceptual errors. Material that can be read aloud is assumed to be recognized without such a queue. If we wish to assume that there is a queue in front of the coder, however, we have to look for imperfect recall of the material immediately after its presentation. That is, if there is not 100% correct recall soon after presentation of the material, we can say that something is lost. If we assume that everything in the working memory is accessible to the retrieval mechanism, and we find that items which were or could have been read aloud are not remembered soon after presentation, we can say that they never entered the working memory and, therefore, were lost from the queue in front of the coder.

Let me summarize briefly the assumptions we are making in order to claim that we are tapping only the queue leading to the working memory:

1. Any material that can be read smoothly aloud is easy enough and presented at a rate slow enough that it will *not* queue in front of the recognizing mechanism, or, for that matter, any earlier processor.

2. All material that reaches the working memory is accessible for retrieval without decay up to the time when it is summarized and reorganized for permanent storage in the long-term memory.

3. Recall of such material that exhibits omission responses soon after the presentation of the material indicates loss from the queue in front of the coder.

The second assumption implies that the response decision component has set a criterion for the emission of a response such that if there is anything stored anywhere in the system, it will be dumped. This is to say that we don't want omissions to reflect a severe response bias such that the subject will not respond unless he is totally certain that his response is correct.

Programming the General Model

The main virtue of the act of programming such a model is the generation of a list of variables that must be specified in order for the resultant system to produce meaningful output. The present model requires the following specifications:

1. A *rate of input* from the previous processor (or from the environment, per discussion above).

2. A *processing time* for each item.

3. A *processing priority*, or queue discipline, specifying which item will be processed first.

4. A *decay rate* and *criterion* for an item being lost to decay.

5. A *maximum queue length* allowed.

6. A *mechanism* which specifies how items are being *interfered* with in the queue, specifying which item will leave so that a new item can enter.

7. A *retrieval discipline* specifying how the stores are dumped, read out, or recognized. This incorporates paced free recall, ordered recall, free recall, and recognition responses.

Variables 1 and 7 are under the control of the experimenter. He can control the type of material and the rate at which it is presented, and set certain requirements for a correct response. The rest of the variables are specifications of postulated internal workings.

Through manipulation of the input and response requirements, we ought to be able to discover the best possible fit of a certain set of reasonable specifications about these internal workings. That is, we expect to find a set of specifications of the variables in the model which will produce output that looks like a subject's output in the same type of task. In addition, we expect to find a consistently close fit when we change the input and output requirements for both model and subject. If we are successful in finding such a set of specifications of the variables in the above general model, we cannot say that we know how a human short-term memory is structured. Rather, we can say that this model is a good functionally equivalent approximation.

The Present Model

To explore the feasibility of such an approach to modeling the learning process, I programmed a very simple set of specifications of the above variables. The set of variable specifications of this simple version is as follows:

1. A constant regular input from the environment.
2. A constant regular processing time, equal for all items. This implies that the material presented is a list of equal and independent items, presumably a list of low meaningful trigrams.
3. A processing priority that follows the prescription "first come first served."[2]
4. A linear decay: a constant amount of decay per unit time and a constant criterion for "lost due to decay."
5. A fixed maximum queue length.
6. An interference priority, called "bumpout," that follows the prescription "oldest item is lost first."

[2] Variable 3 and the equality and independence specification of 2 are comparable to the implicit specifications in the Bower model through the use of the exponential distribution. Here they are made for simplicity, not because we are analytically restricted to their use.

7. Simultaneous retrieval: everything in the queue and the working memory is dumped for output. This is an approximation to unpaced free recall.

The above specifications are written into the program. The following are the parameters that may be set at each run of the program. (The parameter names, as they appear in the program presented in the Appendix, appear in THIS SPECIAL TYPE FONT.)

1. The rate of input in number of seconds per item: INTIME.
2. The rate of coding in number of seconds per item: CODETIME.
3. The rate of decay in the number of seconds per unit decay: DECAYTIME.
4. The actual criterion for "lost due to decay": DECAYLIMIT.
5. The maximum length of the queue, the size of the WAITINGROOM.
6. The time at which recall is requested: RECALLTIME.
7. The list of words, each item including the actual trigram, a variable to indicate the AGE of the item in the system, and the serial position of the item in the list. The serial position is included merely for clerical ease in reading the output. It is never considered by the processes in the program.

Let me give a verbal example of how all this works. Consider a list of length 15 read at a rate faster than the coder can accept and process. The system is illustrated in Fig. 2. The step-by-step analysis is summarized in Table 1. Let the WAITINGROOM be big enough to accommodate six items. The items are read in at a rate of 1 sec per item, processed at 4 sec per item, and decayed every second until they are 7 sec old, at which time they are lost.

Items 1 and 2 enter the system and line up to be processed. The coder

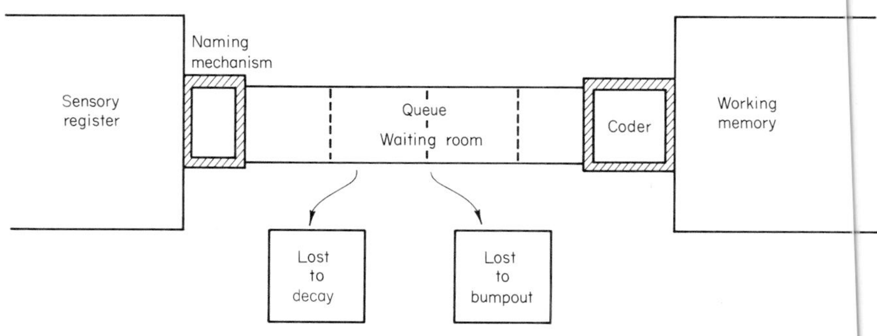

FIG. 2. Queue model of short-term memory.

TABLE 1
Sequential Output of Contents of MEMORY and WAITINGROOM[a]

	WAITINGROOM - Queue								
Time	1	2	3	4	5	6	Coder	MEMORY	
1						–	1		
2						2	1		
3					3	2	1		
4				4	3	2	1	1	
5				5	4	3	2		
6			6	5	4	3	2		
7		7	6	5	4	3	2		
8	8	7	6	5	4	3	2	2	
9	9	8	7	6	5	4[b]	3		
10	10	9	8	7	6	5[b]	3		
11	11	10	9	8	7	6[b]	3		
12	12	11	10	9	8	7	3	3	
13	13	12	11	10	9	8[b]	7		
14	14	13	12	11	10	9[b]	7		
15	15	14	13	12	11	10	7		
									IMMEDIATE RECALL
16	15	14	13	12	11	10	7	7	
17		15	14	13	12	11[d]	10		
18			15	14	13	12[d]	10		
19				15	14	13[d]	10		
20					15	14	10	10	
21						15[d]	14		
22							14		
23							14		
24							14	14	LATER RECALL

[a] Input rate: 1 sec per item. Coding rate: 4 sec per item. Decay rate: gone after 7 sec. Items lost by decay are followed by d. Items lost by bumpout are followed by b.

is not busy, so it can take Item 1 right away. Item 2 must wait. While it is waiting, Items 3 and 4 enter the system. The coder now is finished with 1; it can take 2. Items 5, 6, 7, and 8 enter while 2 is being processed. Item 3 is taken next by the coder. Recall that items are processed on a "first-come-first-served" basis. This leaves a space in the WAITINGROOM; Item 9 fills it. Now the WAITINGROOM is all filled up; that is, the queue at the coder is at its maximum allowed length. When Item 10 arrives, it bumps out 4 according to the prescription "oldest item is bumped out first." Similarly, Item 11 bumps out 5 and Item 12 bumps out 6. Now the coder is finished with 3 and again takes the oldest item in the WAITINGROOM, item 7. Incoming Item 13 fills 7's vacated space, but 14 and 15 bump out Items 8 and 9, respectively. There are no more items being presented (Time 16 in Table 1). If recall is requested immediately, the subject can dump all that is in the working memory *and* the WAITINGROOM. That is, he can remember 1, 2, 3, 7, and 10–15. Recall of Items 1, 2, and 3 constitutes the "primacy effect" part of the bowed serial position curve; recall of Items 10–15 constitutes the "recency effect."

With the particular set of parameters chosen in this example, and with the recall requested immediately after presentation of the last item, we saw no items lost to *decay*. This is because the items entered quickly enough and coding took long enough so that the bumpout process eliminated items before they had a chance to decay sufficiently to be lost. After the presentation of all the items, however, we can see the effects of the decay process. If recall is requested some time after the presentation of the items, say 30 sec, only those items that made it through the coder in spite of decay will be remembered. At that time, the subject will have nothing to dump from his WAITINGROOM, and only part of those items at the end of the list (previously accessible by virtue of their position in the WAITINGROOM) have been coded and stored in MEMORY. In the process outlined in Table 1, a recall requested at Time 24 (a delay from the end of the list of only 8 sec) would show items 1, 2, 3, 7, 10, and 14, with items 11, 12, 13, and 15, lost to decay. After such a delay, the recency effect will have been greatly reduced.

Program Organization and Description

The program that embodies the postulated processes of this working model is written in a string manipulation language called SNOBOL. It was run on The University of Michigan's IBM 7090. The program is made up of three major subroutines, three minor ones, and an executive calling routine. (See the Appendix for an introduction to SNOBOL and an annotated SNOBOL printout.) The three major subroutines, INPUT, DECAY, and CODE, regularly change the values of three stored lists called WORDS, WAITINGROOM, and MEMORY. The subroutines are defined as follows:

1. INPUT: Take the next item from the list of WORDS. Test the WAITINGROOM for capacity. If it is not filled, place the item in it. If it

is filled, execute BUMPOUT subroutine: Find the oldest item in the WAITINGROOM and delete it. Place the new item in the WAITINGROOM.

2. DECAY: Successively take each item in the WAITINGROOM and make its AGE one unit older. If the AGE of an item is greater than DECAYLIMIT, delete it.

3. CODE: Take the oldest item currently in the WAITINGROOM and store it on a list called MEMORY. Delete that item from the WAITINGROOM.

The model postulates that these three processes run simultaneously. The computers we program are all serial processors, but there is a way to simulate this simultaneity. This is accomplished by the executive routine, which determines when each of the three subroutines is to be called. Let me explain briefly. At the end of each execution of each subroutine there is a computation of the NEXT TIME it is to be called. That is, there always is a current value for NEXT INPUT TIME, NEXT DECAY TIME, and NEXT CODE TIME. The parameters read into the program determine how these values are incremented, and thereby determine the *rate* of each process. For example, NEXT INPUT TIME is incremented by an INPUT RATE; when we execute the INPUT process, which takes the next WORD and puts it into the WAITINGROOM (see above), we change the NEXT INPUT TIME by adding to it the constant value called INPUT RATE. The executive routine keeps track of the current TIME NOW. If the TIME NOW matches any of the NEXT TIMEs (i.e., NEXT INPUT TIME, NEXT DECAY TIME, or NEXT CODE TIME), the appropriate subroutine is called and executed. When all three subroutines have been checked and, if it is time, executed, TIME NOW is incremented by 1 and the checking and executing begins again. The simultaneity enters in that in a single TIME NOW, we can execute all three of the subroutines. In real time, they are enacted serially, but in task time, as defined by the TIME NOW value, they are all executed simultaneously.

The Model and the Data

Representation of the Model's Output

In order to compare the results of this model with the data collected and presented in the literature, there is one question that must be answered. What does the model's output represent? The typical representation of data in the literature takes the form of plots of the percent recalled as a function of whatever the independent variable in question is—serial position, meaningfulness, time of exposure, etc. The percentage is merely the number of people that got a certain item right divided by the total number of people who experienced the item. What then is the computer's output? Is it the output of a single subject; does the model contain parameters that can account for individual differences? Or is the output representative of the "typical subject"; is the output such that it may be meaningfully transformed into a measure of the probability of the correct response in a population? My tendency is to favor the single subject representation for the following reason. When we extend this model to include the learning of material with mixed meaningfulness and discriminability, we want to predict according to certain "noticing" strategies. Such strategies are far from universal, and certainly hard to detect from a response measure which sums over various members of a population using widely different strategies. We are looking for subtle changes in a single individual; gross population probabilities obliterate the interesting subtleties.

What then is the locus of the individual differences? Obviously we don't know, but, we will postulate here, for the moment at least, that the locus is the maximum queue length and/or decay rate and limit. We shall leave the coding rate to accommodate changes in an individual's strategy for certain types of material; and the input rate, of course, is determined by the experimenter. By varying these to produce output representative of a sample of subjects, we should be able to fit the model to actual data.

Since we have no actual single subject data in the current literature to compare this model to, we need some additional assumptions about the data that went into the serial position curve. The assumption we must make is that the sloping parts of the curve represent cumulative data. A subject who, in his recency effect, can remember the third item from the end of the list can remember the second from the end, and the last. His data sums with the subjects' whose recency effects extend only two from the end. The result is a cumulative sloping curve. The asymptotic middle comes about *not* because the "strength" of an item in memory determines an equal probability for the correct recall of all center items, as Wickelgren and Norman (1966) would have in their "strength" model of memory. Rather, here the asymptotic middle is postulated to come about because people recall different items systematically and the summing procedure produces the relatively flat area.

The Model's Output

As an initial test, ten different parameter sets were run on the current programmed model. It was hoped that the results would indicate which parameters affected which part of the serial position curve so that systematic experimental variation of the parameters could give firm evidence for this model and its parametric values. Table 2 illustrates the results of the search. The model's output is presented for each parameter set at recall "dumps," both immediately after presentation of the last item and again 30 sec later. Those items that are available immediately but not after a 30-sec delay are noted in parentheses.

First attempts to create some sort of formula which would predict the fate of each item failed miserably. Even with such a simple regular deterministic model, the interaction of the processes is far from simple.

TABLE 2
Items Recalled from a Serially Presented List[a]

Example	Parameters: Experimental I	L	Model C	D	Q	Serial positions of items that can be recalled
A	1	15	3	4	2	1 2 5 8 11 14 15
B					3	1 2 4 7 10 13 (14) 15
C					4	1 2 3 6 9 12 (13) (14) 15
D	3.0	15	3	4	3	1 7 13 (14) (15)
E	2.0					1 4 10 13 (14) (15)
F	1.0					1 2 4 7 10 13 (14) 15
G	.5					1 2 3 4 5 7 8 10 11 13 14 (15)
H	1	15	3	2	3	1 2 5 7 11 14 (15)
I				3		1 2 4 7 10 13 14 (15)
J				4		1 2 4 7 10 13 (14) 15
K				5		1 2 4 7 10 13 14 15
L	1	15	3	4	3	1 2 4 7 10 13 (14) 15
M		30				1 2 4 7 10 13 16 19 22 25 28 (29) 30

[a] Thirteen examples (A—M) of the items that would be recalled with various model and experimental parameters. Items which are available only for immediate recall and not for delayed recall are enclosed in parentheses. [Experimental parameters: I = Input rate (seconds/item); L = List length. Model parameters: C = Coding time (seconds); D = Decay time (seconds); Q = Queue length (number of slots).]

Primacy and Recency Effects

There are a few general predictions which we can make from the output of the model. First of all, indicants of the primacy effect, the number of items in sequence recalled at the beginning of the list, is directly affected by the rate of presentation of the items. Refer to Table 2. In comparing runs that vary only the rate of presentation we see that the runs with slower rates of presentation produce longer initial sequences of items. Now refer to the data collected by Murdock (1962), reproduced in the Appendix of this book and Fig. 9 of Chapter 2, page 57. The experimental procedure required subjects to recall freely words which were presented in lists of varying lengths at varying rates of presentation. Comparison of the curves marked 20-1 and 20-2 (indicating a list length of 20 presented at a rate of 1 sec per item and 2 sec per item, respectively) shows an increased primacy effect in the list presented at the slower rate. In the model's terminology, this means that the faster the items are entering the more quickly the WAITINGROOM is filled up and the sooner the BUMPOUT is executed.

A second thing to notice is the existence of a constant recency effect independent of list length. Returning again to Murdock's data, we note in particular a very stable recency effect for the lists marked 20-1, 30-1, and 40-1—lists of varying length presented at a constant rate. In the model, the ability to dump a full WAITINGROOM is independent of how many items have been presented. In Table 2, note that the change in list length produces a similar constant recency effect represented as contiguous end items.

There is one more simple prediction on which the model and data correspond. Postman and Phillips (1965) collected data very similar to Murdock's except that they varied the list length with delay to recall rather than with the presentation rate. Subjects were required to recall the lists of trigrams either immediately after presentation of the last item or 30 sec later. After the 30-sec delay, the recency effect was eliminated, but the rest of the curve was unchanged. Return for a moment to Table 2. In the output of *all* the sets of parameters except A and K, there is a definite reduction of the number of items recalled after 30 sec as compared with the immediate dump. Those items in the end of the list which are recalled immediately may be dumped from the WAITINGROOM; but items recalled 30 sec later must have made it through the coder; those items which are lost are lost to decay.

Decay and Interference

There is another prediction that concerns inferences about the relative contribution of the decay and interference processes in the queue. The assumptions made in the programmed model allow a fairly simple statement of process interactions. It must be fully understood before we proceed to the prediction. The statement reads:

When the coding rate is held constant:

1. If (WAITINGROOM) $\times$ (INTIME) $<$ (DECAYTIME) $\times$ (DECAYLIMIT) then the decay process doesn't become relevant until all the items have been presented.
2. If (WAITINGROOM) $\times$ (INTIME) $>$ (DECAYTIME) $\times$ (DECAYLIMIT) then the queue length is totally irrelevant. The WAITINGROOM will never be filled up and the bumpout interference never activated.

As an illustration, return to the verbal example given on page 126. You recall that no items are lost to decay until all the items have been presented and the bumpout becomes no longer relevant. This fits Condition 1 above. The waitingroom is size 6; the presentation rate, 1 sec per item; the decay rate is 1 unit of decay per second, and the limit beyond which items are lost is 7 sec. Above, (6) $\times$ (1) $<$ (1) $\times$ (7), the decay process does not become relevant until all the items have been presented. If the decay rate had been faster or the decay limit shorter, we might have had a situation that fit the second condition. Consider the example illustrated in Table 1. If the decay limit is changed to 5 sec instead of the 7 sec used in Table 1, Item 3 decays before it can be coded, and the immediate recall produces items 1, 2, 4, 8, and 12–15. After a delay of 30 sec, only Items 1, 2, 4, 8, 12, and 15 would be recalled. At no time in this condition would items be lost to bumpout. The queue length never exceeds 5, and the waitingroom, which can hold 6, is never filled up. In the above statement, (6) $\times$ (1) $>$ (1) $\times$ (5), so that the queue length is totally irrelevant and all lost items are lost to decay.

Now return to Table 2. Applying the above stated conditions of interaction, we note that runs C, G, J, and K, are those in which only decay is relevant. The rest exhibit the relevance of both decay and the bumpout interference. Because the process that causes items to be lost changes when the end of presentation occurs and that change is obscured in the immediate recall dump, what I want to look at is the number of items from the end of the list which are recalled after the

30-sec delay. In those lists where decay alone is the loss factor, the same level of performance should continue throughout. In the others, however, in which both decay and bumpout are factors, the level of performance first follows determinants of the bumpout process. When the end of the list appears, the decay process's *different* parameters produce performance of a different level. Since the loss due to decay must be slower than that due to bumpout in order for the bumpout to be executed at all, this level of performance, the number of items recalled from the end of the list, should be higher than the asymptotic middle. Note especially set F in Table 2. In the middle portion of the output, one half of the items are recalled. Of the end items, two thirds are recalled. The 30-sec delay need not reduce the recency effect to the level of the middle items.

In the Postman and Phillips data, the curve representing recall after the 30-sec delay remains flat through to the end of the list. In their experiment, subjects were required to perform an interfering (rehearsal preventing) task during the delay interval. However, in my own preliminary work, a replication of Postman and Phillips' experiment with the 30-sec delay left unfilled, the curve again rises at the end. That is, the same end items are recalled more often than those in the middle, though not as often as the immediately recalled end items. Though these data await confirmation, it does seem to lend support to the idea of a change in the operative process that is causing items to be lost. That is, when the coder is not interrupted by some intervening task, the items at the end of a list may remain in the buffer long enough to be coded. Loss here is due to decay, as compared with the case for the middle items, which are constantly subjected to bumpout by succeeding items.

This conjecture suggests several things about the decay versus interference theory debates commonly found in the literature. The effect of either process depends upon the rate of presentation relative to the rate of decay. Interference does not occur alone; decay can appear alone. The evidence for the *joint* existence can be found in the examination of the fate of the items in the last part of a list of items, in the part incorporated in the classical recency effect.

Conclusions

Where to from here? The striking advantage of the model in this form is the number of open doors it leaves. The model as it stands now is encouraging but inadequate. Returning to the list of postulates of the simplified system, I find several deficiencies. A low-level defect is that the model makes overly specific predictions as a result of the assumption that incoming items are equal and independent. Given any two items, any two words, trigrams, numbers, etc., one will always be easier to remember than another.

The model predicts cyclical recall of every third or fourth item in the middle portion of the list. Subjects do not appear to recall in such regular cycles. This suggests that before a subject codes an item he already has decided which items are easier and gives those higher priority than harder ones. The fact that we do not know precisely the variety of priorities used nor the inherent inequalities of items presently keeps us from predicting which incoming item will be stored. However, a computer-specified model can incorporate several hypotheses concerning these processes.

A second questionable assumption concerns the postulated constant coding rate for homogeneous items presented at different rates. Preliminary work indicates that those items that were correctly recalled from a fast presentation are less likely to be even recognized subsequently than items from a slow presentation. This suggests that part of a subject's learning strategy includes a decision of how much average coding time should be allocated to the incoming items. When items are presented in quick succession, he is more apt to allocate less time to each than if items arrive more slowly. This appears to occur even when an alternate strategy, one of choosing an item, coding it fully, and then selecting another, would produce superior performance.

The third and most perplexing defect centers in the assumption that all that is in memory is accessible for recall. We find that subjects recognize items far better than they recall them. Some information stored in memory is either insufficient for a correct recall or else cannot be found. Errors in recall reflect confusions or partially correct information. There is more there than can be dumped. This retrieval problem is closely related to the changing strategies mentioned above. Clearly, an item that has been allocated less coding time will be less likely retrieved at a later time. Consequently, any model that assumes that coding is all or none and that all that is in memory is recalled will consistently overpredict actual performance. When we find a measure of what *is* in memory, we will be better able to be precise about the properties of the entrance processes.

Summary

The problem of attention, information overload, and the loss of items from short term memory is discussed. The model uses the method of computer simulation to explore a simple version of the input properties of a general model of the memory process. Items to be remembered are conceived of as passing through a series of processors until they are stored in a permanent long term memory. Items typically arrive faster than they are processed; consequently, queues arise in front of the processors. Behavior of the items in a queue is postulated to follow certain laws of regularity. Specifically, items decay with time, and incoming items interfere with one another by bumping each other out of a "waiting room" of fixed size. The priority of items taken is assumed in general to be dependent upon a subject's strategy. As an initial simplification, the programmed model postulates specifications intended as first approximations of these processes, e.g., behavior in a single queue, constant coding time, linear decay, and first-come-first-served priorities.

The model makes several strong predictions; for example, the primacy effect varies with changes in the rate of presentation of items, and the recency effect varies with different types of items. The paper discusses experimental evidence bearing on the predictions and considers implications of the postulates and consequential recommendations for exploration of variants of the proposed mechanisms.

Appendix

Introduction to SNOBOL3

The following introduction to SNOBOL is intended to aid those familiar with FORTRAN-type languages to read the text of the actual program. Those who are interested in further details of this language and its more powerful successor, SNOBOL4, should refer to the appropriate language manuals (Griswold, Poage, and Polonsky, 1968).

SNOBOL, like FORTRAN, can operate on numbers and characters, has functions, arrays, and indexing capabilities. But SNOBOL differs markedly from FORTRAN in design and purpose. SNOBOL is primarily a string manipulation language, slow and awkward in arithmetic, while FORTRAN was built for numerical computation.

What is string manipulation? A string is any series of characters, such as this line of print. The operations of string manipulation involve creating, joining, and separating strings, testing their contents, and making substitutions in them.

The general format for *all* SNOBOL3 statements is:

```
LABEL  STRING  PATTERN = REPLACEMENT  /GOTO
```

As we shall see, parts of this format may be missing, subject to default settings. Unlike FORTRAN, there are no fields in which these parts must go, with the exception of the LABEL and the continuation dot starting in column 1, and everything else avoiding column 1.

Let us define each part of the statement by demonstrating an example of a LABEL, a STRING, a PATTERN, its REPLACEMENT, and a GOTO command. Suppose there is a line of print "IS THE THEATER OPEN TONIGHT?." This line of print is a STRING. Since we will want to refer to it, we will associate a name with this string. We shall name this string SENTENCE. Suppose that we did not know the actual contents of the string called SENTENCE and that we wished to see if it had the letters "THE" in it. The operation used is called 'pattern matching' and is the heart of the SNOBOL language. The matching statement is written:

```
SENTENCE 'THE'
```

The sequence of characters SENTENCE is the name of the string on which the pattern matching operation is to be performed. The 'THE' is the pattern for which we are searching. The above statement has no LABEL, REPLACEMENT, or GOTO. The statement is performed immediately after the statement before it (default in the absence of a label); the part of the string that was matched will not be changed (default of REPLACEMENT); and the next statement to be executed will be the one following this one (default of a GOTO). This statement is translated simply to: In the string called SENTENCE, look for the literal triplet 'THE.'

How do we know if the pattern 'THE' was found? In the statement given above, we do not know. Basically, all SNOBOL statements either succeed (S) or fail (F). But if we wish success or failure to leave some mark or have some effect, either the GOTO or an additional operation must be made conditional upon such success or failure. In the following statement, we ask whether the search for a pattern was successful, and we add a GOTO contingent upon that success.

```
SENTENCE 'THE'    /S(OTHER)F(NEXT)
```

That is, if a 'THE' can be found in the string named SENTENCE, the statement labeled OTHER is to be executed next. If a 'THE' cannot be found anywhere in the string called SENTENCE, we will GOTO the statement labeled NEXT. If the GOTO is missing, the control automatically passes to the next statement of the program, regardless of the success or failure of the statement. If the S or F part of the GOTO is missing, the control passes to the statement indicated in the GOTO, again regardless of the success or failure of the statement. For example,

```
SENTENCE 'THE'    /(ELSEWHERE)
```

This particular statement is of no actual use in a program; it serves here merely as an illustration of an unconditional GOTO. Control goes unconditionally to the statement labeled ELSEWHERE, regardless of whether the string SENTENCE has a 'THE' in it.

Pattern matching statements will match only the shortest left-most occurrence of a pattern. As it stands now, the previous statement will find the pattern 'THE' in the second word of the string named SENTENCE. It will not find the THE in THEATER. It will not transfer to the statement labeled NEXT. To find *all* occurrences of a pattern, we need a REPLACEMENT or marker for the pattern once found, and a loop of control back to the searching statement. The most common REPLACEMENT in such a situation is the null string, written '' or simply left blank. This REPLACEMENT serves to delete the matched characters.

```
FIND   SENTENCE   'THE' = ''  /S(FIND)F(NEXT)
```

Here the statement LABEL is FIND, the datum on which the operation is performed is the string called SENTENCE. We search for the pattern on the left side of the = sign ('THE') and, wherever found, replace it with the pattern on the right side of the = sign (the null string, '' in this case). Every time we find the pattern (and do the replacement) we are successful (S); hence, the next statement we do is the one with the label FIND. Thus, we keep repeating the same operation until we fail to find the pattern, in which case we do the statement with the label NEXT.

In our particular example, in which the string called SENTENCE has the contents "IS THE THEATER OPEN TONIGHT?," the above statement will find the first 'THE' in the second word of the string. It will replace that 'THE' with the null string. It will try to find 'THE' again by transferring control back to this statement labeled FIND. After the first successful match and deletion, the string SENTENCE will look like this:

```
IS THEATER OPEN TONIGHT
```

In the second execution of the statement, the pattern 'THE' will match the first three letters of the word THEATER and delete them. After that, the string SENTENCE will be:

```
IS ATER OPEN TONIGHT?
```

The third attempt to pattern match will fail, as there is no 'THE' in the string called SENTENCE. Consequently, control will shift to the statement labeled NEXT.

One of the most useful patterns is the *arbitrary string variable.* This pattern, written **, will match *anything*, including the null string. Suppose we have a string called PARAGRAPH with a paragraph of text as its contents. The statement

```
PARAGRAPH ** ','
```

will match everything up to the first comma in the string called PARAGRAPH. If we later want to examine what we matched by way of this arbitrary pattern, we can give the arbitrary pattern a name, *NAME*, and rewrite the above statement so that we can reference the named string in some subsequent statement. The **'s still means to match anything, but the symbols between them (NAME, in this example) specify the name that is to be given to the string matched by the **. The following two statements:

```
PARAGRAPH *NAME*','
NAME  'THE'
```

together specify a search for the pattern 'THE' in that part of the string called PARAGRAPH prior to the first comma.

As another example of this arbitrary string variable, let us return to the original string called SENTENCE. We could write the following pattern matching statement:

```
SENTENCE 'IS' *MIDDLE* 'OPEN'
```

This statement would look for the shortest left-most occurrence of the pattern 'IS' followed by anything up to the pattern 'OPEN'. It would label that *anything* in the middle MIDDLE. As a result of this statement, the string called MIDDLE would have the contents:

THE THEATER

The simple arbitrary string variable, **, will match a string of any length. If we want to match a certain number of characters, we can constrain this variable. This fixed length is variable is written */'number'* or *NAME/'number'*. For example, to match a six-character string, we write */'6'* or *NAME/'6'*. This pattern can be used in conjunction with other patterns to fix the position of a pattern you wish to find or to pick up fixed length parts from a long string.

Let me illustrate with an actual statement from the programmed model. The statement reads:

```
WAITINGROOM   *FIRSTPART*   *GONE/'6'* ';' OLDEST '/' *LASTPART*
                    = FIRSTPART LASTPART
```

(The dot which starts the second line indicates that this line is simply a continuation of the first line.) This statement translates to read: In the string called WAITINGROOM, find everything up to a six character string which is followed by a semicolon. The semicolon must be followed by the contents of a string called OLDEST, then by a slash, and then by the rest of the string. If this complex pattern is found, call the fixed six character string GONE; call everything before it FIRSTPART; call everything after the slash LASTPART. Now that all parts of the string have been assigned names, replace the old string called WAITINGROOM, with a new string made by concatenating the two smaller strings, FIRSTPART and LASTPART. The statement, if successful, has the effect of deleting GONE, the semicolon, the matched contents of the string called OLDEST, and the slash from the long string called WAITINGROOM. If the statement fails, WAITINGROOM is unchanged, the strings GONE, FIRSTPART, and LASTPART are null (or unchanged, if they had pervious contents) and control shifts to the next statement.

For example, suppose the string WAITINGROOM has the contents; "ABC-01;5/DEF-02;4/GHI-03;3/JKL-05;2/," and the contents of OLDEST is "4." If we execute the statement described above, the string called FIRSTPART will be matched to: "ABC-01;5/." The string LASTPART will have: "GHI-03;3/JKL-05;2/." The fixed length variable GONE will have: "DEF-02." And the new contents of the string WAITINGROOM will be: "ABC-01;5/GHI-03;3/JKL-05;2/."

In addition to such powerful and flexible pattern-matching operations, SNOBOL3 has available many built-in functions, or subroutines. For example, several of those used in the model are:

.NUM(Y)	Test whether Y is a number.
.LE(X,Y)	Test whether X is less than or equal to Y. This is one of many binary comparison operators.
TRIM(stringname)	Chop off all trailing blanks.
SIZE(stringname)	Count how many characters are currently in that string.
SYSPOT	Print the contents of the string named.
SYSPIT	Read a line of the input record.
DEFINE(fn)	Store the code of the subroutine or function. Remember what statement label to enter the subroutine at, and what the function will be called when it is referred to in the main program.

One more operator foreign to FORTRAN is used heavily in the programmed model. It is the '$,' for the operation called *indirection.* If I use the symbol '$' in front of a string name, it translates to mean: Refer to the contents of the string that is *named* by this string. Suppose we have two strings:

The first is named LETTERS, and has "ABC" as contents.

The second is named TITLE, and has "LETTERS" as contents. When I write $TITLE, I am referring to the string ABC, as it is the contents of the string called LETTERS as named by the string called TITLE. That is, ABC is the string named by the string named by TITLE. This operator gives the programmer great flexibility in setting up a statement whose basic structure is constant but whose exact referents vary from time to time. That is, continuing in the above example, we might have another string:

```
NUMBERS = '012345'
```

If we later change only the statement that assigns the contents of TITLE from "LETTERS" to "NUMBERS", all statements with $TITLE in them would subsequently refer to "012345" instead of "ABC".

The Short-Term-Memory-Model Program

The program is written in six chunks. The first five chunks are independent subroutines, or functions. These are executed from commands in the other chunk, the main executive routine. The executive routine determines the organization of the activity of the system as a whole.

In summary, the six chunks of the program are:

1. a minimizer, (the function MIN)
2. a maximizer, (the function MAX)
3. the DECAY process, (the function DECAY)
4. the CODE process, (the function PROCESS)
5. the INPUT process, (the function INPUT)
6. the EXECUTIVE routine.

The functions MIN *and* MAX. The first two functions are included for housekeeping purposes only and have no relevance to the understanding of the model. The minimizer follows the prescription:

1. Check to see if all the items in the list are numbers.
2. Successively compare two items at a time.
3. Keep the smaller of the two to compare with the next item.
4. The last item kept is the minimum of the list.

And the maximizer similarly:

1. Check to see if all the items in the list are numbers.
2. Successively compare two items at a time.
3. Keep the larger of the two to compare with the next item.
4. The last item kept is the maximum of the list.

The third, fourth, and fifth functions are central to the model and its assumptions. I will go through the DECAY function in detail, giving the SNOBOL code as well as a detailed translation of the code. For the other two functions, the code and a general description should suffice.

The function DECAY

The DECAY process is defined briefly in the text. The code for this is:

```
SCF3          DEFINE('DECAY()','WITHIN1')  /(SCF4)
WITHIN1       RUMPUSROOM = WAITINGROOM
              WAITINGROOM *NOTHING/'1'*  /F(LATER)
              P = '1'
START.INDEX   LABELWORD = 'TRI.' P
              LABELAGE = 'AGE.' P
              RUMPUSROOM *$LABELWORD* ';' *$LABELAGE* '/' = /F(BUILDUP.1)
              $LABELAGE = $LABELAGE + '1'
              .GE($LABELAGE,ORIG.DECAYLIMIT)     /S(DISAPPEAR)
UP            P = P + '1'     /(START.INDEX)
DISAPPEAR     DECAYED = DECAYED  $LABELWORD  ';' $LABELAGE '/'
              $LABELAGE =
              $LABELWORD =     /(UP)
```

```
BUILDUP.1      Q = '1'
               P = P - '1'
BUILDUP.2      LABELWORD = 'TRI.' Q
               LABELAGE = 'AGE.' Q
               RUMPUSROOM = RUMPUSROOM $LABELWORD ';' $LABELAGE '/'
               $LABELWORD =
               $LABELAGE =
               .GE(Q,P)  /S(EQUATE)F(REDO)
REDO           Q = Q + '1'  /(BUILDUP.2)
EQUATE         RUMPUSROOM ';/' =  /S(EQUATE)
               WAITINGROOM = RUMPUSROOM
LATER          NEXT.DECAYTIME = NEXT.DECAYTIME + ORIG.DECAYTIME
               SYSPOT = 'THE WAITINGROOM NOW LOOKS LIKE THIS:' WAITINGROOM
               'AND THE NEXT TIME WE DECAY IS TIME ' NEXT.DECAYTIME /(RETURN)
```

Statement SCF3 defines the function DECAY. It uses the DEFINE function to specify that when this subroutine is called it will start at statement WITHIN1. The /(SCF4) simply means that in the initial definition of functions, after defining DECAY, we GOTO define the next function, PROCESS, the first definition statement of which is labeled SCF4.

If we now look at the code which defines the DECAY process, beginning at the statement labeled WITHIN1, we see that DECAY starts by copying the contents of WAITINGROOM to the RUMPUSROOM. This provides a working copy so we do not destroy information while manipulating it. The next two lines of code first look at the string WAITINGROOM to see if there is anything in it. If there is one character in it, we label the one character NOTHING, put the number 1 into P, and go to START.INDEX. If there is nothing in the WAITINGROOM, we GOTO LATER, where we increase the current value of NEXT.DECAYTIME, print out the contents of WAITINGROOM (here nothing) and the new value of NEXT.DECAYTIME, and leave the subroutine.

The DECAY process itself begins with statement labeled START.-INDEX. We begin by setting up a series of labels for the various parts of the WAITINGROOM. That is, we separate the copy of WAITINGROOM (RUMPUSROOM) into various trigrams (TRI.1, TRI.2, TRI.3, etc.) and ages of the trigrams (AGE.1, AGE.2, etc.). Each age of a trigram is made one unit older. Each is tested whether it is now older than the maximum allowed, .GE($LABELAGE,ORIG.DECAYLIMIT). If the age is too large, the control is transferred to the statement labeled DISAPPEAR. We put this trigram on a list so we can later print out those items which decayed away. We then get rid of the appropriate trigram and its age. We transfer to UP, where we increment P value and return for the next trigram and its age. That is, this separating the trigrams and testing their ages is done for each trigram in turn, with control looping back to START.INDEX.

When there is nothing left in the RUMPUSROOM, we transfer to the statement labeled BUILDUP.1 and begin to put the various trigrams and their newly incremented ages back into the RUMPUSROOM. First, Q and P are set to their appropriate looping values. We find the first trigram and its age (TRI.1 and AGE.1) and put them in the RUMPUSROOM, followed by the appropriate separator characters, the semicolon and the slash. That trigram and its age is now deleted, we test for the end of the loop, and either return for the next trigram to put it back in the RUMPUSROOM, or go on to the statement labeled EQUATE.

Since there may be an occasion in which a null (decayed away) trigram is put back on the list in RUMPUSROOM, we have extra ;/'s to get rid of. The statement labeled EQUATE loops back on itself until these are gone. Finally, WAITINGROOM's contents is changed by copying the final RUMPUSROOM into it. We change the value of NEXT.DECAYTIME by the increment ORIG.DECAYTIME. That is, we keep track of the next time this function is to be called. Then we print out the current value of this next time as well as the contents of the WAITINGROOM. After this, control returns to the executive routine.

The operator of *indirection* plays a large role in this and the other functions. Because of the repetitive nature of this "taking apart the WAITINGROOM into its components" I shall explain in detail the three lines of the program beginning with the statement labeled START.-INDEX. The first value of P is 1. The string called LABELWORD then has contents TRI.1 and the LABELAGE has AGE.1. The next statement uses this indirection. It translates to read: In the string called RUMPUSROOM look for *anything* followed by a semicolon followed by *anything* followed by a slash. Call that first *anything* whatever the contents of LABELWORD is. In this case, the first *anything* will be named TRI.1. Call the second *anything*, the one between the semicolon and the slash, whatever the contents of LABELAGE is. In this case, it is called AGE.1. Both of these *anythings*, plus the semicolon and slash, are deleted from RUMPUSROOM.

In the statement labeled UP, we increment the P value to 2 and begin tearing apart the shorter RUMPUSROOM with a new label for each *anything*. First, we set LABELWORD'S contents to TRI.2, and LABELAGE to AGE.2. Then, when we get the two parts of the RUMPUSROOM which are (1) before the semicolon, and (2) between the semicolon and slash, we call them TRI.2 and AGE.2, respectively. When we get to the statement labeled UP, again we increment the P value and loop back to the statement labeled START.INDEX. Thus, this part of the program creates from the RUMPUSROOM a whole series of strings called TRI.1, AGE.1, TRI.2, AGE.2, TRI.3, AGE.3, etc., until the RUMPUSROOM is empty. The flexibility of this pattern matching statement is made possible by this indirection operator.

The function PROCESS

The fourth function is the CODE function as defined in the text. It is here called PROCESS, but is renamed in the text because "process" is an ambiguous term.

1. Check to see if something is in the WAITINGROOM.
2. To find the *oldest* item:
   (*a*) Separate all the AGES from the trigrams and make a list of them.
   (*b*) Find the maximum of the list of AGES.
   (*c*) Find the trigram that had that maximum AGE.
3. Put that oldest trigram and its serial position in the list called MEMORY.
4. Delete that trigram, its serial position, and its AGE from the WAITINGROOM.
5. Change the NEXT.CODETIME (the time CODE is to be called again) by the increment CODETIME (the coding *rate*).

```
SCF4          DEFINE('PROCESS()','PRI')  /(SCF5)
PRI           AGES =
              RECROOM = WAITINGROOM
              WAITINGROOM *NOTHING/'1'*  /F(INCREMENT)
              R = '1'
BEGIN.LABEL   LABELWORD = 'TRI.' R
              LABELAGE = 'AGE.' R
              RECROOM *$LABELWORD* ';' *$LABELAGE* '/' /F(FINDIT)
              $LABELWORD =
              AGES = AGES $LABELAGE ','
              $LABELAGE =
              R = R + '1'  /(BEGIN.LABEL)
FINDIT        CHOSEN = MAX(AGES)
              WAITINGROOM *FIRSTPART* *REMEMBER/'6'* ';' CHOSEN '/'
.             *LASTPART* = FIRSTPART LASTPART  /S(PUT)F(ERROR)
PUT           MEMORY = MEMORY REMEMBER ';'
INCREMENT     NEXT.CODETIME = NEXT.CODETIME + ORIG.CODETIME  /(RESPOND)
ERROR         SYSPOT = 'I AM TRYING TO FIND THE OLDEST ITEM TO PUT INTO '
.             'MEMORY AND CANT.'  /(END)
RESPOND       SYSPOT = 'THIS IS THE WAITINGROOM: ' WAITINGROOM ' AND THIS '
.             'IS IN MEMORY ' MEMORY '. WE WILL CODE AGAIN AT TIME '
.             NEXT.CODETIME  /(RETURN)
```

The function INPUT

The fifth function is the INPUT function as defined in the text.

1. Take the next item from the list of WORDS.
2. Test the WAITINGROOM for capacity.
3. If the WAITINGROOM is not filled up, add this item to the list called WAITINGROOM.
4. If the WAITINGROOM is filled, execute BUMPOUT:
   (*a*) Separate the items in the WAITINGROOM into their respective trigrams and AGES.
   (*b*) Make a list of the AGES.
   (*c*) Find the maximum of these AGES.
   (*d*) Find the trigram with this maximum AGE and delete it.
   (*e*) Put the items in the WAITINGROOM back together again.
   (*f*) Put the new incoming item in the free space in the WAITINGROOM.
5. Change the NEXT.INTIME (the next time this INPUT is to be called) by INTIME (the input *rate*).

```
SCF5          DEFINE('INPUT()','UNDER1')  /(INITIAL)
UNDER1        AGES =
              GONE =
              OLDEST =
              WORDS *TBRU* '/' =  /F(SAYSOME)
              .LE(SIZE(WAITINGROOM) + SIZE(TBRU),ORIG.QUEUE * '9')
.             /F(BUMPOUT)
FILL          WAITINGROOM = WAITINGROOM TBRU '/'  /(MORETIME)
BUMPOUT       WORKROOM = WAITINGROOM
              N = '1'
PEEL          LABELWORD = 'TRI.' N
              LABELAGE = 'AGE.' N
              WORKROOM *LABELWORD* ';' *$LABELAGE* '/'  /F(BIG.1)
              AGES = AGES $LABELAGE ','
              $LABELWORD =
              $LABELAGE =
              N = N + '1'  /(PEEL)
BIG.1         OLDEST = MAX(AGES)
              WAITINGROOM *FIRSTPART* *GONE/'6'* ';' OLDEST '/' *LASTPART*
.             = FIRSTPART LASTPART  /S(FILL)F(ERRORANALYSIS)
MORETIME      NEXT.INTIME = NEXT.INTIME + ORIG.INTIME  /(TELL)
TELL          KO = GONE ';' OLDEST '/'
              SYSPOT = 'THE WAITINGROOM NOW LOOKS LIKE THIS ' WAITINGROOM
.             '. IF SOMETHING WAS BUMPED OUT IT WAS ' KO
.             ' WE WILL DO INPUT AGAIN AT TIME ' NEXT.INTIME '.'
              BUMPED = BUMPED KO  /(RETURN)
SAYSOME       SYSPOT = 'IMMEDIATE RECALL GIVES US : ' WAITINGROOM 'AND IN '
.             'MEMORY: ' MEMORY  /(POSTLIST)
ERRORANALYSIS SYSPOT = 'I CANT FIND SOMETHING TO BUMP OUT.'  /(END)
```

The EXECUTIVE *Routine*

The last of the routines is the shortest in length, the longest in running, and the most important. It is this EXECUTIVE routine that makes the whole thing go.

1. Read in all the input parameters and set all initial values.
2. Set the initial value of TIME NOW.
3. If the NEXT.CODETIME matches TIME NOW, execute the CODE process; if not, go on to the next statement.
4. If the NEXT.DECAYTIME matches TIME NOW, execute the DECAY process; if not, go on.
5. If the NEXT.INTIME matches TIME NOW, execute the INPUT process; if not, go on.
6. If the constant RECALLTIME (time to dump the WAITINGROOM and MEMORY) matches TIME NOW, go to the RECALL process (a few statements later); if not, go on.
7. Now that all processes have been checked and/or executed in this TIME NOW, increment TIME NOW by 1 and return to step 2. above.
8. When RECALLTIME does match TIME NOW, dump the WAITINGROOM and the MEMORY.

```
INITIAL        ORIG.DECAYLIMIT = TRIM(SYSPIT)  /F(END)
               ORIG.QUEUE = TRIM(SYSPIT)  /F(END)
               ORIG.DECAYTIME = TRIM(SYSPIT)  /F(END)
               ORIG.INTIME = TRIM(SYSPIT)  /F(END)
               ORIG.CODETIME = TRIM(SYSPIT)  /F(END)
               ORIG.RECALLTIME = TRIM(SYSPIT)  /F(END)
               NEXT.CODETIME = '1'
               NEXT.DECAYTIME = '1'
               NEXT.INTIME = '0'
               WORDS = TRIM(SYSPIT)  /F(END)
               WORDS = WORDS TRIM(SYSPIT)  /F(END)
               WORDS = WORDS TRIM(SYSPIT)  /F(END)
START          WAITINGROOM =
               MEMORY =
EXECUTIVE      TIME = '0'
JUNIOR.EXEC    SYSPOT = 'THE TIME IS NOW ' TIME '.'
               .EQ(NEXT.CODETIME,TIME)  PROCESS()
               .EQ(NEXT.DECAYTIME,TIME)  DECAY()
               .EQ(NEXT.INTIME,TIME)  INPUT()
               TIME = TIME + '1'  /(JUNIOR.EXEC)
POSTLIST       TIME = TIME + '1'
               .EQ(NEXT.CODETIME,TIME)  PROCESS()
               .EQ(NEXT.DECAYTIME,TIME)  DECAY()
               .EQ(ORIG.RECALLTIME,TIME)  /S(RECALL)F(POSTLIST)
RECALL         SYSPOT = 'I CAN RECALL THE FOLLOWING IF I SAY THEM VERY '
.              'QUICKLY: ' WAITINGROOM ' AND THESE I HAVE STORED FOREVER: '
.              MEMORY '. THESE WERE LOST TO DECAY ' DECAYED 'AND '
.              'THESE WERE LOST TO BEING BUMPED OUT ' BUMPED '.' /(INITIAL)
END
```

References

BOWER, G. H. A descriptive theory of memory. In D. P. Kimple (Ed.), *Proceedings of the second conference on learning, remembering, and forgetting.* New York: New York Academy of Sciences, 1967. Pp. 112–185.

COX, D. R., AND SMITH, W. L. *Queues.* London: Metheun, 1961.

FEIGENBAUM, E. A., AND SIMON, H. A. A theory of the serial position effect. *British Journal of Psychology,* 1962, **53,** 307–320.

GRISWOLD, R. E., POAGE, J. F., AND POLONSKY, I. P. *The SNOBOL4 programming language.* Holmdel, New Jersey: Bell Telephone Laboratories, Inc., 1968.

MURDOCK, B. B. The serial position effect of free recall. *Journal of Experimental Psychology,* 1962, **64,** 482–488.

POSTMAN, L., AND PHILLIPS, L. W. Short-term temporal changes in free recall. *Quarterly Journal of Experimental Psychology,* 1965, **17,** 132–138.

VON RESTORFF, H. Uber die Wirkurg von Bereichsbilgung im Spurenfeld. *Psychologische Forschung,* 1938, **18,** 299–324. (See A. E. Goss and C. F. Nodine, *Paired-associates learning.* New York: Academic Press, 1965.)

WICKELGREN, W. A., AND NORMAN, D. A. Strength models and serial position in short term recognition memory. *Journal of Mathematical Psychology,* 1966, **3,** 316–347.

II

PHONEME STORAGE AND WORD RECOGNITION

6

Acoustic Similarity and Auditory Short-Term Memory: Experiments and a Model

George Sperling and Roseanne G. Speelman[1]

Bell Telephone Laboratories, Incorporated
Murray Hill, New Jersey

[1] Now at Seton Hill College, Greensburg, Pennsylvania.

Introduction[2]

A common tenet in current theories of short-term memory is that items to be reported are rehearsed subvocally prior to report (Broadbent, 1958; Brown, 1958; Conrad, 1967; Glanzer and Clark, 1963, 1964; Sperling, 1960, 1963, 1967). If this is so, then one may expect the acoustic properties of these items—their sound—to influence the number of items that can be recalled correctly. For example, Sperling (1960, p. 21) observed that acoustic confusions (e.g., between B and D, D and T) occurred in a task where stimuli were presented visually and reported in writing, a task in which the items were never overtly represented in an acoustic form. Further experiments showed "that subjects required to memorize sequences of the letters B, P, D, T, etc., do not do as well as when confronted with an equivalent sequence of letters which do not sound so much alike" (Sperling, 1963, p. 31).

Since about 1963, the effect of the sound of verbal stimuli on the ability to recall them has been intensively investigated. The experiments fall roughly into three general classes: (1) experiments that compare memory for sequences of items that sound alike with memory for sequences that do not sound so much alike (Baddeley, 1966; Conrad, 1963; Conrad, Baddeley, and Hull, 1966; Conrad and Hull, 1964; Laughery, 1963; Laughery and Pinkus, 1966; Sperling, 1963; Speelman and Sperling, 1964; Wickelgren, 1965e); (2) experiments that study interference with to-be-remembered items by other items which may or may not sound like the to-be-remembered items (Conrad, 1967; Dale, 1964; Dale and Gregory, 1966; Wickelgren, 1965a, 1966a, 1966b); (3) experiments that are concerned primarily with analyzing response

[2] An account of these experiments was presented to the Eastern Psychological Association (Speelman and Sperling, 1964). An earlier version of the present article appeared as Sperling and Speelman (1967). The procedure and results sections of the article represent the joint work of both authors; the discussions, predictions, and appendices present Sperling's opinions and calculations. The research was carried out at the Bell Telephone Laboratories. The final report was prepared by the first author, much of it being done when he was a visiting staff member at the University of California, Los Angeles, in 1967–8. The authors wish to express their gratitude to Dr. Saul Sternberg and Dr. Donald Norman who contributed many helpful suggestions. Mrs. Judy T. Budiansky wrote the computer program for the graphs in Fig. 11.

errors in terms of the acoustic confusability between a stimulus item and an incorrect report of that item (Conrad, 1962, 1964; Wickelgren, 1965b, 1965c, 1965d, 1966c).

We know from these studies that a string of acoustically similar items is less well recalled than a string of acoustically different items, both with visual and with auditory stimulus presentations. From the interference studies, we know that items that sound like a to-be-remembered item impair its recall more than do items that sound different from it. From the analysis of errors, we know that a whole item, even a simple monosyllable, is not remembered in an all-or-none fashion; its constituent phonemes may be forgotten separately. We know also that items that have a phoneme in common with the correct response item are more likely to occur as errors than items which do not have a common phoneme, and that perceptual confusions between items heard in noise are similar to—but different from—memory confusions in recall.

On the other hand, there are many unanswered questions. How are results obtained with visual and with auditory presentations related to each other? Does interference act directly in memory or only at the time of retrieval from memory? (Is this a useful distinction to make?) Can the results of recall experiments with acoustically similar items be predicted from results with acoustically different items? To answer some of these questions we proceed as follows.

First, we propose a phonemic model of auditory short-term memory. The model is not sufficiently elaborated to predict performance in general, so we later add a set of empirical rules for predicting performance. We also consider in detail the role of rehearsal in maintaining items in memory.

Second, we present the results of a series of experiments in which we measured the differences in memory for acoustically similar and for acoustically different items. In these experiments, we varied the modality of stimulus presentation, the presentation rate, the number of letters presented, and the type of report required.

Third, we use the data of the experiments to examine differences in performance with acoustically similar and acoustically different items, to determine the effect of scoring for items or for positions, to compare performance with visual and auditory presentations, to estimate the capacity of short-term memory, and to assess the role of rehearsal.

Finally, we consider scoring procedures and measures of performance in greater detail. Interpretations of experimental results depend on the scoring method chosen to measure the results. For example, certain classes of interpretation (e.g., partial vs. all-or-none knowledge) require compatible methods of scoring. In other instances, use of the appropriate measure greatly simplifies interpretation. Certain of these methodological considerations have been neglected in the existing experimental literature. Therefore, in the appendices to this chapter we consider the following problems: correcting for the effect of chance guessing, correcting the observed memory span for truncation due to the span's variability, correcting estimates of capacity for the effect of response interference, how partial knowledge about items should be added into a total score, and the effect of scoring with and without regard for the serial position of the remembered item. These results are of general use, even to those who may disagree with the particular theories presented in the paper.

Phonemic Model of Auditory Short-Term Memory

Ultimately, we propose a set of rules for predicting the auditory recall data. A critical concept of the prediction rules is capacity. To provide some insight into the rules, we present first a preliminary model of memory which was developed to deal with capacity (Sperling, 1968). It was not developed further to deal with performance because performance depends on rehearsal and on response-interference, neither of which has been measured in sufficient detail to justify its use in making predictions. On the other hand, when capacity estimates are corrected for response-interference, they are found to be independent of rehearsal, so that predictions of capacity are possible even without information about these factors. Although the model does not relate directly to data, it makes some parameter predictions that can be used by the prediction rules. From capacity, the model predicts the trial-to-trial variability of capacity and the differences between capacity for acoustically similar and acoustically different items. These predictions reduce the number of parameters that need to be estimated in order to apply the rules. In addition, the model provides insight into a number of problems of short-term memory.

The Phonemic Model

BASIC ASSUMPTIONS

(1) When letters are presented auditorily (or when they are rehearsed), all phonemes of the letters are stored in memory; (2) once in memory, constituent phonemes of letters are retained or lost independently; (3) at recall, if only one of the two phonemes of a letter is available, a guess is made from among those letters of the alphabet that contain the retained phoneme in the same position (initial or terminal).

To illustrate the implications of these assumptions, let us consider specifically the actual alphabets used in the experiments of this paper. There were two alphabets each constructed of eight consonants: the acoustically similar (AS) alphabet consisted of the letters *b, c, d, g, p, t, v,* and *z* (pronounced zē); the acoustically different (AD) alphabet consisted of the letters *f, l, m, x, h, k, q, y*. A stimulus sequence was composed by selecting randomly with replacement within one of the two consonant alphabets. Thus, in the AS alphabet, retention of the final phoneme of a letter (ē) is of no value because it does not help to discriminate among the letters of the alphabet. To express the basic assumptions precisely requires some definitions.

DEFINITIONS

Let the most recent arrived phoneme in memory be designated as phoneme 1, the next-most recent as phoneme 2, etc. When letters each consist of two phonemes, the most recent letter contains phonemes 2 and 1, letter 2 contains phonemes 4 and 3, and letter n contains phonemes $2n$ and $2n-1$. Let $p(i)$ be the probability of correct recall of the ith most recent phoneme. Let f_1 and f_2, respectively, be the conditional probabilities of correctly recalling a letter given recall of only its initial or final phoneme. Let f_{12} and f_{00}, respectively, be the conditional probabilities of correctly recalling a letter given recall of both or of neither of its constituent phonemes.

A letter is reported correctly if and only if one of four mutually exclusive events occurs: (1) only its first phoneme is recalled and this phoneme leads to correct identification of the letter; (2) only its second phoneme is recalled, and it leads to correct identification; (3) both phonemes are recalled; or (4) it is guessed by chance when neither phoneme is recalled. The assumption that the memory for each phoneme is independent of memory for other phonemes means that the probability of correct recall of the nth most recent letter is given by the sum of the probabilities of these four events, namely,

$$p(L_n) = f_1 p(2n)[1 - p(2n-1)] + f_2 p(2n-1)[1 - p(2n)] + f_{12} p(2n) p(2n-1) + f_{00}[1 - p(2n)][1 - p(2n-1)]. \quad (1)$$

Evaluation of Eq. 1 requires knowledge of the f's and $p(i)$s.

EVALUATION OF PHONEMIC EFFICIENCIES

When all letters of an alphabet have an equal chance of occurring, we let f_j (the conditional probability of correctly identifying a letter, given only its jth constituent phoneme) be equal to the number of different phonemes of the alphabet that occur in the jth phoneme position divided by the number of letters in the alphabet. We may consider f_j an index of the phonemic efficiency of the jth phoneme position. When $f_j = 1$, the jth phoneme position is totally efficient.

For the AS alphabet, $f_1 = \frac{8}{8}$ (all initial phonemes are different), and $f_2 = \frac{1}{8}$ (all terminal phonemes are e). For the AD alphabet, $f_1 = \frac{4}{8}$ and $f_2 = \frac{8}{8}$. For both alphabets, $f_{12} = 1$ and $f_{00} = \frac{1}{8}$. For simplicity, the double phonemes ks in x and ju in q are treated as single phonemes. The eᴵ phonemes in h and in k are considered not to confuse with each other because they occur in different phoneme positions.

EVALUATION OF $p(i)$

If the memory contained complete knowledge of the first n letters, and zero knowledge of the others, then the probability $p(i)$ of recalling a constituent phoneme i would be given by $p(i) = 1$, $1 \leqslant i \leqslant 2n$ for the first n letters, and by $p(i) = 0$, $i > 2n$, for the remaining letters. In this case, obviously, no difference in memory will be observed for stimuli of different alphabets. In the phonemic model, differences between alphabets result only from *partial* recall of letters. To make an exact prediction of the difference between alphabets requires knowledge of how $p(i)$ varies from 1.0 to 0.

While there is considerable basis for assuming exponential decay processes in memory strength (Atkinson and Shiffrin, 1968; Norman, 1966; Waugh and Norman, 1965; Wickelgren and Norman, 1966; and many of the models in this book), it is parsimonious to avoid the usual dual-parameter description of exponential decay, in which strength decays with one parameter and a second parameter relates strength to $p(i)$. Therefore, it is assumed simply that $p(i)$ decays exponentially with i,

$$p(i) = \int_{i-1}^{i} e^{-x/\alpha}\, dx, \tag{2}$$

(see Fig. 1). This choice of $p(i)$ yields a one-parameter description of the contents of memory in terms of the total number of phonemes α [area under $p(i)$].

The reason for defining $p(i)$ in terms of an integral instead of directly as an exponential (which would be simpler and practically equivalent to Eq. 2) is that the integral definition gives a better intuitive picture of the underlying memory. The abscissa of Fig. 1 may be regarded as space in memory, in which each phoneme occupies one unit of space. Ultimately, of course, it may be desirable to consider that different phonemes occupy different amounts of space in memory and to consider the ordinate of Fig. 1 to represent trace strength [or signal-to-noise ratio (S/N)], rather than probability directly. The advantage of the

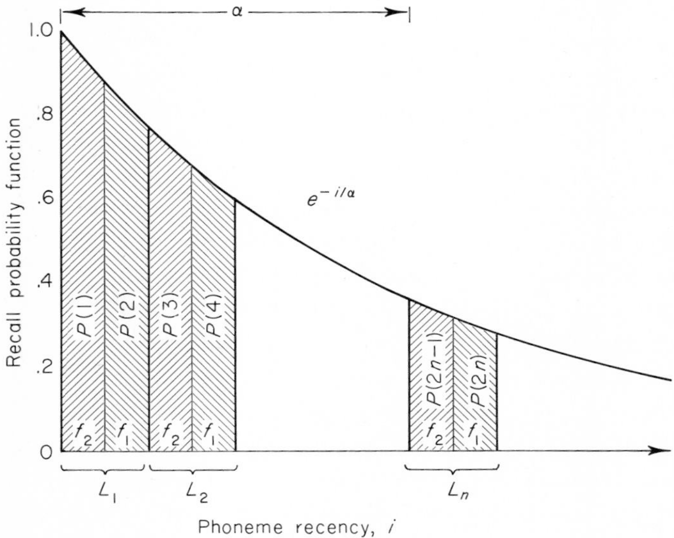

FIG. 1. Theoretical phonemic memory. Abscissa: phoneme recency. The most recently arrived phoneme is numbered 1, the next most recent is 2, etc. Ordinate: recall probability generating function. Shaded areas indicate the probability of recall $p(i)$ of the ith phoneme. The f's indicate the conditional probability of correct recall of the nth letter given correct recall of only its first (f_1) or second (f_2) phoneme. The phonemic capacity α illustrated here ($\alpha \approx 8$) is only $\frac{1}{3}$ of the observed value ($\alpha = 24$).

integral definition of $p(i)$ by Eq. 2 is that it is immediately adaptable to such complications. In any event, the exact form of the decay function is only of second-order importance; the major features of the model are phonemic representation and partial recall.

In the model, there is a strict one-to-one relation between phoneme capacity α and predicted letter capacity C. To derive C for an n-letter stimulus, it is assumed that the n letters occupy phoneme positions 1 to $2n$ of the memory. Application of Eqs. 1 and 2 to each phoneme pair and summing $p(L_n)$ gives the total predicted number of correctly retrieved letters. To compare this number with data, it must then be corrected for chance guessing (to be discussed later); the result is the predicted letter-capacity, C. For example, to anticipate some of the experimental results, if a subject has an apparent capacity of 7.31 AD letters (from a stimulus of 12 AD letters), the model requires a phoneme capacity of $\alpha = 15$. [If the post-stimulus cue (which instructed the subject) also is considered to be in memory, the required phoneme capacity is $\alpha = 24$. The post-stimulus cue is about six phonemes long, on the average, and, being presented last, would occupy the first three letter-positions in memory.]

Once the phoneme capacity α has been determined for one alphabet composed of two-phoneme letters, the model makes an exact prediction of letter capacity for any other alphabet composed of two-phoneme letters. (Generalizing the prediction to more complex stimulus sets than sets composed exclusively of two-phoneme letters would require new assumptions and is not attempted here.) The phoneme capacity, $\alpha = 24$, derived from a capacity of 7.31 AD letters implies an AS letter-capacity of 5.52 letters, i.e., a difference between the capacity for AD and AS letters of 1.79 letters. The predicted difference is virtually the same (1.72 letters) when the cue is ignored.

Further Properties of the Phonemic Model

This section deals with various interesting details and elaborations of the phonemic model. The reader who wishes to follow only the main points should skip directly to the next section.

The model is concerned only with gross similarities among *letters*, whether they have identical phonemes or not. It trivially accounts for Conrad's (1964) observation that an incorrectly reported letter tends to be from the same class as the stimulus letter (i.e., to share a common phoneme). The model is not concerned with whether *different phonemes* are similar or not, although phonemic similarity (as well as letter similarity) plays a role in short-term recall (Wickelgren, 1965d, 1966c). For example, the model makes no distinction between the alphabet (*m, n*) and the alphabet (*m, s*). On the other hand, by generalizing the model so that recall of a phoneme is based on correct recall of the relevant articulatory features, the model could, in principle, handle such data also.

The model does distinguish between alphabets on grounds other than phoneme redundancy. For example, it predicts that *b, c, d* letters are slightly more difficult (about five percent) than *f, l, m* letters because the useful terminal consonant of the *f, l, m* letters is more recent in memory than is the useful initial consonant of the *b, c, d* letters. But it probably underestimates this effect (cf. Wickelgren, 1965e).

REDUNDANCY, INTELLIGIBILITY, MEMORABILITY

There is a nonlinear relation between phonemic redundancy (number of efficient phonemes per item) and item retrievability. That is, retrieval of one efficient phoneme suffices for correct recall of an item. Additional efficient phonemes are redundant, but not necessarily useless. When one efficient phoneme is forgotten, a redundant phoneme still can support correct recall. The phonemic redundancy of digits suggests why digits heard in noise are more readily forgotten than high-quality digits (Dallett, 1964). Digits (most of which contain three phonemes) are highly redundant stimuli, and theoretically should remain intelligible even in noise that greatly reduces the probability of correctly identifying individual phonemes in isolation. In fact, an intelligibility test may be considered as the simplest memory task—recall of one item. In general, then, in simple memory tasks, redundant phonemes provide a margin of safety, a margin which is lacking at low S/N ratios. In a difficult memory task, the redundant phonemes ultimately are needed. Thus, noise digits can suffer in recall, even if originally they were fully intelligible.

More generally, the phonemic model suggests an avenue of approach to an important problem of auditory communications; namely, what character sets optimize performance at particular noise levels? The approach is to find characters such that (1) their constituent phonemes have high phonemic efficiencies and (2) the number of constituent phonemes maximizes a criterion function which weights the values of intelligibility in noise, memorability, and length of message (brevity). As the number of efficient constituent phonemes increases, intelligibility increases, brevity decreases, and memorability first increases to a maximum and then decreases. For example, *A*, *B*, *C* is an inefficient brief code; *Able*, *Baker*, *Charlie* is an inefficient intelligible code. The optimum code obviously depends on the particular performance desired.

REHEARSAL IN THE MEMORY MODEL

This section investigates some consequences of the following assumption about rehearsal: as letters are rehearsed, their constituent phonemes enter into phonemic memory in just the same way as do the phonemes of unrehearsed letters; the sequence of items in memory is determined by the sequence of external and internal inputs; recall is based on reconstruction from all images of a letter in memory; when an item is correctly reconstructed from partial information (e.g., a letter from only one of its constituent phonemes) and then rehearsed, the rehearsed copy contains the full information. Rehearsal is thus particularly effective with redundant codes. The net effect of rehearsal is to make a rehearsed item more resistant to loss, since it has to be lost at two independent locations in order to disappear from memory.

The phonemic model assumes that the only cause of loss of items from phonemic memory is the entry of new items; these push the old items out into the tail of the exponential curve. New items may be new test items or deliberate interference items (retroactive interference). Passive decay (i.e., the effect of time) may be considered as a special case of retroactive interference in which the new items are blank (silent) phonemes. Response interference may be considered a special case in which the new items are the responses. The proposition that rehearsed material in phonemic memory is more resistant to loss thus translates into the hypothesis that rehearsed items are more resistant to retroactive interference, passive decay, and response-interference.

Another consequence of rehearsal is that it is itself a source of retroactive interference. Consider, for example, a rehearsal of the three most recent letters in phonemic memory, designated as A, B, C in order of their arrival. Rehearsal of the 3rd most recent (A, first in order of arrival) causes it to occupy the first letter position. The C and B move down one position, so that B now occupies the 3rd position. Rehearsal of B moves

C to the 3rd position; rehearsal of C restores A to the 3rd position and the cycle is complete. The rehearsed letters now occupy the first three letter positions, the original letters have been moved to positions 4, 5, 6.

Let ϵ be the probability of incorrect retrieval from the 3rd position. The probability that a letter will have been rehearsed correctly then is $1 - \epsilon$. For each of the first three positions, rehearsal reduces by $1 - \epsilon$ the probability that the letter stored there is correct. Because the rehearsed copy has probability ϵ of being incorrect, rehearsal is useful only when ϵ is very small, e.g., for very recent material. It follows that rehearsing long sequences is undesirable; even rehearsal of short sequences is undesirable except when resistance to interfering stimuli is of overriding importance. These considerations are qualitatively in good agreement with our intuitions about rehearsal.

REHEARSAL AND CAPACITY OF THE MODEL

The model gives a good account of the data when the model is assumed to have a mean capacity of 15 phonemes; that is, when the area under the curve of Fig. 1 (the α of Eq. 2) equals 15. In actuality, as illustrated in Fig. 1, there are an infinite number of slots. Thus, if we were to present a stimulus ensemble of 12 letters (as we do, later on), the phonemes of these letters would only occupy the first 24 slots of the model: approximately 80% of the total area under the curve of Fig. 1. Might not rehearsal improve the efficiency of memory by filling some of the remaining slots, thereby using to good advantage some of the remaining 20% of the memory capacity? To anticipate, the answer is *no*; the probability of retrieving information from that part of memory is so low that letter storage would not be improved by more than about 5%, about $\frac{1}{3}$ of a letter.

Maximum use of capacity is achieved when the 12 stimulus letters occupy the 24 most favorable phoneme slots of memory. In general, as we have already noted, it is undesirable to rehearse long strings. Were a subject to rehearse the first group of four letters, we would find that these letters would occupy only about an additional 6.7% of the area under the model's exponential curve. After we correct for the errors that occur in the rehearsal itself, plus correcting for the fact that some of the stored letters are now duplicated in memory, we find that letter storage is increased by less than 5%.

The Experiments

Subjects

Fourteen adult employees of Bell Telephone Laboratories, seven males and seven females, served as subjects. Each subject served for five sessions of approximately one hour each, plus some shorter additional sessions for the control procedures.

Procedures

AUDITORY STIMULI

A stimulus was composed of a sequence of letters selected randomly (with replacement) within either one of two consonant alphabets: an acoustically similar (AS) alphabet (*b,c,d,g,p,t,v,z*) and an acoustically different (AD) alphabet (*f,l,m,x,h,k,q,y*). Every letter occurred in each position of the stimulus an equal number of times in each procedure. The inclusion of different letters having a common phoneme in the AD alphabet (ɛf, ɛl, ɛm, ɛks; e^{I}tʃ, ke^{I}, kju) is unfortunate but impossible to avoid given the restrictions of nonoverlapping sets of items and of exclusion of vowels.

The letters were spoken by one of us (RGS) in a female voice with American pronunciation without any significant regional accent. The letters were spoken in time to a metronome heard through earphones. They were recorded on magnetic tape and presented to subjects through a loudspeaker at approximately conversational speech intensity. The two alphabets were never mixed within a single stimulus. Three presentation rates were used—one letter per second (1/sec), two letters per second (2/sec) and four letters per second (4/sec). The presentation conditions of rate and alphabet were randomly varied from trial to trial.

INSTRUCTIONS

In all procedures, the task of the subject was to write, immediately after termination of the stimulus, as many correct letters as possible in their correct positions on a prepared answer grid-sheet. Subjects were told that in the main scoring procedure only correct letters in the correct positions would be scored as correct, but they were encouraged to guess because there was no penalty for guessing. The temporal sequence in which subjects wrote the letters was not controlled. At the end of each procedure, subjects were asked informally to report any particular tricks they used in performing the tasks.

PROCEDURE I: PARTIAL REPORT

Stimuli were composed of three groups of four letters (all from the same alphabet) followed by the spoken instruction "write one" or "write two" or "write three." The task of the subject was to write the particular group of four letters indicated by the post-stimulus cue. The subjects did not know until the post-stimulus cue which group of letters would be called for (cf. Anderson, 1960; Sperling, 1960). The pause between groups of four letters within a stimulus (and between the last letter and the cue) was equal to the time interval between letters at (1/sec and 2/sec) or to the time interval between three letters (at 4/sec). The sound-duration of letters was less than $\frac{1}{4}$ sec at the 4/sec rate, and increased to almost $\frac{1}{2}$ sec at the 1/sec rate, due to the increased persistence of terminal vowels. Thus, the silent interval between groups of letters was equal to about $\frac{3}{4}$ sec at the 4/sec and 2/sec rates, and to about $1\frac{1}{2}$ sec at the 1/sec rate. Eighteen conditions were tested: 2 alphabets × 3 rates × 3 recall instructions, giving 180 trials in all.

PROCEDURE II: RUNNING MEMORY SPAN

The number of letters in a stimulus was varied haphazardly from trial to trial, i.e., between 10 and 37 letters. Subjects were given no prior indication of the length of a stimulus and there were no intentional intonation cues to stimulus length. Subjects were asked to record the last *n* letters (as many as possible) in their correct positions on a prepared answer grid-sheet (cf. Pollack, Johnson, and Knaff, 1959). Six conditions were tested: 2 alphabets × 3 rates, 60 trials in all.

PROCEDURE IIIA: WHOLE REPORT 12

Stimuli consisted of 12-letter sequence spoken evenly without grouping by stress or intonation. Subjects were told to write all the letters of the stimulus. Six conditions were tested: 2 alphabets × 3 rates, 30 trials in all.

PROCEDURE IIIB: WHOLE REPORT 4–10

This procedure was conducted about two years after all the others. Only seven of the original subjects were still available; the unavailable seven subjects were replaced by new subjects who were matched to them for sex, approximate age, and job classification within the laboratory.

Stimuli were recorded and presented as in procedure IIIa. A stimulus consisted of a sequence of 4, 6, 8, or 10 letters spoken without grouping. A condition consisted of 12 consecutive trials with stimuli of the same length, of the same alphabet, and spoken at the same rate. Stimuli of length 10 were tested only at the 1/sec rate. Twenty conditions were tested: 2 alphabets × 3 rates × 3 lengths (4, 6, 8) + 2 alphabets × 1 rate × 1 length (10), 240 trials in all. The trials were divided into two sessions of approximately one hour each. The sequence of conditions was chosen randomly. Two different random sequences of conditions were used (different recordings) and half the subjects were tested with each sequence.

PROCEDURE IV: SIMULTANEOUS VISUAL PRESENTATION

Letters (about .30 × .35 in.) were drawn in India ink on white cardboard in a 3 × 4 array (Fig. 2). They were viewed binocularly at a distance of 20 in. in a three-field tachistoscope (Sperling, 1965). The viewing sequence was preexposure field, stimulus exposure, postexposure field. The preexposure field was white with a small fixation dot in the center. It was terminated .5 sec after the subject pressed a button to initiate the trial. The preexposure was followed immediately by the stimulus field containing 12 letters. There were three exposure conditions: the stimulus was terminated after .2, 2.0, or 12.0 sec, and immediately replaced by a postexposure field consisting of randomly scattered letter fragments (visual noise). Duration of visual noise was 2.0 sec. The luminance of the white portions of all fields was 23 ft·L. Subjects were instructed not to begin writing until after the letters were turned off.

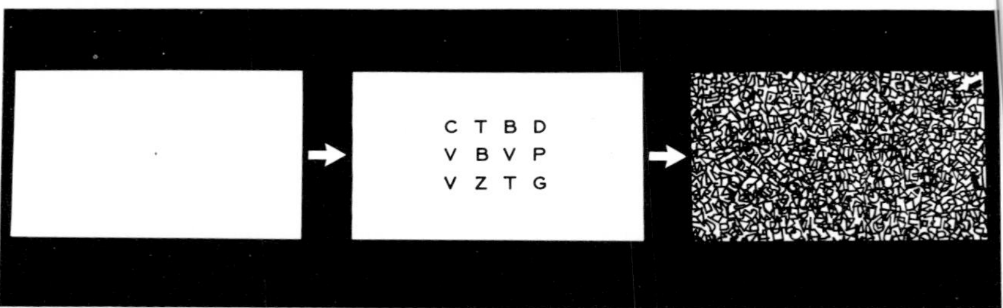

FIG. 2. From left to right, the sequence of stimuli presented to subjects in procedure IV (visual whole report). An AS stimulus is shown.

Trials were ordered in groups of five of the same condition, each group preceded by a sample trial. Six conditions were tested: 2 alphabets × 3 exposure durations, 60 trials in all.

It should be noted that in procedures I, II, and IIIa, trials with different alphabets and rates were intermixed; in procedures IIIb and IV, trials with stimuli composed of the same alphabet spoken at the same rate were grouped together. In all procedures, the various kinds of trials were counterbalanced.

Control Procedures

INTELLIGIBILITY TEST 1

Subjects were tested individually with the stimuli previously used in the partial report procedure. Each subject was instructed in advance to report one particular position from each group of four letters, e.g., the second letter. This yielded three reported letters per stimulus (of 12 letters). Every letter was tested by at least three subjects, and each subject reported 540 letters.

RESULT OF TEST 1

Errors in report occurred only with acoustically confusable (AS) stimuli, and then only when presented at the rate of 4/sec. These were therefore retested by the next procedure.

INTELLIGIBILITY TEST 2

The same stimuli were used as in intelligibility test 1, except that they were rerecorded to increase to several seconds the interval between groups of four letters. Subjects were told in advance to report only one particular letter (e.g., the second) from each group of four letters. Different subjects reported different letters, each letter being reported by at least three subjects. The subjects were told they would be given \$1.00 for a perfect score and \$.50 for a score with only one error.

RESULTS OF TEST 2

The subjects made a total of three errors in the 1260 letters reported. Thus, even with the most difficult stimuli, the AS alphabet presented at the most rapid rate (4/sec), intelligibility exceeds 99%. We conclude that the ability of subjects to identify any of our letters in its context is not one of the limiting factors in these experiments.

Scoring

POSITION SCORING

Except when stated otherwise, all data will be given as corrected position scores. In position scoring, an item must be reported in its correct serial position to be scored as correct. From the raw position score $\hat{R}$, a position score corrected for random guessing $\hat{S}$ is computed as follows:

$$\hat{S} = \hat{R} - \tfrac{1}{7}(N - \hat{R}), \tag{3}$$

where N is the total number of letters reported, $\hat{R}$ is the number reported correctly, and $\hat{S}$ is the corrected score. The cap above $\hat{R}$ and $\hat{S}$ designates that these are sample estimates of underlying population values of R and S. (That $\hat{S}$ is an unbiased estimate of S is proved in Appendix 1.) The corrected score $\hat{S}$ is derived by assuming that an observed score R is composed of S letters, which the subject knows the position of with absolute certainty, plus $R - S$ letters, which the subject writes correctly by pure chance from an alphabet of eight equiprobable letters (cf. Woodworth and Schlosberg, 1954, p. 700). In the partial report procedure, $\hat{S}$ (obtained as above) was multiplied by 3 (because the subject reported only $\frac{1}{3}$ of the stimulus letters) to obtain $\hat{A}$ the estimated numbers of "letters available."[3]

ITEM SCORING

The item score of a response may be defined as a position score obtained after the response letters have been permuted (i.e., rearranged) so as to maximize the position score. In item scoring, inversions of stimulus letters, e.g., writing YX for XY) are counted as correct. The difficulty with item scoring is that chance guessing inflates the item score far more than the position score. (See *Results* and *Appendix 2.*)

Results

MAIN RESULTS, AUDITORY MEMORY PROCEDURES

The results of procedures I, II, and IIIa are summarized in Table 1 and Fig. 3. The main result is that, in all tasks, stimuli composed of

[3] When N letters are presented and j are called for, the estimated number of "available letters" is $\hat{A} = \hat{S}(N/j)$, where $\hat{S}$ is the corrected score Eq. 3 for the response of length j. This calculation assumes each of the N presented letters has an equal probability of being called for in the required response.

TABLE 1
Number of Letters Reported Correctly, Auditory Memory Span, Procedures I, II, IIIa

	Procedure	1/sec	2/sec	4/sec	Mean
	Acoustically different				
I.	Partial report	7.16	7.72	7.38	7.42
IIIa.	Whole report-12	6.00	6.71	4.78	5.83
II.	Running span	4.32	3.04	2.88	3.42
	Mean	5.83	5.82	5.01	5.56
	Acoustically similar				
I.	Partial report	4.75	5.01	4.20	4.65
IIIa.	Whole report-12	4.73	4.34	3.36[a]	4.14
II.	Running span	2.81	2.85	2.08	2.58
	Mean	4.10	4.07	3.21	3.79
	Mean *AD&AS*	4.96	4.94	4.11	4.67

[a] This value represents the mean obtained after deleting data from one stimulus in which 7 of 12 letters were "*b*."

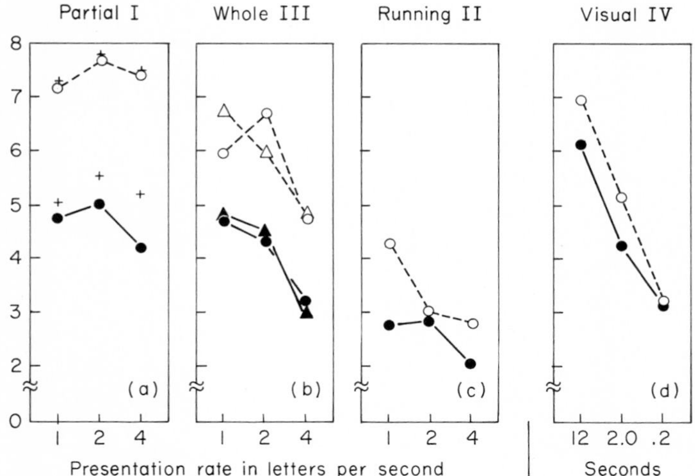

FIG. 3. Mean number of letters reported correctly in various memory span procedures. Abscissa is presentation rate in letters per second for auditory presentations (a, b, c) and exposure duration in seconds for visual presentations (d). Upper curves illustrate data for acoustically different AD letters, lower curves illustrate data for acoustically similar AS letters. The triangles in (b) illustrate averaged scores for list lengths 6 and 8, the circles illustrate scores for list length 12. The + symbols represent the memory capacity as estimated by the method described in the discussion section.

TABLE 2
Number of Letters Reported Correctly, Auditory Whole Report, Procedure IIIb

List length	rate			
	1/second	2/second	4/second	Mean
Acoustically different				
4	3.95	3.99	3.93	3.95
6	5.63	5.50	5.08	5.40
8	6.79	6.58	4.63	6.00
10	6.46	–	–	–
Acoustically similar				
4	3.76	3.63	3.24	3.54
6	4.62	4.69	3.11	4.08
8	5.25	4.43	2.98	4.21
10	5.19	–	–	–

AS letters are reported less accurately than comparable stimuli composed of AD letters.[4]

The results of the auditory experiments with lists of length 4–10 with whole report (procedure IIIb) are shown in Table 2. In procedure IIIb, unlike procedures I, II, IIIa, scores were limited in some cases by the total number of letters in the stimulus.

To see whether the change in subjects or in procedure between experiments IIIa and IIIb affected the results, list length 8 in procedure IIIb may be compared with length 12 in procedure IIIa; both are whole-report auditory tests. The mean number of letters reported correctly in the two AD conditions are 6.00 and 5.83, and in the AS conditions, 4.21 and 4.32, respectively (see also Fig. 3b). These comparisons indicate that the level of performance remained substantially the same after replacement of seven of the original 14 subjects, and the effect of alphabets is substantially the same in both conditions.

ITEM SCORES

The scoring procedure used above was *position scoring:* a response letter was correct if and only if it was the same as the letter in the cor-

[4] An analysis of variance showed all main effects and three interactions to be highly significant. For details, see Sperling and Speelman (1967).

responding position of the stimulus. In *item scoring*, all correspondences between stimulus and response items are counted, irrespective of their position. Whole report data of procedure IIIb were scored by both methods, and an analysis of the difference between the observed position and item scores is given below. The differences between the item scores and position scores are illustrated in Fig. 4. The abscissa represents stimulus length minus the mean corrected position score for each condition. The abscissa thus indicates the mean number of opportunities for item guesses, i.e., the mean number of letters by which the stimulus exceeds the corrected position score. The ordinate represents the mean difference between the uncorrected item score and corrected position score for each type of stimulus, i.e., the guessing success.

The data of Fig. 4 clearly indicate that the difference between item scores and position scores increases almost linearly as a function of the mean number of item guesses, and that the same relation obtains for all presentation rates, stimulus lengths, and alphabets. For example in almost every task, data for AD and AS stimuli differ less from each

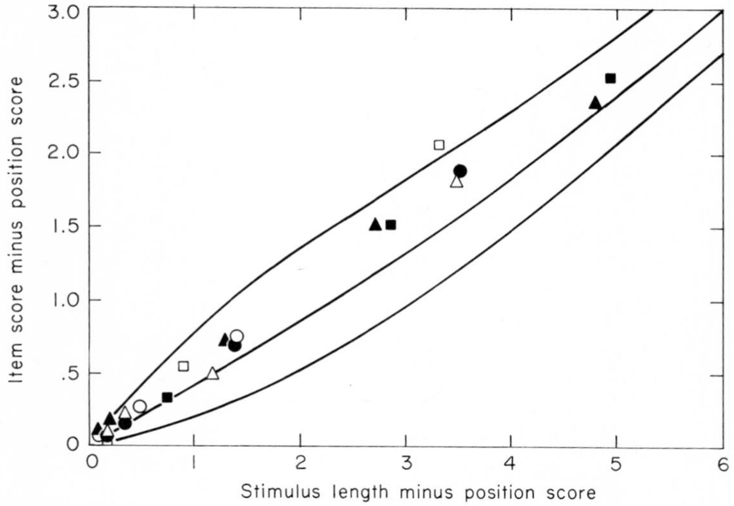

FIG. 4. Difference between item scores (independent of position) and position scores in the whole report procedure. The abscissa represents the opportunity for guessing items, i.e., the difference between number of presented letters and the position score. Unfilled and filled points indicate AD and AS alphabets, respectively; triangles, circles and squares indicate rates of 1, 2, and 4/sec, respectively. Theoretical curves were obtained by assuming that the true difference I between the item-span and the position-span was $I = 0$, 1, and 2 items (lowest, middle, and highest curves, respectively).

other in their item score than in their position score. Figure 4 illustrates that the differences between the item scores for the two alphabets is predicted by the difference between their position scores and does not reflect any new information.

THE EFFECT OF ITEM KNOWLEDGE

Let the mean position memory span $\bar{m}$ be defined as the *position* score that would be observed in the absence of random guessing and the item memory span $\bar{m} + I$ be defined as the *item* score that would be observed in the absence of chance guessing. (Note: $\hat{S}$ in Eq. 3 estimates $\bar{m}$.) The lowest curve drawn in Fig. 4 represents theoretical predictions based on the null hypothesis; namely, it represents the difference between item scores and position scores that would be expected (due to chance guessing) if the item memory span were identical to the position memory span. (The position memory span is assumed here to be distributed normally across subjects with a standard deviation of one letter—see Discussion section.) Although the lowest curve indicates that chance guessing accounts for much of the observed difference between item and position scores, it also indicates that the null hypothesis is untenable. The two curves that bound the data of Fig. 4 were derived by assuming that the amount I by which the item span exceeds the position span for the same task is 1.0 letters and 2.0 letters.[5] Nineteen of the 20 data points fall between these two hypotheses; the one exception is the AD, 4/sec, length-8 condition, where the item span appears to exceed the position span by slightly over 2.0 letters.

If it is assumed that the item span exceeds the position span by $1\frac{1}{2}$ letters (on the average), then inspection of Fig. 4 shows that no predicted item score would be in error by more than about $\pm\frac{1}{4}$ letters—most predictions would be considerably better. We conclude that in these experiments item scores can be predicted from position scores. Because item scores can be derived from position scores, we confine our subsequent analysis to position scores. The relatively frequent presence in memory of two or more items whose positions are not known also provides a simple account (perhaps more plausible than

[5] When a subject's true item span exceeds his true position span by I items, the observed position score—even corrected for chance guessing—may be greater than the true position span. This occurs because the probability of the I items being written in their correct positions (and thus being scored correct by position scoring as well as item scoring) is greater than the probability of a purely random guess being correct. It can be proved that the inflation of the position score by item knowledge does not exceed 1.0 letters. A correction for the inflation of observed position scores by item knowledge is incorporated in the theoretical curves of Fig. 3 (see Appendix 2).

that of Conrad, 1965) for the frequently observed transposition errors (e.g., reporting YX for XY).

MAIN RESULTS, VISUAL MEMORY SPAN (PROCEDURE IV)

At the conclusion of the visual test, each subject was questioned about the strategy he used to remember letters, i.e., whether he rehearsed them in a rote manner or whether he looked for patterns among the letters, formed associations, or tried some other form of coding. For the .2- and 2.0-sec exposures all subjects concurred; they reported rehearsing the letters in a rote, sequential way. During 12-sec exposures, however, subjects differed in their strategy. Based on their replies, subjects were divided into three groups for separate analysis: five subjects who reported using rote rehearsal exclusively (**R**), six subjects who reported using some more complicated form of grouping or coding (**C**), and three subjects who reported both, i.e., a mixed strategy. Typical coding strategies were looking for and noting the location of repeated letters and of familiar letter combinations, e.g., BCD (binary coded decimal), BVD (a brand name), etc.

Table 3 gives the results of the visual memory experiment. Scores of rehearsing, mixed-strategy, and coding subjects are roughly similar at .2- and 2.0-sec exposure durations, and at the 12-sec exposure for

TABLE 3
Number of Letters Reported Correctly, Visual Whole Report, Procedure IV

		Acoustically different Exposure duration			
Subjects	*n*	12.0	2.0	.2	Mean
Rehearsing	5	7.26	5.07	2.99	5.11
Mixed	3	6.28	4.83	3.05	4.72
Coding	6	7.13	5.53	3.63	5.43
Mean	14	6.99	5.21	3.27	5.16
		Acoustically similar			
Rehearsing	5	5.18	4.28	2.76	4.07
Mixed	3	5.51	3.79	3.06	4.12
Coding	6	7.33	4.74	3.67	5.25
Mean	14	6.17	4.37	3.21	4.59

AD letters. At the 12-sec exposure duration, rehearsing subjects show a 2.1 letter deficit for AS letters, while coding subjects actually score higher with the AS than the AD stimuli. [A t-test for the difference between coding and rehearsing subjects at 12-sec exposures gives a t of 2.92 ($p < .01$).]

Discussion of the Experimental Results

Comparisons of Performance with Visual and Auditory Stimuli

Results of visual and of auditory whole report procedures are compared in Fig. 5. The abscissa represents the average number of letters the 14 subjects reported correctly with AD stimuli. The ordinate represents the AS deficit in each task; it is the AD score minus the AS score. In the visual data in Fig. 5, brief exposures are represented at the far left and long exposures at the far right. Figure 5 segregates visual data, indicating separately the visual data of coding and of rehearsing subjects. (Visual data of three mixed-strategy subjects are not represented in Fig. 5; they can be computed from Table 3. The performance of mixed subjects is intermediate between that of rehearsing and of coding subjects.)

We make three general observations (with the exceptions noted below) from Fig. 5. (1) AD scores and AS deficits are strongly correlated. (2) Visual AS deficits are similar to auditory AS deficits at rates of 1/sec and 2/sec but different from auditory AS deficits at rates of 4/sec. (3) Increasing the duration of visual exposures increases visual AS deficits in the same way that increasing the number of letters presented in an auditory stimuli (at rates of 1/sec and 2/sec) increases auditory AS deficits. Varying visual exposure duration does not effect AS deficits in the same way as varying auditory presentation rate. These observations are fully consistent with the visual-to-auditory encoding hypothesis (Sperling, 1963, 1967). The encoding hypothesis states (1) that subjects rehearse letters from a visual presentation at a rate of less than 4/sec and (2) that subsequent memory for the rehearsed letters ultimately is limited by the same factors as if the letters originally had been presented to the ears instead of to the eyes.[6] This hypothesis is considered in more detail later.

[6] Additional support for the encoding hypothesis is obtained from data of some individual subjects. Individual data usually exhibit regularities when they are graphed as in Fig. 5, although subjects vary widely. For some subjects, the data for the visual whole report fall exactly between (*a*) data of the auditory whole report at the rate of 2/sec and (*b*) auditory data at the rate of 4/sec.

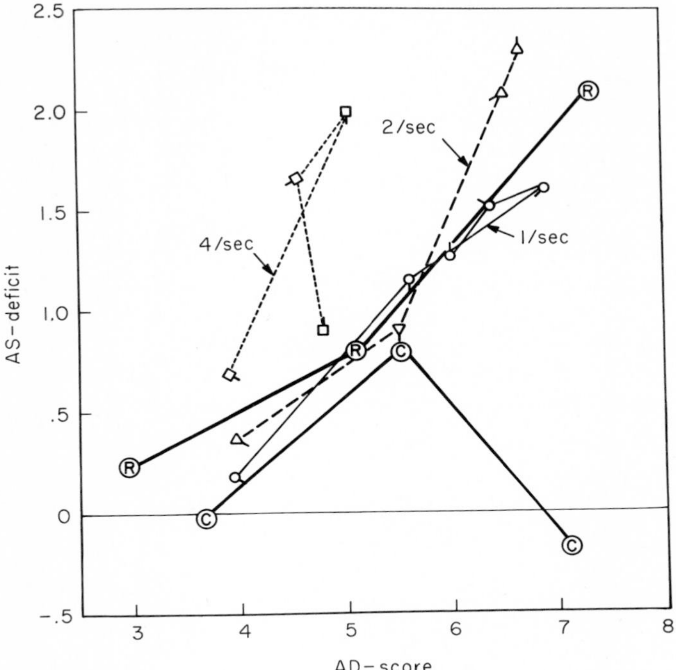

FIG. 5. Comparison of visual and auditory procedures. AD minus AS scores (AS deficits) are graphed against the AD score. Letters (inside circles connected by heavy solid lines) indicate data from the visual whole-report procedure; all other symbols represent data from the auditory whole-report procedure. **R** and **C** indicate scores of rote-rehearsing and of pattern-coding subjects in the visual tasks. The exposure duration is shortest for points at left, longest for points at right. Auditory data are the averages of all subjects; the circles, triangles, and squares represent rates of 1/sec, 2/sec, and 4/sec, respectively. Points representing the same auditory presentation rate are connected, and the rate is indicated. The small pointer emanating from each point indicates the length of the presented list. (The pointer should be interpreted like the hour hand of a clock.)

MEMORY WITHOUT AS DEFICIT

The coding-subject group is a remarkable exception to the equivalence of auditory and visual AS deficits. At visual exposures of .2 sec and 2.0 sec their performance is similar to the rehearsing subjects. However, at 12-sec exposures (where rehearsing subjects show the greatest AS deficit) coding subjects show no AS deficit. Obviously, their mnemonic process of recalling patterns and distinctive combinations of letters does not depend on the sound of stimulus letters in the same way that a rote rehearsal of stimulus letters does. (The AS letters are more frequent in the English language than the AD letters and this may facilitate a coding process based on complex associations.)

That rote-rehearsing and pattern-coding subjects perform similarly at 2.0-sec exposure durations indicates that pattern-coding, a time-consuming mnemonic aid, is not attempted at brief exposure durations. It should be noted here that coding and rehearsing subjects were not segregated on the basis of their data, but on the basis of statements they made about their coding strategy at the conclusion of the experiment, prior to data analysis. (For a similar segregation of subjects on the basis of reported strategies, with substantial observed differences in performance, see also Harris and Haber, 1963.)

ANALYSIS OF OTHER DATA

The analysis illustrated in Fig. 5 (AS-deficits versus AD-scores) may be extended to a study by Laughery and Pinkus (1966). They presented subjects with auditory stimuli of length 6 and 8 as in our procedure III. The main difference was in their selection of presentation rates ($\frac{1}{3}$/sec, 1/sec, 3/sec). Laughery and Pinkus also presented stimuli visually at the same rates. Unlike our procedure IV (simultaneous visual presentation), in their procedure each new letter was superimposed upon and replaced its predecessor. Our analysis of their published data is illustrated in Fig. 6.

Laughery and Pinkus's subjects have lower average scores than ours. To facilitate comparison between their study and ours, we selected the seven subjects with the lowest scores in one of our whole-report experiments (list length 8, presentation rate of 2/sec, AD alphabet) and added their data to Fig. 6.

Inspection of Fig. 6 shows that Laughery and Pinkus's data obtained both visual and with auditory presentations at rates of 1/sec and 3/sec are comparable to the data obtained from our low-scoring subjects at rates of 1/sec and 2/sec. This means that to a first approximation in their experiments, as in ours, AS deficits are predictable from AD scores, independently of the modality of presentation, of the presentation rate (1/sec to 3/sec), or of the length of the presented list (4–12 letters).

Results and Conclusions about Presentation Rate

SLOW PRESENTATION RATES

At slow rates, presentation times can be strikingly long. For example, at the $\frac{1}{3}$/sec rate, a six-letter stimulus requires more than 15 sec for

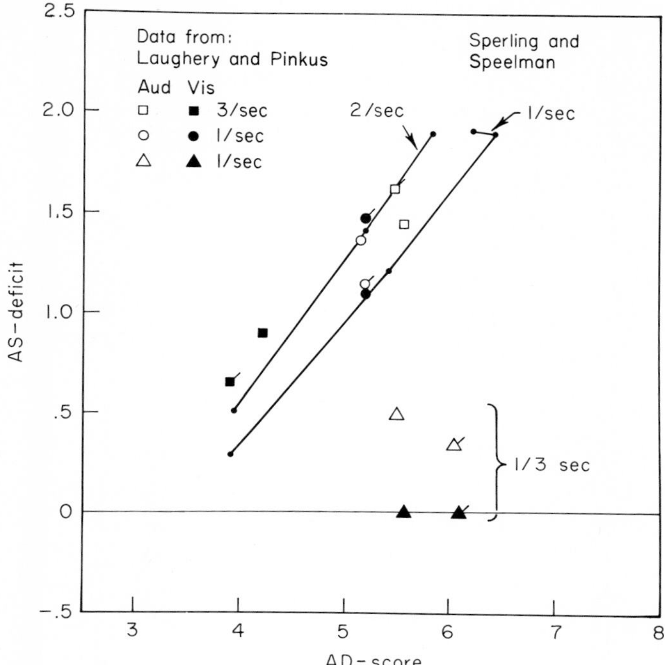

FIG. 6. Data from Laughery and Pinkus (1966). Coordinates same as Fig. 5. Stimuli were of length 6 and 8; length 8 is indicated by short diagonal strokes. Unfilled and filled points represent AD and AS alphabets, respectively; squares, circles, and triangles represent rates of 3, 1, and ⅓/sec, respectively. The solid lines represent Sperling and Speelman's data obtained with lists of lengths 4, 6, 8, and 10. These data are the same as those of Fig. 5, except that they are taken only from the lowest-scoring 7 (of 14) subjects.

presentation, and an eight-letter stimulus requires more than 21 sec The eight-letter stimulus at 3/sec requires only 2.6 sec. It is not so surprising, then, that Laughery and Pinkus's data for the ⅓/sec presentation rate are quite different from their other data, showing no AS deficit for visual presentations and only a slight AS deficit for acoustic presentations.

In our procedures, recall without AS deficits occurred only at very brief visual exposures (where recall presumably was limited by visibility rather than mnemonic factors) and at long visual exposures for coding subjects.

From Laughery and Pinkus's auditory and visual data with ⅓/sec stimuli, and from our visual data with the 12-sec stimulus, we conclude that subjects can recall without AS deficits, but that such a mode of recall requires more time per stimulus item. As a rule of thumb, the time required is about 2 sec per letter in successive visual or auditory presentations, and about 2 sec per correctly reported letter in simultaneous visual presentations. From the coupling of recall-without-AS-deficit to pattern coding in our visual task, we infer that the time-consuming process in tasks that fail to show AS deficits is some form of pattern and/or association coding. The mechanisms underlying the selection of patterns to code, the formation of associations, the storage and retrieval of patterns and associations are far more complex than the mechanisms underlying time-limited rote rehearsal. We are content merely to characterize the conditions under which pattern coding can occur and to note that it is beyond the scope of this chapter.

FAST PRESENTATION RATES

In the graph of AS deficits vs. AD scores (Fig. 5), the 4/sec data fall about one letter to the left of 1/sec and 2/sec data. Our interpretation of this finding is that the 4/sec rate produces an overall performance decrement of about one letter (compared to 1/sec and 2/sec) and that this decrement is independent of acoustic similarity. Later, this observation is given a quantitative interpretation.

MODERATE PRESENTATION RATES

For auditory presentation rates of 1/sec to 3/sec (list lengths of 4–12 letters), for successive visual presentation at 1/sec to 3/sec, and for simultaneous visual presentation at exposure durations of .2 sec—2.0 sec (12.0 sec for rote-rehearsing subjects), the data fall approximately on the same straight line on a graph of AS deficits vs. AD scores (Figs. 5 and 6). This colinearity is interpreted to mean that only one significant underlying factor varies as the many presentation parameters vary. Because the data derived from lists of different lengths, particularly short lists, fall in such a regular order on this line, we propose that the underlying factor is the effective length of a list, i.e., the number of items from the list that the subjects attempt to maintain in memory. For example, in simultaneous visual tasks, the number of effective items is the number of items the subject rehearses. In short auditory lists, all items are effective items. In long auditory lists, we suppose that the effective items are those which are rehearsed plus those at the end of the list.

Although we cannot yet measure the number of effective items directly, we assume that the AD score is a monotonic indication of their number. The high correlation of AS deficits with AD scores is assumed to result from an underlying dependence of both AS deficits and AD scores on the number of effective items.

The stimulus parameters of list length, presentation rate, modality, (but not alphabet), are assumed to determine the number of effective items in the list, as indicated by the AD scores. Because AS deficits depend mainly on AD scores (effective items) and do not show any strong additional dependence on list length, modality, exposure duration, or rate, it follows that one need postulate only one kind of memory to account for all these results. The effective items from all these kinds of lists ultimately are stored in this memory which, because of its large AS deficits, may reasonably be called auditory short-term memory.

Capacity of Auditory Short-Term Memory

In this section, we draw a distinction between the *capacity* of a memory—its maximum possible contents—and the observed *performance* (e.g., whole-report score) under particular conditions. Partial-report procedures give the best estimates of the capacity (see Sperling, 1960). The main advantage of the partial- over the whole-report procedure is that only a few items are called for in a partial report. If reporting these few items interferes with retention of the remaining items, it is no matter, the remaining items are not called for. A second advantage of the partial report is that it samples memory at a more precisely defined point in time than does a whole report, simply because it takes less time to retrieve and to report a few items from memory than it takes to retrieve and to report many items.

When the partial report requires more than one item, then retrieval and reporting of the first item or items, will impair recall of remaining items within the report group. Unless the partial report be limited to a single item, its advantages are only relative, not absolute. By recognizing the inadequacy of the partial report procedure, we can make a correction for it and obtain an improved estimate of memory capacity.

A procedure for estimating a correction factor f is stated and justified in Appendix 1. Basically, f is derived from data of whole reports of four-letters lists. With such short lists, the limiting factor on performance is response-interference, not memory capacity, and therefore f corrects for response-interference. In fact, f is never very different from one here ($1.005 \leq f \leq 1.236$), so that any possible errors in f produce only second-order errors in estimates of capacity.

TABLE 4
Estimates of the Capacity for Letters of Auditory Short-Term Memory

Score	Rate			Mean
	1/sec	2/sec	4/sec	
AD partial report score	7.16	7.71	7.38	7.42
Correction factor	1.014	1.005	1.019	
Est. *AD* memory capacity	**7.27**	**7.75**	**7.51**	**7.51**
AS partial report score	4.75	5.01	4.20	4.65
Correction factor	1.064	1.105	1.236	
Est. *AS* memory capacity	**5.05**	**5.54**	**5.19**	**5.26**
Partial report deficit (*AD–AS*)	2.41	2.70	3.18	2.76
Capacity deficit (*AD–AS*)	**2.22**	**2.21**	**2.32**	**2.25**

ESTIMATES OF MEMORY CAPACITY

Table 4 gives: (a) the partial report scores (numbers of letters available corrected for chance guessing, A, from Procedure I, Table 1); (b) the estimated correction factors *f* for response-interference; and (c) the estimates of memory capacity obtained by multiplying (a) and (b). Table 4 also gives the AS deficits of partial reports (AD score minus AS score) and the AS-capacity-deficits (AD capacity minus AS capacity).

The most significant aspect of Table 4 is that estimates of capacity (even uncorrected partial report scores) are relatively independent of presentation rate (whereas measures of whole-report and running-span performance depend strongly on rate). In estimating the total capacity of auditory short-term memory, it must be remembered that the post-stimulus cue was an auditory stimulus, e.g., "write two." The cue was correctly interpreted in every instance, indicating perfect memory for it. We may conclude that short-term memory can contain 7.5 AD letters plus one post-stimulus cue; this capacity varies $\pm\frac{1}{4}$ letter depending on presentation rate. Memory capacity for AS letters is smaller by 2.25 letters, independent of rate.

The Role of Rehearsal

When stimulus letters are spoken at a slow rate (e.g., slower than 1/sec), or when delays are interposed before report, subjects rehearse letters during the silent intervals. According to the phonemic model, rehearsal occurs because memory decays with time (silent phonemes)—

even when there are no external disturbances—and rehearsal can replace the decaying trace. Rehearsal may have functions for storage in long-term memory, but these do not concern us now. The present questions are: (1) Are rehearsed letters stored in the same memory as unrehearsed auditory letters? and (2) Does rehearsal increase the capacity of short-term memory?

If the answer to the first question were no, then almost certainly the answer to the second would be yes: that is, if rehearsed letters could utilize some new memory—different from the memory for unrehearsed letters—then rehearsal would place at the subject's disposal the combined capacity of two memories. Rehearsal would increase capacity.

If rehearsed letters were stored in the *same* memory as unrehearsed letters, rehearsal still might increase the capacity of memory. For example, imagine a world where spoken letters occur only in conjunction with noise, and at low S/N ratios. If the noise were stored in memory along with the signal, memory for unrehearsed letters would be poor. If rehearsed letters did not contain the noise, the opportunity to rehearse would appear to increase the capacity of memory.

We shall anticipate the conclusion of this section by stating that rehearsed letters are stored in the same memory as unrehearsed letters and that capacity is not increased. To reach this conclusion, we use information about capacity obtained in the last section, and information about rehearsal obtained from introspective reports.

WHAT WAS REHEARSED? INTROSPECTIVE EVIDENCE

Introspective reports of rehearsal in the partial report task are persuasively clear at low presentation rates and paradoxically ambiguous at high rates. At the 1/sec presentation rate, subjects say they rehearse each group of letters in the interval between groups. The silent interval is about 1½/sec, easily long enough to permit rehearsal of the entire previous group. Some subjects say they rehearse the previous group twice (or two previous groups once each) during the intergroup pause. When rehearsal is measured, its rate is found to be three letters per second (Landauer, 1962) and to vary from three to ten items per second (Sperling, 1963). The highest rates are possible only for highly practiced, repeated sequences; three letters per second is a typical rate for new material. Assuming a rate of rehearsal of three letters/second (giving a 2½/sec rehearsal period) implies that the rehearsal overlaps the first letter of the following group. Alternatively, a rehearsal rate of 5/sec would fit the eight letters entirely into the silent interval.

At the 2/sec and 4/sec rates, subjects report that active rehearsing interferes with recall, and that an optimum strategy is to listen passively to the entire stimulus. Whether rehearsal ever occurs in these cases is ambiguous. Particularly at 4/sec rates, subjects report trial-to-trial variations in the "attention" given to particular groups of letters, but it is not clear whether such attention can be equated with the active rehearsal that occurs at the 1/sec rate. From introspective reports, therefore, it is abundantly clear that there is massive rehearsal of stimuli presented at the 1/sec rate, and minimal rehearsal at the higher rates. A rough estimate of the average number of single-letter rehearsals would be 12 to 24 for the 1/sec presentations and less than 4 for the 2/sec and 4/sec presentations.

REHEARSAL, TIME, AND SERIAL POSITION EFFECTS IN PARTIAL REPORTS

Figure 7 shows the accuracy of recall of each report group in the partial report experiment. The result to which we wish to call attention is that the accuracy of report of the first group is virtually independent of

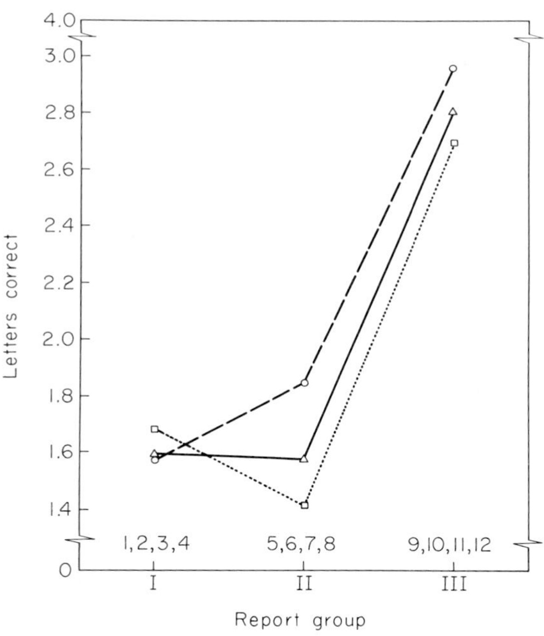

FIG. 7. Mean number of letters reported correctly in each report group averaged over alphabets. The only correction applied to these data is the correction for guessing (Eq. 3).

presentation rate. Calculation of the time from stimulus to response yields some interesting comparisons. At the rate of 1/sec, the first letter of the first group occurs 15½ sec before the cue to report it, as it is followed by 11 letters, three pauses, and the cue. On the basis of Anderson's (1960) data, delays of this length would be expected to interfere substantially with accuracy of report. At the 2/sec rate, the delay of the first item is 8 sec, at the 4/sec rate it is 5½ sec. Therefore, on the basis of time delay from stimulus to report, one would expect a large decrease in accuracy of the first group as a function of increasing delay (decreasing presentation rate). The virtual absence of this expected effect of delay may be explained by the observation we made above; namely, subjects rehearse the first group during the delay. The introspective accounts of rehearsal and the other serial position data thus tend to corroborate each other.[7]

REHEARSAL AND CAPACITY

For both alphabets, the 1/sec rate (most rehearsal) yielded the lowest estimates of memory capacity and the 4/sec rate yielded the second lowest estimates. In fact, these are minor effects, as the capacity estimates are nearly independent of rate. From this observation, and from the observation of massive rehearsal at 1/sec, it can be concluded that when rehearsal occurs, the total amount of material stored in auditory short-term memory is not increased.

Though rehearsal may compensate for passive decay at slow presentation rates, it does not increase estimated capacity beyond that which is observed when rehearsal is minimal or absent (2/sec rate). This conclusion rests on the simple facts that the amount of rehearsal depends greatly on presentation rate, and that memory capacity depends only slightly on presentation rate.

Although 1/sec rates yield the lowest estimates of capacity [based on their lowest partial report score (AD) and second-lowest partial report score (AS)], they yield the highest scores in nearly all other tasks. We explain these results by supposing that rehearsal duplicates and thereby rearranges the contents of memory so that its capacity is optimally utilized for the task at hand. For example, we assume that rehearsing a letter causes it to be entered into memory again. This makes the rehearsed letter more recent in memory (at the expense of the other letters) and means it is stored twice in memory.

[7] For a more detailed analysis of the data of Fig. 7, see Sperling and Speelman (1967).

Dual storage is particularly important when a letter originally is stored in a slot of memory which loses information between the time of storage and the time of retrieval. When a letter has been rehearsed, the net partial information remaining in the original plus the rehearsal storage locations may suffice for correct recall, whereas either location alone might not contain sufficient information. Without rehearsal of short lists, there would be unused capacity—empty locations which are capable of retaining partial information.

When the stimulus list is so long that it occupies the entire useful space of memory, rehearsal of some stimulus letters inevitably displaces others. This may improve performance by increasing resistance of the remaining letters to response-interference. But, even after correction for response-interference in estimates of capacity, rehearsal still will appear to have reduced capacity because duplication occasionally is needless.

Recency and the dual storage of rehearsed letters explain why they are less susceptible to interference by subsequent stimulus letters and less susceptible to response-interference. A similar conclusion (rehearsal protects against interference) is reached by Howe (1965). He presents indirect evidence, very similar to that reported above, to indicate that subvocal rehearsal protects items stored in memory from interference at the time of a vocal report; Howe (1967) reports comparable direct evidence that overt rehearsal protects items in memory from the self-produced interference of an interpolated task.

The effect of rehearsal on utilizing the full capacity of auditory short-term memory must not be confused with the possible role of rehearsal in utilizing other memories. When 3 sec were available to rehearse each stimulus item (or 12 sec for a simultaneous visual stimulus) the data indicated that a different kind of memory became effective (a memory for patterns and associations) with a different dependence on the acoustic similarity of items.

THE LOCUS OF MEMORY FOR REHEARSAL MATERIAL

Are letters which have been silently rehearsed remembered in a different memory system than letters which are heard but not rehearsed? Specifically, is there a memory of the muscular movements (or presumptive muscular movements) involved in rehearsing a letter, a memory which is different from the auditory memory for letters that are acoustically produced at the ears?

Hintzman (1965, 1967) proposes muscular memory because he notes that confusion errors in memory tasks differ systematically from confusion errors in listening tasks. His argument rests on the implicit assumption that the frequency spectrum of internal memory-noise is the same as the flat frequency spectrum of the noise which was used to create listening confusions.

Because the spectrum of speech itself is not flat—it is deficient in high frequencies—a masking noise with a flat frequency spectrum selectively destroys speech discriminations based on high frequencies (e.g., on 2nd and 3rd formants) and leaves discriminations based on low frequencies (e.g., on the 1st formant) relatively intact. In memory tasks, subjects make both kinds of confusions, which implies that the spectrum of memory noise approximates the spectrum of speech. Differences observed between the errors made in listening and in memory tasks (Conrad, 1964) can be explained by the arbitrary selection of the flat-noise stimulus to produce the listening errors.

While there is not yet any reason to suppose that significant muscular memory of rehearsal exists, there are some reasons to doubt its existence.

1. If there were a special memory for rehearsed materials, then rehearsal should increase memory capacity. That is, by remembering rehearsed letters in another memory, the space they occupied in auditory memory would be freed, or at least supplemented, thereby providing greater overall memory capacity. In fact, the opposite was observed: when there was evidence for rehearsal, memory capacity was slightly reduced. This is consistent with the assumption (Sperling, 1963, 1967) that rehearsed letters are remembered in the same memory as unrehearsed, acoustically-produced letters.

2. If memory storage for rehearsed letters were different from memory for unrehearsed letters, then it might be expected to have different properties with respect to the qualities of the letters being remembered. In particular, it might be expected to be less sensitive to acoustic similarity then auditory memory. In fact, a remarkable finding of the partial report procedure was that memory capacity was reduced by almost exactly the same amount (2.25 letters) at all rates of presentation when AS letters were substituted for AD letters, i.e., capacity deficits are independent of rate and therefore of rehearsal. This means that acoustic similarity impairs capacity for rehearsed letters to just the same degree that acoustic similarity impairs capacity for unrehearsed auditory letters. In this respect, at least, memory for rehearsed material is identical to memory for unrehearsed auditory stimuli.

3. It might here be argued that the vocal efforts required to produce various sounds are similar to each other to the exact extent that the produced sounds are similar to each other. Insofar as this is true, motor and sensory memory cannot be distinguished on the basis of sound. It is correct to conclude, however, that memory for rehearsed and unrehearsed letters is qualitatively the same and quantitatively interchangeable. This memory is properly called auditory memory (or auditory information storage) because it depends critically on the sound of the stimuli, even for groups of letters, which according to reasonable inference and introspection, are not rehearsed. There is no need at present to attribute verbal or linguistic attributes to this memory (e.g., Atkinson and Shiffrin, 1968); the data of these experiments can be explained on the basis of acoustic confusability (see below, also Conrad, 1964).

Predictions of Performance

Rules for Predicting Performance

To predict performance directly from the phonemic model, it would be necessary to make more detailed and accurate assumptions about the shape of the phoneme recall function, about the subjects' patterns and rules of rehearsal, about how rehearsed letters are stored in memory, about whether reporting letters is equivalent to rehearsing them, about the effects of time (e.g., silence is a sequence of blank phonemes), and so on. Even if we made all these assumptions, implementing them would require more parameters than could possibly be estimated from the data at hand.

Instead, we have taken an entirely different approach, and attempted to predict the data from the minimum possible number of parameters. In making predictions, we change from the partial-knowledge model to a most nearly equivalent all-or-none model because it offers simpler, more direct predictions. (However, we retain the partial-knowledge phonemic model of capacity to generate two parameters.)

PREDICTION PARAMETERS

The model contains seven estimated parameters. To predict the data of the experiments, the relevant parameters are combined according to a simple set of rules. Many predictions require less than the full set of seven parameters; indeed, it is possible to reduce the number of estimated parameters to five without much loss of accuracy. The seven parameters (and, for convenience, the final estimations of their values) are:

1. letter capacity
   a. AD alphabet (7.31 letters)
   b. AS capacity deficit (1.79 letters)
2. Response-interference parameters for presentation rates of
   a. 1/sec (.70 letters)
   b. 2/sec (1.04 letters)
   c. 4/sec (2.34 letters)
3. Standard deviation of memory capacity (1.22 letters)
4. Running span factor (.59)

PREDICTING WHOLE REPORT SCORES

Subtract from capacity, the AS capacity deficit (if appropriate) and the appropriate response-interference parameter. The result is the predicted mean memory span, $\bar{m}$. For a stimulus of length N, the predicted whole-report score $S(N)$ basically is the smaller of N and $\bar{m}$.

A correction for truncation must be subtracted in computing $S(N)$ whenever $|N - \bar{m}| < 2$ letters. The correction is needed because we assume memory span is distributed normally with a mean $\bar{m}$ and a standard deviation of 1.22 letters.[8] Subjects cannot report more letters than are presented to them, even though their memory span m may exceed N on some of the trials. Hence, we need to truncate the normal distribution at the value of N and to correct for this truncation. The correction is .5 letter when $|N - m| = 0$ and smaller otherwise. (See Appendix 1 for details.)

PREDICTING PARTIAL REPORT SCORES

When a subject makes a partial report of j letters from among N presented letters, the predicted mean number of letters available A is $A = C \cdot S(j)/j$, where C is the memory capacity for the appropriate alphabet and $S(j)$ is the predicted whole-report score for a stimulus of length

[8] Individual (average) memory spans tend to be distributed normally (cf. Pollack *et al.*, 1959). No matter what the distribution of one individual's memory span over i successive trials may be, the overall population distribution (over j subjects $\times$ i trials) is more closely normal than are the individual distributions. The approximation to normality improves as j increases.

j. (This prediction procedure simply reverses the procedure for estimating memory capacity from observed partial report scores. See Appendix 1 for more details.)

PREDICTING RUNNING MEMORY SCORES

The predicted score is simply .59 $\bar{m}$.

SAMPLE CALCULATIONS

We shall illustrate the rules by predicting scores for 4/sec AS letters. (1) Letter capacity for AS letters is 5.52 letters (AD letter-capacity of 7.31 letters minus an AS capacity deficit of 1.79 letters). (2) Mean memory span $\bar{m}$ at 4/sec equals 5.52 letters minus the rate-performance factor of 2.34 letters = 3.18 letters. (Note, the observed memory span for list lengths 6, 8, and 12 are, respectively, 3.11, 2.98, 3.36 letters.) (3) The predicted running memory span is $\bar{m} = 3.18$ letters times .59 = 1.87 letters (2.08 observed). (4) The prediction for list length-4 required a correction for truncation of .17 letters giving a prediction of 3.01 letters (3.24 observed). To obtain the predicted partial report score, the memory capacity 5.52 must be multiplied by 3.01/4.00, giving 4.17 available letters (4.20 observed).

Discussion of the Prediction Rules

CAPACITY

There basically is only one capacity parameter in the rules, the total number of phonemes. The phonemic model derives letter capacities for various alphabets from the phonemic capacity. For convenience, the prediction rules give two parameters for capacity, one for each alphabet. As prediction of the AS capacity deficit by the phonemic model is virtually perfect, only one of these parameters actually needs to be estimated.

Another parameter is saved by predicting the standard deviation of capacity from the phonemic model, rather than estimating it. Predicted values of σ are: 1.43 (AD), 1.56 (AS), compared to 1.22 letters (AD and AS) estimated from data. It happens that the prediction rules are insensitive to variations of σ in this range and goodness of fit is little affected by using one of the predicted values rather than the estimated value.

RESPONSE INTERFERENCE PARAMETER (r)

The phonemic model predicted two properties of response-interference: (1) its dependence on rate (because of the dependence of rehearsal on rate), and (2) its dependence on list length, response-interference being greater for long lists. The first of these properties is explicit in the prediction rules: the parameter r explicitly depends on rate. The second property is implicit: the effect of r depends implicitly on the length N of a presented list. To see this, consider a graph of predicted mean score $S(N)$ vs. N. Figure 8 illustrates $S(N)$ for two values of r, differing by $\Delta r = 1$, e.g., $r = 0$ and $r = 1$. The bottom curve of Fig. 8 gives the difference, which is an indication of how much r subtracts from $S(N)$ as a function of stimulus length. Although r is a constant, its effect depends on stimulus length, becoming important only as N approaches the memory span. The model predicts that partial reports are

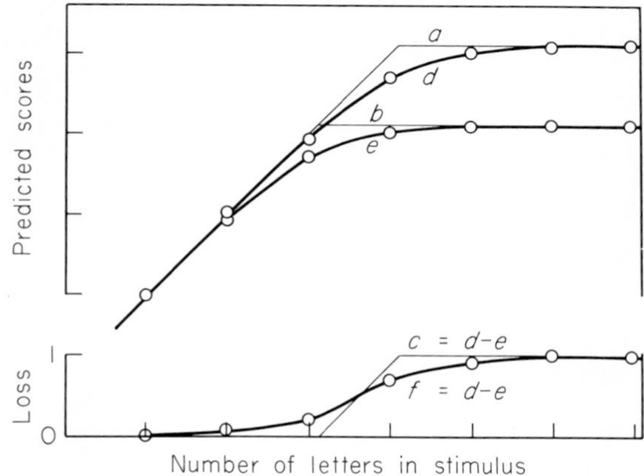

FIG. 8. Examples of theoretical predictions of whole report scores as a function of stimulus length. Curves a,b represent predictions that assume a negligibly small capacity-variance; curves d,e assume a capacity-variance of 1.0 letter^2. The difference in memory span (i.e., difference in response-interference parameter, r) between curves a and b is one letter ($\Delta r = 1.0$). Curves c and f show how the predicted loss in response accuracy depends on the number of letters presented. The ordinate for c and f is the predicted loss. Because the predictions are based on linear equations, the shape of the curve does not depend on the number of letters presented; therefore this number need not be indicated. However, a stimulus contains only integral numbers of letters, therefore predictions are made only at these specific points, indicated by circles. Coordinate markings are spaced at 1-letter distances.

more accurate than whole reports because the effect of r is smaller in the shorter partial report.

EFFECT OF ALPHABET

All differences in performance between AD and AS stimuli derive from the initial difference in letter capacity for these alphabets, and these differences are derived *a priori* from the phonemic efficiencies, f_1 and f_2. The rules translate the initial capacity difference into predicted AS deficits. A large capacity difference does not necessarily imply a large AS deficit in performance. For example, predicted and observed performance on lists of length-3 is virtually perfect for AD and AS alphabets. In the rules, the effect of alphabet is treated functionally in the same additive way as rate. For example, Fig. 8 can be interpreted as referring to two different alphabets.

RUNNING SPAN

In making running-memory reports, subjects typically write the last string of three–four letters first (beginning with the oldest), and then add a string of two to three letters in front of these, and occasionally yet a third string in front of the second. This recall strategy (which may be the only one possible) is inefficient because it unloads the most recent items first. It fails to balance response-interference and recency. The factor of .59 is a *post hoc* empirical estimate of the efficiency of the strategy.

Evaluation of the Predictions

GOODNESS OF FIT

The parameters used in the rules were chosen by means of an iterative optimization procedure which minimized the summed squares of the differences between each of the 38 predicted and observed pairs of values. Figure 9 illustrates a scatter plot of the predicted and observed results. The correlation of the predictions with the observed results of the 38 experiments is $r = .98$. The regression slope is 1.00 and the prediction accounts for .962 of the variance in the data, with a residual error of .27 letters per prediction (expressed in standard deviation terms).

These same parameters are not optimal for predicting the 19 observed AS deficits; nevertheless, they account for .78 of the variance of these

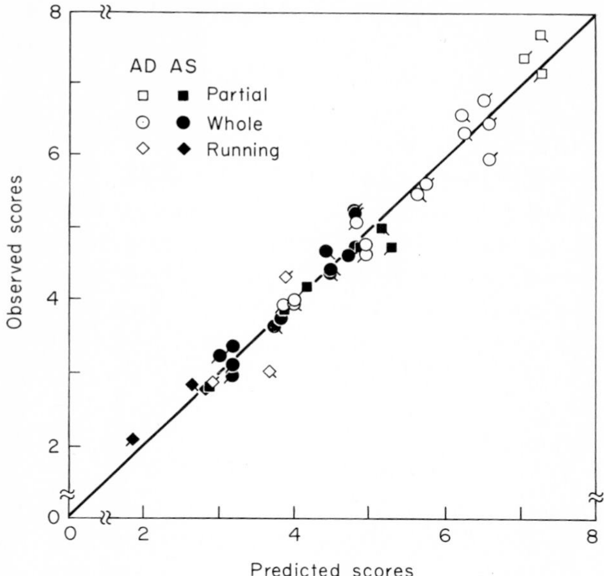

FIG. 9. Scatter plot of the observed scores in the 38 auditory experiments vs. the scores predicted by the calculation algorithm. Presentation rate is indicated by the direction of the diagonal strokes: up-right = 1/sec, down-right = 2/sec, down-left = 4/sec. The constants of the model are: AD capacity (7.31 letters), AS capacity deficit (1.79 letters), response-interference parameter (.70, 1.04, 2.34 letters for 1/sec, 2/sec, 4/sec), running span factor (.59), and capacity variability ($\sigma = 1.22$ letters).

data. Considering the small range of observed AS deficits and their greater error (each is the difference of two scores), this also is satisfactory prediction.

ECONOMIZING THE PREDICTIONS

The model can predict AS scores directly, i.e., without using any data whatsoever from experiments with an AS alphabet. To predict AS scores, six parameters of the rules are estimated only from AD scores, and the AS capacity deficit is calculated from the phonemic model. (The estimated and calculated values are virtually identical.) This prediction accounts for .90 of the observed variance of the 19 AS scores.

The absolute minimum basis for prediction is five experiments; one partial report condition (e.g., 2/sec), three whole reports (e.g., length-8, 1/sec, 2/sec, 4/sec), and one running memory condition (e.g., 2/sec).

The variability may be estimated from the whole reports. The six parameters estimated from such sets of five scores typically predict about .90 of the observed variance of the remaining 33 scores.

The predictions are not sensitive to small changes in parameters. For example, by choosing the memory capacity as 7.5 letters, the AS capacity deficit as 2.0 letters, the effect of rates as 1.0, 1.0, 2.0 letters (1/sec, 2/sec, 4/sec), the running memory factor as .6 and the standard deviation of the memory span as 1.0 letters, the rules still predict .94 of the variance of the original data. This set of seven parameters contains only four simple numbers (7.5, 2.0, 1.0, .6), which certainly brings it within the memory capacity of the reader.

Summary and Conclusions

Recall was tested in 19 different auditory and three visual recall tasks. In all 22 tasks, subjects reported fewer letters correctly when stimuli were composed of acoustically similar (AS) letters than when they were composed of acoustically different (AD) letters.

Subvocal rehearsal was shown not to increase the *capacity* of auditory short-term memory, but to increase the efficiency of utilizing the capacity. Scoring for items recalled, independent of their position, indicated an additional mean capacity of about 1.5 letters (i.e., without knowledge of their position), which was independent of the alphabet, presentation rate, and list length. The relatively frequent presence in memory of two items whose position is not known provided a plausible explanation for transposition errors. Results from visual presentations could be predicted from auditory results by assuming that subjects rehearsed letters of visual stimuli subvocally at rates of less than 4/sec. In presentations that allowed about 2 or more sec per letter, more complex memory mechanisms came into play.

A phonemic model of auditory short-term memory was proposed in which individual phonemes were retained or forgotten independently, a letter being reconstructed from the retained phonemes. The model fully accounted for the effect of acoustic similarity on recall. A set of prediction rules based on the model predicted .96 of the variance of the results of the 2 × 19 auditory conditions.

Appendix 1
Corrections for Guessing, Truncation, Partial Knowledge, and Response-Interference

Correction for Guessing

In this section, we show that the scores, as corrected for guessing by Eq. 3 of the text, are unbiased estimates of an underlying performance factor, the truncated memory span.

DEFINITIONS

Let the length of the presented stimulus be N letters, each chosen randomly without replacement from an alphabet of L equiprobable different characters. Let the memory span, an integer k, have associated with it a distribution function $\varphi(x)$, where $\varphi(x) \geqslant 0$ for all x and

$$\int_{-\infty}^{\infty} \varphi(x)\, dx = 1$$

(see Fig. 10). Let the probability $p(k)$ of x being equal to exactly k letters be given by $p(k) = \int_{k-1/2}^{k+1/2} \varphi(x)\, dx$. The definition of $p(k)$ as the integral of $\varphi(x)$ between $k - \frac{1}{2}$ and $k + \frac{1}{2}$ is in accordance with the intuitive notion of memory span. For example, when $\varphi(x)$ is a symmetric distribution about its mean m, and we say $m = 5.5$, we mean that scores of 5.0 and 6.0 are observed approximately equally often (for $N >> 6.0$ and scores corrected for guessing).

Given that the memory span equals k, the expected score $r(k)$ has two components: a performance factor (the truncated span), $s(k)$

$$s(k) = \min[N, \max(0,k)] \tag{A1}$$

and a guessing factor $g(k)$

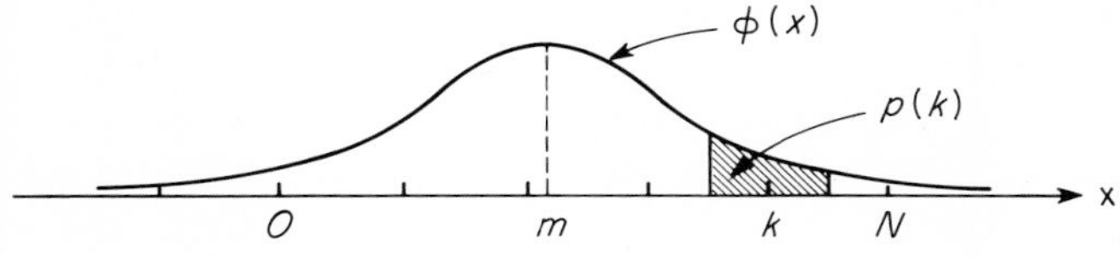

FIG. 10. A memory-span distribution function.

$$g(k) = [N - s(k)]/L, \tag{A2}$$

which results from $[N - s(k)]$ guesses, each with probability $1/L$ of success. We say $s(k)$ is truncated because it equals k only for $0 \leqslant k \leqslant N$, and it equals 0 or N outside this range. The predicted score R is given by the sum over k,

$$R = \sum_{k=-\infty}^{k=\infty} p(k)r(k) = \sum_{k=-\infty}^{k=\infty} p(k)[s(k) + g(k)] = S + G, \tag{A3}$$

where S and G represent the sums of the performance and guessing terms, respectively.

CORRECTION FOR GUESSING

We wish to show that the scores corrected for guessing $\hat{S}$ (Eq. 3 of text) are unbiased estimates of the performance factor S. Given that the memory span equals k, we may write the corrected score $\hat{s}(k) = \hat{r}(k) - [N - \hat{r}(k)]/(L - 1)$. Substitution of $r(k)$ from Eq. A3 for $\hat{r}(k)$, and algebraic reduction gives $\hat{s}(k) = s(k)$; thus, the corrected score $\hat{s}(k)$ is an unbiased estimate of the performance factor $s(k)$. Similarly, by summing over k, it is shown that $\hat{S} = \hat{R} - (N - \hat{R})/(L - 1)$ is an unbiased estimate of S. The corrected scores $\hat{S}$ estimate performance S by "removing" the factor $G = (N - S)/L$, which results from pure chance guessing.

Correction for Truncation

The score corrected for guessing $\hat{S}$ estimates a truncated span S, which depends not only on $\bar{k}$, the mean memory span, but also on N, the number of letters presented. In this section, we show how to compute S from $\bar{k}$. The reader should note that the mean memory span $\bar{k}$ is not exactly equal to the mean m of the memory distribution function because of the quantization of k, but the difference between $\bar{k}$ and m is negligible for $\sigma \geqslant 1$.

The truncated span S is less than $\bar{k}$ whenever there are trials on which the memory span k exceeds N, the number of letters presented. (Some truncation also occurs when $k < 0$, but, with the parameters of the experiments, this effect is entirely negligible.) In the text, $\varphi(x)$ was taken to be normal with mean m and standard deviation σ, so that some truncation always occurs. Given a normal distribution, the truncated span S in Eq. A3 can be given explicitly by

$$S = \sum_{k=n_1}^{n_2} \frac{1}{2} \left[\operatorname{erf}\left(\frac{k + \frac{1}{2}m}{\sigma\sqrt{2}}\right) - \operatorname{erf}\left(\frac{k - \frac{1}{2}m}{\sigma\sqrt{2}}\right)\right] \cdot s(k), \tag{A4}$$

where $n_1 = -\infty$ and $n_2 = +\infty$. There is no appreciable loss of accuracy in Eq. A4 if we take n_1 as the largest integer $< m - 5\sigma$ and n_2 is the smallest integer $> m + 5\sigma$.

The correction for truncation T is used in the text is simply

$$T = \max(m,N) - S. \tag{A5}$$

A useful feature of this definition of T is that it depends only on $d = |m-N|$, being greatest when $d = 0$. Some values of (d,T) are: $(.0\sigma, .381\sigma)$; $(.25\sigma, .270\sigma)$; $(.5\sigma, .183\sigma)$; $(1.0\sigma, .073\sigma)$; $(2.0\sigma, .006\sigma)$. For $d > 2\sigma$, T can be neglected; therefore for $N > \bar{k} + 2\sigma$, $\hat{S}$ estimates $\bar{k}$ directly.

The Effect of Partial Knowledge on Scores

THE ALL-OR-NONE MODEL

The correction for guessing assumed that a subject had all-or-none knowledge, i.e., perfect knowledge of exactly k stimulus letters and zero knowledge of the remainder. We have just shown that the corrected score $\hat{S}$ is given in Eq. 3 of the text is an unbiased estimate of $\bar{k}$. The corrected scores thus are appropriate whenever subjects have all-or-none knowledge.

While subjects may, in fact, have virtually perfect knowledge of the letters in some serial positions of the stimulus, and virtually zero knowledge of letters in other serial positions, there usually are letters at still other serial positions about which subjects have partial knowledge. Partial knowledge violates the assumption of all-or-none knowledge. The aim of this section is to show that the corrected scores $\hat{S}$ given by Eq. 3 also are reasonable to use when subjects have partial knowledge. The strategy in establishing reasonableness will be to show the consistency of the guessing correction with measures of transmitted information.

THE INFORMATION-TRANSMITTED MODEL

The only appropriate additive measure of partial knowledge known to the authors is the amount of information transmitted between stimulus and response (Shannon, 1948). Unfortunately, this measure is impractical. For example, to measure the information transmitted by stimuli of length equal to ten letters (each letter being chosen from an alphabet of eight letters), the experimenter must be prepared to present and to receive any of the $8^{10} = 1{,}073{,}741{,}824$ possible stimuli or responses, and to do so repeatedly in order to obtain the distributions of incorrect responses.

To simplify the problem, each serial position of the stimulus is treated as an independent channel. The information transmitted by a serial position is measurable; the information transmitted by the whole response is the sum of the amounts of information transmitted by each component serial position. This estimate of total information is slightly too low because subjects inadvertently use codes that involve several serial positions simultaneously (e.g., inversions); nevertheless, it is the best measure we have. For the remainder of this section, therefore, we confine ourselves to the analysis of the information transmitted about a single serial position; total information is given by summing over positions.

BOUNDS ON INFORMATION TRANSMITTED

Partial knowledge is revealed in the information-transmitted measure as the amount of information transmitted by incorrect responses. For example, when there is no partial knowledge, all incorrect responses are equally probable and they transmit no information. In this case, the information transmitted $T_{\min}$ is given by

$$T_{\min} = \log_2 L - p \log_2(1/p) - (1-p) \log_2[(L-1)/(1-p)], \quad \text{(A6)}$$

where L is the number of equiprobable stimulus alternatives and p is the uncorrected probability of a correct response.

For the case of maximum information transmitted by incorrect responses, we add the restriction that no incorrect response is more probable than the correct response. The maximum information transmitted, $T_{\max}$ then is

$$T_{\max} = \log_2 L - jp \log_2(1/p) - (1-jp) \log_2[1/(1-jp)], \quad \text{(A7)}$$

where j is the greatest integer $\leq 1/p$.

Let s be the probability of a correct response in the ith serial position as corrected for chance guessing by Eq. 3 of the text,

$$s = p - (1-p)/(L-1); \quad \text{(A8)}$$

s varies between zero and one. To compare the T's with s, we normalize the T's by dividing them by the stimulus information, $H_S = \log_2 L$. (H_S is the limiting amount of information transmitted when recall is perfect.) The normalization gives $P_{\text{min}} = T_{\text{min}}/H_S$ and $P_{\text{max}} = T_{\text{max}}/H_S$. P_{min} and P_{max} are the minimum and maximum possible *fractions* of information transmitted assuming, respectively, the minimum and maximum amounts and information to be transmitted by incorrect responses. Figure 11 shows s, P_{max}, and P_{min}, as functions of p.

Figure 11 illustrates a desirable "betweenness" property of s, namely that s mostly lies between P_{max} and P_{min}. In fact, the following conditions of "betweenness" easily can be proved: (1) $P_{\text{min}} < s$ for all p, $1/n < p < 1$, and for all $n \geqslant 2$; (2) $P_{\text{max}} > s$ for the cusps of P_{max}, except the first and last [i.e., for all p, $1/(n-1) \leqslant p \leqslant \frac{1}{2}$]; and (3) in the limit as $n \to \infty$, $P_{\text{max}} > s$ for all p, $1/n < p < 1$.

The betweenness property of s means that if s is interpreted as a fraction of information transmitted, the fraction usually lies between its theoretical lower and upper bounds. Betweenness means that, when it is not desired to assume all-or-none knowledge, S can be given an alternate interpretation as a reasonable estimate of partial knowledge, i.e., of the fraction of information transmitted.

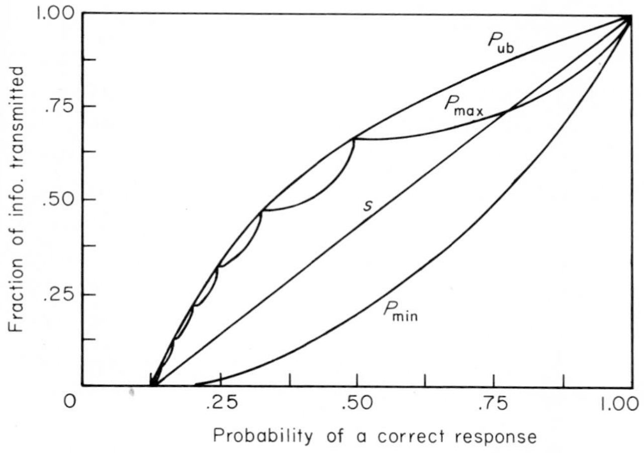

FIG. 11. Fraction of information transmitted vs. p, the (observed) probability of a correct response in a single serial position. The number of equiprobable stimulus alternatives is $N = 8$. P_{max} is the theoretical maximum possible fraction of information transmitted; P_{min} the theoretical minimum; s the score corrected for chance guessing by Eq. 3; $P_{ub} = \log_2 NP$, a simple upper bound that yields correct values of P_{max} whenever $1/p$ is an integer.

In summary, the justifications for using Eq. 3 to correct scores are: (1) there is no feasible alternative computation; (2) interpreted as an estimator in the all-or-none model, it leads to scores appropriate to the mathematical analysis used; (3) it is a reasonable estimate of partial knowledge for partial-knowledge models. This last advantage gives us freedom to use all-or-none and partial-knowledge models interchangeably, depending on which is more convenient in a particular situation.

Correction of Partial Report Scores to Give Estimates of Capacity

THEORY UNDERLYING THE CORRECTION

Consider the case of a subject required to make partial reports of length equal to j letters from a stimulus of N letters. The subject's score A may be less than N for several basic reasons.

A. Some fraction $1 - p$ of the stimulus letters no longer are in memory at the time the report is called for. Perhaps the letters never were stored or perhaps they were stored and subsequently lost. We seek to estimate p, the proportion of letters remaining in memory at the time report is called for. When there are no other losses, capacity $C = pN$.

B. The act of reporting the first and subsequent letters, produces response-interference with the memory of the remaining called-for letters (within-group interference), so that ultimately recall is reduced by some additional fraction $1 - q$. The number of letters available A, i.e., the apparent number of letters in memory, is reduced to qpN (see footnote 3, page 166). The aim of the following section is to estimate q from whole-report data, and then to estimate capacity $C = pN$ from $\hat{A} = \hat{q}\hat{p}N$ by multiplying $\hat{A}$ by a correction factor of $1/\hat{q}$.

C. Various factors related to the cue-to-report reduce recall performance; for example, difficulty in interpreting the cue and possible cue-confusions. Such factors conceivably might be estimated from experiments in which the number and compatibility of cues is varied. Hopefully, they are negligible when the number of cues is small. They are omitted here in estimating a correction factor.

ESTIMATING THE CORRECTION FACTOR

The correction factor is estimated from experiments in which response self-interference is the primary cause of recall errors. This situation obtains in whole report experiments with short list lengths because here the factor of overloaded capacity is negligible. In the ideal case, we would know *a priori* that memory capacity is exactly C letters, and we would obtain whole reports for lists of length j, where $j < C$. Recall errors could not be attributed to capacity overload because $C > j$; therefore, if errors occurred, they would be attributable entirely to response-interference.

Suppose now that C is a statistical quantity which varies somewhat from trial-to-trial. Then, the argument becomes quantitative rather than all-or-none; that is, the more unlikely it is that $C < j$, the more confidence we have in attributing errors to response-interference. (The prediction rules in the text give a full quantitative expression for these arguments.)

The partial reports were of length $j = 4$, so that the response-interference factor is measured from whole reports of length 4. This demands that the memory capacity exceed 4. Memory capacity has not yet been calculated, but we can use the partial report data directly (number of letters available, $\hat{A}$, see footnote 3, page 166) as a conservative lower bound of capacity. Table 1 showed that in all six conditions (2 alphabets $\times$ 3 rates) $\hat{A}$ exceeds 4, i.e., $C > j$. Let $\hat{S}(j)$ be the whole report score or lists of length j. The estimated fraction $\hat{q}$ of letters lost due to self-interference is $\hat{q} = 1 - \hat{S}(j)/j$, so that the estimated correction factor $\hat{f}$ ($\hat{f} = 1/\hat{q}$) is

$$\hat{f} = j/\hat{S}(j).$$

The two major kinds of error in estimating f are: (1) partial rather than all-or-none knowledge of items, (2) not all items have equal susceptibility $(1 - q)$ to response-interference. Happily, these two kinds of error tend to cancel each other.[9]

Appendix 2: Predicted Scores When Items Are Remembered without Knowledge of Position

Definitions

Let $\varphi(x)$ be the distribution function associated with position memory span. Let the distribution function associated with the item memory span be $(x - I)$, i.e., the item span exceeds the position span by I

[9] For more details, see Sperling and Speelman (1967).

items, where I is a nonnegative integer. We wish to calculate R_1, the truncated position score as defined in Appendix 1; R_2, a position score which is higher than R_1 because of an increment resulting from memory of I items (but without memory of their position); and R_3, the item score (i.e., the score obtained after response items have been permuted so as to maximize the position score).

For example, suppose on a particular trial six letters are presented and the memory span is five. This would usually lead to the correct report of only five items. Suppose $I = 1$; one additional stimulus item can be remembered but without any memory of its position. Because only one position on the score sheet remains to be filled after the five letters whose position is known have been written, the additional item always will be written in its correct position. Thus, memory of items even without memory of their position inflates the position score R_2, as well as the item score R_3. This Appendix shows how R_1, R_2, and R_3 are calculated and outlines (without mathematical rigor) the basis of the calculations.

Position Score, R_1

From Appendix 1, we have

$$R_1 = \sum_{k=-\infty}^{\infty} p(k)[s(k,N) + g_1(k,N,L)], \tag{B1}$$

where

$$s(k,N) = \min[N,\max(0,k)], \tag{B2}$$

and

$$g_1(k,N,L) = [N - s(k,N)]/L. \tag{B3}$$

Inflated Position Score, R_2

The position score R_2 is inflated by memory of I items whose position is unknown (g_2), and by pure chance guessing (g_1). R_2 is given by

$$R_2 = \sum_{k=-\infty}^{\infty} p(k)[s(k,N) + g_2(I,k,N,L) + g_1(k + g_2,N,L)], \tag{B4}$$

where s and g_1 are as defined above and $g_2(I,k,N,L)$ represents the expected number of the I items, which are written in their correct position.

The use of g_1 as an estimate of guessing in Eq. B4 assumes that, when items are remembered but written in an incorrect position, their probability of being correct is equal to that of randomly selected items.[10]

To derive an expression for $g_2(I,k,N,L)$, the following definitions are needed. Let B represent the number of positions by which the stimulus length N exceeds the memory span. B is the number of positions the subject fills with guesses or partial guesses. Let A represent the number of items the subject knows (without knowledge of their position) on a particular trial. Then

$$B = \max[0, \min(N, N - k)]$$
$$A = \min(I, B).$$

The response (beyond the position memory span k) contains A items from the stimulus ($x_1, x_2 \ . \ . \ . \ x_A$) and B-A items ($y_1, y_2 \ . \ . \ . \ y_{B-A}$) guessed randomly (with or without replacement). The order of the x_i and y_i is random. The probability that an item x_i finds itself in its originally correct position is simply $1/B$. (Of course, x_i may find itself in a position belonging originally to x_j, but still be correct there by chance whenever $x_j = x_i$. This eventuality is subsumed in the guessing term g_1.) The expected number g_2 of the A items in their originally correct position is

$$g_2 = \begin{cases} 0 & B = 0 \\ A/B & 0 \leqslant A \leqslant B \\ 1 & 1 \leqslant B \leqslant A. \end{cases} \tag{B5}$$

Note that g_2 is not a function of the total number of possible letters L, but only of A/B.

Let the position scores, corrected for random guessing by Eq. 3 of text, be designated as S_1 and S_2, respectively. It is easily proved that $R_2 - R_1 = S_2 - S_1 = g_2$ defined by Eq. B5. A remarkable corollary is that a subject cannot inflate his corrected position score by more than one item, no matter how many nonpositional items he knows, i.e., no matter how much item knowledge he has.

The theoretical predictions of Eqs. B4 and B5 were tested by a Monte Carlo simulation. The empirical results of sampling with replacement from an alphabet of size $L = 8$ differed insignificantly from the predicted results.

[10] This assumption has been proved by S. Johnson (personal communication).

Item Scores, R_3

The predicted item scores are given by

$$R_3 = \sum_{k=-\infty}^{\infty} p(k) \cdot [s_1(k+I) + g_3(k,N,L)],$$

where

$$g_3(k,N,L) = F(A,L) \quad \text{and} \quad A = \min(\max(N-k-I,0),\ N).$$

Here A is the number of guesses at stimulus items, and $F(A,L)$ is the expected number of correct items, scored irrespective of position. It is assumed here, as in the previous derivations, that the number of response items equals the number of stimulus items.

Derivations of $F(A,L)$ have been carried out by S. Johnson (unpublished) and Riordan (1967). The authors are indebted to Dr. Johnson for the values of $F(0,8)$ to $F(8,8)$ which are: .0; .1250; .4414; .8864; 1.4201; 2.0167; 2.6593; 3.3365; and 4.0404.

Figure 4 of the text illustrates the expected difference between item scores and correct position scores as a function of the difference between stimulus length and position score, for three values of I. In treating the data, position scores were corrected for chance guessing by Eq. 3 of the text. For the theoretical curves, therefore, the ordinate of Fig. 4 was $\hat{R}_3 - \hat{S}_2$ and the abscissa was $N - \hat{S}_2$ where $\hat{S}_2$ is $\hat{R}_2$ corrected for chance guessing, i.e., $\hat{S}_2 = \hat{R}_2 - (N - \hat{R}_2)/(L-1)$. The function $\varphi(x)$ was taken to be Normal with mean m and $\sigma = 1$; the curves were generated by assuming $N = 100$ and varying m in steps of .1 from 90 to 105.

References

ANDERSON, N. S. Poststimulus cuing in immediate memory. *Journal of Experimental Psychology*, 1960, **60**, 216–221.

ATKINSON, R. C., AND SHIFFRIN, R. M. Human memory: A proposed system and its control processes. In K. W. Spence and J. T. Spence (Eds.), *Advances in the psychology of learning and motivation research and theory*. Vol. II. New York: Academic Press, 1968. Pp. 89–195.

BADDELEY, A. D. Short-term memory for word sequences as a function of acoustic, semantic and formal similarity in short-term memory. *Psychonomic Science*, 1966, **5**, 233–234.

BROADBENT, D. E. *Perception and communication*. New York: MacMillan (Pergamon), 1958.

BROWN, J. Some tests of the decay theory of immediate memory. *Quarterly Journal of Experimental Psychology*, 1958, **10**, 12–21.

CONRAD, R. An association between memory errors and errors due to acoustic masking of speech. *Nature,* 1962, **193,** 1314–1315.

CONRAD, R. Acoustic confusions and memory span for words. *Nature.* 1963, **197,** 1029–1030.

CONRAD, R. Acoustic confusions in immediate memory. *British Journal of Psychology,* 1964, **55,** 75–84.

CONRAD, R. Order error in immediate recall of sequences. *Journal of Verbal Learning and Verbal Behavior,* 1965, **4,** 161–169.

CONRAD, R. Interference or decay over short retention intervals? *Journal of Verbal Learning and Verbal Behavior,* 1967, **6,** 49–54.

CONRAD, R., BADDELEY, A. D., AND HULL, A. J. Rate of presentation and the acoustic similarity effect in short-term memory. *Psychonomic Science,* 1966, **5,** 233–234.

CONRAD, R., AND HULL, A. J. Information, acoustic confusion and memory span. *British Journal of Psychology,* 1964, **55,** 492–432.

DALE, H. C. A. Retroactive interference in short-term memory. *Nature.* 1964, **203,** 1408.

DALE, H. C. A., AND GREGORY, M. Evidence of semantic coding in short-term memory. *Psychonomic Science,* 1966, **5,** 75–76.

DALLETT, K. M. Intelligibility and short-term memory in the repetition of digit strings. *Journal of Speech and Hearing Research,* 1964, **7,** 362–368.

GLANZER, M., AND CLARK, W. H. Accuracy of perceptual recall: An analysis of organization. *Journal of Verbal Learning and Verbal Behavior,* 1963, **1,** 289–299.

GLANZER, M., AND CLARK, W. H. The verbal loop hypothesis: Binary numbers. *Journal of Verbal Learning and Verbal Behavior,* 1964, **2,** 301–309.

HARRIS, C. S., AND HABER, R. N. Selective attention and coding in visual perception. *Journal of Experimental Psychology,* 1963, **65,** 328–333.

HINTZMAN, D. L. Classification and aural coding in short-term memory. *Psychonomic Science,* 1965, **3,** 161–162.

HINTZMAN, D. L. Articulatory coding in short-term memory. *Journal of Verbal Learning and Verbal Behavior,* 1967, **6,** 312–316.

HOWE, M. J. A. Intra-list differences in short-term memory. *Quarterly Journal of Experimental Psychology,* 1965, **17,** 338–342.

HOWE, M. J. A. Consolidation in short-term memory as a function of rehearsal. *Psychonomic Science,* 1967, **7,** 355–356.

LANDAUER, T. K. Rate of implicit speech. *Perceptual and Motor Skills,* 1962, **15,** 646.

LAUGHERY, K. R. Effects of symbol size on immediate memory. *American Psychologist,* 1963, **18,** 415. (Abstract)

LAUGHERY, K. R., AND PINKUS, A. L. Short-term memory: Effects of acoustic similarity, presentation rate and presentation mode. *Psychonomic Science,* 1966, **6,** 285–286.

NORMAN, D. A. Acquisition and retention in short-term memory. *Journal of Experimental Psychology,* 1966, **72,** 369–381.

POLLACK, I., JOHNSON, L. B., AND KNAFF, P. R. Running memory span. *Journal of Experimental Psychology,* 1959, **57,** 137–146.

RIORDAN, J. A matching problem. *Bell Telephone Laboratories Technical Memorandum,* 1967.

SHANNON, C. E. A mathematical theory of communication. *Bell System Technical Journal,* 1948, **27,** 379–423, 623–656.

SPEELMAN, R. G., AND SPERLING, G. Effect of the sound of stimuli upon short-term memory. Paper presented at the meeting of the Eastern Psychological Association, Philadelphia, April 18, 1964.

SPERLING, G. The information available in brief visual presentations. *Psychological Monographs,* 1960, **74,** No. 11 (Whole No. 498).

SPERLING, G. A model for visual memory tasks. *Human Factors,* 1963, **5,** 19–31.

SPERLING, G. Spatial and temporal visual masking. I. Masking by impulse flashes. *Journal of the Optical Society of America,* 1965, **55,** 541–559.

SPERLING, G. Successive approximations to a model for short-term memory. *Acta Psychologica,* 1967, **27,** 285–292.

SPERLING, G. Phonemic model for short-term auditory memory. *Proceedings of the American Psychological Association,* 1968, **4,** 63–64.

SPERLING, G., AND SPEELMAN, R. G. The effect of sound of stimuli on short-term auditory memory. *Bell Telephone Laboratories Technical Memorandum,* 1967.

WAUGH, N. C., AND NORMAN, D. A. Primary memory. *Psychological Review,* 1965, **72,** 89–104.

WICKELGREN, W. A. Acoustic similarity and retroactive interference in short-term memory. *Journal of Verbal Learning and Verbal Behavior,* 1965, **4,** 54–61. (a)

WICKELGREN, W. A. Acoustic similarity and intrusion errors in short-term memory. *Journal of Experimental Psychology,* 1965, **70,** 102–108. (b)

WICKELGREN, W. A. Similarity and intrusions in short-term memory for consonant-vowel digrams. *Quarterly Journal of Experimental Psychology,* 1965, **17,** 241–246. (c)

WICKELGREN, W. A. Distinctive features and errors in short-term memory for English vowels. *Journal of the Acoustical Society of America,* 1965, **38,** 583–588. (d)

WICKELGREN, W. A. Short term memory for phonemically similar lists. *American Journal of Psychology,* 1965, **78,** 567–574. (e)

WICKELGREN, W. A. Phonemic similarity and interference in short-term memory for single letters. *Journal of Experimental Psychology,* 1966, **71,** 396–404. (a)

WICKELGREN, W. A. Short-term recognition memory for single letters and phonemic similarity of retroactive interference. *Quarterly Journal of Experimental Psychology,* 1966, **18,** 55–62. (b)

WICKELGREN, W. A. Distinctive features and errors in short-term memory for English consonants. *Journal of the Acoustical Society of America,* 1966, **39,** 388–398. (c)

WICKELGREN, W. A., AND NORMAN, D. A. Strength models and serial position in short-term recognition memory. *Journal of Mathematical Psychology,* 1966, **3,** 316–347.

WOODWORTH, R. S., AND SCHLOSBERG, H. *Experimental psychology.* (Rev. ed.) New York: Holt, 1954.

7

A Functional Model for Memory[1]

John Morton
Applied Psychology Research Unit
Cambridge, England

Introduction

A functional model, by the present usage, is one which separates out those processes in the brain which can be distinguished from one another by one of several criteria. The most important of these are the nature of the code in which information is processed, the kinds of in-

[1] Work on this paper was begun while the author was Lecturer and Research Associate in the Department of Psychology, Yale University. While there I benefited from discussions with Professor W. R. Garner and had the opportunity to work with R. G. Crowder who has contributed greatly to this paper. References to "recent experiments" are taken from a forthcoming paper by Morton, Crowder, and Prussin the work for which was split between Cambridge (U.K.) and Yale. M. I. Posner kindly read a draft and helped to disambiguate some of the obscurities.

formation that can interact, and the logical form of the processing operation. In the first instance, the emphasis is on logical distinctions rather than mathematical sophistication in dealing with the microstructure of the data (and so the model has affinities with a grammar) and on relatively gross experimental results. My own preference is to give a general but formal account of a wide spectrum of human performance rather than to account in detail for performance in a limited range of tasks. This is not the only way to increase our knowledge, but it does appear to have the advantages that it discourages overly simple explanations of behavior and keeps clear the distinction between experimental paradigm and hypothetical construct. Thus, the terms short-term memory and long-term memory as used by certain workers in the past turn out to describe only differences in the interval between presentation and recall and do not isomorphically refer to different storage systems, (Baddeley, 1966a, 1968a). Similarly, Proactive and Retroactive Inhibition should be restricted in their application to experimental results that arise from particular paradigms and cannot, according to the present philosophy, be applied as explanations. An effect such as *interference,* however it is manifested neurally, may be applicable to a wide range of phenomena, but it seems to be more useful to attempt to specify the properties of the subsystems within which such effects take place. What the generalizations obscure are the differences between the subsystems, how they interrelate, and the possibility that the separate pieces of behavior upon which the generalization rests have completely different origins and courses.

This paper will first describe a model that was initially developed to account for performance in a variety of word recognition tasks (Morton, 1964a, 1964b; 1969a; Morton and Broadbent, 1967) and in more complex language behavior (Morton, 1964c, 1968a) and has also been used to account for the Stroop effect and similar phenomena (Stroop, 1935; Klein, 1964; Morton, 1969b).[2] The model differs in its treatment of information processing from most of the models devised to account for memory, particularly in the stress placed on the distinctions between the forms of coding in different locations. Consequently, when the model is applied to memory the kinds of explanations that are given for certain phenomena do not coincide wholly with any other account. Since I will try to apply the model to phenomena for which it was not

[2] The Stroop effect is that when naming the colors in which different words are printed, the nature of the words interferes with the color naming.

specifically devised, I will first of all try to explain why it has its particular form and mode of operation. This account is necessarily sketchy; and obvious objections will, I hope, have been covered in the earlier papers.[3]

A Model for Word Recognition

The basic model is shown in Fig. 1. The starting point is the assumption that when a verbal response is available the same final unit operates to produce that response regardless of the source of the information that led to the response. Thus, when you see the word "table," hear it spoken, see the object or are asked to free associate to "chair" or complete the sentence "I put the plate on the ______," the same word

[3] The names given to the various elements of the system have changed since the earlier papers for a variety of reasons, the functions are substantially the same, only the degree of specificity has increased.

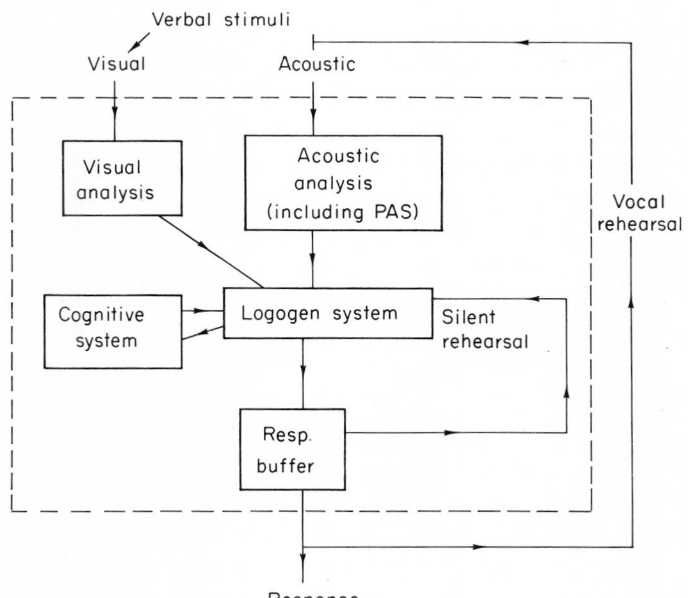

FIG. 1. A flow-diagram of information in the Logogen Model. The dotted line indicates the boundaries of man.

is available as a response (and can be given overtly). The supposed origin of the response is termed a *logogen*, which is the part of the system that produces or leads directly to the instructions to the articulators.

The Logogen System

Each logogen L_i is defined by its output, which can be represented by the set of phonological features $\{P_i\}$, and by the sets of acoustic, visual, and semantic attributes $\{A_i\}$, $\{V_i\}$, and $\{S_i\}$, respectively, (cf. the perceptual and memory vectors in Norman and Rumelhart, chapter 2). The most important defining set is the semantic set. Thus, we would have the same logogen for "table," whether it was printed or handwritten, in spite of the differences in visual attribute sets between the two forms. On the other hand, there would be different logogens for "chop" (to eat) and "chop" (the act), in spite of the fact that the visual and acoustic attribute sets for the two will be identical. It would probably be more accurate to characterize the basic linguistic unit appropriate to the model as a morpheme (Morton, 1968a). There are rather severe unsettled linguistic problems that reflect similar uncertainties (see, e.g., Lyons, 1968). For the present application, however, it will be sufficient to define the logogen in terms of the usual understanding of "word." A logogen is basically a counting device that is incremented whenever there is an input to the Logogen System of an attribute, from any source, which is a member of one of its defining sets. When the count exceeds a certain critical value the appropriate response is made available. It is assumed that sensory analysis of a stimulus proceeds, in general, without reference to subsequent parts of the system, and that the results of this analysis are available to the whole of the Logogen System. If the word "cat" were presented visually, the output from the visual analysis might include the attributes <three-letter word>, <final ascender>, <initial *c*>, <final *t*>, and so on. These items would all be included in the set $\{V_{cat}\}$ of course, and so the logogen L_{cat} would automatically receive an increment for each of these attributes (presumably weighted according to some hierarchical principle). In addition, L_{dog} would be incremented because <three letter word> is part of $\{V_{dog}\}$, and $\{L_{cap}\}$ would be affected both by that and <initial *c*>. The response would be determined by the logogen in which the count first exceeded the critical, threshold value. The appropriate response would then be made available and other responses, in general, would be inhibited.

FACTORS INFLUENCING THE CRITICAL VALUE

The critical value of the count is not the same for all logogens. First of all, the facilitative effect of the prior presentation of a word upon its subsequent recognition (Neisser, 1954; Ross, Yarczower, and Williams, 1956) is accounted for by supposing that following the operation of a logogen its threshold is reduced. Fewer sensory attributes will then be needed to produce the response again. Thus, we would expect that the prior presentation of a word would increase the likelihood of it subsequently being produced as an incorrect response. This facilitation would not be expected to apply to homonyms (Neisser, 1954; Ross *et al.*, 1956) because pairs of words such as "phrase" and "frays" would be represented by different logogens, since they have different semantic and visual attribute sets.

Following this facilitative threshold lowering, the critical value rises more slowly towards its original value. Without such a postulate, the system would rapidly become unstable. It is suggested that the recovery is incomplete and that, within limits, the more a word is used, the lower the resting level of the critical count. The accumulation of such incomplete threshold recovery reveals itself in the word-frequency effect (Solomon and Postman, 1952). The higher the frequency of usage of a logogen, the lower will be its critical value. Thus, for high-frequency words, fewer sensory attributes will be required to produce the response than for low-frequency words. (Within the model, this would apply to both frequency of usage and frequency of occurrence of a word, since the logogen operates in both cases.) Thus, the attribute count required to produce the respective responses would be less in L_{cat}, for example, than in L_{sot}. In the language of Signal Detection Theory, the Logogen Model would predict that the word-frequency effect is due to a difference in criteria between high- and low-frequency words and not a difference in sensitivity. This prediction has been verified by Broadbent (1967) and Morton (1968b). Since the overlap between $\{V_{\mathrm{cat}}\}$ and $\{V_{\mathrm{sot}}\}$ is high, we would expect that when the stimulus *sot* is presented in an impoverished fashion that the response "cat" will often be given, but not vice versa. This account has much in common with the *figural synthesis* model (Neisser, 1967) but without some of its implications.

If, following the presentation of a noisy stimulus, no response is immediately available, it is assumed that some control system causes all the thresholds in the Logogen System to be lowered. The number of times this operation is performed would depend on the instructions to the subjects. This number could be used by the organism in the assignment of confidence ratings to the response. If subjects were forced to give a response on all occasions, even if the stimulus were a dummy (Goldiamond and Hawkins, 1958), then the thresholds in the system would be lowered repeatedly until the first response became available. This procedure avoids the necessity of postulating a decision process, external to the Logogen System, which would have to select one response on the basis of a comparison of the counts in different logogens. In the Logogen Model, the words given as incorrect responses would be determined by the overlap of their sensory attribute sets with that of the stimulus word and the levels of their critical counts. Thus, the system would predict that incorrect response will tend to be more common than the stimulus word (Newbigging, 1961; Savin, 1963), that incorrect responses will share stimulus attributes with the stimulus (Pillsbury, 1897; Vernon, 1929; Savin, 1963; Havens and Foote, 1963; Morton, 1964a), that rare words will be recognized more easily if there is no closely similar high-frequency word (Savin, 1963; Havens and Foote, 1963), and that following an incorrect response, a second attempt will be correct more often than chance (Bricker and Chapanis, 1953).

This account differs from *fragmentation theory* (Solomon and Postman, 1952; Savin, 1963; Newbigging, 1961; Neisser, 1967) in one rather crucial aspect. Fragmentation theory explains all the phenomena mentioned in the previous paragraph by supposing that the parts of the stimulus that are seen clearly serve to reduce the number of alternatives from which a guess can then be made. *Response Bias* in the guesses then favors high-frequency words. While it is not denied that such a reduction in the number of alternative responses can occur, the present model does not require it as a general rule. Morton (1968b) has shown that in order to account for the word-frequency data given by Brown and Rubenstein (1961), it is necessary for even a *sophisticated guessing theory* such as fragmentation theory to postulate differences in sensitivity between high- and low-frequency words as well as response biases, a complication for which fragmentation theory does not allow.

SEMANTIC INFORMATION

The effect of a context on the production of a response is identical in principle to the effect of a stimulus. The context, which can be of any kind, causes what is here called the Cognitive System to send semantic information to the Logogen System. Attributes such as <noun>, <animate>, <male> might be produced by the sentence "He was a drunken ______" and all logogens whose semantic sets contained these items would be incremented accordingly. These increments would effectively reduce the amount of sensory information required to produce the response, the attribute counts from the two sources simply adding without regard to source.

Predictions from the Model

RESPONSE STRENGTH ANALYSIS

Given that there is activity in the system, which is random with respect to a particular recognition task, the average behavior of the system can be predicted by using Response Strength Analysis (Luce, 1959). In this treatment, all potential responses have a strength assigned to them, and the probability of a particular response being made is given by the ratio of the response strength for that particular item to the sum of all response strengths. In Table 1, we have the response strengths for words under three different conditions: with a context alone; with a stimulus alone; and with both context and stimulus.

When a particular context is presented, the counts in different logogens are incremented by amounts depending on the number of relevant semantic attributes produced by the context. In the response-strength table, these strengths are entered as $V_1, V_2 \ldots V_i \ldots V_n$, where V_i is the logarithm of the current count in L_i. When we present a context to a subject and demand a response, we will, by definition, get the most probable

TABLE 1
Response Strengths under Different Conditions[a]

	Response						Total of response strengths
	1	2	—	i	—	n	
Context alone	V_1	V_2	-	V_i	-	V_n	$T = \sum_{j=1}^{n} V_j$
Stimulus alone	1	1	-	α	-	1	$\alpha + (n-1)$
Stimulus and context	V_1	V_2	-	αV_i	-	V_n	$T + (\alpha - 1)\ V_i$

[a] The probability of a particular response in any condition is given by the ratio of the response strength of that response to the sum of the response strengths in that condition.

response most often. This word is regarded as the one to which more of the context-produced attributes are relevant than any other (together with some influence of word frequency). The fact that other responses are also given required that we have some random activity in the system that can increase the count in the logogen corresponding to a less probable word above the critical value before the more probable response occurs. In the response-strength analysis, the behavior of the system is approximately described, the probability of the response i being given by:

$$P_c = V_i/T_i,\ T_i = \sum_{j=1}^{N} V_j. \tag{1}$$

When a stimulus i is presented at a particular signal-to-noise ratio (S/N), the count in L_i will be increased by more than the count in any other logogen. In the table, the relative increase is given by α, where $\log \alpha$ is directly proportional to the actual increase in the count. In general, there will be no systematic relationship between the confusability of any other stimulus and its position j in the table. Note that since performance is predicted in terms of a ratio of response strengths, their absolute values are not important. Thus, all other responses are given a response strength of unity, the logarithm of which is zero, corresponding to no effective increase in the count as a result of the stimulus. The probability of a correct response to the stimulus is given by:

$$P_s = \alpha/[\alpha + (N-1)]. \tag{2}$$

Equation 2 can be arranged as:

$$\text{logit } P_s = \log \alpha - \log(N-1), \tag{3}$$

where logit $P_s = \log[P_s/(1 - P_s)]$, from which we can predict word recognition performance where the number of alternatives is restricted. In Fig. 2, the data of Miller, Heise, and Lichten (1951) are plotted. In this experiment, the subjects were presented with words in noise. The words were drawn from a known vocabulary that varied from 2 through 1000 words in different conditions. In the figure, the best fitting straight lines are drawn. The mean slope is −.82, which compares favorably with the predicted slope of −1.0. For further discussion, see Morton (1969a).

THE INTERACTION OF STIMULUS AND CONTEXT

It has been stated that in the model, the increments due to the context add to those due to the stimulus. In the Response Strength table, the appropriate strengths are multiplied together. Thus, for word i we have

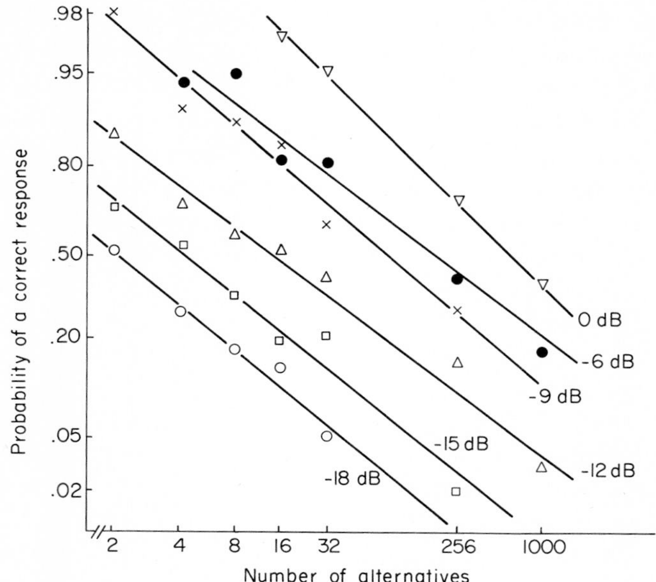

FIG. 2. Data from Miller *et al.* (1951) showing the probability of correctly recognizing a word presented in noise as a function of the number of alternatives. The function plotted is logit $P_n = \log \alpha - \log(n - 1)$, where logit $P = \log[P/(1 - P)]$. The lines are the least-square fit. If they are parallel it indicates that the amount of information available from the stimulus, $\log \alpha$, at a particular S/N level, is independent of the number of alternatives. (Adapted from Morton, 1969a.)

a value αV_i; since the total increment in the logogen count, $\log(\alpha V_i)$, is equal to that due to the context, $\log V_i$, plus that due to the stimulus, $\log \alpha$. The probability of a correct response when both stimulus and context are present is given by:

$$P_{sc} = \alpha V_i/[T_i + (\alpha - 1)V_i]. \quad (4)$$

When we substitute for T_i from (1), V_i vanishes and we get

$$P_{sc} = \alpha P_c/[(1 - P_c) + \alpha P_c], \quad (5)$$

whence

$$\text{logit } P_{sc} = \log \alpha + \text{logit } P_c, \quad (6)$$

where logit $p = \log[p/(1 - p)]$.

By substituting for α from (2), we further obtain:

$$\text{logit } P_{sc} = \text{logit } P_s + \text{logit } P_c + \text{constant}. \quad (7)$$

These equations have been tested against data from Tulving, Mandler, and Baumal (1964) and Rubenstein and Pollack (1963). In both these experiments, the subjects had to recognize words under various conditions where words were presented at different signal-to-noise ratios (S/N) and with different amounts of context (see Morton, 1969a). In Fig. 3, values of logit P_s are plotted against logit P_{sc} from Tulving *et al.* The lines, fitted by eye, are of the predicted slope of unity. Figure 4 shows data from Rubenstein and Pollack. This figure effectively tests Eq. 6, the ordinate representing differences in logit P_{sc} for different (S/N) and different levels of context. On the left-hand side, the context was a part of a sentence and the plot shows that the effect of increasing the S/N (i.e., log α) is independent of the amount of such a context. The right-hand side of Fig. 4 represents a condition where the *context* was the first N letters of the word. Since the information in such a context duplicates some of the information in the stimulus, Eq. 6 would no longer hold. The data confirm our expectations. Thus far, then, the model gives a reasonable account of the data on word recognition and so fulfills the purpose for which it was devised.

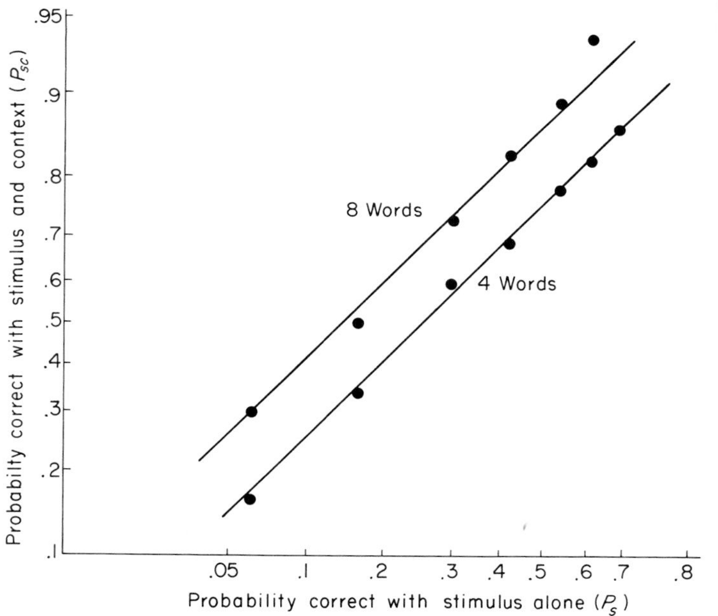

FIG. 3. Data from Tulving *et al.* (1964). Logit P_{sc} is plotted against logit P_s. (Adapted from Morton, 1969a.)

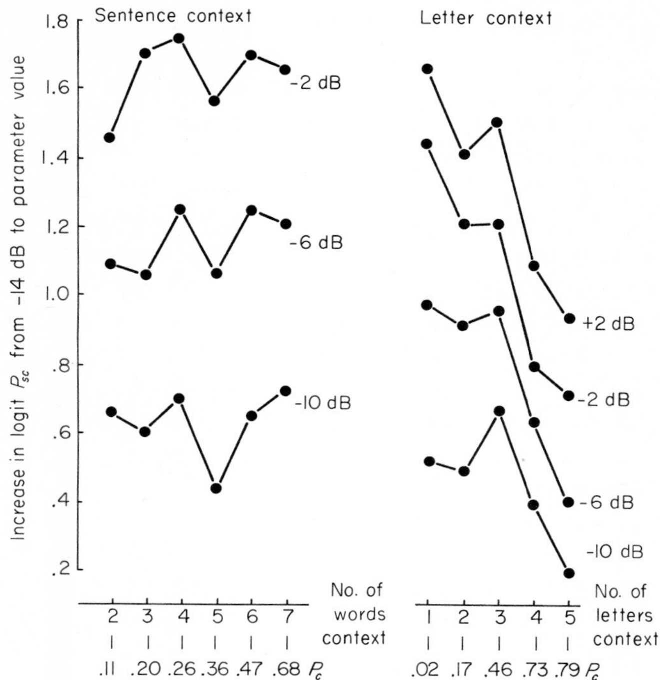

FIG. 4. Data from Rubenstein and Pollack (1963). The left-hand side shows that the amount of information from the stimulus is independent of the amount of sentence context. This contrasts with the right-hand side where the context consisted of letters from the stimulus word. (Adapted from Morton, 1969a.)

The Response Buffer

The Logogen System operates to make a response available. The act of response availability appears to be a sufficient condition for the subjective phenomenon of the *perception* of a word when combined with the general information that particular sensory analysers have been operating. This, together with the indifference of the logogen count to the source of its information, would account for the fact that in reading or in listening to speech we are never aware of the relative contribution of stimulus and context to the phenomena. Following response availability, we can then go on actually to make the response but, of course, need not. In the interval between responses being made available and their being produced, they are in a Response Buffer. The original reason for this construct was to account for the fact that when people are reading aloud, there is a gap between the eyes and the voice, the eye–voice span. This span can be up to five words in length (Morton, 1964d) and one kind of error in reading involves the preposition of a word in the response of anything up to five words. That is, if the words being read are represented by the letter sequence **a b c d e,** the response could be **e a b c d** (Morton, 1964c). Thus, it seemed that all the words in the eye-voice span were available as responses, and some construct was required to allow for their temporary storage. The ear–voice span in shadowing (Treisman and Geffin, 1967) is about the same order of magnitude. Silent rehearsal is seen as the circulating of such information from the Response Buffer back to the Logogen System. Thus, a logogen will not only produce the set $\{P_i\}$, but will also accept it. The difference between this and other accounts of silent rehearsal will be discussed below.

The Cognitive System

OUTPUTS FROM THE LOGOGEN SYSTEM

For verbal material to act as a context, it must in the first place have passed through the Logogen System. For various reasons, it is more convenient to suppose that this is not done via the Response Buffer, but rather that each logogen has two outputs. In the original model, the Cognitive System is responsible in particular for semantic and syntactic analysis of linguistic material. Now it has been observed (Morton, 1964c) that when reading passages of statistical approximations to English or English texts, some subjects make a large number of errors that can only be described in terms of syntactic and semantic analysis. Furthermore, they are frequently unaware of the fact that they have made these errors. This suggested that, while reading aloud, the linguistic structure of the material was analyzed completely and then resynthesized before output. This required that the output from a logogen to the Cognitive System occurred before the output to the Response Buffer. The latter output would be caused by the full semantic description of the item provided by the Cognitive System. The output to the Cognitive System would be in a form that permitted the semantic description of the item to be obtained, for which information from the preceding and, in some cases, the following context would be required. For such a system to work, the value of the count required to produce a semantic output would have to be less than the value required to produce a phonological output.

Where the stimulus is clear and there is no time pressure there would normally be sufficient information from the sensory analysis system to produce both outputs directly, but only in exceptional circumstances would it be possible for there to be an output to the Response Buffer without there also being one to the Cognitive System. From this system it is possible to give an account of *subception* (Lazarus and McCleary, 1951; Dixon, 1958; Brown, 1961; Worthington and Dixon, 1964). By this term is meant the reported phenomena that when a subject is presented with a word usually considered unsociable or taboo, he often reports that he did not see (or hear) it, even though he did, in fact, give an indirect verbal response or change in skin resistance to the presentation. Some of the experiments on this phenomena can readily be explained as *response suppression*, i.e., the appropriate response has been made available but has been consciously suppressed. Such an explanation does not, however, account for all the data. If, however, we assume that for taboo words there is a high response threshold, but a normal semantic threshold then it would be possible for the Cognitive System to have received the semantic description of the word from the Logogen System without there being a response available. The Cognitive System could then react, giving rise to an autonomic response or to the verbal response of an associated word.

Marshall and Newcombe (1966) have described a patient who appears to behave in this way for nonemotional words. If presented visually with the word "storm," he would read it as *thunder;* for "uncle" he read *nephew*. In all cases of misreading, the response was a word closely related to the stimulus (but never, incidentally, an antonym). This indicated that the word had been recognized completely by the Cognitive System, in spite of the absence of the correct verbal response. When the semantic description of the word was sent back to the logogen system, the correct response being blocked, a word with a similar semantic set was produced. The patient was always aware of having produced an incorrect response, and so must have been able to compare the semantic description of the original with that which accompanied his response.

The Cognitive System represents what most people call the long-term store. With letter or digit stimuli, it might not seem particularly meaningful to talk about a *semantic description*; it is, however, sufficient to suppose that the form of such items in the Cognitive System is different from their form in other stores. In addition, the Cognitive System is taken to be responsible for such organizational and associational phenomena as might manifest themselves in a particular task. Finally, from the operation of the system it is required to postulate that whenever a stimulus is recognized information is transferred to the Cognitive System even without rehearsal (cf. Murdock, 1968). The result of rehearsal is to send the phonological description $\{P_i\}$ back to the Logogen System. The effect of this will be to cause the logogen to operate again, repeating the information to the Cognitive System, and so either consolidating the information or making it more accessible (depending on one's theory).

It is claimed that the model in Fig. 1 is about as simple a model as can be devised to account for the data on word recognition. Tentative extensions to more complex language behavior can be found elsewhere (Morton, 1968a). The model has been termed *passive* as opposed to *active* (Morton and Broadbent, 1967). By this distinction, we drew a contrast with certain aspects of analysis-by-synthesis models of speech perception (Liberman, Cooper, Harris, MacNeilage, and Studdert-Kennedy, 1967; Stevens and Halle, 1967). The contrast was, and is, intended to apply only as far as the Logogen System. The evidence in favor of constructive procedures in speech recognition beyond the level of the word is overwhelming. At the word level, such is not the case. An analysis-by-synthesis model would have to predict, for example, that the word frequency effect would reveal itself in the data as a difference in sensitivity (i.e., d') for high-vs.-low-frequency words, and not to a difference in criterion. It was remarked above that the evidence appears to favor criterion differences as the correct account.

Application of the Model to Memory

The only part of the model which has memory as part of its function is the Cognitive System. The other parts of the model appear to store information for varying lengths of time and in varying amounts rather as a by-product of their main functions. This distinction will become more clear in the following sections. What I shall try to do is identify those phenomena that have been found in experiments on memory—particularly short-term memory—which can be accounted for from the mode of operation of the units in the model. This has two consequences: first, it delimits the data which have to be explained by the main memory system; second, it enables us to use memory paradigms in order to study the properties of the units. It is assumed that the subject draws upon all the sources of memory in the model according to their strength, accessibility, and reliability, which will vary with the conditions of the experiment. Very little will be said as to *how* the information is retrieved nor as to how information from the different sources is combined. The stress will be on the forms in which information is coded in the different units, and the conditions under which they may be used. Both of these are determined by the function of the units. Finally, the Cognitive System will be treated in a fairly cavalier fashion. Other chapters in this volume deal with its functional equivalents far more comprehensively than the current state of the Logogen Model would permit.

Sensory Analysis Systems

The Sensory Analysis Systems, visual and auditory, operate to extract significant features from the stimulus. Since such feature extraction cannot be instantaneous, we would expect information to remain in the analysis systems for some time, at some, if not all the levels of analysis. From the properties of the two modalities, we would further expect such storage to be longer for the auditory system than the visual system, particularly at the more complex levels of analysis. The visual and auditory memory systems discussed below refer exclusively to the properties of the Sensory Analysis Systems. Correspondingly, the most simple assumption is made about coding: that only in the respective analysis systems is it meaningful to talk about visual and acoustic coding. This is almost certain to be incorrect where the Cognitive System is concerned.

Visual Memory System

The properties of precategorical visual memory have been described by other people (Averbach and Sperling, 1961; Averbach and Coriell, 1961; Sperling, 1960, 1963; Posner, 1967) and I have little to add. Posner's demonstration of visual rehearsal of letters necessitates the first violation of the assumption just made (Posner, Boies, Eichelman, and Taylor, 1969; see also Brooks, 1968). This is because rehearsal involves generation in the appropriate code and, as stated above, the sensory analysis systems are not granted the power of synthesis. As will be seen, other forms of verbal rehearsal do not violate the assumption.

Precategorical Acoustic Storage

Crowder and Morton (1969) have shown that a wide variety of experimental results can be most simply accounted for by supposing that information can be retrieved and eliminated from the Acoustic Analysis System. This property of the analysis system we called Precategorical Acoustic Storage (PAS). It is proposed that PAS only receives information from the ears (see Fig. 1) and that the material within it is subject both to overwriting and decay, with a maximum useful life of about 2 sec.

The idea of a precategorical store is not new. Crossman (1958) reports an experiment in which he played single words at half-speed on a taperecorder. Providing subjects with a small number of response alternatives improved performance up to 40 sec after the stimulus. Pollack (1959) did a similar study with words played in noise and suggested from his results that a representation of the raw stimulus might last for up to 15 minutes. It is likely, though, that in this experiment, the subjects had coded certain aspects of the stimulus verbally, such as *initial c, two-syllable word,* etc. Such verbalizations could be stored almost indefinitely and could be used to select the response at the appropriate time. In these experiments, and those on the visual trace, such information was all the subject had, as the conditions of presentation were extreme and at the critical interval the stimulus had still not been unambiguously identified. PAS, on the other hand, appears to be operating in a situation where the stimulus has already been clearly perceived once and, in several of the experiments to be described, actually rehearsed aloud. Murdock (1967) has suggested that what is stored in a short-term-memory experiment is an *experimental record,* which can be interpreted in a way similar to PAS. Other references in the literature to *acoustic stores* (e.g., Sperling, 1967; Brown, 1958; Cohen, 1967) fail to make a distinction between articulatory and acoustic effects and so differ from PAS.

THE APPLICATION OF PAS

The properties of PAS enable us to unify a number of experimental findings. These findings are mainly concerned with the immediate serial recall of short, unstructured lists of digits, letters or words at rates varying from .5 to 2.0 items per second. It should be noted that a large number of the findings to be described are consistent with each other inasmuch as any model that will account for one will account for many others. To a certain extent then, this accumulation of evidence is not intended to be interpreted as supporting the present model as compared with all others. The crucial distinction between the Logogen Model and others in the literature relates to the separation of PAS from the Response Buffer. Interference effects in PAS are dependent solely on physical similarity; those in the rest of the system can be functions of semantic similarity as well. There are in addition related differences in the treatment of rehearsal. The differences between various models will be enlarged upon in a later section. In the meantime, I will primarily attempt to show that the model is not inconsistent with a variety of data, and to show how certain data enable us to refine the model beyond its original, fairly loose form. The distinction between data that led to the formulation of PAS and the data that the model *predicts* is occasionally blurred —this corresponds to the state of the relevant information in my long-term memory at the time of writing.

AUDITORY VS. VISUAL PRESENTATION

After the presentation of a list of items the main difference between visual and auditory presentation will be that information relating to the last few items will be present in PAS. It is presumed that little or no useful information remains in the corresponding visual store either because the course of decay is too fast or because, unlike PAS, once a stimulus has been analyzed it is expunged from the system. Apart from PAS, then, according to the present, simplified view, there should be no difference. With either modality, the stimuli are recognized perfectly as they are presented and information concerning their nature is automatically transferred to the Cognitive System. Given that there is equal opportunity or lack of opportunity for silent rehearsal, the information in the Cognitive System should be identical irrespective of the modality. Knowing that performance following auditory presentation is superior we would expect from the model that the advantage, if it arose from PAS, would be restricted to the final serial positions. This is indeed the case (Corballis, 1966).

Figure 5 shows, in idealized form, the serial position error curves that have been found in the two situations (a number of actual data curves are given below). The two curves are instantly recognizable (a fact first pointed out to me by R. Conrad, in 1962). With auditory presentation, performance on the final items is as good as that on the first or second item;

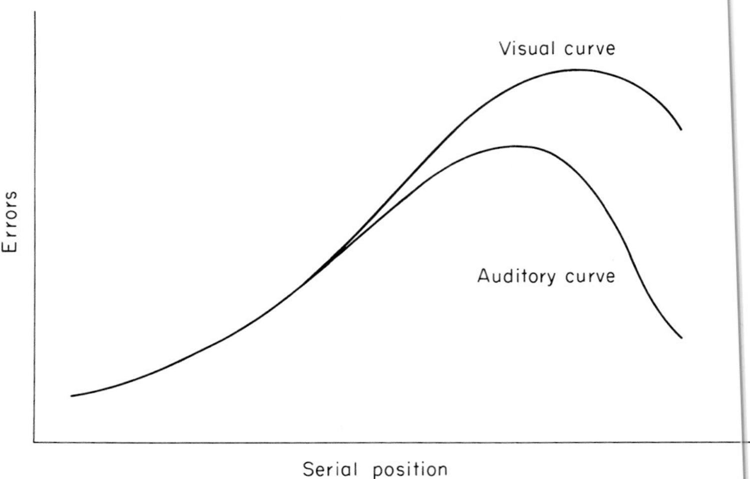

FIG. 5. Idealized serial position error curves following auditory and visual presentation of short, unstructured lists. The difference between the curves is taken to be the contribution of PAS.

with visual presentation, the final item is recalled no better than those in the middle of the list. There is little or no difference between the modalities in performance on the first half of the list. The simplest account of this is that there are (at least) two separate sources of information, one of which, the Cognitive System, reveals itself in the visual error curve. PAS is available only following auditory stimulation and information from it is combined with that from the Cognitive System.

There are at least two ways in which the information from PAS might be made available. It is possible that at the time of recall of a particular item information from the Cognitive System and PAS is combined in the Logogen System (which must always be involved in responses originating from the former systems). Alternatively, the material remaining in PAS after the list has been presented may be automatically sent to the Logogen System while earlier items are being recalled. Such a process could continue until the material has decayed. This repeated output from PAS would cause the appropriate logogen to send an output to the Cognitive System and increase the information there. It would not be necessary for there to be any conscious awareness of such a process. These alternatives, and possible reasons for the particular shape of the visual curve will be considered later.

VOCALIZATION AT PRESENTATION

A number of studies have involved subjects reading the stimuli out loud during visual presentation. Conrad and Hull (1968) presented lists of seven digits visually under conditions of silent rehearsal and vocal rehearsal. The items were then recalled in order of presentation. Their results, given in Fig. 6, show that there is an advantage for vocal rehearsal over the last three items in the list. Similar results have been found by Murray (1966) and Routh (1969). According to the present position, this difference would be accounted for by the information put into PAS following the acoustic feedback of the subject's voice, effectively converting visual presentation into auditory presentation. Further evidence that it is acoustic feedback that is relevant and not, for example, speech-motor feedback, is provided by an experiment of Murray (1965) who showed that vocal rehearsal does not appear to be advantageous when there is a level of acoustic noise in the environment sufficient to drown the subject's voice. Murdock (1967) using a probe technique, has compared visual and auditory presentation and noted that the difference between the modalities is less when the subjects vocalize at presentation. The differences, as with serial recall, were on the final items.

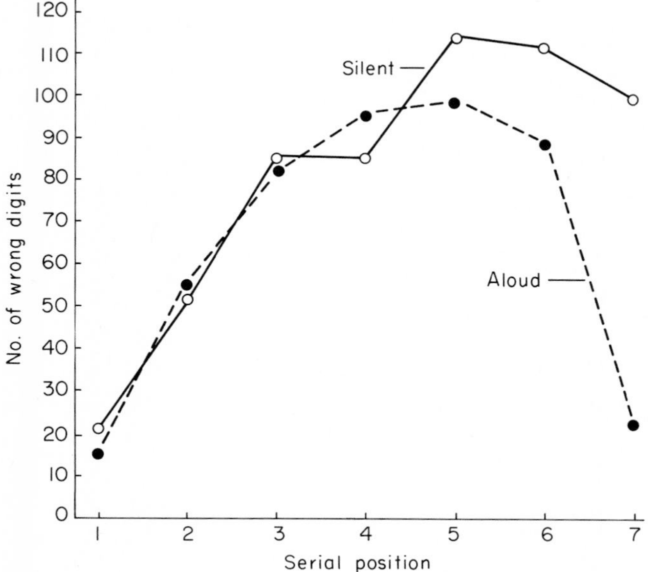

FIG. 6. The effects of silent and vocal rehearsal. (Adapted from Conrad and Hull, 1968.)

STIMULUS SUFFIX AND RESPONSE PREFIX

There have recently been a number of experiments which involved the occurrence of a predictable event between the auditory presentation of a stimulus string and the beginning of recall. In general, this event has either been the addition of the digit *zero* to every stimulus string without requiring a response, a *stimulus suffix*, or the addition of the response *zero* to the beginning of the recall string without it having been in the stimulus, a *response prefix*. The effects of these two seemingly equivalent events are totally different.

The stimulus suffix selectively affects subsequent recall, by far the greatest decrement in performance being on the final items (Crowder, 1967; Morton, 1968c). In effect, the suffix changes the recall curve from that characteristic of auditory presentation to a typical visual curve, though there is some smaller effect on the recall of early items. The response prefix, on the other hand, affects the recall of all the items in the list to the same extent. In Fig. 7 are shown the relevant data from Crowder (1967). On the final item, there is no significant difference in performance between the control condition and the prefix condition, while performance in the suffix condition is significantly worse. This difference means that the effects of the stimulus suffix and the response prefix must be given different explanations.

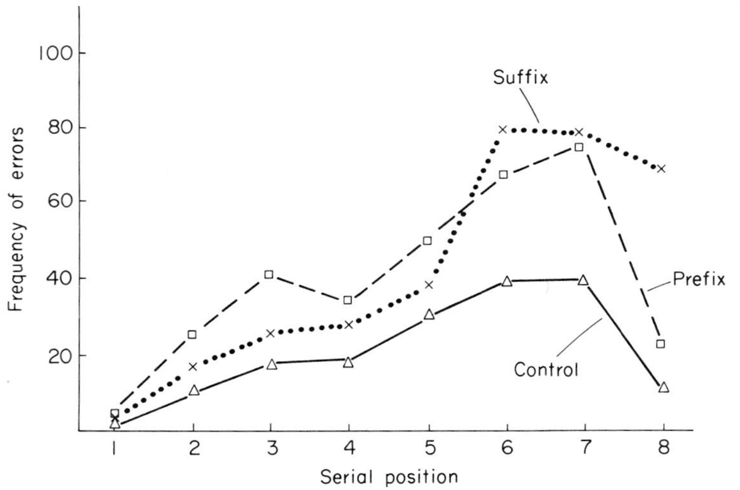

FIG. 7. The effects of a suffix and a prefix on serial recall of auditorily presented stimuli. (Adapted from Crowder, 1967.)

A variety of experiments, mainly by Conrad and by Crowder and his associates, make it clear that the effect of the response prefix comes in the making of the response and not at any other stage (Conrad, 1958, 1960; Crowder, 1967; Crowder and Erdman, 1968; Crowder and Hoenig, 1969). The effect of the stimulus suffix, on the other hand, appears to be most simply accounted for by assuming that it eliminates most of the information in PAS, by, as it were, acting as an additional stimulus item. It should be noted that merely saying the suffix has the same effect as an additional stimulus item does not in itself constitute an explanation, as the position of the additional item is crucial. This is made manifest by an experiment of Dallett (1965), who presented lists of seven items for serial recall. In different blocks of trials, a redundant *zero* was inserted in different positions in the list. When the *zero* was in the final position, performance was indistinguishable from performance on the first seven items of an eight-item list. In other serial positions, however, the redundant element facilitated recall, particularly on the adjacent items. These two effects are most conveniently given different kinds of explanation, the first being the typical PAS-suffix effect, and the other being due to associative phenomena in the Cognitive System.

The main effect of a stimulus suffix, greatly reduced performance on the final items, is consistent and instantly recognizable. It will hereafter be referred to simply as *the suffix effect.*

VOCALIZATION AT RECALL

It has to be supposed that the prefix, although vocalized, does not have a greater effect on the final items through acoustic feedback, because the subjects can partially exclude their own voice from PAS when it is advantageous to do so. The qualification appears to be necessary when vocal recall is compared with written recall. Murray (1966) showed that there was no difference between the two recall methods when the stimuli were presented visually and rehearsed silently but, when the stimuli were vocalized at presentation, recall on the last two items was significantly worse than when the recall was vocal. Crowder and Morton (1969) suggested that this was because the accumulation of acoustic feedback from the response interfered with material in PAS. The difference was very small compared with the suffix effect in spite of there being more potentially interfering events. It remained possible, then, that there was a very small selective effect of a vocalized prefix on the final items in a list that had not been detected. However, Crowder (personal communication) has replicated Murray's experiments and found that even with silent rehearsal performance was worse when the responses were vocalized. It would seem then as though some of the effects of vocal recall at least are not in PAS.

Further Properties of PAS

Since the suffix effect is so large it is a convenient tool to use to study the properties of PAS in more detail.

THE EFFECT OF PHYSICAL SIMILARITY

Recent experiments (Morton, Crowder and Prussin, 1969) indicate that the extent to which a suffix interferes with the final items in the list is a function of the degree of physical similarity between the stimulus list and the suffix. In these experiments, the stimulus was a list of eight or nine digits that had to be recalled serially. The suffix was always redundant and completely known to the subject. The first experiment showed that when the stimulus list was spoken in a male voice and the suffix in a female voice, the suffix effect was greatly reduced. In another study, the stimuli were presented visually under three conditions: with silent rehearsal, with vocal rehearsal, and with the experimenter vocalizing. Preliminary results suggest that when the subject prefixes his recall by speaking the redundant item *zero*, there is a greater effect on recall of the final item following vocal rehearsal than when the experimenter vocalizes. If the subject did not vocalize his rehearsal, the normal visual curve was found and the spoken *zero* prefix to the response had no selective effect on the final items.

These results confirm that the lack of an effect with the spoken prefix in the earlier experiments with auditory presentation was due to the difference between the experimenter's voice and the subject's voice. We do not at the moment know whether a second female voice speaking the suffix would have less effect than a male voice, when the stimulus sequence is spoken by a female, but we would expect this to be the case. It is possible that the disadvantage of vocal over silent rehearsal of auditorily presented material (Mackworth, 1964) can be accounted for in the same framework.

In a third experiment, the intensity of the suffix was increased until it was subjectively twice as loud as the stimulus items. The decrement on final items in this condition was less when the suffix was the same intensity. This suggests that at the point in the system where the effect takes place, intensity does not have an analog representation (such as the amount or extent of neural activity). Instead, it seems as if intensity is coded in some neutral way that can be selected or used as a basis for rejection in much the same way as voice characteristics.

THE LEVEL OF PAS

We have attributed the difference between auditory and visual presentation and the effect of vocalizing at presentation to use of material in the Auditory Analysis System, and we attribute the stimulus suffix effect to the elimination of that material. Within the Auditory Analysis System, there are, however, a number of aspects. To begin with, it is likely that speech features are extracted at a more central part of the system than are more simple acoustic properties such as intensity. One recent experiment has shown that when bursts of white noise of the same, or twice the subjective loudness as the stimuli were presented as suffixes (but not during the stimulus list) there was no effect. This suggests that PAS must be in a part of the Auditory Analysis System that only deals with speech. Further experiments with progressively more speechlike suffixes should help to further delimit PAS.

PAS AND THE TWO EARS

It is possible that PAS information is stored separately for the two ears instead of, or as well as, in a binaural store. Two experiments have tested the degree of laterality of PAS. In the first experiment, the stimulus list was presented monaurally. There were three conditions in which the suffix was presented on the same ear (Ipsilateral), or on the opposite ear (Contralateral) and a Control condition with no suffix. These results are shown in Fig. 8. In the Ipsilateral condition, we have the characteristic *visual* error curve. Performance in the Contralateral condition is superior over the last three items only, but is still worse than the Control condition ($p < .01$, Wilcoxon test).

One possible explanation of this result is given in Fig. 9. We can imagine that the Auditory Analysis System comprises three components, one specific to each ear and one common to the two ears, and that the information comprising PAS can be obtained from any or all of these. A monaural stimulus will lay down traces in the ear-specific part of the system and in the common part as indicated in Fig. 9a. The Ipsilateral

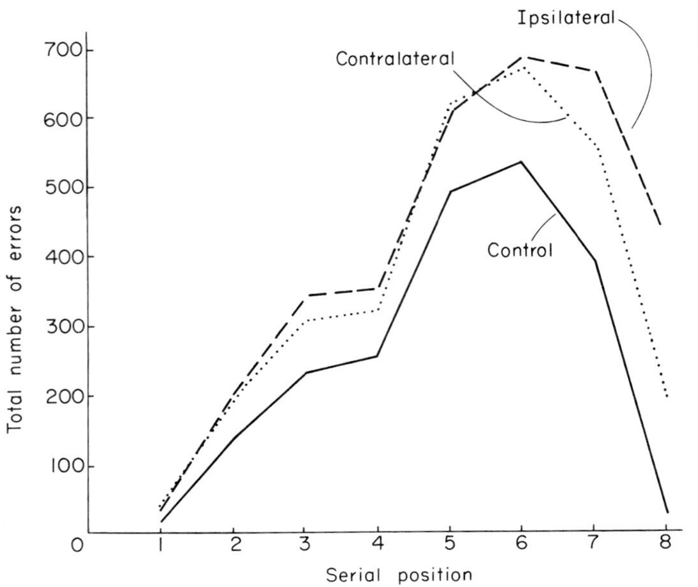

FIG. 8. The effects of a suffix on the same ear and on the opposite ear following monaural presentation. (From Morton *et al.*, 1969.)

suffix would affect both of these to give the visual-type curve. The Contralateral suffix would affect the common part of the system, thereby impairing performance compared with the control condition but would leave the other trace undisturbed, as symbolized in Fig. 9b. This form of analysis leads us to predict that the effect of a monaural suffix on the recall of a binaural stimulus would be intermediate between a binaural suffix and the control, no-suffix condition. The binaural stimulus would leave traces in all three of the components (Fig. 9c), all of which would be affected by the binaural suffix. The monaural suffix would leave one of the ear-specific components unaffected (Fig. 9d). Figure 10 shows the test of this prediction. As different subjects were used in this and the preceding study, no direct comparison can be made between the two sets of error curves. Qualitatively, however, the results fit in with the predictions from Fig. 9.

An interesting negative finding in these experiments is that it made no difference to which ear the stimulus was presented. Apparently the lateralized parts of PAS (if, that is, our characterization of the system is correct) are equivalent (cf. Kimura, 1961; Broadbent and Gregory, 1964a). Work on split-brain patients (Gazzaniga and Sperry, 1967; Sperry

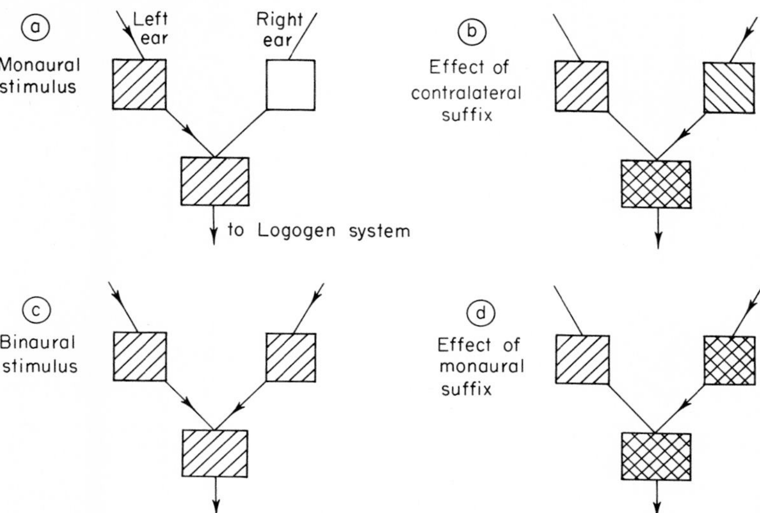

FIG. 9. A three-part PAS theory suggested to account for the differential effects of contralateral and ipsilateral suffixes following a monaural stimulus (*a* and *b*). In *c* and *d*, a prediction is made as to the effect of a monaural suffix on a binaural stimulus. Cross-hatching indicates those portions of PAS that are eliminated by the suffixes. (From Morton *et al.*, 1969.)

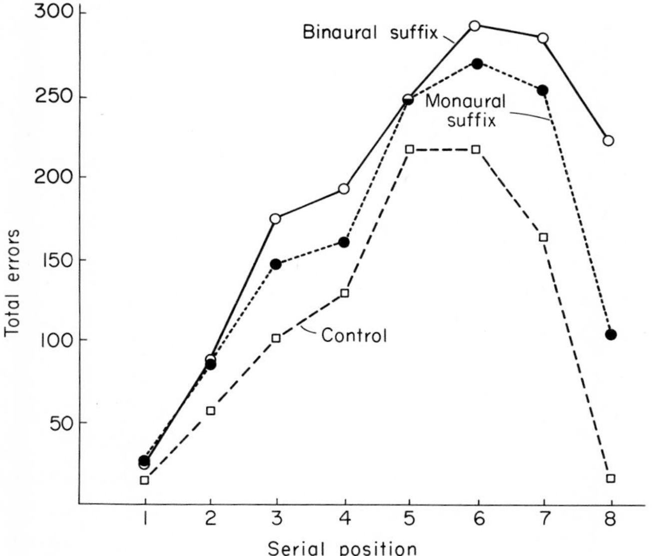

FIG. 10. The effects of a binaural and a monaural suffix on the recall of a binaurally presented stimulus list. (From Morton *et al.*, 1969.)

and Gazzaniga, 1967; Sperry, 1968) indicates that each hemisphere is capable of understanding words. These patients are advanced epileptics in whom much of the tissue joining the two hemispheres has been cut. It had hitherto been supposed that all language functions resided in the major (usually the left) hemisphere. If the name of some object, such as *eraser*, is presented to the left visual field, Sperry's patients, as we would have expected, will deny having seen anything except perhaps just a flash of light. They can, however, find the object from among a collection of other objects, though still without being able to say what the object is. Equally, the minor hemisphere is capable of understanding definitions such as *shaving instrument* for *razor*, though, as with visual presentation, the patients cannot say what it is they have found.

In terms of the present model, such results mean that both hemispheres are capable of performing at least some of the functions of the Logogen System and the Cognitive System. It appears that all the minor hemisphere lacks is the connection between the Logogen System and the Response Buffer. We are still left unclear as to the level or levels of stimulus analysis at which information is transferred from the minor to the major hemisphere in the intact brain nor do we know the nature of the information in the lateralized parts of PAS, but it is clear that any lateralized PAS could contain information of as deep a level of sensory analysis as was found necessary.

It should be noted that any conclusions that may be reached concerning the transfer of PAS information from one to the other hemisphere does not preclude additional transfer at other levels. The ipsilateral fibers from the ears to the auditory cortex presumably transfer relatively uncoded information. Thus, in Fig. 9 each of the lateralized parts of PAS will contain information from both ears (presumably in different proportions) and a monaural suffix would equivalently affect both of the lateralized parts. Equally, we have no reason to reject the possibility of semantic or associative information being used from both hemispheres at the time of recall.

THE TRANSFER OF INFORMATION FROM PAS

Crowder (1969) has produced data which indicate that material in PAS is completely transferred inside 2 sec. He presented subjects with nine digits for serial recall under five conditions, with a suffix either immediately, i.e., $\frac{1}{2}$ sec after the final digit, or after a delay of 2, 5, or 10 sec, and a control with no suffix. In the delay conditions,

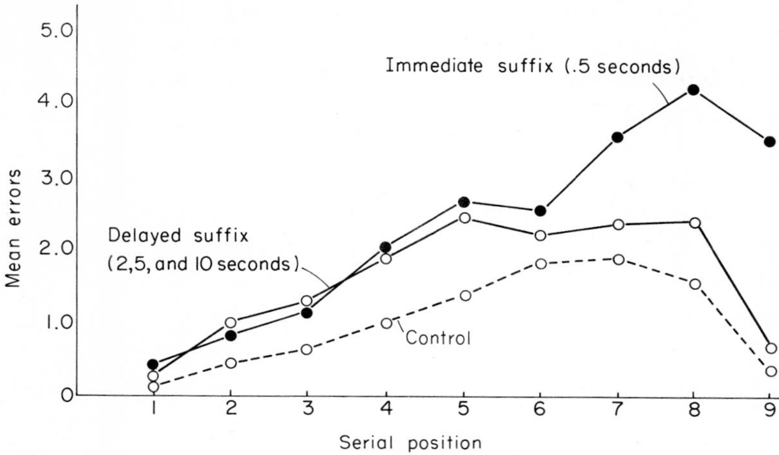

FIG. 11. The effect of delaying a suffix on an auditorily presented stimulus list. (From Crowder, 1969.)

the suffix was treated as a cue for recall. His data are presented in Fig. 11. Performances in the different delay conditions were indistinguishable and have been combined. First of all, it is clear that although the delayed suffix has an effect, only the immediate suffix showed the suffix effect. The difference between an immediate and a delayed suffix is over the last three items as was the change brought about by vocalization at presentation, (see Fig. 6).

Crowder also points out that the change in performance when the suffix is delayed provides another point of contrast with the response prefix since Conrad (1960) showed that delaying the prefix for up to 10 sec did not alleviate its effect. The subjects in Crowder's experiment were tested for five consecutive days. On the fifth day, after 60 trials of the immediate suffix and 180 trials in the delayed suffix conditions, the suffix effect was as great as it was on the first day. This confirms our suspicion that PAS is independent of behavioral strategies.

Parlett (1968) has provided some data that can also be interpreted as supporting the notion that material is transferred from PAS prior to recall. The experiments involved presenting interference material of three items between the presentation of a stimulus list and its serial recall. The interference material was presented after a gap of one second by which time the information in PAS could have been transferred. Parlett showed that when the stimulus material was recorded in a male voice, it made no difference whether the interference was in the same voice or in a female voice. Another of Parlett's experiments involved presenting interference material of a list of either letters or digits following a stimulus list of either letters or digits, the stimulus vocabulary being different from the interference vocabulary. The results showed that when the interference material was the same class as the stimulus material recall was worse. This pattern of results is opposite from the PAS-suffix findings. Accordingly, an explanation in terms other than PAS would seem to be appropriate.

PAS AND DECAY

Posner (1967) has suggested that information presented aurally is subject to simpler encoding than visually presented information. This would account for the finding that an increase in rate of presentation improves immediate memory of auditory material (Conrad and Hille, 1958; Posner, 1964; Mackworth, 1964, 1965; Howe, 1965) but depresses the recall of visually presented material (Mackworth, 1962; Murdock, 1963; Pollack, 1963). It is possible that Posner's explanation is at least partially correct (arguments based on a comparison of speed of reading with speed of listening beg a number of questions). It is also possible that, in addition to being subject to interference, material in PAS decays over time. If this were the case then for the higher rates of presentation there would be more usable information in PAS at the time of recall, leading to better performance (Crowder and Morton, 1969). In line with this, Murray (1965, 1966) has shown that vocalization at presentation is more effective at fast than slow rates of presentation. Note that it is not necessary to assume, as some authors do, that in a sensory store higher rates of presentation will inevitably lead to less information being available (e.g., Norman, 1966; Norman and Rumelhart, chapter 2). This would depend upon the trade-off between decay and capacity, and on the precise nature of the mechanism of displacement or overwriting. Since PAS does have a limited capacity, then if the effect of faster rates of presentation is to make more material available from PAS, the advantage of faster presentation rates should be reduced (or vanish) as the list length increases (Mackworth, 1965) or as the rate goes above an optimum (Aaronson, 1968). We would also expect the same limitations to operate on the advantage of vocalized rehearsal of visually presented items. Slow presentation rate, on the other hand, is likely to favor any condition in which a majority of the information is drawn from the Cognitive System (Posner, 1963, 1964).

The second finding that Posner (1967) cites in favor of his idea is that a subject's ability to delay the processing of one channel of information is better with auditory presentation (Broadbent, 1958; Bryden, 1964) than with visual (Sampson and Spong, 1961). Posner reports an unpublished study by himself and Warren in which this was confirmed directly. Pairs of digits were presented, one auditorily and one visually. Recall of the auditorily presented items was scarcely affected by whether they were recalled first or second. When the visual items were recalled second, however, the number of errors was greatly increased. Buschke (1962) and McGhie, Chapman, and Lawson (1965) have found similar effects with slightly different techniques. The operation of PAS is not inconsistent with such results.

PAS and Selective Attention

Many of the suffix results are strikingly analogous to results in selective attention. To start with, the effect of loudness has an analogy in the experiment of Egan, Carterette, and Thwing (1954). These authors required subjects to select one spoken message in the presence of a second, interfering message. The relative intensities of the two messages was varied, and in general, the louder was easier to follow than the softer. When one of the messages was slightly less intense than the interfering message, however, it was slightly easier to follow than when the two messages were of equal loudness.

The experiments by Anne Treisman provide a number of further points for comparison. Her technique involved the subjects shadowing one message in the presence of a second message. When the two messages were presented binaurally but from different speakers, one male one female, the interfering message was easier to ignore than when the same person spoke both messages, 74% words correct compared with 96% correct in the control condition with no interfering message (Treisman, 1964a). However, when the two messages were presented on opposite ears, there was scarcely any interference from the irrelevant message, even when the two voices were the same, 94% of the words being correctly reported (Treisman, 1964b). It might appear then that the results reported above on the effects of lateralization might be explained in terms of selective attention and Broadbent's (1958) filter model, rather than in terms of a three-part PAS system.

The crucial test is to present the stimulus list monaurally and the suffix binaurally. By analogy with Treisman's results, a filter model would predict better performance with a binaural suffix than with a monaural suffix, since the binaural nature of the suffix could be used as a means of its rejection. By the current theory, on the other hand, there should be no difference between the two suffix conditions since the binaural suffix would affect both the parts of PAS that carry information concerning the monaural stimulus. If there is no difference between the two suffix conditions then we can be fairly confident that PAS contains some lateralized component. If the bilateral suffix has a smaller effect such a notation would have to be abandoned.[4]

At first glance, it appears as though many of the suffix results could be explained in the same framework as those on selective attention. The lack of effect of noise, and when the suffix is at a different loudness or has a different location from the stimulus list could all be given some kind of explanation in terms of the cues available for selection prior to some filter system. In addition, the lack of a suffix effect following a delay could be explained by saying that the filter system had been given sufficient time to adjust its acceptance criteria. There are some problems, however, with such a formulation. To start with, Treisman's experiments showed that a message on the opposite ear scarcely affected performance at all, while a message in a male voice did affect shadowing of a female voice when the two were on the same ear. With the suffix effect, however, the amount of interference between the ears is at least as great as the interference from a voice of the opposite sex. Second, Treisman has shown that the greater the similarity in topic of an interfering message on the same ear the greater the effect. Such an effect is explicitly excluded from PAS. None of the existing suffix experiments are strictly analogous but we recently found no difference between the effect of the suffix *nought* and a condition using random English words. A suffix of the word *recall* had slightly less effect on the recall of the final digit than a binaural *nought* but a greater effect than the monaural *nought*. In addition, Morton (1968c) found the typical suffix effect with a digit following a letter string. This potential difference between the two experimental situations is not crucial since neither Broadbent nor Treisman explain the effect of differences in *response set* (i.e., letters vs. digits) or topic in the same way as they explain the effects of dichotic presentation (Treisman, 1960, 1964a, 1964b; Broadbent and Gregory, 1963, 1964b). In any case, there is one major difference between the

[4] These experiments have now been carried out and with a monaural stimulus there is no difference between the effects of a contralateral suffix and a binaural suffix. The model suggested in Fig. 9 is therefore incorrect.

two paradigms: in shadowing, a message is being ignored while a second message is being received; in the suffix situation, the subjects are instructed to ignore what is effectively the only stimulus present. This contrast is illustrated most obviously by the fact that noise inevitably will affect performance in shadowing, but has not the slightest effect as a suffix.

Response Buffer

Differences between PAS and the Response Buffer

It was suggested above that a number of items can be held in the Response Buffer. These items will always be the last few items made available by the Logogen System. Thus both the Response Buffer and PAS contain information about the last few items. The differences between the two sources are important. In the first place, PAS only contains information following acoustic stimulation. Second, from the comparison of the visual and auditory curves and the effect of the suffix, PAS only contains information about the final three items. Of these, there is most about the last item, less about the penultimate item and very little on the one before that. The Response Buffer, on the other hand, has a greater capacity, and has equivalent amounts of information concerning all the items in it. As previously defined, interference in PAS is a function only of physical similarity. In the Response Buffer, since it is involved in rehearsal, interference is less restricted. Indeed, it takes over some of the functions of a limited capacity system (Broadbent, 1963). As Broadbent remarks, the interference effects in short-term memory "do not seem to depend very much on the nature of the intervening activity," which can be almost any kind of performance "provided that it represents a high rate of information transmission through the nervous system." In this respect, also, it differs from PAS. In the discussion that follows, an attempt will be made to point out the conditions in which one, the other or both information sources are involved.

COMBINATION OF INFORMATION FROM THE RESPONSE BUFFER AND PAS

If recall is serial, information from the Response Buffer cannot be used by the subject, and will be eliminated by the act of recalling items which occur at the beginning of the list. Other types of experiment or instruction, however, would permit information in the Response Buffer to be used. For example, Posner (1964) presented his subjects with eight letters for recall under two conditions. One condition involved normal serial recall; in the other condition, semibackwards recall, the subjects recalled the last four items first and then the first four. With serial recall, his error curves were normal; in the other condition, there was scarcely any errors on the last four items, i.e., the first to be recalled. Murdock (1968) has replicated this result and also showed the effect to be reduced if the subject does not know till after the stimulus which recall method he is to use.

The technique has been used with two variations to test the hypothesis that with semibackwards recall, in spite of the major Response

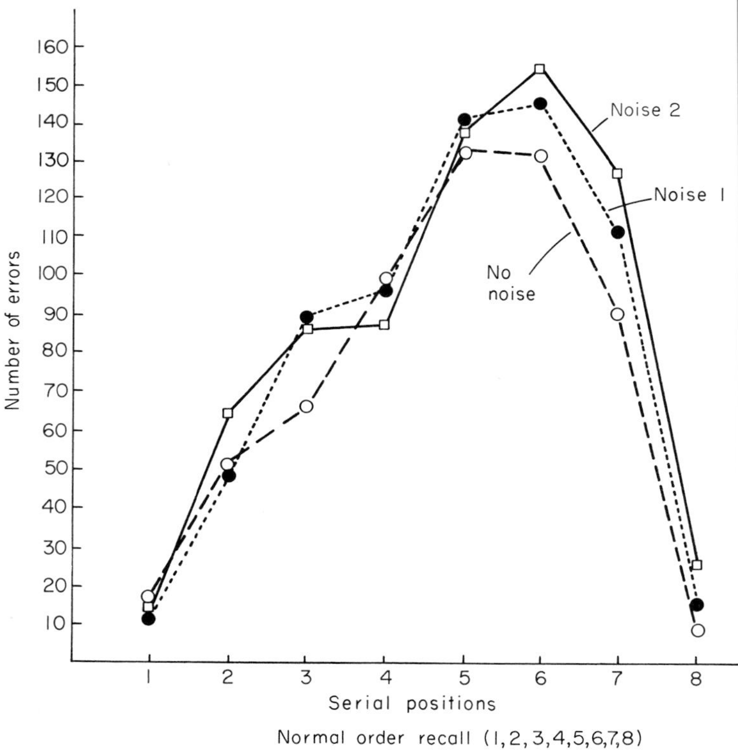

FIG. 12. The effects of low levels of noise on serial recall of auditorily presented stimulus lists. Only on serial positions 7 and 8 are there significant differences between the conditions. (From Morton *et al.*, 1969.)

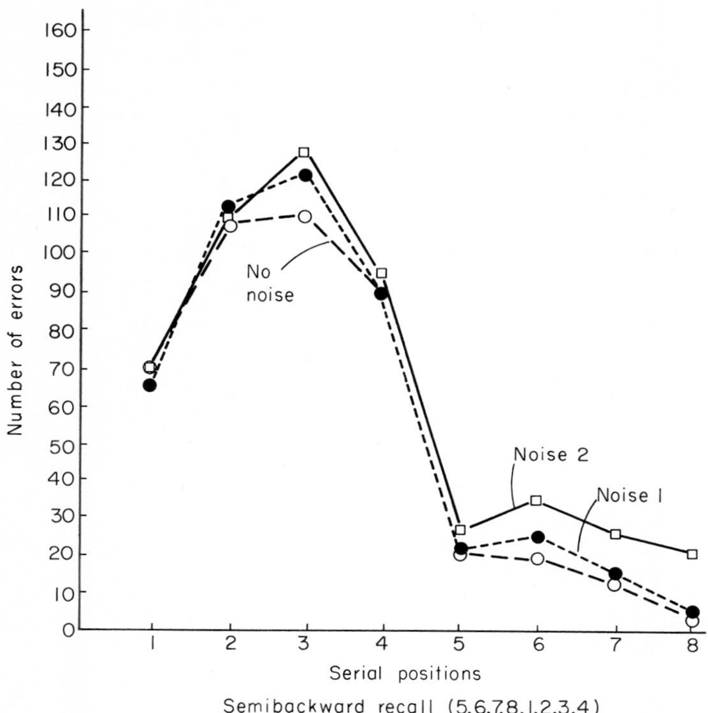

FIG. 13. The effects of low levels of noise on semibackwards recall of auditorily presented stimulus lists. Only on stimulus items 7 and 8 are there significant differences between the conditions. (From Morton *et al.*, 1969.)

Buffer effect, there would be some PAS information available for the final items. In the first of these experiments, subjects were presented with lists of eight digits auditorily. For both recall methods there were three conditions. In two of these conditions the stimuli were played through two levels of noise, the more intense of which was judged to have a negligible effect on intelligibility. In the control condition, there was no noise. The hypothesis was that the noise would increase the effective decay rate in PAS and so affect performance in the final stimulus items. The results are shown in Figs. 12 and 13 and the general shape of the curves agree with Posner's findings. The effects of noise were only significant on the last two stimulus items irrespective of their position of recall.

In the second experiment, eight consonants were presented simultaneously for 2.5 sec and the subjects either read them silently or aloud. Recall was either silent or vocal, serial or semibackwards. The general pattern of the serial recall results agreed with previous findings, with vocalized recall producing the auditory error curve and vocalized recall affecting both silent and vocalized presentation. With semibackwards recall, the pattern was different. The general shapes of the curves were the same as in Fig. 13, showing that the effect of the Response Buffer is not dependent on the modality of the stimuli. The seventh and last stimulus items were, however, recalled worse with silent presentation than with vocalized presentation. The effects of vocalized recall, on the other hand, were restricted to the first four stimulus items, i.e., the last to be recalled.

These results indicate that information in PAS can be combined not only with information in the cognitive system, as suggested above, but also with information in the Response Buffer.

The Response Buffer in Other Recall Techniques

RUNNING MEMORY

In the standard running-memory-span experiment, (Pollack, Johnson, and Knaff, 1959), subjects are presented with a list of items of unknown length. When the list ends, the subject recalls as many items from the end of the list as possible under free recall conditions. With digit stimuli, Crowder and Morton (1969, Expt. I) discovered that subjects could not recall more than five or six items, and rarely made mistakes on the last three items. This is consistent with the hypothesis that material in the Response Buffer is read out first. The two experimental conditions in this experiment involved a stimulus suffix and a response prefix. The stimulus suffix had a small but significant selective effect on the last items in the list indicating, in line with the semibackwards recall data, that some material from PAS was used in the control and prefix conditions.

Free Recall

It has often been observed that when the subject is unconstrained as to the order in which he produces the stimuli, he produces first and best the most recently presented items, (Murdock, 1962; Postman and

Phillips, 1965; Baddeley, 1968a). Representative data are illustrated elsewhere in this volume. In the current model, this would be equated with the results in the previous two sections, the subject being supposed to respond with the items in the Response Buffer. This kind of explanation is similar to that put forward by other people (see below). From the preceding discussion we would predict certain results in free recall. The data from the semibackwards recall and the running memory span experiments indicated that information from PAS could be combined with that from the Response Buffer. Accordingly we would expect that there would be a small advantage of auditory over visual presentation with free recall. Without continued recirculation via the Logogen System, material in the Response Buffer would not be maintained. Thus, we would also predict that intervening activity which prevented rehearsal would result in the final items no longer being recalled best (Postman and Phillips, 1965) nor first (Baddeley, 1968a).

PROBE TECHNIQUES

Much the same line of argument can be applied to account for the serial position curves obtained using the various probe techniques. With the probe technique, the subject is presented with a list of items following which one of the items (a probe) is presented to him and he has to respond with the item that followed the probe in the list. Alternatively, the subject is asked to give the serial position of the cued item or the cue can be the serial position of the item required for recall. Waugh and Norman (1965) showed that recall in the probe situation was a monotonic function of serial position, with the more recent items being recalled better than earlier ones. These authors did not test recall of the first few items and so any primacy effect was obscured. Murdock (1968) did find a primacy effect and showed that the position of worse recall was earlier in the list with the probe technique than with serial recall. In the present frame of reference, such a finding would be accounted for by two factors. First, with serial recall, performance on later items is reduced owing to the effects of preceding responses (by analogy with the prefix effect); with the probe technique, this disadvantage would be eliminated. Second, information concerning the last few items could be obtained from the Response Buffer, a source that, as has been pointed out, is not available with serial recall. Consistent with other results, Jahnke and Erlick (1968) and Baddeley (1968b) showed a reduction or elimination of recency with delay using the probe technique.

From the model we would also expect to find a slight advantage of auditory presentation over visual presentation for the last few items, and no difference on the early items. The data do not confirm this expectation. Murdock (1966) found visual presentation with vocalization at presentation inferior to auditory presentation in the penultimate item and superior on the first few items. He later showed that when visually presented material was rehearsed silently performance was worse than for auditory presentation over the whole list (Murdock, 1967). Norman (1966) showed there were no differences between modalities in the rates of decay of information. The model is clearly not ready to account for the results found with this technique.

The Response Buffer in Relation to Other Models

The Response Buffer has its parallels in other models. It resembles Reitman's "waiting room" (chapter 5), and the Memory Buffer of Atkinson and Shiffrin (1965). One difference from the "waiting room" is that the Response Buffer is the only way to the response mechanisms. In Reitman's model, the Sensory Register, the Working Memory, and Long-Term Memory all have direct access to the response mechanisms. The properties of Atkinson and Shiffrin's Memory Buffer almost without exception apply to the Response Buffer:

1. The buffer has a limited capacity of *items*
2. Items in the store are ordered temporally
3. After the buffer has been filled it stays filled as long as the subject is paying attention (to its contents)
4. Each entering item bumps out an old item
5. Items are always encoded correctly when initially placed in the buffer (as long as inputs are not too fast)
6. Items still in the buffer at the time of test are recalled perfectly
7. An item transferred to a long-term store is still represented in the buffer.

All these properties apply to the Response Buffer. There are, though, some differences of detail between the models in the operation of the buffer and of the rest of the system. It is interesting, however, that in fitting a variety of data, they estimate the capacity of their buffer as being four or five items. This corresponds to the size of the eye–voice span, the original reason for postulating the Response Buffer.

PRIMARY MEMORY

Waugh and Norman (1965) have accounted for some of the results discussed above by invoking *Primary Memory,* which clearly resembles the Response Buffer in its properties. One difference is that Primary Memory comes before Secondary (i.e., Long Term) Memory in the flow of information. The Response Buffer on the other hand in certain respects follows the Cognitive System. In a more recent paper, Norman (1968) has suggested that Primary and Secondary Memory have the same location and constitute a dual-process storage system. Norman's model for attention and memory has close affinities to the Logogen Model in its principles of function. One difference is in the potential use of precategorical storage of auditory information, which Norman does not stress. In a recent paper, Norman (1969) shows that subjects shadowing English words can recognize digits that are presented to the other ear if they are tested immediately. He then claims that the results show that verbal material presented on the nonattended channels gets into Primary Memory. In the present model, this function of Primary Memory. In the present model, this function of Primary Memory could be taken by PAS. The problem is a complex one, however (Deutsch and Deutsch, 1963; Treisman and Geffin, 1967; Deutsch, Deutsch, Lindsay, and Treisman, 1967) and further discussion will have to be postponed.

ARTICULATORY VS. ACOUSTIC CONFUSIONS

The Response Buffer is seen as having the primary function of allowing the production of speech to be programmed efficiently. This being so, it has been assumed that material in the Response Buffer is coded in some phonological units. Confusion errors that occur in the Response Buffer, either in the course of silent rehearsal or in output, should be describable in terms of phonological parameters. Such error patterns have been described both by Conrad (1962, 1964) and Wickelgren (e.g., 1965) for visually presented material. These errors have sometimes been called *acoustic confusions* with the implication that visual information is converted into acoustic information, a model which will be considered below. I have previously suggested (Morton, 1964c) that a more appropriate term would be *articulatory confusions.* Hintzman (1965, 1967) claimed to have produced evidence that appears to substantiate this distinction. Unfortunately, it is difficult to accept his evidence owing to a rather acute conceptual problem. Hintzman's paper showed that in memory for visually presented letters, errors of *place*, such as reporting *B* for *D* or *P* for *T*, occurred more often than errors of *voicing*, such as *P* for *B*. This result he contrasted with Conrad's (1962) and Miller and Nicely's (1955) auditory confusion matrices in which errors of place rarely occur compared with those of voice. Conrad's confusion matrix was obtained by playing spoken letters in white noise. People wishing to support the position that visually presented items are recoded into an acoustic store would claim that the errors are caused by noise or decay in that store. We have no reason to assume, however, that the noise would be *white* or the pattern of the decay random with respect to frequency. As it is possible to produce different patterns of acoustic confusion by using noise with different characteristics (see Miller and Nicely, 1955), we have no way of knowing that our acoustic experiment is the appropriate control. On the other hand, neither are we justified in saying that "the same confusions occur in both cases," (Neisser, 1967). We are left, then, with the logic of our choice. Neisser also says that Hintzman's claim "boils down to an argument for the motor theory of speech perception" (Neisser, 1967, p. 224). This conclusion seems unwarranted in the light of the present model, which supports Hintzman in principle and explicitly rejects the motor theory of speech perception.

In summary, then, the current argument is that items presented visually have to be coded semantically—the province of the cognitive system—and are required in a form from which a response can be made which, in the present system, is an articulatory code in the Response Buffer. If such a system, required for any account of general language behavior, can cope with data on memory, there is no need to postulate *acoustic* coding to do so. The fact that Wickelgren (1965, 1966a, 1966b) has achieved some success in accounting for confusions in memory in terms of distinctive features is largely irrelevant to the present discussion. Neisser (1967) has interpreted Wickelgren's results as representing "an explicit link between speech perception and immediate memory." One might just as well, and with different conclusions, claim that Wickelgren's results represent an explicit link between speech *production* and immediate memory. An attempt has been made to describe the acoustics of speech in terms of distinctive features (Jacobson, Fant, and Halle, 1951), but more recent work has not followed this up and has concentrated instead on regarding distinctive features as the essential element in speech production (Chomsky and Halle, 1968).

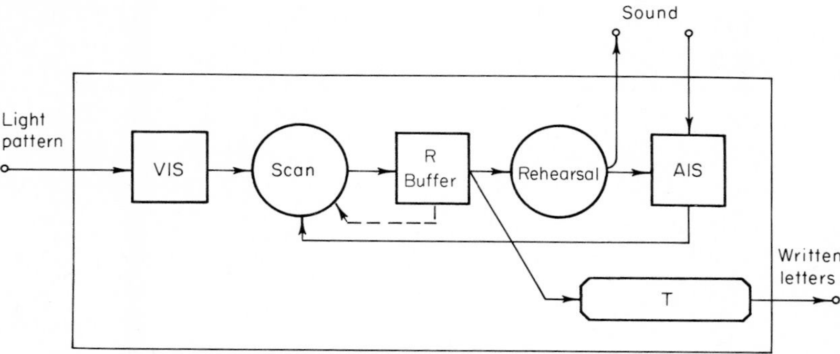

FIG. 14. Sperling's model for memory (1967). The crucial feature for the present discussion is that visual information can be transferred to the auditory information storage (AIS) a feature prohibited in the Logogen Model.

There are, however, other difficulties with models that suggest acoustic storage of visually as well as acoustically present items. One such model, due to Sperling (1967) is shown in Fig. 14. In this model, it is difficult to see at what point there might be an advantage for auditory as compared to visually presented material. The usual explanation is that visually presented material, owing to the necessity of an extra stage of coding, is less efficiently stored in the acoustic store (Posner, 1967; Sperling, 1967; Murdock, 1967). Even if this were the case, we would expect acoustic material to interfere with the acoustic representation of the visual material. In particular, by analogy with the results with auditorily presented material, we would expect that an auditory suffix would selectively affect recall of the final items. Crowder and Morton (1969, Expt. II) showed that this was not the case. In this experiment, however, there was scarcely any effect at all of the acoustic suffix and it might be argued that the subjects were successfully directing their attention to prevent the suffix from entering the acoustic store. Accordingly, Morton and Holloway (1970) repeated this experiment under conditions that ensured that the subjects paid attention to the suffix. The stimulus was a sequence of six visually presented digits for serial recall. There were four conditions, each presented in a block. In one of the conditions, half the subjects had to prefix their recall with a tick and half with a cross. In the second condition, the stimulus was followed by an auditory suffix (the experimenter called out *tick* or *cross* at random) which had to be ignored. In the third condition, the suffix had to be re-

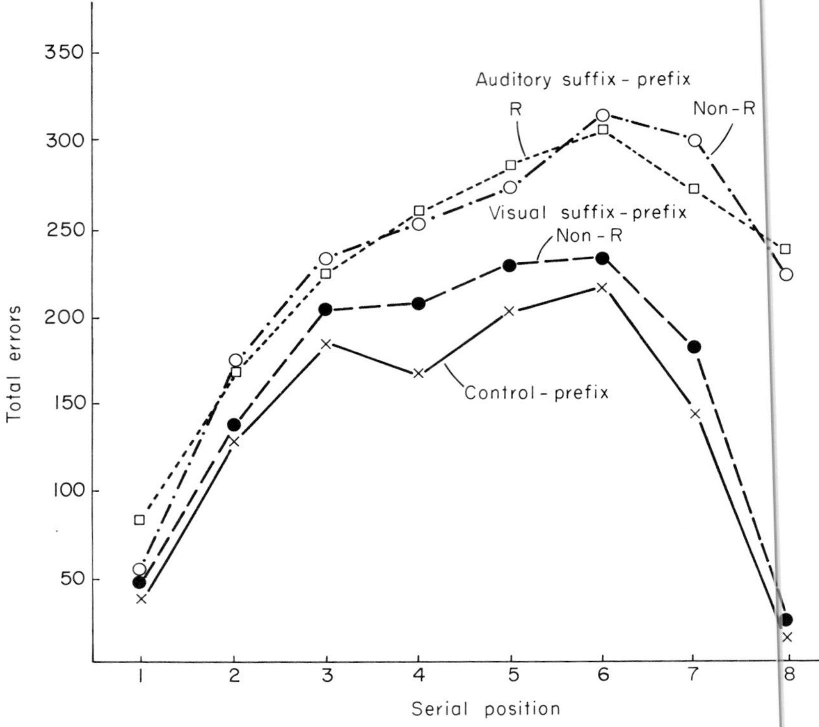

FIG. 15. The effects of a prefix, an auditory suffix, and an auditory suffix–prefix (i.e., a nonredundant suffix that had to be copied by the subject). The characteristic *suffix effect* is absent. (From Morton and Holloway, 1970.) Presentation was visual.

sponded to by the subjects—in effect, it acted both as a stimulus suffix and a response prefix. The last condition was a control condition in which recall was delayed, without interference, for a time equivalent to the response delay in other conditions. The results of this experiment are shown in Fig. 15. The effect of the suffix is almost indistinguishable from that of the prefix, in contrast with the equivalent auditory experiment (see Fig. 7). In addition, in the suffix plus prefix condition, which ensured complete processing of the suffix, there is an equivalent decrement over the prefix condition over all serial positions (except the first which is always good with serial recall). Thus, it seems clear that an acoustic suffix does not interfere with the visual stimulus in the same way as it does with an acoustic stimulus. In Sperling's model, there does not appear to be a way of accounting for this.

In two other experiments, Morton and Holloway showed that a visual suffix has no serial position effect on memory for acoustic material. In the first of these, a list of eight digits was spoken. Following the stimulus list there were four conditions. The control condition involved the subject prefixing his response with always either a tick or a cross. Following the stimulus in the second condition, the experimenter held up a card on which was either a tick or a cross. The subjects had to copy this symbol before recalling the stimulus. This could be regarded as a suffix–prefix condition. In two other conditions, the experimenter spoke the suffix that the subjects had to copy before recalling the stimulus list; in one block of trials the suffix was redundant, the subject theoretically did not have to listen to it but could have merely treated the condition as a prefix condition; in the second block of trials the suffix was randomized and the subjects were instructed to make sure that they copied the correct symbol. The results of this experiment are shown in Fig. 16. To start with, there is only a very small effect of the visual

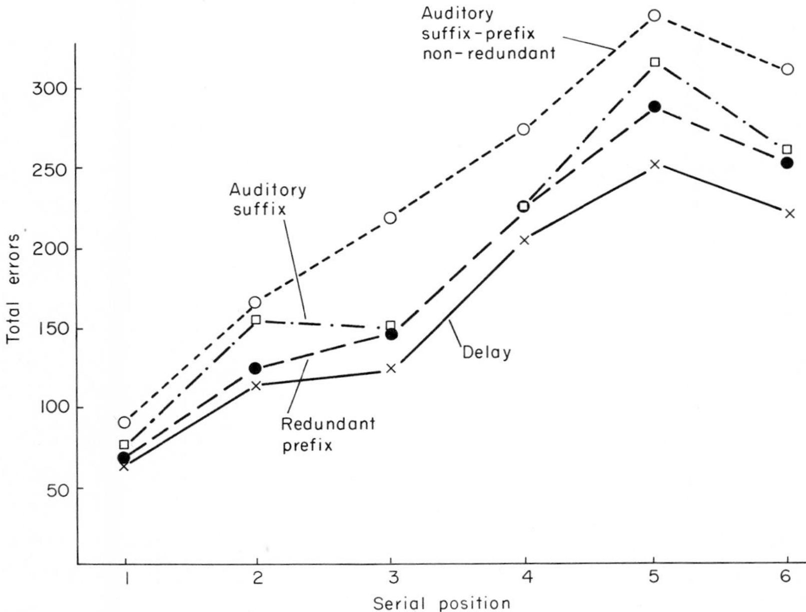

FIG. 16. The effects of a suffix–prefix are compared with the effect of a redundant prefix. A nonredundant visual suffix–prefix has no serial position effect; with the auditory suffix–prefix has no serial position effect; with the auditory suffix-prefix it makes no difference whether the item is redundant or nonredundant. (From Morton and Holloway, 1970.) Presentation was auditory.

suffix–prefix. The difference in error rate from the prefix condition was only significant when the errors over all serial positions were pooled. Second, the auditory suffix had as big an effect when it could be ignored as when it had to be attended to.

There remained the possibility that the absence of a suffix effect with the visual suffix was because the symbols of tick and cross could be simply copied with a minimum of recoding. This was tested by repeating the first two conditions of the preceding experiment but with the words "TICK" or "CROSS" presented as the suffix. As before, this suffix hardly affected recall. Sperling's model, however, makes no provision for excluding visually presented items from the acoustic store, and from such a model we would have to predict a suffix effect in these experiments.

It would, of course, be possible to modify such a model to account for these data while still preserving the notion of acoustic representation of visual stimuli. This could be done by dividing the *Acoustic Store* into two parts with different access channels to the two parts. With the current extension of the Logogen Model, however, such a step is unnecessary.

Cognitive System

The Cognitive System represents what most people call the long-term store. As such many of its properties are discussed in other papers in this volume; one occasional difference is that in other accounts certain features are sometimes ascribed to long-term memory, which in the Logogen Model would be properties of the Response Buffer.

Coding in the Cognitive System

Material in the Cognitive System is primarily coded in a semantic form. The structure of this code is not completely clear but would be contingent upon linguistic considerations (see Lyons, 1968). Kintsch (chapter 11) discusses one system of coding that is compatible with the present model with one exception. He suggests that each word is encoded in memory as a list of markers which are of three kinds, semantic, phonological, and sensory. These markers can be identified with *attributes* in the present model. While it has already been admitted that the Cognitive System will have to incorporate some sensory coding, it is not certain that there must be phonological representation. The suggestion that semantic and phonological codes are coexistent in a Long-Term Store resembles Chomsky's formulation for the structure of *lexical items* in his grammar (see Chomsky, 1967, for the simplest account). In the Logogen Model, semantic and phonological descriptions are related through the Logogen System which acts as a transducer between the codes (see Morton, 1968a, for further discussion). Effects in experiments on memory which have been related to phonological descriptions would here be attributed to the Response Buffer.

The Contribution of the Cognitive System

No attempt will be made here to separate out the functionally distinct units of the Cognitive System. There must however, be a difference between the way in which a speech for a play is stored and the way in which we store information concerning the psychology of memory, to give one clearcut example.

Phenomena such as clustering in free recall (Mandler, 1968), the effects of semantic confusability in long-term memory (Baddeley and Dale, 1966), and the use of idiosyncratic recall cues are all attributed to the Cognitive System. In addition, associative effects and phenomenon such as primacy and finality are considered to originate from the Cognitive System. The finality effect is to be seen in the serial recall curves for visually presented material. It is to be distinguished from recency effects, which are seen in the serial recall curves for visually presented material and in free recall and probe experiments, which are here attributed to the operation of either PAS or the Response Buffer, depending on the experimental conditions. The crucial distinction is that finality effects are a function of position and recency effects are a function of time (Crowder and Morton, 1969).

Since associative phenomena are restricted to the Cognitive System, we would expect indices of associative influence in recall to sharply differentiate recall of the final items following auditory presentation. One such measure has been used by Murdock (1968) who plotted the probability of an item in a particular serial position being correct separately for those cases where the preceding item had been recalled correctly and for those where it was incorrect. Following an error, the probability of a correct response was substantially lower at all except the final position. As such a result is here attributed to information concerning the final item being drawn from PAS, we predict that when visual presentation is used, or when PAS information is eliminated with a suffix, such a differentiation of the final item would not occur. Accordingly, Morton and Holloway (1969) plotted data from their experiments in the same way as Murdock. In Fig. 17, these data are shown. On the left-hand side are data from one of the auditory experiments. The control condition gives results similar to those of Murdock. The suffix–prefix condition differs from this mainly in the last two serial positions following an error. This indicates that recall of these items is susceptible to sequential effects in the suffix condition. On the right-hand side of Fig. 17 are the data from the visual control condition. These curves, from a different group of subjects, show the expected effect.

Since material in the Cognitive System is coded in some *semantic* form we would expect that the acoustic confusability of a stimulus list would have no effect in Long-Term Memory (Baddeley, 1966a, 1968a). However, since the Cognitive System is used in short-term memory, we would expect the semantic confusability of the stimuli to have some effect over short retention intervals (Baddeley, 1964, 1966a,b; Baddeley and Dale, 1966). We would however have to predict that such effects would be greater in the first parts of the list, especially with auditory presentation. The relevant data do not seem to be available.

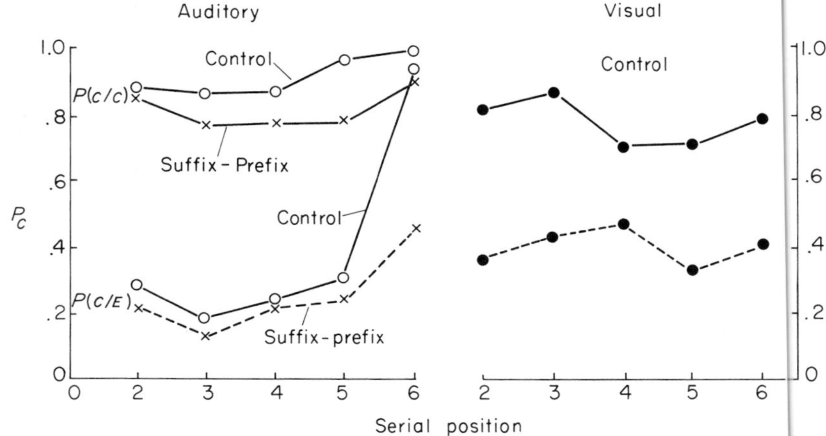

FIG. 17. Conditional effects in serial recall. The functions plotted are the probability of being correct in a particular serial position given that the preceding item was recalled correctly, $P(C|C)$, and given that the preceding item was recalled incorrectly, $P(C|E)$. Only recall of the final item in the auditory control condition appears to be independent of the recall of the preceding item.

Logogen System

The Logogen System is primarily a device for converting sensory information into semantic or phonological information (in language recognition) for converting phonological information into semantic information (in the case of silent rehearsal) and for converting semantic into phonological information (in speech production). Any influence on memory can only be a property of the sluggishness of the system. It is, of course, possible that we can estimate the relative frequencies of occurrence of different words by examining the levels of the critical counts, but that is a rather special kind of *memory*. It should be emphasized that the Logogen System can in no way be regarded as an associative net. There is no direct way of transferring information from one logogen to another. All associative phenomena that involve any semantic relationship are seen at the moment as proceeding via the Cognitive System.

In the original model, information that enters the Logogen System decays with time. It is uncertain at the moment whether the contribution of this information could be very great in the normal memory experiment. However, Morton (1968d) demonstrated a result which is not easily accounted for within any of the other constructs. In this experiment, lists of 16 to 20 single digits were presented to the subjects. At the end of each list, two of the digits were presented to the subject whose task was to state which of the two test digits had appeared most recently. Accuracy in this task is a function of the number of digits between the more recent of the two test digits and the test and also of the number of digits between the two test digits in the list. In the control condition, the test digits only occurred once each in the list. In the main experimental condition, the first of the two test digits had occurred earlier. Two sample lists might be:

Control: 6,8,3,1,8,3,4,**2**,9,**7**,4,8,4,0,1 . . .:2 or 7?
Experimental: 6,8,3,1,8,**2**,4,**2**,9,**7**,4,8,4,0,1 . . .:2 or 7?

Any purely associative theory would have to predict that performance on the experimental list would be superior since the second occurrence of the **2** should add supportive evidence. The Logogen Model, however, makes the opposite prediction. With lists of the length illustrated, the only information relevant to the decision which is required would be the decaying information in the logogens. The logogen that had the more residual information would be judged to be that which occurred more recently. When the earlier digit is repeated, however, the appropriate logogen would have an extra increment of strength since each occurrence of the same item has to be processed by the same logogen. Thus, in the example, for the Control list the strength of the **7**-logogen would be greater than that of the **2**-logogen. In the Experimental list, on the other hand, the information in the **2**-logogen at the time of test would be greater than in the Control condition. The data showed that the prediction from the Logogen Model was upheld. Performance in the Experimental condition was inferior to that in the control condition. A similar result was found by Fozard and Yntema (1966). These authors used pictures as the stimuli, and the time-scale of the experiment was much greater than that of the one just reported. Thus, it would be difficult to attribute their result to effects in the Logogen System. There is no reason to suppose, however, that decay phenomena with a relatively long time scale do not occur in the Cognitive System (see Wickelgren, chapter 3).

Conclusions

Only a few of the complexities of Memory have been discussed. However, the Logogen Model does seem capable of leading us to certain meaningful distinctions between sources of information in memory and of accounting for certain gross effects. In addition, it is sufficiently different from alternative models of information processing to enable different predictions to be made. But beyond a certain point, its method of functioning will have to be made more explicit. The only real conclusion of this chapter is that only a multiple-stage model will have a hope of succeeding.

References

Aaronson, D. Temporal course of perception in an immediate recall task. *Journal of Experimental Psychology,* 1968, **76,** 129–140.

Atkinson, R. C., and Shiffrin, R. M. Mathematical models for memory and learning. Technical Report No. 79, Institute for Mathematical Studies in the Social Sciences, Stanford University, 1965.

Averbach, E., and Coriell, A. S. Short-term memory in vision. *Bell System Technical Journal,* 1961, **40,** 309–328.

AVERBACH, E., AND SPERLING, G. Short-term storage of information in vision. In E. C. Cherry (Ed.), *Fourth London symposium on information theory.* London and Washington, D. C.: Butterworth, 1961.

BADDELEY, A. D. Semantic and acoustic similarity in short-term memory. *Nature,* 1964, **204,** 1116–1117.

BADDELEY, A. D. The influence of acoustic and semantic similarity on long-term memory for word sequences. *Quarterly Journal of Experimental Psychology,* 1966, **18,** 362–365. (a)

BADDELEY, A. D. Short-term memory for word sequences as a function of acoustic, semantic, and formal similarity. *Quarterly Journal of Experimental Psychology,* 1966, **18,** 362–365. (b)

BADDELEY, A. D. Prior recall of newly learned items and the recency effect in free recall. *Canadian Journal of Psychology,* 1968, **22,** 157–163. (a)

BADDELEY, A. D. Delay and the digit probe. *Psychonomic Science,* 1968, **12,** 147–148. (b)

BADDELEY, A. D., AND DALE, H. C. A. The effect of semantic similarity on retroactive interference in long- and short-term memory. *Journal of Verbal Learning and Verbal Behavior,* 1966, **5,** 417–420.

BRICKER, P. D., AND CHAPANIS, A. Do incorrectly perceived tachistoscopic stimuli convey some information? *Psychological Review,* 1953, **60,** 181–188.

BROADBENT, D. E. *Perception and communication.* New York: MacMillan (Pergamon), 1958.

BROADBENT, D. E. Flow of information within the organism. *Journal of Verbal Learning and Verbal Behavior,* 1963, **2,** 34–39.

BROADBENT, D. E. Word frequency effect and response bias. *Psychological Review,* 1967, **74,** 1–15.

BROADBENT, D. E., AND GREGORY, M. Division of attention and the decision theory of signal detection. *Proceedings of the Royal Society (London),* 1963, **B158,** 222–231.

BROADBENT, D. E., AND GREGORY, M. Accuracy of recognition for speech presented to the right and left ears. *Quarterly Journal of Experimental Psychology,* 1964, **16,** 359–360. (a)

BROADBENT, D. E., AND GREGORY, M. Stimulus set and response set: the alternation of attention. *Quarterly Journal of Experimental Psychology,* 1964, **16,** 309–317. (b)

BROOKS, L. R. Spatial and verbal components of the act of recall. *Canadian Journal of Psychology,* 1968, **22,** 349–368.

BROWN, C. R., AND RUBENSTEIN, H. Test of response bias explanation of word-frequency effect. *Science,* 1961, **133,** 280–281.

BROWN, J. Some tests of the decay theory of immediate memory. *Quarterly Journal of Experimental Psychology,* 1958, **10,** 12–21.

BROWN, W. P. Conceptions of perceptual defense. *British Journal of Psychology,* 1961 (Monogr. Suppl. No. 35).

BRYDEN, M. P. The manipulation of strategies of report in dichotic listening. *Canadian Journal of Psychology,* 1964, **18,** 126–137.

BUSCHKE, H. Auditory and visual interaction in immediate memory. *Journal of Psychiatric Research,* 1962, **1,** 229–239.

CHOMSKY, N. The formal nature of language. Appendix to Lenneberg, E. H. *Biological foundations of language.* New York: Wiley, 1967.

CHOMSKY, N., AND HALLE, M. *The sound pattern of English.* New York: Harper & Row, 1968.

COHEN, R. L. The differential effect of stimulus intensity on rehearsed and unrehearsed material in short-term auditory memory. *Canadian Journal of Psychology,* 1967, **21,** 277–284.

CONRAD, R. Accuracy of recall using keyset and telephone dial, and the effects of a prefix digit. *Journal of Applied Psychology*, 1958, **42**, 285–288.

CONRAD, R. Very brief delay of immediate memory. *Quarterly Journal of Experimental Psychology*, 1960, **12**, 45–47.

CONRAD, R. An association between memory errors and errors due to acoustic masking of speech. *Nature*, 1962, **193**, 1314–1315.

CONRAD, R. Acoustic confusions in immediate memory. *British Journal of Psychology*, 1964, **55**, 75–84.

CONRAD, R., AND HILLE, B. A. The decay theory of immediate memory. *Canadian Journal of Psychology*, 1958, **12**, 1–6.

CONRAD, R., AND HULL, A. J. Input modality and the serial position curve in short-term memory. *Psychonomic Science*, 1968, **10**, 135–136.

CORBALLIS, M. C. Rehearsal and decay in immediate recall of visually and aurally presented items. *Canadian Journal of Psychology*, 1966, **20**, 42–51.

CROSSMAN, E. R. F. W. Discussion of paper 7 in National Physical Laboratory Symposium. In *Mechanisation of thought processes*. Vol. II. London: H. M. Stationery Office, 1958.

CROWDER, R. G. Prefix effects in immediate memory. *Canadian Journal of Psychology*, 1967, **21**, 450–461.

CROWDER, R. G. Improved recall for digits with delayed recall cues. *Journal of Experimental Psychology*, 1969, in press.

CROWDER, R. G., AND ERDMAN, H. P. Output interference in recalling digits. Paper presented at the meeting of the Eastern Psychological Association, Washington, D. C., April 1968.

CROWDER, R. G., AND HOENIG, Y. J. Intertrial competition and the prefix effect. *Journal of Experimental Psychology*, 1969, in press.

CROWDER, R. G., AND MORTON, J. Precategorical acoustic storage (PAS). *Perception & Psychophysics*, 1969, **5**, 365–373.

DALLETT, K. "Primary memory": The effects of redundancy upon digit repetition. *Psychonomic Science*, 1965, **3**, 237–238.

DEUTSCH, J. A., AND DEUTSCH, D. Attention: Some theoretical considerations. *Psychological Review*, 1963, **70**, 80–90.

DEUTSCH, J. A., DEUTSCH, D., LINDSAY, P. H., AND TREISMAN, A. M. Comments and reply: "Selective attention: Perception or response?" *Quarterly Journal of Experimental Psychology*, 1967, **19**, 362–367.

DIXON, N. F. The effect of subliminal stimulation upon autonomic and verbal behavior. *Journal of Abnormal and Social Psychology*, 1958, **57**, 29–36.

EGAN, J. P., CARTERETTE, E. C., AND THWING, E. J. Some factors affecting multi-channel listening. *Journal of the Acoustical Society of America*, 1954, **26**, 775–782.

FOZARD, J. L., AND YNTEMA, D. B. The effect of repetition on the apparent recency of pictures. Paper presented at the meeting of the Eastern Psychological Association, New York, April 16, 1966.

GAZZANIGA, M. S., AND SPERRY, R. W. Language after section of the cerebral commissures. *Brain*, 1967, **90**, 131–148.

GOLDIAMOND, I., AND HAWKINS, W. F. Vexierversuch: The logarithmic relationship between word-frequency and recognition obtained in the absence of stimulus words. *Journal of Experimental Psychology*, 1958, **56**, 457–463.

HAVENS, L. L., AND FOOTE, W. E. The effect of competition on visual duration threshold and its independence of stimulus frequency. *Journal of Experimental Psychology*, 1963, **65**, 6–11.

HINTZMAN, D. L. Classification and aural coding in short-term memory. *Psychonomic Science*, 1965, **3**, 161–162.

HINTZMAN, D. L. Articulatory coding in short-term memory. *Journal of Verbal Learning and Verbal Behavior,* 1967, **6,** 312–316.

HOWE, M. J. A. Intra-list differences in short-term memory. *Quarterly Journal of Experimental Psychology,* 1965, **17,** 338–342.

JACOBSON, R., FANT, C., AND HALLE, M. *Preliminaries to speech analysis.* Cambridge, Massachusetts: M.I.T. Press, 1951.

JAHNKE, J. C., AND ERLICK, D. E. Delayed recognition and the serial organization of short-term memory. *Journal of Experimental Psychology,* 1968, **77,** 641–647.

KIMURA, D. Cerebral dominance and the perception of verbal stimuli. *Canadian Journal of Psychology,* 1961, **15,** 166–171.

KLEIN, G. S. Semantic power measured through the interference of words with color naming. *American Journal of Psychology,* 1964, **57,** 576–588.

LAZARUS, R. S., AND MCCLEARY, R. A. Autonomic discrimination without awareness: A study of subception. *Psychological Review,* 1951, **58,** 113–122.

LIBERMAN, A. M., COOPER, F. S., HARRIS, K. S., MACNEILAGE, P. F., AND STUDDERT-KENNEDY, M. Some observations on a model for speech perception. In W. Wathen-Dunn (Ed.), *Models for the perception of speech and visual form.* Cambridge, Massachusetts: M.I.T. Press, 1967.

LUCE, R. D. *Individual choice behavior.* New York: Wiley, 1959.

LYONS, J. *Introduction to theoretical linguistics.* London and New York: Cambridge University Press, 1968.

MCGHIE, A., CHAPMAN, J., AND LAWSON, J. S. Changes in immediate memory with age. *British Journal of Psychology,* 1965, **56,** 69–75.

MACKWORTH, J. F. Presentation rate and immediate memory. *Canadian Journal of Psychology,* 1962, **16,** 42–47.

MACKWORTH, J. F. Auditory short-term memory. *Canadian Journal of Psychology,* 1964, **18,** 292–303.

MACKWORTH, J. F. Presentation rate, repetition, and organization in auditory short-term memory. *Canadian Journal of Psychology,* 1965, **19,** 304–315.

MANDLER, G. Association and organization: Facts fancies and theories. In T. R. Dixon and D. L. Horton (Eds.), *Verbal behavior and general behavior theory.* Englewood Cliffs, New Jersey: Prentice-Hall, 1968.

MARSHALL, J. C., AND NEWCOMBE, F. Syntactic and semantic errors in paralexia. *Neuropsychologia,* 1966, **4,** 169–176.

MILLER, G. A., HEISE, G. A., AND LICHTEN, W. The intelligibility of speech as a function of the context of the test materials. *Journal of Experimental Psychology,* 1951, **41,** 329–335.

MILLER, G. A., AND NICELY, P. E. An analysis of perceptual confusions among some English consonants. *Journal of the Acoustical Society of America,* 1955, **27,** 338–352.

MORTON, J. The effects of context on the visual duration threshold for words. *British Journal of Psychology,* 1964, **55,** 165–180. (a)

MORTON, J. A preliminary functional mode for language behaviour. *International Audiology,* 1964, **3,** 216–225. (b) (Reprinted: In R. C. Oldfield and J. C. Marshall (Eds.), *Language.* London: Penguin, 1968.)

MORTON, J. A model for continuous language behaviour. *Language and Speech,* 1964, **7,** 40–70. (c)

MORTON, J. The effects of context upon speed of reading, eye movements and eye-voice span. *Quarterly Journal of Experimental Psychology,* 1964, **16,** 340–354. (d)

MORTON, J. Grammar and computation in language behavior. In J. C. Catford (Ed.), *Studies in language and language behavior.* Centre for Research in Language and Language Behavior Progress Report No. VI. Ann Arbor, Michigan: University of Michigan, 1968. (a)

MORTON, J. A retest of the Response-Bias Explanation of the Word-Frequency Effect. *British Journal of Mathematical and Statistical Psychology,* 1968, **21,** 21–33. (b)

MORTON, J. Selective interference in immediate recall. *Psychonomic Science,* 1968, **12,** 75–76. (c)

MORTON, J. Repeated items and decay in memory. *Psychonomic Science,* 1968, **12,** 219–220. (d)

MORTON, J. The interaction of information in word recognition. *Psychological Review,* 1969, **76,** 165–178. (a)

MORTON, J. Categories of interference: Verbal mediation and conflict in card sorting. *British Journal of Psychology,* 1969, **60,** 329–346. (b)

MORTON, J., AND BROADBENT, D. E. Passive versus active recognition models, or is your homunculus really necessary? In W. Wathen-Dunn (Ed.), *Models for the perception of speech and visual form.* Cambridge, Massachusetts: M.I.T. Press, 1967.

MORTON, J., CROWDER, R. G., AND PRUSSIN, H. A. Experiment and theory in short-term memory. 1969, unpublished paper.

MORTON, J., AND HOLLOWAY, C. M. On the absence of cross-modal suffix effects. 1970, *Quart. J. exp. Psychol.,* 1970, in press.

MURDOCK, B. B., JR. The serial position effect of free recall. *Journal of Experimental Psychology,* 1962, **64,** 482–488.

MURDOCK, B. B., JR. Short-term memory and paired-associate learning. *Journal of Verbal Behavior,* 1963, **2,** 320–328.

MURDOCK, B. B., JR. Visual and auditory stores in short-term memory. *Quarterly Journal of Experimental Psychology,* 1966, **18,** 206–211.

MURDOCK, B. B., JR. Auditory and visual stores in short-term memory. *Acta Psychologica,* 1967, **27,** 316–324.

MURDOCK, B. B., JR. Serial order effects in short-term memory. *Journal of Experimental Psychology,* 1968, **76,** (Monogr. Suppl. 4, Part 2).

MURRAY, D. J. The effect of white noise on the recall of vocalized lists. *Canadian Journal of Psychology,* 1965, **19,** 333–345.

MURRAY, D. J. Vocalization-at-presentation and immediate recall, with varying recall methods. *Quarterly Journal of Experimental Psychology,* 1966, **18,** 9–18.

NEISSER, U. An experimental distinction between perceptual process and verbal response. *Journal of Experimental Psychology,* 1954, **47,** 399–402.

NEISSER, U. *Cognitive psychology.* New York: Appleton-Century-Crofts, 1967.

NEWBIGGING, P. L. The perceptual redintegration of frequent and infrequent words. *Canadian Journal of Psychology,* 1961, **15,** 123–132.

NORMAN, D. A. Acquisition and retention in short-term memory. *Journal of Experimental Psychology,* 1966, **72,** 369–381.

NORMAN, D. A. Toward a theory of memory and attention. *Psychological Review,* 1968, **75,** 522–536.

NORMAN, D. A. Memory while shadowing. *Quarterly Journal of Experimental Psychology,* 1969, **21,** 85–93.

PARLETT, M. R. Systems of identification and storage of verbal stimuli. Unpublished doctoral dissertation, University of Cambridge, 1968.

PILLSBURY, W. B. The reading of words: A study in apperception. *American Journal of Psychology,* 1897, **8,** 315–393.

POLLACK, I. Message uncertainty and message reception. *Journal of the Acoustical Society of America,* 1959, **31,** 1500–1508.

POLLACK, I. Interference, rehearsal, and short-term retention of digits. *Canadian Journal of Psychology,* 1963, **17,** 380–392.

POLLACK, I., JOHNSON, L. B., AND KNAFF, P. R. Running memory span. *Journal of Experimental Psychology,* 1959, **57,** 137–146.

POSNER, M. I. Immediate memory in sequential tasks. *Psychological Bulletin*, 1963, **60**, 333–349.

POSNER, M. I. Rate of presentation and order of recall in immediate memory. *British Journal of Psychology*, 1964, **55**, 303–306.

POSNER, M. I. Short-term memory systems in human information processing. *Acta Psychologica*, 1967, **27**, 267–284.

POSNER, M. I., BOIES, S. J., EICHELMAN, W. H., AND TAYLOR, R. L. Retention of visual and name codes of single letters. *Journal of Experimental Psychology*, 1969, **79**, (Monogr. Suppl. 1, Part 2).

POSTMAN, L., AND PHILLIPS, L. W. Short-term changes in free recall. *Quarterly Journal of Experimental Psychology*, 1965, **17**, 132–138.

ROSS, S., YARCZOWER, M., AND WILLIAMS, G. M. Recognitive thresholds for words as a function of set and similarity. *American Journal of Psychology*, 1956, **69**, 82–86.

ROUTH, D. "Trace strength," modality, and the serial position curve in immediate memory. *Psychonomic Science*, 1969, in press.

RUBENSTEIN, H., AND POLLACK, I. Word predictability and intelligibility. *Journal of Verbal Learning and Verbal Behavior*, 1963, **2**, 147–158.

SAMPSON, H., AND SPONG, P. Handedness, eye-dominance and immediate memory. *Quarterly Journal of Experimental Psychology*, 1961, **13**, 173–180.

SAVIN, H. B. Word-frequency effect and errors in the perception of speech. *Journal of the Acoustical Society of America*, 1963, **35**, 200–206.

SOLOMON, R. L., AND POSTMAN, L. Frequency of usage as a determinant of recognition thresholds for words. *Journal of Experimental Psychology*, 1952, **43**, 195–201.

SPERLING, G. The information available in brief visual presentations. *Psychological Monographs*, 1960, **74**, (Whole No. 498).

SPERLING, G. A model for visual memory tasks *Human Factors*, 1963, **5**, 19–31.

SPERLING, G. Successive approximations to a model for short-term memory. *Acta Psychologica*, 1967, **27**, 285–292.

SPERRY, R. W. Hemisphere deconnection and unity in conscious awareness. *American Psychologist*, 1968, **23**, 723–733.

SPERRY, R. W., AND GAZZANIGA, M. S. Language following surgical disconnection of the hemispheres. In C. H. Milikan (Ed.), *Brain mechanisms underlying speech and language*. New York: Grune & Stratton, 1967.

STEVENS, K. N., AND HALLE, M. Remarks on analysis by synthesis and distinctive features. In W. Wathen-Dunn (Ed.), *Models for the perception of speech and visual form*. Cambridge, Massachusetts: M.I.T. Press, 1967.

STROOP, J. R. Studies of interference in serial verbal reactions. *Journal of Experimental Psychology*, 1935, **18**, 643–661.

TREISMAN, A. M. Contextual cues in selective listening. *Quarterly Journal of Experimental Psychology*, 1960, **12**, 242–248.

TREISMAN, A. M. The effect of irrelevant material on the efficiency of selective listening. *American Journal of Psychology*, 1964, **77**, 533–546. (a)

TREISMAN, A. M. Verbal cues, language and meaning in selective attention. *American Journal of Psychology*, 1964, **77**, 206–219. (b)

TREISMAN, A. M., AND GEFFIN, G. Selective attention: Perception or response? *Quarterly Journal of Experimental Psychology*, 1967, **19**, 1–16.

TULVING, E., MANDLER, G., AND BAUMAL, R. Interaction of two sources of information in tachistoscopic word recognition. *Canadian Journal of Psychology*, 1964, **18**, 62–71.

VERNON, M. D. The errors made in reading. *Medical Research Council, Special Report Series*, 1929, No. 130.

WAUGH, N. C., AND NORMAN, D. A. Primary memory. *Psychology Review*, 1965, **72**, 89–104.

WICKELGREN, W. A. Distinctive features and errors in short-term memory for English vowels. *Journal of the Acoustic Society of America,* 1965, **38,** 583–588.

WICKELGREN, W. A. Phonemic similarity and interference in short-term memory for single letters. *Journal of Experimental Psychology,* 1966, **71,** 396–404. (a)

WICKELGREN, W. A. Distinctive features and errors in short-term memory for English consonants. *Journal of the Acoustical Society of America,* 1966, **39,** 388–398. (b)

WORTHINGTON, A. G., AND DIXON, N. F. Changes in guessing habits as a function of subliminal stimulation. *Acta Psychologica,* 1964, **22,** 338–347.

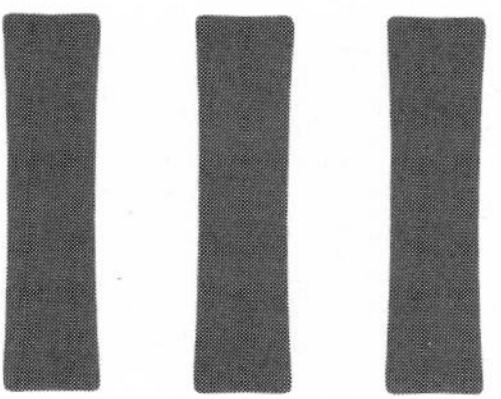

MEMORY FOR ASSOCIATIONS

8

How Associations Are Memorized[1]

James G. Greeno
The University of Michigan

Learning theory as we know it today probably was founded in the seventeenth century, when Hobbes and Locke revived Aristotle's attack on the doctrine of innate ideas. Hobbes and Locke and other empiricist philosophers took the view that knowledge comes from experience. This view requires a learning mechanism, and the empiricists proposed that learning is a process of combining impressions that occur near one another in space and time, or are similar, or contrast with one another. Empiricists argued for the plausibility of a human organism endowed only with elementary sensory (and, presumably, motor) capacities. Complex concepts and sequences of ideas were assumed to develop as combinations of sensory impressions. Thus, the mechanism of association between ideas played an important role in the argument for empiricism, and was therefore part of the justification of the scientific method itself.

It seems safe to say that the belief in association as the elementary learning event has dominated theories of learning and thinking for at least three centuries. The early view that associations form between ideas has been replaced in this century by the idea that associations connect stimuli and responses. But in one form or another, the hypothe-

[1] This research was supported by the U. S. Public Health Service under Grant MH 12717, to Indiana University, and by the Advanced Research Projects Agency, Department of Defense, monitored by the Air Force Office of Scientific Research, under Contract No. AF 49(638)-1736 with the Human Performance Center, Department of Psychology, The University of Michigan.

sis of associationism has enjoyed nearly doctrinal status for most scientific psychologists. Most theorists interested in learning have asked how associations are formed—not whether the basic learning process might be rather different from that described by association theory.

Under the presumption that all learning probably is based on formation of associations, paired-associate memorizing seems to provide the paradigm case of learning in its simplest and purest form. In the framework of association theory, achievements of recall and recognition require relatively elaborate explanations. Learning to recall is sometimes viewed as the formation of connections between responses and some general stimuli, for example, the properties of an experimental room. And recognition is sometimes said to depend at least partly on a learned connection between a stimulus and some general recognizing response which is evoked when the stimulus reappears.

The discussions of recall and recognition included in this volume do not emphasize associationistic ideas. The operative concepts in most of the theories presented here are encoding, storage, and retrieval of items. Rather than asking how associations are formed between stimuli and responses, most of the theories in this volume consider how graphic and auditory stimuli are encoded, how records of stimuli are stored in the subject's working or acquisition memory, and how these records are retrieved and used to generate responses on tests of retention. The theory of memory based on concepts of storage and retrieval evidently gives a rich and illuminating explanation of the processes of recall and recognition, as these are understood at present.

We are faced with an awkward theoretical situation. For tasks involving recall or recognition of lists, concepts of storage and retrieval seem more appropriate than concepts of associative connection. But for paired-associate memorizing, it may seem simpler to theorize using concepts of stimulus–response associations.

In this chapter, I will present evidence suggesting that the concepts of storage and retrieval are also more appropriate than concepts of stimulus–response connections for paired-associate memorizing. The view to which I have been tentatively persuaded is that the task of memorizing associations is not paradigmatic for learning processes in their simplest form. On the contrary, I believe that paired-associate memorizing involves processes that are revealed in simpler form in experiments where subjects memorize lists for recall or recognition. I will not try to discuss these processes in detail—that is the task undertaken by many other contributors to this volume. What I hope to do is to present some of the data that encourage me to believe that their discussions probably describe the basic properties of paired-associate memorizing.

A remark is needed to avoid a misinterpretation. Every theory of paired-associate memorizing has to be an associative theory in that it must explain how subjects come to learn correct responses for stimuli. However, classical association theory makes a specific claim about the nature of the learning process. The theory that this article disputes claims that stimuli and responses are independently manipulable units, and the learning of an association is the formation of a connection between otherwise independent mental entities. In situations that will be considered here, the basic process of forming connections does not provide a complete theory, and we will be concerned with association theory amended to include processes of response acquisition and unlearning of interfering connections.

The alternative theory that I will consider takes a view of association that is basically Gestalt in character. Kohler (1941, p. 493) expressed the idea when he said, "Association is . . . simply coherence within the unitary trace of a unitary experience." I propose that the first stage of memorizing an association involves storing a representation of the stimulus–response pair in memory as a unit. Depending on the materials used, the stimulus or the response or both may already be in the subject's long-term or permanent memory. Borrowing concepts used by Feigenbaum (Chapter 13) and Judith Reitman (Chapter 5) in this volume, the process of storing a pair results in a structure that represents the pair in the subject's working or acquisition memory.

In some situations, successful storage of an item may be all that is needed for successful retention. But in other situations, storage of an item in memory may not guarantee that the subject will be able to perform successfully on tests. In these situations, I propose that the second stage of memorizing involves learning to retrieve the stored item from memory reliably. The process of learning to retrieve could involve changing the stored representation of an item, or discovering relationships among stored items to permit better organization, or some other process. The notion of paired-associate memorizing as a two-stage process of storage and learning to retrieve has been suggested by Estes and DaPolito (1967), although my emphasis on the unitary nature of storage was not explicit in their discussion.

Consider an example. Suppose that one of the items in a paired-associate list is the pair SPIRAL–VIVID. At the beginning of the experiment, the subject has no idea that these two words are supposed to go together—the item is not known. Then at some time, the subject stores a representation of the pair SPIRAL–VIVID in memory. When the stimulus SPIRAL is presented on tests, there is some chance that the subject will be able to retrieve the stored memory structure and give the correct response. But there may also be failures of retrieval, due, perhaps, to other stored items with stimuli similar to SPIRAL, or to requirements for fast responding. If the representation of SPIRAL–VIVID does not permit rapid and reliable retrieval, then further learning is needed, and this is what I am calling learning to retrieve. Once a retrieval strategy for SPIRAL–VIVID is acquired, the subject will be able to respond correctly on tests, and the item will be learned.

I am primarily concerned with arguing that there are two main subprocesses in memorization of associations, and that those involve storage and learning to retrieve. I am less concerned in this paper with issues about the exact nature of storage and retrieval processes. However, some discussion of possibilities is helpful in clarifying the general ideas.

First, regarding the process of storing pairs in memory, Neisser (1967) has argued that storage of information should be viewed as a constructive process relating to a cognitive act. Neisser's argument seems cogent—the mind cannot really be a blank tablet. Furthermore, the nature of the stored memory structure for an item can vary a great deal, depending on what the subject does when he studies it. For example, in studying the pair SPIRAL–VIVID, a subject might form a visual image of a brightly colored design that could appear on a psychedelic poster. Or he might construct an associative mnemonic such as "spiral–viral–vivid." He might select some part of the stimulus, such as its first letter and code "S-vivid." Or he might simply rehearse the pair as it was presented. The information stored by the subject would be different in each of these cases, and questions about the form in which information is stored are very important and interesting. But the notion of storage as it is used in this paper is intended to refer to any representation of the paired associate in memory. The important claim is that an item is stored as a unit, rather than as a connection.

Now, suppose that an item has been stored. On a test, the subject sees the stimulus term of the pair and he has to give the correct response.

There seem to be two ways of thinking about his problem. One common way of thinking about memory involves an analogy with a library or a filing system, or using Miller's (1963) idea, a junk box. An item may well be in memory and not be found on a given occasion. If memory is like a junk box or a filing system, then the process of learning to retrieve could be accomplished by getting the item separated from the rest of the contents of memory in some way, or by getting the contents of memory organized in some systematic way so the subject knows where to look for things.

There is another way of thinking about memory that may be more realistic. Analogies to filing systems or junk boxes make memory seem spatial, with information stored and waiting passively to be found. Another possibility is that memory structures or engrams are functional as well as structural features of the mind. On this view, a stored memory structure becomes active when an appropriate signal is received—the engram may be thought of as waiting for its number to be announced before coming forward. If memory storage involves establishing engrams, then the question of retrieval is the question of whether the engram becomes active when the stimulus is presented on a test. And if it does not with sufficient reliability, then the subject has to set or tune the engram more efficiently so that it will be activated reliably by the presentation of the stimulus.

While these remarks about storage and retrieval processes are entirely speculative, they demonstrate that reasonable general views of the nature of memory are consistent with the claim that memorizing could easily involve two stages that can be called storage and learning to retrieve. Later sections of this paper present evidence that supports this conceptualization.

Statistical Methods

The evidence that will be presented uses measurements of the difficulty of learning in each of two stages in various paired-associate memorizing experiments. These measurements are obtained by estimating the parameters of a Markov model, using results presented in detail elsewhere (Greeno, 1968). The model has four states:

O the state of an item at the beginning of an experiment, applying until the item is stored in memory.

E the state of an item which is stored in memory, but a reliable retrieval strategy has not been acquired and the subject fails to retrieve the item from memory.

C the state of an item which is stored in memory without a reliable retrieval strategy, but the subject succeeds in retrieving the item from memory.

L the state of an item which is stored in memory with a reliable retrieval strategy.

The initial and transition probabilities of the chain are[2]

$$P(L_1, E_1, C_1, O_1) = (t, (1-s-t)r,\ (1-s-t)(1-r),\ s),$$

$$P = \begin{array}{c|cccc} & L_{n+1} & E_{n+1} & C_{n+1} & O_{n+1} \\ \hline L_n & 1 & 0 & 0 & 0 \\ E_n & d & (1-d)q & (1-d)p & 0 \\ C_n & 0 & q & p & 0 \\ O_n & ab & a(1-b)e & a(1-b)(1-e) & 1-a. \end{array} \qquad (1)$$

It will be recognized that this model ignores important temporal features of the memorizing process, discussed in this volume by Norman and Rumelhart (chapter 2), by Judith Reitman (chapter 5), and elsewhere by numerous authors (e.g., Atkinson and Shiffrin, 1968; Greeno, 1967; Peterson, 1966). Present evidence seems to indicate that learning occurs during an interval of time including and following the presentation of the item to be learned. In the experiments to be discussed here, individual items were almost never repeated within short enough intervals to produce effects due to short-term memory.

In the general form of Eq. 1, the model is a little unwieldy. Some simplifications often are acceptable. One simplification results if the first test comes after a single study trial on which the transition parameters are the same as on later trials. Then

$$t = ab, \quad r = e, \quad s = 1 - a. \qquad (2)$$

Further simplifications are possible if the probabilities of acquiring a retrieval strategy and retrieving stored items are the same on the first

[2] In this discussion, I am ignoring the problem of identifiability. The version of the model given in Eq. 1 is not identifiable in the form given, but in every application that will be presented there are acceptable simplifying restrictions that make Eq. 1 identifiable. The assumption that $P(L_{n+1}|C_n) = 0$ is used as an identifying restriction here. In effect, it is assumed that learning to retrieve stored items is a process of strategy selection that occurs only after failures to retrieve.

trial after an item leaves State O as they are on later trials. In that case,

$$b = d, \quad e = q. \tag{3}$$

If the simplifications in Eqs. 2 and 3 are acceptable, the measurements of difficulty in the two stages of learning are straightforward. There are just three parameters, a, d, and p. The value of a measures the difficulty of learning in the first stage. The value of d measures the difficulty of learning in the second stage. And the value of p is the probability of retrieving a stored item from memory before a reliable retrieval strategy is acquired. If the simplifications are not all acceptable the measurements of difficulty in the two stages of learning are less simple. However, summary measures give reasonable indices of the difficulty in each stage. Let Z_1 be the number of trials spent in the State O, and let Z_2 be the number of trials spent in States E and C. The expected values of these variables are

$$E(Z_1) = 1 + s/a, \quad E(Z_2) = (1 - s - t)\ [1 + (1 - rd)/qd] + s(1 - b)\ [1 + (1 - ed)/qd].$$

To obtain the measurements of difficulty needed for the analyses, we need estimates of the parameters of the model. These can be obtained using the method of maximum likelihood. Suppose one item shows a sequence of correct responses (0) and errors (1)

$$X = 1\ 1\ 1\ 0\ 0\ 1\ 0\ 0\ 0\ 0\ \ldots.$$

Using Eq. 1, the likelihood of X is

$$L(X) = (1 - s - t)r(1 - d)^3q^3p^2d + sa(1 - b)e(1 - d)^2q^2p^2d + s(1 - a)a(1 - b)e(1 - d)qp^2d + s(1 - a)^2a(1 - b)(1 - e)qpd.$$

Of course, this is only an illustration. The likelihood of any sequence can be calculated using Eq. 1, in a form similar to the above equation. The likelihood of all the data is the product of the likelihoods of the separate sequences. The estimates of the parameters are those values that maximize the likelihood of the data. For the model we are considering, maximum likelihood estimates cannot be obtained algebraically, but the maximum can be found using a computer search program. We have used Stepit (Chandler, 1965) which uses only a few seconds of computer time to obtain a set of estimates.

To determine whether one or more simplifications of the models are acceptable, likelihood ratio tests are used. The procedure involves finding maximum likelihood estimates of the parameters of the general model, and then finding maximum likelihood estimates of the parameters with a restriction imposed. The value of the likelihood obtained with the restriction will be lower than the maximum likelihood obtained without the restriction, and the ratio of the two values (restricted over general) is called λ. If the restricted version is correct, the value of $-2 \log_e \lambda$ is asymptotically distributed as chi square with degrees of freedom equal to the number of restrictions. In the discussion that follows, when a restriction is called acceptable for a set of data, this means that the likelihood ratio rest for that restriction gave a test statistic with probability greater than .05.

The main analyses involve tests of significance comparing different experimental conditions in the difficulty of the two stages of learning. Likelihood ratio tests are also used in these analyses. Suppose, for example, that we want to test whether two groups differ in the value of a. A maximum likelihood value is obtained for all the data of both groups, with all of the parameters free to vary. A second maximum likelihood value is obtained with a single value of a used for both sets of data. The restricted value of the likelihood divided by the maximum likelihood without the restriction gives a likelihood ratio λ. In this case, $-2 \log_e \lambda$ is asymptotically distributed as chi square with one degree of freedom if the two groups really have equal values of a. Tests can be carried out using more than one parameter, and the degrees of freedom for the chi square distribution equal the number of parameters involved in the test. In this way, we can test whether two groups differ in the difficulty of the first stage of learning, or in the difficulty of the second stage of learning, or in performance during the intermediate stage of the learning process, or in any combination of these characteristics.

Effects of Stimulus and Response Difficulty

Michael Humphreys conducted an experiment varying the difficulty of responses and the similarity among stimuli.[3] The materials he used are listed in Table 1. The four lists were learned by separate groups, using the anticipation method. Subjects were asked to spell the responses. Some summary statistics are given in Table 2. Note that both the stimulus variable and the response variable had reasonably strong effects in the experiment.

[3] A detailed description of the experimental procedures, as well as a full description of the steps taken in analysis of the results, are given in Humphreys and Greeno (1970).

TABLE 1
Lists Used in Humphreys' Experiment

EE	EH	HE	HH
1-HAZ	1-HPF	11-RAS	11-GPS
2-MAK	2-IPW	12-MAK	12-HPF
3-GAW	3-NPE	13-JAV	13-BPC
4-RAS	4-GPS	21-BAQ	21-IPW
5-BAQ	5-JPV	22-HAZ	22-NPE
6-LAN	6-MPA	23-FAC	23-XPO
7-DAP	7-BPC	31-DAP	31-RPK
8-JAV	8-XPO	32-GAW	32-MPA

TABLE 2
Summary Data for Humphreys' Experiment

Group	Mean errors before first correct	Mean errors after first correct	Mean trial of last error
EE	3.10	1.17	5.71
EH	5.06	1.57	8.01
HE	5.28	1.85	8.28
HH	6.64	2.82	11.79

The data of this experiment allow us to test the theory of storage and retrieval learning. Recall that in the theory, the first stage of learning is storage of the stimulus–response pair as a unit. We should expect that this process should be affected by both stimulus and response variables. Then, in Eq. 1, the value of a should be influenced by both of the variables in Humphreys' experiment. On the other hand, the theory says that the second stage involves learning to retrieve items reliably. In Humphreys' experiment, the main difficulty in retrieval might well be elimination of confusion among items with similar stimuli. In this case, the second stage of learning should be influenced mainly by the stimulus variable. In Eq. 1, the values of b and d should be higher for groups with easy stimuli than hard stimuli, but should not be influenced by the response variable.

Now suppose that the theory of storage and retrieval learning is wrong, and associations are really memorized by forming connections between stimuli and responses. A primitive version of association theory would not allow for response effects at all, but association theorists have extended the theory to include an additional process. The most comprehensive treatment of the extended theory is given by Underwood and Schulz (1960). In the extended theory, paired-associate memorizing has two stages. In the first stage, the subject acquires the response term of the paired associate. For a nonsense syllable response, the response learning phase probably would involve forming associations among the components of the response. For responses that were already well integrated, the response learning phase would be a process of increasing the availability of the response in the experimental situation—a process sometimes called formation of a contextual association. The formation of an associative connection or hookup between the response and its stimulus occurs in the second stage of learning.

According to the theory of response-strengthening and hookup learning, the first stage of paired-associate memorizing should be affected mainly by response variables. This means that in Humphreys' experiment, we should expect the value of a in Eq. 1 to be different for groups with different responses, but a should not be influenced by the stimulus variable. In Underwood and Schulz' theory, the difficulty of forming stimulus–response hookups depends on properties of both the stimuli and the responses. This means that in Humphreys' experiment, the values of b and d in Eq. 1 might well depend on both the stimulus and the response variable. A summary of the predictions suggested by the storage-retrieval theory and the response-hookup learning theory is given in Table 3.

The main question, then, is how the parameters of the model varied depending on the experimental conditions. But this question is not meaningful unless the model is approximately accurate as a description of the learning that went on in the experiment. We want to use the parameter estimates as psychological measurements, and as with any psy-

TABLE 3
Summary of Predictions for Humphreys' Experiment

Parameter	Storage-retrieval	Response-hookup
a	Depends on stimulus and response variables	Depends only on response variables
b and d	Depends only on stimulus variable	Depends on stimulus and response variables

chological measurements we have to be concerned with the question of validity. For example, the predictions summarized in Table 3 depend partly on assuming that the stages of learning are approximately discrete and sequential. For example, if the response-hookup learning theory were true, but the stages overlapped, then the model would be wrong but the estimate of a would probably be influenced by both stimulus and response variables.

We cannot prove that the measurements obtained with a model are valid, because we can never prove that a model is accurate. What we can do is to perform tests that have the possibility of rejecting the model if it is substantially wrong. The tests carried out in this case involved comparisons between frequency distributions of statistics in the data with distributions calculated using Eq. 1 with maximum likelihood estimates of the parameters.

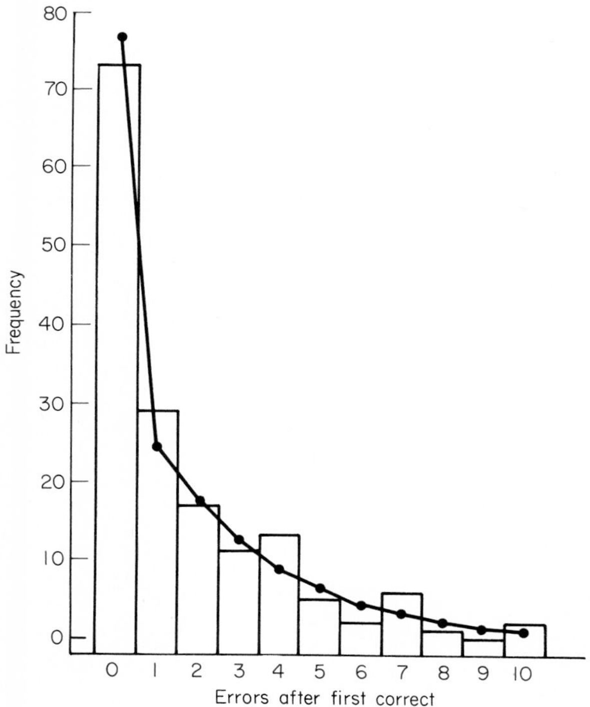

FIG. 1. Theoretical and empirical distributions of the number of errors after the first correct response for Group HE in Humphreys' experiment. The histogram represents the data, and the connected dots show the theoretical frequencies.

For the groups in this experiment, the simplification given as Eq. 3 was not acceptable in one of the groups. Equation 2 was acceptable. Therefore, the goodness of fit of the model was tested using maximum likelihood estimates of five parameters *a, b, d, e,* and *q*.

An illustration of the tests will be given using the group with hard stimuli and easy responses. Figure 1 shows the distribution of the number of errors made after the first correct response on each item. Figure 2 shows the number of trials between the first correct response and the criterion of five consecutive correct responses, which was taken as showing learning. The agreement between the data and these theoretical distribution seems excellent. These distributions involving performance after the first correct response have considerable importance because the model says that an item has to have completed the first stage of learning before a correct response can occur. According to the model, learning that occurs after the first correct response must be all-or-none in nature. The distributions shown in Figs. 1 and 2 test this feature of the data.

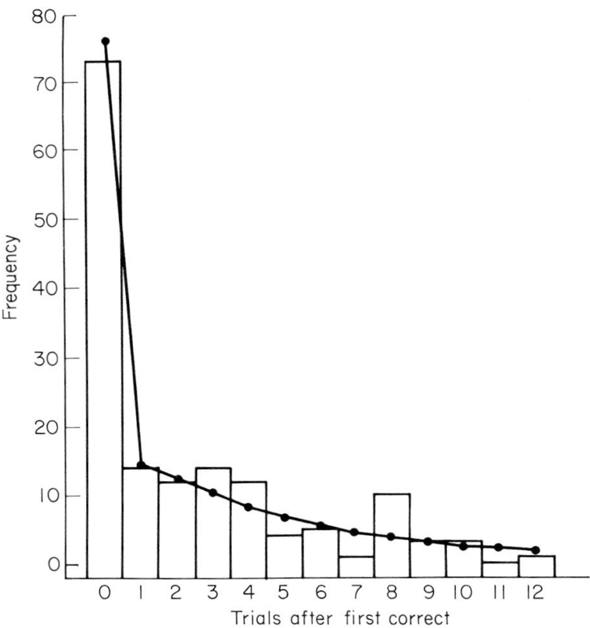

FIG. 2. Theoretical and empirical distributions of the number of trials between the first correct response and the criterion for Group HE in Humphreys' experiment.

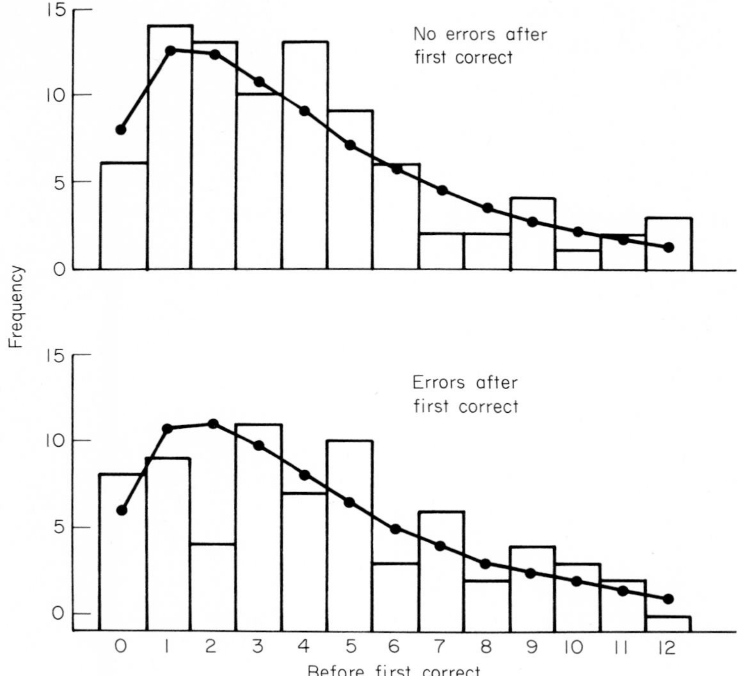

FIG. 3. Theoretical and empirical distributions of the number of errors before the first correct response. The upper panel shows frequencies of sequences with no errors after the first correct response, and the lower panel shows frequencies of sequences with one or more errors after the first correct response.

There are two kinds of sequences that need to be separated for purposes of estimation; sequences that have no errors after the first correct response and sequences that have some errors after the first correct response. Figure 3 shows the empirical and theoretical distributions of the number of errors before the first correct response separated into components. The upper panel has sequences with no errors after the first correct response. For example, a sequence that contributes to the fourth column in the upper panel would be 1 1 1 0 0 0. . . . The lower panel has sequences with one or more errors after the first correct response. For example, a sequence contributing to the fourth column in lower panel might be 1 1 1 0 0 1 0 1 0 0 0. . . . The agreement in Fig. 3 is not as striking as in Figs. 1 and 2, partly because these distributions are based on fewer cases. However, it is still satisfactory.

Figures 4 and 5 show the distributions of errors and trials of the last error for all trials. In effect, these test the assumptions in the model about how the distributions in Figs. 1 and 2 combine with the distribution in Fig. 3. These empirical distributions were not smooth, but the theoretical curves seem to follow the main contours of the data fairly well.

The results shown from Group HE do not include the cases of greatest

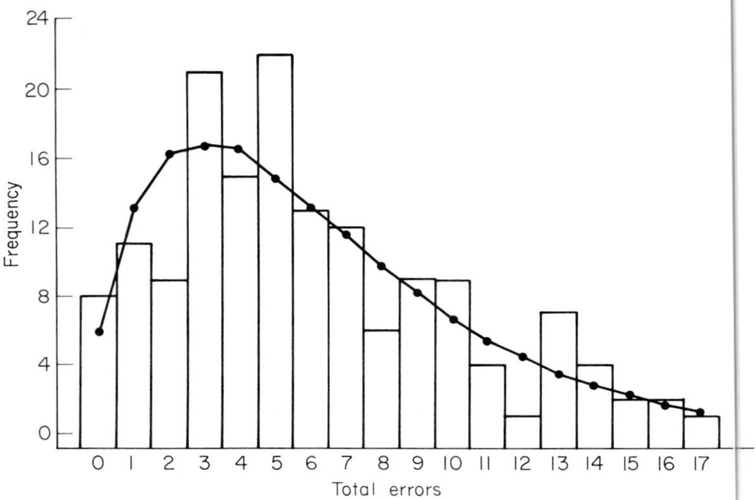

FIG. 4. Theoretical and empirical frequencies of the total number of errors.

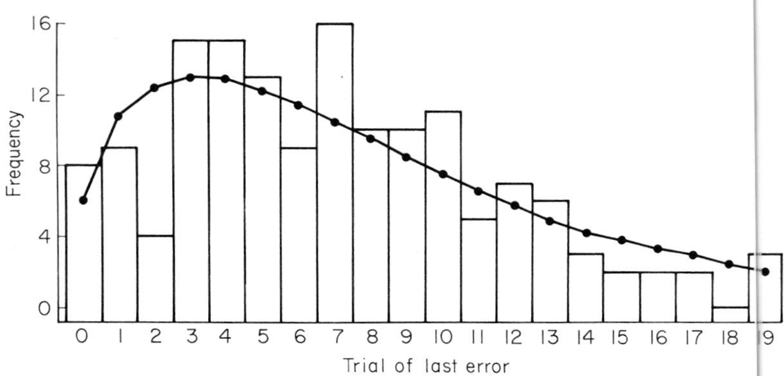

FIG. 5. Theoretical and empirical frequencies of the total number of trials before criterion.

disagreement between data and theory, but they do not include the best cases either. In any event, the real question of the model's validity depends on the overall agreement between all the empirical distributions and all the predicted distributions. Because maximum likelihood estimates of the parameters were used, we know something about the distributions of goodness-of-fit chi-square statistics. Let n be the number of cells in a frequency distribution, and let m be the number of parameters estimated from the data and used in calculating the theoretical distribution, then the asymptotic distribution of the chi-square statistic is bounded by $\chi^2(n-1)$ and $\chi^2(n-m-1)$ (Chernoff and Lehman, 1954). For the four experimental groups, a total of 20 chi-square tests were carried out. One of them was significant at the .05 level using the upper bounds of degrees of freedom, and three were significant using the lower bounds. Statistically, then, the predictions of the model seem to agree to an acceptable approximation with the data. At least, we probably can have reasonable confidence that the parameter values and tests of hypotheses about parameters using the model will not be grossly misleading.

Now recall that the main target of the analysis is to obtain evidence for a choice between two theories of memorizing. One theory says that the first stage is response learning, and should be hard or easy depending on the responses that have to be learned. Another theory says that the first stage is storage of the stimulus–response item, and should depend on both the stimulus and response variable. If the response-hookup theory is correct, we should find that a can be held constant across groups with the same responses. But if the storage-retrieval learning theory is correct, then values of a probably should depend on stimulus as well as response variables. Table 4 has the results of testing the invariance of a across pairs of conditions, using likelihood ratio tests. For example, one null hypothesis is that a has the same value in groups EE

TABLE 4
Tests of Invariance of a

Conditions	$-2 \log \lambda$	p
EE vs. HE	5.97	.015
EH vs. HH	6.69	.010
EE vs. EH	14.23	.0002
HE vs. HH	16.23	.00006

and HE, the two groups with easy responses. The test statistic was 5.97, which has probability .015 under the null hypothesis, indicating rejection of the null hypothesis. A similar result was obtained for the test of invariance of a across groups EH and HH, the two groups with hard responses. The tests involving groups with the same stimuli are included for completeness—they permit rejection of the hypothesis of invariance even more strongly. Since the groups with the same responses cannot be described with the same values of a, the results in Table 4 favor the storage-retrieval theory over the response-hookup learning theory.

The other test involves the prediction suggested by the storage-retrieval theory about b and d. If the second stage of memorizing is learning to retrieve stored items, then b and d should depend on the stimulus variable, but not on the responses. But if the second stage of memorizing is formation of a stimulus–response connection, then the values of b and d probably should depend on both stimulus and response variables. The result to be reported uses the data from all four groups. In addition to testing invariance of b and d, we test the hypothesis that b and d were equal. The theory is required to fit the data of all four groups with any value of a in each group, one value of b and d for groups EE and EH, and a different value of b and d for groups HE and HH. The performance parameters p and e were allowed to vary freely. The null hypothesis is that b and d were equal, and depended only on the stimulus variable. The alternative hypothesis is that all the parameters including b and d differed among all four groups. The test has six degrees of freedom.

The result of the test is in Table 5. The value obtained for $-2 \log \lambda$ was 4.37, which has probability greater than .60 under the null hypothesis. What we found in the statistical analysis is that we can reject the

TABLE 5
Parameter Estimates and $-2 \log \lambda$ Testing $b = d$, Depending Only on Stimulus Difficulty[a]

Condition	a	$b=d$	p	$1-e$
EE	.29	.34	.46	.32
EH	.18	.34	.36	.62
HE	.21	.26	.40	.34
HH	.13	.26	.36	.90

[a] $-2 \log \lambda = 4.37$, $p > .60$.

TABLE 6
Lists Used in Replication of Humphreys' Experiment

EE	EH	HE	HH
P—Touch	P—Delft	FQ—Touch	FQ—Delft
V—Night	V—Blear	VF—Night	VF—Renal
F—Grain	F—Renal	VQ—Grain	VQ—Anode
C—Stand	C—Houri	QV—Stand	QV—Houri
L—Earth	L—Ingot	QF—Earth	QF—Ingot
S—Offer	S—Anode	FV—Offer	FV—Blear

hypothesis of equal values of a across groups with the same responses, but we cannot reject the hypothesis of equal values of b and d across groups with the same stimuli. This fits with expectations based on the storage-retrieval learning theory, and thus favors a choice of that theory over the theory of response strengthening and hookup learning.

The results of Humphreys' experiment have been presented using the literary device of giving the hypotheses first and then the data. This was done for reasons of clarity, rather than historical accuracy. Actually, Humphreys and I had expected to obtain a confirmation of Underwood's theory when we began the analysis, because we had not thought of any reasonable alternative to it. We developed the theory of storage and retrieval learning because the data seemed to disagree with Underwood's theory, at least in the simplified form that we were considering. When a new hypothesis is developed because of a complicated statistical result, it is wise to replicate the study. This was done at Indiana in an experiment carried out with the assistance of Herbert Marsh. We used the same design as Humphreys did, but different materials and procedures were used. The lists learned by the subjects are given in Table 6. Note that the lists were shorter (six instead of eight items), the stimuli were letters rather than numbers, and the responses were words rather than nonsense syllables. Whereas Humphreys' experiment was run using a memory drum with subjects speaking their responses, our replication was run in a computer-based laboratory with stimuli presented on art displays and responses typed on keyboards. Table 7 shows summary data for the replication of Humphreys' experiment. Apparently, the changes in materials and procedures did not eliminate the overall differences due to stimulus similarity and response difficulty, although the effect of response difficulty seems to have been smaller here than in Humphreys' data.

TABLE 7
Summary Data for Replication of Humphreys' Experiment

Group	Mean errors before first correct	Mean errors after first correct	Mean trial of last error
EE	2.66	1.59	4.56
EH	3.93	1.16	5.84
HE	5.02	5.61	13.68
HH	6.19	4.83	13.97

In testing simplifying assumptions of the general model, we found that the simplifications of Eq. 3 were acceptable only for groups EE and EH. The simplifications of Eq. 2 were acceptable for group HH, and nearly acceptable for group HE ($.025 < p < .05$); Eq. 2 was not acceptable for groups EE and EH. Rather than applying the model in its most general (and weakest) form, we used the model with the restrictions that were acceptable in the various groups. The model did not fit as well in this experiment as it did for Humphreys' data. Of 20 tests of goodness of fit, six could be rejected at the .05 level using upper bounds on degrees of freedom, and eight could be rejected at .05 using the lower bounds. For many purposes, this amount of discrepancy would be unsatisfactory, but it probably is all right in this case since we were only concerned to see whether the pattern of results in Humphreys' study would appear again.

Table 8 gives the estimated parameter values for the four experimental groups. Since different simplifying restrictions applied in the different groups, the parameters are not comparable in simple ways. In order to obtain summaries that are comparable, the mean numbers of trials in each stage were calculated using Eq. 4. These figures are also given in Table 8. Note that the mean number of trials in the first stage seems to have been influenced by both the stimulus and response variables, as was true in Humphreys' data. In this study, however, the effect of the stimulus variable seems to have been somewhat stronger than the effect of the response variable. The number of trials required to complete the second stage seems to have been determined mainly by the stimulus variable, as was true in Humphreys' experiment. Thus, the main conclusions that were made on the basis of Humphreys' data seem to have been corroborated in our replication.

It should be remembered that the conclusion of the analysis may depend on accepting the validity of the measurements based on the

TABLE 8
Parameter Estimates and Theoretical Mean Numbers of Trials In Each Stage in Replication of Humphreys' Experiment

Group	a	b	d	e	q	r	s	t	$E(Z_1)$	$E(Z_2)$
EE	.11	.33[a]	.33	.73[a]	.73	.83	.06	.24	1.49	3.00
EH	.17	.30[a]	.30	.75[a]	.75	.85	.27	.14	2.55	3.34
HE	.26	.13	.14	.35	.68	.35[a]	.74[a]	.03[a]	3.90	9.75
HH	.18	.06	.17	.34	.69	.34[a]	.82[a]	.01[a]	5.51	8.51

[a] These parameters were determined by simplifying restrictions.

Markov model, including the assumption of discrete stages. The analyses reported here were carried out using the only two-stage model for which statistical methods have been worked out. It is possible that use of other models might lead to different conclusions. However, if the present analysis is accepted, the conclusion based on these experiments with varying stimulus and response difficulty is that the first stage of paired-associate memorizing is affected by characteristics of both stimuli and responses, but the difficulty of the second stage seems to depend almost entirely on the stimuli. This supports the storage-retrieval theory, since it is consistent with the idea that subjects store the stimulus–response pair as a unit, and then have to develop strategies to retrieve the stored items from memory when they see the stimulus terms.

Analysis of Negative Transfer

The data to be presented in this section were obtained in experiments conducted by Carlton James where prior training produced negative transfer in paired-associate memorizing.[4] The experiments involve comparisons between two conditions. One group learned two lists with the same responses but different stimuli. This is called the A-B, C-B paradigm, and will be referred to here as the C-B condition. The other group learned two lists with the same stimuli and responses, but each stimulus was paired with a different response in the second list than it was in the first list. This is called the A-B, A-B_r paradigm, and will be referred to here as the A-B_r condition.

[4] Details of the experimental procedures and the empirical results are given in James and Greeno (1970).

In these studies, the storage-retrieval theory cannot be compared with the response-hookup theory. The reason is that in both the A-B_r and the C-B conditions, the responses used in the second list are the same as those used in the first list, so there should be no effect due to response strengthening. However, the theory of association learning includes a different factor that should differ between the two conditions of these experiments. In a theory that dates from Melton and Irwin's (1940) study of retroactive interference, negative transfer is explained by the effect of associations that are learned in the first list and must be unlearned before the new associations can dominate performance. In an A-B_r condition, where the stimuli are the same as those learned in the first list, the effect of first-list associations should be quite strong and retard learning by a large amount. In a C-B condition, new stimuli are used in the second list and the first-list associations should have a much smaller effect.

We can construct a version of the unlearning theory that would fit with the two-stage Markov model. Keep in mind that in these experiments, the subject knows the responses from the beginning of training on the second list, since they are the same as those used earlier. This means that any reasonable two-stage theory should assert that both stages of learning involve learning the associations in the second list. Suppose that in State O, the association for a stimulus from list 1 is retained and dominates the subject's performance on that item. The item goes from State O to either State E or State C when the first-list association is unlearned. The transition to State L occurs when the second-list association is learned. According to this conceptualization, the main difference between A-B_r and C-B conditions should be a difference in the difficulty in accomplishing the first, unlearning stage of the memorizing process.

The storage-retrieval theory suggests a different expectation. The task given to an A-B_r group is to learn to use each stimulus from the first list to retrieve a response that is different from the one paired with it originally. In the C-B group, new stimulus cues are used. This leads to the expectation that the main difficulty in A-B_r, relative to C-B, should be in learning to retrieve the new pairs from memory, and the theory says that this occurs in the second stage of paired-associate learning.

Data were obtained from a variety of conditions. In one experiment, each list contained ten pairs of two-syllable adjectives, with two groups (an A-B_r and a C-B group) learning the first list to a criterion of one perfect trial, (*No OT*) and the other two groups learning the first list to the one-trial criterion and then receiving 15 additional trials of over-training (*OT*). In another experiment, each list contained six pairs of two-syllable adjectives. There were eight groups in a 2 × 2 × 2 factorial design. One factor was the main variable—the difference between A-B_r and C-B conditions. A second factor was the presence or absence of a series of pretraining lists (*PT* or *No PT*) each with the same responses as those used in the last two lists, but with different stimuli, and each studied for six trials. And the third factor was the presence or absence of 18 trials of overtraining on the next-to-last list following a criterion of one perfect trial (*OT* or *No OT*).

These experiments were carried out using a memory drum with the anticipation procedure. Stimuli were presented for 2 sec during which the subject tried to give the correct response. Then the response was shown along with the stimulus for 2 sec. There was a 4-sec pause between each cycle in which all the items were presented.

In all, there were 12 experimental groups for this analysis. The simplifying assumption involving the initial vector of the model (Eq. 2) was acceptable in all the groups. Although other simplifications were acceptable in some groups, they were not used in testing goodness of fit or estimating the parameters of the model. The same five tests for goodness of fit were used here as in the analyses described earlier. With 12 groups, there were 60 tests. Three tests were significant using upper bounds of the degrees of freedom, and 15 tests were significant using lower bounds. Thus, the model seems to have fit these data reasonably well.

The theoretical measures of difficulty for the first and second stages of learning are given in Table 9. The values of $E(Z_1)$ for comparable

TABLE 9
Theoretical Quantities for A–B_r and C–B Conditions

Condition	Mean trials in first stage		Mean trials in second stage	
	C–B	A–B_r	C–B	A–B_r
Ten items, No OT	3.94	4.54	2.76	4.12
Ten items, OT	3.50	6.49	2.95	10.05
Six items, No PT, No OT	2.99	2.58	1.28	5.08
Six items, No PT, OT	2.58	3.19	2.70	4.35
Six items, PT, No OT	1.87	1.74	1.55	3.80
Six items, PT, OT	2.48	2.92	1.22	3.59

TABLE 10
Tests of Invariance between A–B$_r$ and C–B

Condition	First stage	Second stage	Both stages
Ten items, No OT	1.4	20.4[a]	21.4[a]
Ten items, OT	29.8[a]	59.5[a]	88.1[a]
Six items, No PT, No OT	1.1	19.7[a]	20.7[a]
Six items, No PT, OT	1.6	9.4[a]	9.6[a]
Six items, PT, No OT	.1	16.3[a]	29.9[a]
Six items, PT, OT	1.9	11.0[a]	32.2[a]

[a] Denotes $p < .01$.

C-B and A-B$_r$ groups seem to show small and inconsistent differences, except for the condition with ten items and overtraining. However, the measures of difficulty in the second stage show large and consistent differences, with A-B$_r$ having greater difficulty in the second stage in every case.

Statistical tests were carried out to compare the difficulty of learning in the A-B$_r$ and C-B conditions, using separate likelihood ratio tests for the two stages. The results are in Table 10. Note that in every case, the difference in the second stage was significant, but the difference in the first stage was significant only in one of the six comparisons. These results seem to justify the conclusion that the main difference between learning A-B$_r$ and C-B lists occurs in the second stage of memorizing.

The results of this analysis provide additional support for the hypothesis that paired-associate memorizing involves storage and learning to retrieve. The hypothesis of unlearning and replacement of associative connections leads us to expect most of the difference between A-B$_r$ and C-B to occur in the first stage. However, in five of six conditions, we failed to find a significant difference in the first stage. In the hypothesis of storage and retrieval learning, it is reasonable to expect the main difficulty in A-B$_r$ to involve retrieval learning, and this expectation is consistent with the finding that most of the difference between A-B$_r$ and C-B was in the second stage of learning.

Summary and Conclusion

I began this article by stating a theoretical question—whether associations are memorized by a process of forming connections between stimuli and responses or by a process of storing stimulus–response units and learning to retrieve them. The preceding two sections have presented evidence that the storage-retrieval theory is a more reasonable hypothesis about the memorizing process. The evidence consists of results obtained by measuring difficulty of two learning stages in various experimental conditions, using a Markov model with the assumption that learning occurs in two discrete stages.

First, it seems that the similarity among stimuli is quite a strong variable in determining the difficulty of the first stage of learning. The difficulty of the first stage is also affected by response variables. Differences were obtained by varying the pronouncibility of trigram responses and by varying the frequency of use of word responses. The first stage of memorizing was not affected in one important case—five of six comparisons between A-B_r and C-B negative transfer conditions failed to show a reliable difference in the first stage of learning.

The second stage of learning was strongly influenced in these experiments by the similarity among stimuli, and large differences in difficulty of the second stage were obtained in comparisons between A-B_r and A-C negative transfer conditions. These experiments have consistently failed to show effects on the second stage of memorizing due to response variables. Pronouncibility of trigrams and frequency of words both failed to produce reliable second-stage differences in these data.

If the measurements presented here are accepted, the findings seem very hard to explain using the theory of stimulus–response connections. Regarding the first stage of learning, sizable effects were found where the theory of connections predicts little or no effect, and effects were not found where the theory leads us to expect them. Specifically, the version of association theory that says the first stage is mainly a process of increasing response availability leads us to expect little or no effect of stimulus variables in the first stage. Yet, the stimulus variables manipulated in these studies influenced the first stage of learning significantly. On the other hand, the version of association theory that says old associations have to be unlearned before new associations can dominate performance leads us to expect a substantial first-stage difference between A-B_r and C-B negative transfer conditions. But all except one of our experimental conditions failed to show this effect.

Regarding the second stage of learning, connection theorists often suggest (and sometimes state outright) that the formation of connections probably comes after other processes like response strengthening or unlearning have taken place. And the formation of connections is often treated as a relatively symmetrical process, which would be expected to be influenced about as much by response variables as by stimulus variables. However, in the data reported here the second stage of learning was affected almost exclusively by stimulus variables. Stimulus similarity had strong effects on the second stage of learning and the difference between A-B_r and C-B conditions was mainly a second-stage effect. Response pronouncibility and frequency of word use failed to show significant effects.

On the other hand, the theory of storage and retrieval learning has features that seem to be quite consistent with the pattern of results obtained in these studies. First, the fact that both stimulus and response variables affect the first stage of learning seems to support the idea that the first stage is just the storage of the stimulus-response pair as a unit. The fact that A-B_r and C-B conditions usually did not differ in the first stage does not seem so surprising if the first stage is storage in memory—after all, both groups of subjects had the same material to store. And the failure of response variables to have important effects on the second stage of learning seems consistent with the idea that the second stage is a process of learning to retrieve. The subject must learn to retrieve each item using the stimulus as a cue. Therefore, similarity among the stimuli and previous use of the stimuli to retrieve different pairs probably should make the process of learning to retrieve more difficult.

The main conclusion of this paper is that basic concepts in a theory of paired-associate memorizing should be storage and retrieval, rather than the concepts of traditional association theory. The present data are certainly insufficient to support a firm conclusion on a fundamental theoretical question. However, to the extent that a conclusion is supported, the conclusion seems to be that the theory of memory has no need for a concept describing a process of association in the sense of connection between mental elements. The processes of information storage and retrieval which seem most adequate for handling recall and recognition memory also seem to be favored for the theory of memory for associations.

Relationship with Other Theories

I have gone to considerable effort to emphasize differences between the storage-retrieval theory and the traditional theory of associative connections. I want to conclude by pointing to some consistencies between the theory used here and others that have been developed recently.

Perhaps the clearest relationship exists between the present two-stage theory and the all-or-none model of memorizing (Bower, 1961; Estes, 1960; Rock, 1957). While the all-or-none hypothesis postulates a single discrete step in learning, the present analysis assumes two such steps. And the statistical machinery used in the present analyses is a direct extension of that used in the all-or-none analyses (especially by Bower, 1961).

The two-stage model of Eq. 1 can be viewed as a generalization of the all-or-none model. Suppose in Eq. 1 that $b = 1$. In the interpretation of this article, this would mean that once an item is stored in memory, it can be retrieved reliably enough to meet the experimental criterion of learning. On this interpretation, learning should be approximately all-or-none in cases where retrieval is easy. And this seems to fit with the facts. Typically, experiments showing all-or-none results use short lists of items and two or three response alternatives that were known by the subjects at the beginning of the experiment. The experimental task then is very close to a sorting task, where there are two or three categories and the subject must learn which category each stimulus belongs in. As the number of categories or the number of items in each category increases, retrieval should become more difficult, and we should expect data to depart from the all-or-none model. And data often seem to be consistent with this expectation.

A two-stage Markov model similar to Eq. 1 was analyzed by Bower and Theios (1964), and they demonstrate that the idea of two discrete learning steps was consistent with data from several experiments. These studies included experiments by Theios where subjects memorized associations and had to adjust to changes in the correct responses for individual items. Kintsch (1963) applied the two-stage model successfully to the results of a paired-associate experiment, but he interpreted the stages as response learning and association-forming, an interpretation that seems to be questionable in the light of results reported here. Another application by Kintsch and Morris (1965) involved recognition and free recall learning, but was consistent conceptually with the present argument. Kintsch and Morris' data supported the idea that when subjects memorize a list of words, the first stage of learning an item permits the subjects to recognize the item and the second stage permits him to recall the item. Storage and retrieval seem like acceptable alternative names for these two subprocesses.

Restle (1964) also proposed a two-stage Markov model as an extension of the all-or-none theory. Restle proposed a trace theory in which learning consisted of acquiring strategies enabling the subject to recall traces. In the first stage of learning, a subject becomes able to recall the response for an item, and in the second stage he discriminates that item from other items similar to it in the list. Restle's theory is like the present theory in that mnemonic records are assumed to represent experiences, rather than connections. And Restle's hypothesis about the second stage of learning as discrimination seems indistinguishable from the present view of learning to retrieve. Restle was not entirely clear about the nature of the first stage of learning—he called it "learning to recall a response," but other aspects of his theory make it seem as though stimulus variables probably would influence the process.

The hypothesis presented here bears an interesting relationship to a recent theory by Martin (1968). In Martin's theory, a major factor in memorizing an association is variability in encoding the stimulus. An hypothesis consistent with Martin's view is that some trials may be required to establish a reliable association between some encoding of the stimulus and the response, and then some further trials may be required to stabilize the encoding. This interpretation of Martin's hypothesis is very similar to the hypothesis proposed in the present article. As nearly as I can tell, the evidence that is presented here does not differentiate between Martin's idea and mine, and the two ideas may be different expressions of the same hypothesis.

The present hypothesis of storage and learning to retrieve also closely resembles Feigenbaum's (1963) model of memorizing incorporated in the program EPAM, and Hintzman's (1968) extension of this work in the program SAL. In EPAM and SAL, the early phase of learning is called image building, and its effect is to store a partial representation of the stimulus and a representation of the response in memory. The later phase of learning permits the subject to discriminate among the stimuli in the list, and therefore to permit reliable retrieval. Thus, I see no important difference between the hypothesis offered here and Feigenbaum's and Hintzman's hypotheses for new learning. On the other hand, EPAM and SAL might lead to predictions about A-B_r transfer that differ from the hypothesis about storage and retrieval that was developed based on James' experimental results.

References

ATKINSON, R. C., AND SHIFFRIN, R. M. Human memory: A proposed system and its control processes. In K. W. Spence and J. T. Spence (Eds.), *Advances in the psychology of learning and motivation: research and theory.* Vol. 2. New York: Academic Press, 1968.

BOWER, G. H. Application of a model to paired-associate learning. *Psychometrika,* 1961, **26**, 255–280.

BOWER, G. H., AND THEIOS, J. A learning model for discrete performance levels. In R. C. Atkinson (Ed.), *Studies in mathematical psychology.* Stanford: Stanford University Press, 1964. Pp. 1–31.

CHANDLER, J. P. Subroutine Stepit. Program QCPE 66. Quantum Chemistry Program Exchange, Indiana University, 1965.

CHERNOFF, H., AND LEHMAN, E. L. Use of maximum likelihood estimates in chi square tests of goodness of fit. *Annals of Mathematical Statistics,* 1954, **25**, 579–586.

ESTES, W. K. Learning theory and the new "mental chemistry." *Psychological Review,* 1960, **67**, 207–223.

ESTES, W. K. AND DAPOLITO, F. Independent variation of information storage and retrieval processes in paired-associate learning. *Journal of Experimental Psychology,* 1967, **75**, 18–26.

FEIGENBAUM, E. A. The simulation of verbal learning behavior. In E. A. Feigenbaum and J. Feldman (Eds.), *Computers and thought.* New York: McGraw-Hill, 1963, Pp. 297–309.

GREENO, J. G. Paired associate learning with short term retention: Mathematical analysis and data regarding identification of parameters. *Journal of Mathematical Psychology,* 1967, **4**, 430–472.

GREENO, J. G. Identifiability and statistical properties of two-stage learning with no successes in the initial stage. *Psychometrika,* 1968, **33**, 173–215.

HINTZMAN, D. L. Explorations with a discrimination net model for paired-associate learning. *Journal of Mathematical Psychology,* 1968, **5**, 123–162.

HUMPHREYS, M. AND GREENO, J. G. Interpretation of the two-stage analysis of paired-associate memorizing. *Journal of Mathematical Psychology,* 1970, in press.

JAMES, C. T. AND GREENO, J. G. Effect of A-B overtraining on A-B_r. *Journal of Experimental Psychology,* 1970, in press.

KINTSCH, W. All-or-none learning and the role of repetition in paired-associate learning. *Science,* 1963, **140**, 310–312.

KINTSCH, W., AND MORRIS, C. J. Application of a Markov model to free recall and recognition. *Journal of Experimental Psychology,* 1965, **69**, 200–206.

KOHLER, W. On the nature of associations. *Proceedings of the American Philosophical Society,* 1941, **84**, 489–502.

MARTIN, E. Stimulus meaningfulness and paired-associate transfer: An encoding variability hypothesis. *Psychological Review,* 1968, **75**, 421–441.

MELTON, A. W., AND IRWIN, J. McQ. The influence of degree of interpolated learning on retroactive inhibition and the overt transfer of specific responses. *American Journal of Psychology,* 1940, **53**, 173–203.

MILLER, G. A. Comments on Professor Postman's paper. In C. N. Cofer and B. S. Musgrave (Eds.), *Verbal behavior and learning.* New York: McGraw-Hill, 1963. Pp. 321–329.

NEISSER, U. *Cognitive psychology.* New York: Appleton-Century-Crofts, 1967.

PETERSON, L. R. Short term verbal memory and learning. *Psychological Review,* 1966, **73**, 193–207.

Restle, F. Sources of difficulty in learning paired associates. In R. C. Atkinson (Ed.), *Studies in mathematical psychology*. Stanford: Stanford University Press, 1964. Pp. 116–172.

Rock, I. The role of repetition in associative learning. *American Journal of Psychology*, 1957, **70**, 186–193.

Underwood, B. J., and Schulz, R. W. *Meaningfulness and verbal learning*. Philadelphia: Lippincott, 1960.

9

Short-Term Memory for Associations[1]

Bennet B. Murdock, Jr.
University of Toronto

In this chapter, I would like to discuss a simple model of short-term memory (STM) for paired associates. It is the fixed-point or fluctuation model previously suggested (Murdock, 1967), and it is a finite-state Markov model which postulates two opposing processes, forgetting and reminiscence. This model in itself is incomplete in that it does not specify what the underlying states are or how they are transformed into observable behavior. I shall first review the model and its domain, then suggest several alternatives that might underlie the observed behavior.

Fluctuation Model

This model applies to paired associates consisting of common English words paired at random. Typical examples are GALLANT-LEGEND, INSPIRE-BRIEFLY, REASON-SUCCESS. The original source for these words was the Thorndike-Lorge (Thorndike and Lorge,

[1] This work has been supported by research grants from the National Science Foundation, the National Research Council of Canada, and the Ontario Mental Health Foundation. I am endebted to Robert S. Lockhart for many helpful discussions and suggestions.

1944) word count, and the 4000 most common words were chosen. By now, the pool has been reduced to approximately 1200 words, all two syllables in length, not more than eight letters long, with contractions, archaic words, homophones, and proper nouns deleted. To insure adequate sampling, lists are constructed by sampling randomly and without replacement from this pool. Whenever possible, each subject is given a different (computer-generated) set of randomly drawn lists to avoid any possible confounding of lists and conditions.

A list consists of some number of pairs, generally six or less, which are presented sequentially. Typical presentation rate is 2 sec per pair. Immediately following list presentation, a probe is presented; the probe is the first word of one of the pairs from the list. The subject is to recall the second word of that particular pair, and usually he is forced to guess if unsure; omissions are not permitted. Following recall the subject may be asked to append a confidence judgment, usually on a six-point scale (from +++ for "sure it's correct" to −−− for "sure it's incorrect"). Only one pair from each list is probed, and the identity of the target pair is obviously not revealed to the subject until the probe is presented. One advantage of this probe technique is that selective rehearsal is difficult; given six pairs, any one of them might be tested.

In any one session, typically 60–72 lists are given to an individual subject, so each of the possible probe positions is tested perhaps a dozen times. One of the nice features of this method is its extreme stability; I once tested subjects for three hours in a row (though with 10-minute pauses every hour) and there was no detectable performance change over the entire session. There is gradual improvement over sessions, but its magnitude is small enough so that it can generally be disregarded. As far as proactive inhibition is concerned, there is little within lists and none across lists (Murdock, 1964), so the marked forgetting that occurs is due to retroactive effects. It is true that naive subjects show more primacy and less recency than practiced subjects, but this difference disappears with surprising rapidity (perhaps one or two lists). However, the present model is intended to apply to the steady-state performance.

According to the model a pair can be in one of two states. To change the terminology slightly, if it is in state A, it is accessible and it can be recalled; if it is in state N, it is not accessible and it cannot be recalled. The use of the term "accessible" follows that suggested by Mandler (1967) and Tulving and Pearlstone (1966). When a pair is presented, it starts a state A with probability p_0 which is generally close to 1.00. With probability $(1 - p_0)$ it starts in state N. Change of state (from A to N or from N to A) is possible whenever a subsequent (i.e., different) pair is presented for study or whenever some other (previously presented) pair is tested. In other words, there is input and/or output interference (Murdock, 1963b; Tulving and Arbuckle, 1963) and here the two are presumed equal.

Transitions in either direction are possible. When a pair goes from state A to state N we may call this "forgetting," and when a pair goes from state N to state A we may call this "reminiscence." The transition probabilities are α and β for forgetting and reminiscence, respectively. Thus, given a unit of input or output interference, with probability α, a pair may go from state A to state N, but with probability $(1 - \alpha)$ it will not; with probability β it may go from state N to state A but with probability $(1 - \beta)$ it will not.

After presentation, the fate of an individual pair is a stochastic process; it fluctuates from one state to the other according to the transition matrix T, where $T = \begin{pmatrix} 1-\alpha & \alpha \\ \beta & 1-\beta \end{pmatrix}$. If the starting state is represented by the row vector s where $s = (p_0, 1 - p_0)$ then, after n intervening items (input and/or output), $p_n = sT^n$. That is, the probability vector for the two states is the nth power of the transition matrix multiplied by the starting-state vector s. The eigenvalues (or latent roots) of T are 1 and $(1 - \alpha - \beta)$ and, provided $0 < \alpha + \beta < 2$, it can be shown (see Goldberg, 1961, pp. 221–228) that

$$p(\mathrm{A}) = \beta/(\alpha + \beta) + (1 - \alpha - \beta)^n[p_0 - \beta/(\alpha + \beta)].$$

Thus, as n increases, provided $p_0 > \beta/(\alpha + \beta)$ the probability $p(\mathrm{A})$ that a pair will be in state A will fall at a rate determined by $(1 - \alpha - \beta)$ and approach as a limiting value the asymptote $\beta/(\alpha + \beta)$.

An example is shown in Fig. 1, where $p(\mathrm{A})$ is plotted as a function of n. The data are represented by the vertical bars which are the means and standard deviations (across subjects) for Expt. III of Murdock (1963a), and the staircase is the model. The estimated value of the forgetting parameter α was .39, the estimated value of the reminiscence parameter β was .13, so the asymptote (dotted line in Fig. 1) was .25. That is, the model predicts that performance will approach as a limiting value $\beta/(\alpha + \beta)$ and this value is the asymptote of the STM retention curve.

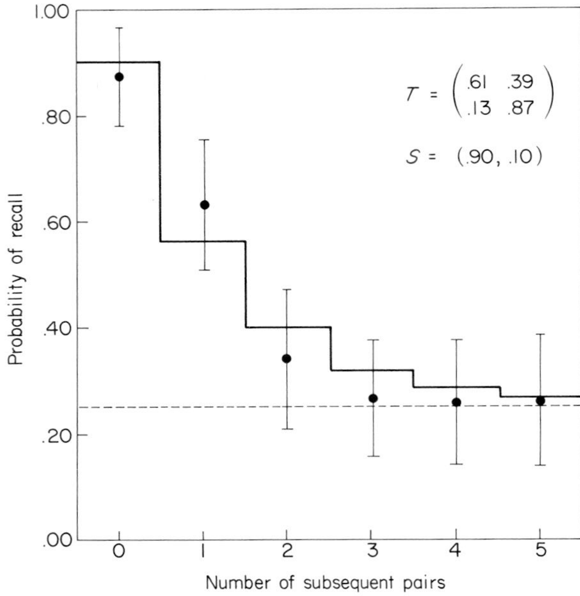

FIG. 1. Recall probability as a function of number of subsequent pairs (data from Murdock, 1967).

The method of estimating parameters was as follows: The drop in recall probability is sufficiently rapid so that one is quite safe in estimating the numerical value of the asymptote simply by mean performance over the first three or four pairs in the list. For these experimental conditions, there is little doubt but what it is consistently of the order of .25 (e.g., Murdock, 1963a). Given this value, one can make a semilog plot of $p(\mathrm{A}) - \beta/(\alpha + \beta)$ as a function of n which, as shown by Eq. 1, will have a slope of $1 - \alpha - \beta$. Then, given the slope and the asymptote, one can solve for α and β. While this is obviously a very casual approach to the estimation problem, as a first approximation the fit seems reasonable and there seems little point now in making use of more precise techniques. The value of p_0 was set at .90 simply because it is a typical value for performance on an immediate retention test under these conditions.

A second example is shown in Fig. 2, which shows data for three individual subjects each tested on 648 lists (Murdock, 1963a, Expt. IV). On the whole the fit is not bad, and there seems to be more individual variation in α than in β. Yet a third example is shown in Fig. 3, which

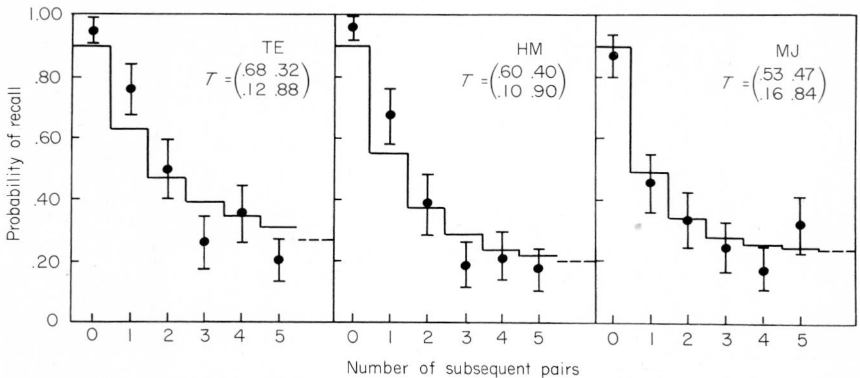

FIG. 2. Recall probability for three individual subjects (data from Murdock, 1963a, Expt. IV).

shows data from a group experiment in which presentation time per pair was varied (Murdock, 1963c, Expt. II). In a between-lists design, pairs were presented either 1, 2, or 3 sec per pair, and the main effect with this experimental manipulation seemed to be that β increased with presentation time but α was not greatly affected. For consistency, p_0 was held at .90 for all three panels of both Figs. 2 and 3, and in some cases (e.g., the first panel of Fig. 3) the fit could be improved if p_0 were also free to vary.

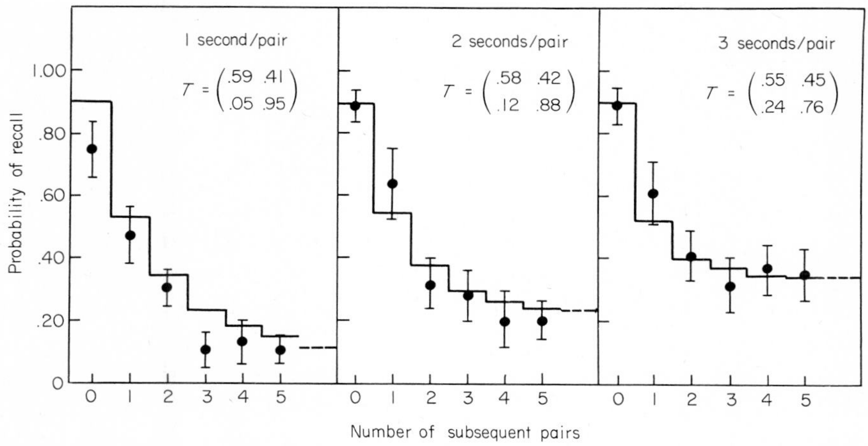

FIG. 3. Recall probability for three different presentation rates (data from Murdock, 1963c, Expt. II).

The simple fluctuation model provides then what I feel to be a reasonable description to account for data on STM for paired associates obtained under the experimental conditions described above. It is obviously not a model of memory in general; it is a model for a particular kind of memory. How does it compare with other models, and what are its strengths and weaknesses?

In comparison with other models (e.g., Atkinson and Shiffrin, 1968; Bower, 1967; Broadbent, 1958; Peterson, 1966; Waugh and Norman, 1965), this fluctuation model does not postulate separate stores (or processes) for short- and long-term memory. In this regard, I would agree with Melton (1963) in his insistence on a continuity between STM and LTM. In fact, I know of no evidence which forces a conclusion of discontinuity with anything like the conviction of, say, the dark-adaptation curve for rod and cone vision (Woodworth and Schlosberg, 1954, Fig. 13–6, p. 370).

Two processes, forgetting and reminiscence, are postulated which occur together over time. Independent evidence for their existence is not available, nor is it immediately obvious to me how it might be obtained. However, pairs are presumed to fluctuate between states, and the probe technique is useful in focusing on and testing the momentary state of any desired pair. Individual pairs are assumed, generally, to start in state A and, over time, migrate as it were to state N. To me, this seems a more reasonable type of model than learning models of paired associates (e.g., Bower, 1961) which say that pairs start in some unlearned state and eventually move to a learned state which is absorbing. The Bower analysis, influential though it has been, overlooks the immediate memory changes that immediately follow presentation, and I am not convinced that absorbing states are really appropriate characterizations for memory or verbal-learning tasks. The extrapolation to the multitrial situation that I have suggested (Murdock, 1963c) says in general that performance on trial $n + 1$ reflects retention from trial n, and more particularly that the same short-term forgetting occurs trial after trial but to a progressively rising asymptote. How the transition parameters α and β change with repetition (indeed, if they do) has not yet been studied experimentally.

What empirical phenomena does this fluctuation model describe or predict? First, it predicts an asymptote in the retention curve that results from the fact that reminiscence is possible. While it is more likely for a transition from A to N than from N to A, at longer retention intervals the larger absolute number of pairs in state N leads to the equilibrium.

The asymptote is deduced from the model, whereas dichotomous models of memory postulate a long-term store and point to the asymptote as an empirical confirmation of the original assumption. The marked recency effect is also consistent with the model, though both its slope and the numerical value of the asymptote will clearly depend upon the values of the parameters α and β. No primacy effect is predicted, and almost never is one found. As noted before (Murdock, 1967), this model predicts quite nicely the slope of the length-difficulty function for single-trial recall of lists of paired associates of lengths from 9–100 pairs. Also, in an Estes (1960) RTT paradigm where a single presentation or reinforcement (R) is followed by two tests (T) separated from each other by other presentations and/or tests, the model predicts that the frequency of NC items [i.e., pairs that were not correct (N) on T_1 but were correct on T_2] should increase with the amount of interference in the interval between T_1 and T_2. There is quite a bit of evidence in the Arbuckle (1964) thesis that is confirmatory.

One of the limitations of this fluctuation model is that it is quite narrow in scope. At this point, I would be hesitant to extrapolate it to single-trial free recall or to tasks with a strong serial-ordering component. There are enough empirical phenomena that are distinctly different for these different types of tasks, and I would rather have a model which is close to the data even at the expense of generality.

The restriction to single presentations may seem unduely severe to some. Lifting this restriction would allow application to the multitrial situation, but would require at least two further assumptions. One assumption would have to be whether repetition laid down an independent trace or simply changed the numerical values of the parameters α and/or β. The second assumption (assuming either the anticipation or study-test procedure) would have to deal with the effect of correct recalls on the subsequent fate of the pair. I shall return to this point shortly.

One possible assumption about the effect of repetition would be that the effect of presentation depended upon the current state of the pair. Thus, repetition would have one effect on a pair in state A, but a different effect on a pair in state N. If this effect were to lay down a second trace in the latter case, but not in the former, and if correct recall could come from either of the traces then perhaps the "Peterson Paradox" could be predicted from the model. This possibility is mentioned only to indicate one possible line of future development; for further discussion of this problem see Greeno (1967).

A second problem with the model is the counter-intuitive suggestion that a pair which starts (with probability $1 - p_0$) in state N can "reminisce" to state A. Unreasonable though it may seem, this assumption has been made, and the only justification is aesthetic: otherwise the model becomes messier.

A third problem, pointed out to me by Robert Bjork (1967, personal communication), is that if the retention interval between T_1 and T_2 in an RTT paradigm is long enough, performance on T_2 should be independent of performance on T_1 and hence (for instance) the NC and the CC proportions should be equal. (As above, N and C represent noncorrect and correct, respectively.) No empirical data are even close; Estes (1960) reports values of .09 and .71, respectively. A possible answer would be that, as suggested by Eimas and Zeaman (1963), a correct recall on T_1 is in some sense self-reinforcing.

There is in fact some supporting evidence that a single correct recall has a disproportionate effect on memory. In two studies (Murdock, 1961) of paired-associate learning using common words and the study-test method, the first study (20 pairs, 32 subjects) showed that probability of correct recall of pairs *as yet unrecalled* was .07, .12, .14, .29, and .29 on test trials 1, 2, 3, 4, and 5, respectively. The probability of a correct recall on the trial immediately following the first correct recall was .68. In a second study (30 pairs, 10 subjects), the recall probability for unrecalled pairs was .03, .12, .11, .21, and .21 for test trials 1, 2, 3, 4, and 5, respectively. The probability of a correct recall on the trial immediately following the first correct recall was .79. There seems to be a discontinuity at the point of the first correct recall, so on this basis, one would indeed expect to find differences between NC and CC proportions in an RTT paradigm.

Enough then for the evaluative comments on the fluctuation model. Let me turn now to a further extension that I feel is needed. Even within the very limited scope of the model, it has no obvious way of accommodating the confidence-judgment findings. Data from a prior experiment (Murdock, 1966) are shown in Fig. 4; these are *a posteriori* probabilities, the probability that the response (recall) was correct given each of the six possible confidence judgments. These data were pooled over all probe positions, but are shown separately for each of the four individual subjects (LB, DO, WS, and AC). Clearly, discrimination is very good; when subjects are sure they are right (+++) they nearly always are, when the are sure they are wrong (−−−) again they nearly always are, and intermediate judgments are monotonically ordered.

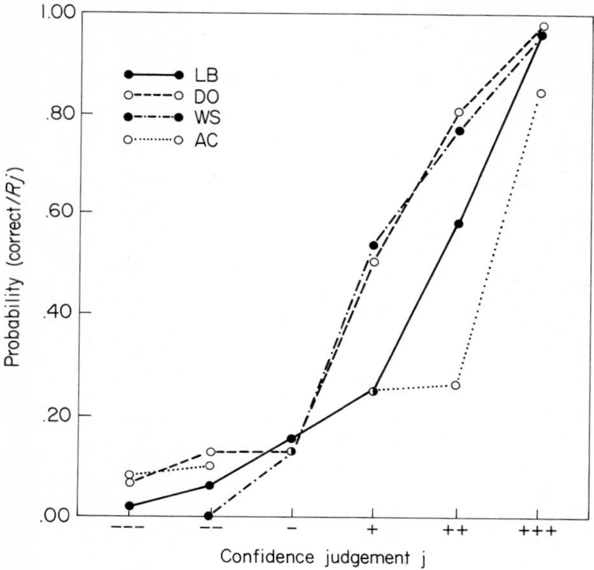

FIG. 4. *A posteriori* probabilities for four individual subjects (data from Murdock, 1966).

In addition to the *a posteriori* probabilities, these data (confidence judgments partioned on the basis of accuracy) were analyzed by methods appropriate to signal-detection theory (TSD). In terms of the TSD model (e.g., Green and Swets, 1966), the conclusion drawn was that there were criterion changes as a function of the retention interval such that, as predicted by the theory, the criterion became more strict as probability correct decreased. However, there were no changes in d'; the value of d' stayed fairly constant around 2.0, regardless of retention interval (probe position).

To digress for a minute, there have been a number of recent applications of TSD to STM (e.g., Bernbach, 1967; Donaldson and Murdock, 1968; Egan, 1958; Green and Moses, 1966; Kintsch, 1967; Murdock, 1965, 1966; Norman, 1966; Norman and Wickelgren, 1965; Parks, 1966). With recognition-memory procedures, the application is quite straightforward; these may be considered Type I or stimulus-conditional procedures (Clarke, Birdsall, and Tanner, 1959) as the *a priori* probabilities are under the control of the experimenter. On the other hand, studies of memory using recall measures would be Type II or response-conditional procedures, and these are more difficult to evaluate in terms of

TSD (Green, 1960). The problem is that, as in word-recognition studies, the subject first has to select a response and then he has to evaluate it.

Then there is the further question of the identification of the parameters. What does one mean by "strength of an association?" If the proper measure of strength is d' then, according to the data just mentioned, one would have to conclude that there was no diminution of trace strength in STM. The accuracy data (probability of correct recall) would clearly seem to be at variance with this conclusion. One possible solution (which has been suggested) would simply be to eschew Type II procedures in STM completely.

I would take a different point of view. I would like to suggest that not only are Type II procedures useful, but that they can provide us with some indispensible information to clarify some of the theoretical issues. Further, I think that consideration of these problems forces us to direct our attention to the underlying states and the decision processes that map them into observable responses.

Decision Processes

The general argument is as follows: the two states, state A and state N, may be thought of as partially overlapping distributions. When a probe is presented, the subject looks inside his head, as it were, and makes an observation based on the current state of the memory trace. On the basis of this observation, he is able to make a response (recall) and compute a likelihood ratio λ. Then λ can be mapped into a confidence judgment. The interval between the presentation of the target pair and the presentation of the probe (more specifically, the intervening interference) determines $p(\mathrm{A})$, the probability that the pair will be in state A. Then, at the time of presentation of the probe, no further changes in state occur; instead, the subject makes an observation and a subsequent decision. It is the nature of these underlying states that must now be considered.

One possibility would simply be to take a continuous strength model (e.g., Wickelgren, Chapter 3) or postulate a "scale of apparent oldness" (Bernbach, 1967) such that pairs in state N are normally distributed along some such continuous dimension and pairs in state A are in a comparable distribution with mean difference of d'. While such an assumption might eventually turn out to be the proper one, at this point it does not seem to me to be very helpful in clarifying or understanding the underlying processes, and at the very least, I think one should consider alternatives. Then perhaps some empirical tests will be possible.

I would like to consider three possible alternatives: a binomial model, a Poisson model, and a geometric (exponential) model. That is, the distributions represented by states N and A might be either binomial, Poisson, or geometric. A rationale for each will be suggested, and some relevant data will be briefly considered.

Binomial

Assume that we have distributions $f_N(\mathbf{x})$ and $f_A(\mathbf{x})$ which characterize states N and A, respectively. To facilitate exposition, assume that $\mathbf{x}$ is some discrete random variable which might represent the *attributes* by which a pair is encoded. Thus, when a pair is presented not only are the words themselves encoded and stored but also attributes which characterize the pair are encoded and stored. Then $\mathbf{x}$ is the number of attributes which characterize any particular pair.

Assume that there are 0, 1, 2, . . . , n attributes that might characterize a pair in state N. This would suggest that what we mean by state N is an incorrect pairing rather than a correct pairing that cannot be found. For instance, in a two-pair list consisting of A––B and C––D, if the words switched and the pairs became A––D and C––B then A––D would be a pair in state N. A pair in state A (e.g., C––D) would differ from a pair in state N in that it would always have exactly k more attributes that would characterize it. Thus, its range would be from k to $k + n$.

Given the binomial, for a pair in state N we have $f_N(\mathbf{x}) = \binom{n}{x} p^{\mathbf{x}} q^{n-\mathbf{x}}$ for $\mathbf{x} = 0, 1, 2, \ldots, n$ and for a pair in state A, we have $f_A(\mathbf{x}) = \binom{n}{\mathbf{x}-k} p^{\mathbf{x}-k} q^{n-\mathbf{x}+k}$ for $\mathbf{x} = k, k+1, k+2, \ldots, k+n$. This would imply that the attributes are binary and independent. The entire distribution for state A is that of state N shifted k steps to the right. These distributions arise when one considers some large number of trials (lists); that is, they are the distribution of attributes over trials.

At the end of list presentation, when the probe is presented the target pair is either in state A or in state N. The subject is assumed to "examine" the memory trace associated with the probe, obtain an attribute count, report out the word associated with the probe, and give a confidence judgment based on the attribute count. If the attribute count is low, the subject may "know" that the response is incorrect, and whether the subject simply says "I don't know" or gives a response with a low confidence (say ———) depends upon what instructions are given. In our experiments, I would rather have a forced response supplemented by confidence judgments than allow omissions.

It is assumed that the subject forms a likelihood ratio λ from the attribute count. This ratio is mapped into a confidence judgment according to some decision rule. A maximum-likelihood rule would say that, given a symmetric payoff matrix, the subject should accept an observation as coming from state A whenever the value of λ exceeded the odds against the occurrence of state A; that is, whenever $\lambda > [1 - p(\mathrm{A})]/p(\mathrm{A})$. It seems unlikely that the subject does in fact follow strictly a maximum-likelihood rule, but on the other hand, the fact that his criterion does seem to change appropriately with retention interval (Murdock, 1966) lends some support to the argument.

If the presence or absence of an attribute is equally probable (and, for maximum informativeness, it should be) then the likelihood ratio

$$\lambda = f_{\mathrm{A}}(\mathbf{x})/f_{\mathrm{N}}(\mathbf{x}) = [\mathbf{x}(\mathbf{x}-1)(\mathbf{x}-2) \cdots (\mathbf{x}-k+1)]/[(n-\mathbf{x}+k)(n-\mathbf{x}+k-1) \cdots (n-\mathbf{x}+1)]$$

for this model. To give a hypothetical example, if there were four attributes and if $k = 2$, then for probe position 6 [$p(\mathrm{A}) = .90$], the maximum likelihood rule would say that any attribute count greater than 1 should be accepted; for probe position 5 [$p(\mathrm{A}) = .60$] any attribute count greater than 2 should be accepted, while for probe position 1 – 4 [$p(\mathrm{A}) = .25$] any attribute count greater than 3 should be accepted. If one wished to compute a numerical value for d' it would be 2.0.

As must be obvious, this attribute model is essentially a binomial analogue of the normal-distribution model of TSD. The horizontal axis would be labeled "number of attributes," rather than energy or voltage, and the random variable is discrete rather than continuous. This model is probably indistinguishable from the dice game described in Swets, Tanner, and Birdsall (1961) if the third die with value 0 or 3 in their example is associated with k in the attribute model.

Poisson

Assume that the underlying distributions are Poisson, with $f_{\mathrm{A}}(\mathbf{x}) = e^{-\mu_{\mathrm{A}}} \mu_{\mathrm{A}}{}^{\mathbf{x}}/\mathbf{x}!$ and $f_{\mathrm{N}}(\mathbf{x}) = e^{-\mu_{\mathrm{N}}} \mu_{\mathrm{N}}{}^{\mathbf{x}}/\mathbf{x}!$ for $\mathbf{x} = 0, 1, 2, \ldots$. The distribution $f_{\mathrm{A}}(\mathbf{x})$ has mean μ_{A} and the distribution $f_{\mathrm{N}}(\mathbf{x})$ has mean μ_{N}, and assume that $\mu_A > \mu_N$. A possible interpretation would be in terms of a copy process (see Bernbach, Chapter 4). For instance, suppose that some small number of copies or replicas of each pair were made, and for each pair the number of copies was a discrete random variable. Not only would duplicates be made when a pair was in state A, but also when a pair was in state N. There would, however, be more copies in the former case than the latter. Then, when presented with the probe, the subject would interrogate memory, obtain a count of the number of copies, and respond on the basis of this count. Since memory holds much else besides these recently established copies, the finding of a copy would certainly be a rare event. A serial exhaustive search of memory for copies seems unreasonable, but parallel search algorithms do exist (e.g., Falkoff, 1965).

To specify the decision process, it would be assumed that the subject would form a likelihood ratio λ from the count reported out from the search of memory. As before, $\lambda = f_A(\mathbf{x})/f_N(\mathbf{x})$ and the likelihood ratio would have to be mapped into a confidence judgment. Speaking generally, the more copies found the more sure the subject could be that the observation was in fact a pair in state A. Again, the difference between state A and state N would seem to be that of correct or incorrect pairings.

It is easy to show that a plot of log λ as a function of $\mathbf{x}$ would be a straight line with intercept $\mu_N - \mu_A$ and slope $\ln(\mu_A/\mu_N)$. This would be an operating characteristic which would not necessitate working with cumulative distributions. By an operating characteristic (ROC curve) is meant the curve traced out when a subject varies his mode of response (acceptance criterion) without any changes in the external parameters of the stimulus situation (Green and Swets, 1966, p. 35). One nice feature would be that each distribution [i.e., $f_A(\mathbf{x})$ and $f_N(\mathbf{x})$] is a one-parameter distribution, and the two parameters (i.e., μ_A, μ_N) could be estimated from this single linear function. However, it should be emphasized that such an ROC plot is in terms of $\mathbf{x}$ (number of copies), so the empirical usefulness of these relations requires knowledge of or assumptions about how this observation (i.e., $\mathbf{x}$) is transformed by the subject into a confident judgment.

Geometric

A binomial model may reasonably be associated with the encoding of associations in terms of attributes, and a Poisson model may describe the number of replicas or copies generated during storage that are observed or counted at the time of recall. The third and last of the three alternatives suggests instead that the underlying distributions are geometric, and these distributions might reasonably result from a search process that occurs at the time of retrieval of information from memory.

Assume that (as in the Feigenbaum and Simon, 1963, EPAM model) information is stored at terminal nodes of a sorting tree. Given a probe the subject follows a path through the tree until he comes to a node where a match may or may not occur. Given a match the subject outputs the response; otherwise he tries again. What constitutes a match is not certain, but it could be, for instance, that the two words of a pair are at a given terminal node and a "match" means that the information stored at the node contains the presented probe.

There is no point to a search process if the target information is known beforehand. Therefore, there must be some number of alternative routes from which the subject must select. Apparently, it is a small number. Within this number, assume that the subject samples randomly and without replacement. Then the number of searches until a match will be geometric with $f_A(\mathbf{x}) = p_A q_A{}^{\mathbf{x}-1}$ and $f_A(\mathbf{x}) = p_N q_N{}^{\mathbf{x}-1}$ for $\mathbf{x} = 1, 2, 3, \ldots$. Thus, the random variable is the number of searches, $\mathbf{x}$. The process is imperfect in that there is some probability of a match with an incorrect pair, evidence for which being the occasional incorrect response with high confidence judgment. However, in general, a pair in state N could, in fact, be considered to be one in which the associative connection (or memory trace) was intact but was not accessible in that it could not be found in the search.

Here the likelihood ratio would be formed on the basis of the number of searches before a match. As opposed to the two preceding models, here a low number would be associated with state A, rather than state N. This discrete process in which the random variable is the number of searches could easily be modified to be a continuous process in which the random variable would be, say, the time to the first match. Then one would have an exponential model as described, for instance, by Green and Swets (1966, pp. 78–81). As they point out, this model has the desirable features that the exponential is a one-parameter distribution and the likelihood ratio is monotonic with the decision axis. (So too the Poisson.)

For an exponential model, the ROC plot should be linear on a log–log plot. That is, if one plots (the complement of) hit rate as a function of (the complement of) false-alarm rate on logarithmic graph paper, the resulting function should be linear with a slope equal to the ratio of the parameters of the two underlying exponential distributions $f_A(\mathbf{x})$ and $f_N(\mathbf{x})$. To make such plots from confidence-judgment data, it is necessary to cumulate distributions in the customary fashion. However, the advantage of an exponential (compared, say, to the Poisson) is that one does not need to know how the underlying datum is mapped into a confidence judgment. Instead, all one needs are the usual TSD assumptions that the confidence judgments are monotonic with respect to the underlying process and not different for states A and N.

Comparison

Here, then, are three alternatives to describe what the underlying distributions of $f_A(\mathbf{x})$ and $f_N(\mathbf{x})$ might be. The binomial, Poisson, and geometric seem to focus attention on processes of encoding, storage, and retrieval, respectively. Obviously, in STM all three processes must occur, but perhaps one plays a larger role in the typical experimental tasks we use. However, the identification of processes with distributions is not necessary, and has been suggested here at least partly to stimulate interest.

What sort of an experimental test of these three distributions might be possible? Clearly the appropriate data are those of paired-associate recall supplemented by confidence judgments. A reasonable approach might seem to be to make ROC plots in the conventional fashion. However, because most distributions do not differ much from the normal and, in fact, approach normality in the limit, in practice, it often works out that underlying Poisson or exponential distributions give remarkably linear functions on double-normal plots. In fact, other distributions also may result in very close approximations to linear ROC plots. Therefore, linearity on a double-normal plot is really a very weak test.

However, slopes are much more revealing. Comparing the two distributions $f_A(\mathbf{x})$ and $f_A(\mathbf{x})$, for the binomial model the variability is the same; for the Poisson the variability of $f_A(\mathbf{x})$ should be greater than the variability of $f_N(\mathbf{x})$, and for the geometric-exponential the reverse should be true. Therefore, double-normal plots might be useful, not in terms of whether the fit is linear but whether and how the slope varies from the 45° line.

One can also examine the distributions of confidence judgments directly. While it is not possible to specify exactly how the likelihood ratio is mapped into confidence judgments, still considerations of symmetry are applicable. For the binomial model, there should be symmetrical confidence judgments in that a high attribute count should lead to as much positive certainty as a low attribute count should lead to negative certainty. Neither the Poisson nor the geometric should be symmetrical. In the Poisson, a low count would lead to negative certainty (i.e., confidence that the observation was wrong) but how many copies are required to elicit a confidence judgment of +++ is not clear. For the geometric, it is the other way around; a match on the first search should lead to positive certainty (i.e., confidence that the observation was wrong), but the number of searches for a confidence judgment of ––– is not clear.

Some relevant data are shown in Table 1. They came from an experiment (Murdock, 1966) in which four individual subjects were tested intensively under Type II conditions (paired-associate recall supplemented by confidence judgments). For each subject at each serial position the distribution of confidence judgments was obtained separately for correct and incorrect recalls. I did the pooling (which is shown in Table 1) as follows: for each subject separately I started with the first and the last probe position. I then combined adjacent positions (working in toward the middle) as long as the distribution at the next position did not seem to be very different from the outside position. While this is obviously a rather subjective approach, I don't think that any great distortion has been introduced by this averaging process. Finally, these early and late distributions were pooled over the four subjects, and these are the data shown in Table 1. The number of observations on which each row is based is shown in the last column of the table. There is no entry for incorrect-late pairs because they were too infrequent (45 in all).

The distributions of confidence judgments for correct responses are

TABLE 1
Frequency Functions for Confidence Judgments for Correct-Late, Correct-Early, and Incorrect-Early Pairs (Data from Murdock, 1966).

	–––	––	–	+	++	+++	N
Correct-Late	.01	–	–	.02	.05	.913	734
Correct-Early	.03	.01	.02	.08	.15	.709	560
Incorrect-Early	.426	.13	.11	.17	.07	.10	540

TABLE 2
Frequencies of Confidence Judgments for Each Subject for Early Pairs Separately for Correct (C) and Noncorrect (N) Recalls (Data from Murdock, 1966).

	LB		DO		WS		AC	
	C	N	C	N	C	N	C	N
+++	82	6	50	2	168	9	97	35
++	15	8	31	8	34	14	2	10
+	4	42	21	26	20	19	2	5
−	6	32	5	17	3	9	0	0
−−	0	26	3	26	0	9	2	7
−−−	2	77	1	10	1	14	11	129
N	109	191	111	89	226	74	114	186

quite sharp both for early and for late pairs. The geometric distribution is not a bad fit for either. In comparison, the incorrect judgments are more variable and (though not shown here) yield more intersubject variation. The fact that the distributions differ for early and late responses can be interpreted as being a manifestation of a criterion shift; for longer retention intervals (early probe positions) the subjects are somewhat more cautious in assigning confidence judgments.

Finally, the data of the four individual subjects for the early probe positions (combined as described above) are shown in Table 2. If one draws ROC curves for each subject in the way that a geometric search-time model would suggest, the fits are really quite good, and the numerical value of the slope does not vary all that much across subjects. However, it is also the case that ROC plots on double-normal paper for the same data yields reasonable fits, which indicates again that linearity is not always a powerful test to discriminate models. It is also true that the data of the individual subjects, particularly for the correct responses, is reasonably described by geometric distributions. Perhaps the strongest statement that one should make is that, all in all, these data are quite consistent with a geometric or exponential search process.

Summary

I have tried to suggest a characterization of the processes which might underlie the observed performance in studies of STM for paired associates consisting of common English words. The fluctuation model is a finite-state model that postulates two states, accessible and non-accessible, with transitions possible in either direction. Transitions occur with input and/or output interference, and the transition parameters are α and β. Simple though this model is, it seems able to accommodate the gross features of the extant data on STM.

To attempt a more detailed characterization of the processes involved, three possible distributions were considered that could generate likelihood ratios which in turn would serve as the basis for the confidence judgments the subjects give in recall. These distributions were binomial, Poisson, and geometric, and they may be associated with encoding, storage, and retrieval processes, respectively. In each case states A and N are presumed to differ in only one parameter of the distribution. Insofar as experimental data are relevant, the indication is that the geometric (exponential) may be the most appropriate.

In closing, let me make one further comment about relationships between measures of TSD and data from Type II procedures in STM. According to the analyses suggested above, the proper measure of memory for Type II procedures would be probability of correct recall, not the d' of TSD. In general, d' would provide a measure, not of "trace strength," but of discriminability. It would reflect the accuracy with which the subject could discriminate between the two states A and N. Thus, it would be quite possible for memory as measured by accuracy data (i.e., probability of correct recall) to be quite poor, yet discriminability (as measured by d') to be quite high. In fact, this is what the data seem to show. So the fact that d' does not change over probe position but recall probability does (Murdock, 1966) is not necessarily contradictory. What the mechanisms are that provide the basis for the discriminability, however, remains to be clarified by further investigation.

References

ARBUCKLE, T. Y. Intratrial interference in "immediate" memory. Unpublished doctoral dissertation, University of Toronto, 1964.

ATKINSON, R. C., AND SHIFFRIN, R. M. Human memory: A proposed system and its control processes. In K. W. Spence and J. T. Spence (Eds.), *Advances in the psychology of learning and motivation research and theory*. Vol. 2. New York: Academic Press, 1968. Pp. 89–195.

BERNBACH, H. A. Decision processes in memory. *Psychological Review*, 1967, **74**, 462–480.

BOWER, G. H. Application of a model to paired-associate learning. *Psychometrika*, 1961, **26**, 255–280.

BOWER, G. H. A descriptive theory of memory. In D. P. Kimble (Ed.), *Learning, remembering, and forgetting*. Vol. 2. New York: New York Academy of Sciences, 1967. Pp. 112–185.

BROADBENT, D. E. *Perception and communication*. New York: Macmillan (Pergamon), 1958.

CLARKE, F. R., BIRDSALL, T. G., AND TANNER, W. P., JR. Two types of ROC curves and definitions of parameters. *Journal of the Acoustical Society of America*, 1959, **31**, 629–630.

DONALDSON, W., AND MURDOCK, B. B., JR. Criterion change in continuous recognition memory. *Journal of Experimental Psychology*, 1968, **76**, 325–330.

EGAN, J. P. Recognition memory and the operating characteristic. Technical Note AFCRC-TN-58-51, 1958 Indiana University, Hearing and Communication Laboratory.

EIMAS, P. D., AND ZEAMAN, D. Response speed change in an Estes' paired-associate "miniature" experiment. *Journal of Verbal Learning and Verbal Behavior*, 1963, **1**, 384–388.

ESTES, W. K. Learning theory and the new "mental chemistry." *Psychological Review*, 1960, **67**, 207–223.

FALKOFF, A. D. Algorithms for parallel search memories. *Journal of the Association for Computing Machinery*, 1965, **12**, 488–511.

FEIGENBAUM, E. A., AND SIMON, H. A. Brief notes on the EPAM theory of verbal learning. In C. N. Cofer and B. S. Musgrave (Eds.), *Verbal behavior and learning*. New York: McGraw-Hill, 1963. Pp. 333–335.

GOLDBERG, S. *Difference equations*. New York: Wiley, 1961.

GREEN, D. M. Psychoacoustics and detection theory. *Journal of the Acoustical Society of America*, 1960, **32**, 1189–1203.

GREEN, D. M., AND MOSES, F. L. On the equivalence of two recognition measures of short-term memory. *Psychological Bulletin*, 1966, **66**, 228–234.

GREEN, D. M., AND SWETS, J. A. *Signal detection theory and psychophysics*. New York: Wiley, 1966.

GREENO, J. G. Paired-associate learning with short-term retention: Mathematical analysis and data regarding identification of parameters. *Journal of Mathematical Psychology*, 1967, **4**, 430–472.

KINTSCH, W. Memory and decision aspects of recognition learning. *Psychology Review*, 1967, **74**, 496–504.

MANDLER, G. Verbal learning. In *New directions in psychology*. Vol. III. New York: Holt, Rinehart & Winston, 1967.

MELTON, A. W. Implications of short-term memory for a general theory of memory. *Journal of Verbal Learning and Verbal Behavior*, 1963, **2**, 1–21.

MURDOCK, B. B., JR. Repetition in paired-associate learning. Paper presented at the meeting of the Eastern Psychological Association, Philadelphia, April 7, 1961.

MURDOCK, B. B., JR. Short-term retention of single paired associates. *Journal of Experimental Psychology*, 1963, **65**, 433–443. (a)

MURDOCK, B. B., JR. Interpolated recall in short-term memory. *Journal of Experimental Psychology*, 1963, **66**, 525–532. (b)

MURDOCK, B. B., JR. Short-term memory and paired-associate learning. *Journal of Verbal Learning and Verbal Behavior*, 1963, **2**, 320–328. (c)

MURDOCK, B. B., JR. Proactive inhibition in short-term memory. *Journal of Experimental Psychology*, 1964, **68**, 184–189.

MURDOCK, B. B., JR. Signal-detection theory and short-term memory. *Journal of Experimental Psychology*, 1965, **70**, 443–447.

MURDOCK, B. B., JR. The criterion problem in short-term memory. *Journal of Experimental Psychology*, 1966, **72**, 317–324.

MURDOCK, B. B., JR. A fixed-point model for short-term memory. *Journal of Mathematical Psychology*, 1967, **4**, 501–506.

NORMAN, D. A. Acquisition and retention in short-term memory. *Journal of Experimental Psychology*, 1966, **72**, 369–381.

NORMAN, D. A., AND WICKELGREN, W. A. Short-term recognition memory for single digits and pairs of digits. *Journal of Experimental Psychology*, 1965, **70**, 479–489.

PARKS, T. E. Signal-detectability theory of recognition memory performance. *Psychological Review*, 1966, **73**, 44–58.

PETERSON, L. R. Short-term verbal memory and learning. *Psychological Review*, 1966, **73**, 193–207.

SWETS, J. A., TANNER, W. P., AND BIRDSALL, T. G. Decision processes in perception. *Psychological Review*, 1961, **68**, 301–340.

THORNDIKE, E. L., AND LORGE, I. *The teacher's word book of 30,000 words*. New York: Teachers College, Columbia University, Bureau of Publications, 1944.

TULVING, E., AND ARBUCKLE, T. Y. Sources of intratrial interference in immediate recall of paired associates. *Journal of Verbal Learning and Verbal Behavior*, 1963, **1**, 321–334.

TULVING, E., AND PEARLSTONE, Z. Availability versus accessibility of information in memory for words. *Journal of Verbal Learning and Verbal Behavior*, 1966, **5**, 381–391.

WAUGH, N. C., AND NORMAN, D. A. Primary memory. *Psychological Review*, 1965, **72**, 89–104.

WOODWORTH, R. S., AND SCHLOSBERG, H. *Experimental psychology*. New York: Holt, 1954.

IV

MECHANISMS OF STORAGE AND RETRIEVAL

10

Repetition and Rehearsal Mechanisms in Models for Short-Term Memory

Robert A. Bjork[1]
University of Michigan

Introduction

Performance in short-term memory situations is, in general, clearly sensitive to variations in conditions of presentation and rehearsal. It is important to consider just what kinds of formal representation of rehearsal and repetition processes are reasonable and possible in models for short-term memory, both to see whether any of the possible mechanisms are supported or ruled out by existing data and, hopefully, to also make more apparent what lines of research are likely to discriminate among the possible mechanisms. This paper is an attempt to outline on the basis of intuition, logic, and current models the likely general mechanisms of repetition and rehearsal in short-term memory, to see any implications of the various mechanisms, and, through a mixture of some

[1] The preparation of this chapter was supported by the Advanced Research Projects Agency, Department of Defense, monitored by the Air Force Office of Scientific Research under Contract No. AF 49(638)-1736 with the Human Performance Center, Department of Psychology, University of Michigan.

relevant data and considerable speculation, to evaluate the relative adequacies of the various mechanisms.

It does not take more than a few minutes staring out the window to decide that the possible number of questions one might ask about repetition and rehearsal exceeds any arbitrary n. Furthermore, considering that items of various kinds might be presented in various ways through various sense modes at various rates and tested in various ways, that the subject may apply various rehearsal strategies to various parts of the item at various times in the retention process, and that each and every one of these variations might alter or change the performance characteristics of the repetition or rehearsal processes involved, it is reasonable to consider only the general classes of possible mechanisms and their implications, rather than to attempt the admirable but imprudent task of considering the specific members of those classes.

The infinite domain of this paper generated by the possible variations alluded to above will be drastically reduced to the point of manageability by several restrictions. These restrictions are intended to isolate, on the one hand, the experimental behavior most amenable to the study of repetition and rehearsal effects, and on the other hand, the most fundamental questions about the representation of repetition and rehearsal in this experimental situation. To other workers in the field, of course, the restrictions will seem all but completely arbitrary.

The experimental situations of primary interest are the Brown–Peterson paradigm (Brown, 1954; Peterson and Peterson, 1959) and its main variations. In this experimental situation, a single subspan item (e.g., a word trigram or consonant trigram) is presented and, after some number of seconds filled with additional presentations of the item, opportunities for rehearsal and/or an interpolated interfering activity of some kind, the item is cued for recall. This general paradigm has, in my judgment, some advantages over other procedures with respect to the questions of interest to this paper. It does not seem as complicated as those procedures that require the subject to remember items at or beyond the memory span and that are thereby heavily influenced by response output interference and other factors, nor does it seem as complicated as the various continuous procedures in which the presentation-test trial structure for an item is interlaced with the trial structure of other items, thereby producing significant and largely unfathomable item interactions. The fact that at any one point in time a subject in the Brown–Peterson paradigm is responsible for exactly one subspan item has the following desirable (simplifying) properties in assessing repetition and rehearsal effects: (a) if the item is presented again, it is reasonable to assume that the subject will attend to it rather than to some other item for which he is also responsible, (b) if there is an opportunity to rehearse, the subject can rehearse successfully whatever he remembers of the item (since the item is easily subspan) with negligible memory loss occurring during the rehearsal process itself, and (c) at the time of recall, the subject can similarly report whatever he remembers of the item with negligible loss in memory occurring in the course of the recall itself.

Organization

The remainder of this paper will be organized around two questions on the representation of repetition and two questions on the representation of rehearsal in models for short-term memory.

Repetition

(1) Should each repetition of an item be conceived of as (a) increasing the strength of a single memory trace, (b) increasing the number of traces of the item, or (c) something else? (2) What kind of model structure is required to predict the significant and complex effects of the spacing of repetitions on performance?

Rehearsal

(1) Does rote rehearsal strengthen memory traces by some process or another, or does rote rehearsal simply maintain items in storage? (2) Does a successful rehearsal of an item operate in essentially the same manner as a presentation of the item?

The Representation of Repetition

What Happens?

Though experience is psychological research shapes one to fear making assertions much stronger than obvious tautologies, it does appear safe to say that the presentation of an item builds up something in memory. The nature of the "buildup," as well as the nature of the "something," is a far less obvious matter. It might be (a) that the strength of a unitary trace of the item is increased (e.g., traditional interference theory; Wickelgren and Norman, 1966), or (b) that the number of traces or retrieval routes (Bernbach, Chapter 4) or conditional elements (stimulus sampling theory) are increased, or (c) that there is some probability that the item goes from a less permanent to a more permanent state in memory (the various multistate Markov models). Although it is clear that these three general mechanisms do not exhaust the possibilities, it is uncertain whether there are any reasonable specific mechanisms that do not fall into one of the three classes. There are, of course, possible representations of repetition which combine the properties of two or all three of the classes (Wickelgren, for example, in Chapter 3 assumes that four different memory traces with very different decay characteristics result from a single presentation).

The problem of discriminating among the three mechanisms mentioned above is formidable. There is not much in the way of relevant data; indeed, it is not clear just what constitutes relevant data. Although the specific representatives of one mechanism-class generally have different implications than the specific representatives of another class, it would be difficult if not impossible to construct a specific model of one class, which in its basic properties, could not be exactly duplicated by a model of another class. For example, with respect to predictions of simple retention curves as a function of the number of repetitions, models of different classes are not necessarily identifiable (for a discussion of the identifiability problem, see Greeno, 1967).

The problem of deriving implications that hold for all models which embody a particular repetition or rehearsal mechanism as opposed to implications that hold for most or some members of the class needs and merits elaboration. Consider Hellyer's (1962) straightforward experimental assessment of the effects of multiple presentations on retention. Hellyer presented consonant trigrams 1, 2, 4, or 8 times and measured retention following 3, 9, 18, or 27 sec of interference. His results are shown in Fig. 1.

If, in an effort to account for Hellyer's findings, one postulates a specific model based on one of the repetition mechanisms listed above, the model will in general make different predictions about the shapes of the curves in Fig. 1 than will some other specific model based on one of the other repetition mechanisms; it is not clear, however, that it is possible to state any one possible property of Hellyer's curves that is

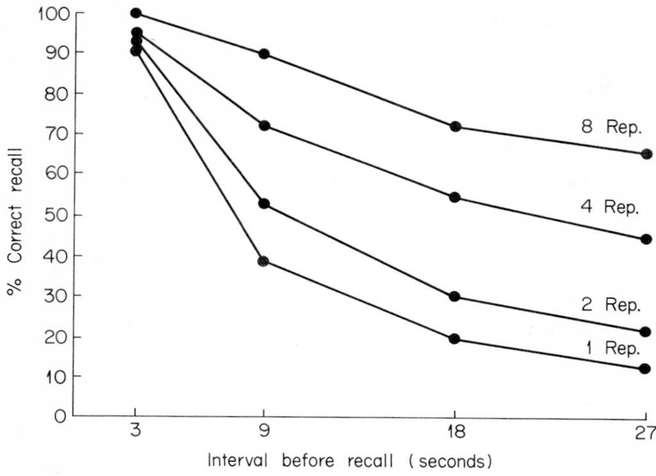

FIG. 1. Percentage of consonant trigrams recalled completely correctly as a function of the number of presentations of the trigram (Hellyer, 1962).

uniquely predicted by all specific models of a given class. To illustrate, consider the following three simple models and their general implications concerning the family of curves in Fig. 1.

Model 1

As a result of presentation, a memory trace is established to a momentary maximum strength sufficient to result in perfect immediate recall. During an interfering activity, this trace strength decreases exponentially with time and the probability that an item is recalled correctly is directly proportional to the momentary trace strength. Finally, each subsequent presentation both reinstates the trace to the maximum momentary strength and increases the resistance of the trace to interference which results in a decrease in the rate of exponential loss of trace strength with time during the retention interval.

This model predicts a family of exponential curves all of which start at unity (when there is no interference) and asymptote at zero (chance performance).

Model 2

The first presentation of an item results in a copy of the item being stored in memory. With each subsequent presentation of the item, there is some probability an additional item is stored in memory—the exact probability is some inverse function of the number of copies already in memory. During each unit of interfering time, any one copy in memory is, independent of other copies, lost from memory with some probability. Finally, if one or more copies of the item are in memory at the time of recall, the item is recalled; if no copies are in memory, the item is not recalled.

This model predicts a family of retention curves that start at unity, go eventually to zero, and become increasingly sigmoid-shaped with increasing presentations.

Model 3

An item is at any point in time in exactly one of three states: not in memory, in short-term memory, or in long-term memory. Items not in memory are not recalled, items in short-term or long-term memory are recalled perfectly. Items in long-term memory are impervious to interference, items in short-term memory are lost in an all-or-none fashion with some probability (greater than zero and less than one) during each unit of interfering time. With each presentation of an item, there are some probabilities p and $1 - p$ that the item, if not in memory, will go to the long-term and short-term states, respectively. If the item is in the short-term state when presented, there is some fixed probability it will go to the long-term state and, failing that, it will remain in the short-term state. An item in the long-term state when it is presented will remain there.

This model predicts a family of retention curves that also start at one and are geometric in shape, but go to nonzero asymptotes, the asymptotes increasing with increasing presentations.

The three models outlined above were chosen so that each of the three types of repetition mechanisms introduced at the start of this section would be represented. In evaluating the models with respect to Hellyer's data, it is clear that the obtained curves do not look like those predicted by models 1 and 3 in that they are not geometric in shape. However, although the increasingly sigmoidal curves do offer general support for model 2 (the multiple copy notion), it is not clear that the curves would go eventually to zero for retention intervals longer than 27 sec, as is predicted by model 2.

The prediction of zero asymptotes differentiates models 1 and 2 from model 3. This prediction seems to be an all but fundamental property of unitary trace strength models, if not of multiple copy models; that is, it is not clear that the concept of a trace asymptoting at some nonzero strength has much meaning, though it might be reasonable to assume that some copies of an item in memory are relatively permanent. The latter assumption, though possibly reasonable, creates a considerably more complex model falling somewhere between the present model 2 and model 3 in its properties. At any rate, Hellyer's experiment did not include long enough retention intervals to decide whether an adequate model should predict nonzero asymptotes or not, and, as Bernbach (chapter 4) stoutly asserts, one should only abandon the notion that at any multiple copies in memory are of a single type under intense pressure from the data.

The fact that Hellyer's data support model 2 over models 1 and 3 does not, unfortunately, imply that the multiple copy mechanism is therefore supported without qualification over the trace-strength and short-term, long-term store mechanisms. With a little ego involvement in either models 1 or 3 and a little practice at repairing models with additional assumptions, it is not difficult to modify either model to account for the general shape of the curves in Fig. 1. Assuming that (model 1) trace strength must decrease to some threshold before it begins to affect probability of recall, that (model 3) there is a sensory store that holds items for very brief periods after presentation, or, for that matter, complicating the assumed effects of the intervening activity in various ways would, among other modifications, make models 1 and 3 more comfortable with Hellyer's data.

Thus, the problem of stating implications that hold for all models incorporating a particular repetition or rehearsal mechanism is a very tough one, and I am not going to face up to it completely in this paper. In a sense, not facing up to the problem is demanded at this point by another consideration: existing data do not generally have the power to test any such possible unique implications. Thus, where it seems appropriate, implications of the most simple and representative members of a class will be evaluated against existing data, if data exist.

Why Does the Spacing of Presentations Matter?

There is now an abundance of evidence from Brown–Peterson-type experiments, from paired-associate experiments, from free recall experiments, from recognition memory experiments, and from other verbal learning procedures as well, that the spacing of repetitions of an item has relatively large and relatively clear effects on both latency and frequency measures of performance. The principal results of existing research on the effects of spacing in short-term memory can be summarized by three findings: (1) In general, performance is significantly better following spaced repetitions of an item than performance following massed repetitions of an item. (2) However, there is an interaction: if performance is measured after very short retention intervals, it is better to have massed repetitions. (3) And there is a limit to the improvements in performance with spacing; as the interval between two repetitions of an item is increased, performance improves to a point and then declines.

Evidence for the first of the three summary statements above is available in two experiments of the Brown–Peterson type (Peterson, 1963; Pollatsek, 1969), and in a number of experiments using paired-associate procedures (Greeno, 1964; Peterson, Hillner, and Saltzman, 1962; Bjork, 1966; Rumelhart, 1967; Bjork and Abramowitz, 1968; and others), recognition procedures (Olson, 1969; Hintzman, 1969), and free recall procedures (Melton, Reicher, and Shulman, 1966). The second finding derives from paired-associate experiments by Peterson *et al.* (1962) and Rumelhart (1967). The third finding derives from paired-associate experiments by Peterson, Wampler, Kirkpatrick, and Saltzman (1963) and Young (1966).

To give all this some sense of specificity, consider first the experiments by Peterson (1963) and Pollatsek (1969). Peterson gave subjects a first presentation of a CVC, had them count backwards for a variable period (1, 3, 6, or 11 sec), gave them a second presentation of the CVC, and had them attempt to recall the CVC after a final retention interval of 6 sec during which they also counted backwards. The obtained proportions of correct recalls are shown below.

$P_1 - P_2$ Spacing interval, seconds

1	3	6	11
.66	.67	.74	.77

Performance improves monotonically with the spacing of the two presentations.

The relevant condition in Pollatsek's experiment is somewhat more complicated. Pollatsek's condition can be denoted $P_1R_1I_1P_2R_2I_2T$, where P_1 and P_2 indicate the first and second presentations of a word trigram,

R_1 and R_2 indicate rehearsal periods of 0, 3, or 6 sec, I_1 indicates a first interference period of 6 or 21 sec, I_2 indicates a second interference period of 9 or 21 sec, and, finally, T indicates a test for recall of the trigram. Pollatsek's results are shown below collapsed over the three values of R_2 and the two values of I_2.

	$R_1 = 0$	$R_1 = 3$	$R_1 = 6$
$I_1 = 6$	.70	.80	.82
$I_1 = 21$	.80	.88	.92

The improvement in performance with increased spacing of presentations is more striking in Pollatsek's data than it is in Peterson's data. Furthermore, there is an improvement in performance with increased spacing independent of whether the increase in spacing results from an increase in the intervening rehearsal period (R_1) or an increase in the intervening interference period (I_1).

The interaction between spacing of repetitions and retention interval was first shown by Peterson *et al.* (1962) who presented subjects with a long, continuous string of study trials and test trials on paired associates. The items of interest were given two presentations separated by zero or four trials on other pairs, and were tested after an interpolated interval of one, two, four, or eight trials between the second presentation and the test. The crossed curves in Fig. 2 show that performance following a short retention interval is better if the presentations are massed and that performance following a long interval is better if the presentations are spaced. Rumelhart (1967) found an analogous interaction between the spacing interval and the retention interval using a continuous paired-associate task in which an individual pair was given six anticipation trials separated by various sequences of interpresentation intervals.

The finding that there is a limit to the improvement in performance following a long interval with increased spacing was first shown by Peterson *et al.* (1963) and was replicated by Young (1966). In both experiments, a single test trial followed the second of two study trials after a fixed number of trials (eight in the former experiment, ten in the latter experiment). Figure 3 shows their results: performance improves with spacing and then declines.

I have taken some time to clarify what I consider the most salient effects of the spacing of repetitions because I consider these effects to indicate better than anything else the sophistication required of any

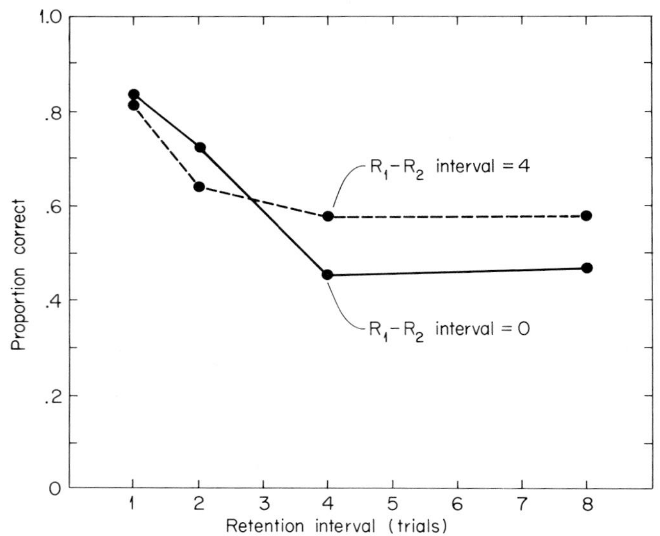

FIG. 2. Mean retention curves for different spacings between a first and second study trial (Peterson *et al.*, 1962).

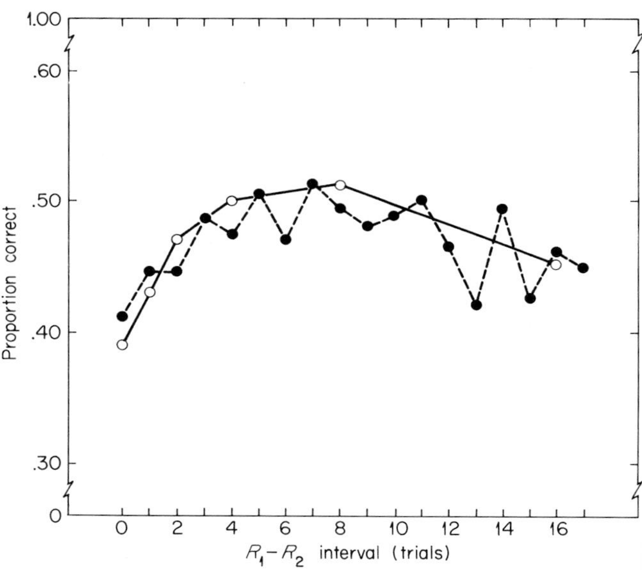

FIG. 3. Proportions of correct responses as a function of the spacing of two study trials (Peterson *et al.*, 1963; Young, 1966). ○—○ Peterson *et al.*; ●----● Young.

repetition mechanism proposed to account in general for existing data. Also, I feel that the data from experiments on spacing of repetitions may have enough power to discriminate among fairly complicated mechanisms. By themselves, the three effects of spacing just summarized rule out a number of otherwise reasonable repetition mechanisms, including, in my view, nearly any mechanism based on the concept of a single memory trace varying in strength along some continuum.

A consideration of the constraints on an adequate theoretical representation of the effects of repetition imposed by the single finding that performance improves with the spacing of presentations will serve both to defend and to clarify the preceding assertions. Any model predicting that the repetition of two different items operates on their respective memory traces in such a way as to preserve at a fixed time after repetition the order of their respective recall probabilities at the time of repetition is ruled out by the spaced vs. massed practice finding. That is, performance following spaced presentations is better than performance following massed presentations, in spite of the fact that the probability of recall measured at the time of the second massed presentation is considerably higher than performance measured at the time of the second spaced presentation. Thus, an adequate model must admit circumstances under which the repetition of one item can be so effective that the probability of its recall might be greater than that of a second item (which was also repeated), even though the probability of recall of the first at the time of repetition might have been a great deal less than that of the second item. Any model that is strictly order preserving in the sense that it always predicts that a repetition will transform the memory for any two items, I and I', with probabilities of recall $P < P'$ at the time of repetition, into memory states at some subsequent time resulting in probabilities of recall, $r(P) < r(P')$, is in trouble. In particular, any model based on an assumption that a repetition increments the current strength or number of traces of an item by some proportion of the difference between the current strength or number and some maximum strength or number seems untenable.

There has now been considerable work addressed to the question of what kind of model structure is required to predict the effects of spacing (Greeno, 1967; Bjork, 1966; Rumelhart, 1967; Landauer, 1969; Pollatsek, 1969). Although most of this work has dealt with paired-associate data, it appears from existing data, that the same general spacing phenomena occur in the Brown–Peterson paradigm as occur in paired-associate paradigms. I will therefore step out with some confidence on the assumption that the theoretical work mentioned above is directly relevant to memory as exhibited in the Brown–Peterson paradigm.

Without going into all the reasons why other notions have been ruled out, it now appears that there are three extant classes of models that have some chance to account for the effects of spacing. The first is a class of Markov models characterized by their Markov properties and the general assumption that an item can be in one of essentially three states of knowledge: not in memory (a guessing state), short-term memory, or long-term memory (permanent). The individual members of this class are defined by various assumptions about transition probabilities which are in turn interpretations of various notions about coding processes, state properties, attentional processes, and the like.

The second class of models are the buffer models of Atkinson and Shiffrin (1968). These models have at their core the notions that (a) there is a fixed capacity rehearsal buffer which operates as a kind of push down store holding a few items at a time and largely determining the properties of the short-term storage system of which it is a part, (b) there is a long-term store out of which items are retrieved imperfectly due mainly to the operation of the traditional mechanisms of associative interference, and (c) the probability an item is represented in long-term storage and/or the strength of its representation in long-term storage are a function of the time it resides in the rehearsal buffer before it is displaced. The last notion constitutes a mechanism through which memory traces consolidate over time, a notion shared with a number of other models (e.g., Landauer, 1969; Norman and Rumelhart, Chapter 2; Wickelgren, Chapter 3; Judith Reitman, Chapter 5); there is considerable disagreement, however, as to the specific nature of the consolidation process.

The third class of models derives from stimulus sampling theory and is based on the notion of stimulus fluctuation (Estes, 1955; Izawa, 1967). These models assume that an item to be remembered together with the context in which it is presented comprise a set of stimulus elements, some of which are active at any one time (momentarily available to the subject) and some of which are inactive (momentarily unavailable to the subject). Over time, there is assumed to be a random fluctuation of any one stimulus element between the active and inactive states.

Rumelhart (1967) has contributed a very thorough theoretical and empirical analysis of these model classes with respect to a continuous paired-associate task. His principal findings are two: (1) that a model he terms the modified GFT (General Forgetting Theory)—which is a modified version of a model suggested and tested by Bjork (1966), which, in turn, is a generalization of models proposed by Atkinson and Crothers (1964), Greeno (1967), and others—accounts very well for his data; (2) that there are specific versions of both the Buffer models and the Stimulus Fluctuation models that are not distinguishable from the modified GFT in his experiment.

Rumelhart's data, as well as Bjork's (1966), offer general support for the notion first suggested by Greeno (1967) that an item already in the short-term state when presented has a negligible probability of going to the long-term state. This notion, in a nutshell, is why these models predict a spaced practice effect. When items are given an immediate or near-immediate repetition, they are either already in the learned state or in the short-term state at the time of their repetition. Hence, the immediate repetition accomplishes little or nothing compared to a spaced repetition which occurs at a time when the item, if not already in the long-term state, is likely to be in the forgotten state from which the probability of transition to the long-term state is relatively high. Although the notion that the probability of transition from the short-term to the long-term state is very small leads to the prediction of a spaced practice effect, it does not predict the interaction between spacing interval and repetition interval shown in Fig. 2.

The modified version of the GFT model suggested by Rumelhart predicts both a spaced practice effect and the interaction shown in Fig. 2. The modification consists of assuming that there is a fixed probability on any trial that a subject will not attend to the item presented, in which case the item will end the trial in the same state of knowledge in which it began. This assumption results in there being a higher probability that an item will be in the short-term state immediately following the second of two massed presentations than there is that the item will be in the short-term state immediately following the second of two spaced presentations. That is, even if the subject does not attend to the second of two massed presentations the item is still likely to be in the short-term state from the first of the two presentations, whereas if the subject does not attend to the second of two spaced presentations the chances are negligible that the item is still in the short-term state from the first of the two presentations. Hence, for suitable parameter values, the modified GFT predicts that performance following a short retention interval is better if preceded by massed presentations than if preceded by spaced presentations because the higher probability of being in the short-term state at the time of testing more than compensates for the lower probability of being in the long-term state.

Unfortunately the modified GFT, and the formally equivalent versions of the buffer and stimulus fluctuation models, are significantly less than perfect. There are at least three problems. First, the assumption that the subject does not always attend to the item presented is suspect. The modified GFT underpredicts the performance on a test trial immediately following a single presentation of the tested item: for typical parameter values it predicts that the probability of a correct response will be between .85 and .95, whereas the data are typically between .95 and 1.00. One might add to the model structure the assumption of a very short-term sensory storage system in order to predict essentially perfect performance on any test occurring within a few seconds of a presentation, but it is likely that the required holding time of the assumed sensory store would well exceed any reasonable expectations derived from existing research on such very short-term sensory storage. Another interpretation of Rumelhart's assumption that subjects do not attend to some items as they are presented which seems more reasonable to me, although it does not solve the present problem, is that the subject chooses on any trial whether to attempt to encode the item in some fashion or not. Although, intuitively, I doubt whether subjects ever (for all practical purposes) fail to perceive an item presented in the normal fashion, I think it is quite likely in continuous procedures that subjects choose on some trials not to make any real storage effort with the item presented.

A second problem is that the modified GFT does not predict the finding (Fig. 3) that there is a limit to the improvement in performance with increased spacing of presentations, i.e., beyond some optimal spacing there is a decline in performance. The model predicts that performance improves monotonically with increases in the spacing of presentations. It may be that one should not assume that the long-term state is permanent, but rather, semi-permanent, with a very small probability of loss from storage relative to that of the short-term state.

A third problem, more tentative than the first two, but also, if it holds up, more formidable, derives from an experiment by Bjork and Abramowitz (1968). This experiment employed a continuous paired-associate task in which some pairs had the following sequence of four anticipation trials. The first presentation (P_1) was followed by x intervening trials on other pairs until the second presentation (P_2). The third presentation (P_3) followed P_2 after y intervening trials, and, finally, the fourth presentation (P_4) followed P_3 after z intervening trials. The following values of x, y, and z were used to generate spacing sequences: $(x,y) = (0,20)$, (2,18), (10,10), (18,2), (20,0) and $z = 2, 8, 20$. That is, $x + y$ was always equal to 20 intervening trials. The principal question of interest was whether the x and y interpresentation intervals were commutative in their effects on performance at P_4. For example, the only difference between the spacing sequences $x = 0$, $y = 20$, $z = 2$ and $x = 20$, $y = 0$, $z = 2$ is the order of the first two interpresentation intervals. Some models predict commutivity in such a case, others do not.

In general, Bjork and Abramowitz found commutivity of the x and y intervals in their effect on performance at P_4. Also, the modified GFT gave a very good quantitative account of the observed performance. However, for the parameter values they estimated, the model does not predict the interaction of spacing interval and retention interval shown in Fig. 2. For the parameter values estimated by Rumelhart (1967), who employed the same general procedure as did Bjork and Abramowitz except for the choice of spacing sequences, the modified GFT predicts the interaction shown in Fig. 2 but does not predict commutivity. Thus, the model can predict the interaction in Fig. 2 and it can predict commutivity, but it can not predict both simultaneously.

An experiment designed to include both the spacing conditions necessary to test for commutivity and those necessary to test for an interaction between repetition interval and retention interval could resolve whether the modified GFT is inadequate or whether, in fact, the two effects do not occur together in paired-associate learning. Should it be possible to obtain both effects simultaneously, a considerable challenge is posed to existing models: no current model, as far as I know, predicts both commutivity and an interaction between repetition interval and retention interval.

The effects of the spacing of repetitions have been discussed in some detail because, as mentioned earlier, their complexity and consistency seem to impose severe constraints on an adequate theoretical representation of repetition in models of short-term memory learning. It seems safe to say that the principal empirical effects of the spacing of presentations on performance rule out some simple repetition mechanisms in models of short-term memory; it seems even safer to say that they do not obviously imply any particular repetition mechanism.

The Representation of Rehearsal

Does Rote Rehearsal Strengthen or Maintain?

There are certainly some among the readers of this paper who are a bit put off by my implicit distinction between rote rehearsal and rehearsal that consists primarily of a search for an effective mnemonic of the to-be-remembered item. Not only do some researchers think that such a distinction has little meaning, but some (e.g., Neisser, 1967, p. 239) feel that it may be misleading to think of rehearsal activity as formally distinct from interfering verbal activities of various kinds. Beyond mentioning the issue, I want to ignore it and to assume that rote rehearsal, i.e., repeating an item over and over to oneself, is a distinct, well-defined activity that subjects find reasonable and commonly do. I do so because (a) it agrees with my introspections and, more importantly, (b) instructions to subjects "repeat the item over and over to yourself" and "try to associate or relate or image the item with or to something you already know" have differential effects on performance.

Brown (1958) seemed to assert, though he has since said that he didn't mean it (personal communication), that the main function of rehearsal is to maintain items in short-term memory and not to somehow strengthen the memory trace of items. In order to investigate this issue, I tested subjects' memory for five two-digit numbers under the four conditions schematized in Fig. 4. Conditions I and III were designed to

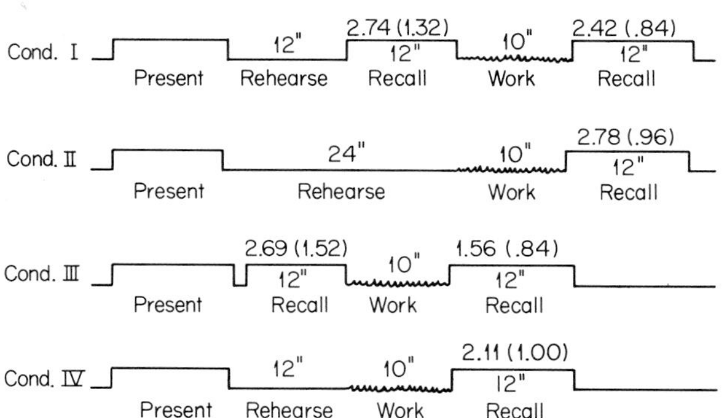

FIG. 4. Mean number of two-digit items recalled correctly in the correct position out of five possible. (The values in parentheses are from a replication of the experiment conducted at the University of Michigan by D. Raymond and L. Hannah in which the subjects were children and four rather than five two-digit numbers were presented on each trial.)

assess by comparison with each other whether a 12-sec rehearsal period prior to a first test for recall (condition I) would make the items recalled on the first test more resistant to the interfering activity interpolated between the first test for recall and the second test for recall relative to the case (condition III) in which there was no such opportunity to rehearse.

A comparison of performance on the final recall between conditions I and III and between conditions II and IV (Fig. 4) illustrates the strengthening effect of the rehearsal periods in conditions I and II. Also in Fig. 5, the higher conditional probability of a correct recall on test two given a correct recall on test one in condition I as compared to condition III illustrates clearly that items recalled on the first test following the 12-sec rehearsal period in condition I are more resistant to the interfering activity than are items recalled on the first test immediately after presentation in condition III. Conditions II and IV

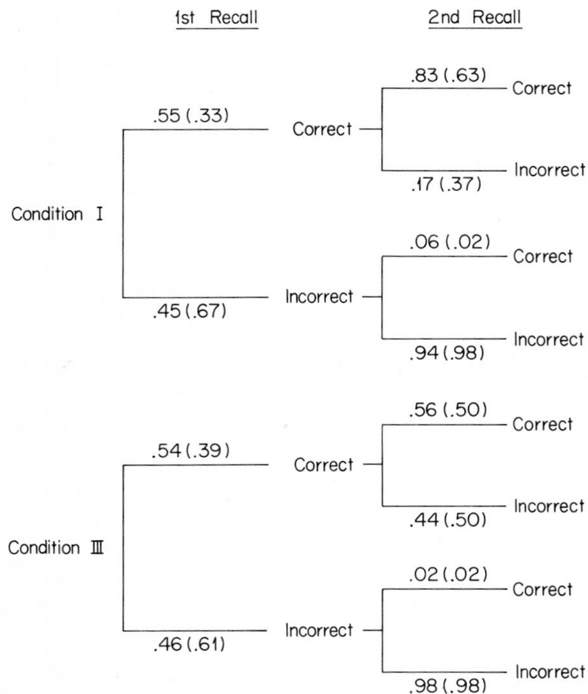

FIG. 5. Conditional probabilities of a recall or nonrecall on the second test given a recall or nonrecall on the first test in Conditions I and III, Fig. 4.

were designed to permit, by comparison with conditions I and III, respectively, an assessment of the relative efficiencies of covert rehearsal and overt recalls in making items resistant to interference, but that, though important, is a different problem (see, e.g., Brelsford and Atkinson, 1968).

There are other relevant data that might be offered to support the contention that rote rehearsal strengthens something, but there doesn't seem to be much question about that, and the question of what is strengthened and how is a good deal more difficult.

Rehearsal: What Happens?

There are several reasonable ways in which rehearsal might act to increase the resistance of a memory trace to interference; they are roughly the same as for repetition. Rehearsal might increase the strength of a single memory trace, it might increase the number of traces of the item, or it might accomplish a change from short-term storage to long-term storage in the state of the item.

Although the ways in which rehearsal and repetition might operate on memory seem similar, it is unlikely that rehearsal and repetition operate in exactly the same fashion to increase the resistance of a memory trace to interference. For example, although rehearsal is less "perfect" than repetition (an item might be lost from memory during the rehearsal period) and, therefore, one might expect that n one-second repetitions would result in better short-term memory than a single presentation followed by an n-second rehearsal period, it might also be the case that a rehearsal period permits more freedom for the subject to achieve a long-term encoding of some kind than does a series of repetitions and, hence, might result in better performance over long retention intervals. In fact, exactly that difference between forced repetitions and covert rehearsal is strongly suggested in the results of a free recall experiment by Glanzer and Meinzer (1967). In this experiment, there was a 3.2-sec interval between the presentations of any two successive words in the list during which, in one condition, subjects were required to give the word just presented six vocal repetitions and, in another condition, subjects were free to rehearse covertly in any fashion they wished. Glanzer and Meinzer found that the latter condition resulted in clearly better recall performance for words presented at the beginning and middle of the list (long retention intervals) than did the former, but that there was no difference in the recall of the items presented at the end of the list (short retention intervals).

There are a number of other possible differences between rehearsal and repetition processes that might be elaborated, but given that there has been no really systematic experimentation comparing the two, there seems little reward in such speculation.

Some hints as to the nature of the rehearsal process as well as some indications of possible differences between the operation of rehearsal and the operation of repetition are provided in the experiment by Pollatsek (1969) discussed earlier. One condition of Pollatsek's experiment was designed to investigate the role of rehearsal in a manner analogous to that employed by Hellyer in the study of repetition effects (Fig. 1) reported earlier. Pollatsek gave subjects a single presentation of a word trigram followed by rehearsal periods of 0, 3, 6, or 9 sec and tested for recall after interference (counting backwards) periods of 0, 3, 6, 9, 15, or 21 sec following the rehearsal. His results are shown in Fig. 6.

The retention curves in Fig. 6 appear to become increasingly sigmoid-shaped with increasing rehearsal and seem to be decreasing to non-zero asymptotes, though longer interference intervals would be necessary to say for sure. In comparison to Hellyer's results (Fig. 1), (a) performance is better overall in Hellyer's experiment (Hellyer used consonant trigrams and Pollatsek used word trigrams) and (b) performance at short

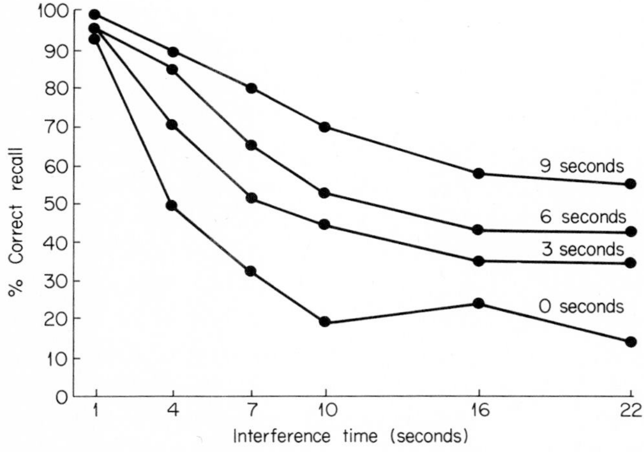

FIG. 6. Proportions of word trigrams recalled completely correctly as a function of rehearsal time (Pollatsek, 1969).

retention intervals in Pollatsek's experiment appears relatively worse and performance at long intervals relatively better than in Hellyer's experiment. The second comparison provides some support for the notion mentioned above that a rehearsal period might be less beneficial on the short term and more beneficial on the long term than are multiple repetitions.

To the degree that the curves in Fig. 6 are in fact approaching nonzero asymptotes, the notion that rehearsal benefits memory by increasing the chances that the item is processed into a relatively permanent storage state is supported. However, if that were the only effect of rehearsal, one would expect that the curves would go to different asymptotes but would otherwise have the same general shape. The systematic change in the shape of the retention curves in Fig. 6 with increasing rehearsal argues that rehearsal affects the short-term storage of an item as well as the long-term storage. As was pointed out earlier for Hellyer's curves, the fact that the curves become progressively more sigmoid-shaped is consistent with the notion that rehearsal adds additional copies of the memory trace to short-term memory. A system combining the multiple-copy and short-term to long-term storage rehearsal mechanisms would give rise to curves such as those in Fig. 6. It might be that during rehearsal the subject can both build up the number of copies of the item in short-term memory (rote rehearsal) or try to achieve a long-term encoding of the item (nonrote rehearsal), and that he does some of each.

Concluding Comments

In contrast to most of the papers in this volume, it has not been the goal of this paper to suggest or test any particular theoretical model of human memory. Rather, this paper represents an attempt to formulate some questions about the formal representation of repetition and rehearsal in models of human memory and to consider the likely alternative representations with respect to those questions in the light of existing data.

At some points during this endeavor, I have felt quite sure that it was overdue and quite worthwhile; at other points, I have been equally convinced that it was premature and frustrating. On the one hand, the current intense theoretical activity seems to be sprouting a number of attractive models (the chapters in this book are good examples). There are large, reliable effects on performance in several different memory paradigms with variations in the conditions of presentation or rehearsal, and it seems only a matter of looking at existing data and theories very carefully to see the general shape of an adequate theoretical representation of repetition and rehearsal. On the other hand, it also seems that for every experimental finding that clarifies some aspect of human memory there is one that questions the integrity of some generally accepted view of another aspect. It is often difficult to derive differential predictions from alternative models, even when they have apparently quite different underlying psychological assumptions. Even when alternative models do make differential predictions, the crucial data are not available.

Depending on how one looks at it, one can see a picture of the human memory system developing bit-by-bit or, one can see a confusing, complex collage of experimental findings, theoretical notions, and unanswered questions. I feel that both views are at least in part veridical and that they together characterize the present state of model building in the area of human memory.

In the remainder of this section, I want to summarize and conclude this paper by stating and elaborating three assertions with respect to the theoretical representation of rehearsal and repetition.

(1) Increases in either the number of presentations of an item or in the time allotted for rehearsal of the item effect both the short-term storage of the item and the long-term storage of the item. Any reasonable doubts that repetition or rehearsal of an item build up the memory storage of the item should be dispelled by Figs. 1 and 6. However, it is at least logically possible that only the short-term storage or only the long-term storage of an item but not both would be strengthened by repetition or rehearsal. Although such systems are logically possible, they appear quite unlikely on the basis of the families of curves in Figs. 1 and 6. In both figures, there appear to be systematic changes in the shapes of the retention curves over short retention intervals as a function of increasing repetitions or rehearsal time, as well as substantial differences in performance at long retention intervals.

(2) The clear but complex effects on performance of variations in the spacing of repetitions of an item indicate the considerable sophistication required of an adequate theoretical representation of repetition. As mentioned earlier, however, the data from spacing of practice experiments may also have enough power to allow one to choose among fairly

sophisticated alternative representations. It would be an impressive achievement to formulate a model that would provide a satisfactory quantitative account of the complex effects of spacing.

As pointed out earlier in this chapter, there are several models that hold some promise of ultimately providing an adequate quantitative account of the spacing of practice phenomena. In particular, the basic Markov structure (termed the General Forgetting Theory) accounts quite well for the first order quantitative effects of spacing during paired-associate learning (Bjork, 1966; Rumelhart, 1967). It might be that modifying the General Forgetting Theory by complicating the short- and long-term state representations within the theory would result in an improved quantitative correspondence between the theory and spacing data that would justify the increase in complexity. For example, one might assume that retrieval from long-term memory is less than perfect or that it is possible to have multiple copies of an item in short-term memory. Although I don't agree with Bernbach (chapter 4) that his single-memory multiple-copy model is any more parsimonious than multiple-memory single-copy models of the General Forgetting Theory type—it seems only a matter of where one chooses to assume complexity within the model structure—his work may well indicate that Markov models have oversimplified the representation of an item within any one type of memory store.

Wickelgren, in Chapter 3, indicates in a general way how his multi-trace strength theory could account for each of the principal effects of spacing summarized earlier in this chapter. Whether Wickelgren's multitrace system could account quantitatively and simultaneously for the effects of spacing remains to be seen.

(3) Although rehearsal and repetition probably operate in the same general way to increase the resistance of a memory trace to interference, they probably do not operate in exactly the same way.

The possible experimental conditions of rehearsal and repetition during a fixed time interval following a presentation of an item vary considerably in terms of how much the subject's behavior is under the experimenter's control. In the case that the subject is free to rehearse covertly, there is very little control; in the case that the subject is required to shadow multiple, rapid repetitions overtly during the interval, there is considerable control. It may well be that the covert rehearsal case provides a better opportunity for the subject to achieve a relatively long-term encoding of the item than does the multiple repetition case which, in a sense, intrudes on the subject. Hence, a period of covert rehearsal is likely to result in a relatively better performance after long retention intervals than is a period of multiple repetitions. The converse, however, is likely to be true for performance following short retention intervals.

The whole problem of formulating theoretical representations of rehearsal and repetition and characterizing any formal differences between the two should be helped considerably by the various current experimental efforts to specify the role of encoding strategies, imagery, grouping strategies, retrieval strategies, etc. in human memory. Hopefully, if this chapter were to be written several years from now, it would be possible to feel quite confident that slowly but surely a picture of the human memory system was developing.

References

Atkinson, R. C., and Crothers, E. J. A comparison of paired-associate learning models having different acquisition and retention axioms. *Journal of Mathematical Psychology*, 1964, **1**, 285–315.

Atkinson, R. C., and Shiffrin, R. M. Human memory: A proposed system and its control processes. In K. W. Spence and J. T. Spence (Eds.), *The psychology of learning and motivation: Advances in research and theory*. Vol. II. New York: Academic Press, 1968.

Bjork, R. A. Learning and short-term retention of paired-associates in relation to specific sequences of interpresentation intervals. Technical Report No. 106, Institute for Mathematical Studies in the Social Sciences, Stanford University, 1966.

Bjork, R. A., and Abramowitz, R. L. The optimality and commutivity of successive interpresentation intervals in short-term memory. Paper presented at the meeting of the Midwest Psychological Association, Chicago, May, 1968.

Brelsford, J. W., Jr., and Atkinson, R. C. Short-term memory as a function of overt and covert rehearsal procedures. *Journal of Verbal Learning and Verbal Behavior*, 1968, **7**, 730–736.

Brown, J. The nature of set to learn and of intra-material interferences in immediate memory. *Quarterly Journal of Experimental Psychology*, 1954, **6**, 141–148.

Brown, J. Some tests of the decay theory of immediate memory. *Quarterly Journal of Experimental Psychology*, 1958, **10**, 12–21.

Estes, W. K. Statistical theory of spontaneous recovery and regression. *Psychological Review*, 155, **62**, 145–154.

Glanzer, M., and Meinzer, A. The effects of intralist activity on free recall. *Journal of Verbal Learning and Verbal Behavior*, 1967, **6**, 928–935.

Greeno, J. G. Paired-associate learning with massed and distributed repetitions of items. *Journal of Experimental Psychology*, 1964, **67**, 286–295.

Greeno, J. G. Paired-associate learning with short-term retention: Mathematical analysis and data regarding identification of parameters. *Journal of Mathematical Psychology*, 1967, **4**, 430–472.

HELLYER, S. Supplementary report: Frequency of stimulus presentation and short-term decrement in recall. *Journal of Experimental Psychology*, 1962, **64**, 650.

HINTZMAN, D. L. Recognition time: effects of recency, frequency, and the spacing of repetitions. *Journal of Experimental Psychology*, 1969, **79**, 192–194.

IZAWA, C. Function of test trials in paired-associate learning. *Journal of Experimental Psychology*, 1967, **75**, 194–209.

LANDAUER, T. K. Reinforcement as consolidation. *Psychological Review*, 1969, **76**, 82–96.

MELTON, A. W., REICHER, G. M., AND SHULMAN, H. G. A distributed practice effect on probability of recall in free recall of words. Paper read at the meeting of the Psychonomic Society, St. Louis, October 1966.

NEISSER, U. *Cognitive psychology*. New York: Appelton-Century-Crofts, 1967.

OLSON, G. M. Learning and retention in a continuous recognition task. *Journal of Experimental Psychology*, 1969, **81**, 381–384.

PETERSON, L. R. Immediate memory: Data and theory. In C. N. Cofer and B. S. Musgrave (Eds.), *Verbal behavior and learning: Problems and processes*. New York: McGraw-Hill, 1963.

PETERSON, L. R., HILLNER, K., and SALTZMAN, D. Time between pairings and short-term retention. *Journal of Experimental Psychology*, 1962, **64**, 550–551.

PETERSON, L. R., AND PETERSON, M. J. Short-term retention of individual verbal items. *Journal of Experimental Psychology*, 1959, **58**, 193–198.

PETERSON, L. R., WAMPLER, R., KIRKPATRICK, M., AND SALTZMAN, D. Effect of spacing presentations on retention of a paired-associate over short intervals. *Journal of Experimental Psychology*, 1963, **66**, 206–209.

POLLATSEK, A. Rehearsal, interference, and spacing of practice in short-term memory. Technical Report, Human Performance Center, University of Michigan, 1969.

RUMELHART, D. E. The effects of interpresentation interval on performance in a continuous paired-associate task. Technical Report No. 116, Institute for Mathematical Studies in the Social Sciences, Stanford University, 1967.

WICKELGREN, W. A., AND NORMAN, D. A. Strength models and serial position in short-term recognition memory. *Journal of Mathematical Psychology*, 1966, **3**, 316–347.

YOUNG, J. L. Effects of intervals between reinforcements and test trials in paired-associate learning. Technical Report No. 101, Institute for Mathematical Studies in the Social Sciences, Stanford University, 1966.

11

Models for Free Recall and Recognition[1]

Walter Kintsch
University of Colorado

This chapter summarizes some arguments which, I believe, are important for the understanding of the processes of recognition and recall and hence for models of these processes. For the most part, the ideas presented here are stated informally and are to be regarded as preliminaries to the construction of formal models. In the first section of the chapter, the question is examined whether recognition and recall involve similar psychological processes or whether there are important qualitative differences between the two. In effect, this section summarizes the arguments for a two-process theory of recognition and recall. In the second part of the chapter, formal models for recognition learning and recall learning are discussed. While the work on models for recognition learning has achieved a degree of maturity, formal

[1] This research was supported by grant MH15872 from the National Institute of Mental Health. I thank Tim Dong who obtained the free-recall data discussed at the end of the chapter, and S. C. Johnson, who kindly made his computer program available for the data analysis.

models for free recall are as yet in their initial stages of development. However, it is hoped that the present report at least contributes towards a sharper definition of the problem and suggests some possible approaches.

Before proceeding, it is necessary to define explicitly the experimental paradigms with which this report is concerned. In a recognition experiment, the experimenter presents to the subject a list of items selected from some homogeneous item pool. Items may be words, numbers, nonsense syllables, or the like. After all items have been presented, the experimenter tests for recognition by presenting the old items plus some new items from the same pool (distractor items); the subject responds with "old" or "new" to each test item. Alternatively, the experimenter may test for recognition by means of a multiple-choice test: he presents one old item plus $(k - 1)$ distractor items and asks the subject to pick out the old item. In a recognition learning experiment, the same set of items, usually in a different order, is presented again. New distractor items are employed for each test. The above procedure is called a list-learning procedure. The standard paired-associate experiment may also be adapted for the study of recognition learning, using either single-item or multiple-choice tests. In a continuous recognition task several hundred trials are given in succession. On each trial either a new item is presented or an old item is repeated. The subject says "old" when he thinks he has seen the item before and "new" otherwise. This procedure is especially suited to control the lag between two successive presentations of an item.

In a free recall experiment the subject is presented with a list of items and is then asked to recall, in any order, as many of the items as he can. In a learning experiment the same list is presented more than once, usually in a different order. The free recall experiments discussed here are always list learning experiments.

Although the operational distinction between recognition and recall experiments is clear enough, in actual practice recognition and recall frequently interact. In a recognition experiment, the subject may respond correctly to some items because he can recall them; on the other hand, in recall experiments where the item pool is small subjects may implicitly scan the set of possible items and respond whenever one is recognized. Experimenters sometimes take measures against such interactions. For instance, the item pool from which recall items are selected if often prohibitively large (e.g., the set of all nouns); or the role of recall in recognition experiments is minimized by presenting so many items that the proportion of items which can be recalled is quite small relative to the proportion which can be recognized. Such precautions guarantee that recall and recognition experiments are at least reasonably pure and to some extent justify neglecting this interaction in the theoretical arguments that follow. Strictly speaking, the models of recall and recognition apply to idealized experiments in which recognition and recall processes do not interact.

Two-Process Theories of Recognition and Recall

A Comparison of Recognition and Recall

It is obvious from our own experience, and it has long been confirmed experimentally, that recognition is easier than recall (McDougall, 1904; Fischer, 1909). However, the problem of exactly defining this "obvious" superiority has proven to be extremely resistant. The basic dilemma was recognized early by Müller (1913), namely that it is not clear how to correct for the frequency of guessing in recognition and recall. The set of alternatives which is considered in recall is presumably greater than in recognition, but it cannot be known precisely. In addition, it is possible that subjects use different criteria in recognition and recall. To date, the problem of comparing the amount recalled with the amount recognized has not been solved adequately. Efforts to use an information theoretic analysis have not been very illuminating (Davis, Sutherland, and Judd, 1961; Field and Lachman, 1966; but note the objections of Dale and Baddeley, 1962).

Instead of being concerned with which is better, recognition or recall, I shall pose the question whether the two involve basically similar psychological processes, or whether there are essential qualitative differences between them. Both hypotheses were formulated rather early in the history of psychology and have had some illustrious proponents. McDougall (1904) stated explicitly what has since come to be known as the threshold theory of recognition and recall. When an item is presented a "sense of familiarity" is aroused. When tested, the subject bases his response on a partially faded trace: low degrees suffice for recognition, while a greater degree of familiarity is needed for recall. The alternative conception is that recognition is a matter of checking the familiarity or response strength of an item, but that recall involves an additional process of search, or retrieval. James (1890) described recall as a search process that terminates when an item is implicitly retrieved; this item is then "recognized" as familiar or unfamiliar and a response is made, or the search process is reinitiated. Müller (1913) explicitly formulated this theory and summarized the evidence in support of it. Historically, the threshold theory rather than the two-process theory has dominated psychology (Postman, 1963; Postman, Adams, and Phillips, 1955). Interest in the two-process theory has lagged, perhaps just because of the introspective appeal of the theory. Only in recent years has the theory been reexamined. Since the threshold theory is generally known (and widely accepted), I shall concentrate here upon presenting the evidence for the two-process theory.

Experimental Variables Which Affect Recognition and Recall Differentially

A large number of experimental variables affect recognition and recall in very much the same way. This is true, for instance, for the important class of temporal variables that have been studied extensively in recent years, such as lag between presentation and test, and massing and spacing of repeated presentations. The experimental evidence for recall has been summarized by Bjork in Chapter 10. No significant change is introduced when retention is tested by recognition rather than recall (Kintsch, 1966; Olson, 1969). This state of affairs, that task variables have the same effect upon recognition and recall, is typical and certainly has contributed to the impression that recognition and recall involve basically the same psychological process. However, there are some experimental variables which have differential effects that a simple threshold theory has difficulty accounting for.

The first such variable is word frequency. It is well known that if a list of items is made up of high-frequency words recall is better than if a list of low-frequency words is used. For example, in a classical study by Hall (1954), recall of infrequent words (1 per million in the Thorndike–Lorge count) is only about 80% of that for frequent words (50–100 per million). Several studies have shown that this relationship is reversed for recognition (Schwartz and Rouse, 1961; Gorman, 1961; Shepard, 1967). Correct recognition is negatively correlated with Thorndike–Lorge frequency. A similar relationship holds when nonsense materials are used: recall is positively related to disyllable meaningfulness, but the reverse is true for recognition (McNulty, 1965a).

Recall is generally better when subjects are given intentional as opposed to incidental learning instructions. (This statement needs to be qualified, in that it is not the intention to learn *per se* which furthers recall, but the fact that the subject tries to organize the learning material for himself when given recall instructions (see Mandler, 1967); however, this does not affect the present argument.) On the other hand, subjects recognize equally well whether they have been told to memorize the material or not. This result was obtained in several studies, starting with Postman *et al.* (1955). A recent paper by Estes and DaPolito (1967) contains a discussion of these studies, as well as some unambiguous experimental evidence. Intentional recall is about 50% more than incidental recall in the Estes and DaPolito study, but recognition performance under the two conditions is practically identical. Recognition, therefore, appears to be quite automatic, while efficient recall presupposes some active, intentional process.

Last, but certainly not least, there is an important difference in the way in which interference works in recall and recognition. Various transfer paradigms have been extensively explored in recall experiments and experimental results are well established in this area (e.g., McGovern, 1964). Parallel studies using recognition testing procedures have appeared only recently and have consistently failed to detect any interference effects between specific associations. For instance, Wickelgren (1967) tested recognition memory for digit pairs embedded in a serial list. He found that recognition of a pair A-B was unaffected by the presence or absence of A-C pairs among the prior or subsequent items. Similarly, Bower and Bostrum (1968) failed to obtain stimulus specific within-list interference in a paired-associate experiment with a recognition testing procedure. Postman and Stark (1969) studied between-list interference in a multiple-choice recognition experiment. They replicated the traditional transfer designs which have often been explored in recall experiments, but did not find comparable effects. Recognition of first-list items (letter-adjective pairs) was almost entirely independent of the nature of the second list which was interpolated between learning of the first list and its test. This is very different from recall. For example, recall of an A-B list was only about 50% when the interpolated list involved the same stimulus terms as the original list but new responses (A-C), compared to a control group which learned a completely new interpolated list (C-D). On the other hand, recognition performance was essentially the same under these two conditions. Recognition, then, appears to be independent of irrelevant alternatives: whether or not an A-B association is recognized depends only upon its own characteristics, not upon other possible responses which might be associated with the same stimulus. Thus, the single item, or the single-memory trace, is an appropriate unit of analysis for recognition memory, while in recall, be it in paired-associate learning as in the experiments above or in free recall, the interrelationship of the items both within a list and between different lists is the most important determinant of performance. The single item is not the proper unit of analysis for a theory of free recall, a point stated very clearly by several previous investigators (e.g., Whitman and Garner, 1962, Tulving, 1962).

Summarizing the experimental evidence so far described, the following differences between recall and recognition need to be considered: less frequent words are more easily recognized, but the more frequent words are best recalled; intention to learn improves recall considerably, but is irrelevant for recognition; finally, interitem relationships play an important role in recall, but for recognition, each item may be considered separately.

The Nature of Two-Process Theory

Given the experimental facts summarized above, what can one say about the nature of the difference between recall and recognition? There is one kind of two-process theory which maintains that the essential difference lies in the possibility of part-responding in recognition: one can recognize an item by recognizing only some small but characteristic part of it, while recall of only a part of the item is usually insufficient to reconstruct the whole item. The importance of this factor was recognized by Hollingworth (1913) and has been demonstrated repeatedly since then. There is no doubt about either the existence or importance of partial recognition. However, it seems to me that this should be regarded as an additional complicating factor, not as an essential difference between recognition and recall. First of all, reconstructive processes in recall are extremely important and well documented (Bartlett, 1932; Bower, 1968. Furthermore, even when the possibility of partial recognition is minimized, a difference remains between recall performance and recognition. Partial recognition is most important in experiments in which poorly integrated stimulus materials are used. Thus, the difference between recall and recognition is a function of how well integrated the stimulus material is. McNulty (1965b) demonstrated this by using statistical approximations to English to manipulate the degree of response integration. He found that the superiority of recognition over recall was most pronounced at low orders of approximation and decreased the more closely actual words were approximated. However, even for the best integrated material where part-recognition presumably played a very small role, there was a significant difference between recognition and recall performance. Thus, partial recognition does not explain all of the differences between recall and recognition testing procedures.

The basic difference between recall and recognition appears to be that recall involves a search process and recognition does not. In recognition, the problem of retrieval is simple: the item is sensorily present and it is a simple matter to retrieve its corresponding representation in memory (although how this is done is by no means obvious); the subject then has some means of judging the newness of the trace (response strength, familiarity); if the newness satisfies some criterion, the subject says he recognizes the item; otherwise, he calls it new; irrelevant alternatives are not considered in this judgement. Whenever an item is presented and the subject pays attention to it, its newness is updated quite automatically. Newness is easiest to evaluate when items are quite distinct and occur infrequently; it is most difficult to keep track of the newness of words that are used very often.

The problem in recall is very different. Items are not sensorily present to be judged for their newness, but they must be retrieved from memory. Retrieval involves getting from one memory trace to the next. What is important therefore are interitem relationships. An item in a free-recall experiment is not retrieved *in vacuo*, but only as a member of a larger structure. To establish this larger structure, i.e., to establish the necessary interitem relationships, intentional activity on the part of the learner is required. Sometimes the appropriate interitem relations are already present and the subject needs only to employ them explicitly in memorizing a list. For instance, it is wellknown that highly interassociated words are easier to learn than unrelated words. Since frequent words are embedded in a richer associative network than rarely used words, they should also be easier to recall. At other times, little or no preexisting structure is apparent in a list, so that the task of constructing a retrieval network is more difficult for the subject, and the resulting structure is less predictable. The main problem of retrieval for the psychological theorist is to discover how the interitem relationships that exist in a subject's long-term memory are employed in memorizing. It is to this question that the latter part of this paper will be addressed.

A similar distinction between recognition and recall-retrieval has been made by Estes and DaPolito (1967). Their results directly support the argument made above that recognition is independent of the subject's intention to learn and hence of particular methods of rehearsal, while appropriate rehearsal greatly increases recall.

If the two-process theory is correct and recognition does not involve search in an important way, then it follows that experimental variables which facilitate retrieval in recall should have no effect on recognition. The most important such variable is structure or organization of the learning material. Several recent experiments indicate that ease of retrieval is not a factor in recognition performance. Dale (1967) asked (English) subjects to name as many county names as they could. The frequency with which each county was named provided a measure of the average availability of that name for this particular group of subjects. Twelve county names that differed widely in terms of this availability measure were used as the learning material in a free-recall and recognition experiment with another, comparable group of subjects. When retention was tested by recall, the probability of recall correlated positively with the measure of retrievability. However, the probability of recognizing a county name was not correlated with its availability. Kintsch (1968b) replicated some well-known experiments that demonstrate that organization of the learning material aids recall, but he also included an experimental condition in which retention was measured by means of a recognition test. The first experiment replicated two conditions from a study of Cofer, Bruce, and Reicher (1966). Both groups were given a 40-word list to recall. The words belonged to four conceptual categories and were selected from the norms of Cohen, Bousfield, and Whitmarsh (1957). For the high-structure group, the ten most frequent words were selected from each of four categories and arranged in blocks by category. For the low-structure group the ten least frequent words were chosen from each category and were arranged in random order. The words were presented one by one, and an immediate recall test was given. The results confirmed the findings of Cofer *et al.* Subjects recalled about 50% more from the high-structure lists than from the low-structure lists.

Half of the subjects were given a recognition test instead of the recall test. The 40 old words were shown along with 40 distractor items printed on a sheet of paper and subjects were asked to identify the old words. The distractor items were chosen from the same set of words as the learning items. For each category, 20 words were selected (either the most frequent ones or the least frequent ones, depending upon the experimental condition). These were randomly assigned to two classes, learning items and distractors. Thus, the only way the subject could tell whether an item was old or not was by a judgment of the newness or familiarity of this particular item. This procedure excluded recognition on the basis of class membership. Class recognition is, in itself, a very important and interesting phenomenon, but I believe that nothing is gained by confusing recognition on the basis of familiarity (item recognition) and class recognition. The latter is closely related to concept formation and involves very different processes than recognition of items drawn from a single, homogeneous set. The results of the recognition tests in Kintsch's (1968b) experiment were clear-cut: there was no significant difference between performance on the high and low-structure lists. This finding did not depend upon the method for correction of guessing. For both classical methods and signal detection methods the two conditions were equal. In a second experiment Kintsch (1968b) extended this finding to a different class of learning materials and to a different principle of organization. The reference experiment here was one by Miller (1958). Miller created meaningless strings of letters that were structured according to certain transition rules (e.g., a *T* can only occur after an *S* and must be followed by another *S*). The same letters in random order provided the learning material for the control condition. Miller found that the structured strings were learned appreciably faster than the random strings. Presumably, the subjects learned some of the rules used to generate the letter strings and thereby reduced the amount of material that had to be memorized by rote. Once the generation rules were known (or at least some of them and not necessarily explicitly), well-formed strings were more readily available than random strings. Kintsch (1968b) replicated Miller's finding, using a slightly different set of rules and also showed that if a recognition test was used instead of a recall test, the superiority of the structured over the unstructured condition disappeared. The distractor materials used in the recall test came, of course, from the same item pool as the learning material—i.e., they were possible strings under the rule system employed in the high-structure condition and random strings in the low-structure condition.

Cofer (1967) studied the effects of interitem associations upon both recognition and recall. His subjects studied six 15-word lists. Each lists had a name. The items in two lists were high-frequency associates to the list name; two other lists were composed of low-frequency associates to the list name, and two lists were zero-frequency associates. After each list was read aloud once, some subjects were given standard free recall tests. As expected, these subjects recalled more words from the high-associate lists than from the low-associate lists, and did worst with the unrelated word lists. Other subjects received recognition tests. They were given a test sheet containing the 15 items intermingled with 15 distractors. The distractors were words given as intrusions in previous recall experiments with the same lists. Recognition performance did not differ significantly as a function of the interitem associative strengths of the lists.

The experiments just discussed, together with the studies reviewed earlier provide fairly strong support for a two-process conception of recognition and recall. Whether they can be integrated into the classical threshold theory is, at this time, an open question, and one that will not concern me here. Instead, I would like to discuss a modification and further development of the two-process theory. The theory asserts that recognition and recall involve basically different processes, with retrieval an important factor in recall but not in recognition. Now consider the following, somewhat stronger model, which could be called the two-stage theory of recall: recall differs from recognition in that it involves a retrieval phase, but recognition is a sub-process of recall; that is, recall is implicit retrieval plus recognition. This is really the theory that James (1890) and Müller (1913) advocated and supported with a wealth of introspective observations. Their arguments are suggestive, but unfortunately they suffer from the weakness of all introspective arguments: what was so obvious to James and what he could so vividly describe is simply not present in everyone's introspection. Bartlett (1932), for instance, rejects the two-stage theory because in his analysis of recall, a recognition subprocess could not always be detected.

Omitting, therefore, the introspective evidence, what other data are relevant to the two-stage theory? Not surprisingly, there is very little. Until the theory is formulated much more precisely than it has been as yet, it is probably impossible to collect really decisive data. Kintsch and Morris (1965) have had some success with a greatly simplified two-stage model. Their model (see also Evans and Dallenbach, 1965) could be called a bare-bones model of recall: two stages are identified, and it is shown that one of these stages is identical with recognition. Their results are suggestive, but all the details remain to be worked out, for both the recognition stage and the retrieval stage.

Although little direct evidence for the two-stage theory is available at this time, it is possible to reinterpret a large number of established research results in the area of verbal learning from the view point of that theory. In an interesting and informative paper entitled "Search and Judgment in Memory," Peterson (1967) has shown how some classical findings concerning response availability and response competition in verbal learning relate to the two-stage conception of recall. He also suggested a model for recall, which, however, like its predecessors, does not go beyond specifying the two stages and assuming plausible learning functions for each.

In the next part of this chapter, extant recognition models will be briefly outlined, and then some ideas for a model of the retrieval process will be discussed.

Formal Models

Recognition

There are two separate developments that must be considered in a discussion of current models for recognition learning. The first stems from the explicit distinction between decision processes and memory factors in recognition performance, following the distinction between sensory and judgmental factors in psychophysics. The second is based upon the application of Markov models to recognition learning data.

The need for a "correction for guessing" in recognition data has always been understood. However, only recently has it become clear that the traditional procedure of correcting for guesses is but one possible method and that there are alternative theories which imply different corrections. An *a*-theoretical approach to the comparison of data with different guessing rates is possible under some conditions (Norman,

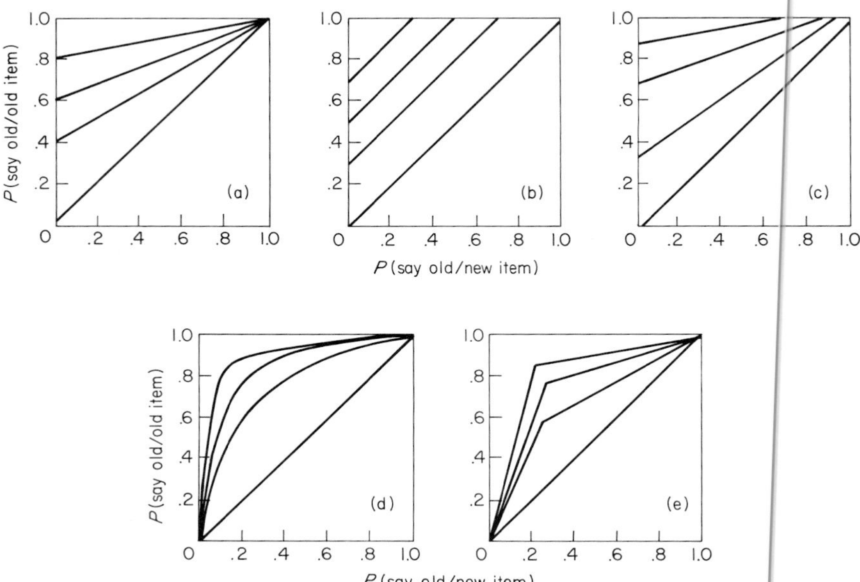

FIG. 1. Operating characteristics for several theories of recognition memory (for explanation see text).

1964), but for the most part, specific assumptions as to the underlying processes must be made. Empirical tests of the alternative assumptions are based upon the shape of the operating characteristics obtained in recognition experiments. A recognition operating characteristic is a plot of the hit rate vs. the false recognition rate under various experimental conditions. Several theoretical operating characteristics are shown in Fig. 1. Figures 1a, b, and c show the operating characteristics implied by the traditional methods of correction for guessing. The three cases have been described by Egan (1958). In general, the traditional high-threshold theory assumes that an item is correctly recognized in a recognition test with some probability p. If the item is not correctly recognized, which occurs with probability $1 - p$, the subject may still guess the correct response with a probability g that depends upon the experimental design. Obviously, g should be about $1/k$ in a well-constructed k-alternative forced-choice test, but the factors which determine g in a single-item test are less apparent. If we let P_s stand for the probability that an item that is, in fact, an old item is recognized correctly, and p_n for the probability that a distractor item is correctly recognized as such, we have

$$P(\text{say old} \mid \text{old item}) = p_s + g(1 - p_s) \tag{1a}$$
$$P(\text{say old} \mid \text{new item}) = g(1 - p_n). \tag{1b}$$

Depending upon the restrictions on the values of p_s and p_n, three special cases may be distinguished. In case I (Egan 1958), we assume $p_n = 0$. With this restriction, the operating characteristic can be easily derived by substituting (1b) into (1a):

$$P(\text{say old} \mid \text{old item}) = p_s + (1 - p_s)P\ (\text{say old} \mid \text{new item}). \tag{2}$$

This relationship is shown graphically in Fig. 1a.

For case II, suppose $p_s = p_n$. In this case, we obtain

$$P(\text{say old} \mid \text{old item}) - P_s\ (\text{say old} \mid \text{new item}) = p_s, \tag{3}$$

which is the traditional correction for guessing. The operating characteristic for case II is shown in Fig. 1b.

Case III is more realistic psychologically than either of the two previous restrictions: the possibility is admitted that subjects may recognize a new item as such (i.e., $p_n \neq 0$), but it is assumed that the probability of this event is less than the probability of correctly recognizing an old item, i.e., $p_n < p_s$. Thus, case III is intermediate between cases I and II and yields operating characteristics of the type shown in Fig. 1c.

Empirical operating characteristics do not look like either Fig. 1a, b, or c. Instead, they are consistently found to be curved and much closer in shape to Figs. 1d or 1e than to the straight lines in the first three figures (e.g., Egan, 1958; Murdock, 1965). For the way in which empirical operating characteristics are obtained, the reader may consult the original articles mentioned above.

Figure 1d is the operating characteristic derived from the theory of signal detection (TSD) as applied to recognition memory. In the extension to memory, only a very small part of TSD is used, and it is somewhat misleading to invoke the name of this sophisticated theory in this connection. Actually, all that is taken over from TSD is the concept of two overlapping probability distributions representing old and new items, plus the decision rule in terms of a fixed criterion. Each item in a recognition experiment has a certain familiarity value (alternately, one could talk about response strength, but the more neutral term seems preferable here). New items have a lower familiarity value than items that have already been presented once. However, there is

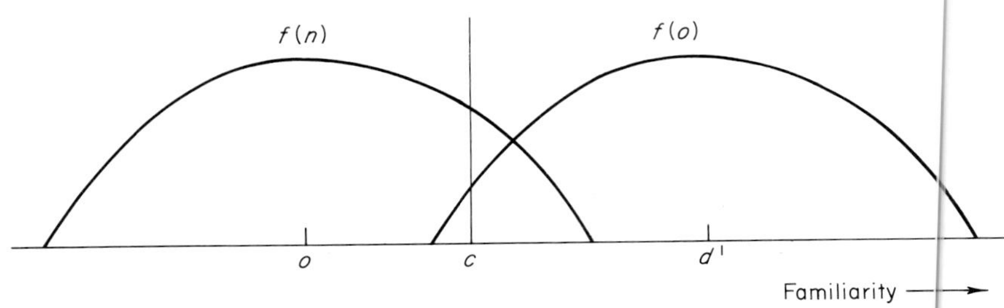

FIG. 2. Familiarity distributions of old and new items and a decision criterion.

noise in the system, and this relationship holds only on the average. Suppose that the familiarity values of new items are given by the probability density function $f(n)$ and that of old items by $f(o)$. Assume further that $f(n)$ and $f(o)$ are both normal with standard deviation equal to one and differ only in their means. On the average, the familiarity of old items is d' standard deviations units higher than the familiarity of new items. In the terminology of Thurstone (1927), $f(n)$ and $f(o)$ are the discriminal dispersions of new and old items. If an item is presented in a recognition test, the subject determines its familiarity value. If this value is higher than some criterion, he says he recognizes the item; if it is lower, he classifies the item as new. This model implies the smooth symmetric curves shown in Fig. 1d as its operating characteristic. Figure 2 summarizes the basic assumptions of the model. The reader should verify that moving the cut-off point for "old" responses from a very low familiarity value to a very high value does indeed produce a function like those shown in Fig. 1d. Deviations from symmetry can be accounted for by several additional assumptions (unequal variances of the familiarity distributions, exponential rather than normal form of the underlying distributions, or by Norman and Wickelgren's 1965 failure-of-attention theory, which will be outlined below).

Since most empirical operating characteristics are curved rather than straight lines, the theory described above with its assumptions of an underlying continuous familiarity or strength scale has been widely accepted. However, it should be noted that a modification of the traditional threshold theory that implies operating characteristics of the type represented in Fig. 1e is possible. In Luce's (1963) low-threshold theory, there are two discrete states for a stimulus trace, each associated with a particular probability of a correct response. For old items there exists a fixed probability that they will be correctly recognized. In addition, some fixed proportion of the new items are also mistakenly recognized as old. The subject is not restricted to these "true" response probabilities and may increase or decrease them according to his biases. If he has a bias for saying "old," he will say so some proportion of the time when he really does not remember the item; his operating characteristic is then given by the upper line segment in Fig. 1e. If the subject has a bias for saying "new," he will say new some proportion of the time when he actually does recognize an item. The operating characteristic for subjects with a "new" bias is given by the lower line segment in Fig. 1e. Hence, the complete operating characteristic consists of two line segments as shown in Fig. 1e. It is extremely difficult and probably impossible to distinguish between the smooth curve of Fig. 1d and the two lines of Fig. 1e on the basis of empirical operating characteristics. This problem has been discussed in detail elsewhere (Larkin, 1965; Wickelgren, 1968). Here it is sufficient to note that Luce provides a theoretical alternative to the assumption that recognition is based upon continuous familiarity distributions. We shall not explore this discrete-state alternative any further in the present paper, since all of the published recognition models employ continuous distributions in one way or another.

Parks (1966) has investigated the subjects' biases in recognition experiments. More specifically, what makes a subject select a particular cut-off point on the familiarity scale upon which he then bases his overt responses? Parks suggested that, with everything else equal, subjects tend to probability match, i.e., they adjust their criterion in such a way that the overall frequency of saying "old" approximately matches the frequency with which old items are presented in the experiment.

An interesting idea has been introduced by Norman and Wickelgren (1965). They relaxed the assumption that all old items have familiarity values according to $f(o)$ as shown in Fig. 2. Instead, they argued that subjects sometimes fail to attend to an item and that such items are not assigned a new familiarity value. Thus, the distribution of old items consist of two parts: a proportion p of the items have density function $f(o)$ and a proportion $(1 - p)$ of the items have density function $f(n)$. The latter are the unattended items. As have been mentioned above, the operating characteristic implied by this model is nonsymmetric.

Norman (1966) and Wickelgren and Norman (1966) have explored a model for recognition that incorporates a short-term forgetting mechanism. They have represented forgetting as an exponential decrease in the strength of items. This work is extensively discussed in chapter 3 by Wickelgren.

The relationship between single-item tests and multiple-choice tests in recognition experiments has been studied within the present framework by Green and Moses (1966) and Kintsch (1968a). According to the model of Fig. 2, the only difference between single-item tests and multiple-choice tests is in the decision rule that a subject employs. His memory is represented by the familiarity value of the test item, and that is the same in all cases. But the decision rule that he employs for multiple-choice tests differs from the criterion rule appropriate for single-item tests. The obvious decision rule for a multiple-choice test is to select that item which has the highest familiarity value. On the average, that will be the old item, but it is, of course, possible that one or even more of the new items will happen to have a higher value than the old item. The smaller the difference between $f(n)$ and $f(o)$, the more frequent such errors should be. Given the distance d' between the familiarity distributions of old and new items, one can calculate the probability that none of the $(k - 1)$ familiarity values of new items are higher than the familiarity value of the old item. These predictions have been quite successful in the studies mentioned. Certainly a very large part of the variability introduced by the use of different recognition testing procedures can be attributed to simple changes in decision strategies as described above.

In summary, one may say that the work on recognition memory that was stimulated by the example of signal-detection theory has been fairly informative. One should not forget, however, that the signal detection framework does not constitute a complete model of recognition. There are other aspects of recognition learning which have not yet been touched upon. Most important, I believe, are the studies concerned with short-term forgetting and spacing and massing of trials in recognition learning experiments. This is not the place to review these studies in detail, but their main impact can be summarized rather easily.

Markov models for paired-associate learning have been most successful in dealing with such experimental variables as the lag between presentation and test of an item and the interpresentation interval in repeated trials experiments. Bjork (Chapter 10) has reviewed both the rather intricate but reliable experimental data in this area and the way in which Markov models can describe this pattern of results. Typically, such a model has three states, as in the upper part of Fig. 3: an initial state, a temporary memory state, and a learning state. The transitions between states depend upon 2 (maximally 3) free parameters, usually

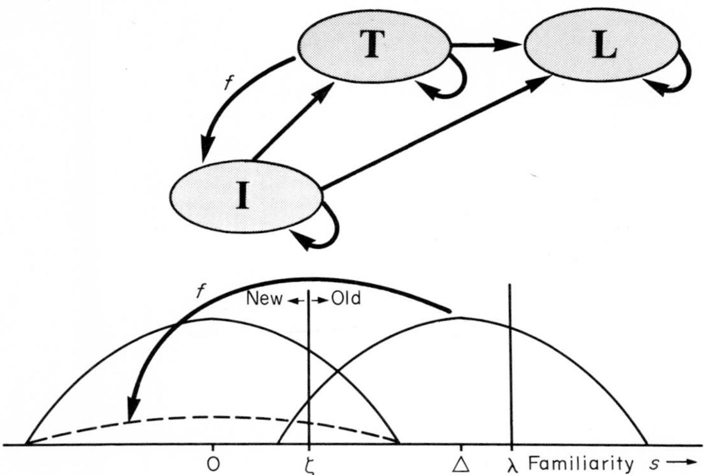

FIG. 3. Two representations of a model for recognition learning (from Kintsch, 1967).

the learning rate and the short-term forgetting probability. Basically these models are concerned with the interaction between short- and long-term memory. Their successful account of lag curves and of the complex effects of the distribution of learning trials implies that these phenomena depend mostly upon the nature of this interaction. With respect to these variables there is no essential difference between paired-associate learning data and recognition learning data. Most of the experimental findings obtained in paired-associate learning have their counterpart in recognition learning (Kintsch, 1966; Olson, 1969). Hence, it is only natural to use the same kinds of models which have been so successful with paired-associate data to account for the effects of massing and spacing of learning and test trials in recognition learning. Apparently, as far as the interaction between short- and long-term memory stores is concerned, there is no important difference between recall and recognition.

The difficulty that arises at this point is, of course, that the Markov models under discussion have discrete states, while we have just found some rather strong arguments for the assumption that recognition judgements are based upon a continuous scale of familiarity. According to the Markov model, one either recognizes an item (whether from short-term memory or from long-term memory is irrelevant here) or one does not, but there is no room for a graded judgement of familiarity. There are several ways to resolve this dilemma. One can abandon the Markov model and work with an incremental learning model. Or one could design a model based completely upon discrete states; it has been mentioned above, that Luce's low-threshold theory is a viable discrete-state alternative that can account for recognition operating characteristics and related findings. As a third possibility the two models could be combined as I shall propose below, so that the attractive features of both are retained. My reason for rejecting discrete state theories is that such theories are contradicted too strongly by introspective reports of subjects in recognition experiments: subjects have a vivid impression of knowing some item very well, or being vaguely familiar with an another item, and of never having seen a third item before. On the other hand, it also seems worthwhile to look for an alternative to pure strength theories. Markov models for recognition learning very elegantly describe a rather complex pattern of experimental results and the short-term—long-term memory distinction has considerable appeal for a variety of reasons, but it is not clear if and how a purely continuous theory of comparable simplicity can do the same job. Finally, there are psychologists who vigorously pursue this approach, as other chapters in this volume attest.

What I prefer is a compromise that permits us to retain the best of both discrete and continuous theories. How this compromise can be achieved has been described elsewhere (Kintsch, 1967; similarly Bernbach, 1967). Only the basic principles will be reiterated here. Suppose that recognition responses are based upon continuous familiarity values as in Fig. 2. The subject's response criterion ζ divides the familiarity scale into two nonoverlapping parts. We shall say that an item with a familiarity value s less than the response criterion ζ is in the initial state I. We shall assume further that there exists a second cut-off point λ, where $\zeta < \lambda$. Figure 3 shows the two cut-off points, together with the distributions of familiarity values of old and new items. It is clear that ζ and λ partition the continuous familiarity scale into three discrete parts. A correspondence can be established between these three segments and the initial state I, the temporary state T, and the long-term state L of the Markov model, as indicated graphically in Fig. 3. The area between ζ and λ corresponds to the short-term state; an item with a familiarity value $\zeta < s < \lambda$ may be forgotten with probability f [i.e., its familiarity value returns to $f(n)$]. If an item has a familiarity value $s > \lambda$, no more forgetting occurs and we can say that the item has entered the learning state. How this correspondence is established in detail is explained in the original source. However, it is important here to realize the principle at work: we have simply taken the framework of a recognition model provided by signal-detection theory and have added to it forgetting assumptions suggested by the structure of the Markov model for recognition. Specifically, the assumption has been added that old items may be forgotten and that the probability of forgetting is a function of the familiarity value of the old item: if this value is high enough (i.e., greater than λ), no more forgetting occurs.

Having resolved the conflict between discrete and continuous models in this way, one is left with a fairly satisfying situation as far as formal models of recognition learning are concerned. A large, systematic body of data can be quite adequately accounted for. However, relative to the remaining problems this achievement is not as great as it seems. We were concerned here only with data from verbal learning studies using a recognition testing procedure. It remains to be shown how relevant such data are to recognition models in general. Secondly, even for this very restricted set of experimental results, all we have is a formal model. The model has nothing to say about *how* an item is recognized; it is not a structural model in the sense that it describes a possible mechanism of recognition. It is merely a device to describe what goes on in a recognition experiment. It sets constraints that future process models of recognition will have to satisfy. As yet there has been little work on structural models of recognition in verbal learning experiments. There has been, of course, a lively interest in pattern recognition in general, but on the whole, this has been divorced from the developments in verbal learning. Some notable exceptions are found in the attempts to write computer simulation programs for verbal learning (Feigenbaum, chapter 13; Hintzman, 1968). Another quite different suggestion as to the possible form that a future process model of recognition could take has been made recently by Anisfeld and Knapp (1968). They suggest that an item such as a word is represented in memory as a complex of features that are time-tagged when presented in the experiment and that recognition is based upon these features. Perhaps familiarity (which in the present paper was used as a purely abstract term) is based upon some kind of a feature count: the higher the proportion of tagged features, the greater the familiarity of an item. A related notion is explored in connection with retrieval processes in recall, and we shall return to the idea of feature-tagging in that context.

The Retrieval Problem

The central problem for a model of recall is to gain some insight into how the organization of the learning material affects recall. The empirical results to which I am referring here are well documented. Any kind of organization of the learning material facilitates recall. For example, the more strongly interassociated the items of a list are, the easier it is to recall them. However, not only direct associations between list members are important, but also indirect links via items which themselves are not on the list of learning items. For a definitive treatment of these problems the reader is referred to Deese (1965). The organization of a list of words in terms of category membership influences recall in a similar way. An experiment of this type was described earlier. A good review of the experimental findings in this area and of the role of associative links among category members has been provided by Cofer (1965). Finally, there is a third source of organization which should be mentioned. When the items of a list are related by any kind of a rule, subjects are somehow able to exploit the constraints imposed by that rule in order to improve their recall performance. The reference experiment in this area is one by Miller (1958), which has already been mentioned.

Associations as well as category membership are determined from norms collected from a large number of subjects. Thus, they reflect relationships that are common to these subjects. However, organization is basically a subjective phenomenon. The particular structure that each subject develops for himself is what matters. Objective organization exploits the very substantial communalities which exist between subjects. Completely ideosyncratic organization, structures, or rules are just as important for recall as structures which are shared by many different subjects. Tulving (1962) and Mandler (1967) have provided important demonstrations of subjective organization.

This brief outline of experimental findings is sufficient to allow us to frame our question more precisely. A model for recall must have some kind of mechanism that makes organized material easier to recall than unorganized material. Two subproblems are implied. First, one must ask how memory is organized, or rather how it could be organized. Only after some kind of answer is provided to that question can one approach the second part of the problem: How is the organization of memory used in a free-recall experiment? It is obvious that subjects do not learn the words presented to them in a free-recall experiment *de novo*. Typically, they know these words very well, and they are merely concerned with remembering them as items of a particular experimental list.

These ideas are not new in the history of psychology. The term apperceptive mass was widely used at one time to refer to a person's organized store of knowledge. Learning in prebehavioristic times was explicitly regarded as a problem of connecting the material to be learned with the apperceptive mass—very unlike writing on an empty tablet! The relationship of the learning material to the apperceptive mass was thought to be the crucial factor determining ease of learning. In fact, one of the very first mathematical models in psychology dealt with these problems. I refer to Herbart's calculus of ideas, which was primarily concerned with describing how new ideas become part of the apperceptive mass (see the reprint in Miller, 1964). The neglect that these ideas have experienced in recent years and the demise of the concept of apperceptive mass may be partly due to the complexity of the problem. There were simply no suitable methods of analysis available. However, it seems worthwhile to resume work on this old problem.

It should also be noted that what I am talking about is not a phenomenon restricted to free-recall learning, nor to the "higher mental processes." A basic characteristic of learning is that there are preexisting structures in the learner's makeup that determine what is easy to learn and what is hard to learn, and what is impossible to learn. These structures are partly genetic and partly experiential, but they are important in classical conditioning of animals as well as in free verbal recall. For instance, Garcia, McGowan, Ervin, and Knoelling (1968) have shown that for rats the taste of a food pellet is easily conditioned as a conditional stimulus (CS) if the unconditioned stimulus (UCS) is a noxious dosage of X rays, but not if the UCS is an electrical shock. On the other hand, the pellet size was a good CS if shock was the UCS, but conditioning was almost impossible if this CS was used in conjunction with X rays. Something in the rat's makeup facilitated the taste—sickness-induced-by-radiation association and made the taste-shock connection difficult to acquire, just as certain verbal associations are easy and others hard to learn for human subjects. For other examples from animal conditioning, see Breland and Breland (1966).

A Tentative Model for Long-Term Memory

What follows are some preliminary and extremely tentative speculations about the structure of long-term memory. They are based upon ideas put forth by linguists interested in structural semantics and related topics, notably Chomsky (1965), Katz and Fodor (1963), Lyons (1963), and Porzig (1950), without, however, being closely identified with any one of these. In the experiments that we are concerned with separate words are usually used as learning material. Therefore, we shall ask how single words could be encoded in long-term memory so that the relationships between words that have been found in psychological experiments as well as in linguistic analyses can be represented.

One possible approach might be to say that words are stored as units and that they are connected with other words through associative links of various strengths. The structure of memory would then be given by a network of associations. I have not followed this approach for two reasons. First, in order to achieve even a mild degree of realism the resulting network of associations would be extremely complicated, and it is hard to see how the redundancy that exists in this network could be exploited to simplify it. Second, even with all its complexity, it is not obvious to me how a purely associative network can represent all relevant linguistic relationships. For example, if a theory admits only associative links, how can it express the obvious differences in the relationships between such word pairs as MELON-FRUIT, NOSE-HEAD, and BREAD-BUTTER?

The model proposed here is a marker theory of memory. Each word is encoded in memory as a list of markers. A marker, at least in the case of semantic markers with which I shall be mostly concerned here, is in general another word. Thus far, the model is an associative network: each entry in memory consists of a list of references to other entries. However, different types of markers will be distinguished. In this sense, the model is no longer an associative network, but it contains different kinds of relationships of which associative relations are one. One can think of the different types of markers as associations with a name, e.g., the "association" between MELON and FRUIT has the name "is a member of class"; the association between NOSE and HEAD is named "is part of"; several different relations hold between BREAD-BUTTER.

Three basic classes of markers are to be distinguished. A word is coded as <S, I, P>, where S, I and P are complex symbols with markers or sets of markers as elements. S is a list of semantic–syntactic markers, and is the chief concern here. I is a list of sensory features or image-markers. P stands for phonetic features; essentially, they are instructions how to pronounce the word. What is meant here can be indicated by reference to the distinctive feature representation of single phonemes. The phonemes of the English language can be described by listing their distinctive features (e.g., Halle, 1964). For instance, in Halle's system, the consonant "b" is characterized by a value of 1 for the features *Voicing, Consonantal, Grave* and *Diffuse,* and a value of 0 for *Nasality, Vocalic, Continuant,* and *Strident.* If *Nasality* is changed to a 1 and all other features are kept constant an "m" is obtained, and so on. Several alternative feature systems have been proposed by linguists, but it is not necessary to make a choice here. More significant is Wickelgren's finding that performance of human subjects in short-term memory experiments actually reflects coding in terms of distinctive features. In particular, Wickelgren observed that the rank order of different intrusion errors in short-term recall could be accurately predicted from distinctive feature models (Wickelgren, 1965, 1966). Thus, the assumption of distinctive feature coding is supported experimentally, at least for the case of single phonemes. It is not clear how this approach is to be extended to complete words, but in principle this seems possible. Perhaps it is sufficient to treat words as concatenations of phonemes; in any case this is a task for the linguist. All that must be assumed here is that some kind of feature representation of the sounds of words is possible. Which phonetic (or articulatory?) system is used is beyond the concern of this paper.

Note an important difference between semantic markers and phonetic features: in a feature system every item is coded in terms of the same set of features, while only relevant semantic markers are used to code word meanings.

The symbol I is vaguely identified with a list of "sensory features." At this time, I have nothing to say about the nature of sensory features or memory images, except that it is absolutely necessary to have some provision for nonverbal memory in a model of memory. Thus, the I-markers are included here simply as a reminder for a task that is to be done. Since our understanding of nonverbal memory is even poorer than that of verbal memory, no further use will be made of this part of the model. Investigations of nonverbal memory are only just beginning to appear in the psychological literature (e.g., Hebb, 1968; Bahrick and Boucher, 1968).

Meaning provides the most important principle of organization in memory. Meaning relations are to be embodied in the list S of semantic–syntactic markers. The meaning of a formal unit (which will be naively identified as a word, neglecting serious problems of definition) is defined by its relationship with other formal units. That is, a word does not have meaning in itself, but meaning in the system is given entirely by context. A formal unit is meaningful because it can be located somewhere in a semantic field. The concept of semantic field (conceptual field, lexical field) has been developed by linguists interested in structural semantics (Trier, 1934, Porzig, 1950). According to Trier, meaning is defined within a field. The meaning of a word is known only if it is contrasted with the meaning of a related or opposed term. As an illustration, consider the way color names are defined: color names are not bound to the physical substratum, the light spectrum, in any precise way. Rather, they are defined with respect to each other, e.g., orange is between yellow and red, but it is not defined as a light of some particular wavelength. Different cultures subdivide the color spectrum in different ways, and even in the same culture, the partitioning of the spectrum is not fixed forever. Changes in the use of the term "brown" since the 18th century have been described by Trier (1934), for instance.

The concept of semantic field is basic to the model. It provides for a definition of meaning without recourse to some substratum of "meaning"; the meaning of a term is determined by the way it is stored in memory—as a list of pointers to other terms. It should also be noted that the distinction between meaning and reference, which philosophers find very useful (Frege, 1892; Quine, 1960), has a natural correspondence within the present model: the relationship of the semantic markers S of one formal unit with those of the other formal units of the system defines the meaning of the unit, while the relationship of the S-markers to the sensory information specified by the I-markers defines reference.

Two kinds of semantic fields must be distinguished. The first relates a set of words that are all of the same form class, i.e., it comprises the paradigmatic relationships. I shall use the term *lexical field* for this type of semantic field. This is the sense in which Trier (1934) originally introduced the term.

A lexical field which is called an *antonymy* is given by oppositions such as MALE-FEMALE, or GOOD-BAD. In the first case, we speak of nongradable antonymy, in the second case of gradable antonymy. Fields with more than two terms are called *contrasts,* following the terminology of Lyons (1963). As an example, I have already mentioned color names: VIOLET, BLUE, GREEN, YELLOW, ORANGE, RED. Frequently there exists a temporal ordering of terms in a contrast field, such as in MORNING, NOON, AFTERNOON, EVENING, NIGHT, or in the many adjective pairs that are used to express the EARLY-LATE opposition in different contexts: YOUNG-OLD, FRESH-STALE, PRIMITIVE-ADVANCED, etc. (Bolinger, 1965). Words which belong to such a set are given a marker $F(X)$. Thus, GOOD will have the marker F(good-bad); ORANGE will have the marker F(color between yellow and red).[2] In general, an F-marker contains the information which is necessary to specify the relative position of a word within a semantic field.

A different kind of lexical field involves *hierarchical* or *sequential* organization. The two most important examples are given by the relation of *class inclusion* and the *part-of* relationship. However, there are many other hierarchical structures which are of importance in memory. Examples are given below.

A hierarchical structure may be represented by a tree diagram. For instance, the hierarchy "country names" may be outlined as follows:

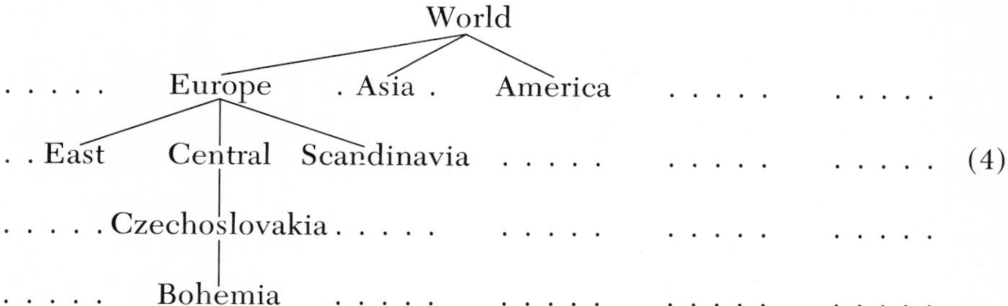

(4)

Each country name has two class markers, one that specifies its superordinate category $C\uparrow(X)$, and one that specifies its direct subordinates $C\downarrow(X_1 \ldots X_k)$. Thus CZECHOSLOVAKIA would be marked as $C\uparrow$ (Central Europe) and $C\downarrow$ (Bohemia, . . .). Most structures of interest are not strictly hierarchical. In a hierarchy, each node is dominated by exactly one higher node. In many structures this is not the case, especially when one is concerned not with socially determined and es-

[2] This is not the only marker of ORANGE, though. The term is tied to the physical spectrum in a more direct way through the related sensory images (I).

sentially arbitrary structures as in the example above, but with real-world structures. One of the problems is that of cross-classifications, which has been discussed by Chomsky (1965). Consider the following example:

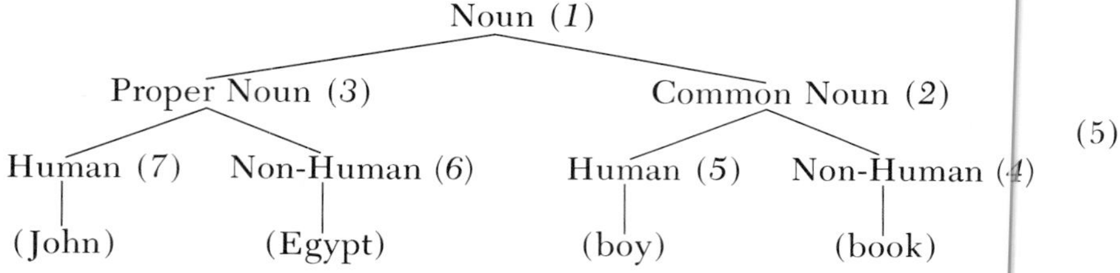

(5)

The tree (5) does not properly reflect the class relationships present. To understand the problem, disregard the verbal description of the nodes and replace them with numbers as indicated. Now it is obvious that the nodes (6) and (4) have nothing in common: the generalization *Non-Human* is completely missed in the formal structure of the tree. However, as Chomsky points out, this only means that tree structures are a poor formal representation for many interesting relationships. A marker theory can handle the problem quite naturally by assigning more than one marker at a time, e.g., BOY would have the markers C(Common Noun) as well as C(Human), and both COMMON NOUN and HUMAN would have the marker C(Noun).

Very much the same holds for the part-relationship. We introduce a marker $P\uparrow(X)$ which says that the entry is a part of another entry X, and $P\downarrow(X_1 \ldots X_k)$ which says that it, in turn, has parts $X_1 \ldots X_k$. Again, we are not dealing with strict hierarchies:

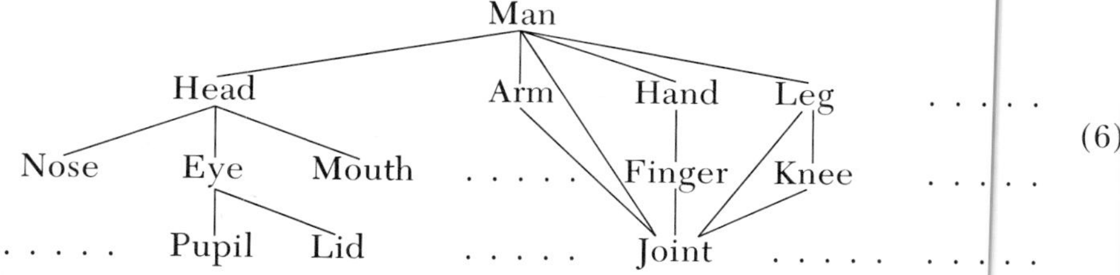

(6)

A detailed discussion of the formal properties of the part-of hierarchy may be found in Bierwisch (1965), from where the above example has been taken.

Besides the well-known cases of class inclusion and the part-of relationship there are other important sequential-hierarchical structures in memory. For instance, it might be necessary to introduce a marker "location" to specify such relationships as a POT is in the KITCHEN, a KITCHEN is in a HOUSE, a HOUSE is in a CITY, and so forth. The problem of cross-classification arises, but it can be handled in the same way as above.

A marker system as outlined here can provide a simple and relatively compact description of logical, semantic, and syntactic information because of the way in which *redundancy rules* can be employed within such a system. First, consider the operation of such rules in the case of antonymy sets. The basic idea here is that an F(X) marker is itself a "word" of the system which has its own set of markers $Y_1, Y_2, \ldots,$ Y_k. We adopt the convention that whenever F(X) appears as a marker, it is automatically extended to include all the general characteristics of the antonymy set. Formally, this convention is expressed by the following rewriting rule:

$$\mathrm{F}(X) \rightarrow [Y_1, Y_2, \ldots, Y_k, \mathrm{F}(X)]. \tag{7}$$

Such rules make it possible to use storage space more economically. For example, consider the antonymy set *color names*: all relevant information of general nature is stored only once (e.g., syntactical markers) and then extended to the individual words by (7).

Redundancy rules are even more important for the description of hierarchical structures. First of all, the general characteristics of a hierarchy need not be written down as markers with every separate word but can be extended to all members of a hierarchy in the same way as it was done for antonymy sets. For instance, any marker P(X) can immediately be subordinated under appropriate grammatical categories by the following rule (after Bierwisch, 1965):

$$\mathrm{P}\ (X) \rightarrow [\text{Count Noun, Concrete, } \mathrm{P}(X)].$$

Secondly, redundancy rules can be used to reconstruct hierarchies. Note that we have stored as a class or part-marker only the immediate subordinate. We now adopt the convention that C(X) and P(X) markers recursively assign all higher and lower order categories to an item. Formally, if XYZ is a part-of chain such as FINGER, HAND, ARM, MAN,

$$\mathrm{P}(X) \rightarrow [\mathrm{P}(X), \mathrm{P}(Y)]. \tag{8}$$

Recursive application of this rule will generate all superordinate markers. The same kind of redundancy rule can be used also for class inclusion and other kinds of hierarchies. Subordination can be handled similarly. Relationships such as those in (6) require multiple markers [e.g., JOINT could be given the marker P(arm), P(man), P(hand) . . . ; a more efficient and a more elegant procedure has been suggested by Bierwisch (1965), but will not be described here].

A completely different kind of redundancy rule that also leads to further simplification of the memory system is the *transformational rule.* Some words may be derived from more basic ones and need not figure as separate lexical entries. Consider, for instance, the relationships GOOD–GOODNESS, BAKE–BAKER, ACT–ACTION, IGNORE–IGNORANCE (examples from Lyons, 1963). These pairs are related by certain linguistic rules (e.g., adjective → abstract noun). Frequently, when a word is derived in this way, it is assigned the markers of the source word, except for changes in the syntactic markers. In some cases (IGNORE–IGNORANCE) changes in meaning occur.

Up to now we have concentrated upon the description of the relationships between items of the same class, i.e., upon *lexical fields.* Now we consider syntagmatic relationships. There exist relations of selection among items that form what I shall call *associative fields.*[3] Much of the meaning of a word is determined only through its use. Associated with each noun are verbs and adjectives, which are part of the meaning of that word and must be listed as special markers. In general associative markers are of the form noun–verb, noun–verb–noun, or adjective–noun. Thus, part of the meaning of HAND is given by such verbs as HOLD or GRASP. Conversely, verbs and adjectives are defined with respect to particular nouns: BITE implies TOOTH, LICK implies TONGUE, BLOND implies HAIR, and RIDE implies HORSE, or in another context maybe CAMEL. Obviously, a model of memory will require a large storage space for this type of information. Great detail is necessary (e.g., the model should know that one can WHISPER TENDERLY, but not WALK TENDERLY; all examples are from Porzig, 1934, 1950). Redundancy rules can achieve less simplification here than with lexical fields. However, no formal problems arise in the model. The difficulty is that so many associative relations will have to be stored. However,

[3] The German terms are much less ambiguous, but I have not been able to find adequate translations. Porzig (1950) distinguishes between *einbegreifende Bedeutungsfelder* (associative fields) and *aufteilende* Bedeutungsfelder (lexical fields). This contrast so lucidly implied by the German is completely lost in translation. Abelson and Carroll (1965) talk about the vertical and horizontal structure of memory corresponding to the lexical and associative fields, respectively.

efficient exploitation of class and part relationships greatly reduces the number of associative markers in the total system.

The final class of markers are *syntactic markers*. Since my immediate concern here is with single words, it is sufficient to mention that such markers exist. A relatively detailed treatment of syntactic markers is available in Chomsky (1965). I should point out that the selection restrictions that Chomsky included under syntactic markers are taken over by the associative markers in the present system.

Before leaving this outline for a model of memory and returning to the problem of recall, a few comments are in order. Note that an important difference exists between the present proposal and Katz and Fodor's theory of semantic structure in the treatment of polysemy. The present system is not concerned with the problem of semantic ambiguity which is central to Katz and Fodor's theory. Our unit is a word meaning, and not a particular letter sequence. Of course, it is often the case that a written word has more than one meaning. In the present model, there will be as many different entries as there are word meanings. Normally, the different meanings of a written word are related in some nonarbitrary way. These relationships will, of course, be reflected in the markers of the various entries. The fact that two formal units have the same written expression, or for that matter the same phonemic expression as in the case of homophones, does not in itself appear to be very significant. Thus, there is no semantic ambiguity in the present system: the semantic field in which the term is embedded disambiguates it completely. Words are ambiguous only if they are isolated from their semantic field, as in the conventional dictionary.

The problem that polysemy poses for a model of this kind should not be underestimated, however. Weinreich (1964) distinguishes 115 sub- or subsubsenses of the verb TURN. This implies that a literate subject must have available many lists of subject–nouns associated with the different senses before he can use TURN properly. Weinreich also points out that the many meanings of TURN are internally structured and can be ordered along three principal dimensions. In some uses, TURN is semantically depleted and receives its meaning almost entirely from other words, such as in "turn the trick," or "turn him free."

Just as one linguistic form may occur in connection with several different markers because it belongs to different semantic fields, different forms may be associated with the same marker. Perhaps it will be useful to introduce a special synonym marker SYN(X) to avoid separate listings in such cases.

It is interesting to speculate on how semantic fields develop. According to Porzig (1934), words are at first defined rather narrowly in terms of concrete associative fields, both in the history of language and in the development of the individual. As it partakes in more and more relationships a word tends to lose its specific content. Selection restrictions are disregarded, and the word develops figurative meanings. In the metaphoric use of a word, restrictions on its use are deliberately violated.

For the memory model outlined here, the semantic-pragmatic distinction has been ignored. Memory must always be regarded in terms of a particular subject, at a particular time—that is, it must be a lexicon and an encyclopedia at the same time.

Retrieval

Given the marker model of long-term memory, it becomes possible to devise a reasonable model for the recall process. Again, the treatment will only be programmatic. In a free-recall experiment, the subject stores the information that a particular word has occurred as a member of the list that is to be memorized. It is not the word itself which is stored, but a reference that the word has occurred. This is the basic assumption of the model; previously, it has been used by Yntema and Trask (1963). Words themselves (in their coded form as a list of markers) are already part of a subject's long-term memory. When a word is presented in a learning experiment, the subject tags the corresponding marker list.

Precisely what the model is supposed to achieve can best be explained by placing it within the framework of the general memory model developed by Atkinson and Shiffrin (1968). These authors distinguish three main *structural components* of memory: Information is selected from a *sensory buffer* and enters a limited-capacity *short-term memory* store. Decay in short-term memory is rapid, unless prevented by active rehearsal. As long as information is in short-term memory, there is a steady rate of transfer of information into a more permanent *long-term memory* store. As soon as it leaves short-term memory, the availability of information in long-term memory begins to decrease gradually. What is selected to enter short-term memory, what is rehearsed, what is transferred to long-term memory is governed by *control processes.* The present model proposes to take over this scheme except for one part: the "transfer of information to long-term memory."

In fact, one could consider the present model as an attempt to state what is involved in that transfer from short-term memory to long-term memory. Just talking about "transfer of information" is surely inadequate, as has been pointed out earlier. It is necessary to specify how existing information is used in this transfer.

When an item such as a word is presented, it enters the system as a sound-pattern (even if the presentation is visual, there is evidence that subjects read words or letters to themselves, i.e., that the effective stimulus is acoustic). This sound pattern is matched with a reference pattern stored in memory, i.e., with a P-matrix. How this match is achieved is beyond the scope of the present paper. It is sufficient to say that the sound of a word identifies the corresponding P-matrix, thereby making accessible the corresponding I and S markers associated with it. Thus, a word is not only identified as a particular sound pattern, but it is "understood." If more than one set of S-markers is associated with the same P-matrix, a selection on the basis of context occurs; in free-recall experiments where there is no context available, selection may occur according to a frequency bias.

If a word is perceived in the sense described above the markers associated with it are automatically time-tagged. Specifically, what gets tagged are the phonetic features involved in identifying the sound of the word presented and the semantic markers that identify the word meaning. We assume that each marker has a familiarity value, and that tagging a marker amounts to incrementing this familiarity value by some amount that depends upon the original familiarity value of the marker. More precisely, we want to make the changes in familiarity values as a result of time-tagging to be like those postulated by the recognition model discussed earlier.

If there is room in the short-term rehearsal buffer, the P-matrix in question enters the buffer; if the buffer is full, the new item enters it with some probability that depends upon a number of factors as discussed by Atkinson and Shiffrin, and apparently also upon the perceptual distinctiveness of the item: the more different a new item is from those already held in short-term memory, the more likely it will be placed into short-term memory. With this assumption, one may be able to account for such phenomena as the "release from proactive inhibition" observed by Wickens, Born, and Allen (1963). Different strategies for deleting old items from the rehearsal buffer have also been described by Atkinson and Shiffrin.

As long as an item is held in short-term memory, "cognitive work" is performed on it to facilitate later retrieval. We distinguish two cases. The first corresponds to the formation of new associations, or rote learning. A word is added as a new marker to some marker list. For instance, if two words A and B are simultaneously held in short-term memory, B may be added as a marker to the marker-list of A. Often A may be some kind of starting symbol, like LIST I, and several words may be connected to it in this manner. The second case is more efficient, and involves the utilization of existing interrelationships among items, i.e., of marker overlap. We assume that the markers of the words held in short-term memory are scanned. If a marker *X* is found that is common to two (or more) words A and B, A and B are tagged in the marker list of *X*. Thus, a system of cross references is built up. Whenever a marker, or a set of markers, is being worked with its familiarity value receives an automatic updating. If no match is obtained, new markers for the words in short-term memory may be generated through the use of redundancy rules, and a search may be made for a match among the newly generated markers. The amount of "working time" available to the subject sets limits upon these processes. If in the available time no match is achieved, the system fails.

Familiarity values are assumed to decay exponentially over time. The older time-tags become, the harder it is to discriminate among them.

Consolidation plays an important role in this model. If the subject is given enough time he may replace a poor retrieval system with a better one, or he may relate items to the system which have only been retained temporarily in the short-term buffer. Clearly, the model implies that, given enough time, a subject should be able to recall even very lengthy lists.

In retrieval the model produces first the words available in short-term memory and those associated with the starting symbol LIST. Then a word chosen at random from those available and its markers are scanned. The marker *X* with the highest familiarity value is selected and the system now moves to inspect the entry corresponding to that marker. The familiarity value of the markers of *X* are determined and if they are above a criterion, *X* is produced as an overt response. The search process is renewed with one of the already recalled words as its starting point. If the recognition check of *X* is negative, the markers of *X* are now scanned in turn, and the whole process recycles. Several stopping rules seem reasonable. For instance, after a number of unsuccessful recognition checks, the search may be stopped completely, or it may be restarted with a different initial item.

Recall cues in this model help to specify the relevant markers that should be used for the search of memory. They must be available at the time of storage in order to be used effectively.

A model like this—if fully developed—could provide an answer to the basic problem of retrieval models. It shows how the organization of long-term memory may be used in learning to recall a list of words: preexisting relations among words guide the search of memory. If two items are part of the same semantic field there is a bridge between them which is used to go from one to the other. Unrelated items may be related through mediators; the recognition check which is also included in the model insures that mediators will not be output themselves.

Clustering in Recall

Having outlined a model for the retrieval process the question arises whether there are data to test this model. Strictly speaking, there are no really adequate data, for the model is not stated explicitly enough to be testable. The only way to evaluate the model at present is through an informal but informed judgment: can it account qualitatively for the semantic relationships which are known to be important and for the principal experimental results of free recall? Obviously, the reader must provide his own answers.

Although no definitive tests of the model are possible at this time I shall report some data analyses in which the attempt was made to recover the structure of semantic relations from free recall data. First, however, some recent work by Miller (1967) must be mentioned.

Suppose a model like the tentative form just outlined provides a fair description of long-term memory. According to that model, the similarity between two words is determined by the number of shared semantic markers. Thus judgments of similarity reflect marker overlap. If the similarity relations among a whole set of items are evaluated, they should be related to the underlying semantic structure. In particular, if the items form a class or part-of hierarchy such relations should be apparent in the similarity judgments. Miller gave subjects a deck of cards with words printed on them and a brief phrase that unambiguously identified the intended word meaning (e.g., PLAY, *fun sport. We often watch the children at play*). Subjects were asked to sort these cards on the basis of similarity into as many piles as they deemed necessary. From the data of many subjects, Miller obtained as his basic measure of similarity the frequency with which word *X* was put into the same pile with word *Y*. The next problem was to determine the structure which underlies the resulting similarity matrix. This was done by using a computer program of Johnson (1967) that extracts clusters of similar items from data of this kind. The program finds the items which are most similar to each other and merges them into a cluster. Then the similarity values are recomputed for the whole table, except that the merged elements are treated as a unit. The same procedure is repeated on the new, smaller matrix until all items are clustered. Obviously, such a procedure insures that the first cluster has the highest intercluster similarity and that intercluster similarity decreases with successive clusters.

Miller applied this analysis to several sets of words and obtained very interesting and promising results. In general, the clustering program generated the kind of clusters which one would expect on the basis of *a priori* linguistic analyses. For instance, such markers as human–nonhuman, or object–nonobject were clearly reflected in the resulting tree structures. However, there were interesting problems. By its very nature, this kind of work will only get at the structure which is common to many subjects. Actually, what determines the sorting is each individual's idiosyncratic organization. Any individual differences will turn up as noise in the present kind of analysis. Nevertheless, Miller's sorting procedure appears to be a very promising experimental technique with which the problem of semantic relationships may be approached, and it provides some empirical support for the marker model previously described.

I have analyzed free-recall data in a similar manner in the hope that this analysis would provide data relevant to the retrieval model of the preceding section. According to the model semantic markers play a crucial role in the retrieval process: given that a word has been recalled, its markers determine which word will be recalled next. Thus, output order in recall should reflect semantic relationships. That it does, indeed, is well known. The clustering of related items in the subject's recall has been extensively investigated (e.g., Bousfield, 1953). I have employed Johnson's clustering analysis to analyze this phenomenon.

Two 16-word lists were used in the experiment. One list consisted of four nouns from each of four conceptual categories (Table 1). The other list consisted of 16 unrelated low-frequency nouns previously

TABLE 1
Output Adjacencies for the Categorized Word List; Trial 1, Blocked Presentation Order

	kangaroo	beaver	buffalo	camel	Ralph	Philipp	Bernard	Dennis	painter	butcher	grocer	janitor	mushroom	artichoke	yam	melon
kangaroo	—															
beaver	49	—														
buffalo	45	82	—													
camel	45	33	—													
Ralph	8	3	13	36	—											
Philipp	11	3	2	0	68	—										
Bernard	13	13	7	7	12	48	—									
Dennis	3	3	3	7	23	36	54	—								
painter	5	5	10	4	11	5	7	30	—							
butcher	3	6	6	7	3	12	3	7	72	—						
grocer	3	7	4	9	9	10	10	8	10	50	—					
janitor	18	3	0	8	23	0	0	8	25	20	30	—				
mushroom	0	0	3	0	3	6	0	3	9	3	14	8	—			
artichoke	0	0	5	0	3	0	3	3	5	6	3	0	75	—		
yam	3	0	3	3	3	3	3	3	10	0	3	3	14	85	—	
melon	3	6	0	3	25	3	6	0	12	12	8	11	12	19	66	—

used by Tulving (1965). For both lists two different presentation orders were employed. The categorized word lists were shown in either random or blocked order; the unrelated word lists were shown either in an order that maximized sequential dependencies (the "high organization" order of Tulving, 1965), or in an order that minimized these dependencies (Tulving's "low organization" order). Words were presented at a 2-sec rate by means of a slide projector. Recall was in writing. All subjects recalled both a categorized list and an unrelated list. Three trials were given with each list, always with the same input order. Subjects were run singly, with between 42–48 subjects per condition. They were instructed to recall as many words as they could without regard to order.

Adjacency measures were calculated on the basis of the order in which the words were recalled. Table 1 shows these measures for the categorized word list when presentation was blocked, trial 1. The higher the entries in Table 1, the more frequently the corresponding row and

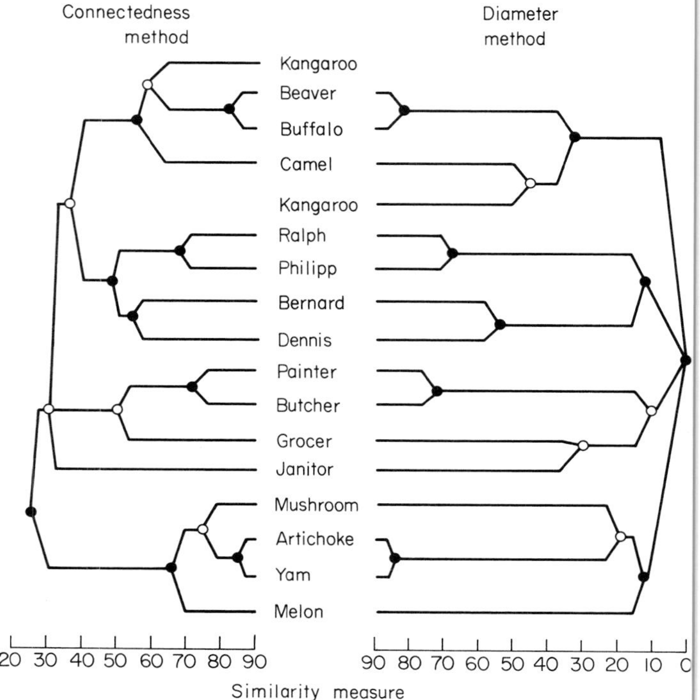

FIG. 4. Cluster analysis of the output adjacencies among 16 words in a free-recall experiment.

column words were recalled together. For instance, the very first entry says that the output adjacency measure for BEAVER and KANGAROO is .49. This value was obtained in the following manner: Of the 37 times that the word KANGAROO was recalled, the word following it in the output protocol was BEAVER 12 times; BEAVER, which also happened to be recalled 37 times, was followed by KANGAROO 6 times; 12/37 + 6/37 = .49. This procedure assures that adjacency measures are symmetric. The adjacency matrices were analyzed with Johnson's clustering program which has been described above.

Figure 4 shows the result of this analysis for the categorized word list, trial 1, with blocked presentation. The analysis was done twice, according to two different methods described by Johnson. If data are noiseless and truly hierarchical, the two methods yield identical results. Thus, the agreement between the two procedures can serve as a check on the validity of the analysis: where the two methods disagree, there is probably no hierarchy to extract. This is important to know, because the program will always form hierarchical clusters, given any kind of data. The results shown in Fig. 4 are quite encouraging. Apparently output order in recall does reflect semantic structure, at least in the sense that items belonging to the same category clustered together. Within each category there seemed to be very little structure of a hierarchical nature, as shown by the disagreement between the two methods of analysis. However, it is possible that there was hierarchical organization, but not enough intersubject agreement so that it was not detected by the present analysis.

When the words shown in Fig. 4 were shown in random order, the hierarchical relationships were not clearly developed on trial 1, but they emerged by trial 3. No hierarchical organization could be identified for the unrelated word lists. These lists were constructed in such a way that whatever objective organization existed was purely sequential, and subjective organization is treated as noise when data from many subjects are combined as was done here.

I have mentioned before that the program identifies clusters in the order of their intercluster similarity. These values for the data of Fig. 4,

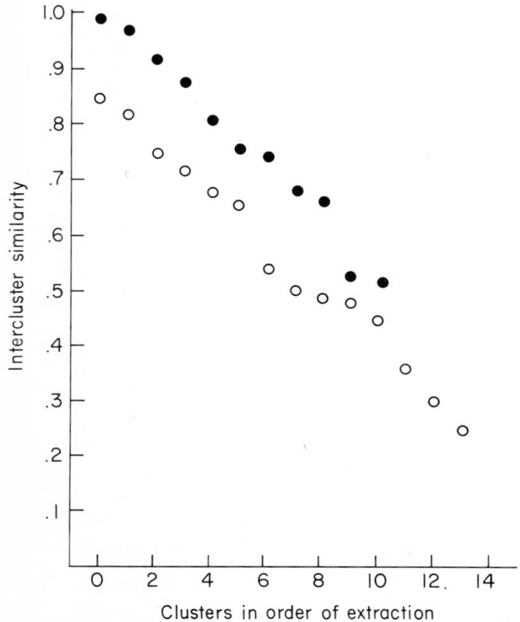

FIG. 5. Intercluster similarities on trials 1 and 3 (for explanation see text).

as well as the values for the third learning trial with the same list, are presented in Fig. 5. Note that organization increases as a function of trials. On trial 3, the clusters have higher similarity measures, and there are fewer clusters, which means that more items are merged at each level.

The adjacency measures in the present experiment were strongly influenced by the input positions of items. Items that were adjacent in input also tended to be recalled together. For instance, the clustering analysis ordered both the blocked category list and the high-organization sequential list according to input order by trial 3. In Fig. 6, this dependency upon input order and the interaction of input order with semantic organization is shown for the random-presentation categorized list, trial 3. The measure of output adjacency plotted on the ordinate is the average adjacency value over all items which are separated by j intervening items in the input order. Two curves are shown: the lower curve is for items that belong to different categories; the upper curve is for items belonging to the same category. Figure 6 shows that items in the same category have generally higher adjacency values, as is implied by such results as those of Fig. 4; second, there is a strong effect

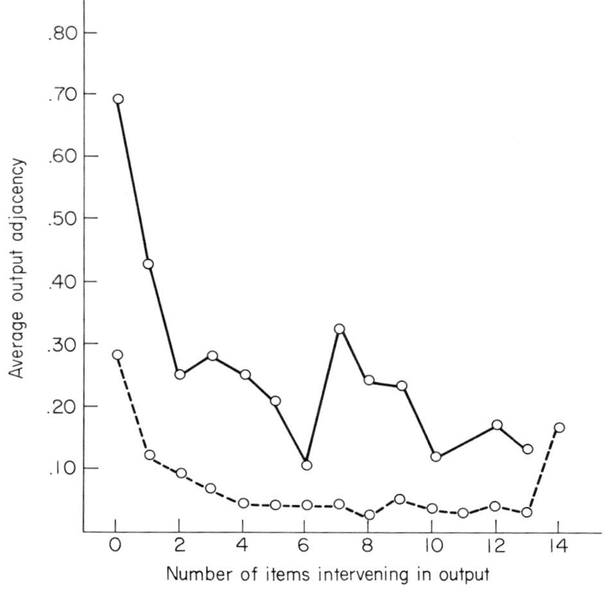

FIG. 6. Average output adjacency as a function of adjacency in input for items which belong to the same category and for unrelated items.

of input order. Items that are adjacent in input or that are separated by only one intervening item are much more likely to be recalled next to each other than items separated by two or more items in the input list. The apparent anomaly for 14 intervening items is easily accounted for. It reflects the relationship between the first and last items of the list.

There are several features in the data that support the model of long-term memory at least qualitatively. Figure 4 illustrates how recall order is determined by semantic relationships. If more complex hierarchies provide similar results the model will be strengthened further. Second, the correlation between output and input order is also in agreement with the assumptions of the model. The model-subject looks for common markers in the word just presented and those still available; the most likely word to be available (in the short-term memory buffer) is, of course, the immediately preceding one. Whether the model can fit functions like those of Fig. 6 quantitatively remains to be determined.

Conclusion

It is clear that the cluster analyses reported here do not constitute a definite test of the model. As far as they go, they support one of the main contentions of it, that output order is in part determined by the semantic structure of the learning material. What has been done here is to provide a framework which hopefully will be useful in the further investigation of free-recall learning. The model outlined here does the job for which it was originally developed: it accounts for what is probably the most essential characteristic of recall, namely that organized lists are easier to recall than unorganized lists. More stringent tests of the model must wait until a more precise version of it is ready for computer simulation. In a general way, however, the qualitative implications of the model appear to be in good agreement with what is known about free recall. Indeed, some quite direct evidence exists that something like the markers hypothesized here is important in memory (Henley, Noyes, and Deese, 1968; Anisfeld and Knapp, 1968). The model also predicts clustering, but not perfect clustering; whether it predicts the right amount of clustering remains to be seen. It places great stress upon what happens at the time of learning, rather than the retrieval process. It has sometimes been suggested that associative relationships among the members of a word list help recall because during retrieval the subject implicitly produces associates of the words already recalled and recognizes the list members among them. In the present model a different mechanism is responsible for the facilitation of recall: if interitem associations are present they facilitate the establishment of a retrieval scheme. Recall cues work the same way: they must be present at the time of storage so that appropriate markers can be tagged. If cues are merely given at the time of recall, they are much less useful in the present model. That seems to agree well with the results of Tulving and Osler (1968) who found that recall cues must be present during learning to be effective.

The model suggested here heavily emphasizes control processes: what markers are tagged, which redundancy rules are used to generate new markers, what words are selected as starting points for the search of memory during retrieval, etc. This gives the model great flexibility, but makes it very difficult to test. However, it can be argued that recall is a very complex process and that this kind of flexibility is just what is needed in a model.

References

ABELSON, R. P., AND CARROLL, J. D. Computer simulation of individual belief systems. *American Behavioral Scientist*, 1965, **8**, 24–30.

ANISFELD, M., AND KNAPP, M. Association, synonymity, and directionality in false recognition. *Journal of Experimental Psychology*, 1968, **77**, 171–179.

ATKINSON, R. C., AND SHIFFRIN, R. M. Human memory: A proposed system and its control processes. In K. W. Spence and J. T. Spence (Eds.), *Advances in the psychology of learning and motivation research and theory*. Vol. II. New York: Academic Press, 1968, 89–195.

BAHRICK, H. P., AND BOUCHER, B. Retention of visual and verbal codes of the same stimuli. *Journal of Experimental Psychology*, 1968, **78**, 417–422.

BARTLETT, F. C. *Remembering*. New York: Macmillan, 1932.

BERNBACH, H. A. Decision processes in memory. *Psychological Review*, 1967, **74**, 462–480.

BIERWISCH, M. Eine Hierarchie syntaktisch-semantischer Merkmale. In M. Bierwisch, (Ed.), *Studia Grammatica V. Syntaktische Studien*. Berlin: Akademie Verlag, 1965.

BOLINGER, D. The atomization of meaning. *Language*, 1965, **41**, 555–573.

BOUSFIELD, W. A. The occurrence of clustering in the recall of randomly arranged associates. *Journal of General Psychology*, 1953, **49**, 229–240.

BOWER, G. H. Originaztion and memory. Paper presented at the meeting of the Western Psychology Association, San Diego, April, 1968.

BOWER, G. H., AND BOSTRUM, A. Absence of within-list PI and RI in short-term recognition memory. *Psychonomic Science*, 1968, **10**, 211–212.

BRELAND, K., AND BRELAND, M. *Animal behavior*. New York: Macmillan, 1966.

CHOMSKY, N. *Aspects of the theory of syntax*. Cambridge, Massachusetts: MIT Press, 1965.

COFER, C. N. On some factors in the organizational characteristics of free recall. *American Psychologist*, 1965, **20**, 261–272.

COFER, C. N. Does conceptual organization influence the amount retained in immediate free recall? In B. Kleinmuntz (Ed.), *Concepts and the structure of memory.* New York: Wiley, 1967.

COFER, C. N., BRUCE, D. R., AND REICHER, G. M. Clustering in free recall as a function of certain methodological variations. *Journal of Experimental Psychology,* 1966, **71**, 858–866.

COHEN, B. H., BOUSFIELD, W. A., AND WHITMARSH, G. A. Cultural norms for verbal items in 43 categories. Technical Report No. 22, University of Connecticut, 1957.

DALE, H. C. A. Response availability and short-term memory. *Journal of Verbal Learning and Verbal Behavior,* 1967, **6**, 47–48.

DALE, H. C. A., AND BADDELEY, A. D. Alternatives in testing recognition memory. *Nature,* 1962, **196**, 993–994.

DAVIS, R., SUTHERLAND, N. S., AND JUDD, B. R. Information content in recognition and recall. *Journal of Experimental Psychology,* 1961, **61**, 422–429.

DEESE, J. *The structure of associations in language and thought.* Baltimore: Johns Hopkins Press, 1965.

EGAN, J. P. Recognition memory and the operating characteristic. Technical Note AFCRC–TN–58–51, Hearing and Communication Laboratory, Indiana University, 1958.

ESTES, W. K., AND DAPOLITO, F. Independent variation of information storage and retrieval processes in paired-associate learning. *Journal of Experimental Psychology,* 1967, **75**, 18–26.

EVANS, R. R., AND DALLENBACH, K. M. Single trial learning: A stochastic model for the recall of individual words. *American Journal of Psychology,* 1965, **78**, 545–556.

FIELD, W. H., AND LACHMAN, R. Information transmission (I) in recognition and recall as a function of alternatives (K). *Journal of Experimental Psychology,* 1966, **72**, 785–791.

FISCHER, A. Über Reproduzieren und Wiedererkennen bei Gedächtnisversuchen. *Zeitschrift für Psychologie,* 1909, **50**, 62–92.

FREGE, G. Über Sinn und Bedeutung. *Zeitschrift für Philosophie und Philosophische Kritik,* 1892, **100**, 25–50.

GARCIA, J., MCGOWAN, B. K., ERVIN, F. R., AND KNOELLING, R. A. Cues: Their relative effectiveness as a function of the reinforcer. *Science,* 1968, **160**, 794–795.

GORMAN, A. M. Recognition memory for nouns as a function of abstractness and frequency. *Journal of Experimental Psychology,* 1961, **61**, 23–29.

GREEN, D. M., AND MOSES, F. L. On the equivalence of two recognition measures of short-term memory. *Psychological Bulletin,* 1966, **66**, 228–234.

HALL, J. F. Learning as a function of word frequency. *American Journal of Psychology,* 1954, **67**, 138–140.

HALLE, M. On the basis of phonology. In J. A. Fodor and J. J. Katz (Eds.), *The Structure of language: Readings in the philosophy of language.* Englewood Cliffs, New Jersey: Prentice-Hall, 1964.

HEBB, D. O. Concerning imagery. *Psychological Review,* 1968, **75**, 466–477.

HENLEY, N. M., NOYES, H. L., AND DEESE, J. Semantic structure in short-term memory. *Journal of Experimental Psychology,* 1968, **77**, 587–592.

HINTZMAN, D. L. Exploration with a discrimination net model for paired-associate learning. *Journal of Mathematical Psychology,* 1968, **5**, 123–162.

HOLLINGWORTH, H. C. Characteristic differences between recall and recognition. *American Journal of Psychology,* 1913, **24**, 532–544.

JAMES, W. *Principles of psychology.* Vol. I. New York: Holt, 1890.

JOHNSON, S. C. Hierarchical clustering schemes. *Psychometrika,* 1967, **32**, 241–254.

KATZ, J. J., AND FODOR, J. A. The structure of a semantic theory. *Language*, 1963, **39**, 170–210.

KINTSCH, W. Recognition learning as a function of the length of the retention interval and changes in the retention interval. *Journal of Mathematical Psychology*, 1966, **3**, 412–433.

KINTSCH, W. Memory and decision aspects of recognition learning. *Psychological Review*, 1967, **74**, 496–504.

KINTSCH, W. An experimental analysis of single stimulus tests and multiple-choice tests of recognition memory. *Journal of Experimental Psychology*, 1968, **76**, 1–6. (a)

KINTSCH, W. Recognition and free recall of organized lists. *Journal of Experimental Psychology*, 1968, **78**, 481–487. (b)

KINTSCH, W., AND MORRIS, C. J. Application of a Markov model to free recall and recognition. *Journal of Experimental Psychology*, 1965, **69**, 200–206.

LARKIN, W. D. Rating scales in detection experiments. *Journal of the Acoustical Society of America*, 1965, **37**, 748–749.

LUCE, R. D. A threshold theory for simple detection experiments. *Psychological Review*, 1963, **70**, 61–79.

LYONS, J. *Structural semantics*. Oxford, England: Blackwell, 1963.

MCDOUGALL, R. Recognition and recall. *Journal of Philosophical Psychology and Scientific Methods*, 1904, **1**, 229–233.

MCGOVERN, J. B. Extinction of associations in four transfer paradigms. *Psychological Monographs*, 1964, **78**, (16, Whole No. 593).

MCNULTY, J. A. Short-term retention as a function of method of measurement, recoding time, and meaningfulness of the material. *Canadian Journal of Psychology*, 1965, **19**, 188–195. (a)

MCNULTY, J. A. An analysis of recall and recognition processes in verbal learning. *Journal of Verbal Learning and Verbal Behavior*, 1965, **4**, 430–435. (b)

MANDLER, G. Organization and memory. In K. W. Spence and J. T. Spence (Eds.), *Advances in the psychology of learning and motivation research and theory*. Vol. I. New York: Academic Press, 1967. Pp. 328–372.

MILLER, G. A. The free recall of redundant strings of letters. *Journal of Experimental Psychology*, 1958, **56**, 485–491.

MILLER, G. A. *Mathematics and psychology*. New York: Wiley, 1964.

MILLER, G. A. Psycholinguistic approaches to the study of communication. In D. L. Arm (Ed.), *Journeys in science: Small steps—great strides*. Albuquerque: University of New Mexico Press, 1967.

MÜLLER, G. E. Zur Analyse der Gedächtnistätigkeit und des Vorstellungsverlaufes. *Zeitschrift für Psychologie, Ergänzungsband* **8**, 1913.

MURDOCK, B. B., JR. Signal detection and short-term memory. *Journal of Experimental Psychology*, 1965, **70**, 443–447.

NORMAN, D. A. A comparison of data obtained with different alarm rates. *Psychological Review*, 1964, **71**, 243–246.

NORMAN, D. A. Acquisition and retention in short-term memory. *Journal of Experimental Psychology*, 1966, **72**, 369–381.

NORMAN, D. A., AND WICKELGREN, W. A. Short-term recognition memory for single digits and pairs of digits. *Journal of Experimental Psychology*, 1965, **70**, 470–489.

OLSON, G. M. Learning and retention in a continuous recognition task. *Journal of Experimental Psychology*, 1969, **81**, 381–384.

PARKS, T. E. Signal detectability theory of recognition memory performance. *Psychological Review*, 1966, **73**, 44–58.

PETERSON, L. R. Search and judgment in memory. In B. Kleinmuntz (Ed.), *Concepts and the structure of memory*. New York: Wiley, 1967. Pp. 153–180.

PORZIG, W. Wesenhafte Bedeutungsbeziehungen. *Beiträge zur Geschichte der deutschen Sprache*, 1934, **58**, 70–97.

PORZIG, W. *Das Wunder der Sprache*. Bern: Francke, 1950.

POSTMAN, L. One-trial learning. In C. N. Cofer and B. S. Musgrave (Eds.), *Verbal behavior and learning*. New York: McGraw-Hill, 1963. Pp. 295–320.

POSTMAN, L., ADAMS, P. A., AND PHILLIPS, L. W. Studies in incidental learning: II. The effects of association value and of method of testing. *Journal of Experimental Psychology*, 1955, **49**, 1–10.

POSTMAN, L., AND STARK, K. The role of response availability in transfer and interference. *Journal of Experimental Psychology*, 1969, **79**, 168–177.

QUINE, W. V. O. *Word and object*. Cambridge, Massachusetts: MIT Press, 1960.

SCHWARTZ, F., AND ROUSE, R. D. The activation and recovery of associations. *Psychological Issues*, 1961, **3**, (Whole No. 1).

SHEPARD, R. N. Recognition memory for words, sentences, and pictures. *Journal of Verbal Learning and Verbal Behavior*, 1967, **6**, 156–163.

THURSTONE, L. L. A law of comparative judgment. *Psychological Review*, 1927, **34**, 273–286.

TRIER, J. Das sprachliche Feld. *Neue Jahrbücher für Wissenschaft und Jugendbildung*, 1934, **10**, 428–449.

TULVING, E. Subjective organization in free recall of unrelated words. *Psychological Review*, 1962, **69**, 344–354.

TULVING, E. The effects of order of presentation in learning of "unrelated" words. *Psychonomic Science*, 1965, **3**, 337–338.

TULVING, E., AND OSLER, S. Effectiveness of retrieval cues in memory for words. *Journal of Experimental Psychology*, 1968, **77**, 593–601.

WEINREICH, U. Webster's third: A critique of its semantics. *International Journal of American Linguistics*, 1964, **30**, 405–409.

WHITMAN, J. R., AND GARNER, W. R. Free recall learning of visual figures as a function of form of internal structure. *Journal of Experimental Psychology*, 1962, **64**, 558–564.

WICKELGREN, W. A. Distinctive features and errors in short-term memory for English vowels. *Journal of the Acoustical Society of America*, 1965, **38**, 583–588.

WICKELGREN, W. A. Distinctive features and errors in short-term memory for English consonants. *Journal of the Acoustical Society of America*, 1966, **39**, 388–398.

WICKELGREN, W. A. Exponential decay and independence from irrelevant associations in short-term recognition memory for serial order. *Journal of Experimental Psychology*, 1967, **73**, 165–171.

WICKELGREN, W. A. Testing two-state theories with operating characteristics and a posteriori probabilities. *Psychological Bulletin*, 1968, **69**, 126–131.

WICKELGREN, W. A., AND NORMAN, D. A. Strength models and serial position in short-term recognition memory. *Journal of Mathematical Psychology*, 1966, **3**, 316–347.

WICKENS, D. D., BORN, D. G., AND ALLEN, G. K. Proactive inhibition and item similarity in short-term memory. *Journal of Verbal Learning and Verbal Behavior*, 1963, **2**, 440–445.

YNTEMA, D. B., AND TRASK, F. P. Recall as a search process. *Journal of Verbal Learning and Verbal Behavior*, 1963, **2**, 65–74.

12

Memory Search[1]

Richard M. Shiffrin
Indiana University
Bloomington, Indiana

A Framework for Search Models

The memory search is one of the oldest concepts in psychology, although one exhibiting somewhat fitful progress over the last half-century. In his *Principles of Psychology* (1890), William James summarizes James Mills' description of the process as follows:

> In short, we make search in our memory for a forgotten idea, just as we rummage our house for a lost object. In both cases we visit what seems to us the probable *neighborhood* of that which we miss. We turn over the things under which, or within which, or alongside of which, it may possibly be; and if it lies near them, it soon comes to view. (Page 654)

In many ways, the conception of the search process to be presented in this paper will be quite close to the views of the earliest psychologists (as represented in the above statement), and quite close also to our own introspections as to the nature of the act. The very obviousness of the memory search may, in fact, have counted against it in recent accounts of memory and learning. This is not to say that the search has been ignored entirely; as we shall see, a number of workers have dis-

[1] This research was supported by the Public Health Service, Grant No. PHS MH 12717-03.

cussed search processes in relation to short-term memory tasks, and Peterson (1967) has extended these discussions in the realm of long-term memory. Furthermore, theoretical and empirical explorations of retrieval processes in memory have taken a large upsurge in the last several years, as the other chapters in this volume will testify. This chapter presents a general and yet fairly simple theory of the search in retrieval, and examines a number of situations in which search models may be profitably employed. It attempts to show that search models can provide predictions for effects about which other models have little, if anything, to say.

The Memory Trace

A prerequisite for any search is a collection of objects through which the search is to be made; in the present instance, the memory traces. A traditional approach defines these traces as a set of images or codes, where the structure of the images is a function of the current task being utilized. Thus, if a series of paired-associates is presented, the subject is presumed to store in memory a series of images, each representing a particular paired-associate item. The memory search could then be said to take place through some subset of these images. The difficulty with this approach is that it is dependent upon the specific task and type of test being used; it would be preferable to define the search upon a collection of objects that would not have to be altered with changes in the task and type of test.

Considerations of this sort make it clear that the images or codes for a particular task are really made up of many smaller units of information (presumably interassociated to some degree) and these smaller units are the objects upon which the search should be defined. For example, in the case of two words being presented on a card for memorization, the units of information stored in memory could include the following: the size and color of the card and the letters; the form of the letters; the orientation of the words on the cards and other visual characteristics; the verbal representation of the words; the meaning of the words; their parts of speech; associates of the words; codes used to link the two words for later recall; and contextual and temporal information that characterize the current situation. These units of information which are stored together tend to be closely associated, so that they are usually recalled together—it is in this sense that they are termed an "image."

We propose, however, that the search be based upon the individual informational pieces. To be precise, the search is defined on some subset of informational units called the search-set. This search-set consists of smaller subsets of information which are the images. The selection phase of the search process consists of selecting randomly one unit of information from the search-set, and then examining the image containing the unit drawn. Suppose that there are n units of information in the search-set, and n_1 of these units make up image A. Then the probability of examining image A on the first search attempt is n_1/n, the number of units in the image divided by the total number of informational units in the set being searched.

Figure 1 gives a schematic view of this process: the informational elements inside the large irregularly shaped area are those in long-term memory; those in the large solidly outlined area (called the search-set) are those through which the search is being made; the information in the small dotted circles is that making up the particular images designated (and is closely associatively connected). Suppose that the stimulus "horse" is the one that has been presented for test. When the search begins, a single element will be selected at random in the search-

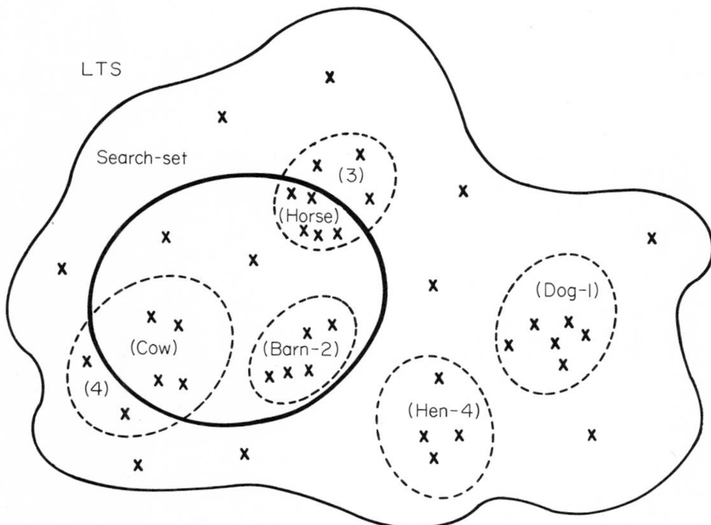

FIG. 1. Organization of long-term store into search-sets and images. Hypothetical structure for a paired-associate task in which images are denoted by dotted circles and units of information are represented by x's.

set (the large circle), and the complex of information associated with it will be examined. The probability of examining the correct image ("horse-3") at the first step in the search will thus be five, the number of informational units in the correct image and also in the search-set, divided by 16, the total number of informational units in the search-set. Thus, the individual units of information are the objects through which the search is made, and not the images *per se*. Nevertheless, in practice it will often be convenient to talk of searching through a particular set of images, with each image having a "strength" proportional to the number of informational units of which it is constituted. The probability of examining a particular image on a particular search is thus the strength of that image divided by the summed strengths of all the images in the set being searched; the rationale for this assumption should remain clear as long as the underlying model is kept in mind.

The view of the memory image propounded above appears quite simple, but this is because the image has been considered solely in relation to the search process. Actually, the structure and relationships of the units of information making up the image have been left unspecified and are not a primary concern of this chapter. We mention here merely a few quantitative approaches to this problem. These include those of Bower (1967b) and Norman and Rumelhart (Chapter 2), in which the units of information are supposed to be representable by a multicomponented ordered vector; and that of Kintsch (Chapter 11), in which the units are arranged in three primary classes, each in vector form, one including semantic–syntactic features, one including phonetic features, and one including nonverbal sensory features. These notions will not be explored further because they constitute a separate problem, and the search process may be examined at a level that is largely independent of the organization of the informational units making up the image.

It is useful at this point to review and introduce some basic terminology. The terms *images* and *codes* will be used interchangeably to refer to interassociated complexes of information stored in memory, as defined by the task and the type of search in which the subject is engaged. This last phrase is important because the subject, by choosing a set of information through which to search, defines the images involved in the search. For example, if the test is for recall of a paired associate, the search may be defined by the subject so that both stimulus and response information make up the images in the set of information being examined; if the test is altered to require stimulus recognition, the subject may alter the search so that only stimulus information makes up the images in the set being examined. In the latter case, the strength of the images will be less than in the former case. The strength of the *i*th image will be denoted by s_i, and will be a numerical measure ranging in $(0,\infty)$, conceptually corresponding to the number of units of information making up the image.[2] The units of information through which the search is made will be called "I-units" and are presumed to have the same sort of existence as the stimulus elements in stimulus sampling theory (Estes, 1959). That is, it is not implied that all I-units are necessarily sampled with equal probability; however, if some I-unit is twice as likely to be sampled as the others, we will conceive of it as consisting of two smaller I-units closely connected. The set of information through which the search is made is called the *search-set* and will have strength $S = \Sigma s_i$, where the sum ranges over all the images making up the search-set. The term *draw* will be used to denote the choice of an I-unit from the search-set at a particular point in the search, while the term *search* will refer to the recursive process in which many draws may be made.

The Memory Stores

The view of the memory system to be described here follows closely that presented in Atkinson and Shiffrin (1965, 1968), and is similar to systems described by James (1890), Waugh and Norman (1965), Broadbent (1958), Neisser (1967), Bower (1967a), and Feigenbaum (1963), among others. There are three different memory stores: the sensory register (sometimes called "very short-term visual memory," and called "iconic memory" by Neisser); the short-term store (called "primary memory" by James, and by Waugh and Norman, and "active verbal memory" by Neisser); and the long-term store (termed "secondary memory" by James). While there is some disagreement on the details, the system to be described is probably representative of these various approaches.

[2] Information is being used in this paper in an informal sense, and not in the technical manner of information theory. However, the strength measure may be thought of as linearly related to the technical measure of information. Suppose, for example, that the I-units represent independent *n*-nary decisions; then increasing the strength by a factor of r will increase the amount of information by a factor of r, in the technical sense.

The sensory register is represented by the very-short-term visual image first investigated by Sperling (1960). This image is an initially highly veridical representation of the impinging visual field. The I-units making up the image fade and are lost from the sensory register after a period ranging from several hundred milliseconds to about a second. Before the image fades, information is transferred from it to the short-term store. Note that transfer implies neither that the original image is affected by the transfer, nor that the information is placed in the short-term store unaltered. In most cases, the information is likely to be acted upon and altered radically by the system; for example, the visual information is often altered into auditory–verbal information for entrance into the short-term store.

The short-term store is primarily auditory–verbal in character and serves as the "working memory." Information in this store that is unattended will decay and be lost within about 15 sec, but rehearsal processes can maintain information here indefinitely. This is the subject's working memory because information transmission to and from the other stores take place through it and are monitored by control processes within it. While any information remains in the short-term store, it tends to be transferred to, and stored in, the long-term store; note that the transfer process does not alter the information in the short-term store.

The long-term store is a more permanent repository for information than either of the others. In Shiffrin and Atkinson (1969), it was proposed that this store is indeed a permanent repository and that information once stored there is never lost—the observed decrements in performance over time and intervening items were ascribed to failures in the retrieval (search) process. It is unnecessary for the purposes of this paper that this assumption be made: the retrieval process would be identical whether or not permanent forgetting occurs. Moreover, note that decrements in performance caused by the functioning of the search process would still appear, and probably be of overriding importance, even if autonomous forgetting unconnected with the search process is a feature of the long-term store. Models with permanent storage of this type have also been proposed by Feigenbaum (1963 and Chapter 13) and Tulving and Pearlstone (1966).

While this paper is primarily concerned with retrieval from long-term store (LTS), it is interesting to note that the recent work on search processes in memory has focused for the large part upon the sensory register and the short-term store (STS). This has probably occurred because, first, the search-set is easier to control in these instances, and second, the latency measure (of high importance in examining search processes) is more accurate at the short values found when dealing with retrieval from the short-lived memory stores.

The Stages of Retrieval

The term *retrieval* shall be used to describe the entire process of information recovery and possible response production, from the inception of the test to the end of the allowable response period. This process shall include initial decisions concerning which memory store to examine, whether to guess without any search whatever, and where in memory to begin the search. If a decision is made to initiate a search, a recursive procedure then begins, which is diagrammed in Fig. 2. First a search-set is selected on the basis of such factors as the stimuli or clues provided in the test, the overall task, and strategies of the subject. A draw is then made from the set of information so designated; that is, some I-unit in the search-set is randomly selected. I-units associated with the selected I-unit are now examined—these I-units will typically make up the structure we call an "image"; the bringing forth of some or all of the information contained in an image is called recovery. The recovered information is then utilized for a further series of decisions. These include decisions governing whether to respond, what response to give, and whether to continue the search. If the search is continued, then the recursion loops back to the executive decision maker for possible selection of a new search-set and continuation of the process.

Prior to examining these stages in detail, it is worth reemphasizing that the basic notions are quite natural and have roots in the earliest writings in psychology. For example, most of these phases of retrieval may be made out in a quote from Hobbes' *Leviathan* upon which William James felt he could not improve:

> Sometimes a man seeks what he hath lost, and from that place and time wherein he misses it, his mind runs back from place to place and time to time to find where and when he had it; to find some certain and limited time and place, in which to begin a method of seeking. Again, from thence his thoughts run over the same places and times to find what action or other occasion might make him lose it. This we call remembrance, or calling to mind. Sometimes a man knows a place determinate, within the compass whereof he is

> to seek; and then his thoughts run over all the parts thereof, in the same manner as one would sweep a room to find a jewel, or as a spaniel ranges the field till he finds a scent, or as a man should run over the alphabet to start a rhyme. (James, 1890, p. 587)

The search scheme described in this paper is quite obviously sequential, or serial, rather than parallel; just one image is examined at a time. The primary justification for adopting this view, apart from quantitative comparisons of specific models, lies in the nature of the input

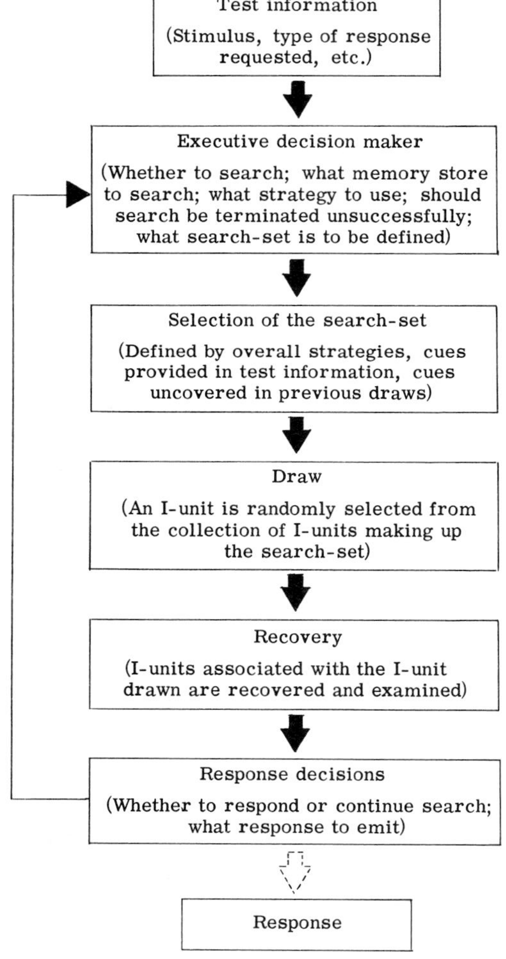

FIG. 2. The search and retrieval recursion.

and output systems. Information input and output to the system is monitored primarily by STS, which is verbal–auditory in character, and our verbal–auditory system seems to operate in an intrinsically sequential manner. Our vocal apparatus forces us to output information sequentially, and if we try to input auditory information simultaneously, it tends either to merge prior to entrance into STS, or to be accepted into STS sequentially. While the above statement is an oversimplification of an extremely complex system, it nevertheless provides a cogent reason why a search for auditory–verbal information in LTS, or a search for any information that is monitored by STS, should be sequential in character. This argument does not necessarily apply to visual information, since visual material is typically presented extended in space rather than time, and is accepted by the system in this manner (in the sensory register, or the visual field). To the extent that an experiment utilizing visual material is monitored by STS, that experiment should exhibit sequential characteristics for the search; yet in such an experiment, there is better reason to expect evidence also for parallel processing. Neisser (1967) argues that this is indeed the case for appropriate experiments in the visual mode. Estes and his co-workers (e.g., Estes and Taylor, 1964) originally had little success with parallel processing models for visual scanning of the sensory register, but more recently have suggested that processing may be parallel, while memory and retrieval may be serial (Wolford, Wessel, and Estes, 1968); Rumelhart (1969), and Norman and Rumelhart (Chapter 2) have also had considerable success with a largely parallel processing model for this situation. Thus, we do not rule out the possibility of parallel processing in selected parts of the memory system in addition to the sequential search with which we shall be dealing.

The Executive Decision Process and Response Decisions

The decision phases of retrieval are treated under a single heading because response decisions are actually a particular subset of the various executive decisions. The response decisions refer to some sort of comparison of the currently recovered information with a standard, a comparison on the basis of which the subject decides two things: whether he has recovered sufficient information to give the desired response, and what response to give. These types of decisions in retrieval have been examined rather extensively, usually in conjunction with the theory of signal detection, and in the context of recognition memory experiments (see, e.g., Green and Swets, 1966; Kintsch, 1967, and Chapter 11; Bernbach, 1967; and Wickelgren, Chapter 3). A typical model assumes that the recovered information (incomplete and noisy) is compared with the stimulus to be recognized; the end result is a feeling of familiarity that may be numerically scaled; the subject decides the stimulus is old or new, depending upon whether the familiarity is higher or lower than a criterion. In these previous models, the decision process has been applied only once, after the search has been completed; in cases where there is only a single loop to the search recursion, these models would of course be congruent to the present one. A single loop search may indeed be reasonable in certain types of recognition situations where the search-set contains only the appropriate, relevant memory image, and no others. In cases where the search loops more than once, it may be important to consider a decision process associated with each loop individually, since this decision process will be of prime importance in determining when the search shall terminate.

The executive decision routine initializes the search recursion by choosing whether to search memory, and then choosing the appropriate memory store. In most cases with which we shall be dealing, STS, or the sensory register, is searched prior to LTS. STS typically contains information recently presented, and in free-recall situations this search order results in the most recently presented items being reported first. In some cases, however, STS may not be consulted. For example, once a list of words to be free-recalled has been learned (stored in organized fashion in LTS), then it is unnecessary to search STS and the words are output in the order in which they are organized in LTS (Tulving, 1962).

Other initial decisions include any overall strategies to be followed. Thus, a decision can be made to scan an iconic image from left to right, from top to bottom, or by some other positional means; a digit string may be recalled in temporal or numerical order; the states of the U.S. may be recalled in alphabetical or geographic order, and so forth. These types of strategies all involve decisions to alter the search-set during the retrieval recursion in a preset and systematic manner. Other strategies could be adopted determining how many draws to make in a particular search-set, or in general, what stopping rule to use.

The most apparent factors governing termination of the search are the expiration of the allowable response time, decay of the information in the memory stores, and recovery of the desired information. The first two factors are quite straightforward, but the last needs more thorough consideration. Whether or not the desired information has been recovered is itself a decision that will probably be governed by some criterion process. If the subject is instructed to respond quickly, then the criterion will be set lower, and the number of draws prior to search termination will tend to be lower; hence the latency will be reduced, but the error probability will increase. Experimental payoffs and other incentives may also be used to change the subject's criterion for acceptance, and hence alter the time until termination.

When should the termination strategies be applied: when an acceptable response is not found, or when an additional response in a series is not found? To begin with, consider the restricted case where a series of draws are being made from the same search-set; some strategy may be in use whereby a number of different search-sets are examined, but a termination rule must be invoked to end the search within each search-set. The simplest termination rule in the event of nonrecovery is the specification in advance of the number of draws to be made; when the response time is quite limited, then the number of draws to be made is externally controlled, since the search will continue until successful or until the allowable response period is over. A rule specifying termination after a fixed number of draws could be used if the search process was difficult or fatiguing, or if small response latencies were of importance. This rule would be less likely to be used if the allowed response time was unlimited and multiple responses were required. Thus, if a task requires the naming of all cities in New Jersey, it would be unreasonable to terminate the search after some prespecified period if city names were still being recovered at that point at a rapid rate. More sophisticated strategies would make termination contingent upon information recovered earlier in the search. These could include repeat counters, successive repeat counters, and successive failure counters. A repeat counter would keep track of the number of draws that resulted in recovery of information already recovered previously in the search. When this number passes some criterion, the search would terminate. A successive repeat rule would be similar, but termination would occur when the number of draws *in succession* which repeat earlier draws passes some criterion. Repeat rules are meant to apply to cases where draws result in recovery of significant amounts of information from the stored images. In certain searches, however, the stored images may be so degraded that recovery following a draw results in little, if any, available information about the stored image. These could be termed null-draws, or failures, and the termination rule could be made dependent upon the total number of these, or the number of these in succession. The choice of termination rule is especially important in the case of multiple recoveries from a large search-set (i.e., all the cities in the United States), since intuitively reasonable terminations such as "ten successive repeats" will result in cessation of the search far before the available images in the search-set are exhausted.

The Draw from the Search-Set and Recovery

The draw is the simplest phase of retrieval, consisting of a uniformly random choice of some I-unit in the search-set. As a result, the probability of examining a particular image within the search-set following that draw is s_i, the strength of the image, divided by S, the strength of the entire set (which equals the sum of the strengths of the images contained in the set). Let d_i be the act of drawing an I-unit from the ith image; then

$$P(d_i) = s_i/S. \tag{1}$$

When an I-unit is selected, the information complex associated with it is examined, and some portion of this information becomes available for the subject's perusal. The information thus examined is not necessarily restricted to that in the current search-set, but may be anywhere in the associative network, or image, tied to the I-unit chosen. To put this another way, the choice if an I-unit merely provides a starting point for recovery of information from an image containing that I-unit. Therefore, recovery refers to that phase of the search in which some portion of the information in a particular image is made available for examination. In applications, the probability of emitting a correct response, if the image under examination indeed encodes the correct response, will be made a function of the strength of the image. Let R_i denote the emission of the response encoded in the ith image, and suppose the ith image encodes the correct response. Then,

$$P(R_i|d_i) = f(s_i^*) = 1 - \exp(-s_i^*).$$

That is, the probability of correct recall given examination of the correct image, is an exponential function of the strength of the image, s_i^*. (The strength is denoted by s_i^*, rather than s_i, to illustrate the possibility that the strength on which recall is based may be larger than the strength on the basis of which the draw was made. In the applications in this chapter, however, these strengths will be assumed equivalent and the distinction will be ignored unless specifically noted.) The exponential function is used both for historical reasons and simplicity; it is a simple way to transform a strength measure in $(0,\infty)$ into a probability value in (0, 1) in the desired manner.

Selection of the Search-Set

A search-set is selected at the start of each loop of the search recursion. The selection of the search-set lies at the heart of the retrieval system, and we shall indicate a few of the major factors upon which the selection depends. These include the task set for the subject, the response required, the clues or stimulus information given in the test, information previously recovered in the search, and overall strategies or biases by which the search-set is systematically altered from one loop to the next. The retrieval system is simplified greatly and becomes easily manageable if the search-set is not altered over the successive draws that are made; fortunately, this is a reasonable assumption in a number of important experimental applications (e.g., single-trial free recall).

An extremely important mechanism governing the selection of search-sets is based upon temporal cues. That is, the search-set is defined so as to be delimited in time. Thus, in laboratory experiments on memory, the images examined in the search are those which have been stored since the beginning of the experiment; in a free-recall task in which the subject is asked to recall all the words of the just presented list, the search-set is limited to those images stored in the temporal period of the most recent list; in a traditional paired-associate list paradigm, this temporal cuing of the search-set also occurs and is called "differentiation." Even in a continuous paired-associate task, there may be a strong tendency to examine recent images in preference to older ones.

In many cases, the composition of the search-set will be determined by the test information presented. For a recognition test or a paired-associate recall test, this information will consist of a presented "stimulus," and the fact that this stimulus may have been presented previously in the experiment. The information about the experiment may enable the search-set to be restricted to "recently" stored images, while the stimulus itself enables the subject to define a search-set containing stimulus related information and hence narrows the possibilities still further. A possible mechanism by which this could occur would involve the subject feeding the system an initial set of I-units and the system returning as a search-set I-units that are jointly associated with the initial set. The initial set could not be too detailed lest a search-set be defined without any members; still, the initial set could easily contain such information as the temporal location sought and major characteristics of the stimulus. In any event, whatever the mechanism by which the selection occurs, a search-set is defined that will have some probability of containing the sought after image (or some I-unit from it). If i is the sought after image, then denote by $p_s(i)$ the probability that this image will be in the search-set. In general, $p_s(i)$ will be higher the higher the strength of the sought after image. In many situations, also, where the subject tends to select the search-set on the basis of temporal factors, $p_s(i)$ will be lower the older the image. In situations such as single-trial free recall, it may be possible to assume $p_s(i) = 1.0$.

Alterations of the search-set during the search will tend to occur either on the basis of information uncovered, or on the basis of a predetermined strategy. The most common example of the search-set altering on the basis of uncovered information is found in the so-called problem-solving search. For example, one may be asked what he wore four days past, or ate four breakfasts past; in either event, the pattern of search will tend to be reconstructive, with a tracing of one's actions backwards in time until the appropriate "context" is found. In other words, a series of search-sets are defined, each older in time, with the information recovered from one helping to define the next. Searches of this sort are common in day-to-day experience, as when we desire the name of an old acquaintance, or the plot of a play seen years previously. This type of search is not restricted along temporal lines; we may find ourselves unable to recall some information until we can laboriously reconstruct the page in the book upon which it lies. In the laboratory, this type of process occurs prominently in experiments on mediation or on chaining of images as a mnemonic device (e.g., Runquist and Farley, 1964; Bugelski, Kidd, and Segmen, 1968).

Let us examine the effects of strategies on the use of the search-set. Consider an experiment where the task is to name as many U. S. cities as possible as quickly as possible. Bousfield and Sedgewick (1944) found that the graph of responses output as a function of time looked like a growth function: the number of cities output in each successive minute was proportional to the number of cities in the set not yet selected. In other words, the number output by time t, $n(t)$, equals $N - N \exp(-at)$, where N is a constant representing the total number in the set and a is a constant representing rate of approach to the asymptote.

To put this problem in terms of search-sets, suppose that there are N cities in a search-set, each with its own strength, s_i. Let the search consist of D draws and suppose that each draw results in output of a city unless that city has previously been output. Then the expected number of cities output in each successive draw is simply the probability of drawing a new city on each draw. If S_d is the sum of the strengths of the cities yet unchosen after d draws, and S is the total strength of the search-set, then the expected number output on the $(d + 1)$st draw is S_d/S. Assuming that draws are made at a constant rate in time, then this implies that the number of cities output in successive intervals of time is proportional to the *strength* of the cities yet undrawn. In the restricted case where all the strengths are equal, this prediction is equivalent to the one stated above by Bousfield and Sedgewick, and will generate the function that was found. McGill (1963) gives a more formal argument demonstrating this point. If, however, the strengths are not equal, the stronger cities will tend to be reported out first (which was found by Bousfield and Barclay, 1950), and the graph of output against time will not be an exponential growth function: there will be too few responses late in the series for such a function.

The subject, of course, might not use a simple random search pattern. If, after responses began to come at a slow rate, the subject began to choose smaller search-sets and systematically examine them (state-by-state, for example), then more responses would be output late in the response series than would be predicted by the random draw model. In general, searching smaller sets which are systematically varied will produce better performance than searching a larger set an equal number of times.

To illustrate this point, consider the miniature situation depicted in Fig. 3. There are four cities in memory, two with strength 1, two with strength 2. There is enough response time for four draws to be made, and these may be made through the search-set consisting of all four cities, or distributed among the two sets consisting of the cities in the two states. Suppose that $Pr(R_i | d_i) = 1$, i.e., any city drawn in the search is reported correctly. Note that $P(d_i)$, the probability of drawing the ith city, equals s_i/S. In the present case, s_i equals 1 or 2, and S equals the

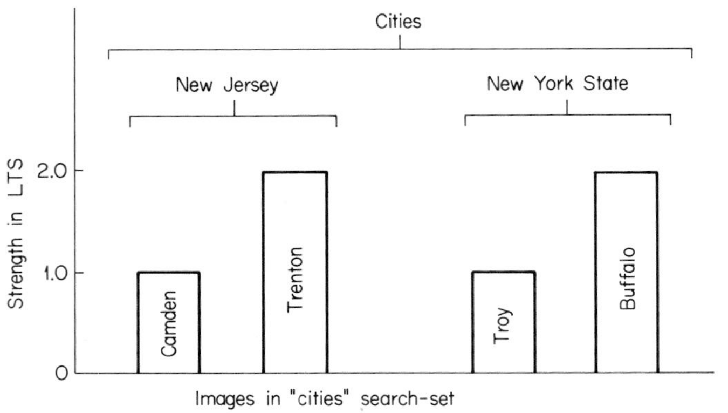

FIG. 3. A miniature example in which LTS consists of city names of varying strength.

sum of the strengths of the cities in any designated search-set. If the four draws are made through the large search-set consisting of all four cities, then $S = 6$. For an item with strength 1 the probability of retrieving it in four draws is $1 - (\frac{5}{6})^4$, i.e., the complement of the probability of not retrieving it on each of the four draws. The expected number of cities recovered, therefore, is the sum of the probabilities for each individual item:

$$[1 - (\tfrac{5}{6})^4] + [1 - (\tfrac{2}{3})^4] + [1 - (\tfrac{5}{6})^4] + [1 - (\tfrac{2}{3})^4] = 2.64.$$

If the search is divided into two parts, the first through one state and the second through the other, there are three possibilities for divisions of the four draws among these sets: 4,0; 3,1; 2,2. Note that S will now equal 3 for any draw. For 4,0, the expected output is $[1 - (\frac{1}{3})^4] + [1 - (\frac{2}{3})^4] = 1.79$. For 3,1, the expected output is $\frac{1}{3} + \frac{2}{3} + [1 - (\frac{2}{3})^3] + [1 - (\frac{1}{3})^3] = 2.67$. For 2,2, the expected output is $[1 - (\frac{1}{3})^2] + [1 - (\frac{2}{3})^2] + [1 - (\frac{1}{3})^2] + [1 - (\frac{2}{3})^2] = 2.82$, which gives the highest mean output. Thus, the most effective search is that in which smaller search-sets are successively examined; this result is quite general and holds in most cases, even when the situation is generalized so as to allow more sophisticated termination rules that allow the recovery probability following a draw to depend on the strength. The best distribution of draws may change with the situation, however. In the above example, if the strength of "Buffalo" were to change from 2 to 10, the best strategy for four draws would be to make one draw in "New York" and three draws in "New Jersey."

Of course we have been defining best strategy here in terms of total images output. There is a sense in which the results are reversed in terms of speed of output. If we look at the expected number of draws until a particular image is output, conditionalized upon the fact that the image is, in fact, output, then this measure will be smaller for the search through the larger set than for successive searches through the smaller sets. To see this for our miniature example, calculate the conditional expectation of the number of draws until a particular city is named for both the 2,2 search strategy and the overall strategy, and for both the smaller and higher strength city names. The conditional expectation is given by the unconditional expectation of the number of draws divided by the probability that the city will be drawn on one of the four draws. In the case of the 2,2 strategy, assume that the initial state searched is chosen randomly. The results of the calculations are as follows: for the overall strategy, the conditional number of draws until success is 2.28 for a city of low strength and 2.01 for a city of high strength; for the 2,2 search, these expectations are 2.4 for a city of low strength and 2.25 for a city of high strength. Thus, for either strength of the memory image, the search is faster for the overall search than for the divided, systematic search.

A finding closely related to these results was reported by Atkinson and Shiffrin (1968). Subjects were asked to name capitals of given states. If a correct answer was not given within five seconds of presentation of the state name, the subjects were then given a hint and allowed 30 seconds more to search their memory. The hint consisted of giving the subjects 1, 2, 4, 12, or 24 consecutive letters of the alphabet, one of which was the first letter in the name of the state capital. Consider the items for which a correct answer was not given within the first five seconds; for these items, the probability correct dropped steadily as the hint size increased from 1 to 24 letters. The average response latencies for correct answers, however, showed a different effect; the one-letter hint was associated with the fastest response time, the two-letter hint was slower, the four-letter hint was slower yet, but the 12- and 24-letter hints were faster than the four-letter hint. The above discussion of search strategies could provide an explanation of these results: when the hint size is small (four or less) a search strategy is adopted in which searches are made successively through search-sets defined by the first letters in the hint. Although this search may be slower than an overall search, when the hint size is small, 30 sec is ample time to make a reasonably complete search through each subset. When the hint size is large (12 or 24), a letter-by-letter search takes too long, on the average, to result in success within 30 sec, and the subject will adopt an overall search; the overall search will result in faster latencies but poorer performance relative to a corresponding letter by letter search.

Summary of the Search Framework

A general theory of memory has been described in which retrieval is formulated as a recursive search. Retrieval consists of a series of loops of a search process. First, decisions are made regarding what memory store to examine, and what search-set to select. The search-set is a collection of units of information (called I-units) arranged in interassociated groups called images. A draw, which consists of choosing an I-unit randomly, is then made from the selected search-set. The image containing the drawn I-unit is then examined and, on the basis of the information recovered, a decision is made either to emit a response, to continue the search or to terminate. If the search is continued, then the next loop of the recursion begins again with the selection of a search-set (often the one utilized on the previous loop). The search continues in this manner until it is terminated by the end of the response period, a response, or the subject's own decision to cease searching.

The basic approach taken thus far has presented the search as an integral part of the retrieval process, applying in some degree to all situations and tasks. As described so far, the search is more a method of framing models of memory than a single testable theory. Therefore, in order to support our argument that the search process deserves to be incorporated in theories of memory, we next turn to a number of experimental situations for which we formulate specific models.

Applications of Search Processes

The memory search is such a pervasive component of retrieval, and depends to such a degree upon decisions of the subject, that no one specific model can be expected to be wholly representative of the data encountered. Nevertheless, individual models appropriately chosen for given situations, each of which fits into the same general recursive retrieval framework, can and do provide predictive power beyond that previously available. We shall try to indicate how search models are able to deal with a large number of variables in a quantitative and qualitative manner. These variables include latencies, error rates, intrusion rates, and second-guessing rates, each of which can be predicted as a function of experimental factors such as the lag (number of intervening items), number of reinforcements, presentation rate, organizational factors, response time, and amount of "proactive" interference. We present an extended discussion of search models for free verbal recall and paired-associate learning.

Search Models for Free Verbal Recall

The free verbal recall situation is an especially appropriate paradigm for the study of search processes because the subject is required to look through all of the "recent" information stored and report out all of the images that can be recovered. The search-set is well defined and can be varied by experimentally controlled factors such as list length. The usual procedure involves the presentation of a series of words at a fixed rate; following presentation, the subject is asked to recall as many of the words presented in the list just seen as possible. In succeeding discussion, the terms free recall or single-trial free recall will be used to refer to a situation in which each list of words presented is different and no list is repeated during any experimental session. Situations in which a list of words is presented more than one time (usually in different random orders each time) will be termed multitrial free recall or multiple free recall.

A representative series of results in a single-trial free-recall paradigm is that of Murdock (1962; see the Appendix to this book and Fig. 9 of Chapter 2). The major effects are the pronounced rise in probability correct for the most recently presented items (the recency effect), the smaller rise for the initially presented items (the primacy effect), the level asymptote connecting the beginning and the end of the lists, and the decreases in probability correct as list length is increased and as presentation rate is increased.

We presume that the recency effect is due to retrieval from STS. The arguments for this assumption are presented elsewhere (Glanzer and Cunitz, 1966; Atkinson and Shiffrin, 1968), but we note one consequence of this assumption here: a period of interfering activity following presentation and prior to recall should eliminate retrieval from STS. One experiment of this type was carried out by Postman and Phillips (1965). When subjects have to do 30 sec of arithmetic between the end of the list and the recall, the recency effect is eliminated. Since the initial and central portions of the curves are unaffected by the intervening task, we may assume henceforth that these portions of the curves represent retrieval from LTS, and it is upon these portions that we shall focus attention.

The basic model proposed for the free-recall situation is quite simple. When the items of the list are presented they enter STS, stay there for a period, and then leave STS. During their stay in STS, they are acted upon by the system, or coded, and information about them is stored in LTS. The result at the conclusion of the list is a series of images of varying strength stored permanently in LTS and several items stored temporarily in STS. During the recall period, the subject first outputs those items currently available in STS, and then commences his search of LTS. Let s_i equal the strength of the image for the word presented in serial position i, and let s_i have a probability distribution with density $f_i(s)$; the value of $f_i(s)$ in a particular case will be called the strength of the ith image. In Atkinson and Shiffrin (1965, 1968), the $f_i(s)$ distributions were assumed to arise from a rehearsal process called the "buffer" in the following manner. A fixed number of words r were assumed to undergo rehearsal at any one time in the buffer; once the buffer had been filled, then each succeeding word would enter and randomly replace one word currently present. The strength built up in LTS for any item was assumed to be a linear function of the time that word spent in the buffer. If r is the buffer size (the number of words able to be concurrently rehearsed), then we have:

$$f_i(s) = \text{prob}(s = \theta t n) = \begin{cases} 0, & n \leqslant r - i, \quad i < r \\ \left(\dfrac{r-1}{r}\right)^{n-1-r+i} \left(\dfrac{1}{r}\right), & n > r - i, \quad i < r \\ \left(\dfrac{r-1}{r}\right)^{n-1} \left(\dfrac{1}{r}\right), & i \geqslant r \end{cases} \tag{3}$$

where t is the presentation time (in seconds) per word and θ is a parameter representing the rate per second at which information is transferred to LTS about an item during its stay in the buffer. Therefore, $tn\theta$ represents the possible values that the random variable s may assume ($1t\theta$, $2t\theta$, $3t\theta$ . . .). The mean of $f_i(s)$ is:

$$E[f_i(s)] = \begin{cases} t\theta(2r - i), & i \leqslant r \\ t\theta r, & i \geqslant r. \end{cases} \tag{4}$$

Thus, the expected strength stored is highest for the first item, decreases until the rth item, and is constant thereafter. The initial items have higher strength because no item can be lost from the buffer until it has been filled, and the buffer doesn't become filled until the rth item is presented. This change in strength over the first few items accounts for the observed primacy effect. We consider an alternative explanation shortly that does not ascribe increased strength to the initial items but which predicts primacy on the basis of a particular type of search scheme.

Although the decrease in mean strength initially, and constant mean strength thereafter, are needed to fit the observed serial position curves, the precise shapes of the distributions are not crucial. Indeed, the distributions given above do not take into account such obvious factors as subject and item differences, and therefore must be considered as approximations. In any event, the entire question of the shape of the $f_i(s)$ is independent of the retrieval scheme used, and readers who wish to reserve judgment concerning the buffer process' applicability in the free-recall situation may conceive of the $f_i(s)$ as unknown distributions which are approximated by the geometric one given above.

The basic search assumption that will be used, at least to begin with, states that the search-set involved during retrieval consists of all the information stored about the items in the just presented list. The restriction to this particular set is presumably accomplished by the use of temporal cues. Each draw during the search is assumed to be made from this same search-set. The model thus composed is quite simple, but we shall see that a more complex model is not needed for the basic free-recall situation.

One problem that is often raised refers to the definition of the functional unit of memory in this situation, or in our terms, the image. For example, if the words are categorized into associated groups, then they tend to be output in clusters from these groups (Bousfield, 1953; Bousfield and Cohen, 1956). One might question in such a case whether an image consists of information about separate words or about separate categories. In the case when common English words are being used with no experimentally preset categorization, we assume that the image consists of information about single words, i.e., the nominal and functional stimuli are equivalent. Alternative models will be discussed later, in connection with categorized free recall.

This assumption does not rule out the possibility that certain random combinations of words input will be stored in closely associated groupings. There is evidence bearing on this question (which shall be examined later) which indicates that serial position is a basis for clustering during output, but that the effect is small on the first test following presentation of unrelated words in random order. Thus, the simple random draw model will be slightly in error when applied to measures involving relations between output and input adjacency, but this error should not affect predictions of overall measures such as serial position curves.

The recovery process will therefore be treated as follows: an image consisting of information about a single word will be examined following each draw; the probability of correct output of that word will then be a function of the strength of the image, as in Eq. 2.

Clearly, the more information stored about a word, the higher will be the probability of recall, everything else being constant. This is an obvious prediction, well supported by the data; manipulations designed to increase storage about some item tend to improve recall.[3] For example, increases in presentation time for a word, or increased number of presentations of a word, improve recall of that word (Waugh, 1967).

In order to complete the specification of the model, the number of draws until search termination must be specified. The simplest case occurs when the recall period is limited by time; in this event, it may

[3] This is strictly true only for single-trial free recall; in multitrial free recall, organizational factors alter the search scheme considerably and situations can be found in which increased strength has mixed benefits, particularly in regards to the learning of the list as a whole. For example, Tulving (1966) has found that if half of a free-recall list has been learned previously, the learning of the second list as a whole may be retarded when compared with the control condition in which half of the list had not previously been learned. In addition, Murdock and Babick (1961) examined a situation in which a single word was repeated from one list to the next (all other words were new) until it was retrieved correctly. They found that the probability of retrieval of the repeated word did not rise with the number of repetitions of the word. It is possible that this result could be explained by subject-item selection effects, but if valid, has interesting consequences for a search theory. In particular, the result could imply that the search is restricted to the temporal range of the most recent list in a very strong fashion.

be assumed that draws are made continuously until time runs out. Thus, we can assume that a fixed number of draws D is made during each recall period. Even when the number of draws made is a random phenomenon, however, the model assuming exactly D draws will probably be adequate, since the variance of the distribution of draws may be fairly small, and D may be thought of as the mean of the distribution.

The model as described to this point, though quite simple, can now be utilized to predict serial position curves from free-recall situations in which rate of presentation and list length have been varied. The probability of correct recall of word i, $Pr(C_i)$, is given by

$$Pr(C_i) = \int_0^\infty \{1 - [1 - P(d_i)P(R_i|d_i)]^D\} f_i(s)\, ds$$
$$= \int_0^\infty \{1 - [1 - s/S(1 - e^{-s})]^D\}\, f_i(s)\, ds. \qquad (5)$$

In this equation, $f_i(s)$ represents the distribution of strengths stored for the ith word; S is the total strength stored for the entire list ($= \Sigma s_i$); and D is the total number of draws made during recall. The term in curly brackets is the conditional probability for the recall of word i, given that word i has strength s. This expression results from the fact that in order for a word to fail to be recalled, it must fail on each of the D draws: the term in square brackets is the probability that the word will not be recalled on any single draw. When the $f_i(s)$ distribution is discrete, as in (3) then we replace the integration of (5) with a summation.

In earlier applications, $f_i(s)$ was assumed to arise from rehearsal processes, and was geometrically distributed as in Eq. 3; s was set equal to θT, where T was the total time an item remained in rehearsal in STS and θ was the rate of transfer of information to LTS. Since the total time that different subjects spent in rehearsal of a given list was constant, S was a fixed and equal quantity for all lists of equal total presentation time and was easily calculated. The model was then fit by a least squares procedure to the data from a variety of free-recall experiments in which list length and presentation time were varied; the conditions ranged from a six-word list presented at 2 sec per word to a 40-word list presented at 1 sec per word, and included the data of Murdock (1962) and Postman and Phillips (1965). The best fit was found when the parameters r (the number of items rehearsed concurrently), θ (the transfer rate of information to LTS), and D (the number of draws made) took on the values $r = 4$, $\theta = .04$, and $D = 34$. The predictions of the

TABLE 1
Observed and Predicted Serial Position Curves for Various Free-Verbal-Recall Experiments[a]

List	Point 1 Obs.	Point 1 pred.	Point 2 Obs.	Point 2 pred.	Point 3 Obs.	Point 3 pred.	Asymptote Obs.	Asymptote pred.	Number of points
M-20-1	.46	.45	.27	.37	.20	.29	.16	.22	2
M-30-1	.38	.35	.30	.28	.21	.22	.19	.17	12
M-20-2	.55	.61	.42	.51	.37	.41	.31	.32	2
M-40-1	.30	.29	.20	.23	.13	.18	.12	.14	22
M-25-1	.38	.39	.23	.32	.21	.25	.15	.19	7
M-20-2.5	.72	.66	.61	.56	.45	.46	.37	.35	2
D-32-1	.46	.33	.34	.27	.27	.21	.16	.16	14
P-10-1	.66	.62	.42	.52	.35	.42	.34	.32	7
P-20-1	.47	.45	.27	.37	.23	.29	.22	.22	17
P-30-1	.41	.35	.34	.28	.27	.22	.20	.17	27
S-6-1	.71	.74	.50	.64	.57	.52	.42	.40	3
S-6-2	.82	.88	.82	.79	.65	.66	.66	.52	3
S-11-1	.48	.60	.43	.50	.27	.40	.31	.31	8
S-11-2	.72	.76	.55	.66	.52	.54	.47	.42	8
S-17-1	.55	.49	.33	.40	.26	.32	.22	.24	14
S-17-2	.68	.66	.65	.56	.67	.45	.43	.35	14

[a] (M = Murdock, 1962; D = Deese and Kaufman, 1957; P = Postman and Phillips, 1965; S = Shiffrin, 1968; point 1 = 1st serial position; point 2 = 2nd serial position; point 3 = 3rd serial position; asymptote = all serial position following the first 3, but excluding the last 15 serial positions if no arithmetic was used, and the number of these serial positions is placed in the column "number of points." In the column labeled "List," the first number denotes the list length and the second number denotes the number of seconds of presentation time per word.)

model were excellent even though the same parameter values were used to predict all the conditions, and the probability of correct recall ranged from .12 to .82 (exclusive of the recency effect).[4] See Table 1.

For these data, Murdock (1962) concluded that total words recalled was closely related to total presentation time. In terms of the terminology of the model, total presentation time determines total information transferred to LTS, and the total amount of information stored in LTS about a list is closely related to total words recalled. The predicted functional relation between total recall and total presentation time is not the linear one suggested by Murdock, but the relation is reasonably close to a linear one over the range of list lengths and presentation rates which were originally examined. Later, Waugh (1967) extended the

[4] For a discussion of the calculations by which the predictions are derived, for the present series of free-recall experiments and also for those yet to be discussed, see the Appendix.

range of list lengths and time per item and found an increasing negatively accelerating relationship as is predicted by the present model.

Waugh's data are shown in Fig. 4 in which average total words recalled, exclusive of the last seven items, are plotted against total presentation time. The last seven items are not used in order to exclude items recalled from STS. The solid line gives the predictions of the model using the previously derived parameter values, and substituting appropriately into Eq. 5. The observed points at a given presentation time represent lists of different lengths whose presentation rates are such that the total presentation time is fixed. Note that the model does not predict exactly the same mean number of words output for all lists where total presentation time is kept constant. For example, if only one word is presented, for any amount of time, mean recall cannot exceed 1.0. Thus, in Fig. 4 several different, but reasonably close, values are predicted for different conditions at a given total time of presentation. In these cases, the average of the predictions was used to draw the predicted curve. Undoubtedly a better fit would be obtained by estimating parameters anew for these new data, but the fit is close enough as it stands to demonstrate that the relationship between presentation time and words recalled is well predicted by the model.

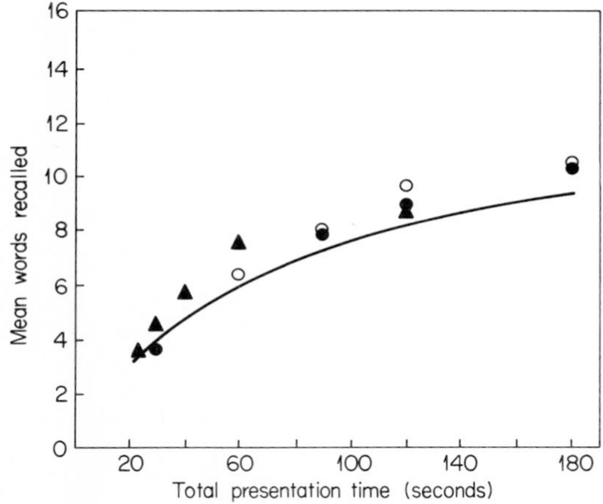

FIG. 4. Mean number of words recalled per list, excluding the last seven items in the list, as a function of list duration. The experimental conditions are as follows: let T equal the list duration in seconds; triangles represent list of T words, 1 sec per word; open circles represent lists of 30 words, $T/30$ sec per word—massed presentations; closed circles represents lists of 30 words, $T/30$ sec per word—distributed presentations. Observed values after Waugh (1967). —— predicted; ○▲● observed.

As list length is held constant and presentation rate is decreased, the model predicts recall probability for word i to increase. This prediction arises because a slower presentation rate results in a larger s_i, and hence a greater $P(R_i|d_i)$, even though $P(d_i)$, the probability of drawing word i on any one draw, is not affected by presentation rate because s_i/S does not change. That is, if time per word is t for list 1 and kt for list 2, then S will be k times larger for list 2, but the probability that an item remains in STS for j seconds in list 1 will be the same as the probability that an item remains in STS for kj seconds in list 2 (since the buffer operates on items and not time). Since s_i is a direct function of the time spent in STS, s_i/S will have the same distribution in the two cases. On the other hand, for a given presentation rate, increased list length will reduce the recall probability for word i, since s_i/S will be smaller at longer list lengths (s_i is constant, and S increases), while $P(R_i|d_i)$ is unchanged. [Remember that $P(R_i|d_i)$ is the recovery probability given that the ith image has just been drawn, and depends only on s_i, not on S.]

The model can easily be generalized to situations where particular words are presented for longer durations than others, or more frequently than others. Probably the simplest assumption to make is that s_i is linearly dependent upon the total presentation time for a word, whether it is presented for an increased duration or an increased number of times. Waugh (1962, 1963, 1967) has investigated free recall under these situations and has found that recall probability for a given word is an almost linear function of the total presentation time for that word, when the total presentation time for the list is kept constant. Figure 5, for example, gives the average probability of recall for words prior to the last seven presented, as a function of the presentation time for the word (from Waugh, 1967). The total time for the whole list is always 120 seconds, but the total number of different words covaries with the number of repetitions of a given word. The solid line gives the predictions of the model based on the previously used parameter values. Although new parameters were not estimated for this situation, the fit is quite accurate, and the more or less linear relationship found in the data is seen to be predicted by the model.

The data in Fig. 5 are based on a design where each presented word is repeated n times. In earlier work, Waugh (1962, 1963) considered the case where only one word in the middle portion of a free-recall list was repeated. The results were comparable to those reported above; the

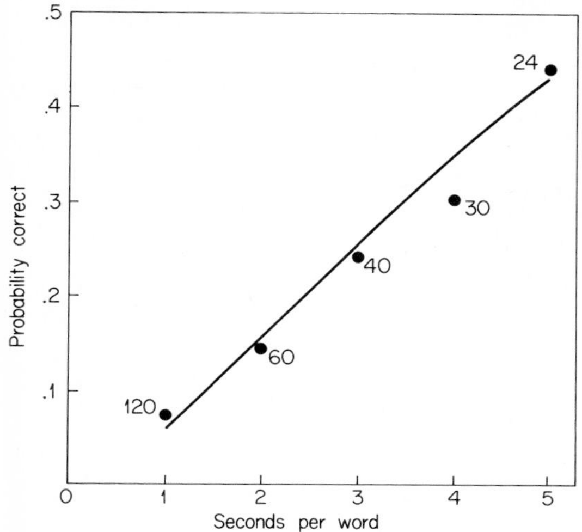

FIG. 5. Probability of recall for a given word as a function of presentation time for that word. [The numbers denote the total number of words presented. The probabilities were estimated across all words prior to the last seven presented. Observed values after Waugh (1967).] —— predicted; ● observed.

probability of recalling the twice-presented word was about twice the probability of recalling a singly-presented word (.35 vs. .17; Waugh, 1963). The predictions of the model (using the previous parameter values) are .38 and .17 for the doubled and single items, respectively. Figure 6 gives the results from Waugh (1962); 50 item lists were presented with four repeated items embedded in the list (in positions 5–46). These four special items were repeated 2, 3, 4, and 5 times, respectively. The probability correct is graphed in Fig. 6 as a function of the number of repetitions; again, predictions were derived using the previous parameter values, and again the predictions are reasonably accurate.

The discussion to this point should make it clear that almost all of the results in free recall which relate to presentation rate and list length, are explicable in terms of a quite simple search model. It has been found that a single set of parameter values can provide adequate quantitative predictions, despite the fact that the data were collected by a variety of experimenters over a wide period of time. All things considered, however, the ability to predict with a *single* set of parameters should probably be considered fortuitous; since the parameters

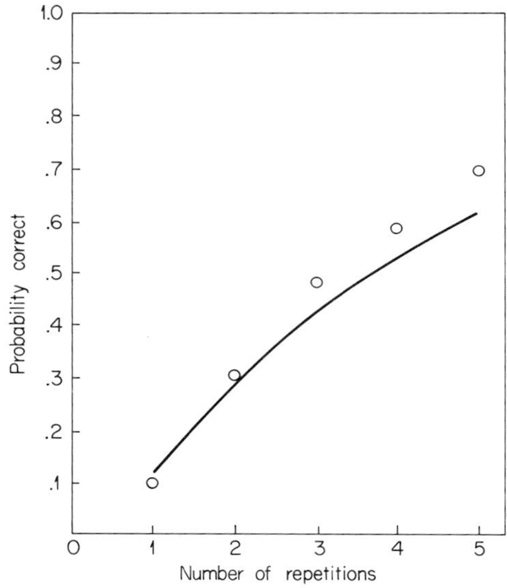

FIG. 6. Probability of recall of a word repeated n times in positions 5-46 of a 50-word list, as a function of n. Observed values after Waugh (1962). OOO observed, —— predicted.

of the model are indeed expected to vary with changing conditions (D, for example, should be larger with response periods of longer duration), the parameters should be estimated anew for each different procedure. The fact that a single parameter set has sufficed is undoubtedly testimony to the high similarity of procedures that have been utilized in the study of free recall.

An Experiment with Successive Response Periods

The search model should be particularly sensitive to changes in the response period, or any other procedural variations that will lead to changes in D, the number of draws made. Unfortunately, simple lengthening of the response period is unlikely to provide the desired manipulation since response termination is often determined by the subject. Interresponse latencies could provide an adequate vehicle for examination of the search assumptions, but such an examination has not yet been carried out. One method that has been used which should result in an appropriate manipulation of D is that devised by Tulving (1967); following presentation, the subject is asked to free recall in the normal fashion, and is then asked to do so twice more. Thus, the subject free-recalls three consecutive times, each response period lasting 30 sec; and the subject attempts to recall all of the words he can (verbally) during each recall period; the presentation rate is 1 word per second and 36 words are presented.

The simplest assumption that can be made in this situation holds that D draws are made during each of the recall periods. A convenient statistic, which should be roughly independent of the effects of retrieval from STS, is the number of new words recalled in the last two recall periods which were not recalled in the first. According to the model, since the list length is 36, this number should be 36 times the difference between the mean probability correct when $3D$ draws are made and the mean probability correct when D draws are made, since the difference gives the probability that any one item is recalled in the latter recall periods, but not recalled in the first. This difference is easily calculated from Eq. 5. (Actually, we should multiply the difference in probabilities by only about 30, rather than 36, since as many as six of the words recalled in the first recall period are recovered from STS and not LTS, and Tulving's data did not exclude words in the recency portions of the list.) Tulving found that 1.58 words were recalled on the last two trials which were not recalled on the first; the prediction of the model, if the previously derived parameter values are used, is that 4.4 new words should be recalled on the last two recall trials. Possible reasons for the overprediction will be considered momentarily, but it should be noted that the qualitative prediction of the model that at least some new words will be recalled was confirmed. In fact, the model predicts that total recall from LTS should be constant for each of the three recall periods, although the individual words recalled should vary somewhat from one recall to the next. The first recall period involves recall from STS as well as LTS, and hence should result in higher recall than the following two, in which recall may be assumed to be limited to LTS; the second and third recall periods should therefore have equal mean total recall at a level lower than that found for the first recall period. This was just the pattern of results found by Tulving (1967):

> . . . the number of words recalled in the third intracycle output phase that were not recalled in the second phase rather accurately matched the number of items that were recalled in the second but not in the third output phase. One might perhaps attribute the occurrence of such a "trading" relation to oscillation at the threshold of recall, but whether we talk about oscillation or about a limited-capacity retrieval system that is insensitive to the content of accessible memory units, the major theoretical problem remains the same—how to conceptualize the events occurring in input and output phases and to account for the effect of these events on availability and accessibility of individual items.

Naturally it is the thesis of this paper that the resolution of this theoretical problem lies in the formulation of appropriate search models of memory. We now consider some of the reasons for the overprediction by the model of the number of new words recalled in the latter two output phases. The initial possibility that comes to mind is that a new set of parameter values estimated for this particular situation would rectify the discrepancy. Without going into the details, however, it may be stated that any set of parameter values reasonably consistent with those already estimated, and which gives accurate predictions for the first output phase, will tend to overpredict the number of new words recalled in the later phases. A second possibility is that the true $f_i(s)$ distributions are not the ones given in Eq. 3; the effect we have been considering varies with the form of the $f_i(s)$ distribution. If, for example, $f_i(s)$ tended to be an all-or-none distribution, with a few items with very high strength, and the other items with very little or no strength, then a large number of draws will almost always result in recall of close to all of the high strength items, and will almost never result in recall of any others; in such an event, the number of new items recalled in additional recall periods would be quite small. This explanation will not be considered further because it is not currently possible to estimate the shape of the $f_i(s)$ distributions and we have no strong reasons for doubting that the $f_i(s)$ distributions are reasonably approximated by Eq. 3.

The most likely explanation is one for which there is a good deal of evidence: during recall, additional information is stored in LTS about the particular items recalled. This fact is strikingly demonstrated in the finding by Tulving (1967) that, under a particular set of conditions in multitrial free recall, recall probability following a series of presentation phases and recall phases may be equal regardless of whether these phases were distributed in the ratio of 1:2 or 2:1. This point is not being questioned here; indeed, it has been commonly assumed in the memory models proposed by this author that all information in STS is continually being transferred to and stored in LTS, regardless of the specific nature of the task at which the subject is momentarily working. If it is true that information is being stored about the recalled words during output, it may well be asked why the model does not assume that the search-set becomes altered during the course of retrieval. The answer lies in the original assumption that the search-set is defined on a temporal basis—words prior to the start of the most recent list are not included in the search-set because of some temporal criterion set by the subject. Similarly, it may be supposed that a temporal criterion is set at the end of the presented list, since it is of no value to the subject to include information in his search-set about words that have already been recalled; indeed, including such information would prove highly detrimental. The situation is completely changed, however, when successive output phases are required; during later output phases, it could prove quite useful for a search to be made of words output in previous output phases. While a search is being made through a search-set consisting only of words previously *output* (defined by temporal factors), no word may be recalled which was not recalled in previous output phases. Thus, if the basic free recall model predicts twice as many new words recalled on later output phases as actually observed, then this may be interpreted as indicating that about half of the draws made during these phases are made from search-sets consisting of previously recalled words. A slight variant of this explanation would hold that the subject, rather than alternating between two types of temporally exclusive search-sets, redefines his search-set on later output phases so as to encompass a larger temporal period, and so that previously recalled words have images of greater strength. This model also would predict smaller numbers of new words output than would the basic model, since a larger proportion of the information in the search-set would be taken up by images of words already recalled.

Rehearsal in Free Recall

The various discussions to this point make it clear that a relatively unsophisticated search model has the power to deal with diverse free-recall phenomena. It is now time to examine the assumptions of the model in more detail. We have assumed that the subject utilizes a rehearsal process called the buffer: There are a number of lines of evidence arguing against the rehearsal buffer assumptions.

Waugh (1963, 1967) demonstrated that recall probability for a word which has been presented two or more times in a free-recall list is not dependent upon the spacing of those presentations within the list (where all the presentations are in the central portion of the list). In order to apply the buffer model to this situation, one must decide what happens when an item is presented which is already in the buffer. If it is assumed that the buffer remains unchanged in this instance, then the model predicts an advantage for the spaced presentations, since a word on its second occurrence cannot supply additional strength until enough time has passed since its first occurrence for it to have left the buffer. An alternative formulation, and the one that has been assumed in making the earlier predictions for this case, holds that each instance of a word, whether repeated or not, enters and leaves the buffer independently; in this case two or more slots in the buffer could be occupied by the same word, and the mean strength built up in LTS for a repeated word would be independent of that word's spacing. This second formulation is suspect primarily because it implies that considerable differences in recall would result between paradigms where a word is repeated twice in succession at a rate of one per second, or simply presented once for two seconds, and this difference is not found in the data.

While the problems raised by Waugh's data cannot be ignored, a number of recent experiments have demonstrated a spacing effect in free-recall; therefore, other evidence is needed before the buffer hypothesis may be rejected. Relevant evidence is found in free-recall tasks where rehearsal is inhibited or directed by an experimental manipulation. A number of studies have demonstrated that forced overt rehearsal of *one* item at a time causes a reduction in the total words recalled (Allen, 1968; Glanzer and Meinzer, 1967). Glanzer and Meinzer (1967) found that overt repetition of words during the intervals between words in the input phase reduced the recall of words prior to the recency range, but left the recency effect largely unaffected. A buffer model would seem to predict just the reverse: a great effect on words to be recovered from STS, and an undetermined effect upon those items to be recovered from LTS.

Other experiments, instead of manipulating the form of rehearsal, have attempted to eliminate it altogether. Murdock (1965) had subjects sort a deck of playing cards into various categories during auditory presentation of a 20-word list presented at a rate of 1 word per second. Presumably, card sorting would interfere with rehearsal, and the most difficult sorting task would result in the greatest interference. The results are shown in Fig. 7. It is clear that the more difficult the sorting task the more depressed is the initial portion of the serial position curve, but the recency effect is unaffected by the difficulty of the interfering task. If the recency effect is largely a result of a rehearsal process, then inhibition of rehearsal should drastically reduce the size of this effect; however, such a reduction was not found.

In order to determine, among other things, whether the various sorting

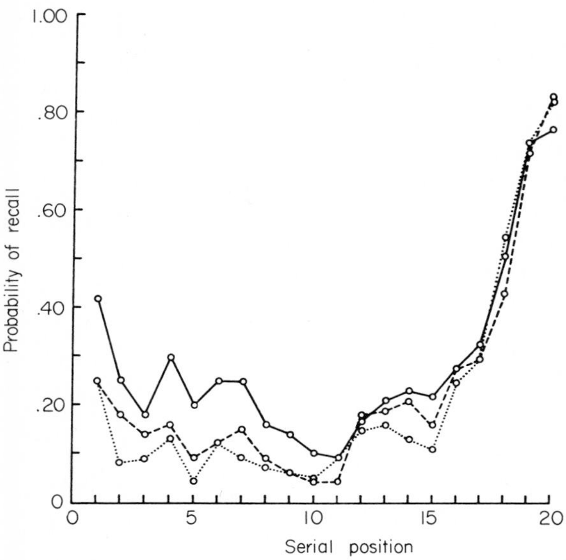

FIG. 7. Serial position curves for free recall of 20-word lists presented at 1 word per second, while subjects carried out one of three subsidiary card-sorting tasks: plain (dealing into a single pile), sorting by color, or sorting by suit (after Murdock, 1965). ○—○ plain; ○– – –○ color; ○ · · · · · ○ suit.

tasks used by Murdock were all too easy to inhibit rehearsal, the following experiment was carried out by George Wolford and the author. Thirty word lists were presented by tape recorder at a rate of 1 word per second. Simultaneously, digits in the range 4–9 were presented randomly via a slide projector at a rate of 1 digit every 2 sec; the subjects were required to keep a running sum of the numbers presented and write down the grand total before attempting to recall the words. Two types of tests were used: in the first, the subjects were required to free recall in the normal fashion; in the second, subjects were provided with a list of 30 pairs of words, and had to identify which member of each pair had been in the list just presented. The distractors used were all different and had never been presented in any list. The order of test of the word pairs was entirely random. Two control conditions were run in which no arithmetic task was used, and there were therefore four conditions, denoted RWN (recall with numbers), RCWN (recognition with numbers), RWON (recall without numbers), and RCWON (recognition without numbers). Forty-four subjects were run in group sessions of about 15 subjects each. Each session consisted of a practice list followed by six lists in each of the four conditions, in random order, (i.e., 25 lists in all); as a result, each of the probabilities in the serial position curves to follow are based upon 264 observations.

The results are shown in Fig. 8; the two curves of interest at the moment are the two in Fig. 8a: free recall with and without simultaneous arithmetic during presentation. That the interfering task was quite difficult is indicated by the extremely low recall probabilities in the central portion of the RWN curve; in this situation, with a very difficult simultaneous task, it is evident that the recency portion of the RWN curve is indeed lowered in comparison with the RWON control. Despite this, the recency effect in the RWN condition is still sizable and this fact would seem to verify the conclusion that the recency effect is produced in large part by retrieval from STS which is independent of rehearsal. On the other hand, the lowering of the recency effect in the RWN condition would serve to indicate that a rehearsal effect is present, but of smaller extent than originally proposed. Another finding arguing in favor of at least some rehearsal will be discussed shortly: adjacently presented words have a higher than chance joint probability of being

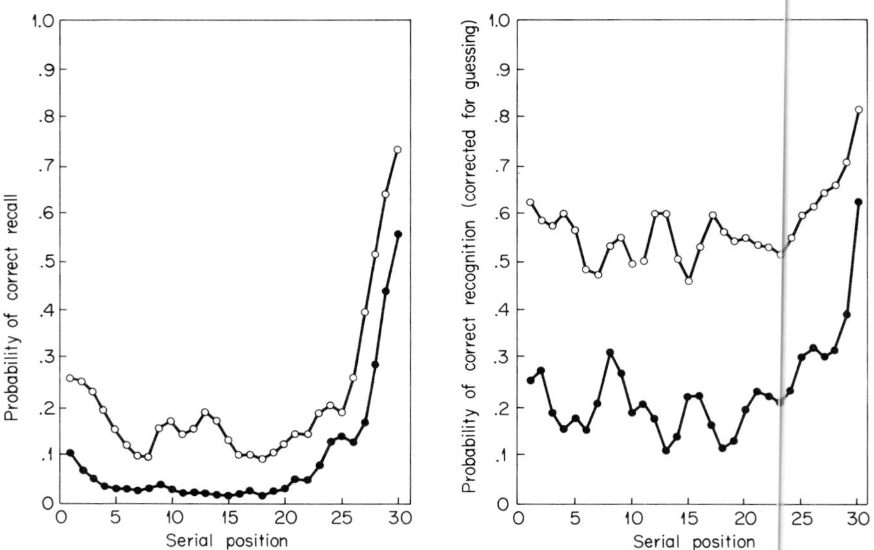

FIG. 8. Serial position curves for 30-word lists presented at 1/sec either with or without a simultaneous arithmetic task; (a) left panel—recall test; (b) right panel—binary forced-choice recognition test. ○–○–○ recall (without stimulus numbers); ●–●–● (with stimulus numbers).

recalled, and are more likely than chance to be recalled together during output. These findings may imply that temporally contiguous items tend to be rehearsed and stored together.

These various findings demonstrate the need for further research to establish the extent of rehearsal processes in free recall, but the proposed buffer process is suspect enough that alternative formulations should be considered. As far as the recency effect is concerned, there is no large problem; the typical presentation rates used are fast enough that the S-shaped recency curve can be interpreted as directly representing decay from STS. A different problem arises with respect to the earlier portions of the serial position curves. Without a rehearsal assumption another method must be found to specify the $f_i(s)$ distribution of strengths stored in LTS, a distribution arising from such factors as differences in codability of the words and so forth. In fact, a distribution would have to be specified arbitrarily, and as long as there is no evidence to the contrary, it is convenient to suppose that the $f_i(s)$ distributions are roughly geometric in form, as given by Eq. 3. The only change needed is that induced by the fact that, in the absence of rehearsal, there is no strong reason for supposing that the mean of the $f_i(s)$ distributions decreases over the first few serial positions. Assume for the moment that the $f_i(s)$ distribution is the same for all i. This alternative model is, if anything, even simpler than the original, but has the difficulty that no primacy effect is predicted. Methods of rectifying this difficulty will be discussed next.

The original free-recall model, and all other models of free recall to date, have the common assumption that primacy results from stored images which are of greater strength for the first few items in the list. It is proposed that a relatively slight change in the search scheme can account for primacy effects, even when the average stored strengths are the same for all items. In particular, assume that at some point or points during the search a draw is made not from the search-set containing all the items in the list, but from a search-set restricted to items near the start of the list. This restriction presumably would occur because the start of the list provides a natural and distinctive cue upon which to define a search-set. It should be clear that such a search will result in a higher recall probability for the initial items; in general, any restricted search will result in higher recall probability for the items in the restricted set as compared with a random search through the entire set. Suppose for example that $D - 1$ draws are made from the entire search-set at random, and one special draw is made from a restricted set consisting of the first item only; suppose also that the presentation time per item is 1 sec. Then the mean strength stored for any item is, according to Eq. 4, $\theta tr = 4\theta$. Based upon the parameter values that have previously been adopted, $E(s_i) = .16$. Therefore, the probability of recovery and output of the initial item following the one special draw is approximately $[1 - \exp(-.16)] = .15$. If recovery is not made on this draw, then the recovery probability for the other 33 random draws is, for say a 40-word list, .14. Hence, the probability of recovery of the initial item in this example would be $(.15) + (.85)(.14) = .27$. Since the actual value observed in Murdock (1962) for this point was .30, it may be concluded that an extremely small tendency to examine selectively the initial items can provide a satisfactory explanation of the primacy effect.

If the search explanation for the primacy effect is correct, then the provision of a distinctive cue at some intermediate point in a free-recall list should result in a pseudo-primacy effect at that point (a la the "von Restorff" effect commonly examined in serial learning). A somewhat different test of this hypothesis is provided by recognition tests. In Fig. 8b, serial position curves are presented for forced-choice recognition performance. If the primacy effect is due to search characteristics, and if we may assume that the recognition test taps memory in a way that is not dependent upon a random search through more than the relevant image, then the primacy effect should not appear in the recognition serial position curves. If the storage hypothesis is correct, then we might expect primacy to remain in both cases and to be larger in the condition without intervening arithmetic. Unfortunately, the data are too unstable to permit us to distinguish between these alternatives. However, Norman and Waugh (1968) did find a small primacy effect for 30-word lists using a yes-no recognition procedure, and these data point to a strength explanation. It may be that further research will show both the search and strength explanations of primacy to be true. Finally, note that the search explanation of primacy might help explain why primacy is not found in short paired-associate lists (Murdock, 1963, Chapter 9).

Relationships between Input Order and Output Order

The possibility that the search-set does not consist of the *entire* set of images of words in the most recent list on each and every draw may be examined in other ways. In multitrial free recall, as the free-recall list becomes learned, the output order tends to become fixed from trial to trial (Tulving, 1962); this fact certainly demonstrates that the search is nonrandom on later trials in the free-recall learning situation. In addition, numerous experiments have shown that items meaningfully related tend to be output together regardless of input position (e.g., Bousfield and Cohen, 1956). It is only on the first recall of a homogeneous list of words randomly presented that the approximation we have assumed is adequate, and even here some deviations from predictions may be found. In particular, it may be shown that words which are in adjacent input positions have a higher than chance joint probability of both being output (but not necessarily output together). To demonstrate this fact, we consider the following statistic: for a given number of items output by a subject on a trial, let Q_2 be the number of pairs of words among those output which were in adjacent input positions, and let Q_3 be the number of triplets of words among those output that were in adjacent input positions. We consider the results from a condition (Atkinson and Shiffrin, 1965) in which 17 words were presented at a rate of 1 word per sec, and a period of arithmetic followed presentation and preceded recall (which eliminated the recency effect). In order to eliminate confounding due to the primacy effect, the recall of words which had been presented in the first three serial positions is ignored in the analysis. The observed values of Q_2 and Q_3 averaged over protocols of equal length are shown in Table 2. N is the number of output protocols of exactly j words in length, where j is the number in the first column of the table. If it is assumed that output is completely independent of input order (for serial positions 4-17), then it is easy to calculate the expected number of doublets and triplets for each j. For doublets, for example, we calculate the probability that a particular pair of adjacent input positions, say k and $k + 1$, will be represented in the j words output [which equals $(j/14) \times (j - 1)/13$] and multiply this probability by the total number of possible adjacent positions (which equals 13). Thus, we have,

$$\begin{aligned} E(Q_2) &= E[\text{doublets} \mid j \text{ words output}] = (j/14) \times (j-1)/13 \times 13 \\ E(Q_3) &= E[\text{triplets} \mid j \text{ words output}] \\ &= (j/14) \times (j-1)/13 \times (j-2)/12 \times 12. \end{aligned} \tag{6}$$

The predictions derived from the expressions in Eq. 6 are also listed in Table 2. It is evident that the observed proportions are higher than those predicted in every instance. The magnitude of the effect may not be startling, but there is no doubt that items that are output

TABLE 2

Number of items Output = j	N	Q_2 = Doublets		Q_3 = Triplets	
		Observed	Predicted	Observed	Predicted
0	—			—	
1	—			—	
2	13	.307	.143	—	
3	16	.750	.418	.250	.033
4	9	1.444	.857	.444	.129
5	10	2.200	1.418	.700	.330
6	6	2.833	2.143	1.000	.660
7	4	3.750	3.000	1.750	1.150
8	5	4.600	4.000	2.400	1.840
9	1	6.000	5.143	4.000	2.780
10	1	7.000	6.418	4.000	3.950
11	1	9.000	7.857	7.000	5.460

[a] The mean number of doubly- or triply-adjacent items in input which are recalled (in any output positions), as a function of the total number of items output. List length equals 17. N is the number of output protocols of j words in length.

tend to be those presented in temporal contiguity. A related finding is that the recalled items tend to be output in such a way that words which were adjacent during presentation are also adjacent in the output protocols. Again, this effect is not of large magnitude for a singly presented list, but becomes quite large after several trials on the same list (Kintsch, Chapter 11).

There are two primary hypotheses to be considered which can explain the relations between input and output adjacency and output probability: both require a somewhat more sophisticated search scheme than the one utilized until this point, and both have some evidence in their favor. In the first, it is supposed that information is stored during the presentation of the list which sometimes links nearby items; then, during examination of an image in retrieval this linking information may be utilized to narrow the search-set on the subsequent draw to include only the information relating to the linked word. This hypothesis proposes that previously stored information is recovered at certain points in the search and then used to redefine and restrict the search-set for the following draw. It is clear that a mechanism of this sort is operating on later trials in multitrial free recall when the output order begins to become fixed from trial to trial. In these multitrial situations, the search becomes increasingly less random, and is governed more and more by linking information which enables the subject to scan successively search-sets of small size (perhaps one word each). Because presentation order is usually randomized from trial to trial in these multitrial situations, it is clear that the linking information utilized is not temporal in nature. Still, we cannot rule out the hypothesis that temporal information is used to control the search in the single-trial situation. This hypothesis holds that the subject utilizes an external strategy to alter and restrict search-sets according to temporal factors; thus the subject may scan first the start of the list, then the middle, and so forth. If there were any tendency to choose restricted search-sets which contained temporally contiguous information, and if more than one consecutive draw were made from this restricted set, then dependence of the output upon input position would be expected. It is well known that the subject can be instructed to search on a temporal basis, as when serial recall instructions are given (Young, 1968), but the extent to which this occurs in free recall has not yet been established. The reader will have noticed that this hypothesis is a more general version of the one proposed for explanation of the primacy effect, which supposed that part of the search might be temporally restricted to the first few items in the list. It should be noted that the hypothesis of a temporally restricted search is not different in substance from the category-restricted search that occurs in categorized free recall. That is, if a series of four-footed animals are presented during input, then the subject may restrict his search at some point during output to "four-footed animals." This kind of restriction is different from the temporal one only in the fact that the category restriction is based upon preexisting associative groupings, while the temporal restriction is based upon information presented during presentation.

Categorized Free Recall

The typical categorized list paradigm consists of the presentation of a list of words already divided into a number of different natural categories (such as "north, south, east, west"); the words of a given category may or may not be presented contiguously. Considerable research has been carried out within this paradigm (e.g., Bousfield and Cohen, 1956; Cofer, 1959), but we focus attention on a few representative studies: Cohen (1963a, 1963b) and Tulving and Pearlstone (1966).

There are two primary approaches to the model which must be considered. The first assumes that the items making up a given category are associated, or coded, together during the presentation period. Of course, the items of a category are already associated prior to the experiment, but this first hypothesis assumes that some additional degree of mediational association takes place during storage. Under this assumption, words within a category are output together with high probability because the search is led from word to word of a given category by information stored during presentation.

The second approach would hold that storage of information about the single words takes place in independent fashion during presentation; however, during recall, previously learned associations between words of a category serve to facilitate recall of that category. Under this second assumption, for example, it may be proposed that the first word of a category recalled allows the subject to generate the category of which that word is a unit; the other words of the category may then be generated one at a time in order that a recognition test may be applied by the subject to each word generated.

These two hypotheses, in one variant or another, have received extensive examination in the literature (e.g., Bousfield, Steward, and Cowan, 1964; Deese, 1962; Bousfield and Puff, 1964; Cofer, 1965, 1966; Postman, 1964; Asch and Ebenholtz, 1962; Tulving, 1966; Kintsch, Chapter 11). The conclusions reached by different investigators have differed considerably, but there is no doubt at present that both processes are active in free recall, the central question being the identification of the relative importance of each in various paradigms. In categorized free recall in particular, both processes are undoubtedly active; nevertheless, in keeping with the general approach of this paper, we shall assume that only the second process applies—that information is stored about words independently during input and that clustering effects result from the search process utilized in recall. We shall see that this process alone can account for many of the effects in categorized free recall.

The model is therefore formulated as follows. Storage of information takes place as before; the mean amount of strength stored for the ith word is linearly related to the presentation time for that word. During recall from LTS, the first draw is made from the information stored about the list as a whole; such a draw will be denoted as a *list-draw.* If a word is then recovered, the subject will generate with some probability (perhaps 1.0), the category of which that word is a member. After a category is generated, the search-set will then be restricted to the members of that category, and depending upon the situation, either the words of that category will be successively generated for recognition, or a search will be made. If the category recovered is *exhaustive* (e.g., "north, south, east, west") then the generation-recognition procedure will probably be used; if the category is effectively *nonexhaustive* (e.g., four-footed animals) then generation of all members of the category will either be impossible or extremely tedious, and at least some of the time a search will be made through the restricted set of members of the category that were presented. We refer to this examination of a category, of either type, as a *category-search* and for the present, we do not specify its length or number of draws. Following a category-search, list-draws are then made until another category is recovered, and retrieval continues in this manner until search termination. There are several possibilities for the termination rule, but we assume that termination occurs after D list-draws have taken place, regardless of the length of the category searches. The model therefore views retrieval in this situation as consisting of two fairly independent search processes, one concerned with recall of categories, and one concerned with recall of words within a category. This view corresponds closely to a similar conclusion reached by Tulving and Pearlstone (1966).

The probability of choosing information relating to a particular word or category on any list-draw is given by the value of strength stored for that word or category divided by the strength stored for the entire list. Now we need to specify the probability of recovering a word once an I-unit relevant to that word has been drawn. As usual, this probability will be an exponential function of the strength, but the information relevant to a single word is assuredly too small to be the strength used in Eq. 4 in the categorized situation. Remember that the recovery process consists of an examination of information associated with the I-unit drawn; in the present case, this information will include information stored concerning the other members of the category, since the various members of a category are strongly interassociated. Thus, it may happen that another member of a category than the one designated by the I-unit drawn may be recalled during the recovery stage; from this member, the category may be generated and a category search then begun. Considering these arguments, let the probability of recovery of *some* word of a category following the drawing of an I-unit relevant to one word of the category be an exponential function of the sum of the strengths of the various members of that category which were presented.

Cohen (1963a) presented 70-word lists at a rate of one word every 3 sec. Each list contained 20 categories of words: five exhaustive (E) categories, three words in number, five *E* categories, four words in number; five nonexhaustive categories (NE), three words in number; and five NE categories, four words in number. The words making up any category were spaced throughout the list. Because the data were reported in a form that included recall from the recency effect, we do not attempt quantitative predictions, but simply compare the qualitative predictions of the patterns of events with the results that were observed. The major results and predictions follow.

(a) Categories E and NE were recalled equally often (category recall refers to the number of categories for which at least one member was recalled). Since the probability of recall of a category depends upon the amount of strength stored for its members, and strength is assumed to be stored word-by-word and independently of categories, the model does not predict differential recall of the two types of categories.

(b) There was a strong tendency for words of a category to be output together in recall. Since the model assumes that a category search is undertaken following each category recovery, this is the natural prediction.

(c) If E and NE categories of equal length are compared, there is a higher probability of recalling any one word from an E than an NE category. Although we have not dealt with recognition, it is presumed that recognition tests yield a higher recovery probability than a corresponding recall test in which the desired response must be constructed. Evidence for this presumption may be seen in the study reported earlier by Wolford and Shiffrin (Fig. 8), in which recognition performance was much higher than recall performance. Thus, a category search in which the members may be generated one-by-one for recognition, will yield higher retrieval than a category search in which it is difficult or lengthy to generate all of the category members.

In another study, Cohen (1963b) covaried the number and type of categories in a list, and presentation rate. First, lists of 10, 15, and 20 categories (35, 53, and 70 words) were compared using both E and NE category types. In addition, 10-, 15-, and 20-word lists consisting of unrelated words were also examined. In all conditions, the words were presented at a rate of 3 sec per word. It was found that the number of categories recalled was higher for the NE and E conditions than for the corresponding unrelated word conditions. For example, the mean number of categories recalled for the 20 category E and NE conditions were, respectively, 12.8 and 12.3, while the mean number of words recalled for the 20-word unrelated list was 9.5. In three additional tests that equated presentation times, the number of categories recalled from a categorized list of N categories and the number of words recalled from an unrelated list of N words were approximately equal.

It is not hard to see that these results are predicted by the model. Whatever the presentation rates, the probability of drawing an I-unit associated with the jth word from among N words presented is the same as the probability of drawing an I-unit associated with the jth category from among N categories presented. In addition, if the total presentation time for the words making up the jth category is equal to the presentation time for the jth word, then the recovery probabilities will be equal. This follows because the strength stored is a linear function of presentation time, and because we have assumed that the recovery probability of a word from category j on any draw will be a function of the total strengths of all the words in category j. Thus, this model predicts the finding that mean total categories recalled and mean words recalled are equal when total presentation time is equalized. For similar reasons, when equal numbers of three- and four-word categories are mixed within a list, more four-word than three-word categories should be recalled; this finding was also reported.

One other result was that the average number of words recalled per category, given that at least one word was recalled, was not affected by list length, but only by category size. Since the model assumes that words recalled in a category after the first are the result of a restricted search, either through the relevant category or the words in the list within that category, list length is predicted to have no effect upon words recalled per category after the first. Let C_p be the proportion of words recalled within a category, for all categories from which at least one word was recalled. A rather surprising finding was that C_p was not a function of category size: "Despite the variations in list length and category size, each recalled E category was represented by approximately 85% of its words. Each recalled NE category was represented by approximately 63% of its words." (Cohen, 1963b, p. 234.)

It is understandable why category size should not have an effect for exhaustive categories. Subjects can generate each member of an E category for recognition. Thus, mean total words of a category recalled (after the first) should be linearly related to the category size. For NE categories, however, such a simple generation scheme may not be possible and a partial search will have to be made. Whenever a random search is made, C_p should decrease as set size increases. Such a decrease was not found, perhaps due to the small range of category sizes examined (3 and 4) and to the fact that relatively common members of the NE categories were selected for presentation. This may have allowed the subject to generate successively the appropriate members for comparison even though the categories were nonexhaustive.[5] Indeed, support for the model's predictions are found in the next study.

An Experiment with Cued Recall

Tulving and Pearlstone (1966) presented 12, 24, or 48 word lists each made up of either 1, 2, or 4 word NE categories. The members of each category were presented successively at one word per second and were preceded by the category label, which was presented for 3 sec. Two types of recall tests were used; in *noncued recall* (NCR) the subjects were told to write down all the words they could remember (excluding category names); in *cued recall* (CR), subjects were given a list of all the category names and then tried to recall all the words they could. Half of the groups were given two CR tests in succession, while the other half were given a NCR test followed by a CR test. The results are shown in Fig. 9a.

Representative predictions of the model were obtained by using a set of arbitrary parameter values (roughly the same as those used in previous applications). These predictions are shown in Fig. 9b. The basic assumptions were the following: First, the category name always becomes available to the subject following recovery of a member of any category; second, either after a category cue has been presented

[5] The situation is even more anomalous than it appears at first glance. The appropriate statistic to be examined is not the one given by Cohen, C_p, but instead is the probability of recall of a word from a recalled category, excluding the first word recalled; that is, the conditional probability of a given word in a category being recalled after the first member of a category is recalled. It is easy to transform Cohen's data into the appropriate values; if n is the category size, and p is the probability reported by Cohen, then the correct statistic has the value $(np - 1)/(n - 1)$. For E categories, this probability has a value of .80 and .78 for four- and three-word categories, respectively. For NE categories, the values are .51 and .45 for four- and three-word categories, respectively. Thus, we find, especially for the NE categories, that recall per word is actually superior for the larger category. Almost certainly this result is anomalous, and may have been caused by characteristics of the particular categories used. In the Tulving and Pearlstone (1966) study, both C_p and the correct statistic decreased with category size as expected.

(in the CR condition), or after the subject has generated a category name on his own (in the NCR conditions), a category search is initiated which consists of five draws through the restricted set of information stored about the members of the category being searched. These assumptions ignore many factors already discussed, such as generation-recognition methods for searching a particular category, but should serve to provide the rough qualitative predictions that are needed.

Comparison of Figs. 9a and b indicates that there is qualitative agreement between the data and the predictions. Cued recall is superior to

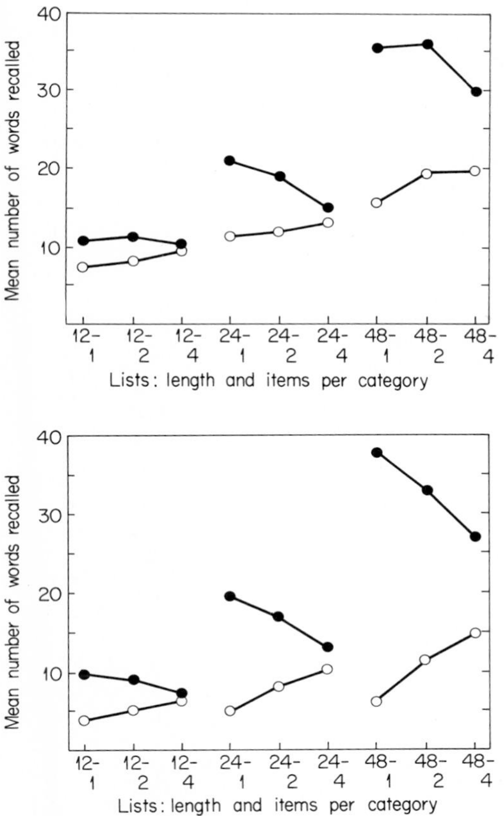

FIG. 9. Mean number of words recalled in the first recall test as a function of list length (upper number on abscissa) and number of words per category (lower number on abscissa) for testing either with or without category names provided; (a) upper panel—observed data; (b) lower panel—predicted values (data from Tulving and Pearlstone, 1966). ● Cued recall (CR); ○ noncued recall (NCR).

noncued recall because the search is restricted to a greater degree (or even eliminated if category size is 1) when cuing is used. In addition, the advantage of cuing increases with list length since the noncued list-search becomes decreasingly effective as list length increases; inspection of the figure reveals this to be the case. For the NCR conditions at a given list length, performance rises as category size increases because a greater proportion of retrieval time is spent in relatively efficient category searches than in list-draws. On the other hand, for the CR conditions, all the draws are made within restricted category searches and the only effect of increased category size is to make each category search less efficient. Therefore, performance is predicted to decrease with increased category size at a given list length in the CR conditions. Note that this effect is somewhat at variance with Cohen's finding that the probability of a member of a category being recalled, given that at least one member was recalled, is not dependent upon category size (for three- and four-member nonexhaustive categories). Indeed, in the present study this probability did drop markedly with increased category size; for example, for the list lengths of 24 and 48, proportion of words recalled per category recalled was about .87 for two-word cate-categories and .66 for four-word categories (or .74 and .55 if we exclude the first word recalled). We could expect this decrease to be the typical result when truly nonexhaustive categories are utilized.

A particularly interesting finding is that the probability of recalling a member of a recalled category does not vary with list length (also found by Cohen, 1966) and is not dependent upon whether the test condition is CR or NCR. These results are predicted by the model since the members of a category recalled after the first result from a category search which is independent of other items in the list.

There are a number of other effects in the data which tend to confirm the proposed search model. For example, in the NCR conditions, words of a given category tended to be output together. An analysis of intrusions showed that noncategorical intrusions were very rare, but intrusions of nonpresented members of a category were relatively common. These intrusions indicate that there is a significant generation-recognition component to the category search, and a more precise model than the one used above should take this component into account. One result not predicted by the model showed that the probability that a category would be recalled, for both the CR and NCR conditions, decreased with list length. In the model, this decrease is predicted for the NCR conditions, but not for the CR conditions. This is because recall of category members, given the category name, should not be dependent upon presented items outside the category.

The second recall test, which was always a CR condition, showed essentially the same results and levels of performance as the first CR recall, regardless of whether the first test was a CR or NCR condition. Thus, a large rise in recall probability took place if a CR test followed an NCR test. This fact and the other results we have been discussing led Tulving and Pearlstone to make a distinction between "availability" and "accessibility." The term "accessibility" refers to items that are retrievable under the momentary test conditions; the term "availability" refers to items that are present in memory and are potentially recoverable at another point in time, or in other test conditions. Of course, this distinction is inherent in any search model; in fact, one of the strongest attributes of a search model is its ability to give precise form to the "availability"–"accessibility" distinction.

Multitrial Free Recall

If a free-recall list is presented a number of times in succession, then two primary effects occur: the strengths of the individual items increase and the interassociative structure of the images in LTS becomes stronger and more highly organized.

The evidence for increasing organization of the information in LTS over trials is unequivocal, based primarily upon an increasing correspondence between output orders on successive trials (Tulving, 1962). This correspondence is marked by a tendency for the subject to develop clusters of words that are consistently emitted together. There are a number of mechanisms by which this increase in organization occurs, but according to the search model they should all result in two effects. First, draws are made from search-sets which, over trials, become increasingly reduced in size. Second, the search-sets are examined successively in an order that becomes increasingly systematic. These two mechanisms lead to marked improvement in recall in comparison with a random search through all the stored images. To put this another way, the primary improvement in performance over trials occurs not as a result of increased information stored about individual items, but as a result of an improved retrieval technique. In one form or another, this basic point has been made in reference to free recall by several authors, including Tulving (1967), Cofer (1965), and Mandler (1967). The same point has been made by Greeno (Chapter 8) for the paired-associate situation, although his conclusion was reached on the basis of a markedly different line of reasoning.

Before concluding the discussion of free recall, we emphasize one point. We have not meant to imply by the discussion of organization in the multitrial situation that such effects are missing on the first trial of the sequence. It has been assumed that these effects are relatively small on the first presentation, and can be ignored without sizable error in situations where randomly selected homogeneous words are presented; in other situations, such as that of categorized free recall, specific search assumptions based upon the proposed organizational structure are incorporated into the model.

Search Models for Paired-Associate Paradigms

The paired-associate situation differs from that of free recall in one primary respect: the search-set is defined in large part by the particular stimulus being tested, and cannot be specified in the model. That is, at test a stimulus is presented and the subject defines a search-set on the basis of the information contained in that stimulus; he does so because he knows that the correct response was initially stored in connection with this stimulus information. The search-set so defined will contain the sought-after image with some relatively high probability, and will probably contain a number of other images whose stimuli are similar in some respect to the tested stimulus. Any one specific image other than the one sought in the search will of course have a probability of being in the search-set which is lower than that of the appropriate image, how much lower being determined in part by the similarity between the two stimuli involved.

For most paired-associate tasks, on any test trial, neither the specific images that compose the search-set nor their total number can be specified in the model. To deal with this problem, we must increase the complexity of the search model. Let $Z_i(j)$ be the probability that the image encoding the jth stimulus will be in the search-set when the ith stimulus is being tested. Then the following statements will usually hold true: $Z_i(j)$ will be larger the more similar are stimuli i and j, lower the longer the lag since the most recent occurrence of stimulus j, and for the case when $i = j$, higher the more information has been stored concerning the jth image.

Just as was the case with free recall, it is initially desirable to apply a search model in a paradigm where the images for different items have relatively low interassociations, or where such interassociations do not affect the search. Perhaps surprisingly, this requirement is difficult to fulfill within traditional paired-associate tasks. In particular, there is a growing body of evidence (not reviewed here) that interitem organization plays an important role in list-structured learning tasks, i.e., tasks in which a fixed set of items is presented over and over again until learned. For such tasks, as Greeno argues in Chapter 8, learning involves considerably more than simple increases in strengths of items; in particular, learning is based upon a growing interitem organization combined with an appropriate search scheme—in Greeno's terms, "learning to retrieve." As a result, these paradigms are inappropriate for a beginning application of search models. Fortunately, tasks are available for which the assumption is tenable that the items are reasonably independent; one of these situations is usually referred to as a "continuous paired-associate learning task" because new items are continually being introduced and old items are continually being dropped.

A search model has recently been applied to two continuous P–A tasks in which a number of independent variables and response measures have simultaneously been examined (Shiffrin, 1968). The experimental variables included the lag between an item's study and test, the number of reinforcements, the total number of preceding items, altering of response members (i.e., proactive interference or negative transfer), and rate of influx of new items. The response measures included the ranking and reranking (following an error) of alternative responses, the proportion correct, the proportion of intrusions and the proportion of "null" responses for both first- and second-guesses, and latencies for responses of all types. On the whole, the model which was applied proved quantitatively accurate in dealing with these variables. Here we now summarize the major points.

Two Continuous Paired-Associate Experiments

Task I: A continuous series of trials was used. Each trial consisted first of a test phase in which a stimulus was presented alone, and then a study phase in which that same stimulus was presented with a response to be learned. Items were given varying numbers of reinforcements (usually 7) at various lags (the lag is the number of items intervening between study and test for an item). The stimuli were consonant trigrams and the responses were the numbers 1, 2, 3, and 4. To respond at test, the subject gave the four responses in the order of their likelihood of being correct; this will be termed the *ranking*. If the response ranked first was incorrect, the subject then was so informed and was asked to give the three remaining responses in the order that he now perceived them to be correct; this is termed the *reranking*. For both ranking and reranking (if necessary) the subject was forced to respond, guessing if necessary.

Task II: A continuous series of trials was used as in the first task. The stimuli were common, short words and the responses were the 26 letters of the alphabet. The subject did not have to respond if he did not know the correct answer; if he did respond and was incorrect, then he was allowed to give a second guess if he wished. Items were given varying numbers of reinforcements at various lags. Almost all items, after a variable number of reinforcements and tests, had their response members altered and were then given several more reinforcements and tests with the new response member. Immediately prior to any study phase on which a change of response was to occur, the subjects were warned that the current stimulus was about to have its response changed. Instructions were to give the most recent response paired with a stimulus; once a response was changed it was never required as a response for that stimulus thereafter, and the subjects knew this.

Before discussing the applications of search models to tasks of the above type, a certain amount of terminology is helpful. When a particular stimulus is presented for test, the image containing the information concerning that stimulus and its correct response will be denoted by the term c-code (c for correct). If the response has been changed, then the image encoding the old and currently incorrect response will be termed an o-code (o for old). All images encoding stimuli not identical to the one tested will be termed i-codes (i for intrusion, since responses generated from inspection of one of these images will be intrusions).

The Lag between Study and Test

The lag between study and test has received considerable attention in recent years, but primarily with respect to the effects of retrieval from STS. Thus, Bjork (1966), Young (1966), and Rumelhart (1967) all demonstrated increasing probability correct as the lag was shortened, but in each case, this increase was attributable to retrieval from the short-term store. Each of these models, in fact, assumed that there was a lower limit to the probability correct determined by the proportion of items that had entered a state of permanent availability. A search model predicts that the probability correct should continue to decrease toward the chance level as lag increases, for any task in which new and homogeneous items are continually being introduced. There are two basic mechanisms which underlie this prediction. The first is an increase in the size of the search-set as lag increases (really, as the total number of input words increases); the second is a decrease in the probability that the c-code will be in the search-set at all. The first mechanism arises because the members of the search-set are determined by similarity to the test stimulus, and the second arises because members of the search-set are determined by temporal factors.

The subject can manipulate the size of the search-set by changing the specificity of the factors determining it, but while a more specific criterion for membership in the search-set will reduce its size, it will likewise reduce the probability that the c-code is included. For any fixed criterion, there will be a larger and larger number of i-codes passing this criterion as the total number of items in memory increases. In the free-recall situation, the size of the search-set affects performance since smaller search-sets gave rise to higher probabilities of a successful recovery prior to search termination. In P–A tasks, an additional forgetting mechanism is present: the larger the search-set, the larger the expected number of i-codes examined prior to the c-code. Because each i-code may give rise to a search-terminating intrusion, larger search-sets will cause decreased performance. These mechanisms alone, however, may be insufficient to explain the observed forgetting with lag size. For one thing, the size of the search-set may be quite small, and only a minimal increase in size may occur as we increase the total number of items presented. In the model that was actually applied to the data, for example, the estimated mean size of the search-set never rose above 5, even after 440 trials and 100 different items. For another, the effects of lag are seen even if we compare tests which are given at equal distances into any session (so that the total number of preceding items is constant).

The primary cause of forgetting with lag is based upon the temporal factors used to define the search-set. In particular, it is assumed that an item's probability of being in the search-set is normally smaller the longer ago the item has last occurred, i.e., the subject tends to search through recent items in preference to older items, everything else being equal. There are two reasons why such a search strategy should be utilized. The first is that recent information is more likely to prove useful, both because the design of most tasks is such that the previous presentation is likely to have occurred recently, and because the subject is bound to have learned preexperimentally that recent information is more valuable than older information, everything else being equal. The second is that the older the temporal period defined for the search-set, the less specific will be the temporal-contextual cues used, and the larger will be the search-set so defined; presumably the subject attempts to limit the size of the search-set. Whatever the justification, however, let us accept the assumption that the probability of an item being in the search-set is a decreasing function of the time (or number of items) since the item was last seen. This holds strictly when no information is available to specify more closely the temporal location of the item; if, for example, we tell the subject the lag of each item just prior to its test, we should expect performance to rise.

The basic lag data for task I are seen in Fig. 10; the probability that the response ranked first will be correct, as a function of the lag between the first reinforcement and test.[6] Since there were four responses, the chance level is .25. It can be seen that the probability is dropping towards chance as the lag increases, but at an ever decreasing rate. Almost all the items retrieved correctly at very long lags are those for which a great deal of strength was initially stored. Also given in Fig. 10 is the conditional probability of a correct *reranking*, given that an incorrect *ranking* was made; the chance level in this case is .33. It may be seen that this "second-guess" probability also decreases toward chance as the lag increases.

The model that was utilized to generate predictions set the probability that a c-code was in the search-set to be a simple function of the strength and "age" of the c-code:

$$Pr(\text{c-code is in search-set}) = Z_j(j) = \frac{s_j}{s_j + B(\text{age})}, \qquad (7)$$

where B is a parameter governing the dependence of $Z_j(j)$ upon "age" and s_j is the strength of the c-code. A most important question arises

[6] In this and subsequent figures, the predicted values from the model which was applied are included in order to demonstrate visually various qualitative features of at least one search model. Since we are not going to present the details of this model, however, these predicted lines may be ignored.

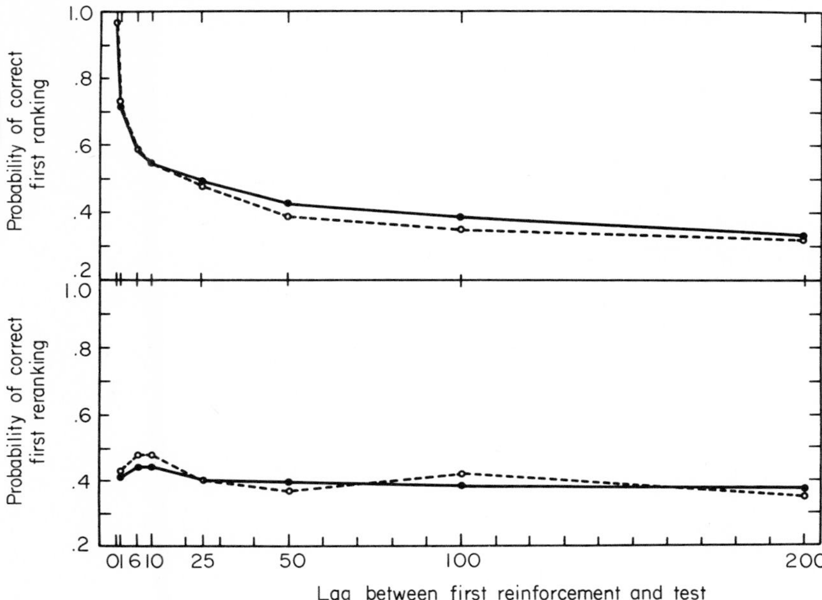

FIG. 10. Probability that the response ranked first is correct (upper panel) and conditional probability (given a first-ranking error) that the response reranked first is correct (lower panel), as a function of the lag following the first reinforcement. (task I). —●— predicted; ––○–– observed.

in the specification of the "age" term; conceivably age could be defined either as total time since last presentation, or lag since last presentation, or the number of new items presented since the last presentation, or the number of unretrievable items since the last presentation. The resolution of this question is important because it determines one of the two basic "forgetting" processes in the model (the other is increased size of search-sets). Thompson (1967) found that intervening well-known items caused much less forgetting than intervening unknown items, but the lags involved were quite small and the result was probably specific to recall from STS. In order to see whether this same result held true for LTS retrieval, lags of a given size (from 10 to 200) were divided into two classes: those for which the intervening items making up the lag had a high average number of reinforcements, and those for which the items making up the lag period had a low average number of reinforcements. The intervening items making up the lags in the first class were presumably well known, and those in the second class relatively unknown. Since task I was not designated to test this question in advance, the two classes of lags did not differ greatly and the resultant effect on recall probability was not large. Nevertheless, recall was found to be significantly poorer when the intervening items had a smaller average number of reinforcements. Thus, we may tentatively generalize Thompson's result to LTS retrieval, and assume that $Z_j(j)$ is a function not simply of the lag since the last presentation, but of the specific nature of the items making up that lag.

Number of Reinforcements

For the most part, the number of reinforcements is a storage variable, and not a retrieval variable, and we therefore will not deal with its effects in this paper. Of course, on the average, the strength stored for an item will increase with the number of reinforcements, but numerous storage models satisfy this requirement, and they will not be expounded here. It is fairly interesting, nevertheless, to consider the effects of covarying number of reinforcements with lag; this was done in task I and the results are shown in Fig. 11. Each panel gives the probability correct for an item with a specific reinforcement-lag history; the lags between successive reinforcements are given in the panels as numbers placed between successive points on the curves. It can be seen that the effects of long lags are much the same following a series of reinforcements as following the first: retrieval is considerably lowered. As seen for item-type 6 in the figure, a long lag (100) following a series of shorter lags (10) causes a considerable decrement in recall probability. This result could be taken to indicate that it is the $Z_j(j)$ probability (the probability that the tested item will be in the search-set), rather than the size of the search-set, which is the predominant forgetting factor in this situation. For if the series of reinforcements at lag 10 is taken to imply that s_j is quite high, then the c-code will be highly likely to be found whenever it is present in the search-set. Thus, the low performance after a subsequent lag of 100 can likely be ascribed to a lowered probability that the c-code has been included in the search-set.

Intrusions

In order to examine intrusions, we must turn to task II, in which responses were not required on every trial. Intrusions occur when an

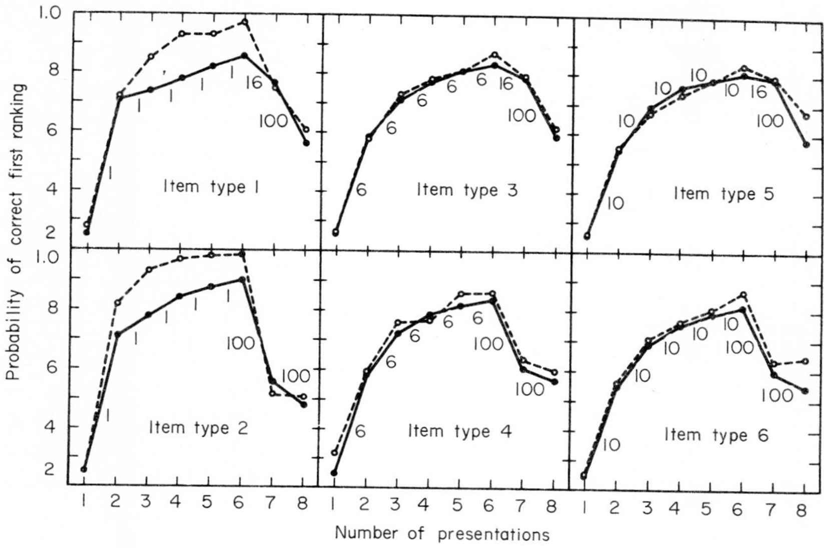

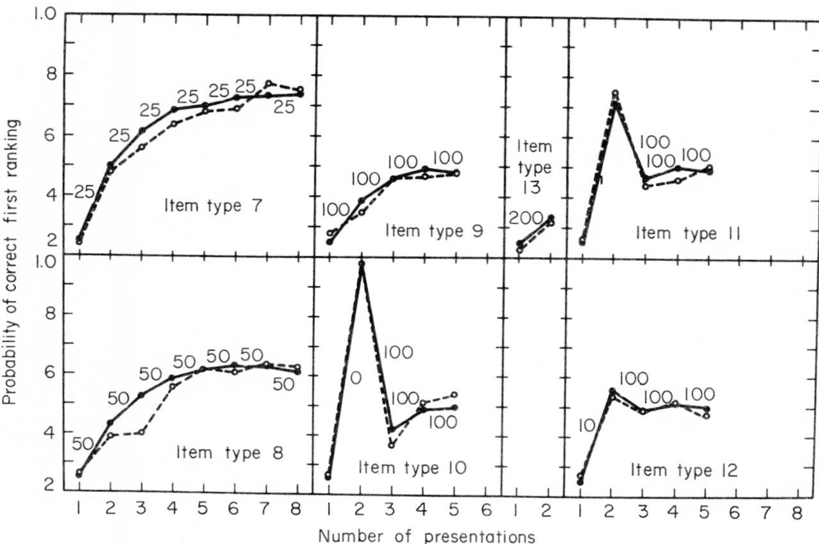

FIG. 11. Probability that the response ranked first is correct for item-types 1-13, as a function of number of reinforcements per item, and successive interreinforcement lags. The small numbers between successive points on the predicted curves give the interreinforcement lags for each item type. (task I). —●— predicted; ——○—— observed.

i-code is included in the search-set and examined, and the encoded response is recovered, accepted and produced (unless this response is correct by chance). Intrusion probabilities are therefore determined by two factors: the probability $Z_j(i)$ that the i-code is included in the search-set, and the probability P_i that the response encoded in the i-code is recovered and produced. $Z_j(i)$ is determined by the similarity of the stimulus members of the *i*th and *j*th items, and by the strength and age of the *i*th item. For most tasks, and certainly for the tasks we are considering, measures for interstimulus similarity are not available. In fact, usually the item in a given presentation position is randomly chosen over sessions and subjects. For these reasons, in many applications a parameter will have to be estimated that controls the average similarity between a c- and i-code. If we consider the dependence upon strength, then we should note that $Z_j(i)$ is a nonlinear function of the strength of an i-code; when s_i is zero, then $Z_j(i)$ must be zero, but if s_i is reasonably large, then it is not all sure that increases in s_i will cause appreciable increases in $Z_j(i)$. The probability, P_i, that the encoded response will be recovered and emitted following the draw of an i-code, is similarly a complex function of the strength of the i-code. In fact, P_i should be an increasing function of the response information encoded, a decreasing function of stimulus information encoded, and some uncertain function of information linking the stimulus and the response.[7]

Taking into account these considerations, we can make two immediate predictions concerning intrusion rates: the first holds that a tested stimulus that has been preceded by a highly similar stimulus (or stimuli) should have a high intrusion probability (and the intrusion should tend to be the response paired with that highly similar stimulus); the second holds that intrusion probability should increase as the total number of presented items increases. The first prediction may be tested most clearly in the case when a response has been altered for a stimulus; in this case the stimulus for the tested item is identical to that for at least one previous item (the o-code). The results may be seen in Fig. 12 in the lower panels. The underlined numbers at the top of each panel give the successive interreinforcement lags *prior* to the change of response

[7] In the model, i-codes were dealt with as follows: any i-code having a strength, s_i, above some minimal level was presumed to have an effective strength s^*, which was used to determine both the probability that this irrelevant code was included in the search-set, and also the probability of recovery given that this irrelevant code was drawn (where both the probabilities are independent of the value s_i). The value s^* was considerably smaller than the average value of s_i, and the difference roughly represented the degree of generalization from the average tested stimulus to the average distractor.

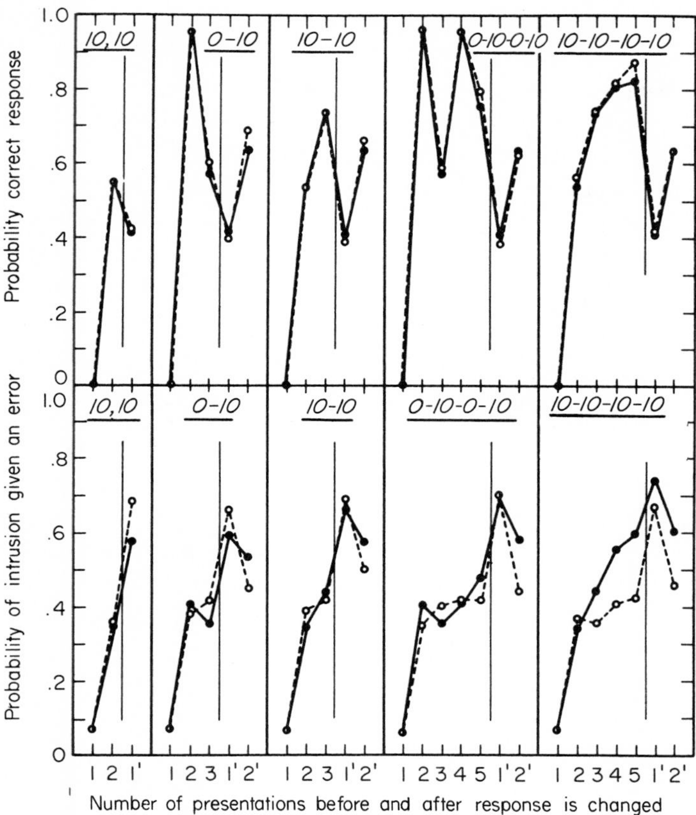

FIG. 12. Probability of correct response and conditional probability (given an error) of an intrusion (as opposed to a failure to respond), as a function of the number of reinforcements prior to and after the change of response; the underlined numbers at the top of each panel give the interreinforcement lags prior to the response change—following the response change each lag is 10. (task II). —●— predicted; --○-- observed.

for an item; following the change of response, all interreinforcement lags were of length 10. The vertical line in each panel indicates the point at which the response is changed for an item. It may clearly be seen that the conditional intrusion rate rises as predicted following the change of response. Furthermore, most of these intrusions (about 5/7 of them on the first trial following the change of response) are the previously correct response for that stimulus. These intrusions of previously correct responses will henceforth be denoted as *old-intrusions*. Other intrusions will be termed *new-intrusions*. Note also that the conditional intrusion rate drops on the second test following the change of response. There are several conceivable explanations for this fact, but the search model predicts it readily since the o-code is older by ten items at the second test in comparison with the first, and the older is the o-code, the less is its probability of being in the search-set.

It can also be seen in Fig. 12 that the intrusion probability on the first test of an item (before it has yet been presented for study) is extremely low, about .07. If a search were made each time a new item was presented for test, then this probability would be expected to be higher than any of the intrusion probabilities prior to the change of response, since the search could never be terminated by a successful recovery. The low probability observed suggests that retrieval in a situation of the present type is really a two-stage process; in the first stage, the subjects perform a recognition test upon the stimulus, and if the stimulus is definitely recognized as being new, then the search terminates at once. The low intrusion rates found indicate that new stimuli are quite often recognized as such; on the other hand, if a decision is made to continue the search (because the stimulus is not recognized as being new) and an intrusion is emitted, then the intrusion rate on the second-guess which follows that intrusion should be very high, since the decision to search memory will presumably remain unchanged. The data strongly confirm this prediction, since the intrusion probability on the second-guess for a new item was about .60, which was as high as, or higher than, the second-guess intrusion probabilities for any other items.

The prediction that intrusions should increase with the number of presented items is also easiest to check for new items (items never presented for study before). Figure 13 gives the average intrusion probabilities for successive blocks of eight new items during the session; that is, the eight new items within a block succeeded one another not directly but after various numbers of interspersed old items. A clear rise in the intrusion rate is seen over the course of the session, a rise that we attribute, in this case, to an increase in the size of the search-set with duration of the session. An alternative explanation, however, could hold that the intrusion rate rises because the probability of making any search at all for a new item increases as the duration of the session increases. The probability of making a search for a new item depends upon the probability of recognizing an item as new, or as old, or neither. If a recognition criterion is used such that a search is made only for

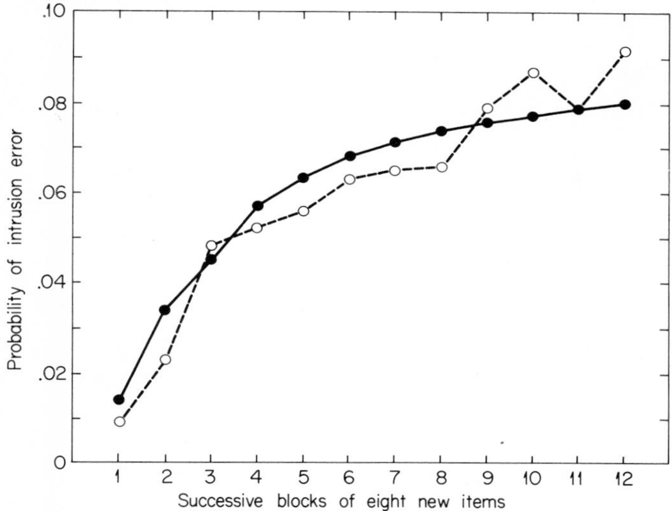

FIG. 13. Probability that a response (intrusion) is given when a stimulus is tested that has not been reinforced previously, as a function of duration of experimental session (individual points are averages over eight consecutive new items). (task II). —●— predicted; ––○–– observed.

items recognized as old, then it is likely that the probability of making a search for a new item will rise over the session. On the other hand, if a criterion is set such that a search is always made except when an item is definitely recognized as being new, then the probability of making a search might not change appreciably over the session. This latter recognition process, which we propose, has been given scant consideration in the literature to date. From the point of view of a search model, however, such a recognition process is quite possible. To recognize an item as new, the subject merely needs to define a search-set that he is reasonably sure will contain at least some information if the item in question has been presented previously, if no information is found in this search-set then the subject can definitely conclude that the item is new. The ability to define such a high probability search-set should depend upon the saliency of characteristics of the stimulus; thus the trigram FKJ is much less likely to be recognized as new than the trigram JFK, given that both are indeed new. These comments are speculative, but the question should prove highly amenable to further research.

Rankings and Second-Guesses

A number of paired-associate experiments have shown that performance on a second response (following information that a first response was incorrect) may be well above chance level (Binford and Gettys, 1965; Bower, 1967b); other experiments have shown that ranking of responses in their order of being correct can result in rankings beyond the first choice which are also above the chance level (Bower, 1967b). The "ranking" result demonstrates that the memory search sometimes results in recovery of partial information about more than one item; two (or more) responses both seem likely to be correct, and the subject ranks them first and second, but sometimes in the incorrect order. The second-guessing result could be explained on this basis, but could also be explained by a model in which the subject initiates a new search of memory once he has been told that he has made an error.

Task I, which utilized rankings and rerankings, should enable us to parcel out these alternative effects. The responses ranked and reranked first should be equivalent to first and second guesses. If the partial information explanation is wholly capable of explaining the data, then we should expect both a ranking effect and a second-guessing effect, and the amount of second-guessing should be predictable from the data are shown in Fig. 14. The abscissa shows the probability of a

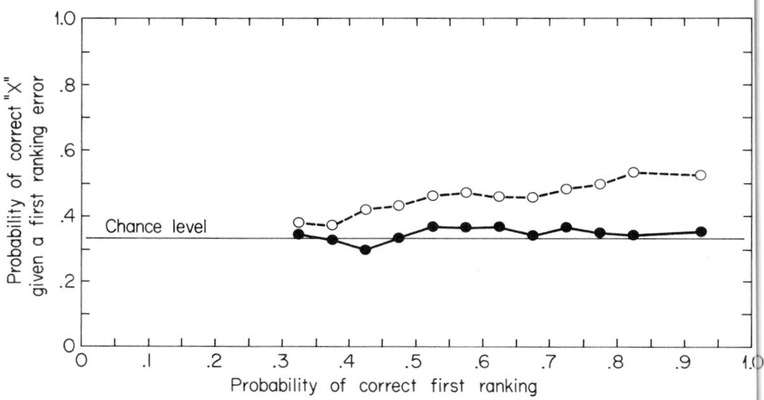

FIG. 14. Probability that the response ranked second is correct, and probability that the response reranked first is correct, both conditional upon an incorrect first-ranking. [A point graphed above the interval $(k, k + .05)$ is based on an average of all trials on which the probability of a correct first-ranking is between k and $k + .05$.] (task I). $x =$ second guess ---○---; $x =$ second ranking —●—.

correct first-ranking, divided into successive intervals which are marked on the graph. For each interval we consider all trials on which the probability of a correct first-ranking lies in that interval. Thus, we partition the 400 trials of any session into classes determined by the probability of a correct first-ranking. For example, interval (.70, .75) determines the set of trials on which the probability of a correct first-ranking was between .70 and .75. We now compute two probabilities: (1) the probability that the response ranked second is correct, and (2) the probability that the response *re*ranked first (the second-guess) is correct. The values of both statistics are computed conditional upon a first-ranking error, so the chance level for each is .33. The results are self-evident; there is a fairly large second-guessing effect, but virtually no ranking effect. This fact demonstrates that subjects were utilizing information to make their second-guess which they were not utilizing to make their rankings. The most likely explanation posits that this information was recovered in a search of memory initiated after the error feedback. The failure to find an appreciable ranking effect was unexpected, but was probably caused by the rapid responding rate of the subjects; apparently the subjects terminated their initial search as soon as the first likely response was recovered (in order to respond quickly), and therefore seldom recovered information about the possible correctness of other responses. Thus, the possibility remains open that under ideal conditions the amount of correct second ranking can be brought up to par with the amount of correct second-guessing; in any conditions, however, second-guessing performance should never be lower than second-ranking performance.

There is only one second-guessing effect from task II that will be discussed here: the probability of giving a correct second-guess following an old-intrusion on the first guess. The results are given in Table 3.

TABLE 3
Conditional Probability of a Correct Second-Guess following an Old-Intrusion

		Successive interreinforcement lags prior to the change of response			
		0 - 10	10 - 10	0-10-0-10	10-10-10-10
Number of presentations following the change of response	1	.31	.27	.23	.27
	2	.54	.50	.51	.39

It can be seen in Table 3 that there is a high probability of a correct second-guess on the first test following the change of response, and an even higher probability on the second test following the change of response. This result has important implications regarding the temporal order of the search. We have been assuming, in accordance with the search model, that draws are made at random within any constituted search-set; in particular, when both the o-code and the c-code are present in the search-set, the o-code is drawn prior to the c-code a good percentage of the time. After error feedback, the search continues and the c-code is often found. It is for this reason that a high correct second-guess probability is expected after an old-intrusion. Although we have not yet suggested such a model, an alternative model in which the codes in the search-set are examined in strictly temporal order, most recent first, is not tenable in the light of the second-guess data. In such a model, an old-intrusion on the first guess would imply either that the c-code was not in the search-set (implying that it was of low strength) or that it was in the search-set but of such low strength so that it failed to give rise to a response when drawn. In either case, the c-code would have low strength and therefore the probability of a correct second-guess would be relatively low; this was not found, however; the probabilities in Table 3 were higher even than those following a first-guess new-intrusion. We may conclude that a *strictly* temporally ordered search through LTS is not tenable. This should be kept in mind because it will have important implications regarding interference, which we will turn to next.

Interference Phenomena

A number of different interference effects are inherent in any search model. We distinguish first between item-specific and nonspecific interference: item-specific interference refers to the case when a single stimulus is paired with more than one response, while nonspecific interference refers to effects caused by similarities among stimuli that are not identical. The distinction is somewhat arbitrary, since differing stimuli can be made as similar to each other as desired, and so-called identical stimuli really differ according to their temporal positioning; nevertheless, the distinction is useful (see Postman, 1961). For either kind of interference, decrements in performance for an item, which are caused by prior presentation of other items, is termed proactive interference; decrements in retrieval for an item caused by subsequent presentation of other items is termed retroactive interference.

In interference terms, the model proposed for free recall predicts both retroactive and proactive effects (nonspecific), and in fact assumes these to be equal. That is, any new item added to a list, whether prior to or subsequent to the item of interest simply has the effect of increasing the size of the search-set by some given amount; the increased size of the search-set then causes reduced retrieval probability.

Item-specific interference has been examined for the most part in list-structured designs, and this fact has made it extremely difficult to separate effects caused by organization over the lists as a whole from effects caused by change of response for individual stimuli. It has sometimes been argued that interference effects found over the lists as a whole (i.e., the A-B, A-C designs) apply to individual stimulus–response connections. Recent work, however, has cast doubt upon this implication. DaPolito (1966) has shown that "interference" effects may be seen for lists when the probability of giving one response to a stimulus is independent of how much has been learned concerning the other response to that stimulus. Further doubt has been cast upon the traditional implications made from list-structured results by findings that recognition tests of performance may fail to reveal interference effects found using recall tests (Postman and Stark, 1969; Bower and Bostrum, 1968).

The position taken by a search model with respect to these results is somewhat intermediate; to the extent that interference is the result of search processes, the effect might be expected to be eliminated through the use of appropriate recognition tests (assuming that the recognition tests bypass the search). On the other hand, recall tests should reveal item-specific interference that holds for individual stimuli, as long as we move from the organizational complexities of the list-structured memory task to a continuous memory task.

Before examining the data, we should consider how a search model handles item-specific interference for a continuous task. Let us initially assume that the probabilities that the c-code and the o-code are included in the search-set are independent and depend only upon the strength and the age of each. Then a certain amount of retrieval loss occurs for each due to nonspecific factors. Item-specific interference arises from those cases where *both* the c-code and o-code are included in the search-set. If we are asking for recall of the response in the c-code, but the o-code is drawn first and the old response emitted, then a proactive interference effect results (P.I.); if the old-response is desired but the c-code is drawn first and the new response emitted, then a retroactive interference effect results (R.I.).

In task II, it was decided to vary the degree of learning of the first response (i.e., the amount of strength stored for the o-code), and then change the response and look for P.I. effects. According to the random draw model, the higher the strength of the o-code, the more often it will be drawn prior to the c-code (when both codes are in the search-set). Thus, increases in the learning of the first response should result in increased P.I.[8] The data are shown in Fig. 12 in the top panels. The probability of being correct at a lag of 10 just prior to the change of response can be seen to vary from .53 to .89. Despite this, the probability of being correct at a lag of 10 following the change of response is essentially constant (.42, .40, .39, .39, .42). Thus, no P.I. is found as a function of the amount of learning of the first response. A general P.I. effect can be seen in that performance at a lag of 10 following the first presentation of the *first* response is about .53, considerably higher than that following the change of response. This general decrease could be due, however, to a decreased probability of storage when the new pairing was first presented (since the subjects were warned at that point that the response was being changed).

This lack of a P.I. effect with amount of learning is unexpected. If the memory search took place in a strictly temporal order, then a P.I. effect would not be expected because the c-code would *always* be examined prior to the o-code; but we have already seen that such an assumption is not tenable (the latency results, to be examined shortly, also rule out such an explanation). Alternatively, we could consider the effects of adding information to the o-code (at the point when the answer is changed) which tells the subject that the answer is now wrong, and not to emit it. If this always occurred, then no P.I. effect would be predicted, but all old-intrusions would also be eliminated. In fact, a large proportion of old-intrusions were emitted in all cases. One tenable explanation posits that the o-code is tagged as being incorrect a variable amount of the time, and that the degree to which this tagging occurs just balances off the P.I. effect for the particular range of conditions examined. From this point of view, the lack of an effect found might be

[8] This task is also referred to in the literature as "negative transfer." We choose not to distinguish between negative transfer and interference for the present type of task.

thought more or less accidental, and it might be felt that an experimental which extends the range of the relevant variables, or alters the task so that coding of an o-code as incorrect is less probable, should reveal P.I. effects as expected. Nevertheless, DaPolito (1966) reported at least one other set of results which confirm those of task II. This discussion of interference does not serve so much to settle any questions as raise new ones, but further research with continuous memory tasks will hopefully lead to a resolution of the current problems.

Latencies

Search models provide a potentially powerful vehicle for the study of latencies. The basic assumption relating latencies to the search mechanism is of extreme simplicity: the latency should be a linear function of the number of draws made prior to response output. In the simplest cases, the only complication that need be considered is the probability that recovery will come from STS; presumably, responses emitted following an STS search will have smaller average latencies than those emitted following an LTS search. For this reason, when the lag is short enough that a significant component of retrieval results from STS, it will be necessary to parcel out probabilistically the short- and long-term components of the observed latency value. Thus, it was found in task II that the latency of correct responses increases as the lag increased from 0 to 10, and this increase can be attributed to a decrease in the probability of retrieval from STS. In this experiment, lags longer than 10 were few, and we therefore cannot tell whether latency increases with lag even when the retrieval from STS is negligible.

There are just a few latency results that shall be considered here. First, the mean latency of correct responses decreased as the number of reinforcements increased, when testing always took place at a lag of 10. This change in correct response latency is a direct prediction of the search model. The greater the number of reinforcements, the greater is the expected strength of the c-code; the higher is the strength of the c-code, the fewer is the expected number of draws before it is examined in the search. This reasoning explains results found by Peterson (1967) and Rumelhart (1967) that mean latencies decreased steadily on trials following the last error for any given paired-associate. Similar reasoning explains why the mean latency of old-intrusions (the emitting of a previously correct response for a stimulus) was markedly less than that of new-intrusions: the o-code has much higher average strength than i-codes.

Correct response latencies after the change of response were markedly slower than prior to the change of response. This result was expected for the following reasons. Following the change of response, a high-strength o-code is likely to be included in the search-set; this o-code may have information stored within it which tells the subject that it is old and incorrect, but it will nevertheless often be examined prior to the c-code, and this examination will increase the mean latency of the correct response. At first glance, it might appear that occasional prior consideration of an o-code will not significantly slow the mean latencies, but this is not so. The predicted mean number of i-codes in the search-set for the model which was applied never rose above 5.0, even on the last trials of the session. The mean number of codes actually examined prior to the c-code is considerably lower than this, perhaps less than 1.0; under these circumstances, the introduction of an o-code into the search-set will markedly increase the mean latency. Further support for these conclusions is found in the following result: the mean latency for correct second-guesses following an old-intrusion (on the first trial following the response change) is slower than the mean latency for correct second-guesses following a new-intrusion. If an old-intrusion is given, the o-code is likely to have a high strength, and hence will tend to be in the search-set again on the second-guess search; it will have been tagged, of course, as being incorrect, but will nevertheless slow the search whenever it is examined.

We shall not discuss latencies further here; the preceding discussion should demonstrate that latencies provide a powerful tool for the examination of the characteristics of the search through the long-term store.

Recognition

Of primary importance to recognition tests is the fact that the actions of search processes may often be verified through the use of recognition tests; whenever the recognition test may be assumed to bypass an extended search, the effects of such a search should be eliminated. There is a fair amount of evidence (e.g., Kintsch, Chapter 11) that recognition tests indeed eliminate extended searches, and we have discussed a number of results which are eliminated with recognition tests and therefore may be attributed to the actions of a search process. These results included interference effects in P-A experiments, the difference between categorized and noncategorized free recall, and the intrusion rates in continuous memory tasks.

It should be noted that a search theory does not propose a sharp dichotomy between recognition and recall tests; recognition tests are supposed to differ from recall tests primarily in the size of the search-sets in the two cases. In appropriately designed recognition experiments, it may be possible to assume that the search-set consists solely of the sought-after image; when this is true, effects depending upon a series of random draws will be eliminated. A considerable amount of work yet remains, however, before it will be possible to identify the set of situations for which this will hold. In task I, for example, each test may formally be considered a forced-choice recognition test, since the stimulus is provided and there are only four possible responses, all well known to the subject. Nevertheless, a number of results indicated that extended searches were taking places; in fact, the model that was applied did not differ from that for task II, in which the response set was much larger. There are several possible reasons why the search-set is not limited in such a situation. The first is based upon the fact that the same responses are used again and again for different stimuli; thus, both the stimulus and response on any test will individually be recognized as having occurred, but the positive recognition will not help the subject decide whether the two had previously been paired. A related possibility is that the test information provided is not complete; although the stimulus and response are available, the code used to store the two is not, and since the retrieval task in this case is primarily to retrieve the code, the test is really one of recall (this hypothesis is closely related to that of Martin, 1968). Other possibilities also exist, and the correct alternative may not yet be known. In any event, it is important to determine which kinds of experimental manipulations lead to search-sets of small size. Although the problem is usually not phrased in this way, a number of current lines of work within the recognition framework are engaged in answering this question.

One final point in connection with recognition should be reiterated. As was pointed out in the discussion of intrusions, the distinction between recognition and recall can be carried over to the test of whether a particular item has *not* been presented. That is, sometimes a search-set can be defined that *should* contain relevant information if the item in question has been presented; if this search-set does not contain the expected information then the item can be recognized as new. If the search-set involved is large, then draws will have to be made from it, and the task will be akin to recall; if the set is small, then an extended search will not be required and the task will be akin to one of recognition.

Summary and Conclusion

A general theory of search and retrieval from memory has been described; in this theory, retrieval is formulated as a recursive search. The stages of the search are seen to correspond fairly close to our intuitions regarding the nature of such a process. These states consist firstly of general decisions regarding what memory store to examine, and what search-set to select. The search-set is a collection of units of information (called I-units) typically arranged into interassociated groups called images. A draw is made from the selected search-set, where the draw consists of the random selection of one of the I-units in the search-set. The next stage consists of the recovery and examination of I-units closely associated with the I-unit drawn. On the basis of this information recovered, decisions are made determining whether to emit a response, what response to emit, and whether to emit a response, what response to emit, and whether to terminate or continue with the search. If the search is continued then the next loop of the recursion begins with the selection of a search-set (often the one utilized for the previous draw). The search continues in this manner until a response is emitted, time runs out, or the subject terminates it unsuccessfully on his own initiative.

Applications of this theory have been discussed in detail for retrieval from the long-term store, as seen in the free verbal recall situation. It is shown that a very simple search model can deal with almost all the available data concerning single-trial free verbal recall, including list length, presentation time per item, and number of presentations per item. A slight generalization of the model allows it to successfully predict the data from a variety of categorized list paradigms. Further extensions to the multitrial paradigm have also been considered.

The search models have also been applied to the paired-associate paradigms. The predictions from the search models have been discussed in relation to a number of commonly examined variables. These include the lag between presentation and test, the number of reinforcements, intrusions, rankings and second-guesses, interference phenomena, and latencies. The discussions are augmented by selected data from two continuous paired-associate tasks.

On the basis of these various considerations, we conclude that the search process merits inclusion in theories of memory. On the one hand, it provides the power to deal with traditional concepts such as forgetting and interference in a new, inclusive, and quantitative manner. On the other hand, it provides quantitative predictions for results, such as intrusions and second-guesses, about which other theories have relatively little to say. For some theories, such as interference theory, the present views may provide an alternative; for others, such as those of Greeno and Kintsch in Chapters 8 and 11 of the present volume, Norman (1968), Atkinson and Shiffrin (1965, 1968), and Shiffrin and Atkinson (1969), the present theory provides a generalization. We admit that the specific models proposed, especially those for the paired-associate situation, are still in the exploratory stage; yet the results to date are encouraging, and the general theory appears to be a promising approach to a number of traditional and recent problems in memory.

Appendix

The predictions for the various free-recall experiments were derived from the following version of Eq. 5:

$$P(C_i) = \sum_{j=1} \{1 - [1 - (j\theta t/S)(1 - e^{-j\theta t})]^D\}\{f_i(s)\},$$

in which $r = 4$, $\theta = .04$, and $D = 34$. (In practice, the sum is taken only to $j = 20$ because $f_i(s)$ is vanishingly small for $j > 20$.) Hence, we have for $i \geqslant 4$, and i prior to the recency effect:

$$P(C_i) = \sum_{j=1}^{20} \left(1 - \left\{1 - \left[\frac{jt(.04)}{S}\right]\left[1 - e^{-jt(.04)}\right]\right\}^{34}\right)\left[\left(\frac{3}{4}\right)^{j-1}\left(\frac{1}{4}\right)\right]$$

(A slight modification of this equation is required for $i \leqslant 4$, but is not given here.) It may be seen that the probability correct for any item is dependent only on t, the time for which it was presented, and S, the total strength stored for the entire list. The value of t in any case is simply the number of seconds per item if the item is presented once, or the number of seconds per item multiplied by n, if the item is presented n times.

The value of S is easy to determine: since θ is the rate of transfer of information to LTS per item per second, the total information transferred equals S equals $4\theta T + W$, where T is the total presentation time per list and W represents additional information stored in LTS after presentation of the list has concluded. In practice, W was set equal to 16θ, which would be the mean amount of additional information stored if the buffer continued to operate after the list terminated. This assumption is rather arbitrary, but for reasonably long lists, the precise value of W is relatively unimportant because it is small in relation to $4\theta T$. Substituting for S in the above equation, we thus have:

$$P(C_i) = \sum_{j=1}^{20} \left(1 - \left\{1 - \left(\frac{jt}{4T + 16}\right)\left[1 - e^{-(.04)jt}\right]\right\}^{34}\right)\left(\frac{3}{4}\right)^{j-1}\left(\frac{1}{4}\right).$$

The values of T and t are of course easy to calculate for any given free recall paradigm, and the above equation was used to generate predictions for the various paradigms discussed in the paper. To calculate mean number output per list rather than probability, we simply add the $P(C_i)$ for the various items in the list.

References

ALLEN, M. Rehearsal strategies and response cueing as determinants of organization in free recall. *Journal of Verbal Learning and Verbal Behavior*, 1968, **7**, 58–63.

ASCH, S. E., AND EBENHOLTZ, S. M. The principle of associative symmetry. *Proceedings of the American Philosophical Society*, 1962, **106**, 135–163.

ATKINSON, R. C., AND SHIFFRIN, R. M. Mathematical models for memory and learning. Paper read at the meeting of the Third Conference on Learning, Remembering, and Forgetting, October, 1965, Princeton, New Jersey. Technical Report No. 79, Institute for Mathematical Studies in the Social Sciences, Stanford University, 1965.

ATKINSON, R. C., AND SHIFFRIN, R. M. Human memory: A proposed system and its control processes. In K. W. Spence and J. T. Spence (Eds.), *Advances in the psychology of learning and motivation research and theory*. Vol. II. New York: Academic Press, 1968.

BERNBACH, H. A. Decision processes in memory. *Psychological Review*, 1967, **74**, 462–480.

BINFORD, J. R., AND GETTYS, C. Nonstationarity in paired-associate learning as indicated by a second guess procedure. *Journal of Mathematical Psychology*, 1965, **2**, 190–195.

BJORK, R. A. Learning and short-term retention of paired-associates in relation to specific sequences of interpresentation intervals. Technical Report No. 106, Institute for Mathematical Studies in the Social Sciences, Stanford University, 1966.

BOUSFIELD, W. A. The occurrence of clustering in the recall of randomly arranged associates. *Journal of General Psychology*, 1953, **49**, 229–240.

BOUSFIELD, W. A., AND BARCLAY, W. D. The relationship between order and frequency of occurrence of restricted associative responses. *Journal of Experimental Psychology*, 1950, **40**, 643–647.

BOUSFIELD, W. A., AND COHEN, B. H. Clustering in recall as a function of the number of word-categories in stimulus-word lists. *Journal of General Psychology*, 1956, **54**, 95–106.

BOUSFIELD, W. A., AND PUFF, C. R. Clustering as a function of response dominance. *Journal of Experimental Psychology*, 1964, **67**, 76–79.

BOUSFIELD, W. A., AND SEDGEWICK, C. H. W. An analysis of sequences of restricted associative responses. *Journal of General Psychology*, 1944, **30**, 149–165.

BOUSFIELD, W. A., STEWARD, J. R., AND COWAN, T. M. The use of free associational norms for the prediction of clustering. *Journal of General Psychology*, 1964, **70**, 205–214.

BOWER, G. H. Notes on a descriptive theory of memory. In D. P. Kimble (Ed.), *Proceedings of the second conference on learning, remembering and forgetting.* New York: New York Academy of Sciences, 1967. (a)

BOWER, G. H. A multicomponent theory of the memory trace. In K. W. Spence and J. T. Spence (Eds.), *Advances in the psychology of learning and motivation research and theory*. Vol. I. New York: Academic Press, 1967. (b)

BOWER, G. H., AND BOSTRUM, A. Absence of within-list PI and RI in short-term recognition memory. *Psychonomic Science*, 1968, **10**, 211–212.

BROADBENT, D. E. *Perception and communication.* New York: Macmillan (Pergamon), 1958.

BUGELSKI, B. R., KIDD, E., AND SEGMEN, J. Image as a mediator in one-trial paired-associate learning. *Journal of Experimental Psychology*, 1968, **76**, 69–73.

COFER, C. N. A study of clustering in free recall based on synonyms. *Journal of General Psychology*, 1959, **60**, 3–10.

COFER, C. N. On some factors in the organizational characteristics of free recall. *American Psychologist*, 1965, **20**, 261–272.

COFER, C. N. Some evidence for coding processes derived from clustering in free recall. *Journal of Verbal Learning and Verbal Behavior*, 1966, **5**, 188–192.

COHEN, B. H. An investigation of recoding in free recall. *Journal of Experimental Psychology*, 1963, **65**, 368–376. (a)

COHEN, B. H. Recall of categorized word lists. *Journal of Experimental Psychology*, 1963, **66**, 227–234. (b)

COHEN, B. H. Some-or-none characteristics of coding. *Journal of Verbal Learning and Verbal Behavior*, 1966, **5**, 182–187.

DAPOLITO, F. J. Proactive effects with independent retrieval of competing responses. Unpublished doctoral dissertation, Indiana University, 1966.

DEESE, J. On the structure of associative meaning. *Psychological Review*, 1962, **69**, 161–175.

DEESE, J., AND KAUFMAN, R. A. Serial effects in recall of unorganized and sequentially organized verbal material. *Journal of Experimental Psychology*, 1957, **54**, 180–187.

ESTES, W. K. The statistical approach to learning theory. In S. Koch (Ed.), *Psychology: A study of a science.* Vol. 2. New York: McGraw-Hill, 1959.

ESTES, W. K., AND TAYLOR, H. A. A detection method and probabilistic models for assessing information processing from brief visual displays. *Proceedings of the National Academy of Sciences, U. S.*, 1964, **52**, No. 2, 446–454.

FEIGENBAUM, E. A. The simulation of verbal learning behavior. In E. A. Feigenbaum and J. Feldman (Eds.), *Computers and thought.* New York: McGraw-Hill, 1963.

GLANZER, M., AND CUNITZ, A. R. Two storage mechanisms in free recall. *Journal of Verbal Learning and Verbal Behavior*, 1966, **5**, 351–360.

GLANZER, M., AND MEINZER, A. The effects of intralist activity on free recall. *Journal of Learning and Verbal Behavior*, 1967, **6**, 928–935.

GREEN, D. M., AND SWETS, J. A. *Signal detection theory and psychophysics.* New York: Wiley, 1966.

JAMES, W. *The principles of psychology.* Vol. 1. New York: Holt, 1890.

KINTSCH, W. Memory and decision aspects of recognition learning. *Psychological Review,* 1967, **74,** 496–504.

MCGILL, W. J. Stochastic latency mechanisms. In R. D. Luce, R. R. Bush, and E. Galanter, (Eds.), *Handbook of mathematical psychology.* Vol. I. New York: Wiley, 1963.

MANDLER, G. Organization and memory. In K. W. Spence and J. T. Spence (Eds.), *Advances in the psychology of learning and motivation research and theory.* Vol. I. New York: Academic Press, 1967.

MARTIN, E. Stimulus meaningfulness and paired-associate transfer: An encoding variability hypothesis. *Psychological Review,* 1968, **75,** 421–441.

MURDOCK, B. B., JR. The serial position effect of free recall. *Journal of Experimental Psychology,* 1962, **64,** 482–488.

MURDOCK, B. B., JR. Short-term retention of single paired-associates. *Journal of Experimental Psychology,* 1963, **65,** 433–443.

MURDOCK, B. B., JR. Effects of a subsidiary task on short-term memory. *British Journal of Psychology,* 1965, **56,** 413–419.

MURDOCK, B. B., JR., AND BABICK, A. J. The effect of repetition on the retention of individual words. *American Journal of Psychology,* 1961, **74,** 596–601.

NEISSER, U. *Cognitive psychology.* New York: Appleton-Century-Crofts, 1967.

NORMAN, D. A. Toward a theory of memory and attention. *Psychological Review,* 1968, **75,** 522–536.

NORMAN, D. A., AND WAUGH, N. C. Stimulus and response interference in recognition-memory experiments. *Journal of Experimental Psychology,* 1968, **78,** 551–559.

PETERSON, L. R. Search and judgment in memory. In B. Kleinmuntz (Ed.), *Concepts and the structure of memory.* New York: Wiley, 1967.

POSTMAN, L. The present status of interference theory. In C. N. Cofer (Ed.), *Verbal learning and verbal behavior.* New York: McGraw-Hill, 1961.

POSTMAN, L. Short-term memory and incidental learning. In A. W. Melton (Ed.), *Categories of human learning.* New York: Academic Press, 1964.

POSTMAN, L., AND PHILLIPS, L. W. Short-term temporal changes in free recall. *Quarterly Journal of Experimental Psychology,* 1965, **17,** 132–138.

POSTMAN, L., AND STARK, K. Role of response availability in transfer and interference. *Journal of Experimental Psychology,* 1969, **79,** 168–177.

RUMELHART, D. E. The effects of interpresentation intervals in a continuous paired-associate task. Technical Report No. 116, Institute for Mathematical Studies in the Social Sciences, Stanford University, 1967.

RUMELHART, D. E. A multicomponent theory of the perception of briefly exposed visual displays. *Journal of Mathematical Psychology,* 1969, in press.

RUNQUIST, W. N., AND FARLEY, F. H. The use of mediators in the learning of verbal paired associates. *Journal of Verbal Learning and Verbal Behavior,* 1964, 3, 280–285.

SHIFFRIN, R. M. Search and retrieval processes in long-term memory. Technical Report No. 137, Institute for Mathematical Studies in the Social Sciences, Stanford University, 1968.

SHIFFRIN, R. M., AND ATKINSON, R. C. Storage and retrieval processes in long-term memory, *Psychological Review,* 1969, **76,** 179–193.

SPERLING, G. A. The information available in brief visual presentations. *Psychological Monographs,* 1960, **74,** (11, Whole No. 498).

THOMPSON, W. J., Recall of paired-associate items as a function of interpolated pairs of different types. *Psychonomic Science,* 1967, **9,** 629–630.

TULVING, E. Subjective organization in free recall of "unrelated" words. *Psychological Review*, 1962, **69**, 344–354.

TULVING, E. Subjective organization and effects of repetition in multitrial free-recall learning. *Journal of Verbal Learning and Verbal Behavior*, 1966, **5**, 193–197.

TULVING, E. The effects of presentation and recall of material in free-recall learning. *Journal of Verbal Learning and Verbal Behavior*, 1967, **6**, 175–184.

TULVING, E., AND PEARLSTONE, Z. Availability versus accessibility of information in memory for words. *Journal of Verbal Learning and Verbal Behavior*, 1966, **5**, 381–391.

WAUGH, N. C. The effect of intralist repetition on free recall. *Journal of Verbal Learning and Verbal Behavior*, 1962, **1**, 95–99.

WAUGH, N. C. Immediate memory as a function of repetition. *Journal of Verbal Learning and Verbal Behavior*, 1963, **2**, 107–112.

WAUGH, N. C. Presentation time and free recall. *Journal of Experimental Psychology*, 1967, **73**, 39–44.

WAUGH, N. C., AND NORMAN, D. A. Primary memory. *Psychological Review*, 1965, **72**, 89–104.

WOLFORD, G. R., WESSEL, D. L., AND ESTES, W. K. Further evidence concerning scanning and sampling assumptions of visual detection models. *Perception & Psychophysics*, 1968, **3**, 439–444.

YOUNG, J. L. Effects of intervals between reinforcements and test trials in paired-associate learning. Technical Report No. 101, Institute for Mathematical Studies in the Social Sciences, Stanford University, 1966.

YOUNG, R. K. Serial learning. In T. R. Dixon, and D. L. Horton (Eds.), *Verbal behavior and general behavior theory*. Englewood Cliffs, New Jersey: Prentice-Hall, 1968.

V

INFORMATION PROCESSING AND MEMORY

13

Information Processing and Memory

Edward A. Feigenbaum[1]
Stanford University

Introduction

EPAM (Elementary Perceiver and Memorizer) is one of a class of computer-simulation models of cognitive processes that have been developed in the last decade. These are models of human information processing in certain learning and problem-solving tasks. This chapter is not intended as a survey of this literature. The reader who wishes to become acquainted with a wide variety of research projects in this area is advised to seek out the book *Computers and Thought* (Feigenbaum and Feldman, 1963).

In this chapter, I shall first sketch briefly the history of the EPAM project, without which the remainder of the discussion is not very meaningful. Next, I will attempt to reinterpret the EPAM theory in terms of

[1] This chapter is reprinted from the *Proceedings of the Fifth Berkeley Symposium on Mathematical Statistics and Probability, Volume IV, Biology and Health, 1966.* (Berkeley, University of California Press, 1966), at the suggestion of the author and with consent of the Regents of the University of California.

an emerging three-level theory of human memory. In the remainder of the chapter, I would like to explore some questions relating to a theory of human long-term associative memory.

Work on the various EPAM models began many years ago. The research has always been a joint effort by myself and Professor Herbert A. Simon of Carnegie Institute of Technology. We have been concerned with modeling the information processes and structures that underlie behavior in a wide variety of verbal learning tasks. These include the standard serial and paired-associate learning tasks, and other not-so-standard verbal learning tasks.

EPAM I was a very simple model—so simple, in fact, that a mathematical formulation, as well as a computer simulation, was constructed. In EPAM I, we postulated a serial mechanism in which the learning of verbal materials took a nontrivial amount of time. We explored the strategies used by subjects to organize their total learning task. The model generated an accurate quantitative prediction of the well-known bowed serial error curve, which plots the percentage of total errors made by subjects at each serial position of a relatively long serially-presented list of words.

EPAM II was a much more comprehensive model. It specified *structures* in which memorized items are stored and retrieved. It specified *processes* for learning discriminations between items; for learning associations among items; and for the familiarization of new items. It specified many other processes for (among many things) responding, attention focusing, and the analysis of environmental feedback. The model generated qualitative and quantitative predictions for more than a dozen of the standard and well-known phenomena of human verbal learning. EPAM II is described in Feigenbaum (1963) and also by Newell and Simon (1963).

The EPAM III model was a reconceptualization and generalization of the processes and structures of EPAM II. It attacked the problem of building up very general associative structures in memory (other than word learning); the association of a familiarized stimulus in an arbitrary number of associative contexts; the construction and storage of internal representations of new stimulus experiences by recognizing and bringing together already learned internal representations (that is, already familiar experiences). With this model, we made certain additional predictions about the effects of similarity, familiarity and meaningfulness in verbal learning tasks. These predictions, as well as a brief description of EPAM III, are contained in Simon and Feigenbaum (1964).

Through the references cited, the reader can pursue the structure of the various EPAM models to the depth motivated by his interests. He would be well advised to be prepared to accept and understand the jargon and notation of the nonnumeric symbol-manipulating computer languages, especially those that deal with list processing.

Information Processing and Memory

Though the quest for an adequate theory of memory is as old as psychology itself, it has been pursued with significantly increased vigor and success in the last decade. This is due in part to increased sophistication in the art of conducting experiments on memory, at the level of neural processes and at the level of psychological processes. In part, it is due also to the desire to explore possible implications for memory theory of the exciting developments in the theory of biological information encoding and storage mechanisms. And, in part, this new vigor is the result of the introduction in the 1950's, and subsequent widespread acceptance of, a new vocabulary of terms and concepts for describing cognitive processes: the language of *information processing* theory. Such terms as buffer storage, coding, retrieval processes, and processing strategy are familiar and commonly used labels, even among those psychologists who do not think of themselves as information processing theorists.

This attempt to bring a reasonable amount of order to the study of memory has been two headed: the search for an adequate description of memory processes and the search for models of the information storage structures that might be involved. This section of the chapter presents the elements of an information processing theory of memory incorporating an integrated set of hypotheses about both information processes and information structures of memory. The EPAM model consists of information processes and structures for *learning* and *performance* in paired-associate and serial verbal learning tasks. The job of the EPAM performance processes is to retrieve appropriate responses from the memory structures when the task so dictates. EPAM has two major learning processes: discrimination learning and stimulus familiarization. The former discovers differences between items being learned and those already learned, and builds up the memory structure to incorporate tests on these differences, so that storage and retrieval can take place with a minimum of stimulus generalization and confusion.

The latter builds internal representations, called *images*, of verbal items being learned. It is an integrative process, in which previously familiarized parts of a stimulus item are first recognized and then "assembled" (according to a strategy) to form the internal representation. As previously mentioned, the EPAM model also contains a number of other mechanisms for attention focusing, organization of the learning task, associative recall, and so forth, which will not be discussed here.

EPAM, as it stands, is a *psychological* theory of certain elementary cognitive processes, framed at the so-called *information processing level*. The primitives at this level are primitives concerning elementary symbol manipulation processes. These primitives are not, at this stage of our knowledge, directly translatable into "neural language," that is, statements about how the processes are realized in the underlying neural machinery. Some fruitful conjectures about this have been made (Pribram, Ahumada, Hartog, and Roos, 1964), however, and more can be expected as increasing confidence in the adequacy of the information processing theory is attained.

An Information Processing Theory of Memory

We proceed now to summarize elements of a theory of memory that the work on EPAM has suggested to us. That part of the presentation dealing with permanent storage is, to some extent, conjectural, since these mechanisms have not been precisely defined or rigorously explored, though they have been suggested by shortcomings in EPAM.

PRIMITIVE POSTULATES ABOUT PROCESS

(a) At the information processing level, the central processing mechanism is essentially *serial*, that is, capable of performing one, or at most a very few, elementary processes at any time.

(b) Each elementary information process takes *time* to perform. To carry out a series of processes requires [by (a)] an amount of time roughly equal to the sum of processing times of the constituent processes. Even for "simple" psychological processes, this processing time may be significantly long when compared with, for example, item presentation rates typically encountered in verbal learning experiments.

These two fundamental ideas are at the root of all EPAM predictions. This is as true of the earliest model, one that predicted only the serial position effect (Feigenbaum and Simon, 1962) as it is of the later, more comprehensive, models (Simon and Feigenbaum, 1964). Neither we nor others has been able to construct an alternate basic formulation that achieves the same results. Postulate (b) we interpret as identical with the "consolidation hypothesis" suggested by McGaugh (1965) and others on the basis of laboratory experiments with animals using electroconvulsive shock and various drug treatments.

The consolidation hypothesis is an empirical generalization. The EPAM theory generates complex and accurate predictions of verbal learning behavior on the basis of an identical postulate inferred from an entirely different empirical base. Taken together, they provide strong confirmation for the basic correctness of the position.

HYPOTHESES ABOUT STRUCTURE

We hypothesize three types of information storage structures:

(a) An immediate memory: a buffer storage mechanism of extremely small size, holding a few symbols. Inputs from the peripheral sensing and encoding mechanisms are held here in a state of availability for further central processing. The immediate memory provides the only channel of communication between the central processes and the sensing processes at the periphery. Central processes may use the immediate memory for temporary storage of internally generated symbols; these then compete for storage with arriving input symbols. The net result of such an immediate memory mechanism is that the total processing system has a very narrow "focus of attention," that is, the central processes can attend to only a minuscule portion of the external stimulus environment at any time.

(b) Acquisition memory: the term is chosen to contrast with long-term permanent store [see (c), below]. It refers to a large working memory for discrimination and familiarization processes. In it are built the internal representations of stimulus objects being learned. In its structure is stored the information necessary to discriminate among the learned objects. This memory has a *tree* structure, called the *discrimination net.* At each nonterminal nodal level is stored a testing process, a *discriminator,* which tests some feature of a stimulus object and sorts the object along the appropriate branch to the next nodal level. The termini of the tree are storage locations at which images, assemblages of symbols constituting the internal representation of an external object, are stored.

It is this memory structure upon which most of the EPAM work has been done, and whose structure is best understood.

(c) The permanent store: this memory structure considered for practical purposes as being of essentially unlimited size, is the long-term permanent repository of the images. The images are linked together in a highly interconnected web of cross associations. Thus, the structure of this memory is not treelike. However, it is plausible that this structure is "indexed" by a discrimination net like the one described above, for efficient cross referencing and searching.

HYPOTHESES ABOUT PROCESS

The theory contains a number of hypotheses about memory-processing activity, only a few of which will be summarized at this point. Others will be touched on in the discussions below.

(a) Working at the level of the acquisition memory, a matching process scans stimulus encodings and images serially for differences on the basis of which discriminators are constructed. The scan is controlled by a noticing order, an adaptive attention-focusing strategy.

(b) Image building in the acquisition memory consists of assembling at a terminal node in an orderly way (that is, controlled by a strategy) *cue-tokens,* which reference other images in the net.

(c) The discrimination net of the acquisition memory over time is elaborated (that is, necessary discriminators and branches are grown) as the task demands finer discriminations for successful performance. The discrimination net is grown in a wholly pragmatic manner, its growth at any stage reflecting what is just adequate for correct performance. There is no attempt at this level to structure or restructure the net for efficiency or logical order.

(d) At the level of the permanent storage, it is hypothesized that a process transfers images, discrimination information, and perhaps even subnets of the acquisition memory to the permanent store, dismantling the structure of the working memory as it processes it. The transferred information is reorganized and tied into the web structure of the permanent store according to an organizational scheme which is more logical and better suited to the long-term retrieval needs of the organism than the pragmatically built structure of the acquisition memory.

Having thus summarized our basic hypotheses about structure and process in a three-level memory, we proceed to describe and discuss each of these levels in more detail.

Further Considerations about Immediate Memory

Our theory holds that the immediate memory is a fast-access, low-capacity storage system whose function is primarily to buffer encoded sensory inputs. We conceive of the immediate memory as being ultra-dynamic, the average length of time of residence of a symbol therein being of the order of seconds, although the stay can be extended under control of a central process by recycling. At any given moment of time, the set of symbols in the immediate memory is *the* operational stimulus environment of the organism. This position is consistent with and contributory to our fundamental postulate that the central processes are basically serial.

The need for such a buffer storage mechanism is twofold. First, since the performance and acquisition processes consume a significant amount of time, it is necessary to hold on to the inputs lest they vanish before any processing can be done on them. Second, buffer storage provides a necessary decoupling of the central processes from the peripheral processes sensing the external environment. This decoupling, relieving the central processes of the impossible burden of instant-by-instant attention to the environment, is absolutely essential because many of the time-consuming acquisition processes are searching or, what is worse, manipulating memory structure and cannot be interrupted at arbitrary times.

It is interesting to note in passing that in large nonbiological information-processing machines (any of the modern familiar digital computer systems), buffered data channels are used for reasons identical with the decoupling argument given above. We cannot here explain the difficulties encountered in operating the early digital computer systems without buffered information transfer. No modern computer system of which we are aware is built without some input/output buffering.

Further Considerations Concerning Acquisition Memory

The acquisition memory is conceptualized as an intermediate level of storage between the ultradynamic immediate memory and the relatively slowly changing permanent store. It is the "working memory" in which the discrimination and familiarization processes classify, and build internal representations of, the current environmental context and the objects thereof. Performance of "current task" is done by referencing the net; images are not stored in this memory indefinitely, but rather, for times of the order of many minutes to a few hours.

It follows that since the information in the acquisition memory is not yet permanently fixed, and since this memory level stores the recently learned context, it might be possible to disturb this memory, destroying its contents, though this would not be so simple a matter as in the immediate memory, where merely a shift of attention suffices. We conjecture that the retrograde amnesia, affecting the memory of recent learning, observed in animals given electroconvulsive shock shortly after a learning trial is a manifestation of just such a destructive disturbance of acquisition memory before the permanent storage processes have had time to operate.

The discrimination net memory of EPAM is our model of the structure of the acquisition memory. When an object is presented to the acquisition processes for learning, the net is grown to provide a unique terminal location in which to build up the image of the object (that is, to familiarize it), if no such location is already available. *Sorting* an encoded object through the discrimination net will retrieve the stored image of the object for further processing or for response generation. The discriminators used in growing the net to make finer and finer discriminations among the objects entering the learned set are constructed from differences found by *matching* processes that compare objects with previously stored images. *Recognition* of an object is the result of sorting the object to a terminal and finding no differences between the object and the image stored there.

Familiarization of an object is done roughly as follows (though we can not go into all the details of the process here). All images (except the so-called elementary images, which are merely stored property strings) are built by listing a set of reference pointers to the net locations of the images of recognized (that is, already familiar) subobjects of the object being familiarized. These pointers are *cue-tokens* of the familiar parts comprising the object. There is only one image for each familiar object in the net, but there may be any number of cue-tokens of this image stored in the context of any number of other images. When an image is processed for some reason, e.g., for generating a response, the tokens of subpart images are used to retrieve the subpart images themselve as necessary. Thus, in summary, an object is familiarized in this memory only by the process of listing tokens of already familiar subobjects. If a subobject can not be recognized in the net, it must first itself be made familiar before it can be used in the construction of the image of the higher-level object.

The image-building processes of EPAM are essentially recoding or "chunking" processes. No matter how complex a stimulus object may be, after the image of that object has been built a single symbol, its cue-token, will be sufficient to signify its presence as a constituent of any other complex stimulus context being memorized. Thus, all stored images turn out to have roughly the same informational complexity (that is, number of symbols needed to represent them in the storage), though, of course, the processing that may have to be done to retrieve details of a particular image may be a complex search. We see here operating the trade-off, often pointed out by computer scientists, between the complexity of the storage representation and the complexity of the retrieval processes. The EPAM model inclines toward simplicity and homogeneity in the storage representation and complexity of retrieval processing. Thus, for example, the response generation process of EPAM is not a simple find-and-output affair but rather a multilayered recursive *constructive* process (Pribram has called this kind of process "*re*membering, as opposed to *dis*membering").

Two additional observations about the discrimination net will be useful. First, the structure of the discrimination net is the embodiment of all the discrimination learning that has taken place during the acquisition of the items stored in the net. That is, there is no separate storage for the information learned during discrimination learning. Second, the net is built by processes that are under the control of a learning strategy. Among other things, this strategy is responsible for the analysis of the information concerning correct and incorrect performance that is fed back to the subject by the experimental procedure. It decides what is causing incorrect responding and what to do about it. It does this by the application of the following "satisficing" heuristic: an addition or change to the net structure or image information that just works (gets rid of the immediate performance problem) is "good enough." As a result, the net is grown in a pragmatic fashion, no attention being paid to the inherent "logic" of the classification task that the net is performing for the system. This heuristic strategy is useful in the short run in that it allows EPAM to learn experimental tasks with reasonable amounts of processing effort. In general, it will not be the best way to organize information for purposes of long-term storage. We shall return to this argument in the next section. These hypotheses about structure and process in the acquisition memory have many interesting consequences in terms of the learning and performance behavior of EPAM. These consequences constitute the validating evidence for the EPAM theory. We shall mention just one result, a rather startling one, since it is a direct consequence of no single process or structure, but is rather a complex consequence of the interaction of many processes and the discrimination net.

The result is this: EPAM exhibits *forgetting behavior* even though there is no destruction or decay of images or tokens stored in the memory. Using traditional labels, this behavior is described as oscillation (in the learning of a single list of items) and retroactive inhibition (in the learning of more than one list).

These two types of forgetting behavior have a single EPAM explanation. The discrimination net must grow to store new items being learned. The cue-token information used by the performance process to retrieve the image of some stimulus item's response associate is generally *just sufficient* to correctly retrieve the response from the discrimination net at the time the association is learned. However, as repetitive trials proceed, and the net grows over time to include new items, this cuing information may become inadequate for retrieving the correct response. In this event, what may be retrieved is a subnet of items (all similar to the correct response) which includes the correct response. A random process then selects a response item from this subnet as a guess. (Note that because of the way in which the net is built, this response, if in error, will be an error of response generalization.) When such an error is made, the processes that analyze the informative feedback can correct it by storing additional cuing information. Within the learning of a single list, when S–R pairs learned on later trials interfere in this way with pairs learned on earlier trials, oscillation results. In multilist experiments, when pairs learned in later lists interfere in this way with pairs learned in earlier lists, retroactive inhibition is observed in the test sequences.

The Long-Term Permanent Store

General Considerations

We have been led to the idea of a permanent associative store of very large size for a number of reasons having to do with conceptual problems of the EPAM theory. On these grounds alone, however, the hypothesis of an additional level of memory is not completely convincing, though some of the problems would be resolved neatly under the hypothesis. The existence of empirical evidence that suggests different storage mechanisms for working-versus-permanent storage is therefore encouraging (Deutsch, 1962; McGaugh, 1965).

The notion of permanence of the storage of symbols in the long-term memory is an assumption for which there is not much empirical evidence. To be more precise about this hypothesis, it is assumed that those symbols upon which a significant amount of processing has been done will never disappear from the long-term storage structure. This hypothesis is not the same as a naive "tape recorder" hypothesis, under which all information sensed is thereby recorded permanently; because of the demands of tasks and the effect of attention focusing processes, some inputs will never receive the processing necessary to qualify them as candidates for long-term storage. The hypothesis regarding permanence is, we think, reasonable at the current state of knowledge. There is no directly controverting evidence, and there is some measure of support from the earlier EPAM modeling efforts, namely, that behavioral evidence of forgetting can be accounted for satisfactorily as *loss of access* to stored symbols caused by dynamic changes of memory structure.

We view the processes of retrieval of symbols from the long-term permanent storage as a problem-solving process. By "problem solving," we mean a process that finds an "answer" path through a large maze of possible alternatives using search-limiting heuristics, as has been widely discussed in the literature on computer simulation of cognitive processes and artificial intelligence models (Feigenbaum and Feldman, 1963). Retrieval times alone would indicate quite a different retrieval process acting in the long-term memory from that involved in the recognition of a familiar object (processes of testing and sorting that are used in EPAM III). Introspection on retrieval episodes, where it is possible to be fairly self-conscious about the underlying processes suggests problem solving—that is, trying out various strategies to guide search, testing hypotheses, exploring particular avenues in depth, piecing together clues in various patterns (as in puzzle solving), a great deal of trial and error searching, and sometimes (as with problem-solving programs) the successful termination of search with great suddenness.

Another phenomenon of long-term memory that needs to be explained is the *fluctuating availability* of the symbols stored therein. Sometimes a particular sought-after symbol can be retrieved quickly and easily; at other times, it may appear irretrievable, no matter how much effort is spent trying to recall it, until some circumstances (or merely the passage of time) appear to "bring it to mind." We shall have some comments about this later in connection with the problem-solving nature of retrieval processing.

An additional and more subtle question that early influenced our thinking about a level of long-term storage involves an adequate explanation of proactive inhibition, to which we now turn our attention.

The memory of an organism at the beginning of a learning experience, it can be plausibly assumed, contains a large number of symbols stored during past learning. How can this total memory context affect associative *recall* in *current* learning? In the present EPAM model, it cannot, that is, EPAM exhibits no proactive inhibition (though there is a "proactive" effect on rate of learning). By the end of the criterion trial the current symbol context is adequately discriminated from previous ones, and no confusion by generalization is possible. In general terms, the problem can be resolved simply by the notion that the recently learned symbols are, over time, assimilated into the total memory context by a transfer process.

Experimental evidence suggests that subjects acquire and use seemingly extraneous features of a stimulus environment in the learning of the task oriented part of the total environment. This information is relevant locally in place and time to the objects of the task. Given a simulated environment enriched with such contextual information, and an augmented list of features for the noticing process to work with, EPAM could learn an experimental task using such local contextual information. The locally relevant information would be used in building discriminators, consistent with the EPAM heuristic that whatever information "works" is satisfactory (for example, the discrimination: "the syllable beginning with the letter R *and* learned 'early' in the experience" versus "the syllable beginning with the letter R and learned 'late'").

Though such information might be useful in speeding up the learning in the experimental session, its utility quickly fades as time passes and stimulus environments change. Local contextual information does not "work" well in discriminating objects and guiding retrieval over the long term.

Processes

Considerations of this kind lead us to suggest a transfer process controlling long-term storage, with these properties.

(a) It "reprocesses" the working memory, copying recently learned images to the permanent store (with the appropriate associative links as determined from the discriminator and cue-token information). In so doing, it makes decisions about temporary versus permanent relevance of the information. It ignores the temporarily relevant information, which thereafter plays no further role. The storage is reused by the acquisition processes in subsequent processing.

(b) It is a *strategy*, in that its decisions concerning long-term relevance may change over time based upon experience with environments or upon instruction.

(c) It is a *low-priority* process. The high-priority processes are those that attend to the demands of the environment and the acquisition of the task. Since it must share with these the processing time of the serial mechanism we have just postulated, and since it must grow a memory structure that is good (useful and relevant) for long-term processing, not merely "just adequate," we conclude that the so-called "consolidation" of the long-term storage will extend over a considerable elapsed time. This time may be of the order of hours, or even days (as suggested by some drug studies), depending upon the activity of the organism and the other information-processing demands it is satisfying, and depending also upon the complexity of the learned task.

It may be that the permanent storage process is slow for another reason, namely that the underlying biological permanent storage process is intrinsically a very slow process. One sees this, for example, in some of the nonbiological memory models that have been constructed. To cite two extremes, the chemical thread-growing memory built by Pask (1961, pp. 105–108) stores information thousands of times more slowly than the fastest magnetic memories of present day computers. Indeed, within a computer system itself, the data rates of the main "working" memory are many times faster than the data rates of the huge "bulk" memories used for secondary storage.

In this connection Chorover's result (1964) showing very fast consolidation is disturbing but not totally at variance with our position, at least for very simple learning tasks. McGaugh, in a personal communication, indicates that his experiments suggest big differences in consolidation speed between simple tasks and complex tasks. On the other hand, Chorover's result is at variance with many previous results in the experimental work on consolidation.

Such a process suggests the solution to the questions posed earlier about the mechanism needed to account for proactive inhibition. It merges the recently learned context with the total symbol context of the permanent memory, and in so doing, throws away some of the discrimination information that was responsible for perfect performance during the criterion phase of the recent learning. The consequence of this is generalization with the symbols of the total memory context, typically for some, but not all, of the recently learned items.

Structure

The structure of long-term memory is viewed here as an extension of the EPAM III (acquisition memory) structures, not as an entirely separate level of organization. The primary memory structure of EPAM III is the discrimination net, described earlier. The images stored at the bottom of the discrimination net are richly interconnected so that usually they form a large and complicated graph. An image is built at the bottom of the net as a collection of tokens for already learned subimages; the subimages are themselves built up in this general way; and so on. In this graph of interconnected images, those that are connected to the discrimination net are said to be in acquisition memory. Others connected into the graph but not directly accessible through the discrimination net are said to be in the long-term store.

Thus, the nodes of the memory graphs are the familiar images of objects. Connections between nodes are either attribute-value links defining relations between images at nodes, or specifically the whole-part relations that are "built in" by the way EPAM constructs images.

There is a simple way of looking at this structure. If the capacity of the long-term store is very great, and if symbols stored permanently therein are to be retrieved without very great information-processing penalties and long search times, there must be multiple entry points to the store. These might be thought of as index points to a large file. The discrimination net of the acquisition memory is, in essence, the *index* to the long-term memory. Under our present conception of storage processes acting in the long-term memory, the discrimination net grows and contracts—it grows during discrimination learning, thereby increasing the number of points at which the net accesses the long-term memory graph, and contracts as the net is reprocessed by the transfer process described above.

The search for images in the long-term store need not be restricted to merely a movement from node to node using whole-part or attribute value relational structure. The discrimination net is always available as an indexing device for selecting a new entry point. Search strategies can be constructed that makes use of this fact, thereby adding an additional "dimension" to the search.

Retrieval from the Long-Term Store by Problem Solving

Stimulus events set up retrieval problems. In the laboratory situation, they are part of the task that the subject is called upon to master. In performance mode, he accesses symbols stored during present and past learning activity. In learning mode, he accesses previously stored symbols to build up higher level images. In our present conception, retrieval of information is either *direct* or by *problem solving.*

Direct retrieval is accomplished in the discrimination net: a path of the net links directly to the image being sought. In the sense described earlier, this directly retrieved image is in the acquisition memory.

If the image being sought cannot be retrieved directly in this fashion, then a problem-solving search for the item is conducted in the neighborhood of the "entry point" given by sorting through the discrimination net the stimulus situation that gave rise to the search. Usually entry to the graph will be obtained at a region containing information similar to the information being sought, since this is how the net and long-term memory graph is built up in the first place.

For this purpose, an adequate problem-solving model is the General Problem Solver (GPS) [Newell and Simon (1963)]. Stated very briefly, GPS solves problems that can be put in the following general form. Given descriptions of an initial problem state and a target state, and given a set of operators for transforming states by reducing differences between problem states, find a sequence of operators that will transform the initial state into the target state.

In the memory retrieval problems being discussed, the initial state is the entry node given by the discrimination net. Some of the extrinsic information that gave rise to the retrieval problem is used up in accessing the appropriate "local" portion of the memory graph. The remainder is available as a description of the target state (the image being sought). This description is the basis for recognizing the target node when it is encountered. Upon encounter, a cluster of symbols is accessed (those associated with the target image), one or more of which may be the sought after symbol(s), for example the *name* associated with the target image. The operators, the means by which states are transformed respond to the various ways of moving from one node to another in the graph.

We wish to conclude this section by looking again at the problem of explaining fluctuating availability of stored symbols in the light of the proposed problem solving nature of the memory retrieval process. GPS, or the Logic Theory Program that was its forefather (Newell, Shaw, and Simon, 1963) or any one of a number of programs (such as Slagle, 1963, his SAINT) that are cousins to the Logic Theorist, are fairly powerful heuristic problem solvers in the sense that, over the domains of their applicability, they solve problems about as complex as people can solve. Yet all of these problem-solving efforts (programs or people) appear to have a common characteristic: the average number of steps in the solution derivations, and in the means–ends reasoning chains, is not large. The longest proof generated by LT was eight steps deep; the average perhaps half that. The average number of steps in GPS means–ends chains for the tasks that have been explored is probably about six. In the well-known Checker-Playing Program (Samuel, 1963) and in some chess-playing programs, analysis proceeds four half moves deep in the "look ahead" search.

Suppose that in memory retrieval problems, under a GPS-like regimen, comparable limits on "solution complexity" were to be encountered (a reasonable assumption). Then on some particular retrieval attempts, searches may be unsuccessful (subjectively, frustratingly so) because the item being searched for is not within the "span" covered by the problem solver from the entry node given it by the index, that is, the discrimination net. In other words, the selected entry node was not "close enough" to the target node for the "path length to solution" to be within the bounds of average depth of search. The sought for item is thus inaccessible unless a better entry node is selected.

One way to achieve a better solution is to postpone the retrieval problem for some time, awaiting the circumstance (testing periodically) that the contact nodes of the discrimination net with the memory graph will be more favorable. This is a possible solution because in the normal course of events, the discrimination net is expanding and contracting under the impact of the changing environment, as described earlier. Thus, we have here a possible explanation for fluctuating response availability, even in the absence of a conscious retrieval strategy.

However, deliberate strategies are also ways of inducing shifts of entry nodes. Some strategies, for example, might employ early or intermediate products of search in various arrangements as inputs to the discrimination net for new entry node selections. Another strategy which appears to be commonly used is the systematic generation of "stimuli" (produced and used internally), which we would interpret as a search for an appropriately "local" portion of the memory graph in which to search for a particular item. A common example of this is the trick of "going down through the alphabet" when trying to remember the name of some object. This strategy is very much a trial-and-error process, like most other heuristics, but it often works. Here we have another piece of the explanation for fluctuating availability of stored symbols, this time strategy-directed.

There are other general inferences one could make from a model of the type that views memory retrieval as a problem-solving process, but discussion of these is best postponed until after a computer simulation of the model is written and tested.

Conclusion

In this chapter, I have proposed a three-level theory of memory:

(a) an immediate memory of very small size, in which information is stored for very brief intervals, which acts as a buffer storage to decouple the input (peripheral encoding) processes from the central processes and as a temporary storage for central processing;

(b) an acquisition memory, a working memory with the structure of the EPAM discrimination net, in which discrimination learning takes place and in which the internal representations of stimulus objects are built;

(c) a permanent storage in which the internal representations are organized and stored for long-term retrieval.

The EPAM model is a precise formulation of the immediate and acquisition memories, and we have been able to demonstrate and validate the consequences of these parts of the theory. The theory of the permanent storage is a logical extension of EPAM suggested to the theorist as a resolution of certain difficulties with the present model. Since it has not been precisely described or tested by means of computer simulation, it is offered in a tentative spirit.

The discrimination net of the acquisition memory is viewed as an index to the permanent storage. Retrieval of information from the permanent storage is viewed as a problem-solving process, along the lines of the General Problem Solver model.

References

CHOROVER, S. L. Neural information processing and memory. In J. L. McGaugh (Chm.), Information processing and memory. Symposium presented at the American Psychological Association Annual Meeting, Los Angeles, September 1964.

DEUTSCH, J. A. Higher nervous function: The physiological bases of memory. *Annual Review of Physiology*, 1962, **24**, 259–286.

FEIGENBAUM, E. A. Simulation of verbal learning behavior. In E. A. Feigenbaum and J. Feldman (Eds.), *Computers and thought*. New York: McGraw-Hill, 1963. Pp. 297–309.

FEIGENBAUM, E. A., AND FELDMAN, J. (Eds.) *Computers and thought*. New York: McGraw-Hill, 1963.

FEIGENBAUM, E. A., AND SIMON, H. A. A theory of the serial position effect. *British Journal of Psychology*, 1962, **53**, 307–320.

MCGAUGH, J. L. Facilitation and impairment of memory storage. In D. P. Kimble (Ed.), *The anatomy of memory: Proceedings of the first conference on remembering, learning, and forgetting*. Palo Alto, California: Science and Behavior Books, 1965. Pp. 240–291.

NEWELL, A., SHAW, J. C., AND SIMON, H. A. Empirical explorations with the Logic Theory Machine: A case study in heuristics. In E. A. Feigenbaum and J. Feldman (Eds.), *Computers and thought*. New York: McGraw-Hill, 1963. Pp. 109–133.

NEWELL, A., AND SIMON, H. A. Computer simulation of cognitive processes. In R. D. Luce, R. R. Bush, and E. Galanter (Eds.), *Handbook of mathematical psychology*. Vol. 1. New York: Wiley, 1963. Pp. 361–428.

NEWELL, A., AND SIMON, H. A. GPS, a program that simulates human thought. In F. A. Feigenbaum and J. Feldman (Eds.), *Computers and thought*. New York: McGraw-Hill, 1963. Pp. 279–293.

PASK, G. *An approach to cybernetics*. New York: Harper, 1961.

PRIBRAM, K., AHUMADA, A., HARTOG, J., AND ROOS, L. A progress report on the neurological processes disturbed by frontal lesions in primates. In J. M. Warren and K. Akert (Eds.), *The frontal granular cortex and behavior*. New York: McGraw-Hill, 1964. Pp. 28–55.

SAMUEL, A. L. Some studies in machine learning using the game of checkers. In E. A. Feigenbaum and J. Feldman (Eds.), *Computers and thought*. New York: McGraw-Hill, 1963. Pp. 71–106.

SIMON, H. A., AND FEIGENBAUM, E. A. An information processing theory of some effects of similarity, familiarity, and meaningfulness in verbal learning. *Journal of Verbal Learning and Verbal Behavior*, 1964, **3**, 385–396.

SLAGLE, J. R. A heuristic program that solves symbolic integration problems in freshman calculus. In E. A. Feigenbaum and J. Feldman (Eds.), *Computers and thought*. New York: McGraw-Hill, 1963. Pp. 191–203.

14

What Does It Take to Remember?

Walter Reitman[1]
The University of Michigan

[1] I should like to acknowledge valuable comments on drafts of this paper by John Brown and Judith Reitman, and by Bruce Roberts, Richard Sauvain, and Daniel Wheeler. I also want to thank Professor Wendell R. Garner and Professor Donald Taylor for discussing several of the arguments presented here with me. Portions of the paper were written while I was a participant in a seminar on modeling, and I want to thank the other participants of the seminar, in particular, Professor Robert Bjork, Professor James Greeno, Professor David Krantz, and Professor Keith Smith, for ideas and information that found their way into the discussion presented here. I owe a particular debt of gratitude to Bob Bjork for two years of patient and good-humored efforts to educate me, usually in the face of great odds. To preserve the peace at Michigan, I should add that none of the foregoing comments imply any endorsement of the views outlined in this paper. Much of the work described here was made possible by support received under USPHS Grant No. MH12160, which I should like to acknowledge with appreciation.

The Segregation of Memory

Computer simulation models of psychological processes often have a terrible time sticking to their subjects. Take GPS, the General Problem Solver, for example (Newell and Simon, 1963; Ernst and Newell, 1969). GPS certainly solves problems. But it does a variety of other things as well. It is a jack of all trades. If we keep close track of its behavior as it solves problems, we find that it actually spends most of its time moonlighting as a memorizer, pattern recognizer, and language processor on the side (Reitman, 1969c).

It is easy to see why. The complex symbol sequences GPS produces are meant to approximate the detailed behaviors of human problem solvers. Real behavior, whether we label it problem solving, pattern recognition, or learning, depends upon the human information processing system as a whole. Problem solving cannot be simulated without considering such other aspects of cognitive activity as pattern recognition and the storage and retrieval of information. The treatment of these other aspects may have to be simplified if we are to make progress with the questions of most concern to us, but they cannot be ignored altogether.

The same holds for models of memory. Memory behavior is a function of an integrated system for processing information. As we show below, for example, subjects working at memory tasks may use quite complex systems of strategies in acquiring, storing, and accessing information. If our main concern is memory, it is natural and necessary to limit our treatment of these other aspects of human information processing. In doing so, however, it is important to keep in mind certain consequences of these restrictions in scope. At best, the models that result will ignore interesting questions. At worst, if simplification goes too far, or if the processes involved are too interrelated to separate, what remains is no more than an arbitrary and artificial problem. Research on memory that focuses on such problems is not likely to help us to understand the original questions of interest. Far from clarifying memory behavior, simplification carried out this way serves mainly to blind us to what is really going on.

Simplification in Research on Problem Solving

The first part of this paper deals with certain kinds of simplifications that have become almost conventional in experimental studies of memory. Before turning to them, however, it may be useful to see how memory is handled in an information-processing model concerned primarily with another aspect of cognitive activity. The example illustrates some of the simplification options one has available in constructing simulation models. It also demonstrates some of the drawbacks associated even with the most reasonable efforts to segregate memory problems from other problems of human information processing.

Models of human problem solving such as GPS are mainly concerned with methods, strategies, and heuristics. The goal has been to discover and reproduce individual heuristics and the modes of organization enabling systems of these heuristics to solve complex problems. To expedite exploration of problem-solving methods and organization, such systems typically make do with simplified treatments of other cognitive functions: perception, learning, language use, and certain aspects of memory. GPS, for example, automatically stores and retains substantial amounts of information it may need at some subsequent stages of the problem-solving process. Unless deliberately destroyed, all such information is guaranteed to be accessible, if and when required.

This simplifying assumption of a perfect memory might not be a bad first approximation to the special case of a careful, highly organized thinker working without time constraints and with an unlimited supply of pencils and paper. The main value of the assumption, of course, is to permit the investigation of problem solving to proceed without having to consider complications arising from information loss. But for anyone concerned with forgetting and confusion as it occurs in the laboratory and in everyday life, the simplification results in a memory model far too powerful to serve as a realistic general account of how humans store, retain, and retrieve information.

It must be emphasized that we are talking about one model and a particular kind of simplifying assumption with respect to memory. It would be wrong to conclude that all information-processing models ignore the problems of capacity limitations and information loss. There are several models, notably EPAM (Feigenbaum, Chapter 13) and the models developed by Laughery (1969) and by J. Reitman (Chapter 5), which are specifically directed to these aspects of learning and memory. It would be equally wrong to assume that information processing models of other aspects of cognitive activity simplify away all memory problems. Some of our most interesting and detailed representations of the structure of the information stored in memory occur in such models (see the discussions of graph models and active memory models below).

Our point, then, is simply to illustrate one kind of reasonable simplification procedure, one which in this case has the effect of separating research on memory from research on thinking. To restate, GPS avoids the problems of information loss due to such factors as noise or capacity limitations by postulating a memory that cannot suffer unintended losses of information. As a result, the memory model embedded in the system is of limited value to those working on forgetting and information loss, since it is, in effect, immune to the consequences of interference and decay.

Simplification in Experimental Studies of Memory

Studies of thinking and problem solving such as GPS have given us more explicit conceptions of the means by which humans apply an integrated system of strategies to a broad range of problems. They constitute frameworks for thinking about mediating processes in cognitive activity, and about such problems as attention allocation as a function of goals and strategy system structure. It is important to recognize the tactical value of the simplifying assumptions that made it possible for these investigations to come this far. At the same time, it may well be that further progress in understanding thinking will require closer attention to the phenomena of human memory. The next advances may require models that take full account of information-processing limitations, models concerned with the details of how everyday information is acquired and then effectively brought to bear in subsequent cognitive activity (Reitman, 1969a).

Given these concerns, it might be expected that those interested in thinking could make good use of the data and models resulting from current experimental investigations of memory. The work often employs conceptions of human information processing (see, e.g., Norman, 1969) closely related to those underlying simulation research on thinking, and its main concerns are precisely those problems of capacity limitation and information loss we observed to have been simplified out of models such as GPS. As it turns out, however, the simplifications involved in producing these memory models and data typically are quite severe, raising questions about their relevance to everyday memory phenomena, particularly those of interest to the student of thinking.

The simplification process characteristic of current experimental research on memory begins with the choice of the subject's task. Consider some of the differences between everyday memory activities and the memory tasks required of subjects in the laboratory. Little of what we recall under everyday conditions is deliberately rehearsed for that purpose. Under everyday circumstances we take in information not as an isolated operation, but in conjunction with and in the course of other ongoing activities. Typically, that information consists of facts, statements, and patterns, not isolated nonsense syllables and words. It is easy to understand how the differences between laboratory tasks and everyday memory activities come about. They arise from the experimenter's desire to simplify and standardize inputs, to reduce the number of task and subject variables involved in storage and retrieval so as to make the remaining variables easier to induce from the data. This amounts to treating the laboratory task as a tool for decoupling a memory subsystem from the larger system of cognitive processes subjects use in their everyday activities. As we shall see, however, it is doubtful that most such tasks achieve this decoupling.

The simplification process is carried still further in the models developed to account for the data produced in laboratory studies of memory. Storage and recall in the laboratory task setting at least sometimes may appear to involve only the few simple and straightforward processes such models typically assume. At other times, however, it clearly calls forth constructive activities, conjecture, hypothesis testing, and search operations which involve strategies and patterns of organization fully as complex as those used in solving problems. Very likely, furthermore, the process systems in the two cases overlap and interact substantially. In this light, the memory models produced by the simplification process we are considering are of little help to the investigator interested in other aspects of cognitive activity. They eliminate the everyday context of memory and ignore the problems he is concerned with.

Some memory investigators will accept in principle the view suggested here, yet consider the simplifications made to be justified by the results achieved. It is in the best traditions of science to work intensively within single paradigms in order to test a model. Furthermore, it is accepted practice to justify a particular model mainly in terms of how well it fits the data from a set of experiments within a relevant paradigm.

Once within this cycle, however, devising paradigms to test models, then justifying the models solely by how well they fit the paradigm data, it is easy to get lost in a closed loop. We lose sight of the original phenomena of interest. We cease to be concerned with the adequacy of customary simplifications to the basic questions we presumably want to answer in the long run. Since recent experimental and simulation work has expanded our conceptions of cognitive activity and the range of methodological options available to us, now may be a good time to come up for air. There is no denying the need to simplify, but it may be useful to pause, suspend judgment, reexamine what seems to be going on, and take a detached look at present working assumptions and their consequences.

What Do Subjects in Memory Experiments Do?

It has been known since before the turn of the century that the behavior of experimental subjects often includes efforts to cope with the requirements of the laboratory tasks they are presented with. They actively problem solve while learning. To the extent that this goes on, the decoupling we spoke of earlier evidently is less than perfect. Most memory models assume, however, that the laboratory task successfully decouples memory from the rest of the cognitive system. It would be helpful, therefore, to have some more detailed information on this point. By applying protocol collection methods normally employed in problem-solving studies to several different memory tasks in use in our laboratory,[2] we have been able to observe and record subjects' behavior more extensively. The following brief account, based on the protocol of a subject participating in a typical free recall experiment, will give some idea of what we find.

The subject is presented with a series of fixed-length lists of words,

[2] I am indebted to Elizabeth Ligon, Judith Reitman, Jane Tanner, and Daniel Wheeler for helping to provide the data, and to Peter Headly and Dick Nordrum for writing the computer control programs for the experiments.

one word every few seconds. Once an entire list has appeared, the subject recalls as many of the words as he can, in any order. We ask him to note and comment on what he is doing, or trying to do, during both presentation and recall.

Evidence from Protocol Data

Examining the resulting protocol, we find that much of the subject's time is spent in working out and testing various coding and retrieval strategies. As he acquires experience with the task, he becomes sensitive to list length and begins to differentiate among the parts of the list. He notes that if he can judge when a list is within six or seven items of the end, he can try to retain the last few items by constant repetition of the final sequence as it is presented. Gradually, he learns to switch to such a procedure at that point. Within the main body of the list, he experiments over trials with a variety of coding strategies. At one time or another, he concentrates on the sounds of the words; on the meanings of the words; on forming associations between consecutive words; on classification and categorization procedures; and on imagining physical and conceptual schemes into which words may be inserted as they are presented.

The subject finds some items easier to recall than others, and words presented in subsequent lists sometimes remind him of items in previous lists he was unable to recall. He thus obtains a certain amount of feedback on his performance as the experiment proceeds, and he spends part of his time using that feedback to locate and try to improve inadequate strategies. At one point, for example, after working with a strategy involving imagined visual scenes, he notes that the words "feat" and "skill" were lost, apparently because his associations to them were not concrete and hence nothing in the visual scene he had constructed reminded him of them. He then wonders whether changing abstract words like "feat" to more concrete equivalents, for instance "feet," would improve his performance. At another point he notes that he can recall the image he set up, but cannot figure out what word it stands for, and he instructs himself to try for more highly differentiated images. At still another point, he reports himself unable to retrieve a whole complex of images he thinks he set up, and he resolves in subsequent trials to construct multiple interconnections among scenes to increase the likelihood of getting from one to another when he wants to retrieve them.

DATA LIMITATIONS

There are several important restrictions upon the use to be made of such data as these. We used only two or three subjects in each experimental setting. We do not think our subjects, mainly graduate students interested in memory, are typical, or that all subjects do these things. Many subjects in a typical memory experiment may be unaware of mnemonic devices. Perhaps they simply look at the stimuli as they are presented or repeat them to themselves.

We cannot even be sure our subjects do the things they describe. They do not come with systematic strategies for observing or terms for reporting what they do. We know that much goes on they are unaware of, unable to tap. We have, for example, protocols from one subject working with CVC trigram stimuli in a paired-associates learning task. This subject firmly and insistently reports multiple occurrences of the same stimuli, possibly because of stimulus selection factors (Underwood, 1963) or auditory confusions in coding, when not a single stimulus has been presented more than once. If subjects can make such perceptual and judgmental errors about external events, there is every reason to expect their protocols to contain at least some statements about their own activities which are incomplete, erroneous, and on occasion even directly contrary to fact.

INFERENCES ABOUT MEMORY BEHAVIOR

Though subjects sometimes may be wrong in assessing what they are doing, however, we ought not rule out the possibility that they occasionally are right, and that their reports contain valuable clues to what is going on. To document this possibility, we can cite not only the observed ability of subjects to improve their performance, but collateral lines of evidence as well. Winikoff (1967) has shown that protocol reports can be highly predictive of behavioral data, and there are several studies that indicate that memory performance can be varied substantially by general verbal instructions about what subjects are to do. Bower (1969), for example, has shown that instructing subjects to memorize by forming connected images results in substantial improvement in performance.

It is no big jump from such results to suggestions about the possible uses of experience and the potential efficacy of self instruction. From his own experience, a subject may learn, for example, that a particular coding strategy requires more time than the spacing of the stimuli allows. Having discovered that, he perhaps may try to modify the coding strategy. Alternately, he may combine it with a strategy of ignoring incoming stimuli which are presented while the coding of a prior item still is going on. Whether a subject's interpretations of his prior behavior and its results are right or wrong in any given case, his conclusions and consequent self instructions can be expected to affect his processing of subsequent items.

Even the subject who reports nothing cannot be presumed to be doing nothing. Quite the contrary: once we accept some form of process model, with a set of capacities and capacity restrictions, it is hard to see how we can avoid assuming a control system that organizes and manipulates those capacities in response to the requirements of each new experimental task. It may well be that in contrast to what we have seen in these protocol data the strategies of many subjects are simpler and fewer in number (looking at the words, repeating sets of them, etc.). But there would seem to be no good reason to rely on chance in this respect when, as we shall see, it is possible to reduce strategy variance directly, by instruction and training.

Relation to Problem-Solving Protocols

Not surprisingly, the data we have obtained resemble, in many ways, typical protocols collected from subjects working at problem solving tasks. For many subjects, and not just those working under thinking aloud conditions, the memory tasks that confront them define problem situations. The initial problem is to perform to some criterion (perhaps "as well as I can"). This may lead to a second problem, one of developing procedures for performing well in this particular task situation. Some subjects also may face a third problem, involving figuring out how to allocate their time and cognitive capacities between the first two.

We do not want to argue this problematic character of the laboratory task situation too strongly, at least not on the basis of our data. We asked subjects to provide protocols, and such instructions may have emphasized this aspect of the task. It should be noted, however, that the limited memory performance data collected under these conditions do not deviate in any obvious ways from data collected without protocol instruction. Furthermore, though subjects asked to state what they were doing or trying to do only *after* the end of an experiment give much sketchier and presumably less reliable reports, these subjects also report similar attempts to work out effective ways for dealing with their tasks.

CONCLUSION

In sum, generous allowances for the inadequacies of protocol data probably are appropriate in the present case. Nonetheless, it seems clear from these materials that at least some subjects spend a good part of their time not on the memory problem immediately before them, but in learning what they can do, and how their actions interact with the parameters of the particular task before them.

Decoupling Reconsidered

Since it appears reasonable to assume that subjects can develop and utilize a variety of strategies, let us accept the assumption for the moment and see what it implies. We observed that the laboratory tasks normally employed in the study of memory can be interpreted as being intended for the purpose of decoupling a memory subsystem from the rest of the subject's cognitive apparatus. Apart from the value of any laboratory situation in standardizing the environment, the point of these particular tasks depends upon the assumptions (1) that such a simpler decouplable memory subsystem exists, and (2) that the tasks in fact substantially decouple it, inactivating the rest of the subject's cognitive system.

If these assumptions are incorrect, then far from simplifying a subject's cognitive activity, such tasks may complicate it. A subject who has no simpler memory subsystem capable, say, of memorizing nonsense syllables, may feel obliged to try to develop effective procedures for dealing with them. In that event, his performance at any time will reflect a mix of his developmental efforts and his provisional strategies of the moment.

As he acquires experience with the task and his strategies for it, the subject's developmental activity may damp out and his procedures may become more stable. We can encourage the subject to stay with one strategy (see the section on strategy control), and we can try to determine, at least by direct inquiry, whether he believes he has done so on any particular trial. But unless we take such deliberate measures and perhaps even if we take them, there is little guarantee of such stability. At any moment the subject may become dissatisfied with his performance, or get a new idea he wants to work out, and elect to change to some other way of doing the task.

Even if the subject settles for one strategy and does not vary from it, there is little reason to regard the data he produces as the output of the simple decoupled memory system envisaged by some current models. At the very least, it should be treated as the output of that subsystem operating in conjunction with the particular strategy the subject has chosen.

If different subjects choose different strategies, or an individual changes from one strategy to another, then trying to induce the structure of a general decoupled memory component from data aggregated over such variations would appear on its face a difficult task. There is no more reason to expect such an effort to succeed than to expect, say, that we could induce the hardware or software organization of some unknown computer from an examination of its outputs aggregated over different unknown programs. We can assume that the subject's output, like the computer's, respects the constraints defined by the basic processes generating it. But there is no reason to think our analytic tools capable of inducing those processes from such data, particularly if in applying those tools we insist upon ignoring the evidence for the existence of strategies and for the ability of subjects to vary existing strategies and to generate new ones.

The reason for this is simple: if the outline of cognitive activity presented above holds, then most current analysis techniques are inappropriate. Strategy change cannot be regarded as an additional variable in some overall additive model of behavior. Such models cannot accommodate the relation between strategies and basic processes. That relation is not additive; it is conditional. Strategy systems are not stationary behavior sources in the short run. A strategy achieves its effect by turning basic processes on and off, by changing their parameters, and by redirecting them to other subjects. When strategies are changed, all of these effects also are changed.

It is true that aggregated data from memory experiments sometimes do produce interesting results. In some cases, this may reflect the stabilizing effect of the training subjects receive. In other cases, however, such results probably depend more upon properties of the task than of the subject. For example, the finding that low association value nonsense syllables are more difficult to memorize than familiar concrete nouns may mean nothing more than that over comparable populations of subjects, however varied the individuals' strategies, the differences between the two types of stimuli are sufficient to produce a strong main effect.

Studies of task variables, for example those having to do with the meaningfulness of words, have yielded important findings that any process theory of memory must take into account. But these results so far have added little to our knowledge of the basic processes of memory *per se*. In particular, they hardly argue against the conclusion we have drawn from the data discussed above. To the extent that these data reflect what subjects do in typical memory experiments, there is little reason to believe that such experiments in fact decouple a distinct memory subsystem or yield information useful in drawing inferences about such a subsystem.

Decoupling in Retrieval

The discussion of decoupling so far has focused on coding and storage processes. The same kinds of considerations apply to retrieval. The simplest model of retrieval behavior is in terms of a single retrieval process. This process is treated as a unitary primitive. It is not analyzed into a complex of component processes. The process takes some cue, stimulus, or retrieval request as input and produces one or more items from memory (or perhaps no item) as output. To study this process is to attempt to discover functional relations between properties of the input, including relevant aspects of the total environmental context, and properties of the output, including the case of failure to retrieve.

For several reasons, most investigators add at least one additional stage to the model, to account for what happens when the basic retrieval process fails. In its simplest form, this second process takes the form of a random mechanism that perturbs or jiggles the storage system between primary retrieval attempts.

Postulation of a mechanism that randomly perturbs traces when the basic retrieval process fails may be a useful theoretical simplification. In fact, however, it seems reasonable to suggest that retrieval behavior involves a good deal more than this two stage model would admit. If I cannot remember where I put my keys, I may try to visualize or construct for myself typical situations involving my use of the keys, in an effort to contact an appropriate memory trace of relevant recent activity. If that succeeds, I next may attempt to construct the outcome of that activity, as a way of generating hypotheses about the likely location of the keys. Each of these hypotheses then may be used in conjunction with the basic retrieval process (e.g., do I remember leaving the keys in my office door, in the car ignition, etc.).

Whatever we take to be the best formulation of the primary retrieval process, the intervening activity determining the individual retrieval operations very likely involves complex strategies for manipulating information. Furthermore, use of these strategies presumes subsidiary calls on the hypothetical basic retrieval process, for example, to secure information about habitual activities involving my keys for use in constructing hypotheses about their whereabouts. Once again, there is no *a priori* reason to regard such strategies as necessarily employing only one such process, or indeed to anticipate any sharp boundary distinguishing these strategies from those involved in such other cognitive activities as problem solving.

Simple Models of Memory

There are several obvious virtues in a segregated treatment of memory, one that postulates only a few capacities and a minimal set of processes or states to account for the formation of associations and the retrieval of information. Other things being equal, such a treatment is much easier to grasp and test than an explanation invoking complex systems of strategies, strategies more or less indistinguishable from those involved in other cognitive activities, strategies that must be specified individually in great detail before predictions can be made. Even more important, if such a treatment is tenable then whatever we learn about these basic processes has direct and immediate predictive significance over the whole memory domain.

If the experimental and protocol data discussed above have some validity, however, learning and recall may involve processing networks far more complex than such simple models envisage. Furthermore, as we noted above, even if these networks do depend upon a small set of basic processes, unless differences among strategies are very limited, we cannot expect statistical manipulations of aggregated experimental data to wash the gold free. It is possible to regard the evidence for complex strategy systems as epiphenomenal, a delusion certain subjects share with susceptible psychologists. If we credit that evidence, however, it is hard to be optimistic about general memory models simple enough to be specified in full by a few capacities, a few basic processes, and a set of interrelations one can flowchart on a single page.

Strategy System Conceptions of Memory

If simple memory models are too restrictive, it is possible to view memory behavior as the product of a complex strategy system operating with substantial amounts of stored information. This metaphor suggests several research goals. We can study the rule and strategy systems subjects use in coping with memory tasks. We can try to relate the learning of strategies and choices among strategies to individual and task variables. And we can seek to find out how strategy systems are built up and organized from underlying basic processes. Each of these objectives has its own advantages and limitations.

Describing Strategy and Rule Systems

Good descriptions of the rule or strategy systems people use can be a valuable teaching aid. They should prove useful in aiding us to discover any fundamental invariants underlying human information processing ability. They also focus our attention upon the properties and requirements of the tasks we present to our subjects.

We should note, however, that it is possible to give an accurate description of strategies for carrying out some complex activity without necessarily specifying for the system under investigation the actual functional organization of the processes realizing such strategies. The distinction is fundamental and must always be considered in evaluating what we are getting in a particular psychological model or description. Fitts (1964, p. 249), discussing an early artificial intelligence system, the autopilot, notes that "it is more than a coincidence that the pilot's job, in many respects, corresponds to that of an autopilot, and that the variables which are considered by the design engineer in perfecting an automatic control system are analogous in many respects to the task variables which affect the . . . pilot." The autopilot embeds a theory of the environment in which the pilot operates. If both pilot and autopilot cope with that environment successfully, the strategies of the two systems may be similar at many points. But that is not to say that the autopilot necessarily is a good model of the process organization of the pilot as he behaves in that environment.

The same point may be illustrated from the computer simulation literature. Often such models embed useful representations of the strategies people use. It is difficult to know what can be concluded about these strategy system descriptions, however, other than that they reflect the internalized properties of the environments upon which they operate. How much of the Simon and Kotovsky (1963) sequence extrapolation model, for instance, is about the psychological processes in sequence extrapolation as opposed to the structure of the sequence extrapolation task? Could the sequence extrapolation task be carried out by *any* information-processing system whatever so that it did not require detection of cycles? If not, if cycles must be found in one form or another in order for the problem to be solved, then it appears that "humans find cycles" is a psychological proposition only in a weak sense. It follows from two basic assertions, (a) that the human information-processing system is a subset of all information-processing systems, and (b) that *any* information-processing system must find these basic structural units if it is to solve the problem. In this case, the model remains relevant to psychology by dint of proposition (a), but there is nothing about it *specific* to humans or psychology.

Detailed exploration and description of individual strategy systems is valuable, both for its immediate applications, e.g., in teaching better ways of thinking, and also as a first step towards more satisfactory theories of human information processing. But such descriptions are a long way from an adequate theory of the invariants peculiar to the information processing capabilities of human beings.

Investigating How We Learn and Choose among Strategies

Once we accept a strategy system metaphor as a framework for thinking about memory, it is natural to ask how strategies and rules are learned, and how we choose from among the strategies we know in carrying out some task. In investigating these problems, however, it is important to avoid paradigms which are inappropriate to the strategy system concept.

We might be tempted, for example, to investigate how the learning of a particular strategy varies with some property of the task. Or we might ask how the choice among strategies depends upon certain motivational or personality characteristics of the subject. If we attempt to investigate these questions using conventional paradigms, however, we are in effect ignoring our assumptions about the strategy systems generating our data. Unless the strategies involved are simple and few in number, we are unlikely to be able to answer such questions using analytic techniques which treat changes in the dependent variable as some additive function of the variables we manipulate.

The very formulation of a problem of choice among strategies can be misleading. If our protocol data are reliable, subjects do not always have to choose among available strategies (except in the logical sense). They may develop new strategies from earlier components and prototypes. This problem of strategy proliferation might be ignored were it true that strategies could be classified into a few basic types. But we have little reason to be sanguine about such a prospect on the basis of past experience. If the system for generating new strategies is of the same order of complexity as the system for generating new sentences (and they surely are closely related), then strategy classifications probably will not account for any more variance than simple sentence taxonomies do.

Finally, even the notion of a personality variable is contaminated by inappropriate conceptions. After all, most such variables are measured by tests which produce the desired scores only by dint of the same additivity assumptions we rejected earlier.

Thus, though the goals we are dealing with here may be quite reasonable, we need to be careful about the methods we use for achieving these goals. In a subsequent section on strategy control procedures, we return to these problems in more detail.

Specifying Basic Processes for Retrieval, Search, and Recognition

The idea that individual strategies are important already has a good deal of acceptance in research on learning and memory. Many investigators, for example Bower (1967), informally assume that subjects can switch among strategies as a function of changes in experimental conditions. Atkinson and Shiffrin's model (1968) allows for changes in the way certain capacities are employed as a function of a subject's choice of strategy. Should that conception prove insufficient, it now is possible to go well beyond the treatment of strategies as unitary elements. We can use information-processing languages (see the description of SNOBOL in the Appendix to Chapter 5, by J. Reitman) to specify the details of individual strategies and even the means by which strategies can be modified and developed.

Any such attempt raises some difficult questions, however. Since these questions also for the most part apply to the simplified models discussed earlier, it will be worthwhile to make them explicit. In brief, (1) we need to ask how one defines individual processes and strategies appropriately; and (2) we must examine more closely the relations between these basic processes and the strategies or programs that use them.

As an instance of the definitional problem for basic processes, consider again the hypothetical basic retrieval process discussed previously. Is it reasonable to assume only a single unitary process? If we look at current computer systems, we find many different labels for retrieval operations: list search, table lookup, hash coding, direct addressing, indirect addressing, content addressing, inverted file retrieval, etc. To be sure, the processes these terms refer to overlap; different levels in the hardware–software hierarchy are involved; and the variations in terminology also in part reflect differences in data storage formats. Furthermore, since the underlying organization of information processing in humans probably is very different from that in computers, these concepts do not necessarily apply directly to what goes on in human heads. People may use some of these procedures, or perhaps none, relying instead on other as yet unknown mechanisms. But since there is no single retrieval process in the relatively well-ordered world of computers, it is hard to see why there should be just one in man.

Kintsch, in chapter 11, argues for a two process model of retrieval. As he points out, such a conception can be traced back at least to William James. There is a recognition process, and there is recall, which involves both recognition and a preceding search or location process as well. Such a conception has intuitive appeal, and Kintsch gives a good summary of the evidence in its favor. But it is not easy to reduce such a conception to a set of well-defined operations. Consider first the search aspect. To what extent can we lump together what goes on when you try to recall (1) your name, (2) how you kick a football, and (3) the present location of your car keys? If we use introspective evidence as a guide, the first seems an immediate automatic response. The second may require constructive internal replay prior to our being able to produce a verbal description. The third, as we have seen previously, quite likely involves complex operational sequences under the control of some general strategy system. Is any unitary search process, with a single set of characteristics and input–output relations, likely to cover all three cases?

Relation of Retrieval to Perception, Pattern Recognition, and Problem Solving

How are we to distinguish the concept of a basic recognition process from notions such as matching, or from the operations that go on in perception? Luria (1968) describes one case in which information retrieval regularly appeared to display characteristics we associate with perceptual activity, and Luria's detailed account emphasizes these similarities repeatedly. His data come from a very exceptional individual, a professional mnemonist who appears to rely primarily upon perceptual coding. Thus, we cannot rely upon them too heavily in drawing general conclusions. But this intimate relation between perceptual operations and certain kinds of retrieval has been known, at least on introspective evidence, for thousands of years. The ancient mnemonists were careful to advise students to avoid shadows, lack of contrast, and inadequate spacing in setting up mental images (see Norman, 1969; Yates, 1966), presumably because these "perceptual" factors were believed to affect retrievability. Bower's recent work (1969) provides indirect support for this idea in that it demonstrates the efficacy of appropriate visual imagery in coding and retrieving paired-associate words. It will be interesting to see whether further experiments which deliberately vary instructions to subjects in order to manipulate these "perceptual" factors confirm the old precepts in detail.

Viewed in this light, the whole question of basic retrieval processes shades imperceptibly into perception and pattern recognition on the one hand, and problem solving on the other. The complex interrelations between memory and other cognitive activities mentioned at the beginning of this paper become more explicit. But all this is of little help if our main concern is to define some basic memory processes. For as an examination of typical pattern recognition and problem solving programs demonstrates (good examples are: Minsky and Papert, 1967; Ernst and Newell, 1969), such accounts also involve mixtures of perceptual, memory, and problem solving elements at least as complex as those we have been considering here. In fact, it is not far wrong to regard the *differences* among memory, pattern recognition, and problem-solving investigations as mainly differences of emphasis. Memory investigations, for example, often are concerned with retrieval of single unvarying items, like words, while pattern-recognition research tends to focus upon recognition of elements that have been transformed or combined with other elements. The two types of investigations also typically differ in the emphasis given the generative aspects of recognition, that is, the ability of a system to recognize new combinations of elements. Otherwise, however, they have a great deal in common. In view of this overlap between memory research and the modeling of other aspects of cognitive activity, we should expect a more adequate exchange of information across the conventional boundaries to be of general benefit. But these intricate interconnections among the various aspects of cognitive activity help make identification of an adequate set of basic processes difficult to achieve.

Distinguishing Processes from General Functions

As the foregoing observations imply, the difficulty in formulating basic processes adequately has been a problem for some time in programmed models of psychological activity. Programs in such areas as learning, pattern recognition, concept formation, and problem solving have postulated basic processes. There even is reasonably good agreement about the information processing functions any such program must carry out: matching, testing, and comparing; forming associations; searching and retrieving; and so on. But as yet there have been no explicit formulations of these processes general enough to permit incorporation of the same process in different models and programs, wherever the function in question is called for.

If we limit ourselves to general functions, however, as opposed to explicitly formulated processes, we may be lumping together very different ideas without making adequate distinctions among them. Matching, for example, refers to a general function that can take substantially different forms. Any statistical program will involve frequent matching of one number to another, to determine whether a limit has been reached, a subroutine has been repeated the right number of times, and so on. We also find the term matching used to refer to such complex processes as that which goes on when people recognize faces. They are said to have done so by matching the perceptual input to information patterns stored in memory. Each usage of the term in reference to the general matching function may be appropriate. But we do not want to assume that the processing details across so broad a domain necessarily are similar.

Terminological confusions involving a failure to distinguish process and function uses of a word cause problems both in the simulation and the experimental literature. Simulation models sometimes are claimed to be theories of general functions, when, in fact, they do no more than embed a particular process that carries out that function in some very narrow context. In the experimental literature, terms such as encoding, memorizing, filtering, searching, retrieving, deciding, selecting, etc., often are employed in widely varying senses, or without clear specification of the sense intended. As one example, we saw previously that retrieval of information may involve one or more basic retrieval processes. But retrieving information in general requires a great deal more than a retrieval process. It presumes an extensive network of strategies, control mechanisms, and other basic processes as well. At one moment a term like coding or retrieving or searching will be used to label some specific postulated process. At the next, with no explicit indication of the change of meaning involved, it is taken to refer to some broad function taken as a whole. It becomes a name for the total behavior to be explained.

General functions such as matching, searching, etc., even apart from explicit representations of corresponding processes realizing these functions, are valuable conceptual starting points. By themselves, however, they are of limited use to psychologists interested in models characterizing the peculiarities and specific properties of the basic processes underlying human information processing.

Defining Individual Strategies

The difficulties inherent in formulating sets of distinct strategies are much simpler to state. It mainly is a problem of deciding where one strategy ends and the next begins. As noted in discussing the protocol material summarized previously, subjects appear to have considerable ability to modify old strategies and develop new ones. There is little reason to hope, therefore, that some standard set of strategies can cover the variety of options available to any individual. Furthermore, once we accept this view, it follows that unless we also know how particular subjects construct, modify, and choose among strategies, some or perhaps most of what we learn about a particular strategy may apply only to that strategy. It has no necessary predictive significance across situations or subjects.

Distinguishing Basic Processes from Strategies

Though the development of computers has contributed substantially to the present stock of psychological ideas concerning memory, recent advances in computer system organization have hardly simplified the problems involved in formulating these ideas. We already have considered some of the difficulties for the notion of basic processes raised by the multiplicity of such processes one finds in modern computer systems. The organization of these systems suggests another difficulty as well, one having to do with the boundary between basic processes and strategies or programs.

Modern computer systems are multilevel organizations. Thus, a basic operation at one level may well be a substantial program at some lower level. Furthermore, some present day systems permit programming in languages (microprogramming languages) that enable users to alter functional connections among hardware elements. Thus in effect they permit us to redefine the basic operations of the system right at the hardware level. If we allow ourselves to think in terms of such systems, the line between basic processes and the programs utilizing them rapidly becomes obscure.

Speculating on human information processing organization in this light, one may imagine that though we operate with strategies defined over underlying processes, we also are capable of redefining or reorganizing those processes when the habitual strategies that use them prove inadequate. If humans do possess such capabilities, it would for example explain the failure so far to provide any single process account of the Neisser–Sternberg data on the way that subjects search through lists (see Neisser, 1967; Sternberg, 1967). In other words, the extensive training subjects get in such an experiment may lead to development of an appropriate set of strategies and processes. At the level described by existing models for these data, however, there need be no simple correspondence between the strategies and basic processes developed under one set of experimental conditions and those developed under some other set of conditions.

This possibility also might be useful in thinking about visual prism data. These data seem to suggest that after extensive experience with distorting lenses subjects actually reorganize their perceptual activity (as opposed to learning to interpret their way around the distortions) in such a way that the visual field appears normal despite the induced alterations.

A third phenomenon that may be relevant comes from observations of language learning. We assume that a normal child can learn the phonemes of any human language if he is exposed to them early enough and grows up in that linguistic environment. Phoneme boundaries divide the many possible variations in speech sounds into limited sets of categories. These categories do not, in general, correspond from one language to another. Thus, nonnative speakers of a language, not having a command of the relevant phonemes, may have considerable difficulty hearing and making speech distinctions which are obvious to native speakers. Is it reasonable to regard the phonemes of a language as basic operators in speaking and understanding that language? If so, we should recall that the particular phonemes for a given language are acquired through experience. Furthermore, though it takes a great deal of effort for an adult to acquire a full phonemic command of a foreign language, it sometimes does happen.

Some Problems and Paradigms for Research on Memory

In the foregoing sections of this chapter, we have seen that each of the conceptions of memory and of the goals of research on memory we have considered mixes advantages with substantial unresolved problems. Simple models can be tested by experiments. Some give good fits to restricted sets of data. Yet if our protocols can be trusted, such models typically simplify out too much. In our view, memory is not a simple decouplable system; it is more like a complex interconnected collection of structures, processes, strategies, and controls. Memory behavior does not depend solely upon a memory subsystem; it reflects the activity of the human cognitive system as a whole. In this view, simple models are of limited use as aids to a general understanding of memory.

Strategy system conceptions come closer to the phenomena they are meant to explain. They run into problems of definition and testing, however. We do not know how basic processes should be specified. We are not yet able to deal with the development, modification, and proliferation of individual strategies. We still cannot distinguish clearly between basic processes and the sets of strategies operating with them. We can be encouraged by the conceptual, methodological, and empirical achievements of the past decade, but we still have a way to go.

Many of the questions discussed above, however, cannot be resolved at the present time. The investigator of memory behavior must simplify. He cannot continually worry about the relation of retrieval processes to those involved in perception. He cannot be put off by the possibility that basic processes may not really be basic in any absolute sense. The most he can do is to remain aware of the possibilities he has excluded in the course of devising a manageable set of concepts and goals for his research.

Let us agree, then, to turn for the balance of this paper from the kinds of questions we have been considering to a discussion of some more practical research implications of the approach developed in the foregoing sections. The discussion which follows deals with three areas of research which stand out as relatively promising in the light of this approach. Work in each of these areas, on the structure of information in memory, on how that information is processed, and on strategy control procedures, illustrates the developing coincidence of interests between simulation and experimental investigations. Each also offers significant opportunities for sophisticated combinations of simulation and experimental techniques.

What Is the Structure of the Information Stored in Memory?

Thinking back to the origins of such primary tools as the list learning and paired-associate paradigms, we can recall a time when our single goal was to discover general laws of learning, functions displaying basic relations between input variations and variations in performance. Some investigators believe this goal substantially achieved. Learning is all-or-none, long-term forgetting is due to interference, and so on. Whether this belief is true, other goals gradually have been added to the list of research problems on memory. We now try to explain not just how information is acquired and what happens to it once it is in memory. We also increasingly seek to give an explicit account of the structure of information in memory and to describe how it is processed.

Such questions once were dismissed as matters for philosophy. But they recur. They are part of the disputes among associationists, behaviorists, and the new breed of psycholinguist. They are implicit in research on judged similarity, and on free and controlled association. And they have erupted back into research on verbal behavior, for example in studies of clustering.

It is generally agreed that the clustering phenomenon reflects interrelations among items in memory. We are unlikely to explain clustering unless we represent these interrelations in our account. But how detailed should such a representation be? Clustering is one manifestation of interrelations in memory, but hardly the only one, or even the most significant one. The primary behavioral manifestations are the things we say, the statements we make about things and the relations among things. A very simplified representation of relations among items may be sufficient to explain clustering phenomena. In the long run, however, if we want to explain the structure of information in memory as evidenced in verbal behavior, the representations we need will have to be powerful enough to account for what we know and say.

The need for more detailed representations of information in memory is increasingly widely recognized. Greeno (1969) discusses several interesting possibilities, as does Kintsch in Chapter 11. Indeed it is difficult to see how some of the most promising empirical work can be pursued much further without representations of this sort. As an example, we refer again to Bower's work, which demonstrates that interrelating items in images or sentences makes for substantial improvement in retention and subsequent retrieval. At some point, we will want to know why particular images and relations work better than others. It will be hard to answer such questions without representations of the information involved. Conversely, once we have such representations we can ask important theoretical and applied questions about language, comprehension, and the ways in which acquisition of new information depends upon the information already stored in memory.

Graphs and Networks

Present efforts to develop such representations, for example the discussion by Kintsch in Chapter 11, center around structures that may be regarded as *graphs*. These are systems of nodes, corresponding to items or elements in memory, interconnected by links which are taken to stand for various sorts of relations among the items. The first languages deliberately designed for the purpose of formulating such structures, termed information processing languages (IPL), were developed by Newell, Shaw, Simon, and their associates more than a decade ago (see Newell *et al.*, 1964, for details). For simulation purposes, the IPL languages have now largely been superseded by more convenient and powerful tools (for example, the SNOBOL language described in the Appendix to Chapter 5). The ideas involved, however, remain the most promising approach to this representation problem yet proposed.

In most psychological applications, little if any use is made of the mathematics of graphs or of literal drawings of graphs on paper. The power of the concept as a psychological research tool results from using it to define a set of conventions for the representation of information. In practice, much the most powerful way to use a graph representation of any interesting body of information is to define the concepts of nodes and links in terms of the data structures and processes of some computer language, the list structures of IPL, for example, or the strings and string processes of SNOBOL. It then becomes possible to set up and investigate far more substantial and complex systems than any one could reasonably hope to state and investigate on paper. In fact, then, those who use graph representations of information often turn out to be thinking in terms of structure and process concepts derived from experience with a computer system for representing and manipulating graph specified information.

A generalized statement of graph concepts and a detailed introduction to their use is contained in Reitman (1965). This source illustrates how both simple and complex concepts in memory may be represented by graphs or networks of interconnected items. It describes how such memory representations may be used as a base for models of concept attainment, similarity judgment, and problem solving. And it sketches out ways in which such representations may be applied in accounting for comprehension of verbal statements and the integration of newly acquired information into existing memory structures.

The most fully developed application of a graph scheme to the representation of interconnections of items in memory is found in the work of Quillian (1966, 1967), who developed a completely specified network of interconnected word concepts together with a program capable of mediating among these interconnected elements. Given two words or items represented in the memory network, the program is able to find and output detailed descriptions of the relations between them. Furthermore, these outputs are not simply lists of mediating elements. They are detailed and exact statements of complex relations. To be precise, the program output is a set of statements corresponding to the answer a subject might give if asked to describe the relations between two words or concepts from memory.

From the foregoing description, it should be evident that graph representations are a powerful tool for describing information structures in memory. They enable us to specify in detail formulations of the sort Kintsch describes. Furthermore, since they are easily realized with simulation languages and techniques, we are able to evaluate such formulations by determining just what they do or do not account for. With respect to such models as that Shiffrin describes in this volume, for example, such languages offer a convenient and powerful means of specifying in detail both the processing mechanisms and the structures in memory such a model postulates.

Most computer simulation research with general graph models has been restricted to sufficiency tests. It has attempted to determine what such models could account for (concept attainment, similarity judgment, problem solving, language production, etc.). There has been little empirical work relating detailed predictions from these models to laboratory data on human performance. Certain experimental paradigms, for example those used in the study of clustering or the role of hierarchies in memory (Mandler, 1967), obviously are relevant. But these paradigms have not been applied in conjunction with highly specified models of the sort just described. Hence we cannot draw any conclusions about the adequacy of these models with respect to such data. Sophisticated combinations of simulation and experimental techniques are now beginning to be explored in these areas (see, e.g., Collins and Quillian, 1968). However, the potential inherent in mating experimental procedures with information processing and simulation concepts and techniques still remains largely unexploited.

The significance of such a development would be hard to exaggerate. We come to these problems from an interest in the storage of information and its retrieval from memory. In the most general sense, however, we are dealing with the information base for perceiving, judging, and thinking, as well as remembering. In short, we are concerned here with fundamental problems of cognitive structure, the basis of all aspects of human cognitive activity.

RELATION TO NONPSYCHOLOGICAL WORK

The examples we have been discussing deal explicitly with psychological problems. In terms of their abstract structure, however, such models also are related to a large and active research effort centering around problems in information retrieval, generative linguistics, artificial intelligence, and computer science. Those interested in learning more of these interrelations may find useful the general descriptions of

Ash's (1968) TRAMP system for information retrieval and Reich's (1969) linguistic information-processing system given in Reitman (1969a, 1969b, respectively). See also Minsky (1968).

It is important to be clear about the relation between the psychological and nonpsychological aspects of the models we have been discussing. In particular, the relation involves no necessary assertion of basic similarity between humans and computers. The fundamental information-processing mechanisms in the two cases seem to me clearly very different. But similar problems of information representation arise in both cases. Furthermore, since both involve the storage and processing of verbal materials, the representations developed in the two cases may be expected to be related. Consequently, though systems such as those Kintsch and Quillian describe eventually must be validated against detailed human data, it is not surprising that at this stage they do not differ in any fundamental way from systems one might propose for handling corresponding artificial intelligence or information retrieval problems.

Some readers will interpret this as evidence for the close relation between problems of human and artificial intelligence. For them, the relevance of related work outside the psychological domain will be obvious. Others will regard these similarities as indicating the inadequacy of models like those just discussed. Until such models can be rejected on empirical grounds or subject to comparison with some as yet unspecified alternatives, however, they would seem to offer the most viable approach to problems of memory structure now available to us.

How Are Memory Structures Processed?

A model of information structure is only a component of a general theory of memory. We also need an account of how stored information is used. This problem defines the second broad research area we wish to consider. It may be possible to evaluate the representational adequacy of a memory structure model taken by itself. But a test of a theory of mnemonic behavior is a test of a system of coupled assumptions about structure and process together.

We touched on process considerations in discussing the role of strategies in retrieval. In this section, we are interested in problems of underlying process organization. We would like to know, for example, whether mnemonic behavior is a strictly sequential activity, or whether it involves parallel processing of some sort. If some form of parallel processing is assumed, we need to know the constraints it is subject to. After all, serial processing is well defined; but parallel processing is a term that can be applied to all forms of organization which deviate from strict serial order in any way whatever. Hence, it tells us little to assert that mnemonic behavior is generated by a parallel processing system unless at the same time we describe the operation of the system in some detail.

Experimental Tests of Assumptions about Memory Structure and Process

An information-processing model specified in sufficient detail to be simulated has one great advantage. All of its assumptions are explicit and hence, at least in principle, testable. I do not mean to suggest that such a model is easily proved or disproved as a whole on empirical grounds. In general that is difficult to do, for reasons I have outlined at length elsewhere (Reitman, 1967). However, it is sometimes possible to obtain direct experimental evidence bearing upon individual assumptions.

To illustrate how the explicit specifications required for programming a model can lead to experimental tests with broadly significant results, consider certain assumptions included in some of the models developed by Simon and his associates. These models assume that some kinds of information are stored in simple lists, which are processed serially from head to tail. Simon and Kotovsky (1963), for example, describe a concept induction and sequence extrapolation model in which the alphabet is represented as a linear string. In every case, it is assumed that this string is entered at the beginning.

An experiment by Sanders (1965) suggests that this set of process and structure assumptions is inadequate. Instead, his data are consistent with a conception of the alphabet as a random access string. The time subjects need to respond with a letter some fixed distance from a stimulus letter varies with the direction of movement and the number of intervening letters, but not with the position of the stimulus letter in the alphabet. Further evidence against the sequentially processed linear string idea comes from studies by Gough (personal communication, 1968) and Pollack (1967), who show that subjects make faster order judgments about pairs of elements such as letters when the elements normally are remote from one another (e.g., c and r) rather than when they normally are close together (e.g., p and r).

The Functional Organization of Memory

Many psychologists would disagree with a treatment of memory in terms of strict serial processing. Neisser (1967), for example, argues for a parallel processing conception and summarizes a considerable amount of experimental evidence generally supporting such a view. Unfortunately, most parallel processing conceptions are vaguely specified. Even those few which are relatively well defined are difficult to test. In view of the importance of the idea, however, it may be useful to consider it briefly and to make note of the modeling efforts relevant to it.

In addition to the experimental evidence Neisser cites, there are two additional classes of considerations that might incline us toward a parallel processing conception. The first comes from observations of programs designed to carry out complex operations involving large amounts of interrelated information. Such programs often experience a difficulty that shows up as a search problem in game playing, pattern recognition, and problem-solving systems. There are too many alternatives to evaluate, and humans notice things more quickly than we can account for in terms of our current conceptions of search strategies. In language translation it appears as a question of semantics: the human knows and is able to use more than we are prepared to encompass in our programs. I prefer to think of it as a problem in the organization and use of human memory. That is equivalent to the formulation in terms of search if we assume that memory is a passive storehouse of information, waiting to be interrogated by retrieval processes under the guidance of some search heuristics. But the problem looks very different if we assume, instead, that human memory is active, as Hebb (1949) suggests. Then our task is not so much to develop new and better search strategies but to devise explicit models of how such a memory might be organized and operate.

BIOLOGICAL EVIDENCE

A second difficulty with serial processing conceptions of memory is the biological evidence to the contrary. Recent work on cell genetics, for example, reveals an astounding amount of independent local activity even at a molecular level. Witkin (1966) discusses cellular subsystems apparently capable of patching up damage to genes caused by ultraviolet radiation. Lwoff (1966) describes how the fate of individual cells infected by virus particles depends upon complex mechanisms determining "whether a repressor or the key enzyme responsible for autonomous multiplication is formed first." "An organism," he writes, "is a molecular society and biological order is a kind of social order." Jacob (1966) discusses research designed to discover "how molecules find each other, recognize each other, . . . transmit the signals which modify the activity of their neighbors," and he writes of genetic material as containing "not only the plans for the architecture of the cell, but also a program to coordinate the synthetic processes, as well as the means of insuring its execution." All of this, note, is attended to well below the level of individual cells. At every higher level the story is the same. The firing of sensory cells is determined by events within them and at their boundaries. The heart beats, food is digested, and wounds are repaired all without the intervention of some omnipresent central processor. In fact, as Eliza Doolittle might have observed to Henry Higgins, most everything within us seems to go on quite nicely without our willing it.

There seems no reason to believe that the activity of our billions of neurons or of the information-processing components they form is organized differently. In fact, if the functional organization of the human information-processing system roughly parallels that of a digital computer, with its passive repositories of information and its one or two serial processors mediating all activity, then the great unsolved problem is how, out of the local changes in our billions of neurons, that form of organization is achieved. If current programs fall short in the ways we described, it may be because almost without exception they embed the strategy systems inferred from human behavior in functional organizations very different from those the biological evidence suggests mediate such behaviors in man. The corollary is that it is alternative forms of functional organization we ought to be investigating in our programs.

The limitations of present programs do not necessarily imply a fundamental flaw in the information-processing approach or even in the modeling languages now available. The problem is rather the inadequacy of our concepts of functional organization. As the programs briefly described below demonstrate, it is quite feasible to simulate other modes of organization using current computer hardware. True, for example, that hardware operates serially and utilizes a passive memory. But just as we may represent three-dimensional objects in two dimensions, by means of conventions for interpreting the relations among the lines on our sheet of paper, so we may specify conventions allowing us to simulate parallel systems with serial machines. The difficulty is not one of hardware or of the limits of our computer languages, but of ideas: we don't know what to say.

Active Memory Models

We have space only for a brief description of two examples of active memory systems. The discussion should, however, convey some idea of the possibilities for developing conceptions along these lines.

We begin with the Argus model (Reitman, 1965). Argus is a mixed system. Memory for concepts consists of a graph or network of interconnected elements. Each node in this network has levels of facilitative strength and inhibitory strength associated with it. When the strength level reaches some criterion, the node becomes fully active and capable of diverting attention to itself. Strategies in Argus are under the control of a serial executive process modeled upon GPS. Strategy activity affects the level of activity at relevant nodes, and node activity is capable both of altering the activity of related nodes and of interrupting the executive. The main purpose of the model is to provide a basis for thinking about autonomous memory activity as a source of attentional shifts and as a factor contributing to problem solution.

REICH'S MODEL

A system which goes even farther than Argus, in that all information processing is accounted for by a network of active memory elements, has been developed by Reich (1969, in preparation; see Reitman, 1969b, for detailed description). Reich's program is a model of language processing. It implements a theory of linguistic information processing being developed by Lamb (1966). Linguistic knowledge is treated as a network of relationships in memory. In this respect, it is similar to the graph models discussed previously. But since all activity in Reich's system is a property of the network itself, the model is distinctly different from conceptions of memory activity cast in terms of search and transformation routines operating upon passive stores of knowledge.

Grammatical knowledge is embedded in a network consisting of interconnected nodes of several types. Each node becomes active whenever it receives an appropriate signal pattern from nodes connected to it. In the passive memory of a serial processing system, such operations would be carried out one after another by a central processor. Here node functions anywhere in the system go into effect directly, as soon as the appropriate inputs are present. Many nodes normally will be active at any given time. Becoming active, a node propagates a message to each node it in turn connects to. Thus, each node is a function or operator that carries out its information processing activity whenever it receives the pattern of input information appropriate to nodes of its type. This is the sense in which the network is not only a storehouse of information, but also the processor of that information. This is why I have referred to the memory employed in this model as consisting of active elements. The conception of memory here is very different from the idea of a passive store of information operated upon by an external central processor which retrieves and transforms the information stored.

Since we can approximate such active memory models in a digital computer representation, however, there evidently is at least a rough equivalence between the active and passive conceptions of memory. Given this equivalence, one might wonder whether the active-passive distinction is really fundamental.

Such an interpretation of the correspondence seems to me to miss the point. In principle, if only we were persistent enough and could afford it we could simulate all of the information processing that goes on in our bodies on a serially processing digital computer. But there is no obvious reason to think of our bodily activities this way, and to do so is to risk ignoring fundamental questions about the means by which the simultaneous multilevel activities of our cells and organs are coordinated and integrated. The same applies to memory. We can simulate an active element memory on a serial computer. But the simulation is motivated by a desire to be able to think about problems of memory integration, coordination, and control that do not arise in a serial system.

TESTS OF ACTIVE MEMORY MODELS

The foregoing descriptions may be useful in adding to our stock of ideas for thinking about the processing of information in memory. To the extent that they are shown through simulations to generate behaviors similar to those they are meant to explain, they tell us how things might be. It would be nice if we could test the key assumptions in such systems directly, as we were able to test the idea of a serially processed head-to-tail list in the case of the Simon and Kotovsky model. Unfortunately, it is not now clear what such tests would be. Given the importance of process organization in a theory of memory, however, a successful combination of experimental and simulation approaches in this area should pay high dividends if it can be achieved.

Controlling Subjects' Strategies

The third research area we wish to consider is one in which it is possible to be more specific about appropriate paradigms. Many of us subscribe to a view that regards human behavior as the product of a complex information-processing system. We recognize that variations in strategies over time and from one subject to another occur and affect our data. Yet we continue to run our experiments with little or no reference to the effects of these strategy variations; it is hard to see why.

Perhaps the answer has to do with attitudes about experimental procedures that are remnants of an earlier conception, one regarding behavior as mainly stimulus determined. As we noted previously, the goal of research, according to this conception, is to establish general laws relating manipulations of selected experimental variables to variations in consequent behavior. All other aspects of the stimulus situation are held constant as much as possible, and variations in behavior that do not depend upon the experimental manipulations are treated as error variance. We discussed the drawbacks of the analytic methods associated with this conception above, in the section on decoupling. Now we return to the problem, to see whether we can improve the basic experimental paradigms to make them accord better with our present conceptions of behavior. The goal is to find ways of modifying and reinterpreting these paradigms to enable us to take account directly of variations in strategy over subjects and over time.

Strategy Control Paradigms

It is easy to cite cases in which paradigm development along these lines already is taking place. One example is Bower's current work on imagery, already referred to several times previously. A crucial aspect of this work is direct control of strategy variation by means of experimental instructions. Control subjects are allowed to memorize the paired associates in any way they wish. The experimental group, however, is specifically instructed to do so using images in which the elements in each pair are interrelated. Other examples of this sort of technique could be cited, but its use is not widespread and it certainly has not been pushed to its limits. Let us see what further steps might be taken along these lines and what the advantages and disadvantages of such a development might be.

Keeping for the moment to the imagery problem, if subjects can be instructed to use images, and if the experimental evidence demonstrates a significant improvement in performance as a direct consequence of such instructions, perhaps the next step might be to restrict strategy variation still further by more elaborate and detailed instructions about what to do. We might specify the kinds of images subjects are to use. We might even try to describe how such images are to be obtained and formulated.

Should it appear that our specifications are becoming too complex, we can try to shape the subject's behavior gradually. We can begin with a simple instruction. Once the subject is able to carry that out, we can add another step, then still another, and so on.

A STUDY OF DIRECTED FORGETTING USING STRATEGY CONTROL

The use of complex instructions and training procedures such as these may appear to require a good deal of faith in our subjects' willingness and ability to cooperate. It is possible, however, to combine these procedures with experimental controls that enable us to assess the efficacy of strategy control training and instructions directly. To illustrate, let me briefly describe a study Jane Tanner and I are carrying out, in collaboration with Robert Bjork and Keith Smith.

The problem is to elucidate the processes that go on in directed short term forgetting, a phenomenon Bjork (1970) and others have demonstrated in several previous studies. In the typical Bjork paradigm, a trial consists of a single presentation of from one to eight trigram-word pairs. After each such presentation, the subject is shown the trigram from one of these pairs and asked to recall the corresponding word.

On some trials, an "instruction to forget" is given to the subject at some point during the presentation of the sequence of trigram-word pairs. This "instruction to forget" takes the form of a special prearranged signal. In some of Bjork's studies, the signal is a change in the color of the background against which the trigram-word pairs appear. In our study, it is a change in the position of the pairs with respect to some constant reference line. The first few pairs may appear below the line, for example, followed by the balance of the pairs presented above the line or vice versa.

The subject knows that if the signal occurs during a given trial, he will not be tested for recall on any of the pairs that were presented prior to the occurrence of the signal. Thus, he can forget those pairs and concentrate on remembering only pairs presented after the signal occurs. To obviate the possibility that some subjects simply will wait for the signal and then attend only to the pairs that follow, the experiment includes a substantial proportion of trials on which no signal occurs. In such cases, the subject may be tested on any of the pairs presented on that trial.

The effects of such a signal are quite striking. In particular, it wipes out substantially all the proactive inhibition effect presignal items normally would have on those that follow them. Let us assume, for example, that on some trials we have presented three initial pairs, then the forget signal, and then four postsignal pairs. Now we test recall on the third postsignal pair by presenting the trigram and asking the subject to respond with the appropriate word. This result may be compared with recall of the third pair on trials in which four trigram-word pairs are presented alone, with no signal and no presignal pairs preceding them. When we make such comparisons, we find that recall performance under the two conditions is essentially indistinguishable.

Given such results, it is natural to wonder what the subjects are doing when the forget instruction appears. What happens to memory for the presignal items? The Bjork paradigm unfortunately does not permit a direct investigation of this problem. Recall of presignal items cannot be tested without violating the meaning of the signal.

There are several ways in which one might try to get around this difficulty. In our study, we use a combination of training procedures and strategy control instructions. Subjects first learn to perform the standard Bjork task. Once they can do so, we explain that we also are interested in what happens to the presignal items, and that we occasionally will test recall of those items. Such tests are distinguished from regular tests of postsignal items by prefacing the stimulus with an asterisk. Subjects are told that we are mainly concerned with the postsignal items, and they are asked to behave just as they were behaving in the first part of the experiment, prior to the introduction of the asterisked tests. In other words, they are specifically asked to behave as if the asterisked tests were not going to occur.

After the experiment, each subject is questioned systematically to determine whether he thinks he succeeded in carrying out the instructions. Many subjects say that they were unable to do so consistently. Since we do not have any basis for expectations about the behavior of these subjects, we put their data aside without examination, for analysis at a later time. Many other subjects claim to have behaved as requested, however. Preliminary analyses of data from these subjects indicates that their performance varies little if at all from the performance of subjects in the standard Bjork experiment. We do not yet know whether our data will contribute to a better understanding of the effects of the forget instruction, but the results obtained so far clearly demonstrate the value of strategy control procedures as an experimental tool.

Advantages and Disadvantages of Strategy Control

The foregoing experiment has been described as a modification of Bjork's experimental design, a modification involving the introduction of techniques for strategy control. It is interesting to note, however, that the original design itself assumes that subjects can be instructed to exert a degree of voluntary control ("forgetting" or "not forgetting") over their mental activity. Thus, Bjork's studies, like Bower's work on imagery, reflects the gradual alteration in our notions of reasonable experimental procedure that has resulted from the growth of strategy system conceptions of behavior. In that respect, the experiment just described merely goes a few steps further. It assumes that humans are capable of developing and utilizing more complex mental strategies, it encourages development of the desired strategies through appropriate instructions and training, and then it compares resulting performance with performance in a reference condition, to assess the efficacy of the experimental procedures directly.

Though they may grant that the results we have described can be obtained through strategy control techniques, some investigators may want to question the value of the results themselves. Perhaps all we have found out when we use such shaping methods is that some subjects will do what we ask them to. Since the procedures we are proposing are rather different from the more usual method of placing a subject in a situation, presenting a task, and recording the results, it may be useful to consider the rationale for strategy control in more detail.

The objection just mentioned may make good sense from certain viewpoints, but it seems inconsistent with an information-processing conception of the sort we are working with here. Our goal is to secure information about the basic structures and processes underlying memory behavior. Given that goal, we want to find experimental manipulations that will help us to achieve it.

There are several ways of working toward this goal. One approach is related to a common technique of linguistic analysis. The linguist[3] looks for what cannot be said. He observes, for instance, that one can say "John wrote the letter in an hour," but not "John wrote letters in an hour." The linguist then looks for related examples, and subsequently tries to induce the general linguistic variables that determine these restrictions on what can be said. In a somewhat similar way, the psychologist interested in the basic structures and processes underlying behavior may choose to focus upon the limits of performance. If subjects find it impossible to carry out certain classes of tasks, it may be reasonable to search for some basic limitation or constraint that is responsible.

Strategy-control procedures are another tool for getting at these basic constraints. We specify what the subject is to do as precisely as possible in order to learn more about the means by which he does it. Just as the linguist may vary his test sentences and the situations to which they apply, so the psychologist can vary both the strategy and the task to discover the significant factors and determine their effects. But we cannot vary strategies unless we control them in the first place. Furthermore, if we do not control strategy variations, if instead we let each subject do his own thing, and change things at will without our knowing, the resulting data are likely to be far too confounded to provide useful information on basic processes.

If strategies can differ, why not reduce this uncontrolled variation as much as possible? Why permit each subject to decide how he will do the task before him? True, our data then represent normal uninstructed behavior, but is that really what we want? Given our interests, why perfer data contaminated by the innumerable accidents of background and experience that determine normal behavior?

[3] I want to thank David C. Bennett for a very interesting discussion that provided both the general point and the specific example.

Perhaps another analogy may be helpful. Suppose we are interested in determining the basic anatomical structures and processes underlying skilled physical performance. We could begin by selecting 100 randomly chosen college sophomores and putting them through a battery of athletic tests. We also could study performance on some of the tests in more detail, observing, for example, how success in getting over a high bar varies as a function of changes in the height of the bar. Alternately, however, we could begin by training each subject to perform a given task in some standardized fashion. Once performance has stabilized, we then collect data for each subject. With uncontrolled differences in task procedures thus substantially reduced, would we not then be more likely to secure data that would permit us to induce the underlying anatomical factors and the way they work?

It is interesting to know how individuals vary as a function of innate differences and prior experience. If we are not mainly concerned with individual differences, however, why allow them, particularly those reflecting not basic capacity factors but casual differences of training and experience, to complicate our problem? If we are trying to determine general properties of the human information-processing system, what reason is there to study average unconstrained behavior?

It is true that we no longer get information reflecting the normal distribution of strategies in an uninstructed population if we constrain strategies. Perhaps that distribution implies something significant about human information processing. If there is reason to suspect this in some situation, it clearly is worth studying. In most cases, though, we cannot distinguish this possibility from other much less interesting ones. Some subjects will have come across imagery as a way of holding things in mind; others will not. Some subjects will have come across making up a story as a mnemonic; others will not. Some subjects who know one or another such technique will assume they can use it in the experiment; others, noting that the experimenter didn't explicitly say they could use it, will not. Maybe they are supposed to stare at the words. When these are the consequences of a failure to control strategies by training and instruction, the resulting distributions of strategies are of no interest. All we have done by not controlling strategies is make it difficult to get much from the resulting data.

Strategy control runs counter to some standard statistical modes of thought in that it depends upon an unwillingness to treat strategy change as a source of error variance. But as we have seen, those modes of thought are themselves inconsistent with an information processing conception of behavior. According to that conception, behavior is not to be accounted for in terms of a set of additive components. It is generated by a system in which some of the components (the strategies) switch other components on and off at various times and as a function of the outcome of prior processing. If this view is correct, there is little reason to stay within the framework of the additive components approach. We want instead to work out new ways of discovering what subjects can and cannot do. Then, once we have some interesting performance well defined and constrained, the problem is to understand the means by which it is achieved.

Summary

This chapter has examined some conceptual and methodological interactions between information-processing investigations of cognitive activity and current attempts to build models of memory. An information-processing program intended to generate behavior simulating human thinking, for example, necessarily includes assumptions about the organization of information structures in memory, about access and acquisition strategies, and about the basic storage and retrieval processes in terms of which such strategies are defined. Often, however, it is difficult to divide the elements of such a system into two distinct subsets, those having to do with memory and those not.

In addition to outlining a few of the more interesting ways in which memory may be treated in such models, we consider some of the implications for experimental research mainly concerned with memory behavior. For example, do current paradigms actually permit conclusions about memory independent of its interrelations with other cognitive functions? We discuss evidence indicating that at least some subjects in typical memory experiments spend substantial amounts of time working out and using strategies that may enable them to perform better in the particular experimental setting. To what extent need research on memory take account of such activity? What are the conceptual and methodological options open to the investigator at this point? If he is willing to view memory as an aspect of a more general system of cognitive processes, he may be able to make use of relevant ideas about information structure, process organization, and strategy control, and the chapter concludes with a discussion of ways in which these ideas might be applied in research on memory.

References

Ash, W. TRAMP. CONCOMP Project, University of Michigan, 1968.

Atkinson, R. C., and Shiffrin, R. M. Human memory: A proposed system and its control processes. In K. W. Spence and J. T. Spence (Eds.), *Advances in the psychology of learning and motivation research and theory.* Vol. 2. New York: Academic Press, 1968.

Bjork, R. A. Positive forgetting: the non-interference of items intentionally forgotten. *Journal of Verbal Learning and Verbal Behavior,* 1970, in press.

Bower, G. H. A multicomponent theory of the memory trace. In K. W. Spence and J. T. Spence (Eds.), *The psychology of learning and motivation.* Vol. 1. New York: Academic Press, 1967. Pp. 230–325.

Bower, G. H. Mental imagery and associative learning. In L. Gregg (Ed.), *Cognition in learning and memory.* New York: Wiley, 1969, in press.

Collins, A. M., and Quillian, M. R. Retrieval time from semantic memory. BBN Report No. 1692, July 14, 1968, Bolt, Beranek and Newman, Inc., Contract No. F33615–67–C–1982, Aerospace Medical Research Laboratories.

Ernst, G. W., and Newell, A. *GPS: A case study in generality and problem solving.* New York: Academic Press, 1969.

Fitts, P. M. Perceptual-motor skill learning. In A. W. Melton (Ed.), *Categories of human learning.* New York: Academic Press, 1964.

Greeno, J. G. Psychological representation of structured knowledge. Paper presented at the meeting of the American Education Research Association, 1969.

Hebb, D. O. *The organization of behavior.* New York: Wiley, 1949.

Jacob, F. Genetics of the bacterial cell. *Science,* 1966, **152,** 1470–1478.

Lamb, S. M. *Stratificational grammar.* Washington, D. C.: Georgetown University Press, 1966.

Laughery, K. R. Computer simulation of short-term memory: A component-decay model. In J. T. Spence and G. H. Bower (Eds.), *Advances in the psychology of learning and motivation research and theory.* Vol. 3. New York: Academic Press, 1969.

Luria, A. R. *The mind of a mnemonist.* New York: Basic Books, 1968.

Lwoff, A. Interaction among virus cell and organism. *Science,* 1966, **152,** 1216–1220.

Mandler, G. Organization and memory. In K. W. Spence and J. T. Spence (Eds.), *Advances in the psychology of learning and motivation research and theory.* Vol. 1. New York: Academic Press, 1967, Pp. 327–372.

Minsky, M. L., *Semantic information processing.* Cambridge, Massachusetts: MIT Press, 1968.

Minsky, M. L., and Papert, S. A. Research on intelligent automata. Status Report II, September 1967, Project MAC, Massachusetts Institute of Technology, ONR Contract NONR–4102(02) and ONR Contract NONR–4102(01), Advanced Research Projects Agency, Office of Naval Research.

Neisser, U. *Cognitive psychology.* New York: Appleton-Century-Crofts, 1967.

Newell, A., and others. *Information processing language-V manual.* Englewood Cliffs, New Jersey: Prentice-Hall, 1964.

NEWELL, A., AND SIMON, H. A. GPS, a program that simulates human thought. In H. Billing (Ed.), *Lernende Automaten.* Munich: Oldenbourg, 1961. Republished: In E. A. Feigenbaum and J. Feldman (Eds.), *Computers and thought.* New York: McGraw-Hill, 1963. Pp. 279–293.

NORMAN, D. A. *Memory and attention.* New York: Wiley, 1969.

POLLACK, I. Structure of memory search. In *Mental Health Research Institute 12th Annual Report.* Ann Arbor, Michigan: University of Michigan, 1967. Pp. 20–21.

QUILLIAN, M. R. Semantic memory. Unpublished doctoral dissertation, Carnegie-Mellon University, 1966.

QUILLIAN, M. R. Word concepts: A theory and simulation of some basic semantic capabilities. *Behavioral Science,* 1967, **12,** 410–430.

REICH, P. A. Unpublished doctoral dissertation, University of Michigan, 1969, in preparation.

REITMAN, W. R. *Cognition and thought.* New York: Wiley, 1965.

REITMAN, W. R. Modeling the formation and use of concepts, percepts, and rules. In L. Lecam and J. Neyman (Eds.), *Proceedings of the fifth Berkeley symposium on mathematical statistics and probability.* Vol. IV. Berkeley: University of California Press, 1967. Pp. 65–79.

REITMAN, W. R. The uses of experience: Open statements, ill-defined strategies, and intelligent information processing. In J. Hellmuth (Ed.), *Cognitive studies.* Vol. 1. Seattle: Special Child Publications, 1969, in press. (a)

REITMAN, W. R. Information processing models, computer simulation, and the psychology of thinking. In J. F. Voss (Ed.), *Approaches to thought.* Columbus, Ohio: Merrill, 1969, 243–286. (b)

REITMAN, W. R. The conceptual bases of simulations of higher mental processes. In J. Mehler (Ed.), *Cognitive psychology handbook.* Englewood Cliffs, New Jersey: Prentice-Hall, 1969, in press. (c)

SANDERS, J. W. Unpublished manuscript, Psychology 550, University of Michigan, 1965.

SIMON, H. A., AND KOTOVSKY, K. Human acquisition of concepts for sequential patterns. *Psychological Review,* 1963, **70,** 534–546.

STERNBERG, S. Two operations in character-recognition: Some evidence from reaction-time measurements. *Perception & Psychophysics,* 1967, **2,** 45–53.

UNDERWOOD, B. J. Stimulus selection in verbal learning. In C. N. Cofer and B. S. Musgrove (Eds.), *Verbal behavior and learning: Problems and processes.* New York: McGraw-Hill, 1963.

WINIKOFF, A. W. Eye movements as an aid to protocol analysis of problem solving behavior. Unpublished doctoral dissertation, Carnegie-Mellon University, 1967.

WITKIN, E. M. Radiation-induced mutations and their repair. *Science,* 1966, **152,** 1345–1353.

YATES, F. A. *The art of memory.* Chicago: University of Chicago Press, 1966.

Appendix: Serial Position Curves

Many of the papers in this book use illustrations of the serial position curve, either to make their theoretical arguments or to demonstrate the fit of their model to experimental data. Two experiments seem to be the most popular in providing sources of data for these purposes: Murdock's (1962) paper on the serial position effect of free recall, and Phillips, Shiffrin, and Atkinson's (1967) paper on a probe-type recall experiment. Although these data are popular with the model testers, the actual probabilities associated with them are not readily available. Thus, to get numbers that can be tested, it is necessary either to request the data from the original experimenters or to approximate them by laboriously converting the points on the published graphs back into probabilities, a technique that is as inaccurate as it is time consuming.

To help future investigators, the original data from these two experiments are collected together here in this Appendix. There are sources of data, of course, other than the two experiments presented here. Papers that were used in the book are Postman and Phillips' (1965) study of the temporal changes in free recall, Wickelgren and Norman's (1966) recognition memory study of different list lengths, and Yntema, Wozencraft, and Klem's (1964) study of the effect of list length and pretation rate on recall.

The Postman and Phillips data, in some sense, do not need to be fit, for their point is that the recency effect of a serial position curve disappears when there is a long (filled) time interval between presentation and recall. Given that they have made this point well, Murdock's data can then be altered to eliminate the recency portion of the curve whenever this prediction of the model needs to be tested. The data of Wickelgren and Norman (1966) are contained in their original publication, and so do not need to be reprinted here.

Interpreting the Predictions of a Model

Before presenting the data, it would seem to be appropriate to issue a word of warning to the model builder about the conclusions that can be drawn from a demonstration that the model describes the serial position curve. Any model of memory that discusses both short- and long-term aspects of memory, whether it assumes the existence of one, two, three, or four memories, must be able to describe the shape of the serial position curve. It is a test of manhood, and every model that wishes to be taken seriously must eventually pass that test. Thus, although it is a *necessary* condition that any model be able to describe these data, it is not a *sufficient* condition for the acceptance of that model. In addition to this type of curve fitting, a good model will have psychological reality—it will be possible to make psychologically meaningful statements about each of its processes and parameters. Thus, the model will handle many different classes of data, not simply those which come from one standard experimental paradigm. In addition, it will exhibit reasonable sets of estimates for the parameters: the ways that the model parameters vary across subjects and experimental conditions should agree with the nonmathematical psychologist's intuition about the effect of these variables. Finally, the model should be able to make specific predictions about performance on new types of experiments, hopefully with the new predictions coming directly from parameters which have been estimated from previously performed experiments. None of the models presented in the present volume meet all of these tests, although some of them show signs that future revisions will bring them closer to these goals.

We can draw an analogy here between the present day attempts of the modeler of memory to fit the serial position curve and the attempts of the mathematical learning theorists to describe the learning curve when their field was first flourishing. Learning theorists soon discovered that many completely different models would describe the learning curve of the same experiment equally well; they had to develop other ways of distinguishing among models. We, too, are beginning to discover that different models describe serial position curves equally well. Thus, like our predecessors, we must learn to evaluate models by other, more stringent criteria. A useful source of information about the techniques of assessing the validity of models is Sternberg's (1963) chapter in the *Handbook of Mathematical Psychology, Volume 2.*

Murdock's Data[1]

PROCEDURE

Six groups each had a different combination of list length and presentation rate. These six combinations were 10–2, 20–1, 15–2, 30–1, 20–2, and 40–1; the first number indicates list length and the second number indicates presentation time (in seconds) per item. Thus, 10–2 means a list of ten words presented at a rate of 2 sec/item. Notice that the first two, middle two, and last two groups were matched for t, total presentation time (20, 30, and 40 sec, respectively).

For each group there were 80 different lists. The lists were constructed by randomly selecting words from the (approximately) 4000 most common English words (Thorndike and Lorge, 1944, G count of 20 and up), except that homonyms, contractions, and archaic words were excluded.

Group testing was used. Lists were read to Ss either at every beat (presentation rate of 1 second/item) or at every other beat (presentation rate of 2 sec/item) of an electric metronome set at a rate of 60 beats/minute.

After each list there was a recall period of 1.5 minutes. The Ss wrote down as many words as they could remember in any order that they wished. Each recall period was terminated by a verbal "Ready" signal which preceded the start of the next list by 5–10 sec. All groups were given 20 lists per session and four sessions; successive sessions were spaced 2–7 days apart. Nothing was said about rehearsing while the lists were being presented.

In all, there were 103 Ss, students of both sexes from the introductory psychology course who were fulfilling a course requirement. Exact Ns by group are shown in Table 1. (Murdock, 1962, p. 482)

RESULTS

The results are summarized in Tables 1 and 2. Illustrations of the serial position curves can be found in Fig. 9 of chapter 2 (Page 57). The value for the asymptote of the curves is the complement of the value for v given in Table 2 of Murdock's paper. Murdock says that they were ". . . determined from the mean recall probabilities averaged over the flat portion on each serial position curve."

Note that in the free-recall experiment, the order in which the subject

[1] I thank Bennet B. Murdock, Jr. for sending me the copies of his data sheets which were used to make Tables 1 and 2 and allowing them to be published here.

TABLE 1
Summary of Murdock's Serial Position Curves

Group	No. subjects	Obs. per point	Asymptote	Number of words recalled	
				Mean	SD
10–2	18	1440	.452	6.39	.76
20–1	16	1280	.148	6.87	1.16
15–2	19	1520	.378	8.25	1.40
30–1	19	1520	.186	8.82	1.98
20–2	15	1200	.270	8.53	2.08
40–1	16	1280	.115	8.24	1.08

TABLE 2
Data from Murdock's Serial Position Curves

Condition	Percent recall (listed in order from serial position 1 to n)									
10–2	68	56	48	45	45	57	67	70	83	95
20–1	46	27	20	15	16	15	15	15	21	22
	23	21	23	25	29	39	61	74	83	95
15–2	63	51	45	40	38	38	39	39	42	49
	57	61	79	87	98					
30–1	48	30	20	18	20	20	18	17	20	19
	19	19	18	18	16	15	20	18	18	18
	20	20	23	24	33	39	52	74	89	97
20–2	55	42	37	34	28	30	28	26	23	27
	29	32	29	38	38	43	57	74	87	94
40–1	30	20	13	12	11	11	12	13	12	09
	15	12	10	10	11	13	11	10	13	10
	11	10	11	15	14	12	12	15	14	14
	17	17	15	22	27	38	51	72	84	95

reports back the words affects the probability of correct report for the words in the last portion of the serial position curve. See Waugh and Norman (1965) for a discussion of the effect that this has on Murdock's data.

Phillips, Shiffrin, and Atkinson's Data[2]

PROCEDURE

The Ss in this study were 20 females. They were drawn from a pool of Stanford University students who had expressed an interest in participating in psychological experiments, and were paid for their services. Each S participated in five sessions, each session lasting approximately 1 hour. The first session was a practice session, designed to familiarize S with procedure and to eliminate practice effects. Three display sizes ($d = 8, 11, 14$) were used in session 1; the next three sessions were also restricted to these three display sizes. The last session for each S employed five different display sizes ($d = 3, 4, 5, 6, 7$).

The experiment involved a long series of discrete trials. On each trial a display of d items was presented. A display consisted of a series of $2 \times 3\frac{1}{2}$-inch cards containing a $\frac{3}{4} \times 1\frac{1}{2}$-inch colored patch in the center. Four colors were used: black, white, blue, and green. The cards were presented to S at a rate of one card every 2 sec. The S named the color of each card as it was presented. A metronome was used to maintain a constant rate of presentation for each display. Once the color of the card had been named by S, it was turned face down on a display board so that the color was no longer visible, and the next card was presented. After presentation of the last card in a display, the cards were in a straight row on the display board: the card presented first was to S's left and the most recently presented card to her right. The trial terminated when the E pointed to one of the cards on the display board, and S attempted to recall the color of that card. The S was instructed to guess the color if uncertain and to qualify her response with a confidence rating. The confidence ratings were the numerals 1, 2, 3, and 4. The Ss were told to say 1 if they were positive, 2 if they were able to eliminate two of the four possible colors as correct, 3 if one of the four colors could be eliminated as correct, and 4 if they had no idea at all as to the correct response. These confidence ratings will be designated R_1, R_2, R_3, and R_4. Each display, regardless of size, ended at the same place on the display board; that is, displays began at different places on the display board, and hence Ss knew, from the position of the first card, how long each display was to be.

Each S was given two complete blocks of displays in each of the first four sessions. A block consisted of one display for each serial position in each display size. Thus there were $(8 + 11 + 14) = 33$ displays per block, and a complete session involved the presentation of 66 displays. During the fifth day each S was given five complete blocks of displays. A complete block in the final session consisted of $(3 + 4 + 5 + 6 + 7) = 25$ displays; hence, the total session involved the presentation of 125 displays. Each serial position of each display size was selected as the test position exactly once per block. The presentation order of displays (display size and test position) was randomized within each block; furthermore, the cards and their order were determined randomly for each display.

At the beginning of the second session, Ss were told the proportion of correct responses that they had achieved for each of the four confidence ratings. They were reminded at that time that the "ideal" proportion correct was 100% for a confidence rating of R_1, 50% for R_2, 33% for R_3, and 25% for R_4. No further information feedback was given concerning the confidence ratings during subsequent sessions.

[2] I thank Richard C. Atkinson for providing me with these data and allowing them to be published here.

RESULTS

> The overall proportions of correct responses for Sessions 1 to 4 were .66, .72, .73, and .72, respectively; each point is based on 7920 observations. Since the proportion correct is reasonably stationary for the three sessions following the practice session, it is assumed that performance in Session 5 (involving different values of d) is comparable to that in the three preceding sessions. In subsequent analyses, the data from Session 1, the practice session, will not be included. (Phillips, *et al*, 1967, pp. 306–307)

The results are presented in Table 3. Note that Phillips *et al.*, plot their serial position curves backwards, with serial position 1 representing the last item in the list. For an illustration of these data, see Fig. 1 of chapter 4 (page 105). To see what these same data look like when plotted in the conventional manner, see Fig. 10 of chapter 2 (page 58).

TABLE 3
Data from Phillips, Shiffrin, and Atkinson[a]

Display size	Obs. per point	Serial position	$Pr(C_i)$	$Pr(R_1)$	$Pr(R_2)$	$Pr(R_3)$	$Pr(R_4)$
		1	1.00	1.00	.00	.00	.00
3	100	2	1.00	1.00	.00	.00	.00
		3	1.00	1.00	.00	.00	.00
		1	1.00	1.00	.00	.00	.00
		2	1.00	1.00	.00	.00	.00
4	100	3	.99	.98	.02	.00	.00
		4	1.00	.98	.02	.00	.00
		1	1.00	1.00	.00	.00	.00
		2	.99	.99	.01	.00	.00
5	100	3	.96	.95	.05	.00	.00
		4	.97	.95	.05	.00	.00
		5	.98	.98	.02	.00	.00
		1	1.00	1.00	.00	.00	.00
		2	.98	.99	.01	.00	.00
		3	.95	.95	.05	.00	.00
6	100	4	.94	.86	.14	.00	.00
		5	.93	.91	.08	.01	.00
		6	.97	.93	.06	.01	.00

Table 3 (Continued)

Display size	Obs. per point	Serial position	$Pr(C_i)$	$Pr(R_1)$	$Pr(R_2)$	$Pr(R_3)$	$Pr(R_4)$
		1	1.00	1.00	.00	.00	.00
		2	.97	.98	.02	.00	.00
		3	.93	.93	.07	.00	.00
7	100	4	.89	.83	.14	.02	.01
		5	.83	.71	.27	.02	.00
		6	.82	.81	.18	.01	.00
		7	.95	.85	.12	.02	.01
		1	1.000	.992	.008	.000	.000
		2	.975	.975	.025	.000	.000
		3	.933	.908	.075	.008	.008
8	120	4	.892	.733	.225	.033	.008
		5	.817	.592	.292	.117	.000
		6	.733	.575	.342	.050	.033
		7	.800	.667	.258	.067	.008
		8	.908	.733	.208	.050	.008
		1	1.000	1.000	.000	.000	.000
		2	.967	.933	.058	.008	.000
		3	.933	.808	.183	.008	.000
		4	.767	.633	.233	.108	.025
11	120	5	.633	.417	.383	.150	.050
		6	.608	.367	.450	.117	.067
		7	.658	.325	.375	.233	.067
		8	.592	.350	.425	.133	.092
		9	.550	.325	.442	.175	.058
		10	.567	.425	.375	.167	.033
		11	.742	.475	.433	.067	.025
		1	1.000	1.000	.000	.000	.000
		2	.967	.942	.058	.000	.000
		3	.892	.808	.158	.033	.000
		4	.717	.617	.342	.033	.008
		5	.708	.417	.417	.133	.033
		6	.617	.400	.367	.158	.075
14	120	7	.458	.183	.375	.308	.133
		8	.400	.192	.425	.258	.125
		9	.433	.217	.392	.233	.158
		10	.450	.208	.433	.267	.092
		11	.467	.192	.517	.183	.108
		12	.508	.233	.467	.267	.033
		13	.475	.242	.500	.175	.083
		14	.642	.392	.475	.100	.033

[a] Proportion of correct responses and proportions of each confidence rating for the five smallest display sizes.

References

MURDOCK, B. B., JR. The serial position effect of free recall. *Journal of Experimental Psychology,* 1962, **64,** 482–488.

PHILLIPS, J. L., SHIFFRIN, R. M., AND ATKINSON, R. C. The effects of list length on short-term memory. *Journal of Verbal Learning and Verbal Behavior,* 1967, **6,** 303–311.

POSTMAN, L., AND PHILLIPS, L. W. Short-term temporal changes in free recall. *Quarterly Journal of Experimental Psychology,* 1965, **17,** 132–138.

STERNBERG, S. Stochastic learning theory. In R. D. Luce, R. R. Bush, and E. Galanter (Eds.), *Handbook of mathematical psychology.* Vol. II. New York: Wiley, 1963.

THORNDIKE, E. L., AND LORGE, I. *The teacher's word book of 30,000 words.* New York: Columbia University Press, 1944.

WAUGH, N. C., AND NORMAN, D. A. Primary memory. *Psychological Review,* 1965, **72,** 89–104.

WICKELGREN, W. A., AND NORMAN, D. A. Strength models and serial position in short-term recognition memory. *Journal of Mathematical Psychology,* 1966, **3,** 316–347.

YNTEMA, D. B., WOZENCRAFT, F. T., AND KLEM, L. Immediate serial recall of digits presented at very high rates. Paper presented at the meetings of the Psychonomic Society, Niagara Falls, Ontario, 1964.

Author Index

Numbers in italics refer to the pages on which the complete references are listed.

C

D

E

F

G

Y

Z

Subject Index

A

I

L

M

N

O

S

T

U

V

W